The Ethiopian ambassador Endalkachew Makonnen serving up the stew

Well Vale

Turia

Photo call with Mabel Strickland, the 'Queen of Malta', in the centre

...cond from right, front. Christopher Lee second from left, front

WEST HILL BAKERY STORES

Opening day of Gulzaman's grocery store

OH, WHAT A
LOVELY CENTURY

OH, WHAT A LOVELY CENTURY

One man's marvellous adventures
in love, war and high society

Roderic Fenwick Owen

SPHERE

First published in Great Britain in 2021 by Sphere

1 3 5 7 9 10 8 6 4 2

A CIP catalogue record for this book
is available from the British Library.

Hardback ISBN 978-0-7515-8302-1
Trade paperback format ISBN 978-0-7515-8301-4

Abridged by H. Boursnell
Abridged and edited by E. Barrett

Typeset in Bembo by M Rules
Printed and bound in Great Britain by Clays Ltd, Elcograf S.p.A.

Papers used by Sphere are from well-managed forests
and other responsible sources.

Sphere
An imprint of
Little, Brown Book Group
Carmelite House
50 Victoria Embankment
London EC4Y 0DZ

An Hachette UK Company
www.hachette.co.uk

www.littlebrown.co.uk

I would be most unhappy to think that any parts of this long memoir should be cut on grounds of 'decency', for those bits are essential.

Roderic Fenwick Owen, 1921–2011

Contents

Editor's Note

The travel writer and biographer Roderic Fenwick Owen (1921–2011) lived a most unusual life, filled with travel, adventure, pleasure and people. It was possible for him in a way it wouldn't have been for most: he was born into a wealthy, notable family and his connections and education opened doors for him, as did money in later life and the continuing power of the British Empire overseas, even in its decline. He understood this; he didn't take any privilege for granted, making the most of them in a way few surely did – to see more of the world, to understand the people he met there, and to be generous to the people he loved. This is why his story is so richly compelling, set against a backdrop of a world undergoing immeasurable change.

Having kept diaries and journals all his life, the private memoir he transformed them into in his seventies for his family to keep ran to almost a million words. The book you are holding in your hands is closer to 200,000. Abridging it was difficult! Some aspects, such as details of his finances and the organisation of his trips, were easier to take out. But with regard to the rest it was a case of choosing the most vivid stories that would build a complete picture of his fascinating life. Like film scenes cut by directors at the editing stage, some of those lost were wonderfully entertaining but had to remain on the cutting room floor because they weren't necessary to the narrative; I hope Roddy would forgive this pruning. In his covering note to his memoirs, he made mention of abridging the books for a wider audience (indicating that perhaps his powers of fortune-telling, as he at one point made use of in Tahiti, really were as good as he advertised them). His only request if this were to happen is on page v: that nothing be cut on grounds of 'decency'. Throughout this book you will hear how much it meant to Roddy to finally be in a decade where he could talk freely about sex and relationships, having had to hide that part of his life in all his other books up to that point. So that was the compass with which abridgements were made; no story was cut on those grounds – indeed those parts are so riveting it was no hardship to keep them in.

But if his life was extraordinary and 'of its time', it was also ordinary and timeless in many ways too. He was looking for love and purpose, as perhaps we all are – those were the reasons he went all over the world, befriending everyone he could wherever he went. He knew the same tragedies and faced many of the same hurdles we can all recognise. Indeed, hearing him recount details of far-flung places is evocative; his brushes with 'history', both recent and distant, enthralling; and his experiences with famous and notable people titillating. But it's often the people you might not have heard of before that add the most colour to Roddy's story. Regular people who lived captivating lives in a century that feels more remote to us with each passing day, presented without rose-tinted nostalgia and pride on the one hand or embarrassed, disdainful shame on the other, as are so often applied to the period now as we – the generations who inherited or outlived the twentieth century – try to make sense of it.

Roddy was such a practised author that he did not leave many holes in his memoirs that needed to be filled in, though you will find footnotes added to provide the reader with more context where Roddy assumed knowledge. The holes that exist centre on what happened to some of the characters in the book after they left Roddy's own life story; we would invite anyone with information about any of the people mentioned herein to get in touch with us via info@littlebrown.co.uk, and we have included a list of repeat 'characters' at the back of the book to assist with this. We would love to hear more about them.

Inevitably, in the telling of his own story, Roddy gives away many private details about these people's lives. Those details have been verified wherever possible – but in lots of cases this wasn't an option, given that the majority of the individuals discussed have now died. In any case, readers – like historians considering source material – are invited to remember that there are two sides to every story, and sometimes more. Luckily for us, Roddy's side is like a good vodka martini: dry, strong and often too much fun. As Roddy concluded in the original covering note to his memoirs: 'I trust that readers will find the subject-matter as entertaining as I did whilst living it.'

I trust that you will, too.

E. Barrett, January 2021

part one

growing

1921-39

1

At 6.30 a.m. on 27 March 1921 – Easter Sunday – a delivery boy from Harrods rang the bell of a white porticoed town house in Prince's Gardens, Knightsbridge. His cargo was an enormous chocolate egg tied with blue ribbon, which was opened on the chequered hallway tiles to reveal a boy called Roderic. What a lovely surprise all round!

Doubts first began to break the surface as to the validity of the story because of my debut being so early in the morning – when Nanny might have been up and doing, but surely not my parents? Perhaps only Nanny had to be there for the Opening of the Egg? She seemed to be the only really important person on the scene at all other times.

My parents were Bettina Rawnsley, daughter of the High Sheriff of Lincolnshire and the niece of Hardwicke Rawnsley, one of the founders of the National Trust; and George Fenwick Owen, bespectacled and moustachioed. They had met almost eight years and one world war ago in September 1913, two months after my mother's grand coming-out ball at 20 Grosvenor Gardens, where Princess Marie Louise* and 800 guests had been in attendance. Until this point, Bettina had felt attached to an Alwyne Hobson but she'd gone off him at a shooting party on Raasay, a small island nestled between the mainland of Scotland and the Isle of Skye that her parents frequented in summers. Bettina decided she didn't find Alwyne exciting enough, and when she passed him the cup from which she'd been drinking and he wiped the brim before taking a sip, she declared him ungallant.

Conversely, nothing was boring about George Fenwick Owen. He was the nephew of renowned Victorian trend-setter and 'Gentleman Jockey' Major Roddy Owen, who won the Grand National in 1892 on Father O'Flynn. His mother was Maya Fenwick Owen, a notable harlot in Edwardian society. As George's uncles and elder brother had already departed this world, he and his mother were left very well off, living

---

* Princess Marie Louise of Schleswig-Holstein, a granddaughter of Queen Victoria.

at Brantham Court in Suffolk. The house was a fine example of mock-Tudor on the grand scale: mullioned windows throughout, and oak – oak everywhere in the form of panelling, flooring, even cupboarding. The front door was of oak so massive that on being opened it 'whooooshed' as it pushed air backwards and forwards.

Upon meeting George, Bettina found they had plenty to talk about, swapping stories of Big Game in Africa (at the time, 'safari' sadly meant hunting lions, buffalo and other exotic-seeming animals). Such a proven sportsman was naturally asked to Well Vale, the Rawnsley family pile in Lincolnshire, for the shooting; and naturally he acquitted himself better than any of the other guns. So glamorous a character was sure to own one of the early motor-cars. In it, he arranged to drive Bettina to Lincoln, but on the way a tyre burst and they had to turn tail and come back. George was cross and he lost his temper. For Bettina, the moment was a watershed: either she had to mind, most dreadfully, or she had to accept him as he was, temper and all. She knuckled under without protest, thus precipitating an era of a new 'understanding'. At the end of January 1914, George booked all the seats in an entire First Class compartment on the train going from London to Well Vale. Pulling down the blinds, he bribed the guard to see that they weren't disturbed, and then he made his move; which is to say he proposed, and was accepted.

My maternal grandmother, Maud, wrote in her diary: 'Betty told me at night they were engaged. We all went out hunting. I came down early to breakfast and offered my heartiest congratulations to George. He is so nice; she could not have chosen anybody I could like better.'

They were married in St George's, Hanover Square – down the road from Liberty's – and their cousin Alice Godman lent them a huge redbrick town house, 45 Pont Street, for the wedding reception, it having a large ballroom perfect for the occasion.

In Paris for the first stages of their honeymoon, Bettina was suffering from that arch-wrecker of romance: such a cold that she could hardly breathe. She recovered in time to enjoy a long trip across Imperial Russia on the Trans-Siberian railway – in those days a dream of comfort for those who could afford to travel in style. They went on to Japan, with Bettina's maid – a severe Scotswoman – always in attendance. Amongst the Ainu, the maid spent much of her time dutifully holding up sheets to shield her employer from men wetting the paper walls of more than one rustic inn with their fingers – the idea being to make them transparent enough to be seen through, on the pretence of 'never having seen a European without their clothes on before'.

In Bettina, however, a child had begun to stir – my oldest sister Morvyne Mary Martia – effectively spoiling much of the enjoyment of prolonged travel abroad. They returned just before the outbreak of the Great War, in good time for my father to be sent to Gallipoli and Palestine, get a bullet through his heart, and survive – or I would never have been born.

According to the traditional rhyme, 'The child that is born on the Sabbath Day / Is Bonny and Bright and Good and Gay', and with it being an Easter Sunday, the omens were therefore excellent – the rhyme perhaps a little too literally specific, had anyone cared to give it a thought, which no one did.

In my early days, life had no shape; and what form it took was what others enforced. I remember it included perpetual dressing and re-dressing: a sailor suit or a furry Peter Rabbit get-up for walks in the park, and velvet Little Lord Fauntleroy knee-breeches (with buckles) for coming down to tea in the drawing-room.

Meals were arbitrary; they had to be eaten when brought to the nurs-ery, not when hunger struck. Nanny-discipline could be harsh; food unwisely left on the plate might turn up again at the next meal, and the next. On more than one occasion the congealed remains of fatty meat and fried parsnips – both *bêtes noires* of mine – were saved and produced triumphantly a day later. If I were sick I might even be forced to take the little pile of vomit back into my mouth. It never occurred to me to complain to a higher parental authority, which certainly wouldn't have approved of such goings-on.

I was a shy child, dating from my first attempts at speech, which had been marred by persistent stammering. A specialist had advised my mother to make me burst into song when confronted by a difficult word. I well remember piping up in a thin treble, eyes bulging with tears, crimson in the face. Terrified at the time, I was of course so effectively cured as to become the very opposite of tongue-tied when older.

In spite of any drawbacks, life in the twenties for an upper-class child was very pleasant. After Prince's Gardens, so convenient for walks around the Serpentine in Hyde Park, we 'took' houses in the country. Nothing need be bought, for the simple reason that on one side of the family there was Brantham Court, and on the other Well Vale: the redbrick Georgian manor house set within seven acres of parkland on the edge of the Lincolnshire Wolds that my mother's brother, my Uncle Dick, was to inherit from my grandfather.

We came to rest at rented Rempstone Hall, in Dorset, off the Corfe Castle/Swanage road on the Isle of Purbeck. The hall comprised two very different-style houses cemented together, one being a grey stone farm-house with a slate roof dating from the seventeenth century, the other a redbrick mansion from the eighteenth and nineteenth centuries. Its heaths stretched down to Goathorn Quai* on Poole Harbour and Japanese deer could be seen in its woods. Rempstone's garden was long and elaborate, with a 'gwyle' (a wooded walk where beech-nuts proliferated) and a pond where frogs spawned in huge, glutinous bunches, the males apparently bent on digging claws into, then suffocating, the luckless females. Myriad glow-worms sparkled in tinselly showers and bats wheeled and squawked. When we were allowed to sleep out, as we sometimes were on warm summer nights, we would wake at sunrise, camp-beds wet with dew, ravenous for breakfast which no one wanted to get for us at such an unearthly hour.

There was plenty of mischief to be had and my sister Genissa – two years my elder – and I were just daring enough to partake in some of it. One summer in Alford, the town nearby Well Vale, we conducted a series of raids on a shop, taking toys to give to a labourer's children at Park Farm, by whom we were thought quite extraordinarily generous. Our mother found out before the shop-keeper did; he was so surprised when we were forced to confess and make restitution that he took no other action. Having learnt not to steal, we'd been taught a lesson in the value of money. Having some would make stealing unnecessary; yet how were we to get hold of the essential stuff? We hit on the idea of going to Lambert the butler and asking to borrow a shilling for this or that guest. As leaving-tips were generally lavish, it was to be supposed that Lambert regarded what was slid into his discreetly outstretched palm at the end of a stay included a repayment. It took some time before we were found out and severely punished, but it was worth it at the time. Summers at Well Vale also gave us the opportunity to play tennis on both an upper and a lower court; and when we tired of tennis there was boating on the lower lake – boys rowing, girls sitting back, trailing fingers through weedy green water.

We even had a governess we liked, a Miss Evelyn Oxley, whom I affectionately called Tocky for a reason that escapes me now. When my eldest

---

* Better known as Goathorn Point.

sister Morvyne was sent away to boarding school, Tocky was employed by my mother mainly for Genissa, but also to give me a good grounding before prep school. She was wonderfully warm and both of us felt a great deal more towards her than we probably did our parents at that time.

The only fly in the ointment – a small one, at that – was my father's behaviour, which seemed to grow worse as the twenties rolled by. I had the usual boy's fear of his father, possibly because he was so large and so seldom visible, spending much of his time at the Bath Club, doing goodness knows what. Such disjointed memories as I have of him are mostly connected with that prime mystery, sex, about which I knew nothing. An early memory was, when very young, crawling under the dining-room table, irresistibly drawn towards the V-shaped gap between his legs. He was wearing a rough brown tweed knickerbocker suit, so it must have been winter. I crawled up and put my hand nearer and nearer, without actually touching, thrilling to the thought of being so near and yet so far. I must have known that actual contact was forbidden, probably from being ticked off for playing with myself 'down there'.

On went my game, whilst the grown-ups droned on and on, until I simply could not resist a tiny touch: a hardly noticeable prod, so gentle, in fact, that it passed unnoticed. Emboldened, I had another go, this time with a kind of stroking jab. Fatal! My father jerked his knees together with a 'What the Devil!' and a downward swish of his arm, which I dodged. Encountering no resistance, he banged his knuckles against the underside of the table, followed by words quite meaningless to me, that early in life. I was hauled from my 'cave', smacked, and sent up to the nursery.

Far from being dampened, my curiosity was stimulated. Whilst romping each morning on the four-poster where the two giants lay, I would manage to clutch forbidden parts, under the guise of flopping uncontrollably about. There was no fun to be derived from touching my mother, as she seemed to have nothing there but a fold of flesh; but my father was a different matter, because when pressed 'accidentally', something squashy moved like a bunch of grapes between his legs. It was such a large appendage that it seemed to belong to a different order of creation from my own little winkly thing. I found it fascinating and rolled about all the more, unrebuked because no one realised what I was up to.

A much later event was, in its way, a sequel. We used to bathe from a hut in Studland Bay, my father and I retreating to change behind a towel rigged up across the hut, whilst the girls changed on the other side. I wanted to study my father in detail, but as he always turned his back on me, my curiosity was always thwarted. So I conceived the idea of crawling about, pretending to look for a dropped comb; it gave me the chance of looking up under the towel which was all that he was wearing. I spied fleshy things hanging down irregularly, though without much hair, as he wasn't a hairy man. When my ruse was detected he kicked out and I seized his leg, pulling him off balance and giving myself a wonderful close-up, had I not been too distracted to take it all in as we rolled together on the floor.

But not all my memories of him are quite so genial. Though wounded in body he was still whole, and as children we had no way of knowing how the war had affected his temper, if it had. We were given to understand that he had always been a man to quarrel with his closest companions. He couldn't blame his wife, for she was completely faithful to him – not that we grasped what being faithful meant. But from what hints were gleaned from the incautious comments of grown-ups unaware that their words were being lapped up, her example was one which he was constitutionally incapable of following, it seemed. They shared enough interests to gloss over some of the difficulties: Old Master drawings, gardening and Egyptology, the latter leading to contacts with Howard Carter, discoverer of the burial chamber of Tutankhamen. And he remained rich enough to enjoy the many opportunities for shooting which came the way of a man with a notably 'straight' (if short-sighted) eye, even if the game were no longer so big as before. But he couldn't resist the temptation to become richer still, via the Stock Exchange.

Little did anyone guess where that would lead him.

———

2

By the time I started prep school in 1930, when I was nine years old, we were 'ruined'. The fall-out of the Great Crash of 1929 affected many people across the world, most of all the unsuspecting average Joe; my father was not one of those, but he was affected nonetheless. He had been dabbling on the stock market – I couldn't understand exactly how; selling stocks he hadn't bought, or buying shares without the money to pay for them. Whatever he'd been up to, life changed somewhat thereafter: no more Rempstone Hall and Japanese deer. 'We shall have to manage on what used to be my dress allowance!' said my mother bitterly. We moved into Kingston House, on top of a hill overlooking Corfe Castle.

Considering that we were ruined, it was odd that we still had a cook, a maid and a chauffeur-gardener; but in those days servants were paid so little that there was nothing too extraordinary about that situation, it seemed. Ruined parents could also afford to send their children to Summer Fields school in Oxford, where I spent most of my time from 1930 to 1934. Summer Fields had been started in 1863 by the Victorian fitness enthusiast Archibald Maclaren, or rather by his wife, the redoubtable Mrs M. My grandfather Walter had been their sixteenth pupil and the second from Summer Fields to win a King's Scholarship to Eton. Both precedent and expectation were therefore upon me, whether I knew it on my first day or not.

Perhaps some boys believe, or can be hoodwinked into believing, that they are happy at school. I wasn't, and no one could persuade me otherwise. Mrs Williams, the Headmaster's wife, was maternal – but for her, the first days at Summer Fields would have been terrifying. Little beings utterly unaccustomed to standing on their own feet were like tyros pushed into a pool at the deep end without having been taught how to swim. It was then that Mrs Williams proved her worth: large of bosom; comforting and consoling; breath reassuringly redolent of those lovely silver balls scattered on cakes.

Up to the very moment of parting from my mother I was cosseted, the centre of attention, even more so than usual on account of impending farewells. The next, I was being propelled through a door leading from Mrs Williams' cluttered drawing-room into the Head's study which smelt of strange, strong brilliantine. To a boy, Mr Williams was as old as the hills and as terrifying, his complexion a mottled ruby-red and his Adam's apple as prominent as a pointed egg. His nose was the most remarkable feature – bony, protruding in a way seldom seen amongst the living, the nose of an embalmed corpse (I would have thought, had I ever seen such a thing, which I hadn't). But his voice was worse than all those combined, starting with a bagpipe drone, an '*Mmmmnnn*' acting as a carrier for something more awesome to come. His study would prove to be the throne-room of judgement on future occasions – either a verbal ticking-off preceded by a glare, or there might be a cane propped against his desk, and then we knew we were in for a beating.

On that first day I was swiftly handed over to a monitor, who couldn't have been more than thirteen. With that grave oldster I passed, for the first of many times, through a baize swing-door and into a corridor vibrant with shouts and thuds: the school in all its bareness.

The transition was apocalyptic. I reacted accordingly, with an uncontrolled 'GOSH!' A few yards away, another new boy was sobbing. It helped make up my mind: I wouldn't, however much I felt like it. 'You can blub if you must,' announced the prefect airily. My answer was to blush, deeply and all-envelopingly, all over my face and down my neck, spoiling my grand gesture of dismissing the idea of crying as a childish absurdity. Blushing has always been my Achilles' heel, flaring up when least wanted.

I was given a desk for my 'things', such as they were. A locker was also assigned, which did everything except lock, presumably to allow the masters to check its contents. I quickly discovered that there was no cubic inch of privacy to be had anywhere in the school. Beds were arranged in dormitories; meals took place in a dining-hall with a top table for masters; even 'ablutions' were semi-public, in what was called 'The Vinery', where door-less cubicles were separated from the main area only by swing-barriers. The Vinery was glass-roofed, warmed in winter by a Valor 'Perfection' paraffin stove which, we quickly found, had one great virtue: a piece of lavatory paper placed on the circlet of dewdrop-shaped holes at the top would turn brown and eventually catch fire, ascending, aflame, in an upward swirl of hot air before fluttering in ashes to the stone floor.

If home life had been a tangle of rules and regulations, school life was all of that with knobs on. We were all sorted into one of four leagues: Maclaren, Case, Moseley or Congreve. But why was one supposed to feel loyalty towards one's 'league', when nobody was allowed to choose which he wanted to belong to? It was all very mysterious. League marks could be won by a variety of means – good behaviour in class, skill at work or games, ability to invent, compose or draw, et cetera. Making up a crossword puzzle was an easy-scorer, I soon discovered. Feeble was the youth who couldn't do anything to gain recognition.

It was, of course, a clever system of 'Divide and Rule' (on which, we were assured, the greatness of first the Roman and then the British Empire had been founded). It took in most boys, but not me. I couldn't identify with my league, which happened to be Moseley. Even at that age I adopted the unusual view that it didn't matter which league came top at the end of term, a quirk which has followed me throughout life: in competitions where success depends on the efforts of gifted individuals, I have never cared which country wins what event, being solely interested in the person themselves, regardless of nationality.

Every morning at Summer Fields began with a cold dip, boys lining up to plunge into a bath under Matron's gaze. The shock to the system was considerable – an important part of the '*corpore sano*' ideal, we supposed. My chief memory of it (beyond the startling discomfort) was that almost every boy, like me, was circumcised. It was rare to find an odd one out, shamefacedly washing his tiny parts in an enamel basin. After breakfast, another queue would form in Matron's room for spoonfuls of some tonic or other, 'Radio Malt' being the favourite, closely followed by sharper-tasting 'Virol'. It was infra dig to go tonic-less into lessons; few were bold enough to risk the disgrace.

An abiding memory from the first days was when we were gathered together in the largest classroom (called 'New School') by Mr Williams for a pep talk. The gist was that we should never forget that we were 'gentlemen', which meant following certain rules unless we wanted to be considered 'oiks'. Prohibitions greatly outweighed encouragements. For instance, unlike boys from the Dragon School in central Oxford – we were on the outskirts – we must never wander about in shorts, unless for games. Shorts at all other times were 'common'. We were being indoctrinated with a lasting over-regard for 'proper' tribal dress, a concern that would follow us throughout life, assuming (I thought then and think now) far too much importance.

We were also cautioned against 'talking smut', which could only lead to indulging in smutty acts, whatever they were. I longed to know more.

Now that memory has taken a back seat, a golden glow suffuses Summer Fields days. I can remember how much I disliked being there without being able to recall exactly why. It seems so heavenly in retrospect.

Swimming, for instance. We would be taken on a conducted walk through fields to a special bathing-place, owned by the school, on the banks of the Cherwell, where the mud was held together by the roots of willows. It was slippery down the bank, murky in the water, yet the whole circumstance of the outing – undressing and putting on little slips of red cotton, jumping in and landing on the uneven, muddy bottom and plopping up and out again, reeking of methane – was unforgettable. It wasn't luxurious, it wasn't comfortable; but what did that signify, compared with the joy of flinging off clothes out of doors, where they were normally worn?

Then there was the 'Hay Feast', a *lupercalia*, when masters playing at being boys could be rolled about in the stubble as boys from each form defended their 'nest' of hay previously stacked in heaps to dry. The feast got into its stride when packets of food and drinks of lemonade (made from vivid yellow crystals, gloriously synthetic) were handed around before we linked arms to tramp back to the school singing, 'One man went to mow, went to mow a meadow!'

Other walks had a higher moral purpose. We might be led in crocodile up the Banbury Road past the War Memorial. There we would be told to doff caps, 'in memory of the brave men who gave their lives so that you boys can stand here today'. It made us wriggle with unease. The thing which meant so much to our elders meant nothing to us, so how could we be grateful? We were not to guess that in years to come the boot would fit, that our dearest friends, perhaps we ourselves, would be the ones being commemorated.

I had a menagerie of friends, some famous to me, such as James Fletcher. Innocently we would climb into bed together to carry on conversations in whispers, far into the night. His parents lived at Ardmulchan Castle, near Navan in Ireland, which sounded wonderful.

And some famous to others. There was a young man of mystery, tall for his age, thin, his voice (with nasal overtones) smooth and more than a little ingratiating. He wasn't good at organised games, preferring golf, which he also wasn't much good at. He sat for a scholarship to Eton but didn't come high enough on the list to secure one, so went to Wellington. When his middle name was found to be 'Carandini', it 'proved' that he must be an ice-cream merchant, though he claimed (in vain) that his Carandini was a *conte* of high degree. What with one thing, what with another, he was the butt of many a rag, as incapable of defending himself against taunts as against fists. All in all, hardly the most memorable lad in the school. Yet such were the schooldays of a future Count Dracula, a wily Fu Manchu, Frankenstein's creature and a whole list of other Hammer horror heroes. He was Christopher Lee, least sinister of boys.

The career of another future actor was more predictable. Unhesitatingly, Patrick Macnee was cast in leading roles in our school plays. He was Brutus in *Julius Caesar* when I was merely the one-liner, 'Cinna, a poet'. Watching him in *The Avengers*, so long, long afterwards, I would remember him declaiming: 'You sticks, you stones, you worse than senseless things! Knew you not Caesar?' At Summer Fields he was an average type (if such a thing exists), but with a raucous voice strong enough to be audible in the back row of the stalls.

Then there was Peter Solomon, a small boy with a large head and carroty hair who told vivid stories. I would team up with him on walks in order to hear a recital of such wildly unfamiliar events that I finally accused him of making it all up. Russia was always the background, with sleigh-rides through the frozen wastes of Siberia complete with wolves. He told me that his grandfather was Grigori Benenson, the richest and most powerful Jew in St Petersburg before being brought low by the Revolution. Subsequently, a fiend of a woman had thrown acid at his face, scarring him for life. Could all that really be true? Yes, every word. Ousted from control of the Lena gold-fields, the family had mounted a lawsuit against Barings for something like £20 million. Meanwhile Peter's mother, Flora, who'd previously never lifted a finger, had persuaded Marks and Spencer to make her their Welfare Director, where she proved brilliantly innovative.

(Later, at Eton, Peter would be known as 'Solomon-Benenson', later still as 'Benenson'. In that guise he would help found Amnesty International, a subsequent career no less original than his mother's – or indeed his grandfather's.)

There were also peers to dislike. We named one boy 'Signor Pomposo'. He was Julian Amery, whose father had been a Cabinet minister. In school debates, he was always leaping to his feet, pontificating. At the age of ten his future career was clearly mapped out. Some twenty years later he'd become a Member of Parliament, and later still a leading figure in the Monday Club.*

Although I knew nothing of them at the time, fearful things were happening back at home, things which would alter our lives completely. My mother let the ball drop when she took me out for lunch at my great-aunts' house. Fanny and Ethel lived in Norham Gardens, near the University Parks. We were eating delicious fishcakes prepared by their cook, Mrs Nott. Fanny handed me a cut-glass jug of home-made lemon barley-water, removing its cover of gauze weighted down with coloured

---

* The Monday Club was formed in the sixties by Conservative politicians, in response to the Conservative government veering too far to the left (in the eyes of the club's members). It is most famous for its stance against non-white immigration to Britain.

beads as she did so. I was pouring myself a glass when my mother said, 'Of course I dismissed that woman at once, but by then it was too late!'

'What woman?' I asked innocently.

Looks were exchanged all round. Evidently something was up.

'Oh well, I suppose he has to know eventually,' my mother went on. 'I mean Miss Oxley, who else?'

'You mean TOCKY?' I asked in bewilderment and dawning despair. My use of the childish name drew furious glances. Too late, I realised my mistake, biting back tears whilst having to go on pouring out the barley-water – quite a feat, and rather beyond me as it happened. Over the highly polished table spread a pool needing to be mopped immediately. In the confusion, my own emotional upset went unremarked. But what a storm of emotion it was! I had adored Tocky. So, apparently, had my father, though not as much as me, I felt sure. He'd run off with her and left my mother and his children behind.

I went back to Summer Fields and told Matron that I'd overeaten (plausible) and might throw up. I was hastily led into the 'sick-room', given a kidney-shaped bowl and left to nauseate alone. Once on my own I burst into tears and wept uncontrollably, stimulating myself to fresh outbursts by muttering the word 'Tocky' whenever sobs flagged. It wasn't him that I missed; it was her.

I was found by the under-matron, who sat on the bed and told me about Mallory and Irvine climbing Mount Everest back in '24. Why her story should have been so comforting I had no idea, but comforting it was. So much so that in future moments of great stress I would sometimes revert to a reverie of mountaineering, my mind losing itself in an imaginary, but intense, physical effort on sunlit, snowy slopes.

Later, in a furious show of siding with my mother, I wrote to my father, demanding to know why he'd run away with a woman who smelt of fish. It was a thing which I had never noticed about Tocky, but I'd heard my mother say so. To increase the drama, I put that little gem on a postcard. I can't imagine what my father made of it, since my previous letter to him had blurs on the writing-paper caused by tears at the thought of never seeing Miss Oxley again. Quite possibly, he didn't care. He seemed content to wash his hands of us three children, never asking the court for 'access', whilst off he went to Italy with his Evelyn, touring for months and months on end in a top-down Lancia.

———

3

What effect my father running off with the governess had on me, I couldn't tell – everything seemed so odd, it was impossible to pick out one aspect on which to concentrate. I developed an extraordinary hatred of mud and dirt, which led to me disliking the muddiest and dirtiest game of all, rugger – which in later life, too old to play, I would love to watch. So intense was my strange loathing that during the rugger term each year thereafter I managed to work myself up enough to affect my health. A soaring temperature guaranteed that such psychosomatic whimsies had to be taken seriously. Off I would be pushed to the 'San' (known as 'Newton') in an ancient sedan chair lined with buttoned red leather fraying at the edges. It was almost worthwhile being a 'non-walking' case in order to be eligible for a ride in it.

During those weeks of illness I was also given a jigsaw puzzle of the Flying Scotsman, which had far too many same-shaped bits. I remember Great-Aunt Fanny came to visit and swooped on a gap which had eluded my keenest endeavours, filling it with pieces plucked from the table as adroitly as a hen pecking at grains of corn.

For some children, the demise of their parents' marriage might have an adverse effect on their education, but overall it only served to spur me on. Thanks to Tocky's tuition, when I'd started Summer Fields I'd had such a head start over other boys my age that I was moved up twice in the first term. Then my progress had slowed and the teachers started to write me off as an inattentive idler. Perhaps remarkably, all of my teachers were nice, especially the two sisters known as 'The Miss Hills', Miss Hill *ma* and Miss Hill *mi*, who took the two lower forms. Both taught the piano, both sang in the Bach Choir. Miss Hill *ma*, formidably plain, was the more dominant, Miss Hill *mi* the sweeter. They acted as female buffers between the unfamiliarity of being in a class at all and a full exposure to the nearly-all-male school life. As soon as a boy felt sure enough of himself to try and bully Miss Hill *mi*, he was on his way. When he dared challenge Miss Hill *ma*, he'd arrived.

The only exception within the nice ranks was Geoffrey Bolton, nick-named 'Boltosh', whose temper, we were told, had to be excused on account of shell-shock. When roused, he would gobble like a turkey. For a long time I managed at least to keep on the right side of the ogre, eventually falling from grace in a blaze of publicity over the self-marking of a Latin lesson. Each boy in the small class was supposed to say exactly how many things he'd got wrong. When it came to my turn, I admit-ted to eight.

'EIGHT?' demanded Boltosh incredulously. 'Only eight mistakes ... OHHHH, WHAT a lie!' He flung a pencil at me, which didn't score a hit; but absolutely on target was the undeniable fact that my mistakes must have numbered at least twelve.

Alas! his roar had been like a line of blank verse, incantatory, infinitely copyable. To my extreme dismay it was taken up by other boys and shouted back at me next day. Some seniors conceived the mischievous idea of 'con-vening a court' in a changing-pavilion in order to 'try' me. It would have been highly unpleasant, but for two factors: I'd previously sucked up to two of the strongest boys in the school, because I admired them; and another, the all-but head boy called Harland, was bound to be on my side because we knew each other during the hols.

Proceedings were cut short by the school bell and I was delighted when one older boy came up to me immediately afterwards, saying, 'It must have been perfectly dreadful to be in your shoes!' – a phrase with lovely overtones of good usage. He was Timothy Bowes-Lyon, the future Queen Elizabeth II's cousin, with a large head and excellent manners, but so slow in the uptake that he was considered simple. ['He's a royal godson!' I was informed, as if that explained everything.] I'd liked him before; I doted on him thereafter.*

---

* Roddy disclosed more about Bowes-Lyon later in the original memoirs: 'As a boy, he couldn't have been more delightful to the pariah of the moment. When I learnt what fate befell him I regretted even more strongly that he'd been removed from Summer Fields; for had I been in touch with him from boyhood on, I might have helped. He was eventually sent to Stowe, at that time bracketed with Bryanston by being thought of as a 'dustbin', taking boys who couldn't pass the entrance exams into stricter public schools. Then drink did its worst; and matters weren't improved when he became the 14th Earl of Strathmore in 1949. The slide downhill continuing, he fetched up in a drying-out clinic where he met a barman's daughter, a nurse who became his wife. Had she given birth to a boy after Timothy's death, the child would have been the 15th Earl; but it was a girl, who lived no longer than a few weeks. Eight years later, as if to complete the unhappy story, the widowed – and from that day childless – mother died by her own hand. Poor, polite Bowes-Lyon!'

Yet Boltosh couldn't keep me down and, interestingly, my father's appalling fall from grace kicked me into action. I began working, really working, to such an extent my teachers agreed I might have a chance of gaining the one thing Summer Fields prized above rubies: a scholarship to Eton.

In June 1934, I was one of a select few to be sent, with others from schools throughout England, to sit for one of the fourteen or so Eton scholarships yearly on offer. We stayed at the White Hart in Windsor and sat a test in the blue-carpeted neo-classic School Hall before being interviewed by a viva voce board. It was terrifying to be confronted by such elderly faces, but their questions were calculated to cause no further alarm. Their last question to me was about the books I liked to read.

'Anything from Edgar Wallace to the Bible,' I piped up.

'In that order?' one of them asked.

'Yes, sir, in that order,' I said, fearful in case I'd been too bold, awarding only second place to the sacred. But it made them laugh.

We had time to make copies of our papers for later scrutiny by Boltosh. After studying mine, he wasn't particularly encouraging, saying that my chances were no more than 'fair'. We were allowed to go home after our gruelling ordeal, to await results. All the greater was my surprise in mid-June when my mother triumphantly read out a telegram – from the bully himself – which went:

CONGRATULATIONS! RODDY HAS WON
6th SCHOLARSHIP.

The effect was instantaneous: I walked on air, heart thumping, mouth dry, retching with excitement. No hour in my life had been as fine as this and the day was mine, all mine; I could do what I liked, even to the extent of gorging on any number of scoops of ice-cream, actually made with real cream, from the Worth Farm Dairy in Swanage. Doubly welcome, not so much because sixth place went one better than my beloved grandfather's seventh, but because it was two better than my Uncle Dick's eighth.

Uncle Dick, my mother's brother, had never liked me, which seemed to originate from him taking personal offence (as did my grandmother, Maud) over my dislike for riding and hunting. My grandfather Walter, whom I adored, was a Master of Foxhounds of the Southwold Hunt so to them it was a slight that I didn't want to take part, even though the truth was his involvement was the sole mitigating factor. I idolised my grandfather and was tormented by having to make a stand against his most cherished sport. But I couldn't enjoy it. On the day of my debut two foxes were chased and killed, one of the masks being awarded to me so that I could be officially 'blooded'. Eager fingers snatched the head of a fox from hounds leaping and baying in a frenzy of excitement. Blood was carefully smeared on my face, using the fox's brush, whilst avuncular old hunt followers dwelt on the importance of never washing it off, but letting it fade naturally away. It was then that I realised beyond all doubt that this was not for me and never could be. Similarly, I couldn't stand to shoot, even though I'd inherited my father's straight eye. It wasn't the killing I couldn't bear – I would willingly shoot any number of birds and rabbits for the pot – it was the way people behaved whilst on a shoot, the organising of it in the name of sport, which I found so jarring. The prevailing heartiness of the day guaranteed that I would feel out of things, the only really enjoyable feature being the shooting lunch, sometimes out of doors, more often in a room on a tenant's farm. Delicious; and even better for grown-ups, who had drink to stimulate their appetites.

Sadly, throwing myself into the eating wasn't enough for my Uncle Dick, so securing the Eton scholarship was viewed as potential reparations for my bloodsport shortcomings.* My sister Genissa sent a letter to my mother from Malvern with regards to the news (she was at St James's† in Worcestershire where she would eventually become Head Girl): 'It is too, too wonderful of Roddy he really has done frightfully well, and such a sell to Uncle Dick, thank heavens!!!'

The icing on the cake was when Boltosh magnanimously admitted: 'I feel that my first duty is to apologise for casting doubts on Roddy's ability to rise to an occasion.' But then he had to go and spoil it by adding: 'There is one thing which he MUST learn before he goes to Eton, and that is to be more dependable. At the moment he is, with one exception, the last boy in fifth form I would choose to do a job of any sort for me – not because I doubt his willingness or his ultimate ability to do it, but simply because he does not seem able to look after himself or to think what he has got to do, where he has got to do it and what he needs to help him do it . . .' For such a damaging opinion my

---

* It was important to Roddy's family that Dick liked Roddy because Dick and his wife Susan had no children, so Roddy – as his only nephew – was his natural heir.

† The school still exists, now as Malvern St James's.

mother never forgave him: it was too close to echoing what my uncle thought of me.

Beastly, BEASTLY Boltosh! I thought, working myself up into a frenzy of indignation. *If it's the last thing I do, I'll prove him wrong!*

And so my days at Summer Fields came to an end. There was still fun to be had. I remember a distant cousin of mine, Henry Thurrold, pointing out a passage from the Old Testament referring to men pissing against a wall. To my exceeding delight, I soon found an even more startling reference to that supposedly shocking function in 2 Kings, Chapter 18, verse 27: 'But Rab-shakeh said unto them, Hath my master sent me to thy master, and to thee, to speak these words? Hath he not sent me to the men which sit on the wall, that they may eat their own dung and drink their own piss with you?'

Happy days indeed when such Biblical admonitions seemed the height of naughtiness!

We would eventually discover that the Lord God of Hosts had far worse in the way of punishments up His sleeve for offences we were too young to know anything about. The 'sin' of Onan had already become familiar at second-hand, when a couple of years before a senior called Kay obliged with a demonstration of exactly what the Bible so graphically described, there before our very eyes.* Unable to follow suit, we weren't entirely sure what the fuss was about. When we played with ourselves, nothing happened except for an erection and a lovely tingle; never this white stuff to show for it. But with regard to the Cities of the Plain,† the first time that we realised what all those men had been up to was when Mr Williams gave us his 'Leaving Lecture', which, under pain of punishment, we were forbidden to divulge to our juniors.

---

* Onan's sin was 'spilling his seed'. He features in Genesis in the Bible. His father Judah told him to sleep with his sister-in-law, Tamar, as her husband, Onan's elder brother, had died. Onan didn't want Tamar to bear his children because they wouldn't be considered his descendants, so when he had sex with her he withdrew before ejaculating. God killed him in punishment – although it is sometimes argued that the punishment was for disobeying his father rather than 'wasting' his semen.

† The Cities of the Plain refers to five cities mentioned throughout the Bible (and other religious texts), which included Sodom and Gomorrah, places which in modern times became negatively synonymous with homosexuality. God destroyed the cities with brimstone and fire after some men of Sodom asked Lot to hand over his male guests (who were actually angels) so they could 'know them'. Lot offered the men his virgin daughters instead, but the men refused. Lot was rescued by the angels and told to leave with his family and not look back; his wife did, and was turned into a pillar of salt.

His strictures included not just THOSE MEN, but Lot's delightful daughters, too. Disgraceful! We came away with the conviction that there was something nasty about sex, taking place, as it evidently did, far too close to other, genuinely unclean functions. Was the aim to put us off indulging in such practices until we were too grown-up to care? If so, it was a very English way of going about things. And a complete failure, of course.

4

My father's desertion continued to cause me personally very little grief. I missed our chauffeur more than him, having conceived a passion for uniforms provided that they were worn by the right person.

Some other aspects of the divorce provided unexpected benefits. My father really had lost all his money. He had to be rescued by his thrice-widowed mother, my grandmother Maya, who was prepared to allow him £550 a year (a sum much larger than it sounds today, but nothing compared with the £10,000 p.a. he'd once enjoyed). But to promote the divorce, she settled a sum on us three children amounting to £900 p.a. which meant we were now better off. Maya's lawyers were the trustees and so they decided when and what for we received anything, but, subject to their whims, I had some control of my own purse-strings for the first time ever. In practice, at that moment, it meant little; but the theory was a delight.

Whilst my father would later abandon dearest Tocky for Beni, the daughter of one of the trustees no less (and with whom he had two girls, Sarah and Jane), I took the continued celibacy of my mother for granted. She often invited my sympathy, referring to Miss Oxley as 'a servant in my pay', as though that made betrayal worse. I failed to see why. I thought she was really rather lucky to have got rid of such a quick-tempered – and newly poor – husband.

I was too young and ignorant to understand how galling it must have been for her, deserted by the one and only man in her life. She told us that she might be getting an offer of marriage from a middle-aged Naval bachelor called Hume; but as he was a bore of bores, we didn't think she could be serious. Rather more on the cards was Reggie Boothby, a King's Messenger who owned a fine Georgian house near Spilsby; but he had only one eye and I had the distinct impression that he was fonder of me than of her. In fact, he married an heiress and produced the required children before running off to Scandinavia to live on a boat with another man – so I may have been right.

My mother would have said yes to a godfather of mine, Lord Arthur Woodbridge, had he thought of asking her; but he didn't, having acquired a satisfactory mistress to whom 'nobody was ever introduced'. His tobacco factory for Churchman's cigarettes was in Ipswich, and he lived in a vast and luxurious – but fake – house called Abbey Oaks, not all that far away. It was his generous habit to take lady friends shopping and buy them something they fancied. He once gave my mother a very pleasing set of Victorian dining-chairs, as the result of a visit to Woodhall Spa.

And so life continued. My mother didn't like Kingston House, but true to form, I preferred it to the far grander Rempstone Hall we'd lived in before (similarly, I was the only one in our family to prefer the darker Victorian Brantham Court to the imposing Georgian Well Vale). Kingston House was built of grey Purbeck stone, splendidly castellated, and it had the most wonderful view not only of the ruins of Corfe Castle but of wide swathes of heath beyond, stretching as far as Poole Harbour.

It had been designed in the late nineteenth century by the Earl of Eldon's pet architect, Street, as the new vicarage to go with a new church a few yards further down the hill. I could never see why Eldon thought that a village as small as Kingston could do with a second church, but that was his affair. Since the vicar was content with the old vicarage near the old church, we were the ones to benefit. We were tenants of Eldon's son, Sir Ernest Scott, who lived at Encombe, a huge and sprawling grey Georgian house tucked into the encircling hollow bowl of land between Swyre Head and St Aldhelm's Head, approached through thick deciduous woods.

Ernest Scott – 'Ernie' as we called him – gave us permission to wander all over his estate, which included not having to pay 6d at two check-points. Ernie was a small man with thin hands, eccentric in spite of having been in the Diplomatic Service where, I would have thought, all eccentricity might have been ironed out. Not so. He was obsessed with a desire for economy. To avoid using his car he would bicycle for miles, even in full evening dress, black patent-leather shoes in a basket on the handlebars.

We could bathe, if we so wished, in Freshwater Bay below Encombe, where a small waterfall trickled over grey-black cliffs of Kimmeridge clay to join the natural breakwaters of more grey-black shale leading out to sea. It was a beautiful place for picnics; you reached it along woodland paths where wild garlic grew in such profusion that when trodden on it scented all the surrounding air. Those deserted woods, from the very beginning, were marvellously exciting and became much more so with the approach of adolescence. If I had time – when coming back from using Ernie's squash courts – I would leave the track and bounce on my bicycle over rough ground, strewn with shrubs, to a thicket where I could remain unseen, even by a stranger approaching to within a few yards. Once there, I would throw off all my clothes at top speed, as if to prepare for a ritual. Naked, I would moon about and, if the ground were not too sodden, lie down amongst green shoots of wild garlic in sheer joie de vivre.

I thought my experiences unique; and of course I was wrong, although it took several years before I found out that any number of boys had once wanted to behave as I'd behaved, also thinking themselves unique. The difference was, they usually hadn't dared indulge: through lack of opportunity; for fear of being caught; even from prudery too deeply engrained to be lightly cast aside. Thank goodness for Encombe woods.

5

All teenage boys are ripe for rebellion given the right conditions; my parents' divorce was quite possibly a seed, and Eton was definitely the soil.

Eton was as grand as any Oxbridge college – or rather, as it's so large, a good portion of either one of the universities – and no wonder: it was established by Henry VI in the fifteenth century as a way to enable poor, clever children to go to Cambridge. Over time, children with parents who could pay were allowed to attend, until they outnumbered everyone else. Those on a King's Scholarship, as I was, were considered to be the poor, clever children. We were 'Collegers' owing to the fact the scholars were originally housed in College whilst the fee-paying students paid to stay in town; this made us 'Tugs', short for 'Togati' ('the gowned'), and we enjoyed many traditional privileges. As the school owed its founding to our forerunners so we occupied much of the ancient parts. We walked daily across the expanse of School Yard, under Lupton's Tower – the redbrick clocktower grander even than the entrance to Hampton Court Palace – through Cloisters and up well-worn steps into Hall, there to sit on benches at long tables of solid oak. On our way we would pass a pump, with a silver cup attached to it by a chain, from which we could drink deep draughts of ice-cold water. (After my time, the cup was stolen and the well condemned as a hazard to health, although generation after generation of poor scholars had cheerfully used it without ill effect.)

In antique living quarters, new arrivals were put into a 'chamber' divided into 'stalls', door-less but with heavy green baize curtains. At the centre of the chamber there was a space with a fireplace of ample proportions and a table deeply scored with lines and dents – public space, cheek by jowl with the cubicles. Although a cubicle was no substitute for a room of one's own, an unwelcome intruder could be banished by the tradition of calling out 'STALL CURTAINS!' three times. We were looked after by a maid, Grace, and an old man called George, who grumpily woke us each morning and later made our beds.

We Tugs wore a black gown which separated us from other boys in the school (known as Oppidans, so called because originally their lot were not housed in College but paid to live in town, and *oppidum* is a Latin word for town). It might have been a badge of honour. It wasn't. It simply indicated that we were 'too keen', unathletic 'swots' (a word which didn't form part of the school's idiosyncratic vocabulary). We were assumed to be poor, not that it mattered greatly. Money, as such, played a very small part in Eton life. Pocket money was what counted and poorer parents, as a rule, were more prodigal than the richer ones. Thanks to the divorce settlement, I was already responsible for arranging my own finances; in which way I was luckier than other boys, who had all that done for them. The worst thing about being a Tug was that black gown, which created an instantly identifiable minority. Good practice for some aspects of later life, perhaps, but who wanted a preview?

I quickly forgot my promise to prove Boltosh wrong. By the end of my first 'half' – as terms were known at Eton – I was faced with a truly dreadful situation. At 'Trials' (exams), marks for all subjects were lumped together, the total being used to decide each scholar's place on the ladder. As I was rotten at maths and could only solve the simplest algebraic problem by learning whole pages of equations by heart, I soon realised that I was done for. However hard I worked I could never come near the top again. No luck in games either. I could kick a nifty football, but Eton didn't go in for soccer, preferring its own 'Field Game', a hybrid unknown to the outside world. Neither squash nor tennis, which were my games, carried high prestige.

And so I couldn't compete at work, nor at their idiosyncratic play; and I couldn't retire to lick my wounds in private because there was no real privacy. My reaction was to change from being docile and hard-working into an idle rebel. It reached a point where grown-ups began getting seriously concerned. They tried one so-called remedy after another. Sternness: 'If you don't conform, you'll be beaten.' Understanding: 'We know what it's like for a growing boy; you're just at the awkward stage.' Indifference: 'If you're determined to go to the Devil, we'll have to wash our hands of you!' None of those techniques of adult desperation worked, of course.

Luckily, there were a few favourable outside influences. My beloved grandfather sent a brace of pheasants to our learned Provost, Monty James, his school contemporary. The following Sunday the great man, writer of superb ghost-stories, who was said to be able to read a book at the rate of turning over a page, asked me to a delicious full English breakfast in his comfortable lodgings. I prattled away, sixteen to the dozen, and he repeated the invitation several times each 'half'.

As I could impress (some) grown-ups, given the right opportunity, what about having a go at impressing older boys who, owing especially to the system of 'fagging', held all of the power? We weren't allowed to mingle with boys more than one 'election' higher, i.e. senior by more than a year, but 'Love Will Find a Way', theme song from the operetta *The Maid of the Mountains*, was echoed in many a heart. Love certainly would find a way for someone used to hearing that his fair curls were 'wasted on a boy'. I planned to open the campaign by ingratiating myself with anyone who might possess (or come to possess) power over me.

With most, I failed, but others responded in what I was naive enough to think was a strange way: they blushed; they stammered; one put his arms around me; another manfully gripped my shoulders. Over such enthusiasts I acquired an instant, effortless mastery – rather exciting. So this was love? How little I'd known about it before! It seemed that everyone not positively hideous was up to similar pranks, the key word being 'worship'.

'You WORship him!' one little horror would shout at another.

Or, more thrillingly: 'He worships YOU!'

Worship could take the oddest forms: sometimes the worshipper did no more than gaze adoringly from afar, at pains to avoid the slightest contact; sometimes with a directly opposite effect, by inflicting punishment on the grounds that there must be 'no favouritism'. [I saw through that excuse straight away, even before reading Freud's *Totem and Taboo*, from which I learned that people's apparent motives were seldom their true ones – a startling theory which, in a sense, changed my life.]

I was a late developer, which had caused me much anxiety in the past. When my body, to my relief, started going the way of all schoolboy bodies, I learnt what made other boys blush and grope. I was soon at it too, though in a mawkish sort of way, not quite sure what I was supposed to do. For instance, Billy Ednam* begged me to stand absolutely still against a wall, facing him. Towering above me, trousers down, wriggling like an eel, he would be gripped by a paroxysm of sex, after which he'd abruptly leave the room, without a word; whereas John Tweedie did much more, with grunts of delight and without guilt-ridden after-effects. I soon learnt that semen had a smell as individual as BO. It had never occurred to me before, having never experienced enough of it to make comparisons.

Tweedie bought gramophone records for me, 'When My Dream Boat Comes Home' being a particular favourite. If we met in Rowlands, the school shop, I'd be stood waffles and 'strawberry messes' – as many as I could wolf down.

Then there was an older boy called Chadwick who wished me to 'experiment' (as he put it) with the end of an umbrella – a mystifying procedure which ended with the ferrule breaking through the seam of his tightly stretched trousers, drawing blood. He yelped, and for the next few days went about looking pensive before suggesting a repeat performance, to which I turned a deaf ear. Avoiding pain, not inflicting it, was my aim.

---

* Later Viscount Ednam, the 4th Earl of Dudley.

6

Life at Eton was never dull. In summer, when not rowing as 'Wet-bobs' or playing cricket as 'Dry-bobs', we could frequent the Music or the Drawing Schools, or go for long walks through Windsor. Few worked seriously except for the Tugs, and Tugs (like monks in a secular world) made up for the prevailing spirit of indolence by working overtime. How lucky I was to be a Tug! I wish I'd thought so then.

One of my favoured pursuits was considering religion, as I was at the right age to be confirmed. By default that meant Church of England. My family inclinations were towards middle-of-the-road Anglicanism. Because of this, I confessed to a fondness for 'High' practices, complete with clouds of incense. I liked to be different. One of my strongest and purest differing attitudes to my family was on the subject of war: I'd thought about it seriously and come to the conclusion that it was wrong. In spite of this, I joined the Corps, as a good contingent of Eton boys did, succumbing to pressure from my grandmother, and to some extent from my mother, both of them anxious to prove to Uncle Dick that there was stern stuff in me. More reflection led me to decide that I should never have listened to advice so blatantly against the grain of my nature, so I soon resigned from the Corps and joined the Peace Pledge Union. Becoming a pacifist caused the most extraordinary upset which seemed to anger almost everyone, both at school and at home, so to that extent it was a triumph of self-assertion.

My chase for Catholicism brought me into touch with the school's Reverend Robin Hudson, an added inducement being that his sister had married the Duke of Richmond. The Rev., I was astonished to find, promptly developed a crush on me, even going so far as to take me up to London one evening, allowing me to select which show we'd see. I chose the Empire, Shepherd's Bush, chiefly in order to hear 'The Two Leslies' singing 'Ain't it grand, to be bloomin' well dead!' They made a lower-class funeral sound so mournfully comic that I could almost agree with them. The Rev. was appalled by my lack of taste, for which reason

(I supposed) he gradually dropped me from his affections. But it may really have been because, little prude that I was in spite of all my own transgressions, I edged away from the hand reaching out to pat my knee.

My other experiences with clergymen were of a completely different kind. Spurred on by my distant cousin Henry, the one from Summer Fields, also at Eton, I wrote to all the reverends with titles, just for the fun of seeing how they'd reply to my supposedly serious request for details of local ghost-stories. Many answered, some at great length.

Canon Antony Deane, living, on account of his official post, actually within the walls of Windsor Castle, was another distant cousin, so of course he was one of my priestly targets for Sunday tea when there was nothing more interesting to do.

Other places to take tea included the fashionable Cockpit, or the less fashionable Nell Gwyn up near the Castle, where 'ladies' served cream teas on fine ironstone crockery. At Nell Gwyn's I met Marlene Dietrich. She looked as singular as she did on her posters: frizzed blonde hair, high arched eyebrows, deep eyelids and obvious cheekbones. I stared at her, eyes bulging, then strolled over to talk, without asking for an autograph. She seemed to enjoy it; and perhaps she did. An Eton boy was a scalp, of a sort – she wasn't to know that I was only an unimportant Tug.

I welcomed the rare – very rare – occasions when my father turned up in the open Lancia with my once-beloved Tocky, now his somewhat embarrassed Evelyn, before he left her for Beni. We would drive out somewhere and have whatever meal the occasion demanded. He seemed like an amiable stranger, good for a tip if for nothing else. I can't remember ever asking him about his wonderful pre-war expeditions. Perhaps they wouldn't have interested my self-centred self at that time. I was more concerned with the way in which I had suddenly shot up (apparently after being stung by a wasp at the back of my neck) nearly nine inches in a year.

School memories can be boring for those not sharing them, a stricture applying equally to mine. However, there are a few more which deserve a mention. I made friends with Derek Beecham, close relation of the famous conductor Sir Thomas. Together we composed popular songs – music by him, lyrics by me. We frequented Chloe's, in the High Street, where the large (and partly moustachioed) proprietress let us thump out tunes upstairs on an upright piano and didn't mind if we smoked. We were amazed when she was placed out of bounds, not on that account but because boys were said to have been encouraged to indulge in 'spiritual experiences amongst other things' on her premises. Just what was one, and, even more, what was the other, we wondered? To us she'd been a motherly soul with a fine selection of home-made cakes, never once inviting us to any other kind of séance.

Apropos of smoking, I didn't inhale, but was hooked all the same. I would buy by weight a selection of fat and thin cigarettes and would visit an antique shop not far from Chloe's which had the name 'DAISY' in flowing script above the door, relic of a former existence as a tea-shop. The ancient proprietor would let me light up as we sat at the back of his shop, allowing plenty of time to stub out an end on the (rare) occasions when a customer wandered in. The old man loved to impart his expertise, in which way I learnt about verge watches, Baxter prints and other fascinating things.

Eventually I did inhale, after which I really became addicted. The new necessity led me into folly, though not of a sort which I ever could have imagined; it provided the worst example of a Great Betrayal since my father's desertion. Stephen Spring-Rice, two elections my senior, occupied 'Upper Tower', a room having direct window-access to the college roof. He showed fondness towards me. I knew the signs, and as proof he invited me to climb out and join him in lighting up, out of sight (and smell) of the rest of the world – which I did gladly. But one evening, on going to his room and finding no one there, I clambered out on my own and was duly discovered by him, up to our second most favourite pastime. To my complete bewilderment, he suddenly turned 'pi', saying that he'd have to report me – WHICH HE DID. I was given a wigging by the Master-in-College, then a beating by a member of our 'Library', yet Spring-Rice escaped scot-free!

On coming to my room when I was still smarting from the cane, he asked anxiously, 'You didn't mention me smoking, did you, Roddy?'

'Of course not, Stephen. I'm not a sneak like you!'

He expressed surprise when I refused to have anything further to do with him from then on.

It was not the only time I was told off for something; indeed my sole extenuating feat whilst I was at Eton – winning the Loder Prize for Declamation (an award for reading from memory) – was rather obscured by all the hoo-ha I created when I painted my 'room'.

Somehow I was never caught over weekend trips. Bicycles provided a standard means of getting away from school, but there were other methods for the ingenious. Julian Peck, nephew of Monsignor Ronnie Knox (author and Catholic priest), and I cadged lifts to Ascot, our goal not being the racecourse but the hotel Berystede, where we'd have a leisurely lunch with a bottle of Niersteiner and tiny glasses of Green Chartreuse to follow. Round about the time of the coronation of King George VI, the patriotic management flew a number of Union Flags, one of which I took to the top of the tallest evergreen, securing it firmly with gardening twine. For years it remained in place, a magnet attracting me back to the Berystede to see if it were still defiantly fluttering. Until one day, without explanation, it was to be seen no more.

'Wet-bobs' and 'Dry-bobs' had their special days of glory. We were allowed out of school to go to Henley for the Regatta and to Lord's for the Eton and Harrow match. Dry-bobs and Wet-bobs were also the star performers on the 4th of June, Founder's Day, when visitors strolled about on Agar's Plough and Upper Sixpenny, pretending to watch cricket but actually meeting and greeting old friends before going to the river to see the boats, interspersed with picnics from cars parked on the field facing the Fives courts called Lower Sixpenny.

Before six o'clock struck there would be a concerted rush to School Yard for 'Absence' to be read out, when boys had to answer to their names being called. Those who'd missed seeing people they'd hoped were looking for them might surface in a flurry of overheated fathers, mothers and sisters, introducing and being introduced. It brought the boys back under the Masters' control, if only temporarily, after which they might disperse into nearby hotels such as the Bridge.

The next public show would be a floodlit Procession of Boats best seen from a bank opposite and beyond Fellows' Eyot, the whole area being enclosed within a fence, with admission by a limited number of tickets only. Experience taught us that the only way to get 'front row' seats on the river bank was to arrive really early, complete with rugs and picnic-basket, then occupy the time with eating and drinking. There followed an interlude, midge-resonant, before darkness began to fall. Then at last a first boat would heave into sight; then another, and another. The crews weren't in their usual whites, but in coats splendidly frogged, wearing straw boaters entwined (traditionally by their girl-friends) with garlands – a scene surpassing anything from *HMS Pinafore*. As the young men came into view, they obeyed their cox's orders to stand up by numbers. They'd rise, two by two, oars held upright, wobbling as the last oars left the water. Gracefully they would doff hats, replace them, then let their oars smack the water to allow them to sit down, two by two, before rowing away from the floodlights into the enveloping darkness. It might happen that a wobble would become too extreme and a boat rock from side to side, even to 'swamp', to a chorus of boos and cheers from the bank.

The procession was officially ended by *Monarch*, a boat with a crew of ten instead of the usual eight, inexpertly manned by an ex officio crew including the Captain of the School (always a Tug), the Captain of the Oppidans and other worthies who might (or might not) know one end of an oar from another. In *Monarch* they were so careful to maintain their dignity that swamping was unheard of.

The procession over, the crowds would grow restive, small groups sitting on the grass starting to sing 'WHY are we WAIting?' Champagne corks, aimed by those who'd brought bottles with them, popped and flew into the river. Other rival songs might start up and peter out ... until at last a *THUDDD!* sounded from across the water, followed by a *WHOOOOSH!* as a first rocket soared into the sky.

On the opposite bank men could be seen purposefully trotting about with tapers, lighting this or that pre-planted piece: waterfalls of coloured fire pouring into the river, emitting screeches, bangs, or both; Catherine wheels revolving, hissing; fiery novelties leaping and howling against a background of lesser rockets, released in clumps. And so it would go on until suddenly an obviously superior rocket would be heard thumping into the sky, on its own, bursting high above the trees, spraying elaborate multi-trails of stars. Full of hope, someone in the crowd would shout: '*ONE!*'

Another rocket more spectacular than the first, a bang, then a second bang creating not one but two sprays of stars ... and the gang who'd shouted '*ONE!*' would be joined by others shouting '*TWO!*', news spreading through the crowd eager to greet a third with a roar of '*THREE!*' A four-burster, a five-burster, and the crowd would be in ecstasies, hoping against hope for a six-fold explosion, which was rare, because it was so expensive. A seven-burster, rarest of all, was reserved for an ultra-special occasion only.

As the final shout died away, there would come a fizzling splutter from a set-piece displaying an immense FLOREAT ETONA and another splutter from an equally huge representation of exploding royalty. The show being at an end, an addictive aroma of spent cartridges would drift from the bank opposite, where red and green flares, cunningly set behind bushes, continued to illuminate a scene of packing-up. A crowd united in contentment would slowly gather up rugs and picnic things and plod towards the entrance-gate, showing none of the urgency which had characterised their stampede on arrival.

Could anything have been more precisely satisfying than such a spectacle from start to finish: in the background the dark red floodlit towers of College, and a foreground of fireworks reflected double in the river? Many thought of it as the greatest show on earth; so many extraordinary parts going to make a unique whole.

———

7

On board TSS *Letitia* in 1938, having joined at Toulon in the French Riviera and with the first stop of Messina in Sicily behind us, my mother, sisters and I listened to a talk on the part played by General Franco in the Spanish Civil War. Halfway through, a young woman with fair hair and a round face stood up and defiantly announced, 'I want to marry Adolf Hitler.'

The thirties had been rolling by, and with it history, gathering pace and size it seemed, or at least in hindsight. The young woman in question was Unity Mitford, on board with her mother (who seldom emerged from her stateroom) and two of her infamous six sisters. Ten years later, Unity would die as a result of an illness inflicted when she tried to kill herself after war broke out between her beloved Germany and England.* One of the other Mitford sisters, Diana, married Oswald Mosley, leader of the British Union of Fascists. Fascism, not just in Germany, experienced something of a heyday in the thirties. I remember an awful old man in green tweeds and a pork-pie hat was often to be seen in Eton High Street, selling copies of *The Blackshirt*, which many of us bought out of curiosity – it contained instructions

---

* The official cause of death, in May 1948, was meningitis caused by the bullet that remained lodged in her head after the suicide attempt.

to take to the streets in procession, waving placards and giving the Nazi salute, which seemed to me a daft way of carrying on purely to annoy one's elders.

That summer, delightful cruise around the Hellenic sites complete, we stayed with Granny Rawnsley at Claxby Hall in Lincolnshire. My dear grandfather, Walter, had died whilst we were away on TSS *Letitia* two years previously in 1936. I was devastated. Unlike most grown-ups, he'd always been patient with me, his coaching helping towards my better scholarship, his love and regard for the awkward boy that I was contributing no end to improve my shaky self-esteem. We heard that in his last ramblings he claimed to have seen his brother, John the farmer, coming to fetch him. John had died not long before Walter – in a dentist's chair, fatally gassed whilst merely having a tooth extracted.

Afterwards my grandmother Maud, the Rawnsley dowager, removed herself from Well Vale of her own volition, to avoid making her son, my fearsome Uncle Dick, and his coldly elegant wife Susan wait (as she put it) 'for dead men's shoes'. Claxby was Well's dower-house; Dick and Susan had lived in it whilst they waited for Dick to inherit. My grandmother took with her to Claxby the knack of creating the grand-yet-homely atmosphere which had formerly characterised Well, whereas Susan quickly contrived to turn Well into a chilly imitation of what, in her day, had been Claxby. It was a wonderful illustration of what a powerful influence one person can have on a place.

One afternoon some cousins, the Cheales family, came to play tennis with us and they brought with them a German au pair, Budi von Mach, a boy of seventeen, like me. In those days an au pair was simply someone from abroad staying and learning the language, in return for accepting someone back for the same amount of time. There was no question of the guest working his/her fingers to the bone for a pittance, which was what au pair arrangements would involve post-war.

Budi turned out to be a blond bombshell, Teutonic to his fingertips, and on and off the tennis-court various opportunities presented themselves for friendly touching and gripping. In a tiny bathroom behind the room downstairs where we changed there was just him and myself, sponging ourselves down after a final game before tea. The room, smelling of wet mackintoshes, was seldom used for other purposes, but on that day it was filled with a warm aroma of honey carelessly extracted only that morning; we had to tiptoe, laughing, around sticky pools on the lino floor. It was the third week in August, round about my grandmother's birthday, the traditional time when Archer the gardener relieved the bees of their surplus stores.

Budi insisted on me coming to Germany next spring, to his parents' flat in Ulm, on the Danube. Germany at that time was a land of horror for the Jews, and not too well regarded by others, either, who – even so – failed to grasp the true extent of the situation. I knew a certain amount about what had been going on from my old friend Peter Benenson, who was at Eton with me, and in particular from his mother, Flora. She had successfully persuaded a listening Marks and Spencer to provide jobs for large numbers of female German-Jewish refugees. (Another of her impacts on the history of her adopted country was to help unmask the double agent Kim Philby, who was a notorious spy for the Soviet Union.)

But for Flora's concern, refugees would have meant little to me. In common with others, I tended to discount tales of woe recounted in heavily accented, accusatory tones, loaded with self-pity; such an act seemed so un-English. It would come to seem reprehensible, but it was the honest prevailing attitude, as only those alive at that time will remember – and they might prefer to forget.

With Budi in prospect, I ignored the worst aspects of Hitler's regime, as many tourists visiting foreign countries today bury their heads in the sand over the policies of respective rulers. Young Germans were romantic figures, drifting about Europe in ultra-short shorts, super-bronzed and super-fit – the *wandervögel* (although officially the Nazis had outlawed such wholesomeness when they came to power in 1933). To us with our pasty faces, in our flapping, high-waisted 'longs', they were truly fascinating, liberated where we were fettered. Even more intriguing, those tanned demi-gods emerged from a background of notorious post-war decadence, envied by those of us who came from strait-laced homes – which most of us did. I could hardly wait to enter such a promising milieu.

The journey out was a joy. There was I, getting on and off trains and boats on my own, wrestling with a strange language on my own, finally in unfamiliar surroundings on my own. At no time was there a person in authority at hand to check what I did or how I did it. I was finding out what life could be like, away from home and away from school. It was even sweeter than I'd imagined.

Ulm, in southern Germany, on the border with Bavaria, proved to be a picture-postcard place of tall houses topped with orange pointed roofs

almost as tall again, snug around Ulm Minster which boasted a spire
that made it the tallest completed church in the world. It was as if God
had pinched the place between thumb and finger and pulled upwards.

Colonel von Mach and his family were squeezed into a flat heavy
with Biedemeier furniture which had come from a grander home. The
Colonel had married 'beneath him', but had married money. The money
had vanished in the turmoil of the mark's inflation following the Great
War, but he'd struck real gold in his homely wife, for whom children,
cooking and the Church were the principal things in life. In reduced
circumstances she came fully into her own, seldom grumbling except
over such minor matters as the difficulty of obtaining cream (which had
disappeared from the shops when butter was rationed as part of Hitler's
'Guns before Butter!' campaign).

Worse things passed without open comment, discussed with scowls
only when old friends met to drink together. The Colonel disapproved
of the Nazi inanities but was forced to hide his feelings. Informers were
much to be feared, especially informers from within the family group.
A new and alarming spirit was at large, as it had been for years in the
Soviet Union. Children were being encouraged to sneak on parents
showing the slightest sign of deviating from the Party line. The sort of
youth who loved dressing up in uniform and marching about could be
a menace for miles and miles around. Fortunately, the elder von Mach
boy, who at that moment was serving his time in an *arbeitsdienstlager*
(compulsory work-camp), was an 'Earnest Bible Student', a semi-pacifist
organisation much frowned-upon by the authorities. Budi was probably
weak enough to have been tainted by Nazi doctrine, but parental influence over him was strong enough to prevent any such thing.

I was warned about that, with a request that I shouldn't admit to
having been warned, when I asked whether I might be allowed to attend
classes at Budi's school. Go back to school when I didn't have to – was
I mad? No, I had an ulterior motive. I'd gone there to meet Budi one
day and instead of hanging about outside had walked in and been taken
to his classroom, where an English lesson was in progress. The master,
thinking to show off, came out with the classic 'How now, brown cow?',
then asked me to comment on his accent, which was all wrong, though I
had more sense than to tell him so. My tact led to me being asked to give
a short lecture on the pitfalls of English pronunciation, before sitting
down to join the class for the rest of the lesson. As it happened, I was
put next to – squeezed up against – a strongly built lad with Titian-red

hair, short-cropped over a freckled forehead. His name was Werner, and I was much taken with everything about him, especially when I noticed that from his perspiring body wafted a fragrance, entirely natural, of flowers and spices. No more was needed to make me his ardent admirer.

By chance, Werner could do with my help. He wanted to improve himself and, to put it bluntly, he was no intellectual. But he was the school champion at practically every form of sport, which meant that he was highly regarded by the other boys, though pointedly not by the English master, who seemed to enjoy sneering at him for being such a dunce. 'Werner's parents are nobodies!' said Budi, an admission acting as a spur rather than a deterrent to my increasing regard.

When Werner shyly asked 'Will you go walks with me, speakink English?' the stage seemed set by Fate for my contentment. The only fly in the ointment was Werner's exceeding lack of forthcomingness; it was a hard slog to keep a conversation going. By way of compensation, whenever he practised any form of sport we could discuss that.

Our first attempt at swimming together was unforgettable. We didn't go to a pool but to the banks of the Danube, which in Ulm was mud-coloured, not blue. The river flowed at a tremendous rate so the dodge was to jump in, be swept rapidly downstream, and emerge at a distance where there was another bathing-point. It looked *haarsträubend* (hair-raisingly) dangerous, and I was no swimmer, having only with difficulty passed the school test. Werner was determined not to let that stop us. 'I'll look after you,' he promised. 'Dive in!'

I dived, or rather jumped. Mud-coloured water near the bank was flowing more steadily than the current in mid-stream, but it was swirling with some force, which I wasn't used to. Once in, I looked for Werner and to my horror saw him nonchalantly engaged in conversation, hands on hips, with a boy on the bank, whilst I was being rapidly borne along and away. I struggled in vain against the water; my head went under, and when it emerged Werner was nowhere to be seen. Desperately threshing about, I soon realised that he was already no more than a few yards away; then in front, he was such a superb swimmer. The current sent me spinning into his arms. Seldom had I been as thankful for anything as I was for that. I came near to fainting, not from shock but from sheer relief.

Next day, the School Sports Day took place. My hero triumphed in event after event, trotting back to me each time to be praised and patted. I was in continuous transports of delight, even if it took place on a ground so hung with black-and-white swastikas on red backgrounds that it might have been the setting for a Party rally.

All day and all night, soldiers were drilling and marching through the street immediately below my first-floor window. I watched in amazement; they looked so happy, which I should certainly not have been, doing what they were doing. The scent of limes in full blossom hung heavy in the air. Germany in 1939 – militaristic and sure of itself.

Into the room slipped Anni, the von Machs' maid, who brought me a pot of tea each afternoon (good of the family to let me have such an expensive luxury on a regular basis). Finding me standing by the window she moved closer, then closer still, pushing against me, gesturing down the street towards a huge-crated object draped in camouflage-netting. 'Look, look!' she squeaked. '*Dicke Berthe! Dicke Berthe!*' It was the famous gun which during the First World War had caused consternation by lobbing shells into Paris from German lines seventy miles away.

Anni stared at Big Bertha, then at me. She was as transparent as a tropical fish and I had the instant, automatic response of a teenager to a touching hand. A thought flashed through my head: *I'm bound to be a disappointment compared with that massive barrel protruding from its netting!*

But if Anni thought so, she didn't say so. Our innocent little flirtation continued unchecked.

My walks with Werner were doomed all too soon to end, because I was all set to leave the von Machs. One Hans Siemers had come to Ulm to see his old friend, the Colonel. I was told that he was rich, from a family firm and from property in Hamburg. Frau von M. made special efforts to give him the best of everything, including strawberries crushed into sparkling white wine – one of the most delicious drinks in the world.

'Come to Hamburg and stay with us!' said Herr Siemers in an expansive mood after a superb dinner. Naturally I agreed enthusiastically. There was to be one last chance of being with Werner before that: the outdoor festival of *Sonnenuntergang*, when the young would get together to affirm allegiance to the Fatherland. The occasion being a Hitlerjugend ('Ha-yot') celebration, I would have to be smuggled in by Budi, dressed up in their uniform of khaki shorts, khaki shirt and loose tie, so as not to cause comment.

The 'Going Down of the Sun' festival appeared to me to be an up-to-date celebration of a Pagan Midsummer Night's Eve, involving the Ha-yot and the comparable organisation for girls, the Bund Deutscher Mädchen (BDM), in a romantic mish-mash of being young and patriotic and together. We marched in columns to the hill selected for the purpose and there sat down. As the sun started sinking we sang songs, like Boy Scouts at a jamboree. A leader, far down below, shouted through a loud-hailer for what seemed ages before giving an 'Akela-the-Wolf' call to all us Mowglis.

My presence went undetected until near the end, when an unpleasant-looking older man started making a fuss about the stranger in their midst. Budi said nothing, staring nervously at the ground. Werner simply strode up to the man and grabbed hold of his shirt, shaking him from side to side. 'Fock off, *Scheiss!*' he said in purest Anglo-German. 'FOCK OFF!' The man stood his ground for no more than a second, then sloped away, muttering.

8

Budi and I went by train to Hamburg 'hard class', as it was called, and hard it was. Ordinary seats in pre-war Germany could be very uncomfortable. Frills were for foreigners, not for the toughened bottoms of the Third Reich, was the assumption.

Cinemas were the same. I watched Leni Riefenstahl's *Triumph of the Will** on a wooden tip-up in a cinema devoid of decoration whilst I was out there. As for the film, it was astonishing by reason of its technical brilliance: parade after parade, brilliantly montaged, Hitler's every appearance stage-managed to make him seem more than human. I wondered where I'd seen such a technique before and came to the conclusion that it was exactly how Mae West was presented, in every film she made. In essence, a bunch of anonymous characters would be

---

* The *Triumph des Willens* is often cited as a famous example of a propaganda film. Released in 1935, it showed scenes of the 1934 Nazi Party Congress which had been attended by over 700,000 people.

shown clamouring for the star to appear. At last, when the clamour had become persistent enough, there she'd be: corseted solid; feathered and bejewelled; filmed from only the most flattering of angles. A masterpiece of comic overstatement, made even more telling when she opened her mouth to sing, for what emerged from that slinky face was a thin, twangily nasal sound, a parody of a parody.

What emerged from Hitler's mouth was indeed the Triumph of a Will – his will: undiluted hysteria, male militarism, madness and despair; the mutterings of a character out of a Joseph Conrad novel, without a trace of humour. The difference between Mae West and the Führer was that he meant his nonsense, to the last syllable, whereas she, presumably, did not. Once having made that comparison, I was preserved from being taken in, in spite of the fervent crowd-feeling generated at his every appearance.

In Hamburg there was great stir and bustle. A KDF ('Strength through Joy') ship was about to arrive at the docks. SA troops in brown shirt-sleeves – their 'proletarian' uniform – were staging a rally to greet the factory-heroes returning from the holiday which they were supposed to have earned by working far harder than they had to. It all sounded bogus to me, as it did to my host, who bore little love and even less regard for a regime which had dented his finances. The Siemers family had once been of considerable importance in the commercial history of Hamburg. Their shipping-line had contributed to its growth and they had owned a swathe of land on the outskirts, ripe for urban development. All to no avail. Under threat of confiscation, Nazis dominating the city council had served a Compulsory Purchase Order, enabling 'the People' to acquire the land for a pittance. As some kind of sop, the new suburb was permitted to bear the name Siemershöhe. The family were angry but far from ruined, continuing to live at Geffckenstrasse 19, a detached villa in a large garden, with a staff to look after them.

Hans Siemers had a daughter called Carola who was determined to be considered elegant. I thought her wonderful. My trouble was that I'd come to Hamburg with Budi, with whom I was bracketed, and sophisticated he was not. I'd never required anything like that of him before, so he must have been bewildered by the way I wanted to quit his side to cleave to Carola. Nice, honest Budi! I didn't behave well towards him, I regret to say.

Carola knew a number of men who liked nothing better than rushing about in fast cars, drinking and partying. Even better, nobody expected me to pay for anything – quite the gear change from Ulm where I'd understandably been presented with a bill at the end of each week by the hard-up von Machs. Carola took me to grown-up places such as the bar of the Vier Jahreszeiten Hotel where I saw two tarts sipping Danziger Goldwasser. Both were plump and wore 'Robin Hood' hats (popularised by Deanna Durbin)* on hair which fell, as fashion demanded, in a tightly frizzed heap over padded shoulders. Another evening, she took me to a 'Dancing' which boasted '*Tanz am Licht*', a floor made of glass lit from below. There she taught me to rumba, rhythmically quivering to the music, scarcely moving, hemmed in by rhythmically quivering, scarcely moving others. How elegant it seemed!

One particular dance was a 'must', though only behind closed doors: 'The Lambeth Walk'. To me, it was an ironic joke, but to them it was mandatory. All the smart young things had somehow obtained a record to play whenever they could, regardless of, or perhaps because of, the Führer's detestation of 'Afro-Jewish degeneracy' – scarcely the first description coming to mind when considering Cockney exuberance.

Hamburg that summer was hot, cloudy and humid. I lay about in the garden with Budi but could seldom sunbathe. As for lolling indoors, the Siemers family had an established habit of going after lunch into a small sitting-room to lie down on an ottoman covered in a Turkish carpet. All of us: Herr Siemers, still chewing the end of a cheroot; his *Frau*; Carola; Budi; and myself – and, if he were home on leave, Georg, elder son, pride of them all. We didn't talk. We simply got on with the business of dropping off to sleep, which most of us did within minutes.

Georg was currently doing Military Service. He was a correct young man and no Nazi. He told me that Hamburg, with a tradition of being a free port, hadn't taken kindly to being under Socialist control, even when Socialism was called 'National Socialism' and was purporting to be different.

One day he happened to hear Carola humming the song 'Under the Red Lanterns of St Pauli'. He said: 'I guess Roddy ought to see the place.'

'Maybe at his age they won't let him in,' was her answer.

They exchanged looks of utmost complicity, from which I felt excluded. However, it was agreed that Georg would take me there next

---

* A Canadian actress and singer famous in the 1930s and 1940s for her appearances in musical films.

day. To add to the mystery, his father was on no account to be told where we were going.

When we reached St Pauli it didn't look anything much, except for being both sleazy and glittery. Our goal, which was a street called something like Winkenstrasse,* seemed strange because at either end it had barriers of overlapping corrugated-iron to keep it hidden from accidental public view. Men who might have been police stood in front of the barriers, looking tough.

'They are there in case of trouble,' said Georg. 'Chuckers-out!'

Casually we strolled on through, hands in pockets.

What a sight on the other side! Rows of what might have been mistaken for shops, except that in each window sat a woman – or women – in various stages of undress, engaged in activities more usually associated with being behind locked doors. Some, perhaps worn out by keeping up an endless show of provocative behaviour, were indulging in homely pursuits, such as knitting. One was even doing a crossword, sucking at her pencil, frowning with the effort. A motley mix of men, mostly in pairs or gangs, some in uniform, were wandering along; pointing, sometimes laughing.

In front of many of the doors stood touts, drawing extra attention to what couldn't possibly be overlooked. On seeing us, a sad-eyed ponce shouted: 'Have a good time while you're young, *junge mensch*!' Behind him his merchandise wriggled about on a chaise-longue, and seeing that she'd captured our attention, stretched out a fat leg and lifted her skirt to display underwear of a kind which, in my innocence, I didn't know existed: a mass of frills where no frills were needed; and where they should have been, a diamond-shaped gap, lined with fur. Georg bandied words with the tout. I couldn't follow what they were saying, but I was pointed at, which made me want to sink into the ground, then frowned at, which was perhaps worse.

We strolled on. 'What was all that about?' I asked, concealing my relief that a bargain hadn't been struck.

'She was prepared to make a special price for you,' said Georg. 'Or rather, she was until I told her keeper you had the clap. Then she didn't seem so keen!' Of course, he may have been having me on, but it made

---

* This is probably a misspelling of 'Wilkenstrasse', or 'Shop Street', which was another name for Herbertstrasse, a famous street in St Pauli's red-light district that still exists in much the same capacity today.

me realise what risks the women ran. 'They go for a check-up each week,' he said. 'If they don't, they'll be arrested and made to have a medical, so on the whole they prefer to obey regulations.'

For the next half-hour we wandered slowly up and down, gawping, soon ignored by the touts. By not appearing shocked, I may have been something of a disappointment to Georg. It was an act, for in fact my mind was in a turmoil, but I wasn't going to let on. He called my bluff by asking whether we had such streets in London, and I didn't know quite what to answer. I told him that I was sure they existed, but needed a lot of finding.

'It's never easy to find what you really want in life,' he said, looking steadily at me. Annoyingly, I blushed, in an all-over-everywhere way. I couldn't say exactly what I sought. I didn't really know, myself; not this, at any rate. But then – what? Perhaps an inkling of my true nature made me blush even harder.

I wanted to stay on in Hamburg, and had even found a German teacher, Frau Fera, prepared to charge nothing provided I took her around the city and out on the ferry-boat to Blankenese. But as the news became more and more threatening my mother grew more and more alarmed. She sent would-be cryptic telegrams, advising 'Your friend Roddy' to return immediately, by air. It was a clever bribe, because she knew how keen I was on flying, ever since going for a spin (for 10s 6d) in one of Sir Alan Cobham's open bi-planes at Skegness. The final decider came when I'd been issued with a ticket to visit Heligoland and it was suddenly cancelled, on grounds of 'military security'. Things were obviously getting serious.

It was desperately sad, dragging myself away from Budi and the Siemers family, without a final goodbye to freckle-faced Werner; but it had to be done. I was lucky to get a seat on a Lufthansa flight which was the air equivalent of a slow train: it landed at four different places before putting down at Croydon. Not a moment too soon. Before the week was out, war was declared and Germany became the enemy. Everyone said so; it had to be true. But I would never be able to echo that hatred of a whole people which propaganda urged us to express. The von Machs and the Siemers were no more responsible for the actions of Hitler's government than children are for the actions of their parents; the fight was between the grown-ups, and everyone else, no matter which 'side' they were on, served only as collateral damage.

part two

war

1939-42

9

The outbreak of war disrupted everything for us, as it did for everyone else; and like everyone else, we soon settled down to it as though it were the most natural thing in the world.

In the chaos, I went up to Oxford. I'd sat for a Balliol Exhibition and failed to win one – not surprising considering the gap in formal education which had resulted from a far more educational time in Germany. However, on the strength of my performance I was allowed in without having to take a further entrance exam.

I'd spent most of my intervening time between Germany and Oxford with my good friend Hallam Tennyson. We called ourselves the 'Doves' and we were the most platonic of friends, incredible as it may have appeared to those who knew us. Physically we were very unalike: me tall and smiling; he smallish, habitually with a quizzical frown on his face. We were convinced that his great-grandfather, Alfred Lord Tennyson, had been inspired to write 'In Memoriam' to honour what passed, in his day, as just such a friendship with Arthur Hallam.

Our sudden, tremendous amalgamation grew out of pacifism and tennis combined – an oddly potent mixture. The pacifist part came from our shared belief; the tennis, largely by accident. We'd met at a tournament in Lincolnshire, at Bayons Manor, belonging to Hallam's cousins, the Tennyson d'Eyncourts (who also happened to be very distant cousins of mine), the d'Eyncourt part of their name being a sham, as romantic as the medievalism of their Victorian castle with its mock ruin. In partnership for two years running we became the Junior Doubles champions of Lincolnshire, with me winning the Junior Singles as well; but our triumph extended no further than the county. At Junior Wimbledon, Hallam was knocked out straight away and I followed suit, losing to a Chilean who went on to become runner-up to the winner. The Chilean had excelled at net-play, whereas I, like Hallam, was best on the baseline; but above all, we'd been eliminated so quickly because we hadn't practised enough, nor were we really fit.

All that notwithstanding, we were soon speeding at our Dove-most around Dorset on a second-hand motorbike for which I'd paid £18, exchanging restricted confidences with every passing mile. With the benefit of hindsight, it was curious that such confidences entirely omitted confessing to any form of sexual activity, since such was, at our age, our main preoccupation.

The Doves went up to Oxford together, mutually disapproving of the war. It should have been a strengthener of bonds and was, to some extent, but Oxford's heady atmosphere showed how different our tastes in friends could be.

He wrote to me saying: 'Dove R. expects every sacrifice from Dove H. (who, alas mad bird that he is, is willing to give it) though he (Dove R.) is not willing to do anything too inconvenient in return. Write, if only to assure me, my bird, that this is not so. Selfish as we are I think that to each other our selfishness is non-existent because we are ONE. I claim no virtue, the merging of our two personalities has just happened – mystically, incredibly, and I doubt if even He could explain its fundamental cause.'

I deserved the reproach. As I was the one most bewitched by novelty, I was, in a sense, most to blame for seeing more of my new friends and less of him. I was almost off my head with relief at finding Balliol so congenial. In the past, exercising little control over my daily life had been a kind of hell: Summer Fields the worst; Eton rather better; and now Oxford, so heavenly as to be beyond compare. Of course, there were some rules to be observed, but even those could be circumvented. I should have been 'gated' for hardly ever eating a meal in Hall. I wasn't, because my infrequency made the authorities forget that I existed.

On account of the war, I elected to take Medicine instead of the usual subjects. There again, my attendances were so infrequent that I wasn't missed. Dissecting out the cranial nerves of a dogfish ought to have roused my keenest interest. Instead, I plumped for a life of pleasure.

A tiresome parrot-cry on many lips was 'DONTcher know there's a WAR on?' Indeed I did, adjusting my sights accordingly. What was the point of working hard for a degree, what was the point of anything, much, when the Germans seemed so obviously to be winning? That idea – that certainty, rather – made a mockery of every normal aspiration. The future would be full of suffering, so why not make hay before the bad times began? It was an apocalyptic moment in history, with the world crashing about our ears. To pretend otherwise seemed ludicrous.

Such hedonism combined with pacifism must have appeared incongruous to my elders, though I found no difficulty in reconciling the two. The College buttery had pre-war stocks of wine at pre-war prices. It didn't take me long to devise small Sunday morning parties for a few new friends. 'Oh, what a good idea!' they'd all agree when handed glasses of champagne poured over crushed strawberries. For the first time in my life I knew what it was like to be a sought-after host; and the knowledge was sweet.

Older friends had come up to Balliol, for instance Peter Benenson,* sharing a room with Conrad Scott-Forbes (later to become a TV and film actor). With them I deliberately knocked back glass after glass of whisky to see what effect it would have, until obliged to take my whirling head outside to be sick. So this was IT? I'd often wondered. Learning to take advantage of the stage just before becoming completely blotto, I got less drunk more slowly in the company of John Lincoln, an athletic Australian. We fell asleep together on his floor, to the sound of Fats Waller singing 'Ain't misbehavin', savin' mah lurve for you!'

As a freshman, I had to share rooms with a stranger, an owl-eyed Northerner whose passion was train-spotting. I contrived to exchange him for John Edye and then suffered the fate of having John exchange me for a better friend of his, Walter Salmon. What mortification! I wasn't used to such a rebuff. It took me down a much-needed peg or two. John Edye ('Archie' to his friends) doubly distinguished himself: he became an object of adoration to an Egyptian called Sabri, who bought him a gold cigarette-case; and at the same time he invited a young woman, Margery Gardner, up from London to a party. Margery Gardner? Wouldn't that name ring a bell a few years later? Of course – the poor girl was to end up as one of the murderer Neville Heath's mutilated victims.

Parties, parties, parties. Possibly the Eckstein river-jaunt was the most talked-about. Our host hired a steamer which carried us, drinking our heads off, up to Abingdon and back. As we passed through the locks, onlookers offended by seeing the *jeunesse* being so outrageously *dorée* shouted insults, but changed their tune when offered free drinks as the boat slowly rose or fell.

Then, Wayland Dobson and Iona Knabenshue threw a famous

---

* This is the last we see of Peter; in Roddy's original memoirs he looks for him at an Oxford reunion some decades later but he hadn't attended.

'Husband and Wife' party; Wayland as the wife, Iona the husband. At its height the lights were switched off and stayed off, for any of us to get up to anything we fancied – a daring ploy for those days.

Fighter pilots from the nearby RAF station frequented the bar of the Randolph Hotel. There, instead of the girls they liked to say they were seeking, they might find me, ready to be bought drinks. Their minds weren't really on sex. They needed someone outside the Service to listen to their cheery tales of 'shows' and 'prangs' which, beneath the banter, weren't cheery at all. I didn't make the most of my opportunities, generally failing, through ignorance, to follow up the necessarily tentative leads I'd be thrown – but listen I did.

What with one thing, what with another, no wonder that I fell at the first hurdle of my medical course – not that it worried me in the slightest. Instead I took up a new role as an artist at the Slade School, which had conveniently been 'evacuated for the duration' to join the Ruskin in Oxford's Ashmolean. I'd developed a sudden artistic zeal on account of being taught to use powder-paints by Stella, artistic Arthur Churchman's (Lord Woodbridge's) granddaughter, whilst staying at their estate of Abbey Oaks.

I was astonished by the sight of a girl standing nude in front of the life-class and still more astonished by a male model posing discreetly in a jock-strap, as if his private parts were unpresentable.

'He might at least have put on a clean one!' whispered a man at the easel next to me.

'I only wish he'd take the bloody thing off!' I replied, then had to go and spoil things by blushing.

Through art classes I met, always wrapped in a sari, Vilasini Gorakshakar ('Vil'), a Rajput from India. I chose to 'respect' Vil instead of trying to get her into bed, whereas I shamelessly pretended already to be sleeping with Diana Marriott, a red-headed Colonel's daughter; so evidently I had a lot to learn, in spite of thinking myself adult and sophisticated. Still, there were many agreeable lessons which a wartime Oxford version of *La Vie Bohème* could teach a young man as open to new experiences as I was.

There was so much that was new in the way of people, so much to be grateful for. Mary Stanley-Smith, known as the Queen of Ship Street, set an unforgettable example. Sleeping-space on the floor of her tiny, uncomfortable house was never denied to any friend requiring it: 'Where there's room in the heart, there's room in the house!' was her motto. I took it to heart for ever, aware that it would have an immeasurable impact on life.

At around the same time, I started teaching painting to children with learning difficulties. They adored making powder-paint puddles in cake-tins and splashing the crude colours on to lining-paper – good cheap fun for all. As a spin-off, I dared expose some of my own works at a 'Free Finland'* exhibition and sold one (of a galleon) to Kay Dick, the journalist and author.

When not otherwise engaged, I went about more and more with Vil, who was shortly to return to India. We travelled up to London and stayed one chaste night (at her expense) amidst the gilded glories of the Ritz, then went on to Liverpool to join her sister. Liverpool was grey, as was the Adelphi Hotel, where again I stayed at her expense and where an odd event took place. My eyebrows happened to be very light-coloured, almost invisible against a tanned forehead. Vil declared that they would look nicer if touched up with her mascara, which she went ahead and did – or rather, overdid. As we sat drinking tea in the hotel lounge, a young Army officer left his group of other officers, came over, and asked to borrow an ashtray, addressing me as 'Madam'. By the way he kept looking back and grinning it was obvious that he was doing it for a bet.

'Do I look like a madam?' I asked indignantly.

'W-well, n-no, now I see you close up,' stammered the man, turning scarlet.

I turned an even deeper red, then felt the blood draining from my face.

'You've gone all white!' said Vil, clutching my sleeve as the officer withdrew, apologising. 'I was afraid you were going to hit him.'

'As a pacifist, I couldn't very well do that,' I said.

I was still puzzling over the disquieting incident whilst seeing Vil on board her ship and, not that I knew it then, out of my life.

All that time, pacifism sat oddly on my shoulders, but it sat genuinely. It was my main philosophical problem, threatening to loom larger as conscription loomed nearer. I knew that the day would come when I would have to tackle it head-on.

---

* The Soviet Union had invaded Finland towards the end of 1939; war between the two lasted until March 1940 (which is why the war is better known as the 'Winter War'), ending with a treaty in which Finland ceded over 10 per cent of its territory to the USSR.

10

In late summer 1940, the Doves learnt that they could join a body called 'The University Ambulance Unit' which was being formed by a fellow student, Miles Vaughan-Williams. He was arranging for a few kindred spirits to take over Hawkspur Camp near Great Bardfield, in Essex, there to be taught advanced first-aid by a pacifist doctor. As well as Hallam, we were joined by Oliver Wrightson (another Old Etonian friend) and Hubert Fox, a good friend of mine on account of his ability to languidly drawl comic, incisive comments. The prospect seemed like great fun and so my sole anxiety was that I didn't much like what I considered to be Miles's calculating bossiness, although I recognised that without it he couldn't have organised the scheme so thoroughly.

Hawkspur consisted of a few wooden huts scattered about a field sloping off a quiet country lane. Creature comforts were minimal – bunk-beds, outdoor trench-latrines amongst the nettles and so on. Had it rained, the going would have been frightful, but in high summer the countryside was at its best, the mud at its least. Nobody complained; in fact nobody dared complain, for fear of being thought 'uncommitted'.

Even in so remote a corner of an English field, the natives from the nearest pub twigged, within five minutes, that 'UAU' stood for 'Bunch of Conchies'. But it also proclaimed that this bunch meant business, strictly confined to the humanitarian; so perhaps we weren't wholly bad.

Overhead, the Battle of Britain was being fought; tiny specks roaring and whining in the blue sky. Inevitably, a plane crashed near Hawkspur and by chance I was the first on the scene, bumping across country on my motorbike. It was one of theirs and it hadn't exploded or caught fire. A young German was still in the cockpit, as dead as could be but looking quite undamaged except over his chest, where blood was seeping through his flying-jacket. He was as blond as Budi von Mach and not much older. I tried unsuccessfully to undo his harness; then, yielding to an impulse, nuzzled him gently. He was still warm. My mind went blank. Why couldn't I see him simply as a dead enemy, which was what he was, after all? Why think of him as a living man?

Others came panting up, full of scorn. 'Serve him right!' said one of those new arrivals. 'Serve the bugger right!'

I said nothing. I couldn't trust myself to open my mouth without giving offence.

Another tried surreptitiously to pull a ring from the pilot's finger, saying defiantly, "E's got no further use fer it!'

But the hand was already too swollen and the ring wouldn't come off.

'Shame on you!' said an older woman.

I thought: *This is what it means to be English.*

Some days later:

'I'm a natural ash-blonde,' said Peryl to Oliver, almost before I'd had time to get off my motorbike. 'People think I've gone prematurely white. I haven't, of course, but no one will believe me.'

'And this machine is a Francis-Barnett,' I said. 'It's awfully heavy, because of the armour-plating. They built it to look streamlined, that's why. Actually, it's rather sluggish.'

Far from being as inconsequential as they sounded, our remarks – I realised later – were full of hidden suggestions; not that it was obvious to someone as inexperienced with women as myself.

I had arrived at a house called 'Once Upon a Time', near the village of High Easter, with Oliver Wrightson riding pillion, in order to look up Peryl, Marchesa di Montagliari – his brother's friend, and possibly more than a friend, whom he'd never met before.

Cottage and chatelaine could have come straight from the pages of a novel by Dornford Yates.* The ash-blondeness of the owner was a suitable match for oak beams, 'limed' to make them silvery, picked out against pale pastel colours on walls painted blue and green downstairs, pink upstairs. For someone like the Marchesa to be living in such tweely named, tweely thatched surroundings, there had to be an explanation; and so indeed there was. 'Once Upon a Time' had been an amusing bolt-hole, to be dashed down to for weekends with smart friends. With the outbreak of war, it had become an only home; unvisited, off the beaten track.

I flicked the parking pedal down with my foot. The machine all

---

* Dornford Yates wrote bestselling thrillers and humorous novels in the 1920s and 1930s.

but fell over and I had to wrestle with it, getting my hands covered in grease. The day was hot. Forgetting about fingers, I fished in a pocket for a handkerchief to wipe my sweaty brow. The hanky turned grey.

'You look like a couple of garage-hands!' said Peryl (though Oliver was still perfectly clean), pulling us inside to mop me up.

A query to be got out of the way immediately was the title of 'Marchesa'. As Peryl was obviously English, she must have married into it; and so she had. 'It used to be such fun, having a handle to one's name,' she wailed. 'But now it's HELL, sheer hell! I spend half my time explaining to morons behind desks that I'm not a bloody foreigner. Franco was, of course, so he's safely tucked away on the Isle of Man, poor lamb!' (Enemy aliens were interned there, under Home Office Regulation 18b.)

Oliver and I tried our best to look sympathetic, but really I agreed with the rule. I might be a 'bleedin' conchie', but that didn't imply that I wanted spies running around on the loose. Our own position was fragile enough without rushing to the support of potential agents, however innocent they were supposed to be.

Lunch was simple and delicious. We tucked into prodigious quanti- ties of salad, dressed superbly. Peryl said: 'I use tarragon vinegar, that's the secret.' But she had also used sugar, mustard and mint, combined in exactly the right proportions with a hint of coriander – beautifully un-English.

Whilst we ate, she gave glimpses of life as it had been. 'We'd drive down here in the Daimler on the spur of the moment, with hampers from Fortnum's and a crate of champagne.' [*Pure Dornford Yates!* I thought again, *except that the car would have been 'The Rolls'.*] 'Franco adored entertaining. In fact, I soon found my friends deserting me ... [pause for us to express incredulity] ... because he was always the life and soul of the party, which was easy enough for him. I was the one who had to be business-like.'

The business to which she referred was a dress-shop in Carlos Place, off Grosvenor Square: BATIK, by Vanek, which she had started whilst bearing the name of her first husband, Squire Van Neck. She'd moved directly from a country life of tweeds and sport into that diamond-hard, cut-throat world – and done rather well in it. She told us the secret of her success: 'I was the first person to insist on a proper foundation garment. I don't mean just stays or a corset, but something capable of controlling those awful female figures all the way from here' – saying which, she got up from the table and dabbed at her neck – 'to here!' – indicating what, to me, seemed an indelicate area. As if on cue, I blushed; then, noticing her noticing, went deeper red. I was astonished to see the very faintest tinge of pink suffusing her face; it made me turn a deeper rose-madder and pull out my handkerchief in an attempt at concealment. Of course, it had to be that same hanky, grey with grease, which had been such a bother before.

'Now you'll need another wash,' she said. 'This time I think we'd better use Vim.'

She pulled me after her into the kitchen, shutting the door, leaving Oliver sitting by himself. Grabbing a canister of Vim from the shelf, she put an arm round me, drawing us together so that the hand holding the Vim was sandwiched between our bodies. I was thrilled to bits, also slightly alarmed; however, not too shy to venture a kiss, more of a peck. It wasn't enough by half. Peryl seized my head and plugged our lips together, firmly and expertly. She quivered. I tingled and got an erection. When at last there was an opportunity to speak she said, 'Now we know why we both went so red, don't we?'

To have a blush equated with sexual prowess was a new and welcome interpretation of my much-loathed weakness. It was exciting, too, to think that nothing more than the thickness of a door separated the way we were carrying on from a completely oblivious Oliver. When our clinch came to an end my hands were sprinkled with Vim, steered under a hot tap and dried on a dish-cloth.

We returned to the dining-room with an air of detached insouciance. But Oliver wasn't so easily taken in. When Peryl left the room to make coffee, he whispered, 'I say, what was going on between you two? You took ages!'

'She couldn't find the Vim,' I said lamely.

'Oh I see. I thought from your blushes you must have been up to something.'

When the time came for us to leave, the motorbike wouldn't start, however much I kicked down the pedal. Peryl had to fetch a bottle of precious petrol, which finally did the trick. 'Better love hath no woman,' she said, 'in these days of rationing. But anyhow, come again as soon as you can!'

Once the Francis-Barnett was ticking over – or, rather, sputtering over – we could legitimately kiss goodbye before roaring back to the puritan atmosphere of Hawkspur, where it was assumed as a matter of course that we would have spent our time off going for a healthy ramble.

That evening there was an advanced first-aid demonstration. One of us had to strip down and have his thigh bandaged by each in turn all the way up to his crotch. For the 'patient' to have displayed embarrassment would have been considered false modesty. In my newly awakened amorous state, there wouldn't have been anything false about my reaction to having such sensitive parts handled, so I declined the honour of being the guinea-pig.

And so to bed, in a communal bunk-house, on hard wooden slats.

––––––––––––

11

The sequel was swift to follow.

It was possible, though difficult, to be rung up by the outside world. Normally the camp telephone went unanswered because no one would be in the 'office' when there was work – and there was always work – to be done elsewhere. Nevertheless, a couple of days later I was informed, in a loud voice in front of everyone, that 'A foreign lady phoned and wants you to call her back.'

The message was delivered with great disdain by our doctor, a dour Northerner, the suggestion being that it was mere frivolity.

Peryl proceeded to draw me into a plan for us to meet in London. The ensuing nights were filled with erotic dreams, alternating with a few 'naked-in-public' nightmares. In recompense, I threw myself into all sorts of tasks, the lowlier the better, even offering to take a spade and enlarge the latrine-trench.

Trains to London were running almost normally, sporadically halted by a continuing Battle of Britain. The sight of those little single-seater aeroplanes twisting and diving in combat made me profoundly uneasy. It wasn't that I was afraid to join their ranks, but was I justified in accepting their protection, when I hadn't asked for it? What right had I to be enjoying clandestine appointments down here, whilst they were fighting and dying up there?

Before reaching the station I saw a tiny toy in the sky twirl and tumble, emitting smoke, so I stopped by the side of the road with my motorbike still running. Above the noise it made I could hear a dron-ing, which stopped when an engine spluttered, re-started and cut out. There was an ominous silence, until the earth shook with the shock of an explosion. One of ours, or one of theirs? Being on a slight incline which would make re-starting easy, I risked switching off. In the deafening silence, I heard the birds singing their hearts out against the high-pitched whine of telephone wires. Nobody else was about. It was as if nothing had happened. But it had, and I knew it had; there was a pillar of smoke in the distance to prove it.

It took hours to reach Green Park by Underground, where the esca-lator wasn't functioning. I'd expected the capital to be full of khaki-clad soldiers, but there didn't seem to be all that many about. The normality of London was slightly appalling after what was happening in the skies over Great Bardfield.

My rendezvous with Peryl was in the Park Lane Hotel, of which I knew nothing. The black marble and glass of its entrance was intim-idating for someone who wasn't particularly clean, unsuitably dressed and out of their depth: in short, me. None of that seemed to matter to my 'date'. She was sitting in the lounge craning her neck, clearly very relieved that I'd turned up. At the first waft of my presence, she said, 'Let's go straight upstairs, shall we?'

I followed her into the lift. She was wearing a pinky-purple tweed skirt, rather long. Far from concealing, it drew attention to her legs. I watched them pouncily gliding ahead of me down the passage and wondered what there'd be higher up.

I was soon to find out. My excitement became intense when I realised that something was due to take place then and there, that we were to undress at once and get on with it. I could hardly breathe, let alone speak.

And then the awful let-down. In mid-embrace I shrivelled to noth-ingness. As I squirmed about, trying to hide my condition, the air-raid sirens went, loudly from somewhere in the nearby park. My life-savers. 'Damn!' said Peryl. 'Damn! Damn! Damn! We'll have to go down to the shelter. It's in the basement, I believe.' As we flung on clothes, I was speechless with relief.

In the lift we met other hotel guests, a rum lot. Two of the women wore hats and the men with them were so small that I towered over them like a crane.

One of them joked: 'What's the betting the bar's shut?'

We all laughed.

'If they haven't, I'm for a gin-and-it, with a dash,' said Peryl. 'We'll both have one.'

'Or two, or three, or more!' sang out the same man automatically, without looking as cheery as his words suggested.

There was a bar, and it did have what Peryl wanted. The 'dash', I discovered, meant absinthe, hinting at degradation of the most sophisticated French kind: just what an inhibited Englishman needed at that moment. As I downed mine, I felt it taking effect as if in rhythm with the thuds and bangs of anti-aircraft guns stationed in Hyde Park. By the time that the 'All Clear!' went – which was very soon, the whole thing being a false alarm – I was floating on a cloud of aniseed into the lift, along the passage and back to her room. We tumbled on to the bed to resume what had been so providentially interrupted, but with this difference: I was like iron.

When it was all over, my crude thrusts were quickly forgiven. 'You must admit, that's the best time you've ever had with any woman!' said Peryl triumphantly. She couldn't have said anything more welcome. It stimulated me to unburden myself of a confidence, *the* confidence as far as I was concerned: 'I'm afraid I don't know a lot about women. You see, you're the first.'

'Am I? Am I really? . . . I mean, really? You're not just saying that to be polite?'

'Yes, or do I mean no? REALLY!'

'You must have played about at school?'

'Of course I did, but that was with other boys.'

'Well, darling Wumphus, seeing as how you've been so open with me, I'll let you into a secret,' she said. 'I've got what's called "the Cleopatra Clutch". I tell you, it's something very few women have, or even know about, but it's one of the most important things in the world. When I grip a chap, he stays gripped; that's why you found it so good. You may never come across another woman with the Clutch in your whole life!'

She was right: I never have. Nor has any other woman ever called me 'Wumphus', or invited me to call her, even more shamingly, 'Wimphy-Boo'.

———————

12

After training at Hawkspur, Miles arranged for the UAU to be deployed as 'Shelter Marshals' or 'Rest-Centre Supervisors' during the first Blitz on London. Such responsibilities were utterly unfamiliar to most of us, as was the area to which we were sent: it was not so much an 'East' as a 'Deep' End.

Those who found themselves suddenly being looked after by a bunch of mostly middle-class conchies were the epitome of old-fashioned, working-class 'Cockney sparrers', chirpy in disaster yet without a speck of gratitude for anything done to help them. We were regarded as fruit ripe for the plucking – except that on the whole we were too penniless to be worth bothering about, in spite of our genteel accents. (Although fellow Hawkspur man Noel Currer-Briggs had access to a Tudoresque mansion alongside Regent's Park, where we fetched up sleeping on parquet floors in intervals between one job and another.)

When busy, we really were busy. When the Blitz began in earnest, landmines (dropped by little parachutes) created homelessness more efficiently than bombs; and that was where we came in. Each day brought its straggle of the bombed-out – women mostly, clutching their few belongings done up in sheets, pillow-cases and tattered curtains. Once arrived, they sat around in our bleakly hygienic rest-centres, tucking into tinned salmon and sliced white bread, with nothing to do but listen to the cinema organ played by Sandy MacPherson, eternal prime-time broadcaster of those early days of war. By night, the new arrivals would have to be fitted into existing shelters, where they were unlikely to be welcomed by 'residents' already complaining of overcrowding.

As representatives of Authority, we were in focus for traditional suspicions. Being conchies didn't help; for why weren't we clenching fists like the rest? What was in it for us? Must be something, or we wouldn't be larking about in their manor, that was for sure. Spies, most like!

Such sentimental illusions as I may have had about the nobility of 'the workers' were quickly dispelled, allowing me to appreciate their many sterling qualities without viewing them through rose-coloured spectacles. I wasn't disillusioned so much as re-illusioned by the reality. My new feelings were encapsulated in a short, sharp report, a record of exactly what had happened one day in the early autumn of 1940:

> 5.30 in the morning, East End. People pushing aside a curtain of black-out cloth hanging over the entrance to the rest-centre. 'Name please?' – 'Morgan'. 'Address?' – 'Swanfield Estate'. 'Children?' – 'Four . . . Ag, she's 12, Betty 9, Bobby 6 and Doreen 5 . . . (a nervous fumble at a stained tie) . . . and the Missus, y'know, she's, well, expecting another in May . . .'

Gradually the hall fills. At one end a rudimentary kitchen, where a 'Soyer' keeps itself and exasperation at boiling-point. Who'd be the next to volunteer for the post of soup-stirrer and washer-up? Young Jimmy would. Smiling, sprightly young Jimmy would even empty the emergency loos, the 'Elsans', without demur. Soon Jimmy was everyone's favourite; based on his willingness to tackle all kinds of work, the one prized quality of the moment.

After a week, Jimmy said he was engaged to a girl in another rest-centre. What could be done? He had no money and no clothes: 'Gone, a'course, when the flat went up in smoke, an' me wiv nuffin but what I stand up in!'

Everyone started collecting for Jimmy's wedding. Pennies and sixpences from those who at last had someone worse off than themselves to feel sorry for. 'Loaves and fishes!' said a grand old character known as 'The Duchess' (reputed to have as much as £50 'put by') when she heard that the collection amounted to nearly three pounds. 'Loaves and fishes, that's what it is. A sign and a miracle!'

The next thing was to get Jimmy a ring. Someone arranged it through a charitable Society. Then the rest-centre Supervisor – myself, aged 19 – managed to put in for a civilian suit and a special allowance of £10. The stage was set. All was ready.

Alas! Jimmy vanished and was nowhere to be found.

'Bugger 'im,' said 'The Duchess'. 'I would fancy another cup!'

After dealing with so many homeless, it was ironic that I should find myself with nowhere to lay my head. Our house on the Isle of Purbeck had been quickly commandeered by the Army. My mother (who should have known better, considering that this was her second war) let us leave behind a cellar stocked with wine and chests-of-drawers full of clothes. Needless to say, everything was systematically looted. However, she also told Moore, the gardener, to bury the best of the family silver under a flagstone just inside the greenhouse. 'Where the Huns won't be able to get at it,' she said.

Our home, for the duration, was to be my grandmother's dower-house in Lincolnshire. In Well Vale, a longish trudge across the park, my Uncle Dick, himself too old to fight, considered conchies to be the lowest of vermin. As he already disliked and distrusted me, it must have seemed providential, finding such justification. I didn't relish the thought of being exposed to his contempt, so stayed on in blitzkrieged London when hostilities momentarily died down and the UAU found itself at a loose end.

Where to go, in town? Hallam had an honorary 'Aunt Corkie' in Glebe Place, in Chelsea, said to be the most wonderful of family friends, a prop and stay in times of trouble. Well, perhaps she'd been all that in the past, but after a week she made it clear that she didn't want a couple of idealistic young men, hopping with East End fleas, encamped on her for a single day longer. At which point I thought of my other grand-mother, Maya Fenwick Owen, in Brantham Court, who never came to her London house. So to 6 Chesham Street in Belgravia Hallam and I went: an ordinary town house with a dog-leg drawing-room on the first floor. The caretaker, a shirt-sleeved Mr White, lived in a basement which had never been 'done up', surrounded by the sort of dilapidated furniture usually to be found below stairs. Mrs White had another job nearby, as store detective for Harrods; and their daughter, working in the Foreign Office, was engaged to an officer. All of them entered into the spirit of the times. Since the house apart from the basement was supposed to be unoccupied, they had to hide us in a gloomy back room, but by day I could wander up to the drawing-room and do my painting, poring over huge sheets of cartridge-paper laid directly on to the moss-green carpet. Hallam, meanwhile, took himself daily off on a bicycle to do social work in the East End.

My use of poster-gouache paints was a continuation of what I'd begun doing at Abbey Oaks. Some of my efforts must have passed muster because two were later accepted for an 'Artists of Fame and Promise' exhibition at the Leicester Gallery, and two were taken on hire by a university lending scheme. Even Mrs White was fairly polite about them, which meant a lot to me, considering how frank she was about everything else, including her husband's performance in bed. 'I still oblige White on occasions,' she said. 'But I don't mind telling you, it's force-work!'

Hallam considered that I ought to be doing the same sort of social work as himself; it was the first real rift between us. I didn't want to do any more good for the time being and I refused to feel guilty about it. Guilt, however, did surface over one set of happenings. Every now and then I would go out and pick someone up. After Peryl, it wouldn't be a girl, but a man.

On the moving staircase at Piccadilly I was approached by an Irishman of my own age called Kieran Tunney, living as 'the ward' – so he said – of an octogenarian, Leslie Pyke, in the house in Culross Street which had once belonged to Mrs Willie James.* He was already starting to write plays (he became rather famous at one point), his first effort being a musical entitled *Boola-Bonga*.

He wasn't my one and only. I bumped into an Army officer in a bookshop and then met another, Bobby Pinder-Wilson, who went as far as paying for my ticket to visit him in Portsmouth, where he was stationed. For such purposes I assumed the Oscar Wilde-ly bogus name of 'Sebastian Sand', thinking that it was no more than a temporary divergence from the norm. The whole of society seemed to be in a state of flux, so why not me too, over anything I fancied?

It turned out Hallam was up to similar larks; but incredible as it may seem, I had no idea of that at the time.

13

A call to renewed pacifist action came swiftly. The UAU, disbanding for want of employment, was suddenly given an opportunity to

---

* Mrs Willie James was a celebrated hostess in the Victorian and Edwardian eras, throwing parties for the elite of the day, including Edward VII and the King of Spain.

join, en bloc, a body called the BVAC (British Volunteer Ambulance Corps), and it was under the control of a blond-bearded artist. Perfect!

Soon, at the stately (but ugly) pile of Barrowby Hall near Garforth, Hallam and I were being taught how to maintain ambulances and/or the patients they were designed to carry. As usual, I found machines harder to understand than humans, especially those machines. Even on warm mornings the chances were that the self-starters wouldn't work. No, they would have to be shoulder-wrenchingly wound and wound, fiercely kicking back; then for several minutes they would have to be 'run in', wasting precious fuel. However, the job was the job, and that was that.

After a short training session at Barrowby, we were sent to Army bases unaware of the true nature of what was about to hit them. I was parted from Hallam when Miles and I were despatched to a regiment in West Hartlepool. The phrase covering our status was 'Graded as Officers'. By then we were in khaki, in what looked exactly like an officer's uniform, except that instead of pips it sported a glittery, braided flambeau. Over it I wore an ankle-length teddy-bear coat, bought for £3 10s 6d at a sale at Elliston and Cavell's in Oxford. So richly impressive did I look that the Colonel to whom we reported addressed all his remarks to me; at which Miles, the brilliant organiser, was greatly put out. The Colonel recognised that he had to make the best of the strange creatures inflicted on him so at first we were fed, though awkwardly, in the Officers' Mess, before being told, with heavy politeness, that 'perhaps we'd be happier making our own arrangements'.

We weren't dependent upon the regiment for transport, having our own ambulance, so we could drive about the town searching for a billet. Finding what we thought was a suitably respectable district, we knocked at random on a door. A smiling Mrs Sutton appeared. Our request flustered her. She said that she didn't want to seem unpatriotic, but she had only one spare bedroom and it had only a double-bed. Would we mind sleeping together? Miles and I looked at each other in dismay. Neither of us would have minded, provided that it had been with the right person, but he was no more right for me than I for him. In order not to burn our boats we said we'd enquire elsewhere and let her know; but as no other house admitted to having so much as a single bed to spare, we returned perforce to Mrs Sutton. 'One thing I can guarantee,' she said. 'There'll always be plenty of fish for your tea, because that's what we are – Sutton's Fish.' And so they were, the whole family: Mrs Sutton and her daughter working full time in the shop, and the young son going in to help out. We'd fallen on our feet.

Tucked up in bed with Miles that first night, I pondered how extraordinary it was to have a complete absence of feeling towards someone with whom I was forced by circumstance to be entwined. Huddling together for warmth, we struck no kind of spark. At last I was able to understand something which had always puzzled me – how, in days of yore, travellers had thought nothing of sharing beds with strangers in country inns. Miles was no stranger, of course; simply not a friend.

The Colonel sent us to Sick Quarters to see what his Medical Officer would make of us. The MO was a blotchy-faced, red-nosed man, reeking of booze. At first sight a tricky brute, he was in fact courteous and delightful, if occasionally short-tempered when provoked by the stupidity of his orderlies. We could be useful, he said, if we were prepared to act as male nurses at moments when nobody needed our ambulance – which was most of the time. Being conchies, we naturally agreed to help in any way and at any hour. 'Splendid!' said the MO. 'We have a couple of men in with scabies. Ever dealt with it before?'

In those days the standard treatment for scabies was to dab the body all over with sodium bisulphate, let it dry, then dab all over again with a solution of hydrochloric acid – which effectively released sulphuretted hydrogen, traditional constituent of schoolboy stink-bombs. No scabies-insect, however well established, could stand up to that dreadful smell of rotten eggs for long; but neither could the operator. My first patient that day was a soldier from the Pioneer Corps with the shaven head of an old lag. He was shy about taking his pants down, but not half as shy as he was soon to be when I dabbed his privates this way and that, where the infestation was at its worst. He looked desperate, went rapidly hard, looked desperate again, then decided to make a joke of it: 'Must be doing us good, sir!'

'That's the nearest you'll come to anything good for the next few days,' I said, trying to strike the right jokey note. But apparently I sounded too much like an officer for it to work.

Pretending to be at ease, he began whistling 'Music, Maestro, Please' out of tune.

Poor thing! I thought, *but poor me, too: so eager to please, and so inept!*

Our debut in society had a northern flavour all of its own. Nice Mrs Sutton went daily to Binns to sip coffee and be joined by this or that crony. Of those, two were very definitely personalities: Mrs Coulson and Mrs Dyer, wives respectively of a bank manager and a ship's chandler. Mrs Coulson's tongue was celebrated for miles around for being quite, quite poisonous. Mrs Dyer ('Rosalie'), on the other hand, was big-mouthed in a different way: full of hoarse endearments and warm, warm of heart. Rosalie had a chorus-boy friend, Bobby, no longer young but tolerated by Mr Dyer as presenting no threat to his marriage. I succeeded in seeming too normal for Bobby to let his peroxided hair down in front of me. To my surprise he showed signs of extreme jealousy when I stayed on, one night, to sleep on the sofa in Rosalie's sitting-room. He needn't have worried; I was far too sozzled to respond to her motherly caresses.

All seemed to be proceeding smoothly, until rumours about 'who we really were' began to spread. Mrs Coulson was one of the first to say, to Mrs Sutton, that we were 'shirkers'. A distressed Mrs Sutton came to us hoping for a denial. What were we to say? We might indeed be as worms beneath the feet of decent folk, but long before being called up we had consistently tried to do what we conceived to be our duty. Mrs Coulson was hardly an example of a keen war-horse, yet she felt fully entitled to look down on hard-working us. Nevertheless, the accusation rankled. Perhaps we should have counted ourselves lucky not to have been handed whole sacks full of white feathers; though in fact everyone else made a point of saying that they 'didn't mind' – which wasn't quite what we wanted to be told.

After that, West Hartlepool became unendurable. So when we heard a rumour that the BVAC might soon be dissolved, I greeted it with relief. It left the way open for entry into the Friends' Ambulance Unit (FAU), top-of-the-heap of all pacifist organisations, if they would have me.

14

It was not the best of moments to be summoned to appear before the Conscientious Objectors' Tribunal, but that was how things turned out in 1941. We conchies faced three arbiters, of which one (Mr Justice Hargreaves) was an actual judge; another was a superannuated trades union official and another unmemorable. Their main purpose was apparently to find out whether our objections were 'religious'. If so, well and good; but if not, then why not? My own (interrupted) leanings towards the Quakers hadn't progressed far enough for me to make that claim. I had to trust that they would appreciate my honesty in refusing to cite such grounds. Vain hope! 'Application rejected!' was the verdict.

Before prison gates finally clanged behind the unsuccessful there was an appeal procedure to be gone through. Whilst waiting for that slowly turning mill to do its grinding I heard that I'd been accepted by the Friends. Had they been quicker off the mark, I might never have realised how unfairly conchies could be treated, if they didn't fit precisely into a preordained pigeon-hole.

Hallam, also accepted by the Friends' Ambulance Unit, was sent with me and a handful of others to Guy's – not to their main hospital in central London but to a substantial section evacuated to Orpington to the south-east of Greater London. Once there, we were distributed wherever most required, which at first meant acting as emergency stretcher-bearers, on call night and day. As that vital job had diminished in importance since the debacle of Dunkirk* was out of the way, we were increasingly sent to the wards and the operating theatre as unskilled dogsbodies.

Being self-inflicted, our hours were long, sometimes beyond reckoning. As pacifists, we felt we had to work ourselves to the bone and to be seen to be overworking, to show the world what we were truly made of. I found myself in an orthopaedic ward, where dreadfully wounded veterans of Dunkirk were making a slow recovery.

A potentially tense situation arose. How might those brave men, ruined forever by war, react to having a declared non-belligerent nursing them? In fact, it wasn't tense at all. There was only one incident the whole of my time there and that was when a civilian started shouting abuse, yelling that he wasn't going to have this, wasn't going to put up with that, from a bloody conchie. The outcome? Seldom could a man have been more firmly squashed by those whom he was hoping to impress. My favourite patient, an ex-merchant seaman deprived of the use of his legs by a German torpedo, demanded to be wheeled over to

---

* The Battle of Dunkirk – which resulted in the Allies being forced to retreat back to England via civilian rescue boats, as well as navy ships – had taken place in May–June 1940.

the offender's bed, to give the man a roasting he would never forget. I was so touched, the tears came into my eyes.

My saviour, the seaman, was often moody and difficult to handle. I had to learn by experience never to appear condescending, but so much had to be done for him: lifting him on to a bedpan; lifting him up again; wiping him; gently setting him down – always to his embarrassment, however much we pretended that it was all in a day's work. I came to understand and forgive the bright jocularity of nurses; for what else would serve, in certain situations? Yet I tried not to copy their traditional manner, tempting though it was.

He particularly enjoyed being given a bath, which involved wheeling him into the one bathroom for the whole ward and manhandling him, with great difficulty, into the bath itself. He liked to say that it made him feel sexy, but those parts of him had also been affected by paralysis. Would I ever forget that agonised face, the sudden gleam of a smile, the sad, uncontrollable pout? No, never.

His behaviour was so different from the way Paddy Gorman, an Irish Guardsman, carried on a few beds away. Paddy had a smashed knee-cap, doubly serious for him because he was a keen footballer. He wriggled appreciatively when I rubbed what was delicately called his 'back' with methylated spirits, then patted on powder to prevent bedsores. Grinning conspiratorially, he made it clear that he wanted more intimate attentions (which I would have given him like a shot, had the standard screens provided more privacy). Pre-op, he hung on to my hand, squeezing it as I helped wheel him into the theatre.

I became known as 'King of the Sluice', a post for which there was absolutely no competition. The sluice was a deep porcelain sink with an extra-wide hole down which everything unpleasant was routinely poured. Its wooden side-flap provided a support for the nastiest job of all, scrubbing a 'plaster bed' with Dettol so that it could be re-used. Plaster beds were needed to keep smashed limbs rigid whilst they seeped quantities of blood and pus. Dissecting out the cranial nerves of a decaying dogfish was a bowl of roses compared with cleaning up a plaster bed after a really purulent wound. However, before coming off duty, I would see that the sluice was as sparkling as if nothing foul had been anywhere near it – a job as nauseating as anything I'd ever, voluntarily, undertaken in my life. For a saint, it would therefore have been the most satisfying; but I was no saint.

The words 'coming off duty' had a welcome meaning for other

hospital workers, but not for me. I had admitted having learnt how to cook at a Boy Scout camp, which was enough to turn me into Chief Chef from then on. It involved not just preparing the food but drawing rations from hospital stores run by a foxy little man who dispensed everything as though it came from his own private larder. By my second visit he was beckoning me over to this or that shelf where, on the pretext of 'pointing things out', he'd press himself against my back. Next, he was patting, then pinching. I couldn't claim to be thrilled, but when I found that a pat was worth an extra tin of veg, and a pinch an extra tin of pilchards, I was prepared to play along, pro bono publico. 'Rations are showing a great improvement since you took over' was the verdict. I didn't choose to explain why.

The whole thing started to take its toll. I was desperately tired and overworked and many ordinary things were getting on my nerves, as for instance the behaviour of nurses: the way they'd bustle up and down, pointlessly feigning busy-ness when calm efficiency would have been better; or the way a senior would give a junior a ticking-off, particularly if it could be done in front of a personable male patient. Little unkindnesses, little jealousies; that hospital world was overflowing with petty tyrannies in which I neither had, nor wanted to have, a part. It was almost as if I'd been put on stage in the wrong play, without being given a chance to rehearse my lines. Extreme exhaustion allowed little time to mull over such muddled ideas, but they were stirring within me and wouldn't let themselves be ignored for long.

Hospital life provided plenty of variety in other directions. I was sent to the theatre, to help keep instruments sterile. The first operation which I attended, duly masked and gowned, was an intricate affair involving switching the function of tendons in a man's wrist. To the theatre sister's astonishment, I watched dispassionately whilst a quick incision opened up a wound like a mouth, instantly dabbed with swabs and dilated with forceps. 'Most people who aren't used to it feel queasy. Some have even been known to faint at the first cut,' she said. She wasn't to know that I'd witnessed slashes far more shocking back in a Balliol bathroom, when a friend of mine had tried to take his own life.

I was less stolid when given a leg, which I'd just seen amputated by hack-saw, to take down to the 'dump' to be burnt. Wrapped in a red rubber sheet, the limb seemed to weigh a ton. The old man in charge chucked the parcel carelessly on to a smouldering pile of old dressings, where it heaved and charred, as if still partly alive. It ought to have been properly incinerated, but this was wartime and there was nobody to object.

Guy's Hospital (Orpington) had taken over an existing infirmary, a workhouse. The part where most of us worked was an annexe, consisting of wooden huts linked by covered corridors, makeshift from outside but tolerably well equipped within – the best that could be afforded. The original inhabitants had been allowed to stay on and creep incongruously amongst the spick-and-span nursing staff. I volunteered to remain on duty over Christmas 1941, so was involved in helping serve a proper, elaborate dinner to those old inmates. It pleased me at the time and would please me even more later to reflect that I could claim to know exactly what was meant by 'Christmas Day in the Workhouse'. A heart-rending occasion, shot through and through with determined jollity; once experienced, never to be forgotten.

So much to learn, from those days and nights of too much work and too little leisure. So much to learn.

Oddly enough, a growing reputation as an economical cook was what removed me from Guy's, Orpington. The FAU had a detachment at the Middlesex Hospital; some thirty of us living communally in the oldest of wards, green-tiled and permanently reeking of carbolic.

My catering allowance was only 2s 6d per head, per day. With extra kitchen help on a rota basis I scraped, not peeled, mounds of potatoes and each evening made old-fashioned porridge from oats, heating it early next morning in a double saucepan. I plied my captive customers with fried liver coated in flour, because nothing was cheaper or more easily obtainable than offal. For a second course, stale confectioner's cake at a knock-down price could be masked with custard to make it palatable. Lord Woolton, at the Ministry of Food, would have been proud of my variants on his infamous 'carrot pudding'.

For some reason difficult to fathom, cooking revived my interest in girls, all but stymied by over-exposure to too many nurses. On an afternoon off – for at the Middlesex I did at last have such a thing – I met Bridget Chetwynd on a bus going all the way from Tottenham Court Road to South Kensington for 4d. We got on well and she told me that she was doing typing for Peter Quennell, literary and social historian, for fun. I found her brilliantly amusing and sophisticated, though relatively uninterested in sex. However, like Mrs White, she was prepared to 'oblige' someone she fancied for other reasons.

After that, I was sent to a rest-centre at Stoke Newington. For a change, we weren't at all busy; in fact none of us knew quite what to do next. Hitler had apparently grown tired of sending bombs to fall on Stoke Newington, let alone Slough. We huddled, ready for the worst, and the worst never came. For days on end, checking stores once a week was our most strenuous task. At first, such inactivity seemed heavenly, but it soon palled.

I wandered about in nearby Islington, having heard that the Children's Care Committee were looking for helpers. They welcomed even such a one as myself with open arms; so I could be busy once more. Islington, as those who were to 'discover' it in the sixties would agree, was full of wonderful squares and gardens, once grand, but since fallen into decay. The war contributed its quota of shabbiness by producing sporadic bomb-damage. Nothing was repaired for years, so there was nothing to stop the buildings from going steadily downhill. My job was to visit parents of 'maternally deficient' children who were playing truant from school, and to dish out benefits where necessary (no one ever wanted to accept these 'hand-outs', however necessary they might be). But the time of idleness had stimulated thoughts and feelings which might otherwise have lain dormant. My new work at Islington merely postponed the central problem: was I right to go on doing what I'd been doing, when I no longer felt like doing it?

I pondered and pondered, by day, wondering and wondering, by night sleepless. There was much agony to endure, but the new demands of conscience, like the old, couldn't simply be ignored. I was slowly being driven to the conclusion that I was no longer a conscientious objector.

Precisely at that moment, as though on cue, I was summoned to appear before the Appeals Committee, a much more informal body than the original Objectors' Tribunal. They didn't hector or harangue. On the contrary, a few quiet, sensible people went carefully into my record of voluntary service and decided that of course I must remain with the Friends.

They used the words 'of course', which was thoughtful of them. It was most welcome, but in the circumstances an unfortunate way of putting it. The new directive was as impossible for me to follow as the tribunal's harsher one. I had refused to join the Forces for my own good reasons. Now I would have to refuse to continue with my saviours, the Quakers. Hardly was the ink dry on the Appeals' verdict than I was handing the Friends' Ambulance Unit my resignation. Fantastic as it seemed, I would have to end by joining up. 'Fighting for King and Country?' By no means! Fighting for myself, for my own desperately-trying-to-be-honest self.

Meanwhile, with no reason to continue bearing the burden of the world's woes on conscience-stricken shoulders, I could set about enjoying life, as I'd done so enthusiastically at Oxford, but with a difference: I was at large in London when all the conventions were breaking down. What in the world could be more enticing for a young man than that?

———

15

By this point it was 1942, and I was but twenty years old. For the time being I would continue my work for the Islington Care Committee and remain with the Friends. As I was still stationed at the Middlesex, my thoughts turned to finding a place to live nearby. The district was nicely central, no more than a fifteen-minute walk from Piccadilly Circus – the hub of everything, I thought. I began visiting such agents as were still operating in Blitz conditions, enquiring after modest rooms, a cut just above the lowest hostel accommodation. Such places were available at between 12s 6d and 15s 6d a week.

The rooms I was sent to see were almost always at the top of a house, that being where a bomb would strike first. I was not overly keen on a room in Cleveland Street, to one side of the hospital, but was prepared to take it because it was only one floor up: a charmless oblong lit by a gas-jet projecting from a side-wall; off it a cubby-hole with a sink and draining-board and just enough space for a gas cooker (which wasn't supplied, though the agent said that one could be bought second-hand for £2 19s 6d from a shop next to Maples in Tottenham Court Road). That was all. No bath, indeed no bathroom in the whole house, and only the one lavatory on the ground floor, shared by everyone. To top all else, there was a peculiar frowsty smell on the stairs, of geraniums wrapped in old socks. I wondered where it was coming from. All the same, I moved in, glad to have a place of my own again at last.

Bridget Chetwynd, by then a part-time lover, lent basic furniture: a wardrobe painted pink; a table; a rickety chair; a double-divan bed; and some ancient cooking-things encrusted with the grime of years. Not that I cared. Anything capable of use was good enough for me. Of much more immediate concern was what happened nightly when I turned off the gas-jet. I would feel itchy, then scratchy. With the gas-jet on again, a score of insects could be seen scurrying back into cracks in the wall. Dark-brown, groovy-backed, each with a seafarer's rolling gait, they would advance in line towards the bare floorboards, making for my bed. It was my first encounter with bed-bugs.

Evidently the bugs didn't like the gas-light, so I kept it hissing away, which made the room unbearably hot and the bites itch even more. After the first night I procured four cylindrical cigarette tins, poured in paraffin, and humped each divan leg into a tin, creating an oily, impassable barrier. I had to be careful not to let the bedclothes (a sheet, a bolster covered in ticking and two dog-blankets) touch either the wall or the floor.

On settling back, I found to my horror that some of the more enterprising bugs had learned to climb upside down across the ceiling above the bed and let go at just the right moment – an incredible feat of applying newly acquired knowledge, placing them high on the ladder of Natural Selection. When squashed, they emitted a brown ooze responsible for the all-pervading frowsty stink on the stairs. In future, that smell would be a valuable warning signal. But what was immediately to be done?

I talked it over with my downstairs neighbour. She was extremely reticent; she wouldn't use the word 'bug', but referred to the infestation as 'dirty'. 'I've hired a roomful of furniture from Catesby's,' she whispered, as though unable to admit to it out loud. 'It wouldn't do for them to find out!' (Catesby was in Tottenham Court Road. It had never occurred to me that furniture could be hired from a shop. How they'd come to regret that policy, in certain cases!)

The house was owned by the hospital, so I persuaded them to fumigate the place, though they only did my room and of course one of the bugs survived and managed to find its way into my neighbour's; their negligence was extraordinary, to be excused only by 'DONTcher know there's a WAR on?' I heard later that even large-scale fumigation mightn't have sufficed. Bugs were capable of moving sideways as adroitly as up and down. Further enquiries revealed that there were several 'bug-lines' running through London, crossing and re-crossing the smartest and most expensive streets. Their exact location was said to be a house agent's most closely guarded secret.

At this point my mother took a hand. She was so appalled by my account of the bed-bugs that she offered to lend me the extra, if only I would get myself a proper flat. For 19s 6d a week, Farnham and Coigley assured me that I'd be getting 'a different class of property' – two rooms and a combined bathroom/kitchen at the top of a house in Nassau Street, opposite the casualty entrance of the Middlesex. When I saw it, I was enchanted by its leaded rooftop, to which only my flat had privileged access – private enough for sunbathing naked. I took the flat at once.

'We don't need a formal lease. Drawing one up would simply be a waste of money,' said the cunning agents. 'We can just have a Gentlemen's Agreement.' I was too thrilled with the new flat to find such a remark suspicious; and anyhow, I foresaw making £1 a week by letting one of the rooms, furnished, to a Friend tired of communal living over the road. It was to be my first experience as a landlord, of prime importance because it set a pattern for true independence, of never again being subject to the whims of the respectable – a valuable influence in life from then on.

When I returned Bridget's things, I was afraid that their sojourn in Cleveland Street might have made them 'dirty', so I was greatly relieved to hear that the fumigation had done its work. I missed her huge bed most, because it meant that I would be sleeping on the floor. Other bits of furniture flowed in quite unexpectedly. My father (of all people), now with Beni in Thurloe Place, contributed some of the contents of a Bosham cottage where he'd formerly nested with 'my' Tocky. The best pieces I acquired were reserved for the lodger; my own comfort was of secondary importance.

My mother came to London for war-work, but I saw very little of her. She was made a Corporal – a low-sounding rank, but denoting that she was in charge – of a Red Cross detachment based on Grosvenor Crescent, delivering ambulances. When they decided that they would prefer a younger woman for the job, she returned to Lincolnshire to become a SAAFA (Soldiers', Sailors' & Airmen's Families Association) representative for the Combined Forces Families charity, not far away from where my sister Morvyne was (at that moment) a land-girl. My younger sister, Genissa, was a Naval Voluntary Aid Detachment nurse at Haslar before being sent to Ceylon. All the family members were beavering away, doing their bit; all except me.

For once, I didn't feel in the least guilty. I'd been working such exceedingly long hours as a conchie that I felt entitled to a well-earned rest. And as for danger: with anti-aircraft guns raining down shrapnel as we walked the streets, I was fatalistically convinced that nothing could touch me. When nothing did, it seemed to be a vindication of faith rather than foolhardiness. I strode out and about at all hours in the black-out, revelling in new-found freedom.

16

I'd been like a moth to Bridget's flame, instantly attracted to her brilliance, regarding her as the fountain-head of sophistication, although even at that early stage I recognised that her writing, as marvellously funny as herself, tended to be all on one wavelength. She seemed stuck in a groove of depicting Evelyn Waughish characters in Evelyn Waughish situations. She seemed to know 'everybody'. Through her, I was soon hobnobbing with the literary critic Cyril Connolly (not much) and the poet Brian Howard (rather more). The literary scene had been unknown to me, and I was much drawn to it, possibly because it contained people eager to discuss what no self-respecting Friend would so much as mention.

Brian Howard,* especially, liked to shock and startle. What a treat! His attitudes were original and amusing, to me at least. Why did he bother to cast his pearls at my feet? I honestly didn't know, but I took it all in my stride. There were numerous dinners at La Belle Meunière and other Charlotte Street restaurants, which included shaming rows with waiters and other drunken scenes, all fascinating for me and costing nothing, of course, as I had no money.

---

* Brian Howard was an interesting, if Marmite, character. In a letter to a friend, Evelyn Waugh admitted he based '2/3' of a character who popped up in his books under different names on Brian. Waugh would later say that as a young man he'd been 'dazzling' but that he was 'constantly attacking people with his fists in public places' in later life. When Roddy knew him, Brian was in his late thirties and had clearly started entering this phase.

Brian was living in a flat in Hallam Street, a solid-looking place belonging to his mother (who ran Floris, the scent-shop in Jermyn Street, with steely efficiency). He would invite me along for an evening. Usually there'd be someone else there, too. 'Aha!' he would say. 'Here comes the Quaker Governess! May one ask what you're going to disapprove of today?'

'You, to begin with!' I might reply. And we'd go on from there.

One incident stuck in my mind because it involved a recently developed hobby. I'd started collecting old gramophone records, which could be bought for 2d or 3d each in local junk-shops. However scratched and indistinct, they appealed to me by evoking the twenties, a decade before my time and all the more precious for that reason. Brian adored them too; but then, he was of their period. My 'Flamin' Mamie, the Two-time Vamp' ('The Hottest Baby in Town') was possibly his favourite.

One day, Brian asked me to bring along 'Some of These Days', sung by Sophie Tucker; not her later rubbish but the throaty, original version for which I'd paid a whole 6d. We put it on his gramophone and Brian mimed it à la Sophie, becoming a Red Hot Momma himself. He said, 'I want you to ring the number I'm about to give you and say, in a very ordinary voice: "This is the Musical Telegram Company. We have been instructed to play the following Musigram for you. Are you ready . . . ?"' That was his cue to start the record going:

Some of these days
You're gonna feel so lonely . . .
You're gonna miss ma huggin'
You're gonna miss ma kissin'

. . . and so on. The plan was to wait for it to run its course, when I was to hand over the telephone for him to add: 'And serve you right, YOU HEARTLESS BUGGER!'

At first, all went well. The man at the other end answered and waited. But halfway through he replaced the receiver with a bang, leaving us with nothing but the dialling tone. Brian was – or claimed to be – heartbroken. Actually, I felt that it had increased his enjoyment by providing the perfect excuse for a scene, sprawled in a chair, legs outstretched, Sephardic face racked with misery. 'Oscar would have appreciated the torments I suffer!' he groaned. 'But what's that to a prim young Quakeress?'

The restaurants to which he took me were technically allowed to charge no more than five shillings a head. In fact, by means of a 'cover charge' and other ruses, they managed to bump up a bill to ten or more shillings. Even so, they provided good value, far beyond my means. In particular, The White Tower (which had been Stulick's 'Eiffel Tower' in my favoured twenties)* produced a moussaka so amply satisfying that they were accused of using cats to eke out their meat-ration. But for Brian, I would never have gone to such places and thus missed the tail-end of a sample of pre-war life, to be treasured later.

When I had perforce to feed myself, all the skills learned with the Friends came into play. Porridge continued to be a daily staple, cheap and nourishing. In a workman's café in Goodge Street I could get a substantial breakfast (with bacon) for 9d and a better one for another 2d. Allowing for a twenty-fold multiplication, such prices were reasonable beyond belief from today's viewpoint.

Nassau Street was in the heart of a district later to be dubbed 'Fitzrovia', the Fitzroy Tavern† being at its centre. Naturally, I gravitated to it of an evening, never having seen anything like it in my life before; an added advantage being that no Friend would be likely to cross its sinful threshold. So much was to be written about 'the Fitz' that it was to become part of the mythology of London low life. Its ceiling was stuck with bags of coins ('for our annual children's outing') and one could always count on Paul, a pianist with straggly hair, beard, earrings and bangles pre-dating the hippies. (Apropos of Paul, I learnt that he was famed for drawing intensely sado-masochistic pictures of lobsters pinching, with gigantic claws, outsize parts of naked men and women.)

To me, the most interesting feature was the presence of two presiding bar-flies, both women, both with a favoured coterie whose function was to keep them continually supplied with drink – spirits, for choice, but a lowly half-bitter would do if nothing stronger were on offer. They were Nina Hamnett and Sylvia Gough, as unalike as could be except for that

---

* The Eiffel Tower was a hotel and restaurant on Percy Street, frequented by the likes of George Bernard Shaw, the painter Augustus John and Edward VIII before he was King, among many others. It became The White Tower in the 1940s, remaining until the nineties. Today, you can find a Vietnamese restaurant on the site called The House of Ho.

† The Fitzroy Tavern was a popular haunt for George Orwell, Virginia Woolf, Dylan Thomas, George Bernard Shaw and other famous literary types.

shared weakness. Nina, having written *Laughing Torso*, was capable, if not too far gone, of telling intriguing tales of pre-war Bohemia, but she was likely to break off in mid-flow if she spied a sailor. She could then be brutally direct: 'I'll have you know, young man, I'm good for a fuck!' Then, peering with boot-button eyes into a prospective victim's face: 'That is, if you're not looking for SOMETHING ELSE!' On the whole she was intelligent and gave good value for the money spent on her.

Sylvia Gough, on the other hand, had been 'a beauty', boasting of having been a chorus-girl before marrying a General. Whereas Nina was a lady, Sylvia had learnt to be lady-like – one difference between them. Sylvia had acquired an upper-class trick of throwaway speech, which could be very amusing. She was not as slovenly as Nina, usually to be seen in a brown coat trimmed with fur, in those days a patent of respectability. Sylvia liked to 'talk grand', about people she'd known who were smart rather than artistic.

I preferred Sylvia, perhaps partly because she preferred me. I enjoyed her reminiscences, true or false, of country-house weekends, whereas I had not the slightest wish to hear what pranks Gaudier-Brzeska, or even Picasso, had got up to with Nina. So, when Sylvia happened to ask me, one Saturday evening, to put her up for the night, I said yes.

In the basement of Nassau Street lived our caretaker, Mr Fitch. Normally in braces and shirt-sleeves and reeking of BO, on Saturdays he would tog himself out like a masher at the halls around the turn of the century: brown suit, floral button-hole, bowler hat with turned-up brim, silver-mounted stick and all. Sylvia and I encountered Mr Fitch at the front door, bidding an elaborate good night to a lady friend.

'Ah! Goo–DEEvening!' said Sylvia grandly, before giving vent to a burp and being violently sick. 'Beg pudden!' she intoned, smiling roguishly as she plunged towards the stairs, leaving me to make what apologies I could.

Chasing Sylvia upstairs, I had to abandon her in the flat and rush back with a cloth and a jug of hot water. Mr Fitch rounded on me furiously, but I kept silent as I cleaned up the mess, trusting to my actions to calm him down. Luckily his lady friend, overpainted and ultra-refined, was still hanging about. Helpfully, she declared, 'Ay think your mothah may have eaten somethink to disagree with her!' which tied his tongue. When I got back upstairs, I found Sylvia already stripping off her clothes, revealing pink satin cami-knickers, far from clean. Questing about, she demanded, 'Where's the bed? My God, I can't see the bloody bed!'

'Of course you can't,' I said crossly. 'That's because there isn't one.'

'Must have a bed ...'

'No "must" about it. We sleep on the floor, here.'

Eyeing me with deepest suspicion, she crawled, without undressing further, under the heap of bedclothes where I normally slept myself. I retired to the lodger's room, which happened to be empty.

Next morning, to my horror, I found that she'd bled on to the bottom sheet. 'Darling, I ought to have given it a mench – I think I may have caught the clap from that stinker Dermot! 'Member, we were talking about him last night? Too shaming! Anyway, one thing I can positively guarantee, it isn't the syph. Promise!' She indignantly refused my porridge – 'Never touch the stuff!' – but was glad of a cup of strong tea and a piece of cheese (on the ration, therefore precious).

On her way out, she tripped on a stair and sat there, wailing. For a moment I feared (unworthily) that it might be weeks before I'd be shot of her. I underestimated her stamina. 'Just a bruise, darling, nothing to worry about. See you this evening!'

Not if I can help it! I muttered to myself, managing a foolish grin. Traces of last night's excesses were still clinging to the front doorstep. That would mean a formal visit to the caretaker, to abase myself even more humbly, in true Quaker style. I found him once more in shirtsleeves, reeking of an evening's excesses on top of his usual smell, and with a hangover too. Even so, I realised that I didn't really mind anything that had happened, it had all been so strange and compelling. I could regard it as the baptism of a true Fitzrovian.

———

17

As I drew further apart from the Friends, I began dipping first a toe, then my whole self, into the world of London night-clubs, entirely because Bridget had become one of the team responsible for the social gossip page of the *Tatler*. She had perforce to pursue her quarry to The Four Hundred, The Suivi and The Nuthouse, which she didn't enjoy doing on her own, so she asked me to be her companion. She found it boring, but I was as keen as could be, so keen that Elma Warren, holding sway over 'the Nut' in thick, black-rimmed glasses, encouraged me to come whenever I could, 'on the house' even without Bridget.

On such occasions I was expected to pull my weight by going round the tables where American airmen from the Eagle Squadron sprawled in a manner which would eventually be stigmatised as 'macho', encouraging them to drink up and order expensive food. The Eagles were forerunners of American Forces Over Here. They were superior and pleasantly naive. Few of us had met their like before. They would lavish money on drink and talk about treating the club hostesses 'like queens', but as the girls were forbidden to take on private business before closing time – 4.30 a.m. – rare were the boys in powder-blue who could survive till then with libido intact.

How could I remain uninfluenced, exposed to the exciting turbulence of a wicked world after the anxious calm of conscientious objection? I could see and hear myself changing under the impact of all those new people and new things. The war with which I'd been grappling daily seemed to recede into a background of occasional bangs, flashes and wailing sirens. It was sometimes hard to remember that I was still living in the same old England.

Alas! I had only the same old bank-balance, depleted by such mundane matters as gas and electricity bills and a bare minimum spent on food. Even with a lodger it was hard to make ends meet when they had to include the sort of life I was leading. Under such circumstances, my standards of morality and behaviour took a nose-dive. I began putting things down on my mother's account at Harrods. When she found out, she was extremely annoyed – rightly so, though I didn't want to see that at the time.

As things turned out, I didn't have to look far for a new source of income. It turned up, lisping, on the doorstep, in the shape of ex-Slade School Marcus Grischotti (who had been discharged from the Army – rather curiously, for wetting the bed – and was now training as a wireless operator in the Merchant Navy). I was glad of his presence, reviving, as it did, memories of my friend Vil Gorakshakar and all those other pleasant Oxford moments. He moved in to sleep, like me, on the floor.

Then his half-brother Barry appeared, having suffered a genuine nervous breakdown working for the Censor in Bermuda. And shortly after that, a third brother, 'Wigs', in the process of being cashiered for embezzling regimental funds. Wigs was over-fond of drink, and when drunk his character underwent a dramatic change: he would become sly and bellicose, a fearful mixture. I couldn't fit him into Nassau Street on a permanent basis, but during his short stay he contrived to steal at least one of my suits, possibly two, for pawning round the corner. Perhaps I should have put up a 'House Full' sign when people kept on arriving – friends, or friends of friends, hoping for a roof over their heads 'just for the night'. With Mary Stanley-Smith's precept in mind, I wouldn't turn anyone away unless they were too awful for words. Helpings of porridge could be stretched to fill almost any number of mouths and comfort was minimal; but who minded, in wartime?

The downside was I couldn't get on with my painting, or indeed with anything except endless chat, punctuated by playing a selection of twenties records, stacked eight at a time on an automatic turntable bought for £9 in West Hartlepool. Just then, I happened to come across Jacqui, who I'd met during my time at Stoke Newington Rest-Centre, and was asked to dinner at her place in Gloucester Gate Mews, the other side of the park.

'Watch out, shee'th after you!' lisped Marcus.

So much the better! I thought. *At least it'll get me away from here, for a moment.*

Jacqui had certainly earned her descriptive name of 'petite blonde'. She was five-foot-nothing and as blonde as could be, with pinky highlights which she imagined suited her. She talked with a slightly Welsh accent. As a social worker, she had been almost as incongruous as myself. However, it turned out that she wrote poetry – hence the dinner, when we were to discuss her verses as much as anything. I duly arrived with an overnight bag (the usual kit at that time, in case air-raids made travelling back across London too hazardous). Her 'houselet' was everything that Nassau Street was not: it was clean; it had fitted carpets everywhere except in the kitchen; in fact, in house agents' terms, it was thoroughly 'bijou'.

We sat down to a newly arrived 'Lease-Lend' tin of sausage meat, a lump of tasty stodge much meatier and less sausagey than it sounded, being American. Then we sat on a chaise-longue in her sitting-room, which was not much wider than a corridor, reading her 'works' out loud, which led to a more intimate interchange. I was taken by surprise by feelings which, with Bridget, had lain dormant; feelings recalling my success, after a fumbling approach, with Peryl in the Hyde Park Hotel.

Here again the anti-aircraft guns boomed and rattled from a park –
Regent's Park – and a siren sounded. But neither of us was inclined to
seek an air-raid shelter.

'Shall we go into the bedroom?' said Jacqui eventually.

Her bedroom was by far the largest room in the houselet, equipped
with fitted cupboards and with a bathroom off, as warm as toast from
thermostatically controlled electric central heating. For the rest of that
night I saw no reason to shift; nor next day; nor the following night. We
ate our way through her hoard of precious tins as though there were no
tomorrow. Only the realisation that my absence might be causing grave
concern in Nassau Street brought about a move.

Marcus greeted me uneasily. 'All I can thay ith – THE GYPTHY
WARNED YOU!' he lisped.

'But I've had a wonderful time.'

'Tho you thay. But will you thtill be tho thrilled when you thmell
the orange-blothom? Thath where ith all leading.'

'I'd better ask her here,' I said. 'She won't survive the shock of our
slum for long.'

There I was completely wrong. Far from 'doing a Snow White' and
chasing us out with bucket and broom, Jacqui seemed to relish the
untidiness, the continual noise, above all the comings and goings. I
only managed to shift her back to her own home by having a telephone
at last installed, so that she could ring up and invite herself back at any
moment. This relieved my unease at being delayed like an overdue
foetus in the thermostatically controlled womb of Gloucester Gate
Mews. Marcus didn't have to issue his warnings. I was well aware of
what could lie ahead, unless I were careful.

———

18

With sails set to catch the wind from whatever quarter it blew, I
rocked randily towards 27 March 1942, my twenty-first birthday.

The only cloud on the horizon was the prospect of being called up.
I'd decided on the Air Force – not as a pilot (I didn't care for hunting

foxes, let alone Germans*) but an observer, seated at a flight-desk, working out courses and times of arrival. Poor as I'd always been at maths, such elementary geometry shouldn't be beyond my powers. I set aside the question of how to go about it the better to concentrate on the coming moment when the Key of the Door would be mine.

In the eyes of the world, to reach the age of twenty-one was to achieve maturity; yet, on the brink of becoming officially adult, I felt the same as ever, inside. Still, it was to be a very special anniversary, marked with a coming-of-age-party, which was to begin at Martinez, the Spanish restaurant near Piccadilly Circus, and end up in The Nuthouse, and paid for by family, thank goodness.

I woke up on the 27th to Jacqui preparing a proper breakfast of bacon and eggs. (She had insisted on staying at my place in order to 'do it' on the day, which meant a minute after midnight, so that we could then get some sleep.) As a treat I'd hired a Daimler, with a chauffeur in uniform protected from us by a glass partition, who ferried Jacqui home and me to the bank to deposit a cheque from one of my godfathers for £50! I drew out £15, the largest sum in cash I could ever remember having in my pocket. Later, the Daimler took me, sitting in solitary state, to the Grosvenor, where Merrie, Lady Rawlinson,† a great old chum of my grandmother's, was giving a lunch for the birthday boy. Grandly I pressed five shillings into the chauffeur's hand for him to get a bite to eat.

Eventually Marcus, Jacqui and I went in full evening rig to the Empress Club, in Dover Street, where my mother was staying. 'Roddy's Night Out' had officially begun.

At the sight of Jacqui, my mother blanched. It was their first meeting, and they weren't likely to have much in common. Nothing had prepared her for the special hair-do Jacqui had gone to the hairdresser's to achieve earlier in the day, which was indeed sensational: imitation violets scattered

---

* Roddy did go through all the tests to become a pilot, but it was his eyesight that let him down – something he confessed he was relieved about, given his reason here: he didn't want to shoot down other men anyway. But he was upset with regards the short-comings of his sight, which he blamed on the 'Dame' (the matron) at Eton. She hadn't let a teenage Roddy seek treatment quickly for pink-eye because 'Trials' (exams) were about to start. Though Roddy's grandmother Maya paid later for him to be treated by a London specialist, he believed by that point the damage was done, as his eyesight never completely recovered.

† Merrie Rawlinson was the wife of the 1st Baron Rawlinson, who was a leading General for the British in the First World War, in particular at the Battles of the Somme and Amiens.

over ash-blonde waves, pink-highlighted, drenched in lacquer to keep everything in place. When first asked to admire it, I had to pretend to be lost for words. I hardly dared think what effect it must be having on another woman. Granny Rawnsley behaved rather better, seeming to notice nothing unusual. Awkwardness was quickly dispelled by Marcus, who was generally able to keep the ball rolling in any company.

Apart from the hiccup of Jacqui's presence, it interested but appalled me to find myself back in favour with my grandmother and other relations on three counts: I'd 'come to my senses'; I'd 'seen the error of my ways'; I was about to 'fight for my country'. All three explanations happened to be incorrect, but why try explaining?

At Martinez we were joined by Bridget Chetwynd, promising to write us up. Elma Warren was going to be thrilled, that was for sure. When the time came for us to leave our paella and Spanish fizz, we were able to walk round to the Nut, which was in a basement in Regent Street. Elma greeted us with enthusiasm, tempered with financial acumen: 'We'll put on something special for you tonight, and then perhaps we'll see our photos in the *Tatler*?' As usual, Bridget and I were admitted free, but the others had to pay their pounds. 'How very good of her to let you in for nothing because it's your birthday!' said my grandmother, unaware. I didn't disillusion her.

We were led into the dim, low-ceilinged room hung with lines of what looked like washing: corsets and other more glamorous underclothes were strung out overhead, creating an atmosphere of abandon. At the further end, beyond a tiny dance floor, a band of men who looked elderly to me – they'd have been in their early thirties – tinkled and banged and blew. I knew them all, of course; but again, that was something I didn't choose to let on.

I welcomed a chance of talking to the dancers, Antonio and Rosaria. I'd only ever smiled at them before. Antonio was sinuous, with a farouche look about him, very appealing. Emboldened by the occasion, I asked for his address and mentioned that I might drop by and see him, perhaps even the next day. 'Please, not too early!' was his reply, eyes flashing.

The band struck up with one of my favourites (I'd asked them nicely), 'Happy Days Are Here Again', following it with 'If I Had a Talking Picture of You-hoo', one of Janet Gaynor's songs, popularised by Ruth Etting.

'Ruth Etting had just the right waily quiver in her voice, missing in more modern singers,' I said knowledgeably.

'As a fully paid-up gangster's moll, I daresay she did!' said Bridget.

Soon they were striking up 'Happy Birthday to You!' which reduced the entire club to bemused silence, then mild hand-clapping when the spotlight swung on to a bowing, smiling me. Glasses were waved, toasts were drunk. 'All the more for Elma,' said Bridget. 'She's getting her money's-worth out of us tonight.'

Then the lights dimmed, insofar as they could: they were too dim already to see clearly what we were drinking. The spotlight switched to Antonio and Rosaria as they began their routine of elaborate 'oriental' movements to the strains of 'Chanson Hindou'. I'd seen it several times before, but I still enjoyed the bendings over backwards, the jerky neck movements from side to side. They gestured constantly in my direction, Antonio all but presenting me with his bare, gyrating belly-button. 'He thinks you'll be standing him drinks later on,' said a cynical Bridget. She didn't know what plans I had for later on still.

Another of the acts, Al Burnett – bat-faced, more than slightly sinister – was ushered on stage with a fanfare. He started with his usual opening song:

> *Once I was a barmaid, down in Drury Lane,*
> *My master he was good to me, MY MISTRESS*
> *WAS THE SAME!*

All right so far, including:

> *Along came a sailor, in coat of navy blue,*
> *He'll climb the rigging like his father used to do.*
> *But then what? The chorus:*
> *Frigging in the rigging, frigging in the rigging,*
> *Frigging in the rigging, he'd ECK-all else to do!*

I breathed a sigh of relief at the use of that word 'eck'. Al couldn't always be relied upon to slur over the obvious. Glancing at our table to make sure that we were clapping, he launched into 'Leicester Square', one of his most risqué numbers, breaking off only to shout 'Well, you asked for it!', then continuing, to the tune of 'The Lambeth Walk':

> *Any time you're Leicester Square, all the boys are girls down there,*
> *You'll find them all . . . doing the Fansy Walk!*

Again, the tactfulness of substituting an 'f' for a 'p'. I looked round at Granny Rawnsley. She was smiling vacantly. Everything was passing above her head.

> *There's a little one there called 'Queenie' . . .*
> *And a MASSIVE BRUTE, called 'Teeny' . . .*

went on Al, with gestures to match. For the final exit, he put one hand on his hip and with the other pretended to swing a handbag. For 1942, that was pretty strong medicine. My mother was looking baffled, Granny Rawnsley still smiling vacantly, actually beating time. 'I've always liked that Lambeth thing,' she said. 'They seem to enjoy themselves so much, doing it.'

I discovered later that my mother had spent a miserable evening, fearing that at any moment I would be announcing my engagement to Jacqui. Her relief, when I didn't, was enormous. She might not have minded so much had she known that I'd been chatting up Antonio. As things turned out, there would be little reason for her to worry. Calling at his flat in Old Compton Street at midday, I found him still in a dressing-gown. Daylight was none too kind to a pale, lined face which had looked so smooth and ruddy under a spotlight. I fled, making what excuses I could.

I was definitely not going to get engaged to Jacqui. Now that the key of the door had officially become mine, there was all the more reason to be sure of turning it in the right lock.

But what lock was that? I just had no idea.

19

On 1 June 1942, an otherwise glorious summer's day, it arrived: the document summoning me into the Army. However, I'd already decided to go the whole hog and become one of 'The Few'; even if, by then, to be a member of an RAF flying crew meant being one amongst many.

Luckily, I had a lever to make this a reality. Whilst slowly walking between Martinez and The Nuthouse my grandmother had mentioned Group Captain Morven Cavendish-Bentinck and the fact that he was 'in Sheffield, looking after Air Cadets. It suits him because he can easily get back home, although of course Welbeck [Abbey]*'s been taken over and they're all crouching cheek by jowl in one wing.'

I knew of Morven, of course. He was the excellent (but not excellent enough) pupil of the classical pianist Irene Scharrer† (I was acquainted with Irene's son Ian Lubbock), and younger son of the animal rights activist Winifred Cavendish-Bentinck, Duchess of Portland. Certainly worth writing to. I sent him a boyish letter, calculated to appeal, and the effect was stunning: I was invited to lunch, when we might 'go into the question more thoroughly'.

Dressed in what was known as 'Sunday best' I presented myself at Sheffield's most superior hotel, where the Group Captain was obviously a valued customer. A whole unrationed pigeon each was on the menu. I seized it in my fingers.

'Splendid!' said Morven approvingly – a signal that we were home and dry. We hardly mentioned my threatened call-up. 'I can arrange for you to present yourself here. That'll side-step the Army thing,' he said. 'Now tell me, what have you been up to lately?'

What indeed hadn't I been up to, these last months? I thought it better not to embark on even a limited version. (I was wrong. Morven would have loved louche details, the loucher the better, but I wasn't to know that.) Instead of describing hectic times in the Fitzroy, I dwelt on my months of worthy but pedestrian toil in the UAU, the BVAC and the FAU. He could scarcely suppress a yawn as the initials came tumbling out.

'I'm told there's lots of fun in London these days,' he said, his chin (shaven, but still rather blue) quivering. 'Ian Lubbock seems to think so, anyway.'

'Oh, Ian,' I said reprovingly. 'I've heard he's too fond of men!' What

---

* Any words in square brackets within this book were inserted by Roddy.

† Irene Scharrer (1888–1971) reminds us that, even in Edwardian times, women could be part of the celebrity that has always followed music. She studied at the Royal Academy of Music and gave her first concert in 1904 (aged just sixteen); she would give many more until she retired in 1958. She would often play four-handed compositions with the even more famous Myra Hess (who toured various European countries, as well as America).

induced me to come out with such a preposterous statement I didn't, and would never, know. Was it because I thought that this was what I was meant to say to a very senior RAF officer?

Hardly were the words out of my mouth than I regretted them heartily, so heartily that I started blushing, which in turn reduced Morven to a jelly; he wobbled visibly, assumed a worried look and asked earnestly, 'Is he? Is he really? I wouldn't know . . .'

The remainder of our lunch proceeded with reserve on either side. Oh, how I could have kicked myself! The stupid truth was that until then I didn't connect equivocal goings-on with 'respectable' people. Evidently I had a lot to learn.

In spite of the absurd contretemps, the lunch fulfilled its objective. Army calling-up papers were mysteriously squashed. A switch to the RAF was made, as promised. I awaited a new summons to serve my country via Sheffield.

But first, I had to end things with Jacqui. One night I had a 'wedding nightmare' (well known to psychologists) in which I'd all but reached the altar before realising that it was a ghastly mistake – a salutary warning. The very next morning we talked it over. I had to assure her that there wasn't 'another woman', but that I simply couldn't continue. She didn't make a scene, but simply packed up and went back to her tidy cocoon. I had to hope that she was better off without me; and I may have been right.

In August I was summoned to present myself in Sheffield for induction into the RAF, where the new intake was then sent straight to a camp outside Warrington, to be immersed in a life unimaginably remote from ordinary existence. Every move we made was accompanied by shouted orders, every shout prefaced by profanity. Even in the East End I'd never heard its like. Shocking? More than shocking: a series of blows, almost physical in their intensity, battering the mind into submission. Was this how to make men out of raw recruits? If it were any comfort, it must always have been so. But it wasn't much comfort.

I rushed to a telephone booth to ring up Bridget in London and soon heard her drawly voice answering: 'Poor Roddy! It must be too, too ghastly! Can't you find some warm and cosy character to "show you the ropes", as they say? I mean, that's what's supposed to happen in all the best stories.'

I was interrupted by a man hammering on the door with angry

gestures: 'Ere, mister! Git a move on, there's uvvers in the queue!' I noticed he called me 'mister'. It meant that although we were all alike and in uniform I hadn't become 'mate'. Our English class system had triumphed even over HMG's most determined act of levelling-down. What it boiled down to was that I could never hope to be 'one of the lads'.

Being used to a background of twenties gramophone records, I wasn't bothered as much by the continual noise as were some. Lack of privacy at night, also, was manageable for one accustomed to sleeping on a floor in the company of (if not with) comparative strangers. But not having enough palatable things to eat came as a surprise, considering how unfussy I was about food. Every other meal consisted of 'individual meat pies', gristle enclosed in a soggy crust, supplied, we decided, by hard-faced men doing well out of the war. The alternative was 'bread-and-scrape', meaning margarine, which might or might not be overscraped with a pinky goo purporting to be jam. The remedy was a visit to the NAAFI, where spam and chips were to be had at a very low price; but few of us had been provident enough to bring much money along.

And, search how I might, I couldn't find so much as one of Bridget's 'warm and cosy characters' to take me under his wing. Instead, I found that I was the one to be sought out by a would-be-superior intellectual who expected me to join him in despising the 'clottishness' of everyone else. I wouldn't. Why shouldn't they be clots, if that were what made them tick, especially as some of the least brainy were often the best-looking?

I was getting used to the rules of underdog military society when we were posted to an ITW (Initial Training Wing) in Blackpool – a slow train journey through unfamiliar blast-furnaces and industrial slag-heaps. As we drew into the station, some of the lads cheered. They didn't cheer for long. We were marched raggedly through mean streets behind South Shore, where the meanest of boarding-houses offered façades identical in greyness to the pavements. Formed into platoons, each platoon was directed into this or that billet to be housed and fed by the boarding-house keeper: always a woman, always penny-pinching, usually with a smaller, subservient husband in the background. It was as if we'd been thrust into one of Gracie Fields' earlier films, but without her perky hoots to inspire us to keep our peckers up. If they'd ever had hearts of gold, unattractive dealings with unattractive lodgers had long since scarred them. They were simply ghastly.

We slept as many to a room as the housekeepers could squeeze in. We were fed on 'brawn', a sludge embedded in reddened jelly, or else on 'cottage pie' of unknown provenance, with occasional 'treats' of sausage. No meat passed our lips which hadn't been adulterated in some way with extraneous matter, not even masked by herbs. Hot water came on twice a day, but woe betide the dare-devil who tried to run a bath! What basins there were reeked of drains, which was only to be expected, considering that for years they'd been used as *pissoirs*. When drenched in Jeyes Fluid they retaliated by emitting a prolonged, ineradicable stink.

Our training was not particularly irksome, even though it entailed rising early to trot up and down the promenade doing physical jerks, which some of the men found hard to bear, especially the married ones, missing their morning cuddles. I knew what they meant, but I wasn't missing mine; it was rather a relief to wake and find myself alone in bed.

Our Corporal-in-charge singled me out to be Platoon Leader. Not that it made much difference – we were all equally 'A/C2s', Aircraftsmen 2nd Class – but he needed someone to carry the can when things went wrong. His decision thus to elevate me caused mutterings. This late in the war we were of all ages, the eldest being a grey-beard of forty-two, nicknamed 'Uncle'.

'Why didn't you put Uncle in charge?' I asked the Corporal.

Answer: 'You're an educated sort of bloke, I could spot you a mile off!' Which actually didn't please me much. It was one more proof that I still wasn't fitting in.

We were in a prime spot for entertainment when Wakes Week came and went. Thousands of girls from northern mills poured into Blackpool intent on one thing and one thing only: getting a man in uniform. We undistinguished airmen were jostled as we stood at the bar of our local by girls eager to pay for our drinks. Everyone wanted a 'dog's nose', a pint of beer followed by a 'chaser' of gin – a lethal combination, guaranteed to make the whole object of the exercise incapable of response. Outside the pub, the pavement would end up slippery with vomit, and girls clutching their prey (to prevent him from falling) would find nothing but a limp un-achiever, unable to perform the expected 'knee-trembler' against the sea-wall of Blackpool's pebbly beach.

Aside from that, there wasn't much temptation to stay out late, but if we happened to be out when our horrible landlady had decided to lock her front door, we would have to resort to one of the places advertising 'GOOD BEDS, 1/6d and 2/6d', of which there were several in the streets behind South Shore. At the cheaper rate – all that was available one night – I had to share a bed (flannel sheet, cotton twill coverlet, bare bolster, no blankets) with a tramp who wet the mattress and of course, poor thing, pretended he hadn't. I got up early and fled, hobbling through deserted streets, keeping an eye out for military police nearing the end of their night-shift.

I hobbled because boots were bothersome, rubbing blisters on our heels. We all suffered; Uncle, with lumbago, more than most. On one unpleasant occasion we were lined up for injections – typhoid, tetanus, TAB – shoved into us by needles growing blunter and blunter; possibly sterilised each time, but more likely not. We all survived, so it can't have done us much harm. One of our sergeants delivered himself of a memorable, ringing endorsement: 'When they ask you lot what you did in the fucking war, you fucking tell 'em you spent the happiest days of your lives marching up and down the fucking front at Blackpool with sore fucking arms!' For once, it seemed an accurate assessment of our predicament.

Within weeks we were supposed to have been transformed into proper airmen, with proper airmen's ideas in proper airmen's bodies. Perhaps, superficially, some of us were. If so, it didn't help the authorities to decide what to do with us. We kept marching up and down the promenade, or else we were detailed to go to the sergeants' quarters, there to shine brass buckles, or 'blanco' belts.

Some of the men complained at having to do such menial work. I enjoyed it, especially when it entailed chatting up a PT sergeant whilst he was back in his billet, changing out of his white shorts. (We had only been issued with dark blue ones.) He would become almost human, boasting about what he'd already done/would do with his girl. By pumping him for details, I could get him excited; and excitement would lead to the beginnings of an erection, when we would both pretend that nothing unusual was happening. I never could have imagined that there might come a time when I could refer to such a thing openly, in writing, for in those days even to mention it in passing would have been dangerous. How welcome they were, those little flashes of sex, lighting the gloom of our otherwise darkling existence!

———

20

One day I was sent for by the Commanding Officer, an Air Commodore no less, who wished to know why my name wasn't on the list of prospective officer-trainees.

'Having been a conscientious objector, sir, I thought I might not be regarded with much favour.'

'Well, in the ordinary way, you'd have been right. But I see that an application has already been made on your behalf.'

'Sir, I had no idea . . .'

'You didn't? *Hmmmm* . . . Anyhow, it comes from Sheffield, where it seems you have an influential friend vouching for your character and capabilities.' He glanced up at me with what I recognised, from romantic novels, as 'a ghost of a smile playing about his lips'. 'So, with your permission' – another smile – 'I shall see that you are sent off on a – let me see – Flying Control course.'

That was how I came to be posted to a camp outside Bridgnorth, for a cart-before-the-horse period of learning the ins and outs of Flying Control before becoming the officer administering its mysteries. An odd way round of doing things, I thought, but not half so odd as one of the earliest confidences with which we were entrusted, the existence of a network known as 'Radar'. In common with nearly all England, I had previously supposed that men from the Observer Corps lay in wait on cliff-tops, reporting the approach of enemy planes. So they did; but their efforts were insignificant compared with what radar could show those huddling indoors over a cathode-ray tube screen in an Operations Room. Exact position, identification of friend or foe, radar could manage the lot – a marvellous, top-secret system at the time.

Our job in Flying Control, we were told, was to handle take-offs and landings, and see that nobody 'pranged'; but there was far more to it than that. The whole airfield, in a general sense, was ours: the ground services such as the fire-engines and the runway lighting system, as much as the communications. Only the weather wasn't under our control – and meteorology was something which we were required to know a lot about in the way of cloud formations, wind, rain and snow. We had to be able to judge the height and distribution of a cloud-base and in misty conditions assess visibility in terms of yards, not just as it was happening, but in advance.

Primarily, we were there for when things were going wrong. We might have to prepare for a 'pancake', an emergency crash-landing, or 'talk down' a pilot forced to descend, 'blind', through cloud. Above all, we had to be prompt and decisive in firing a red 'Very' light, an action automatically putting a stop to everything happening in the air and on the ground, forcing aircraft coming in to land to go round again, or aircraft about to take off to swerve from the runway. A Flying Control Officer had to be sure of his capacity to summon up enough nerve to snatch the Very pistol and fire without hesitation. It was probably the hardest lesson of all for us to absorb; failure could mean the difference between salvation and disaster. At our lectures I took copious notes, describing our duties word for word.

On evenings off we would walk into Bridgnorth, to visit one of its old-fashioned pubs. I soon saw that the intelligent thing to do was to buy our hut-sergeant drinks, then say, 'Couldn't manage another, Sarge,' when it was his turn to shout.

When we took our exams at the end of the course, nearly all of us passed. I duly reproduced our lectures, relying upon a traditionally excellent short-term memory. My new chum the hut-sergeant was impressed: 'It won't be long before I'm calling you "sir", Rod.'

'Largely thanks to you, Sarge!' I answered unblushingly.

Here, at long last, was a real-life version of the 'warm and cosy character' foreseen by Bridget. Alas, the exigencies of Service life would split us asunder before he had much time to show me the ropes, or anything else for that matter. Such a pity, when things were turning out so well!

I was thereafter posted to Cosford, where I worked so hard I passed my training with flying colours – in actual fact, second from top, with particular commendation for a convincing parade-ground manner, of all things. In between we were given leave. I travelled by train to London in a compartment packed to overflowing with troops behaving as if the cameras of posterity were recording their every move. Cheerful jocularity was the prevailing style; that and slumber, sprawled one against another. Which war was it, the first or the second? It could have been either.

What I wanted above all was the company of people 'speaking my own language' – without any prim- or proper-ness – which meant, first and foremost, Bridget. On arrival in London I made directly for 10 Selwood Terrace. Alas, Bridget had a full house so suggested I try Shirley Cocks, who was fond of me. Shirley was a nice warm creature, running to fat, busy writing plays, so far without success. Her husband Barney, Clerk to the House of Commons, seemed to rue his choice, but at a distance, because she was living on her own in 88 Charlotte Street. I was desperate for the company of a woman, after being so exclusively amongst men, so I was delighted when Shirley invited me round. It was all very casual and unplanned; but in those days we were like that, in between the wailing of a siren and the 'All Clear!' There was nothing particularly odd about my behaviour, nor about hers. All things considered, it was a wow of a time – my last fling as an ordinary aircrafthand before facing the positively larval challenge of turning from man into officer.

Next stop, Lincolnshire, where my mother and sister were living with Granny Rawnsley. Morvyne had arrived at 'an understanding' with an RAF officer, billeted at Claxby, in charge of the top-secret Skendleby Radar Station (to me secret no longer). He showed me round his hush-hush outpost as one equal to another; he seemed a jolly young man once he stopped being technical, very much a Northerner. Sadly, whilst he was away in India, Morvyne broke off the engagement and returned his ring – an example of what was known as a 'Dear John' situation, when those flung together by the war realised, before it was too late, that wartime propinquity was no excuse for a life-long commitment.

My homecoming ought to have been triumphal, on all counts. Ex-conchie, ex-gentleman-ranker, I could almost be considered fit for decent society. But I was wrong if I thought that my wicked uncle would view me with any more understanding, let alone favour. He was far from pleased. He wasn't quite sure why I must still be disapproved of, but he sensed that there was something in me deeply antipathetic to his most cherished prejudices; only, for the moment, my shortcomings were hidden behind a veil of 'proper behaviour'. (He was right, of course.) My grandmother, on the other hand, was simply delighted. All had been forgiven. Her 'treasure' (Miss Herrington, otherwise known as 'Auntie') dished up a stuffed shoulder of veal, a passable version of the fatted calf.

———

21

My first posting as a Flying Control Officer was to Jurby, on the Isle of Man, in Training Command – softest of all situations. There the islanders were living off the fat of the land, unrationed, in the midst of plenty. To add to the cushiness, I travelled as an officer, First Class, something I hadn't done since the market crash of 1929/30 had turned us into poor relations overnight.

At Jurby, the control tower was equipped in the standard manner, with two sorts of radio/telephone (r/t): one, on which we spoke, with a range of no more than a few miles; the other (w/t) far-reaching, but only for the 'dits' and 'dahs' of the Morse code. Take-offs and landings were radio-controlled, though in an emergency there was also a man standing by to flash a green or red light at the end of the runway. Things could quickly go wrong, largely because short-range communication by voice was subject to fading, even complete inaudibility. If several aircraft were trying to talk at the same time, the one nearest, or with the most powerful set, drowned out the others, creating chaos.

As a junior, I expected normally to be a simple No. 2. But when my No. 1 went to answer a call of nature, or was busy with any number of administrative duties, I found myself left alone, to sink or swim. It wasn't long before I was in sole charge when a top-of-the-range emergency threatened: a tiny single-seater attempting to land in the wrong direction and in the path of an incoming aircraft. I rushed, I grabbed the Very pistol, I fired. Up shot a red star, yet still that wretched little single-seater floated downwards like thistledown, against every indication given by the wind-sock. Mercifully, the incoming Anson was being piloted by a capable old hand. When barely a hundred feet above the runway he gathered speed and zoomed up, shouting over the radio, 'What the HELL was that for, eh?'

'A THING without a radio!' I replied, so shaken that I could hardly get the words out.

Next moment, a cheery voice broke in saying, 'Sorry old boy, my radio wasn't switched on!' I then saw the pilot taxiing along to a point near the foot of the tower, getting out and coming up to see me. He was a visiting Group Captain, a high-ranker covered in medals. 'Sorry old boy!' he repeated. 'Awfully sorry and all that!' What sort of strip was I supposed to tear off such a contrite demi-god?

Away from work, station life at Jurby would have been enviable had it not been for Squadron Leader Bell. Bell was my immediate control tower senior, an ex-pilot with years of experience, unwillingly seconded to training. He despised the wingless, he was 'almost a gent' and he yearned to be young again – a witches' brew of discontent, simmering away, ready to boil over at what he (rightly) guessed was my lack of special regard for his wingly qualities. He irked me so much that I decided to request a posting elsewhere, if possible overseas, so as to put the greatest conceivable distance between Bell and myself.

Staying put at Jurby came equipped with so many benefits that my request must have seemed madness to many. We were eating better than anyone else in England and driving about on limitless petrol. I was even able to arrange for my mother and Genissa to visit me by de Havilland Dove, on one of the few civilian flights still operating. My sister's arrival caused two of the pilots to become quite friendly towards me, for the sake of getting an introduction. Also on the Isle of Man, under Regulation 18b, was Franco, Marchese di Montagliari, though I had no wish to seek him out. It would hardly be fair to confront him with the news that his wife, last seen two and a half years ago, had bounced about with me in the Park Lane Hotel and elsewhere.

Thinking of Peryl – a thing I hadn't done much, lately – it occurred to me to telephone her next time I was in London, which happened sooner than I thought. After a brief spell in Dumfries I was informed that I would be transferred from Training Command for Service Overseas without delay and that I must take Embarkation Leave forthwith. It would not just be another hello but a hail and farewell to Peryl, my first affair. With anticipation, but also with a certain amount of apprehension, I travelled down to London in officer's First Class comfort.

I went straight to Nassau Street. Marcus had completed training as a wireless operator in the Merchant Navy and was afloat on a job, so I had the flat to myself. *Perfect for Peryl!* I thought as I picked up the telephone. A cracky voice answered: 'Once Upon a Time!' I recognised it as belonging to Peryl's mother, a long-suffering but sharp-eyed old dear. I made myself known, and the next moment was hearing 'WUMPHUS!', that shaming pet-name. 'Wumphus, where are you? More to the point, what are you?'

I told her, to the accompaniment of suitable gasps. She said that she would come up to London at once. Then I made the mistake of saying that my flat was bed-less. She put on what I instantly remembered as her calculating voice: 'Oh I see! Yes, I see what you mean. We obviously can't stay there, can we? Perhaps you'll book a room in a hotel, in any name you like so long as it's not mine; and of course you must let me be responsible!'

Not much difference in her, I thought; the changes were all in myself.

Even at that juncture I got things wrong by selecting a modest boarding-house in Bayswater for our rendezvous. Peryl wasn't having any of it: 'I'd sooner try the Mapleton, in Piccadilly Circus,' she said decisively, refusing even to unload her bag from the same old Daimler as before. 'They tell me it's where the tarts all go, but at least it's central.'

So to the Mapleton we went, to see for ourselves that what she had said was true: tarts were everywhere. I was fascinated.

However: 'You've become someone entirely different,' Peryl said accusingly when we were established. 'You're no longer the faun who danced naked in the moonlight for me.' (I'd almost forgotten that episode, it seemed so long ago.) 'I hardly know what to say to you ...'

She'd hit the nail on the head; we'd become strangers. I was no longer the over-sensitive boy but posing as a rough, tough grown-up, blunted by the RAF. She was old enough to be my mother, but I'd always known that. She was dressed, as usual, very smartly, too smartly for the middle of a war: a two-piece frock of white dots on a tan background, with a hat like a dish of the same material – a real dress-designer's choice, as was to be expected. Nothing very novel about all that ... so the change, as she said, was in me. Even though the 'Cleopatra Clutch' was working as never before, when we parted I was never to see Peryl again.

In Nassau Street, I found Marcus, back early from his ship. 'Thunk without trathe!' he wailed. 'I thall never get over it!'

He was very friendly, and I responded favourably when he raised the question of what was going to happen to my flat whilst I was overseas. I said that I'd ask the agents to let him take over the 'Gentlemen's Agreement'. (When I did, they promptly added an extra half a crown a week to the rent.) Our reasoning was that I might get killed, leaving him flat-less, so I handed it over to him on the understanding that if and when I were to return unscathed, he'd hand it back to me.

'Of courth!' he said, with tears in his eyes. 'Overtheas, OVER-THEAS . . . I'm tho thorry you're having to thuffer what I couldn't even bear the thought of!'

'I don't look at it like that,' I said. Still, I put my things away in various drawers sadly. They looked paltry in daylight, yet I was really sorry to be bidding them farewell for an unknown length of time. Then, decks cleared, I was ready to sail into the sunset, my new address an Army Post Office (APO) number 'somewhere overseas', exactly where being a secret.

Arriving at the port of embarkation, I was told by the first man I met that we'd be going to North Africa. Within a couple of days we were heaving towards Algiers in a troop-ship packed with men (in crowded and uncomfortable quarters) and officers (in relative luxury, four to a cabin).

'Have you a nickname?' was almost the first question my cabin-mates asked.

'Yes,' I replied unblushingly. 'Friends call me "Rags". You can too, if you like!' So that was evidently how I wished to present myself, just then. It was a spur-of-the-moment decision, hard to explain. Perhaps I thought that it sounded casual, with overtones of manly good-humour – which was not exactly how I would have described myself, if asked.

part three

an officer abroad

1943-7

22

Officers crowded into the ship's lounge, where a woman of uncertain age sat at a baby grand piano in full evening dress: embroidered silk top, black tubular bottom, sensible shoes. *Ding dang dang DONG!* she went, thumping out the Warsaw Concerto, *GerDING dang DONGGGGG!* It was purest schmaltz, yet with echoes of a world in upheaval – which was what ours was, just then.

From somewhere close at sea there came a *WHUMPHHH!*, followed by *CRUMP-WHUMPHHH!* As British officers, we merely looked at each other with eyebrows raised.

Someone murmured knowledgeably: 'Depth charges. Must be German subs about.'

The pianist went on playing, whilst further *crumps* and *whumphs* rocked the ship, one very near indeed. Were we going to be hit? No, apparently not. Some of us had a slight feeling of anti-climax.

No more depth charges. Amidst a storm of clapping, the pianist pounded to a close. A senior officer rose to his feet and owlishly commended her for her bravery. She beamed and was about to push her luck with an encore when ship's bells and hooters signalled 'Boat Drill'. We bustled off, morale heightened.

It was a hot beginning of July in 1943. The men stripped to grey 'issue' underpants (those being the days before jockey-shorts came into favour) and inevitably over-exposed themselves to the sun. Others huddled in a hold playing interminable games of 'Housey Housey', later to spread to a significant section of England's elderly as 'Bingo'.

What we were not allowed to do was to keep a diary. 'It might fall into the wrong hands,' our Commander said. 'And that might cost men's lives.' Attentively we listened, and I was naive enough to believe that it was my patriotic duty to comply. After the war was over, when our seniors could hardly wait to rush their carefully documented daily reminiscences into print, my consolation had to be that service overseas, when not lethal, was on the whole pretty boring. What highlights there were, were easily remembered. Even so, during the years to come, the confidence trick played upon us juniors made me cross, gathering momentum as an irritant when more and more war-bestsellers hit the bookshops. *I'll mention it somewhere, if I get a chance!* I resolved. This is that chance, here and now.

When our baggage was being off-loaded on to the dock in Algiers, the tin trunk containing almost everything I owned fell from a grab-net into the water, to be stolen at high speed by a gang in league with the crane-men. They struck lucky: my gun formed part of the booty. Since I had no intention of getting into trouble for its loss, I was to pass the rest of the war unarmed – a suitable state for a former pacifist.

Algiers in summer was hot beyond belief. When we moved out to Hassan Dey, we moved in sweating clumps, in lorries shielded from the sun by khaki coverings doing their best to suffocate us. Hassan Dey was a camp set amidst scrub and pine trees on the seashore. It could have been delightful, in other circumstances. As it was, 'ablutions', perched on a mound of sand known as 'Mount Ararat', consisted of a wooden box with eight seats in a row, unprotected even by strips of canvas. Flies abounded. We were given the same food daily: bully-beef and biscuits, the biscuits toughened by dehydration, the beef unrefrigerated, disintegrating in lumps of ooze on our plates. Of course, it couldn't be long before we all succumbed to dysentery, when the advantage of siting the camp near the shore became clear. Officers and men alike could be seen running to the beach, stripping off as they ran, to plunge into a cleansing sea.

Our conditions were largely due to lack of organisation, as I saw when I hitched a ride to Algiers and came across an American Officers' Club. Emboldened by memories of the Rainbow Room, an American Officers' Club in London I'd sneaked into a fair bit during my time, I strolled casually in, chatting to a neat-looking Captain in smart pinky-fawn trousers. With him I sat at a properly laid table and was served with bully-beef. But this was bully with a difference: thin slices, chilled to a snowflake, on a bed of cos lettuce. A jug of Thousand Island dressing was passed round. Normally I wouldn't have fancied it, but here it tasted of ambrosia. The Americans looked so clean, smelling of scented soap, in no way comparable with our sweaty lads reeking of carbolic.

'Just arrived?' they asked politely. 'Right now, the war's over in these parts.'

It was true. The whole long Mediterranean shore of Africa had been liberated, and on 10 July the Allies put the matter beyond doubt by landing in Sicily. Algiers was wasting no time in exploiting the situation as best it could. Due to the swamping power of the dollar, inflation was rampant. Some 'commodities' rose to the occasion by increasing their intake a thousand-fold, notably the brothel industry. Although the Casbah, a crumbling quarter of the city, was officially out of bounds, two houses standing just inside its confines were ever-open for Allied customers. Of the two, one was for the men; the other, the Sphinx, was reserved exclusively for the officers.

I made my way into the Sphinx, past a standing screen of military police joking amongst themselves but doing nothing to stop us. Inside, a madame rattling gold bracelets pointed to three scrawny houris sitting on a padded bench. They were only, as it were, the advance guard. Others were to be found downstairs, beyond the point where a second madame sat at a table selling tickets, at £1 each, for 'L'Exhibition', whatever that might be. I paid and was shown into the basement, a surprisingly large and smart room with a mirrored ceiling reflecting a central, beige-padded area. Benches banked up all round (except where interrupted by another entrance) already held a number of American officers, loudly chatting as if to display a confidence they didn't feel. An awkward silence would be broken by a guffaw, followed by another silence. We were all waiting, waiting . . .

At last, six girls, dressed in pink powder-puffs and nothing else, rushed screaming with simulated pleasure on to the central padded area, waving what looked like small rubber truncheons. 'Dildo! Dildo!' they shrieked, strapping them on, displacing the little that was already there. So those were dildos? I'd never heard of such toys, much less encountered them. A performance followed, which only ended when a very drunk American was invited to join in but for obvious reasons couldn't perform. 'POUFF!' shouted the ringleader finally. 'INUTILE!' This angered one of the man's friends: 'Hey! Looky here, he ain't no goddam inutile, you goddam whore!' Things might have become ugly, but the upstairs madame came down to promise 'a rain-check' for the disgraced non-performer. Some officers stayed on, for obvious reasons. I preferred to leave without further ado.

Soon after, I was posted to Grombalia in Tunisia. To reach the 'Great Gromboolian Plain' we were put into a train which took four days to puff its way to Hammamet. I occupied my time assisting a Czech doctor on his rounds during the perpetual stops, my Ambulance Unit experience proving useful, this far from home.

Grombalia was no more than a bakingly hot point on the map, a temporary landing-strip in a setting of dried earth scattered with olive trees. Our camp was entirely tented, with what was called an 'EPIP' marquee for the Officers' Mess. In such ad hoc accommodation I supposed that dress would be informal, so I turned up for my first evening meal in shorts and ankle-socks. Totally wrong! Our Wing Commander Horgan reprimanded me and sent me back to put on 'longs'.

I was their first Flying Control Officer, and they didn't much want one. Before I came on the scene they'd managed by having a man on the runway with an Aldis lamp, flashing for take-offs and landings.

As we were dropping bombs in support of troops operating in Sicily, I was virtually a night flying controller, which involved sitting in a three-ton lorry with a W/Op and two radios: r/t for talking, w/t for longer-range Morse communications. As on the Isle of Man, the short-range r/t kept fading and failing, causing chaos; but this was chaos in war conditions. When that happened, as it inevitably did, far too often, angry pilots would come storming round to the control truck to 'tear me off a strip', declaring that the old Aldis lamp system was far superior – as indeed, in many ways, it was. They might find me brewing tea over a Primus stove and be offered a mollifying cuppa. (I ran the Primus on high-octane aviation fuel – dangerous, of course, but I had no alternative.)

Once all the sorties were safely home I could doze, to be woken perhaps by a stray caller from another unit demanding an emergency landing. Far worse were the nights when I waited and waited for our own aircraft to ask permission to land, when not quite all had returned safely. Frantically I would wind the handle of the field telephone, trying to raise any HQ or Ops Room for news of our missing men. More often than not there'd be no news at all, whilst the night sky grew steadily lighter . . . and still no sound of an engine.

When we were told that our Wing would be stood down for a few days, I was so exhausted from working nights, writing reports and checking the runway come sunrise, and then struggling to sleep in the heat, that I hardly felt capable of going into Tunis. But go I did, hitch-hiking on military lorries, although it was not what officers were supposed to do. I found my way to the RAF Officers Hostel, the

Majestic, where I could enjoy a proper bath and a proper bed, in that order. How tired I was!

Tunis looked charming, a French Regency Cheltenham framed by date-palms. I was too tired to go out on the town. Instead, sleep swooped down on me, the first really sound sleep since arriving in North Africa.

———

23

On returning to Grombalia, I heard that 326 Wing was being transferred to Gela, southern Sicily, by which time overwork had so sapped my resistance to disease that I succumbed to both malaria and sandfly fever, simultaneously. A spell in a tented field hospital cured me of any tendency to luxuriate in leisured sickness, so fearful were the smells, so comfortless the beds jammed cheek by jowl together in rows.

Sicily was followed by a push forward into the toe and heel of Italy, coming to rest, briefly, outside Taranto. At Brindisi, 326 Wing (night-flying Bostons and me) merged with 232 Wing (daytime Baltimores). So at last I was not the only controller; I could reckon on working long, but not impossible, hours.

During the second week in September 1943 the Allies landed at Salerno and the Italians signed a 'Short Instrument of Surrender'. By the end of that month we had gained control of Naples, on one side of formerly enemy territory, and the plain of Foggia, with its potential airfields, on the other. As far as we were supposed to be concerned, the surrender 'made no difference'. 'The Wops' became 'Non-belligerents', not Allies. The rule was 'No fraternisation!', as it had been when we arrived. Vain hope! Our men pursued their former practice of chasing every girl in sight with renewed vigour. But now they were starting to see a signorina as a friendly human being rather than as a Venus fly-trap.

In spring 1944 I was sent to Sorrento, to the Hotel Cocumella, taken over for the specific purpose of providing local leave. We trailed in khaki-coloured lorries through Avellino and over a snow-girt spine of hills before reaching a battered Naples and 10,000 ragged urchins.

Leaving all but the most persistent behind, we carried on to Sorrento, gleaming in the springtime sun, warm and inviting. The orange trees were in blossom, their fragrance enveloping us as we looked around at an undamaged holiday promontory.

Girls loitering in twos and threes returned our stares. But we wanted baths and drinks before grappling with love's hand-maidens. By chance, I was put into a room with Chris, an untypical Spitfire pilot as agreeable as he was good-looking. I was in luck. When buffed-up and well fortified, we strolled into the street towards a trattoria of the simplest sort, set in an angle of the road. Hardly had we gone more than a yard or two before two girls converged on us: Columba Minervini, olive-dark and straight-nosed, and Gianna di Jura, a tip-tilted ginger monkey. Both were five-foot-nothing, but there was rather more to Columba in the way of shoulders and hair.

Chris couldn't speak a word of Italian, so I had to do the interpreting, using what few words I knew, eking them out with dog-French. Both girls spoke German after a fashion, though they didn't want to admit to it. I told them that we couldn't care less, after which they eagerly accepted an invitation for a bite to eat at the trattoria. In double-quick time they demolished huge piles of spaghetti, but with a grace of manner that was truly captivating. It was the first of several meals *à quatre*, paving the way for a visit to Capri after permission had been sought from an elderly parent in a fur coat reeking of moth-balls. Away we went, in one of the few civilian ferries still running, a steamer groaning with over-laden Caprese, as if from the pages of *South Wind* by Norman Douglas.* None of us was as sea-sick as his famously liberal-minded bishop.

The girls knew of a place to stay (possibly where they'd stayed before, with a Fritz or a Friedrich). We were shown two rooms, one with a double-bed and the other with two singles. I would willingly have shared the double-bed with Chris, and it wouldn't have been in the least like sleeping with Miles in West Hartlepool, but Columba and Gianna put us firmly into the two-bedder room.

Next evening, back on the mainland, a dance was held in the Cocumella. We officers lurched drunkenly about, disdaining sweet-meats in favour of copious draughts of Asti-Spumante. Maudlin from

---

* *South Wind* was a successful novel of its day, published in 1917. It is set on the fictional island of Nepenthe, which was based on Capri. Thomas Heard, a bishop returning to England from Africa, was its central character.

drink, I wandered into the hotel gardens which stretched to the top of precipitous cliffs. There was a bright moon in a sky delicately strewn with clouds. The sea sighed and glittered silver, far down below. Orange blossom blew heavy in the air, an almost tangible presence, all-pervading. It struck me then, that even with all the splendour spread before me, I wasn't truly happy. Something was lacking; what most hearts yearned for wasn't at all what I was seeking. I sobbed aloud, alone.

Having reached the plain of Foggia, we were bogged down for months in support of an Army held up by Germans resisting unexpectedly stiffly, considering how minimal was their air support. We lived in tents in the middle of mud, not sorry to remain untouched by enemy bombardment which would have added immeasurably to our woes. My job increased in importance when the Americans, in Liberators and Flying Fortresses, came to join our 'advanced' Wing. Once or twice a gigantic aircraft would explode spectacularly on the PSP (pierced steel plate) temporary landing-strip, bringing into play all the aerodrome control systems which were my responsibility. The numbers of aircraft to be dealt with daily made it even more imperative that I should have the nerve to fire a red Very light without a moment's hesitation, when necessary.

I liked the newcomers. A visiting American pilot called Wray took me up in a twin-tailed Lightning, converted for photo-reconnaissance. We swooped and rolled through the sky at high speed, piling on the Gs, whilst in the transparent nose I pretended to remain imperturbable when actually anything but. I was truly grateful to that American. None of our pilots would have encouraged a similar trip – there was a coolness between ground and air. Hence the relief, the extravagant joy, when fliers like Wray or Chris were so genuinely friendly.

We were still stuck in Foggia when I had news from home: my some-what estranged grandmother Maya had died, at well over ninety. Such sorrow as I felt was dispelled by the news that the £300 p.a. – a large sum in those days – which she had promised to leave to me had been switched to Anna, the Swiss maid. Ours had been a strained relation-ship, and I didn't at that time know what malice she'd shown towards my mother in letter after letter to her wounded son before I'd even been born, which strained it further in memory. However, there was one remark for which I could genuinely thank her: 'You may often feel embarrassed, Roddy, BUT YOU NEVER NEED BE SHY!' It stuck in my mind forever after, often providing solace in moments of spine-tingling inferiority.

———

24

Like flies buzzing round a juicy carcass, Desert Air Force next descended upon Caserta, coming to rest at Marcianise, two miles down the road to Naples. A runway and 'dispersals' of PSP were quickly constructed by the Pioneer Corps; and, for a change, I had an actual tower for Control purposes. We were encamped, as usual, in a nearby field, a former orchard.

Half a mile up the road, the Royal Palace of Caserta was empty when we arrived, but would soon be filled by MAAF HQ (Mediterranean Allied Air Forces Headquarters) uprooted from Algiers. Two American fighter squadrons of Thunderbolts, including an all-Black unit, found a temporary home with us, as did a squadron of reconnaissance Mosquitos. The Americans introduced me to a new form of control, a system of 'buzzing' the tower in formation before breaking off, automatically spaced, for a series of quick, safe landings. It looked terrifying, but like many things favoured by 'those Yanks', it was actually highly effective.

Since I had a Bedford three-tonner at my sole disposal, Naples was within easy reach of our camp. I didn't try to return to Sorrento. The Isle of Capri was more attractive, because I knew that there was a Rawnsley house in Anacapri, Dil Aram, belonging to the Canon's* son, Noel, who'd married an American poetess, Violet Cutbill. Though they were cousins, I didn't know them well. The last time I'd seen Violet was at the funeral of Great-Aunt Ethel, drifting about in tulle and indulging in affected Italian phrases. However, I realised that I might be in a position to do them a service, whilst contributing to my own welfare.

American forces were about to take over the entire island as a rest-camp for their troops. I took the trouble to seek out and interview the biggish-wig responsible for commandeering alien property, in order to

---

* The Canon being Canon Hardwicke Rawnsley, co-founder of the National Trust.

beg him to lay off Dil Aram. 'Lucky you reached me!' he drawled. 'I can't say our boys are too particular when we take over places, especially as regards the furnishings.' He filled in a prohibition notice, suggesting that I go straight over to Capri and stick it up on the door of the house myself, to make sure. I was even given a permit to cross whenever I wished by an American military ferry. I needed no second prompting.

I hadn't penetrated to Anacapri with Chris and the girls, so the heights were new and enchanting. I only had to ask for the house owned by English people to be told: 'Everybody knows the English signora's place. You go along this stone-walled track, through orchards you can only reach on foot.'

Eventually I came to what looked from the outside like a typical Italian cottage. Inside, it was just as typically English. Lurking in the garden terraced steeply downhill was the signora's servant, a native treasure with an archaic grin called Domenico, so shy that he would only speak in a whisper. He managed to convey that he could do everything, including cooking, if I would send him out to buy the food. To his great satisfaction (and awe) I pasted up my notice saying that Dil Aram was English property which couldn't be 'sequestrated'. Then I settled down to strumming on the baby grand, pulling books from the shelves and generally lounging about. That evening Domenico produced a simple but delicious meal, washed down with coarse, metallic wine from the slopes of Vesuvius. This was the life.

With Norman Douglas's *South Wind* ever in mind, I had high hopes that a few eccentrics might have managed to survive the war, untouched. I questioned Domenico. He mentioned two women, both over eighty, living at Casa Surya, at a point near where the track branched off for Dil Aram. They were Emilie van Kerkhoff and Miss Suart, ancient girl-friends, Indonesian-Dutch. I found Casa Surya without much difficulty, and the old girls living in reduced circumstances, supplies from Holland having inconveniently dried up. They were on very short commons indeed, so I spent a long time chatting, leaving them with a wad of Allied Military Currency (which looked bogus, but which was in fact accepted with alacrity wherever troops were stationed).

I saw what I could of those old dears in the short time available. Emilie subsequently wrote one of the nicest letters imaginable. Needless to say, it was undeserved. At the risk of being (rightly) accused of patting myself too keenly on the back I cannot resist a substantial quotation:

Partir, c'est mourir un peu – yes, for him who goes and
for him or her who remains. I am not going to write you
long letters, nor have you to answer them if you don't
feel like it – Just a few things I want to say now. I had
lost the melody of life in these last hard years. And now
something is again singing within me. That has been
your influence, dearest. You gave me from your youth
and strength, you gave me your confidence. I hope that
I could give you something from my deep inner peace –
you have been sent to me just in time and I will be more
courageous now and perhaps feel stronger. I know that
you will never do anything unworthy of yourself. The
same pride which lives in me is yours also . . .

Such encouraging words! Well worth coming to Anacapri for. I knew
that I could never live up to her high opinion, but at least I could try.
Emilie's incentive would always be there, urging me not to forget what
ought to be done, however often I failed to do it.

I couldn't wait to return; which I did, several times, joyfully seeing
my two Dutch dolls. I also started entertaining. With Domenico as 'staff'
I was able to spread a net for the American Commander, asking him to
dinner with the two English Naval officers who were on Capri in some
official capacity or other. In fact, I was rapidly becoming part of the high
society of the moment. My hospitable impulses served me well when one
afternoon I missed the boat returning to Naples and had to ask the Navy
to rush me over to the mainland in time for night duty at Marcianise.

A minor mishap was responsible for a delightfully unexpected adventure
round about this time. I was on my way to Naples when my three-
tonner broke down. I hitch-hiked, chance placing me in the back of
a truck full of American GIs. I was squeezed up against a sturdy body
in shiny khaki belonging to Sgt Joe Birmingham, to whom I chatted
so democratically that, as he later admitted, he never guessed I was an
officer. We got on famously. When we reached Naples, I suggested that
we might go about together. 'That'll suit me fine!' he agreed.

Emboldened by signals which seemed to be coming directly from the
Fates themselves, I confessed my rank and bore him off to the Officers'
Club, where he looked so well dressed that no one spotted what he was.
Obviously we couldn't stay the night there, so after a day of exhaustive

sight-seeing we managed to find lodgings in a house of utmost (apparent) respectability. They had just the one room free, and it had lace curtains, lace bed-spread and lino on the floor, though it reeked rather of Jeyes Fluid.

Came the night. We climbed into the double-bed and I was wondering how best to set about what I had in mind when 'OUCH!' I felt what had to be a bite, then another, then another. I couldn't believe it, but my old friends the bed-bugs were on the prowl, a familiar frowst-and-geranium stink battling against the masking smell of disinfectant. I turned on the lamp. Hiding until ready to emerge, several of the creatures were scrambling over the mattress beneath the under-sheet.

I was being abundantly bitten. Joe, due to some mysterious chemistry in his blood, was not. He lay unscathed in his clean khaki underpants, with never a bite nor bump, none too pleased to be roused not by stroking but by scrabbling and scratching. My skin's fearful itchiness made me neither a good companion nor a romantic one. In the morning I longed – how I longed! – to see him again on some less disturbing occasion, yet difficulties in the way of such a plan were legion. His unit was about to move to one of the many landing-strips on Foggia; he hadn't been told which and had no means of letting me know. The Fates were perhaps already regretting their burst of benevolence.

As war risks diminished, entertainments proliferated. The film of *Wuthering Heights* came to Caserta and was very well received. Marlene Dietrich, dressed in khaki slacks, also arrived to entertain the troops. I was one of the crowd (otherwise of Americans) watching with some incredulity as she sat on an improvised stage with a saw bent between those famous legs, coaxing it to howl out the latest tunes. She appealed to the audience to come up and make requests. I needed no second bidding, pushed my way to the front and greeted her with: 'You won't recognise me, but I was the Eton boy who talked to you in the Nell Gwyn tea-rooms in Windsor, years ago.'

'But of course I remember you very well, darling. You haven't changed a bit!'

It was my cue for: 'Nor have you, Miss Dietrich!'

Mutual hypocrisy established, she asked what tune I'd like her to play.

'"Always",' I said.

'That's not an easy one, you know.'

I did know: I'd tried it out on the baby grand at Dil Aram and had been baffled by its change of key in the middle. However, she gamely attacked it with her saw, to the delight of military men far from home who desperately needed to feel – against all the evidence – that those left behind were continuing to behave as the song suggested.

———————

25

The monastery of Monte Cassino continued to block the road to Rome. I couldn't understand why the Benedictines had picked such a site for their great foundation. It controlled the entire Liri valley, making it inevitable that any army advancing from the south had either to take or subdue it; no middle course was practicable. The Allies were bound to see the building crowning such a strategic hill-top not as a glorious historical achievement but as a menace. How they grew to hate that source of ever-watchful eyes!

I could see for myself, when our ALO (Air Liaison Officer) took me to the hills above Venafro to have a look at the supposedly stagnant battlefield. Spring had scattered successive layers of green over buildings scarred by bombs, hiding even the obtrusive coils of wire connecting innumerable field telephones. Everything was very quiet and still. Nothing shattered the peace until a gun on the German-controlled slopes opposite opened up, prompting retaliation from our side. After a period of whistling bangs, silence again, penetrated by the song of birds for whom spring conveyed quite another message. Everywhere we trod, we felt – and no doubt were – overlooked by the enemy. The village of Cassino was completely wiped out by intensive bombing raids and the monastery itself damaged. But who could blame the soldiers who saw it as a menace to their lives? The accepted answer, ever since, has been: 'All posterity!' If all posterity had been there at the time, under continual sentence of death, it might have been forced to conclude that there were other points of view to be considered.

On a pink-washed wall a sign in black Gothic capitals announced: *WEIN MUSS ALT UND MÄDCHEN JUNGE SEIN!* ('the wine must be old and the girl must be young'). The sort of sentiment to appeal to any soldier from any army. *Poor foreign man!* I mused. *So like us!* A diary found on Monte Cassino read: 'I want so badly to get home to my wife and son. I want to be able to enjoy something of the beauty of life again. Here we have nothing but terror and horror, death and damnation.' Graffiti-artist and diarist could have been one and the same.

After five months,* the Battle of Monte Cassino was finally won by the Allies. Path cleared, Rome was ours in June 1944. I hitched a ride into the Emerald City the day after it fell and continued to go whenever I could. Rome for me was not just a city of triumphal arches, girls flinging flowers and all the other ingredients of an Entry of the Gladiators. I made straight for Piazza Madama (backing on to Piazza Navona) to seek out Marjorie Scaretti, formerly Marjorie Jebb,† whom I had encountered often at Well Vale given she was a friend of Uncle Dick's wife, awful Aunt Susan. Time to display English solidarity.

I rang. Nothing happened. I banged. Nothing happened. Then windows rattled, voices called out, and I heard the sound of a bolt being drawn back. When the door was opened by a servant I saw Marjorie halfway up the stairs, obviously preparing to be 'out' should being 'in' involve risk. As it was, I was greeted with far more rapture than I had expected, being referred to, in front of the servant, as 'Cousin' Roddy. Intercepting my surprised look, she explained, 'I would be very glad of an English cousin in the days to come. We aren't out of the woods yet!'

This was a new, more human Marjorie. She offered me a hot bath – always the first thing we warriors wanted – and was not too dismayed when I left behind a gentian-violet trail of Castellani's Tincture, with which I'd been vainly trying to treat an outbreak of athlete's foot.

I'd been told that she had married the Banca di Scaretti, so I knew that she must be very well off. Besides the Piazza Madama house there was a former Medici castle, il Trebbio, at the foot of the Futa Pass outside Florence. After my technicolour soaking Marjorie said, 'I'm going to take you to Vittoria, Duchess of Sermonetta. She's very grand and so's her *palazzo*, which was once an amphitheatre, of all things.' How changed was this Marjorie! Could she really have been such a great friend of my aunt's? She asked tenderly after that cold demon, which forced me to reply with hypocritical enthusiasm. I even began to wonder whether Susan might have nicer hidden depths, thus far successfully concealed from my mother, sisters and myself.

---

* January to May 1944.

† The notable British diplomat Gladwyn Jebb's sister.

La Sermonetta was most amiably civilised and *grande dame*. She dealt in amusing remarks: 'One opens one's last tin of sardines and dips into one's capital and we manage somehow, in spite of having such idiots over us. We implored Mussolini not to drag us in, but he wouldn't listen. You'd think he was having an affair with one of those awful Hun generals, the way he carried on!'

I listened agog. I'd never heard a smart older woman referring so casually to sexual peccadillos – never, save for Sylvia Gough and Nina Hamnett at the Fitzroy. In those days, such things were seldom mentioned in polite English society, being more characteristic of 'the Bloomsberries'.* But I was discovering that Roman society adored attaching scandalous motives to every aspect of everyone's behaviour. The more respectable they were, the more these Roman ladies loved scandals, real or invented; it didn't seem to matter which. I wasn't particularly surprised when a fattish old/young man (I think, her nephew) sidled up and pinched my thigh in front of her, squeaking, 'Naughty! Naughty!' Vittoria didn't turn a hair: 'It's the uniform, you see. Naturally he had to steer clear of the Huns, so now I suppose he feels as liberated as the rest of us!'

Then, with practised chic, she turned to other topics. I felt so at home, even more so when I learnt (as I quickly did, from no lack of amused, eager informers) that the Duchess, grand as she was, was nevertheless Signor Scaretti's *maîtresse en titre*, which Marjorie was said to accept with equanimity. Truly remarkable!

Meanwhile, we were continually attacking Germans, but by this point in the war we (the RAF) were never being attacked back. Our 'advanced' landing-strips might suddenly be called upon to cope with such a volume of air-traffic that at Fano I was congratulated on handling one movement, in or out, every one and a half minutes (a record only to be exceeded at the height of the Berlin Airlift;† not that I realised at the time what a record standard I was setting).

A sort of control tower had been constructed, where I sat with my

---

* The Bloomsbury Group – Virginia Woolf, E. M. Forster et al.

† For almost a year from 1948 to 1949, the Soviet Union blockaded West Berlin on the ground from the Western Allies (Berlin being in Soviet-controlled East Germany). British, American, Canadian, French, Australian, New Zealand and South African forces instead had to supply the citizens of West Berlin with necessities by air – at one point delivering over 12,000 tons in a day.

own wireless operator and an American W/Op Sergeant to help deal with a squadron of their Mustangs. Sarge was imperturbable and from Milwaukee – a combination guaranteeing super-loud remarks in an accent sometimes difficult to interpret. He was there when a Spitfire, encumbered with two 500lb bombs, veered from the runway on take-off and headed straight for us ... and just missed. Apart from the expected 'JEEZ!' he merely observed: 'If that guy had scored, it woulda been "Hooray for me and fuck you!"'

'I don't think he'd have had much time for that,' I said.

'Hell, lootenant, that cock-sucker, he'd uv made time!'

I was given a fright of a different kind when low cloud obscured our whole field. We were sitting in the tower doing nothing, because nothing was flying, when an anxious American voice was heard requesting an emergency landing. The only thing to do was to land him by means of a 'Controlled Descent through Cloud' – a lesson taught (theoretically) at Jurby and never put into practice since then. I thanked God for our greatly improved r/t sets, which made communication more effective than it had ever been on the Isle of Man. With an assurance which I was far from feeling, I 'talked him down' over the next ten minutes. 'Can you see us yet?' I kept asking, to which the reply was always: 'No, sir! Can't see a goddamned thing!' – until at last we could both see and hear our lost sheep, descending low over the runway, all set for a perfect landing.

The pilot came round to see me, first gripping my arm, then giving me a prolonged hug. 'You saved my life!' he said, over and over again. 'I've never been so scared!' As there was a spare room where we were quartered, I put him into it; and there I found him, fast asleep, when I came off duty. 'If there is anything I can ever do for you in return, I'd do it!' he said, eyes shining with gratitude. 'Anything!'

What temptation.

My lot had plenty of time on their hands. Save for those actually involved in the fighting, the war was fast becoming a pleasant interlude. Things were going well elsewhere, the invasion of Normandy soon putting paid to German V-weapons developed just too late.

On one pretext or another we were able to make long journeys through a subdued and hungry Italy, bearing bully-beef and blankets, with cigarettes – even the foul 'V' brand issued to us – always the chief medium of exchange. As Mess Secretary, it fell to me to ensure a supply of wine. Away beyond Jesi, the village of Casa Cantonara produced a new pressing of red wine which both sparkled and tasted of strawberries, but only for about a fortnight after travelling.

Our new Air Liaison Officer was Captain Lord Kitchener, so shy that he put up with being called 'Kitch', when he must have hated it. Like all ALOs he had his own transport, whereas I was still stuck with a three-tonner, so with him I visited tiny San Marino, where we called on the Regent and were told that we were free to wander wherever we wished. Such activities were known as 'swanning about'. Whoever could, did. When I was told early in 1945 that a Flying Control Refresher Course was going to be held in Cairo, it sounded like the super-swan of all time, so I made sure of being included.

On the way back from the Middle East, I might be able to trace Sgt Joe, perhaps carry him off to Anacapri, bearing gifts for my two dear old Indonesian-Dutch ladies. Everything was going swimmingly, I reckoned, as I set off for Egypt, deaf to the hollow laugh with which the Benevolent Ones decided to greet those cherished plans.

———

26

In preparation for the refresher course I grew a moustache – no easy matter for one who was no Esau. But I wanted to look more manly and I thought that for the sake of my job I needed to look more mature, both things coinciding with a hope that I would impress Sgt Joe, whilst at the same time allaying his fears of what others might think of our friendship. Before flying to Cairo I had the sense to obtain a leave pass, in case there might be a chance of travelling onwards to Luxor.*

My companion, Squadron Leader Howson, my senior and I were sent upon arrival to stay in a tented camp in Heliopolis. I happened to have an honorary great-aunt conveniently at hand in Heliopolis, Bonté

---

* Luxor, on the Nile, famously contains the ruins of an Ancient Egyptian city (known as Waset, Nut or Thebes) and has therefore been a tourist trap for decades.

Elgood. She'd been one of the earliest lady-doctors, her husband Percy being Chief of Police. Together they had helped crush (so they hoped) the traditional trade in hashish. Percy Elgood was dead, but Bonté was very much alive and a figure to be reckoned with in Anglo-Cairene circles. My mother and Morvyne had found her most helpful when they'd gone out to stay with Uncle Dick and Aunt Susan (Dick's old regiment having been stationed in Egypt for much of 1926 to 1935). When their hosts had proved unwilling to take much trouble to introduce them to people, Bonté had done her best to make up for it.

I'd known her all my life, but tended to identify her more with my uncle and aunt than with my grandmother because of latterly always seeing her at Well. Considering that she'd known the Vale in its heyday under my beloved grandfather, I could only hope that she hadn't been taken in by the chilly smartness of the new regime; for if so, she might be inclined to disapprove of me.

Her house, Villa Beata, was only a short walk away from our camp. It was a comfortable Italianate villa, with a tower and a lawn of crab-grass which required little or no mowing, just plenty of watering. The door was opened by a well-trained Nubian servant in a long white djellaba and red tarboosh. Bonté welcomed me with open arms, obviously not at all influenced by anyone else's opinions. I was warmed and thrilled by such a reception, expanding like a desert flower after a few drops of rain, just before my twenty-fourth birthday.

The letter she wrote to my mother survived, so I can quote extensively from it:

March 30th, 1945.

My dear Betty,

Your letter arrived just when I was going to write to you to tell you what pleasure Roddy's arrival here has given me. He rang up at once, even before he went to camp (about ten minutes away from this house) – and during the few days he has already been here I have seen him daily, as he comes in and out as he likes and sits and reads if I am not there. He is a fine upstanding fellow, and it is easy to talk with him about everything. You would be even more pleased with him than perhaps you already are. His understanding of the world is good and there is an element of forbearance and attentiveness to his surroundings which is not so usual. On his birthday I found him waiting for me when I came in to lunch with a friend (Lady Spinks, whom Susan will remember) and we

*made a little celebration for him, from which he had to rush off to his course
again. I need not say that the first evening he (and I!) talked of Well and the
Manor and all the dwellers therein so dear to him . . .*

By 'the Manor', she meant Claxby. As for the reference to Well, I
can't imagine how I managed to convey an impression that all 'the
dwellers therein' were equally dear to me. I must have wriggled out of
actually saying so, somehow.

What a relief, to encounter such a heart-warming honorary great-
aunt! After my semi-nomadic life her house seemed a miracle of
comfort. Bonté entertained incessantly: amongst others, Sir Robert
Gregg, who had a fine collection of tomb ornaments and statuary, Sir
Somebody and Lady Rowlatt, and James Baxter, Adviser to the Bank
of England. I wasn't always the perfect caller, unfortunately. There was
one dinner with the Beeleys from the Chancellery where guests started
pontificating about Germany.

'I'd shoot the lot of 'em!' said one.

'Oh, I don't know,' argued another. 'I'd just have them all castrated!'

I sat quietly tucking into pieces of cold fowl (scrawny, as all the
chickens of Cairo were in those days); but then they made the mistake
of seeking my opinion.

'Well, if you ask me, I think that those who are so keen on killing every single German had better go to Germany and do the job
themselves.'

Dead silence. A nervous laugh from Mrs B. and a chuckle from her
husband Harold, who agreed with me. It hadn't been the most tactful
of remarks for the dinner-table. I was forgiven on account of my uniform, no doubt.

Plenty of those whom I met remembered my uncle and aunt from
his 12th Lancer days. 'It wouldn't be often that Cairo saw anyone of
such distinction and taste,' said Bonté. There we were, back to that old
conundrum: why, oh why had they always been such ogres as far as I was
concerned? Life-long ogres, past, present and – as I rightly foresaw – in
the future as well.

I had money in my pocket and, for once, things to spend it on. The
Service paid for most things in life and my pay had been piling up,
on top of which I had my share of the divorce settlement trust, which
the trustees were doling out equally to my sisters and myself. To my

amazement, I found that Allied Military Currency was selling on the streets of Cairo at a tremendous discount, halving its value. I could easily afford to take back enough with me to Italy to satisfy every prospective need.

When the course ended, Howson and I decided to move into the city centre, to a room opposite the Carlton hotel. Almost as quickly, we moved out. The reason? Bugs again! I obviously had some deep attraction for them. It impelled me to cash my leave-pass straight away and join an overnight train to Luxor under the old-fashioned auspices of the travel company Cook Wagons-Lits, acting for the YMCA. Howson couldn't come with me, because he'd neglected to apply to his own unit for leave. I was the sole representative of the RAF in Luxor, in the Savoy hotel, all the rest being Army. The only sense in which the war intruded was that we were in uniform, though by general consent no one took any notice of rank.

Luxor burst upon me, as it had burst on so many over the years, like a strangely sinister thunderstorm. My Eton education had taught me that the Greeks were the arbiters of every kind of taste; Western, that is. Yet here were buildings slanted at odd angles, covered in depictions of gods with the heads of animals offering gifts to this or that Pharaoh. Surely it should have been the other way round: sovereigns placating the gods, if only with a contrite heart? A seated ruler presiding over a pile of penises cut from conquered soldiers suggested that to incur the wrath of the Pharaohs might have been rather too bold a move.

There weren't many others trailing round the tombs and temples, so wherever we went, our group was the largest. Our party wasn't, on the whole, much interested in what the guide had to say. The prevailing desire was to be conveyed (in a horse-drawn *gharri*) back to the Savoy bar, there to indulge in increasing tipsiness whilst being waited on, hand and foot. I wanted a great deal more than that; I wanted to soak up new experiences, no matter what. The massive Temple of Karnak seemed to vibrate through my body from the moment when I first walked down the Avenue of Sphinxes. I lingered behind our chattering group, gazing enraptured. It wasn't long before such eccentric behaviour attracted the attention of our guide, Ali, who kept darting back to sweep me into his flock again, until I begged him to desist.

He smiled. 'I see you are different from others. Would you like I show you Luxor by moonlight this evening?'

'Oh yes!' I answered, looking at him for just about the first time. He was no oil painting, dressed unbecomingly in a far-from-clean white djellaba overlaid by a black cloak. It was impossible to tell his age, because his head was wrapped in a white turban, also far from clean. I supposed him to be thirty or thereabouts.

There was a splendid moon that night. Ali duly turned up at the Savoy, looking very neat and smart. For fear of a reprimand, he wouldn't accept a drink at our bar, but stopped at a sleazy place in the souk, where he had three in quick succession, explaining that as a good Muslim he shouldn't really be downing anything at all. He was already swerving when we reached Luxor Temple, where he exchanged rapid words with an ancient guardian before handing him money.

'How much?' I asked.

'For you, nothing!' he said with a great show of indignation.

This will cost me more in the long run! I thought to myself. Not that I cared.

A line of asterisks might once have been called for, at that juncture; but not here and now, and not from me. In spite of being so experienced, I was also genuinely naive. Ali pattered on about Anubis and hawk-headed Horus, Lord of the Far Horizon, and spoke of Rameses the Second, mighty Pharaoh at whose command rose so many monuments to (his own) glory. Moonlight could only penetrate to roofless parts of the long temple, so Ali had to shine his torch to illuminate cavalcades of figures deeply incised into the stone walls. Seen like that, they seemed to jump about, as if alive. Had they spoken, the effect could hardly have been more startling. And the heat was terrific. Luxor had spent all day soaking up the rays of a blazing sun and the temple was projecting them back at us in waves – spicy, yet with more than a hint of petrol and donkey-dung.

We came to a wall depicting the doings of the greats and grands of Upper and Lower Egypt. I was shown the god Min, Lord of the Erect Phallus, with his chief attribute protruding parallel to the ground, long and thin.

'You like Min?' asked Ali eagerly.

'Well . . . yes, I suppose I do! I think it's a remarkable—'

My wafflings were brought abruptly to an end by Ali standing against me, rocking to and fro, breaking off to whisper, 'Not here!' Clutching my arm, he trotted me towards an open, roofless area where two gigantic stone figures – of Rameses the Second, inevitably – sat half in moonlight, half in shadow. Behind one of them was a dark, all-but-concealed gap. There he let himself go; and I didn't object in the least. What was happening was a million miles away from any kind of ordinary life as I'd known it and Ali was doing nothing I didn't welcome. The dream-like surroundings of the ancient temple, the swollen lotus-columns, trappings of high seriousness, combined to make the memory of it something to be treasured, even though the reality was sordid.

'I like you!' declared Ali a few minutes later. 'For you I will leave my job with the YMCA. We will hire a sailing-boat and we will go in this boat down the Nile.' It sounded delightfully pre-war. I had to mention straight off that my leave was limited. He seemed prepared for that: 'Then you must take sick-leave. You're an officer, they will believe you.'

'Not a hope!'

'We shall hire a cook,' went on Ali. 'And a boy to look after the boat. We will have great enjoyment.'

'I'm sure we would. All the same, it just can't be done.'

'Ah no, no,' he said glumly. '*In sh'Allah* you will say it can be done!'

On our way back to the Savoy, he insisted on stopping and having three more drinks in rapid succession. They affected him unpleasantly: he became stony-eyed and he began boasting about what he'd done with me, which I didn't much like. When we parted I was feeling distinctly queasy, sore and with a cold coming on. By next morning, the cold had fully developed – a real corker, my eyes running, nose squelching. My new moustaches tickled like mad, damply drooping rather than manly.

As I'd known for some time past, masculinity and femininity were already distributed haphazardly in my nature. There was nothing to be done about that, even if I'd wanted to. Why then complain? Indeed, who was I, a creature of a mere handful of years, to argue with eternal Min, great aspect of a greater god? In spite of feeling so ill, my spirit was bubbling away. I had to keep it all to myself, of course. I dared tell no one of my adventure.

Upon heading back to Cairo two days later, I saw Ali at the station and offered him a large tip, which he rejected, until I persuaded him to take it on grounds that if I should return he would be put to the expense of making arrangements. He came specially to see me off, he said; but of course there were the others to be seen off as well. It was hardly the moment for a display of anything much.

Back in Cairo I rejoined my Squadron Leader. He couldn't wait to tell me: 'You've no idea how disgusting these Egyptians can be! I was caught short down by Kasr-el-Nil barracks, so I went into this public lavatory, filthy place. A man there looked as if he knew me; I thought he might be someone from camp. Anyway, he said he had many English friends and wanted to talk English, so I took him for a drink in one of those street cafés. Next thing, he was patting my bum!'

'Oh?' I asked a little too eagerly, quickly remembering to add: 'Good heavens! Then what?'

'Told him to bugger off, PDQ. I wasn't playing any of those games!'

'What was the chap like?'

'That was the funny thing. Seemed a decent sort, said he was keen on football. Shows you never can tell . . .'

All the same, his eyes sparkled as he told his story. It had enlivened some dull moments for him otherwise spent in the Carlton bar, drinking their special brand of 'John Collins': gin and lemonade stirred with a pink syrup tasting of marshmallows.

With me back, he wanted to see the Pyramids, so we duly took a crowded 'Brown Tram' out to Giza. En route, he nudged me: 'Can't say I like the way these men shove themselves up against one!'

The lady doth protest too much, methinks, I methought.

At that time, visitors were still allowed to climb the Great Pyramid. Locals hung about, offering to help haul a climber up and over the huge blocks of stone from which a smooth top-dressing had long since been removed for use elsewhere. For those in the know, there was a right way and a wrong way up, using age-old hand-holds. I would have found the attempt impossible without the help of two lithe Egyptians, one to push and the other to pull. Even so, it was exhausting in the boiling heat. The reward was exhilaration, not just from the moment, but from the idea that each climber was linked to other climbers far in the past: my grandmother, Maud; my great-uncle, Canon Hardwicke Rawnsley; and his great-aunt, the Arctic explorer Sir John Franklin's second wife, Jane. The man who'd climbed with Jane had (naughtily) engraved her name up there, though I didn't know that at the time, or I would have looked for it.

Howson tried to have a go, unassisted. He started off, then stopped, having second thoughts, which stimulated me to continue. He didn't mind being left; he waited patiently at the foot of the Great Pyramid, pestered by the usual pesterers. He was a good companion, really, never asking and never wanting to know a thing about me. I rewarded him by loaning him my feverish cold, with interest.

It was time to go back to Italy. Howson wanted to return via Rome, whereas I was determined to try my luck in Foggia, hitching a ride without the slightest difficulty. Rolling up my newly acquired wad of cut-price Allied Military Currency in an empty Balkan Sobranie tin, I landed and booked in at the Foggia Officers' Club. Naturally I left all my gear at the desk before setting out to hitch-hike to Joe's possible address, one of the numbered airfields controlled by the US Army Air Corps.

I drew a blank at the first, then at the second field. Yes, Joe had been there, but had gone. Where to? Nobody knew. What did this Englishman – hold on, English lootenant – want with him? What had he done? 'Nothing. Just a pal!' I had to answer with studied carelessness, heart pounding. Ironically, my lift back to the club was in a jeep driven by a major making every effort to be more than friendly – to which, in normal circumstances, I would have responded whole-heartedly. But as it was, there I sat, bumping along, grimly thinking: *Here I am, in the middle of nowhere, going nowhere, having come all this way for nothing.* A consolation was that I would soon be on my way to Anacapri, to bring more light into the lives of my dear old Dutch.

Not until I was alone in my room did I discover that the Fates had taken a decisive hand. The oval-cylindrical Balkan Sobranie tin was in the bag where I'd left it; but instead of bank-notes, there was a scrunched-up chog of paper from an old copy of *Stars and Stripes*. All my plans came crashing about my head. Fortunately, it had only been my 'extra' money in the tin. I had enough to proceed to Naples and on to the Isle of Capri, but not much, not nearly enough, to spare for those two deserving darlings in Casa Surya.

On that visit to Anacapri, my behaviour was muted. I never heard a word of reproach from Emilie for not being able to shower her with further notes of Allied Military Currency. On the contrary, she presented me with a wooden puppet of the comic Indonesian god Djongelan. 'He's the jester,' she said. 'He goes to all the feasts of the gods and gets up to no end of mischief, tipping over their drinks and scattering their rich food. But they always forgive him, because he amuses them. A little like you, Rudi dear, at times!' Would there ever be an end to her insight? I was able to do one more thing for them, at least, by going to their Consul in Naples and informing him of their plight. The Consul promised to look into the position, not just theirs but that of other Dutch citizens in need, to see that they didn't starve. I had to assume that he was a man of his word.

It was my last contact with the magical island, but it was not the last I heard of Dil Aram. When Domenico passed the news to Violet Rawnsley that 'a cousin' had been staying, she wrote in greatest indignation: 'I never gave anybody permission to use my house!' In the States, where she was spending a safe war, she was far from places where her country's soldiery was let loose upon foreign property; whereas I, who had seen GIs flinging furniture from Canzone del Mare (the house belonging to Gracie Fields) down on the rocks of Capri, had no illusions.

27

News from all fronts grew daily more fantastic: Germany was crumbling; Germany had an atomic V2 up its sleeve; *Der Führer*, from his 'Eagle's Nest', would fight to the bitter end, surrounded by elite remnants of a defunct SS. Ever more extravagant stories flew. Meanwhile, I made my way up north to our new landing-strip at Milano Maritima, on the coast beyond Rimini, in time to celebrate victory in Europe on 8 May 1945.

With the war at an end, people's minds started turning to employment after 'demob'. It made me realise that I'd never had a job, as such, busy as I'd been throughout the war and working exceptionally long hours. I had no inkling of what being a 'nine-to-fiver' was like.

Post-war jobs were very much in the wind. My mother wrote, mentioning that I'd once said that I might try for the Diplomatic Service and that if so, she was all for it. I felt constrained to reply decisively and at length. Years later, I discovered that she had preserved it carefully, as an historic document:

July 3rd, 1945. 239 Wing, Desert Air Force, C.M.F.

　　Darling Mung,

　　I thought I'd made my position quite clear. Obviously I hadn't. Here it is, then.

　　I don't intend to join the Diplomatic either now or at any time, unless for the sake of finding a new setting for a story.

　　I'm not the Diplomatic type. I disapprove of what they do. I loathe their means and methods of going to work. I hate the endless intrigues of a Diplomatic career. I couldn't be unobtrusive and respectable if I tried.

One isn't alive just in order to surround oneself with a straitjacket. I don't want to be a success, I have no ambition. The only thing which would mean anything to me would be the feeling that I have written something entertaining or painted something good. If this means I shall have to live in a pigstye [sic] instead of in furnished Diplomatic apartments in a foreign hotel, well and good. If it means I may be going hungry sometimes, instead of eating a seven course official dinner, well and good.

I don't expect the contrast will be so glaring (not if I can help it). But I am at least prepared to live wretchedly. One thing I understand more and more each day is that provided one has the minimum standard of something over one's head, a bed, and occasional meals, one can be just as happy as anyone with far more . . .'

I went on to say that I knew her own enthusiasm for writing was swamped 'by the demands of society life and marriage' and that I hoped she'd therefore support me in not making the same sacrifice, and claimed it was her fault that I liked art, having always taken me to picture galleries. All in all, the sort of letter which I hadn't written since pacifist days, and as pompous as those mostly were.

The authorities didn't know what to do with any of us in the meantime. It transpired that the Department of Aircraft Safety wanted to enquire into Flying Control systems in advanced units, and since I'd become known for sitting scribbling an appallingly bad detective novel in my tent instead of jollificating in the Mess, the chance was offered to me. As I travelled about, Terry Lancaster came with me. Terry, a peace-time journalist, had secured the plum job of writing the history of DAF. He was excellent crude company in spite of being – to my dismay – a red-hot Socialist. He was later to become well known as 'Man o' the People', writing abrasive editorials for that paper under the banner slogan 'The Things that Matter to You and Me', complete with a photograph of himself in what could best be described as 'tough, sincere mode'.

He came with me to Chiusi to call on one of my introductions, the Contessa Ottiere della Chaia. There we found what Terry called a classy woman, pacing about in a large town house, explaining away the lack of furniture by saying, ruefully, 'It wasn't the Germans we had to hide it from, but your troops!' We offered to take the family out for a picnic in Terry's jeep, using for that purpose some of the tins of bully-beef

with which we were liberally supplied. The Contessa tactfully declined
to accompany her daughter and two of her teenage girlfriends, having
decided that the presence of so many was itself sufficient chaperonage.
Away we scorched, with me driving, showing off by going faster than
was necessary.

Sitting in the back, Terry, the smart operator, swiftly got his arms
round two of our passengers, provoking giggles and squeals. Our picnic
took place on a knoll under some trees, and as we became flown with
wine (provided by the girls) we began petting – nothing very 'heavy', but
enough to let them play about with us, comparing this and that whilst
pretending innocence. I was pleased with my new role of toying and
kissing without more serious consequences.

On another occasion we were driving along when we saw a villa with
a lovely garden. 'Let's ask to be shown round!' I suggested. A flattered but
puzzled chatelaine went off with me, eager to explain what the different
plants were in Italian, whilst Terry (as if in a Restoration comedy) was
chatting up her pert young maid, indoors.

'What transpired?' I asked quietly when he rejoined us.

'Oh, we managed a quick poke, in what little time there was!' he said.
He was indeed a smart operator.

My subsequent report on Flying Control systems didn't please my
superiors, who considered it far too critical; but they could do nothing
because I'd already by-passed them by sending it direct to Air Ministry.
However, it had put me on the map as a writer.

'You'd better do the DAF history with Lancaster,' they suggested.

I didn't take too kindly to that idea, not seeing myself as a co-author,
much as I liked Terry.

'Then how about a spot of Mountain Rescue?' was the next suggestion.

'Lovely. Just the job!' I enthused.

I didn't have to know anything about mountaineering, which was
just as well, considering that I'd never climbed anything higher than
Ben Alligin.* Instead I was required to set up an organisation in which
others would be doing all the hard work; in short, it was what an officer
was created for. I could largely invent what I had to do: procure a three-
tonner; stock it with bully-beef and blankets; go with a driver to remote
hill-villages on the Italo/Yugoslav border; call on the local top-dog;
arrange for a team of rescue volunteers; leave goodies as evidence of

---

* Better known as Beinn Alligin, a mountain in the Highlands in Scotland.

further goodies to come; then vanish in a cloud of dust and exhaust fumes in the direction of the next valley. Simple really!

The scope for patronage was immense. In each village we would be feasted and plied with *vino*. I wasn't ever by myself, having been allotted the sort of driver I might have prayed for, a young Corporal called Sanderson who'd learnt the facts of life in the Boys Brigade. He was exactly my type – matter-of-fact, though shy. During our wanderings we might be stuck in some remote place, in a rudimentary inn where we had to share a bed. Such felicity made me tense, to the point of suffering aches in strange places, until relieved. Sanderson took it all in his stride. I rather wished he'd been with me on the occasion when, driving alone for once, I stopped to give a lift to a girl with shorn hair – mark of a collaborator – who tearfully shrieked: 'Help me, help me to escape my tormentors! I will give myself to you, if you will carry me a few miles up the road!' I let her climb in, but politely declined the favour.

Although happily employed in my own plum job, I was put on tenterhooks by hearing, from Terry, that he might not want to tackle the DAF history after all. Should that be the case, the next in line would be me. It would raise problems of its own, for as peace progressed I was drawing further and further away from a habit of wartime obedience. I could see clearly that to write the sort of book which was then being envisaged – a catalogue of triumphs unsullied by the mistakes of superiors – would be impossible for me. Such eyewash would be valueless, yet how best to convince those who might soon be holding my literary fate in their hands? To avoid explosions of wrath, I would have to tread as delicately as if through a minefield.

Mountain Rescue was like a holiday to me, but as if that wasn't enough, I was offered another welcome break: accompanying my (new) Squadron Leader to Vienna to try and persuade the Russians to conform with Allied rules of aircraft safety at the shared Vienna (Schwechat) airfield.

My new Squadron Leader was what Americans would unerringly have dubbed 'a lovely guy'. Fair, smiling, modest, Tony Hudson wasn't a senior officer by nature, so to have him as one was a delight. We set off in an open jeep to drive through the Semmering Pass, just as the Bora, a freezing wind from the Steppes, was starting to blow in earnest. Thawing out at an inn taken over by the military for such transients as ourselves, I was further delighted to find Tony moving the two beds together to form one big double on grounds that it would be 'more friendly'. Alas, my rising hopes were dashed by his exceptionally matter-of-fact way of saying good night and turning his back on me as soon as we lay down. Apparently he meant exactly what he said.

He had to revert to being the Squadron Leader as we trailed round offices in Vienna horribly overheated by tiled stoves behind double-glazed windows. In contrast, through the streets of the city whistled the Bora, doing its best to turn our brains to ice. As I saw it, my role was to back Tony up, whatever he said or did. We both enjoyed the element of theatre in that, and possibly as a result became as effective as we were pretending to be.

The three we needed to influence were: a large extrovert with a booming laugh, ostensibly in command but actually no more than a figure-head; a thin intellectual with long black hair (unusual for those times), suspicious of everything; and a handsome woman, highlighted blonde, who turned out to be a Colonel in the KGB. We would take them to our Officers' Clubs and fill them with drink – filling ourselves, of course, at the same time. We would seize glass after tiny glass from a huge round tray, downing each at a gulp. Vodka was the preferred tipple, but very often it would be some sticky liqueur, likewise liberated from an already over-liberated zone.

They greatly enjoyed our clubs so we only went to one of theirs once, which had taken some persuasion on our part. It was called the Hofberg, a battered building whose huge doors stood open to admit a throng of Russian officers in uniform and their women, some of whom carried trophies obviously looted from neighbouring shops. One girl was wearing five hats, perched one atop another like a pagoda.

Red Army soldiers stood guard both inside and out. Those in the street tried to bar our way, till over-persuaded by our three sponsors. But other soldiers standing at the top of the grand staircase refused to let us in, shouting that it was forbidden. Our trio argued and argued; then, to our astonishment, admitted defeat, their high rank cutting no ice. After such a contretemps the very least that they could do was ask us back to their own quarters. We drove to a nondescript hotel which, on the inside, was full of gilded furniture, swags and mirrors.

More trays of drinks in tiny glasses accompanied by pickled green tomatoes and sardines. The disgusting feast was served up by a thick-set woman who pulled me aside to mutter, in passable English, 'Look at those uncivilised animals, those thieves who have stolen our country!' Realising how she'd taken me by surprise, she added: 'I am Estonian. I am not deceived by robbers, nor must you be!'

Her words caused me a twinge of unease for carousing with her country's enemies. And I felt further twinges, of another kind, when the thin, suspicious officer produced, apparently out of nowhere, a camera, tripod and floodlight, announcing his intention of snapping us for 'souvenirs'. Such elaborate equipment simply didn't match the suggestion that it was all impromptu.

We were invited to hug and nuzzle the KGB Colonel, to the accompaniment of flash after flash. They hadn't reckoned on me not minding being compromised with a tarty female, so I toyed and kissed with reckless enthusiasm. With Tony and the other two I was more circumspect, rejecting bear-hugs with a show of indignation, ostensibly prepared to do no more than link arms, like old comrades on a spree. Nothing could have pleased me more than the idea that every compromising print would find its way into the Kremlin archives, creating a potentially valuable false impression.

Next morning – or rather next midday, so late were our awakenings – our hosts looked hang-dog, declaring that they'd been thoroughly shamed by our experiences at the Hofberg. As if to compensate, they displayed an extraordinary willingness to accede to all our requests for a joint system of Flying Control. 'Da! Da!' they repeated as we drove out to Schwechat field. To make it official, they said, through an interpreter (previously we'd communicated through a sort of German-English mix, plus vodka): 'We understand the need to compromise. There have been too many near-misses between ours and yours.' We could hardly believe our ears.

But it was a fact. They agreed to the Allied system, even to the extent of using English wherever possible; and they meant it.

28

At last, after much shillying and shallying, come December 1945 I was officially being offered the job of 'leg-man' for the history of Desert Air Force. I accepted the job of roving reporter with enthusiasm, hoping that it might lead a step further, to actual authorship. I was sufficiently emboldened to issue an ultimatum: I wouldn't let them refer to me as 'the chap writing us up', or even as the man helping 'compile' the book. I was the author.

Having established that criterion without causing more than minor offence, I could proceed to an important point, which was that my priority ought to be to cover the ground over which DAF had flown. It would involve an immediate return to the Middle East. I was soon employing the usual techniques of aerial hitch-hiking, reaching Cairo (first by Dakota, then by Liberator), ready for Great-Aunt Bonté's overflowing hospitality once more.

I needed her assistance and didn't underestimate her capabilities. She happened to be a close friend of the Air Officer Commanding, Air Marshal Medhurst. Spared the protocol of writing in for an appointment, I found myself in his august presence, saying how helpful it would be if I were to be flown hither and thither at will.

'In fact, you simply want a magic carpet,' he replied, reaching for his pen. 'I think we might manage that.'

Next thing, I was clutching a letter headed TO WHOM IT MAY CONCERN, ordering everybody in the world to assist me.

Whooping with joy, I rushed back to tell Bonté, but she was pre-occupied. She was expecting King Farouk's uncle, Prince Mohammed Ali, to arrive at any moment for tea. It seemed that he was far more important to her than the King. I couldn't quite follow why at that moment but later learned the reason. King Farouk had been under a cloud with us since the battle of el-Alamein,* when our tanks had been sent to the gates of Abdin Palace to prevent him fleeing the country. Official circles maintained a wary friendship; others didn't. Prince Mohammed Ali, on the other hand, was regarded as loyally pro-English, even if he would insist on proclaiming his patriotism in French.

'He likes people to laugh at his jokes,' Bonté told me. Hanging in the air was an unspoken wish that I'd behave myself by joining in the applause for every royal jest, regardless of whether I found it funny or not.

Her behaviour, when the moment arrived, was educational. She swooped low in a curtsey and called him 'sir', chatting away freely after that, occasionally pulling his leg. She had to do it in French, that being

---

* The battle in 1942 was decisive for the Allies; it not only thwarted the threat to important British holdings such as the Suez Canal, but was the first crucial success for the Allies in a year, serving to bolster morale.

the language he preferred. Mohammed Ali was ancient but spry, fond of the sound of his own voice. When he turned his attention on me it was as awe-inspiring as being caught in the beam of a searchlight. Described as 'an historian', I felt like an impostor, blushing deeply (of course); whereupon the old thing tried, with practised skill, to put me at my ease. I so appreciated his efforts that though I knew them to be prompted merely by politeness, I found them taking effect. Next thing, I was holding the floor with what I hoped was an amusing account of what was happening in Italy, until I had to be turned off like a tap, in mid-spate, in order to allow one of the other guests a chance to get a word in edgeways.

Nobody seemed to mind. It was evidently what they expected of a young officer from the outer fringes of a war which had so nearly engulfed them in disaster. Before the royal party swept away in a cavalcade of bannered cars, the goodbyes, like the greetings, were back to being formal – a flourish of 'sirs' and curtseying.

'Thank you, Roddy dear, you played your part very nicely,' said Bonté. 'This has been quite a red-letter day for you, hasn't it? One you're not going to forget in a hurry, I'm almost sure!'

The Medhurst letter produced an immediate twentieth-century magic carpet in the shape of a clapped-out Anson. A crew was rather more difficult to conjure up because Christmas was coming. All the same, four of us took off from Heliopolis on 9 December for the short hop to Alexandria.

For the first time since being posted overseas, I was legitimately keeping a diary. I scribbled: 'The strips of country field near Alex become so regularly rectangular that they resemble parquet, moss grown, with gaps caused by dead straight irrigation canals making grooves in which a giant might catch his foot. Houses squat, fungoid. Over Rosetta we see buildings looking like water-towers.' Was there an advantage to be gained from making notes as boring as that? None that I could see.

I felt extraordinarily privileged to be exploring new places. The same could not be said for my press-ganged crew, a threesome of Flight Sergeants, who weren't interested in going anywhere; they would far rather have stayed in Cairo. They had no desire to meet anyone apart from other aircrew, or eat anything except English food. Much of their energy seemed devoted to talking about, or planning, their next cup of tea. I failed to see how I could make them better-disposed towards our odyssey, and it distressed me beyond measure.

On the road to el-Alamein next day, we passed a bleak hut with a sign announcing 'The Camel's Head'. It was more like the camel's back for me. My crew clamoured to stop for a cuppa and once inside were granted exactly the kind they craved: thick, dark brown, heavily laced with sweetened condensed milk – the 'char' of a thousand desert brew-ups. Our stop served one purpose: I discovered that a permit was required to visit the battlefield and that it should have been obtained in Alexandria. The military policeman conveying that information was actually rather apologetic. My men were delighted; the prospect of things going wrong brought a smile to each face. But blessed or unblessed by the Army Bureau, I intended at least to have a glimpse of el-Alamein and, as luck would have it, we were unchallenged as we looked around. Near the South African memorial a sign said that the English and German minefields had been no more than 400 yards apart. We trusted that all the mines had been lifted.

Beyond was the English cemetery, makeshift, and with a makeshift car park bordered by a corrugated-iron shed marked LATRINE. As one man, my crew made a dash for it. I was glad they did, because it left me free to contemplate, on my own, the white-painted crosses stretching out in regular lines. I was suddenly overcome, feeling the tears pricking my eyes, overwhelmed by the thought that each cross marked a grave and that in each grave lay the remains of a body, perhaps no more than an arm, a leg, or a shred of khaki stained with blood. Eventually, when the cemetery had been properly tidied up, it might become a quiet sanctuary for the living, not (as it was at that moment) a place of pre-constructed pits into which anonymous fragments of the Glorious Dead were being trundled, daily. I hastily pulled myself together as my crew emerged from the latrine hut with over-elaborate looks of disgust, waving arms to shoo away flies.

Towards el-Daba there was a third cemetery, in its way the most poignant of all, a last resting-place for tanks of all nations. Battered beyond repair, the iron monsters had been dragged here to suffer the humiliation of being cannibalised to provide spare parts for those still battling on. There were light Italians with pitifully thin armour-plating, massive American Shermans, Allied and Axis relics, witnesses to Rommel's defeated pride and Monty's* victorious vanity. All, alike, had been taught the lesson that the desert 'paths of glory lead but to the grave'. All were rusting silently – yet not in utter silence. A breeze played idly with loose flanges of metal, twanging and thumping as if on some grotesque piano. Sand had begun to drift across the wrecks, settling deep into hollows where men had once crouched uncomfortably.

Whilst my crew sat half in, half out of the staff-car, yawning their heads off, I wandered alone through the echoing loneliness of the tank cemetery, towards a mosque as ruined as everything else, undergoing repairs by a few *fellahin*. Birds flew, twittering, to perch near the roofless dome, scattering messes over threadbare carpets which had been placed on the uneven floor.

'Now that the war is over, we can come here once more for *selah*,' said one, speaking English. 'We thought the Germans would win, but Allah decreed otherwise.'

So He did, I thought. *So He did, or I wouldn't be here!*

29

After that we headed to Siwa Oasis, 200 miles inland, by way of Mersa Matruh, once a seaside resort – as no doubt it would be again – now a deserted ghost-town of ruined shops and a beach wired-off with warnings against unexploded mines. A Captain in charge there recommended Siwa as 'one of the queerest places under the sun – you're sure to love it!' which is why I decided on the detour. Luckily it had been much used by the Long Range Desert Group, so I had a legitimate reason for going there.

From the air the journey looked simple, but rough. A macadam road gave way to a plethora of sandy tracks, running parallel with one another

---

* Erwin Rommel was the General in charge of the German troops; Bernard Montgomery was in charge of the British troops. Roddy finds Rommel to be an impressive character (more to come on this). Whether one agrees with him or not, it's not an unusual opinion: he was lauded as such at the time and in the immediate years after the war by Allied press.

over swathes of hardened mud and scrub. We arrived over fantastic rock formations, whorls and pagodas high enough for us to fly level with their flattened tops, guarding the straggling palms of Siwa. Two hills, with hill-coloured huts clinging to their sides, rose up from a sandy central arena. Some of the higher huts were roofless, like wasps' nests ripped open, and untenanted, suggesting a population in decline.

There was no runway, though there was a flag fluttering to do duty as a wind-sock. We came in to land on the longest available clear space, on a surface which looked as if it had been sprinkled with flat white stones. Fortunately, looks were deceptive; the stones were cakes of salty mud which crackled and *vroomed* underfoot like the 'singing sands' of Studland Bay as we walked into a welcome. The impromptu welcoming committee consisted of a truck and a uniformed Sergeant, pumping hands and shouting '*Sayeeda!*' He'd been instructed to take us straight to his leader, the Mamur.

The good man said that he would have food bought and sent round to us, together with one of his servants to deal with it. Next day he'd take us on a guided tour of the oasis. Kindness could hardly have been extended further. We were to stay in the Government Rest-house originally built for King Farouk, who'd refused to budge without a full complement of luxuries. Failing the King's presence, it was bare of all but essentials such as hard wooden beds and a dusty sofa or two, which exercised such an attraction for my crew that they flung themselves down and were soon happily snoring. This left me free to set off on my own across the salt-caked dried mudflats towards the larger of the two hills we'd seen from the air. This was the metropolis, where huts were piled, higgledy-piggledy, floor on roof on floor, off a 'street' winding upwards. The sun was preparing to set. In the distance, flat-topped pagoda rock formations were still glowing golden, a deep, dramatic yellow ochre.

Skirting a graveyard like a petrified forest of stone stumps, I reached an escarpment honeycombed with huts, where village elders sat gravely in their robes, as if cooling off after a bath. They flashed their eyes in answer to my '*Sayeeda!*', but without replying. I followed a goat up an alley-way, until a figure in black darted out from behind a bead curtain and hauled the animal indoors. Higher still, a young girl, head uncovered, brushed past me in a skilfully intimate way before disappearing behind another bead curtain. She'd been naughty, I could guess. Ripples of laughter indicated that she was recounting her adventure to an audience of other girls, respectably out of sight.

Strewn with tiny balls of goat-dung, the sandy alley went winding upwards through sand-coloured walls, pierced by slits, presumably windows too high to be looked through save from inside. I might have been in a gigantic termite mound, capped by a rocky summit; which was where I found a man in mauve-striped pyjamas, sitting on a ledge. He was youngish with pencil moustaches and long-lashed, liquid-looking eyes.

'Me Hakim,' he announced.

'Lovely!' I said.

His reaction was to jump to his feet and ask: 'Top?'

I nodded. He scrambled up to the highest ledge, helping me up too. By then, a monstrously enlarged sun was sinking as rapidly as a lift. For a few moments we shared a marvellous, panoramic, golden view of Siwa, whilst from a mosque already in shadow a muezzin called the faithful to prayer.

I looked at him questioningly. 'Oughtn't you to be on hands and knees, or something?'

He shrugged. 'I am a Coptic gentleman!' Unspoken was: *And that's why I trouble to climb up here to watch the sun go down. You wouldn't find a Muslim doing that!*

He didn't bother to hide how superior he felt. He was an excellent source of information about things which the Mamur might have found too shocking to mention. I egged him on, eager to hear more. The gist of what he said was:

Ethnically, the Siwans were Berbers, coming originally from Tunisia. There were only about 4000 of them, so it was all the more remarkable that they'd developed their own strange customs from which no one had (so far) succeeded in dislodging them. Between adolescence and the moment of actually acquiring a wife, young men were encouraged to find an official boyfriend, to whom they were then regarded as being 'married'. Far from being condemned, the practice was recognised as the prime protector of young girls, who might otherwise lay themselves open to seduction. 'Some of our visitors find this custom too tempting and want to join in,' admitted the doctor. 'So now Siwans pretend that it doesn't happen any longer. But that's not true. It does, and you may be sure I don't mind talking about it.'

I bet you don't! I thought. *Nor having a go yourself, I'll be bound!*

He took me back to his house for thick, sweet, mint-flavoured tea in tiny glasses. He left me fondling a fuzzly black dog called Dora whilst he attended to a couple of patients. When he returned, he told me that the bitch had been abandoned, sadly, by an Englishman. I pumped him about Siwa's contribution to the war effort. 'Oh dear!' he said, rolling his eyes. 'We had to put up with a very different sort of visitor in those days.'

In 1940, 1941 and 1942 there'd been Australian and Egyptian troops in the oasis, then four months of Italians and Germans. The Italians had used as many as twenty-seven aircraft to bomb the villages, when women had learnt to run out of their houses and scatter amongst the palm trees.

When I got back to the Government Rest-house, I found an argument in progress about whether to open a tin of pineapple.

The Mamur and Hakim – who turned out to be Siwa's doctor, an important man – collected us next day in a 1935 Ford. We drove down raised causeways between strips of cultivation, slippery tracks which were soft on top, hard beneath, as if made of soap soaked briefly in water. To either side were straggly canals, or gardens of fruit and veg fenced-in with palm-fronds. However haphazard it might all look, every single thing that grew was somebody's property.

We saw the date-enclosure, where men were allowed to eat all they wished, provided that they left by sunset. And the olive-oil press, worked by a man walking in a circle, pushing a lever to roll a stone against a stone ledge, forcing out a dark liquid, as turgid as blood. 'Like butchers, olive-oil pressers can't be buried with the rest of us,' said the doctor. I asked why. 'Because everyone knows they are naughty rascals!'

We arrived at the wells, *raison d'être* of the oasis, dark emerald pools with huge bubbles rising to the surface all the time and bursting. It was the custom, we were told, for a bride to take a dip on the eve of her wedding, without using soap, the bubbles alone being considered enough to make her clean. I put my hand in to taste a drop of the water. It was faintly fizzy, like Eno's Fruit Salt.

Some way off, half a dozen women were bathing, all but their heads covered in shifts of blue-striped cotton, with overcloaks of mauve. They weren't going to let our presence pass without theatrical protest, which took the form of throwing one cloak over all four heads and bobbing up and down, caterpillar fashion.

Before the day was over I asked the crew for a favour. Would they mind taking the Mamur and the Hakim and the rogue pro-British

Sheikh living nearby up for a spin over Siwa? They hesitated – when did they ever not hesitate, over any request of mine? – but conceded. At the last moment we included the Sheikh's driver, he pleaded so hard. His naivety added greatly to our enjoyment; he was convinced that when we banked, the Earth was tilting and not us. 'So small! So small!' he kept shouting above the noise of the engines. When we flew low over his own house, he wrestled about to get a better view, which might have put us off-balance, so it was just as well that we'd strapped him in.

30

Our next flight along the coast gave some idea of the Western Desert: brown distances interspersed with small harbours, the sole connecting link a thin, uneven road. It was difficult to understand why anyone had wanted such barren wastes. I doubted whether one in a hundred of our men (or, for that matter, the enemy) had had the vaguest idea of what purpose they were serving in careering backwards and forwards between Egypt, Libya, Tunisia and Algeria.

With new knowledge acquired from reading intelligence reports, I gathered that troops needed supplies which only ships could bring; and ships needed harbours, which had to be protected by troops. By capturing large areas of desert, aircraft gained airfields from which they could fly to protect ships bringing the troops' supplies through the Mediterranean. The whole process seemed to go round and round in a circle. Why protect that sea-route in the first place? Apparently, because it was 'the road to India'. At which point my mind boggled. I couldn't understand why such a route should have been considered so overridingly important in a war against Italy and Germany. Evidently I needed to be taught to take a more global view – difficult for one who was only just starting to grapple with local considerations.

Tobruk, in Libya, demonstrated what many people thought the desert war had been about. In the harbour there were said to be 147 wrecks, mostly hidden under water. During General ('Electric Whiskers') Graziani's advance, it had become a symbol of Allied resistance, holding out against all odds. Long after the event it was difficult to see what such gallant defiance had achieved, except to foster a legend of grit and pluck, with particular reference to the bravery of Australians and South Africans. When Rommel swept through like a forest fire, Tobruk had tried to hold out again, then was overwhelmed.

Humbled by the thought of the hardships endured by men heroically battling, it nevertheless didn't stop me from being busily concerned with problems of where to stay and where to eat in reasonable comfort. Catering arrangements in Tobruk were on a large and successful scale: for officers, The Ladybird; for other ranks, Windy Corner; for non-European troops, The Chop Shop. There was even a bathing-beach reserved for 'Officers and Sisters', proving that no time had been lost in creating those divisions dear to the military heart, in order that everyone should know exactly where they were supposed to stand.

Flying on, I could see why Mussolini had formerly coveted Cyrenaica,* for the whole *jebel* region beyond Halfaya looked green and fertile. Little harbours like Derna were inviting; and the ruined colonnades of Cyrene were evidence of a classical (therefore commercial) importance stretching back into history. We landed at Benina aerodrome, firmly under Allied control, where my crew raced off for steak and chips.

My eccentric desire was to taste the waters of Lethe, River of Forgetfulness, then to remember what it had been like – an attractively self-contradictory project, to be achieved by visiting a cavern famed as an entrance to Hades.

I prevailed upon a fitter to bring a couple of Tilley lamps and come exploring with me. We were to find that others had made the pilgrimage for other purposes: steps led (via a crevice in the red earth) down through coils of dried faeces to a flattish green area strewn with empty tins and cartons. If ever there were a place better forgotten, this was it.

A hundred and twenty feet underground, water ran sluggishly through a grotto; and at a decrepit landing-stage, there had once been a raft. Had it been Charon's ferry on the river Styx, I might have considered throwing an obol, or even an Allied Military Currency note, into it, but the raft had sunk to the bottom and nobody had bothered to dredge it up again. I dabbled my fingers in the semi-stagnant water encrusted with white scum, then put them to my mouth, encouraged by seeing that a greenish prawn, six inches long, had managed to survive in the fetid shallows.

---

* The eastern coastal district of Libya.

I apologised profusely to the fitter for dragging him along on such a disappointing expedition. 'I don't suppose you'll remember much about it, one day?'

'Oh no, sir, this is something I'll never forget!'

So much for Lethe's fabled attribute.

Crew disbanded (the magic carpet broke down around the desert monument 'Marble Arch'), my last stop on my tour for research purposes was Malta, the great prize of the Mediterranean, which controlled the Sicilian narrows and had remained unconquered. The islanders were proud and pleased with themselves, fondly remembering the three Gladiator planes *Faith*, *Hope* and *Charity*, which for a time had provided the sole air-shield against the enemy. It was a good moment to be British; we could hardly have been more popular.

Having finished what I'd come to see, and more – key names were names no longer, but places which I would be able to describe – I returned to Rome on Christmas Eve. There was time for a few more adventures: staying with the Air Officer Commanding and his 'court' in an Austrian castle; and learning to ski in Cortina where the food alone would have staggered anyone arriving fresh from rationed England (*mont-blancs* of cream scattered with chestnuts, vol-au-vents bursting with chicken breasts, abundant hams, thin slices of foie gras – I had seldom seen such displays, even at a Hunt Ball, pre-war). But by 1946, Blighty was calling and it was time to go home.

31

How we were looking forward to England, Home and Beauty! At least, some of us were. Others, dreading to find themselves unemployed following demob, were not so sure. 'Civvy Street' with its shops, pubs and cinemas sounded fine, but not so fine without cash to spend or a roof overhead. On returning to the place of their dreams, servicemen who'd endured years of hardship in war-torn countries abroad were flabbergasted by the discomforts still to be faced in the mother country. Rationing

continued unabated: scraps of meat; scrapes of butter; morsels of cheese –
even less than when they'd left. The cry of '*Vae Victis!*' – Woe to the
Conquered! – needed standing on its head. 'Woe to the Victors!' seemed
to fit the bill better. So much for winning a long and costly war.

I was of course one of the lucky ones who was able to postpone my
demob indefinitely due to the DAF history, and lucky to like the job and
have a regular income. Somewhere to live proved trickier. When I turned
up in Nassau Street, prepared to let Marcus stay on for a while, I was given
the dustiest of answers. 'It'th my flat now!' he lisped. 'But of courthe you
can thtay here free until you find thomewhere of your own.'

I gasped, I felt physically sick, not just sick at heart. I'd handed over the
flat to him to make his life easier, should my own be forfeited overseas.
And now he was clinging to the letter of a wartime tenancy law and
refusing to hand it back. It was the second time that I'd been shockingly
betrayed by a former friend, being reported for smoking by Stephen
Spring-Rice at school being the first instance. The shock was absolute,
like running into a lamp-post in the black-out. 'I don't think I'll be staying,' I said, as soon as I could bring myself to speak.

I couldn't shake the dust of Nassau Street from off my shoes then and
there, because more or less everything I owned in the world was stored in
drawers and cupboards; some pieces of furniture, too. I had to continue
to have dealings with Marcus; but I wasn't going to let him get away
with it entirely. 'It will do you no good in the end!' I said, in a voice of
doom. As I spoke, I saw, in a flash, that what I had said was prophetic. If
he were capable of doing this to me, to whom he owed so much, then he
would surely do the same to others. There was no need for me to curse
him; he'd done that for himself. 'I'll let you know in due course when
I'm ready to pick up my things.' And then I didn't slam, but gently closed
the door on the past.

I poured out my woes to Bridget, who came up with a brilliant idea:
'Ian Lubbock is looking for someone to share his dive. Let's give him a
ring!' Ian Lubbock, you might remember, was the fellow I described as
being too fond of men when I was sucking up (badly) to Group Captain
Morven Cavendish-Bentinck.

Ian, now an actor, lived in Holland Park, in the basement of No. 19,
a flat belonging to his mother, the classical pianist. In consequence, an
enormous concert grand piano blocked part of the back room which was
to be mine; and an ageing theatrical with powdered cheeks called Maurice
Berkeley occupied a smaller front room with yet another piano in it. Ian's

room controlled the entry to the only bath – an awkward arrangement when he happened to be sharing his bed with another. Somewhat to my amazement – because it meant that I must have got him all wrong – this other, at that moment, was Irene Worth, the actress known not only for her superior stage technique but for her connection with the difficult director Gabriel Pascal. Which must have been why he didn't seem to mind too much that his wife, Lys, lovely but of minimal brain-power, had run off with clever Cyril Connolly.

I fell gladly into my new digs – paying Ian £3 a week, the right amount for those days – along with my collection of ancient gramophone records. With those familiar sounds for a background I might have imagined myself back in Nassau Street, though I missed the last-minute guests flaked out on the floor, the ten-minute walk to Piccadilly Circus and the local Fitzroy and its disreputable clientèle.

I couldn't afford a car, even had one been obtainable. So, like Ernie Scott back in Dorset, I rode everywhere on a bicycle, even when going out to dinner, all togged up in a dinner-jacket. Each day I would cycle to the offices at Cadogan Gardens and eagerly go through piles of files. That they contained precisely the sort of propaganda against which I'd been inveighing before taking on the history didn't matter. I didn't intend using them, except to check facts.

I set to work bombarding anyone who might have anything interesting to contribute with requests for interviews and/or documents. Some 70 per cent replied; and of those, no more than 5 per cent came up with something worthwhile. From that 5 per cent I learnt an essential lesson: to friends and families, the memory of those killed in action was sacred. Those who mourned, and would mourn perhaps for the rest of their lives, didn't deserve to have salt rubbed into their wounds by any words of mine. For their sake, the truth might have to be bent a little, at times, in unimportant ways. It was a humbling consideration, not to be ignored even in the quest for that Holy Grail of historians, accuracy, on which I was setting such store.

In quest of the truth in all other respects, I was prepared to stoop to low tricks. Air Historical Branch contained a category of top-secret Cabinet files (known as 'Punch') to which I was forbidden access. I schemed to nullify such an absurd ruling. My friend José was working in Central Registry, through which such files passed when requested by official historians under the direction of Denis Richards. I used to take José to lunch sometimes, which was how I discovered that she would usually go and 'powder her nose' for quite a time before going out. On days when she was going out but not with me, I could manage to be alone in Registry long enough to purloin the files I wanted, carry them up to my room, scan them quickly, bring them back sandwiched between other files, and replace them exactly where I'd found them. I considered that the ends definitely justified the means; for how else could I have avoided making the most elementary mistakes, such as assuming that Montgomery and Tedder* were always in harmony? I was thrilled to discover that I had chapter and verse for claiming that those two Supremes were at variance on almost every plan of High Command, Tedder always proving right.

A thing which never failed to amaze me was the puerile language used by the high-ups: 'Good hunting, chaps!' or 'Tally-ho!', etc., as if they were sportsmen. I liked it in a way for being so British, but I could imagine it driving our Allies round the bend. The more I delved through files licit and illicit, the quicker I became at extracting nuggets of information relevant to my purpose, understanding at last how the Provost Monty James back at Eton had been able to read a book at the rate of turning its pages. I never quite reached that standard, but was soon not so far off.

Whilst my history plodded towards completion (the more I researched, the more terrifying the project became. I was such an amateur. How had I ever had the nerve to suppose that I could marshal so many facts to make a cohesive whole?) Hutchinson's also agreed to publish my very poor detective novel *The Flesh is Willing*, which I'd started in my tent at Brazzaco. It had an intricate plot involving a séance and a naive young man, wrongly assumed (by some) to be myself. The dream of being a real writer was coming true at last.

32

The winter of 1946/7 was one of the coldest on record. Venturing on to the ice on the Serpentine in Hyde Park, I fulfilled a childhood urge by

---

* Arthur Tedder was Marshal of the Air Force and was a crucial figure during the war in the Mediterranean and North Africa.

being able to walk across to 'Peter Pan's Island'. In Holland Park, Ian turned
out to be tight when it came to heating, so I froze. Ex-Squadron Leader
Tony Hudson had nowhere to sleep one night in London, so I invited him
to stay (in my bed, whilst I took to a mattress on the floor). Such was the
discomfort of the best I could offer that he left after a single night.

I was saved by a cousin of whom I hadn't heard till then: Aelwyn
Howard-Williams. Aelwyn lived opposite St Augustine's Church in
the basement of 94 Queen's Gate, and he informed me that a Lady
Udney, living on the first floor, was looking to move out; once she did
I moved immediately into her battered but grandiose flat. The front
room had three French windows leading on to a balcony, sittable-on
because it extended over a large entrance-porch. Badly constructed
partitions cut across the elaborate cornices of what had once been a fine
drawing-room, thereby creating a sitting-room, a thin, high bedroom,
a claustrophobic hall with one leaded window leading nowhere but into
the sitting-room, and a small kitchen. The bathroom, being up a few
stairs, made the flat feel like a maisonette. A separate room at the back
would do splendidly for letting purposes. How wonderful it seemed –
even better than Nassau Street. Needless to say, my new flat offered so
many opportunities that it became known to my friends as 'Slut Hall'.

Cousin Aelwyn continued to 'crouch', as he described it, 'down
amongst the dustbins', surrounded by splendid antique furniture. Every
now and then he would spot a painting by de Wint, buy it for next to
nothing and sell it to the Usher Gallery in Lincoln. Perennially hard up,
he was an expert fortune-teller, known widely as 'Willie-the-Witch'.

Meanwhile, my sister Genissa wrote from the frozen wolds of
Lincolnshire that Granny Rawnsley had tripped over a dog in Skegness
and fallen on to a broken bottle. High drama! In her own particularly
animated way, Genissa described what happened as Uncle Dick was
driving both back to Claxby:

> *Granny suddenly said, 'I can't stand it any longer, do drive faster
> Dickie.' I thought she meant her leg was bleeding, but no, it was
> just that she wanted to spend a penny so badly!!! Suddenly just
> after we passed the Radar Station and had reached the steepest
> and most slippery part of the Hill she said, 'Stop at once I can't
> wait.' Before she could scramble out and I could hobble to her she
> began to tiddle in her nicks poor thing and we had a dreadful
> scene half in and half out of the car with Dickie being completely*

useless in helping me pull down her nicks!! So she arrived back
here soaked through and frozen with cold, having a slight rigor. I
got busy with hot water bottles, tea and bath towels and she soon
cheered up. Oh the foolishness of her Age in not telling me she
wanted to get out until the very last moment of her endurance . . .

Was this what we would all come to eventually, I wondered?

Claxby was now Genissa's home, after serving in Ceylon as a nurse. It was also the base for Morvyne, mostly away studying singing in London, and for my mother, deprived of Kingston House post-war. None of them were happy to continue the arrangement indefinitely, so we drove all over the county looking for a place of our own.

When we finally lit upon a suitable house it was not in Lincolnshire, but in Sussex, a former Priory with twelfth-century chapel and refectory, Elizabethan brew-house and Georgian wing. As if to compound architectural confusion, 'Tudorbethan' half timbering, dating from the twenties, protected a drip-stoned three-gabled front. It was called Langney, Langney with an 'n', one of those names sure to be wrongly spelt (with a second 'l' instead of an 'n') by anyone not already in the know. Without informing the agent, Morvyne and I went to look it over and, seeing a downstairs lavatory window open, climbed in. The rooms looked to be in unusually good shape, having just been painted, which for those days was unusual. Immediately post-war, repainting was against the law; but that hadn't worried its owner, Countess Hollender – a Papal title, so we were informed – who'd bought it as a speculation. She had already ripped out a drawing-room chimney-piece, which she'd sold separately, replacing it with a pebble-dashed horror; worse still, she'd disposed of a fine oak staircase, putting nothing in its place. What was on the market was what was left over after such depredations.

We purchased the Priory in the names of us three children. Technically, from then on we 'let' it to my mother, an arrangement which caused her no pain but which kept it from having to be sold when she died. So there we all were, settled once more – or, at least, for now – after the long sojourn of war.

If there is a closing chapter to my wartime tales, it seems appropriate that they should be about the German friends I made in the spring of '39. It took some doing, but I finally tracked them down, to hear that Georg Siemers had never returned from service on the Russian front and that Budi von Mach, dear chubby, blond Budi, had been killed in action in Russia on 13 February 1942, aged twenty-one. His mother wrote: 'I am astonished that you are writing novels now, that would have made much pleasure to Budi. I am dreaming often of him, and then I hear him laughing, he was always happy . . .'

I laid her letter down and howled, more for that enemy than for many an English friend.

Sophisticated Carola had survived, though Hamburg had been grievously destroyed.

There was no one left to give me news of that champion of champions, red-headed, freckled Werner.

part four

the south seas

1948-9

33

With a foreword by none other than the Marshal of the Royal Air Force, Lord Tedder, *The History of Desert Air Force* finally appeared on the bookstalls in September 1948, where it achieved no more than a moderate success.

Getting Tedder to supply the foreword had been my idea, asked of him when I interviewed him. I then seized the opportunity of a second interview to ask for another favour, telling him that I'd seen, in a dream, that I was the writer of his 'Life'. Had it been anything other than the truth I wouldn't have dared approach him with such assurance. He was somewhat taken aback. 'Plenty of other biographers have asked for my Life,' he said. 'Why should I choose *you*?'

'Because the dream said so.'

'In that case, I have no alternative,' he replied, eyes twinkling (as they often did when he wished to disguise his true thoughts). 'All right, go ahead and do your worst!'

It was a real triumph. Authors had been angling for Tedder for some time, meeting with a blank refusal. Just why he favoured an unknown such as myself no one could understand; and I didn't go about explaining. (My grandmother was exceedingly proud and enthusiastically told Uncle Dick the news, hoping, as ever, to endear me to him. 'Don't you believe it!' Uncle Dick said to his cold consort, my aunt Susan. When my grandmother protested, he was heard to add: 'He's having us on!' What little respect I had left for him dwindled.)

Tedder replied equally favourably to my next idea, which must have come as even more of a shock to him. I asked, 'Would you mind, sir, if I don't start on your Life for at least a year?'

'Mind?' he said quizzically. 'Why should I mind? Only too relieved . . . but may one ask *why*?'

'The South Seas have me in thrall,' I told him. 'I'm longing to go, before it's too late.'

Before entering the Royal Flying Corps in the First World War,

Tedder had been a District Officer in Fiji, so his reply was a hearty, 'Now that's something I *can* understand!'

The desire to drop everything and start travelling was not as sudden as it seemed. Restlessness had been my lot for quite a while. The South Pacific, that ocean of dreams, had been making its presence felt ever since the armistice, with particular emphasis on Tahiti. Before having any chance of going there it had been an obsession. Late at night I would murmur a witch's invocation to her broomstick: 'Horse and hattock, ho and away!' adding, 'Ho and away for Tahiti!' Then, for good measure, I would intone a triple '*OM MANI PADME HUM!*' to get the Lord Buddha on my side as well. The dream whirled through my brain like a tornado, for if such a thing were anywhere to be found, I was convinced, like so many others in the past, that the South Seas contained the Earthly Paradise.

Yet I really knew very little about Polynesia. I *did* know that a white Norwegian ship, *Southern Cross*, was one of the few vessels regularly calling in at Papeete, port and capital of Tahiti. I saw in an evening paper that she had arrived in London, so that was the signal for me to visit the Norwegian Seamen's Hostel in Bayswater, to seek out a crew member. Nobody asked whether I were a seaman, let alone a Norwegian. Within a few minutes at the bar I was talking to Erlang Erlandsen, wildly attractive, everybody's idea of blond male comeliness, and, as luck would have it, a sailor aboard *Southern Cross*, which would be sailing the following day. I had no time to lose.

Erlang said that he'd always wanted to visit a typical East End pub. The fame of Charlie Brown's* had spread to Oslo, so I promised to take him. Not having a car, we would have to go by tube and bus. 'No, no,' he said, 'we take taxi!' – and at his expense. I could see why 'every nice girl loves a sailor'. When foreign, they were prepared to do the paying, whereas English ones, more worldly-wise, had cottoned on to the fact that the world was full of punters willing to pick up the bill for Jolly Jack Tar – if only one could be found before a run ashore ended.

At Charlie Brown's there was the usual din and potter of a rattling

---

* Charlie Brown's was a nickname for the legendary Railway Tavern in Limehouse, Tower Hamlets, so called because Charlie Brown had been the landlord of the pub for almost four decades until his death in 1932 (when 16,000 people were said to have lined the streets to watch his funeral procession). Sailors from all over the world visited the pub, Charlie Brown's generosity and firm hand earning him the title 'King of Limehouse'. The pub was demolished in the seventies for construction of the Docklands Light Railway, but you can visit Charlie Brown's roundabout nearby.

good beery time. 'You join our ship!' urged Erlang as we sipped our beer. 'I tell you, you come on board, Erlang hide you until too late to throw you off, yes?'

'Yes!' I yelled back. 'Yes, yes of course!' For a glorious moment, it even seemed possible.

'Tahiti! Tahiti! Tahiti!' whispered Erlang within an inch of my ear, his face glowing.

I asked: 'How do you say "I love you" in Norwegian?'

*Ja enske dai,** it sounded like.

'Then, *Ja enske dai, ja enske dai, JA ENSKE DAI!*'

And so indeed I did; but at such a time and in such a place my plea was unlikely to prevail. Spotting a lonely prey, a pub harpy closed in asking for a cigarette, then for a light from Erlang the magnificent, Erlang the – alas – too easily cajoled. Soon she had slipped into a position between us, fumbling his trousers, shouting hoarse endearments.

'I go with her,' he said, turning to me. '*Ja enske dai*, you understand, but I go fuck with her. Mean nothing!'

I had to accept the situation. I would never see Erlang again ... but how his words rang in my ears!

The scene of a second push towards Tahiti was the Turkish Bath in Russell Square. I would often go there by night, marvelling at the waste of space. There was room for clients to drift about under some extraordinary architectural features, pillars carved with niches for painted stone figures bearing painted shields. The Gothic atmosphere was almost ecclesiastical; or might have been, had it not been for some most unecclesiastical goings-on. Perhaps a few were there simply to get clean; if so, it was hard to distinguish which from whom.

Visibility in the steam room was as impenetrable as a London fog. Out of the thick mist loomed an athletic young man, who sat himself down on the slab next to me with the usual opener: 'D'you come here often?'

'Probably not half as often as YOU do, Bill!'

'Good God, it's Roddy!'

Bill McLean was an old school friend, once cherished. We had constantly sat together in 'Div', which meant that he was a year older than me, because King's Scholars, unlike Oppidans, started life in Upper School, missing out Lower School altogether.

---

* Roddy didn't have Google Translate to clarify; the Norwegian for 'I love you' is *Jeg elsker deg.*

Whatever Bill had been searching for, it wasn't someone like me (except as a last resort). However, he found it more amusing to talk than to go on prowling, so back he came with me to Queen's Gate for a chatty breakfast. We didn't have too much to catch up on as I'd encountered him, on and off, when he'd been living in an expensive haunt of smart bachelor's digs in Half Moon Street.* Since then he had married Daška Ivanovic of the Yugoslav shipping family.

What a paladin was Bill! His career had been full of the dash and brilliance of a John Buchan† character. He'd been one of a Special Air Services élite, based in Cairo, famed for their casual competence. He'd been dropped into Yugoslavia, to help direct the exploits of Partisans when (again like a Buchan character) he'd been betrayed by a bunch of 'lefties' in the Bari HQ. Money, in millions, had always surrounded him, though his mother's extravagance had put a temporary stop to that. To cap all else, he was about to stand for Parliament.

I mentioned Tahiti, I mentioned Erlang and his ship. 'There's more than one way of killing a cat!' said Bill. 'I know Stanley Cayzer pretty well, he comes out shooting. His family owns the Clan Line. Not that Stanley has much to do with that side of things, but he might be useful. Shall I sound him out?'

Bill was as good as his word. He invited me to dinner in Gloucester Square,‡ Daška eyeing me with a certain suspicion, as if unable to understand why I seemed to be such a friend of her husband, being poor and of no obvious use to his career. After dinner, Stanley was stolid, but Doussa, his Egyptian wife, was dancing about like a firefly, glittering with *entrain*. I spent much of a most entertaining time trying to match her. When Bill asked Stanley if he could help me, Doussa jumped up from her chair and danced over to her husband, patting his face. 'Now then, Stanley dar-leeeing! Of course we must help this awful young man!' So of course he had to promise that he would.

––––––––

* Half Moon Street is in affluent and central Piccadilly, a stone's throw away from Green Park.

† Author of *The Thirty-Nine Steps*, the first of the novels featuring all-action hero Richard Hannay.

‡ Gloucester Square is in Paddington, another affluent and central part of London, this time a stone's throw away from Hyde Park.

34

Lovely Doussa Cayzer! Obedient Stanley! I was offered the job of Assistant Purser on *Clan Urquhart*, without pay; in fact I had to contribute £45 towards my keep, all the way Down Under. By then my interest in the Fenwick Owen divorce settlement had dwindled to about £200 p.a. and would dwindle further from being in typical trustee gilt-edged stocks, but it would be enough to get me out to Tahiti. I was also able to keep Slut Hall going in my absence by letting the spare room to a couple of men, which paid for the rent of the whole. Thus fixed, I was all set and ready to go.

On a cold November day in 1948 I joined *Clan Urquhart* in Liverpool for my sinecure of a post. My immediate boss, Kit the Purser, was an old hoofer who had deserted the halls for the sea when he found it too hard to do high kicks to order. He was a fount of knowledge and wickedness. 'There aren't many in this ship your old uncle can't do what he likes with!' he boasted on the third day out, eyes glinting from behind blue-tinted spectacles. 'Just let him know the score and he'll put you wise!'

The crew were Goanese, gentle, super-polite. Our Captain was hardly that – he was famous for an ability to outdo even the Australian wharfies in his command of lingua-bloody-franca. So of course he had a heart of gold.

Any work which I was doing being voluntary, time hung heavy on my hands. I read and re-read a copy of *Wide World*, articles on Angkor, Tibet and Easter Island being particularly fascinating. Would I ever manage to see any of them? All, for different reasons, seemed impossibly difficult to get to. I was roused from inaction by the jollifications, dear to the crew, to celebrate 'Crossing the Line' – which in this case meant the Equator. Great fun was had by all, dressing up in makeshift female garb – outrageous camping under the guise of hearty horse-play.

We called at Fremantle, Adelaide and Melbourne, dropping off a mixed cargo of tinted bathroom suites, before I left the ship in Sydney, booking into Brown's Hotel, where I had to share a room with a stranger, a sheep-rancher from Queensland. 'Come up north and spend a few weeks with me!' he urged. It was my first taste of the Great Aussie Friendliness, and it was an effort to decline with thanks, but I was determined to make sail for more remote islands and needed to put all my efforts into finding that passage instead.

Come New Year's Day 1949, I was aboard SS *Rona*, blowing a cloud of smoke ahead of her on a following wind, steaming through a gap in the reef towards the Suva waterfront. As we passed into the still waters of the lagoon it was intermittently misty; the green hills of Fiji rose, separated by layers of cotton-wool cloud, towards peaks of naked rock. Even wrapped as it were in gauze, the slopes glowed an emerald green. Tír na nÓg* itself couldn't have been greener.

We were met by a smart young man from Government House, impeccably dressed in spotless white ducks, coated, collared and tied as if the damp heat didn't exist. To cap it all, the Garrick Hotel (at which the W/Op kindly dropped me) looked like something out of one of Somerset Maugham's atmospheric stories: potted palms, brass ash stands, rattan chairs and a strong smell of beer and feet – fascinating in its own sleazy manner. It enjoyed two great advantages: it cost very little and was far from respectable – twin virtues for the beachcomber which I was shortly hoping to become. I looked around me with interest, wondering how soon I might manage to find someone to batten on; for whoever heard of a Joseph Conrad character – which was how I was beginning to see myself – paying his own way?

That evening the hotel played its part by putting me at a table with a florid, dark-haired man in his early thirties; good-looking, but running to seed and very drunk. His name was Ian Graham and he was the Burns Philp local manager, living a few miles outside Suva. Naturally I'd heard of Burns Philp, the biggest shipping agency in the (British) Pacific. And here was this weighty character inviting me to come back home with him. 'That would be lovely!' I said, matching him drink for drink.

I'd guessed that we would be in for some serious whiskying and that I might be asked to stay the night. What I hadn't realised was that Ian's house would have only one bed in it, a single. We were jammed together, chastely, willy-nilly, because he was too drunk to do anything

---

* One of the names for the paradisiacal 'Otherworld' of eternal youth and beauty in Irish mythology.

but flake out in mid-fumble. Unfortunately, he was also too far gone to be roused by calls of nature. The result, next morning, was a sopping mattress only discovered when his 'boy' came to call us – tactful touch – with two cups of tea. An embarrassed Burns Philp manager then tried his best to get over the awkwardness of the moment by explaining how unusual it was for a man such as himself to have a Fijian looking after him. 'They don't make good servants, in fact they don't make servants, period! That's why most of us employ Indians.'

The 'us' meant 'us Europeans', though that description was questionable. Actual Europeans were few in number in the islands; 'Europeans' tended to be Australians (sometimes) or New Zealanders (more likely). Most of the islands' inhabitants were Indians, whose ancestors had been brought in to grow sugar cane for the CSR.* Few had been content to remain for long 'in their proper place'. Industrious and successful, much of the business life was in their hands, whilst their numbers had increased so dramatically that they would soon be outnumbering the native Fijians, who seemed uninterested in carrying on a trade. Inhabiting islands where everything grew in abundance and lagoons, conveniently protected by coral reefs, were alive with fish, natives had found it unnecessary to work hard for the basics of life. Naturally they didn't make good servants: the very idea of regularity in any shape or form was alien to them, exceptions being made for love and war.

The Fijians most immediately to be seen in the streets of Suva were the police, splendidly masculine even when wearing the *sulu*, a skirt snipped into a diamond pattern at the hem. Point-duty might have been specially designed to show them at their best; they obviously got a kick out of the admiration of onlookers for the quick, smart movements required for the job.

In spite of – perhaps because of – such a disastrous start, Ian hadn't finished with me. He kindly 'took me in hand', which meant an introduction to the Defence Club. From outside, it was a simple tin-roofed wooden shed. Inside, it was like an Officers' Mess, Pacific brand, hung with flags, trophies and photographs of past presidents. To the accompaniment of much back-slapping, a fan whanged round and round overhead. Conversation was jokey, concerned with how badly this or that fine fellow had behaved at a previous night's drinking session.

---

* Colonial Sugar Refining Company.

Since Ian favoured it so much, it was unlikely that we would become soulmates.

However, he kept up the good work by being extremely helpful where I needed help most. In his position he could easily arrange for my onward transit to Tahiti, something which at that time wasn't easy, because nothing was going direct. One sole copra-boat was plying between Tonga and Tahiti, and it would be the only one for several weeks, so I would first have to get to Tonga.

My plans seemed to be maturing nicely in this direction when other things slotted into place. I'd been given an introduction to a couple living in Suva, the Witheringtons, and they invited me to dinner.

They lived a fairish walk away, beyond Government House. Strolling along, I passed a wired-in compound where Fijian men with frizzy hair were horsing about, stark naked. I was amazed, supposing that prudish missionaries had put their collective foot down firmly on that sort of thing. With women, the missionaries seemed to have had more success: shapeless 'Mother Hubbards' – reaching nearly to the ground, like night-gowns – were everywhere to be seen. Eagerly I approached the compound and engaged the Fijians in conversation. They were soldiers. I would of course have stayed longer, but I didn't like to be too late for my dinner-hosts at our first meeting.

The Witheringtons were almost as improbable as the nude soldiers. They'd been theatrical agents in Soho and had all but gone bust. They'd come to Fiji with the vague, but traditional, idea of 'starting a new life in the Colonies'. In Suva they were running an import/export business, presumably with some success, since every so often they would make enough to travel abroad for a fortnight. Their scheme was to live frugally from day to day, except for one meal a week when they indulged themselves with a five-course affair, two sorts of wine (French, not Australian) and brandy and liqueurs. That was the meal to which I had been bidden, so it was just as well that I hadn't lingered too long in other company.

They wanted to talk about England and things theatrical and I obliged (they claimed to have heard of my former housemate, Maurice Berkeley, but I had the feeling that this was only a polite pretence). Towards the end of a convivial evening they exclaimed, as if with one voice: 'It's Lindsay for you, Lindsay Verrier! We'll send him a wire, if you like.' Lindsay was a doctor living on Fiji's other main island, Vanua Levu, in the remote 'bush'. 'He'll really tell you what's what,' they said. 'He's sure to take to you, being a writer. He's a great one himself for playing with words!' The good doctor sounded exactly the sort of person I was looking for.

35

Lindsay Verrier's telegram of reply to the Witheringtons went:

AM STAYING NADURI WHERE FRIEND WILL BE WELCOME AND WILL SEE WHEELS GOING ROUND STOP HE SHOULD COME LABASA HOTEL AND COLLECT MY LETTER AND ENQUIRE MY LOCAL ARRANGEMENTS STOP MINIMUM LUGGAGE SAY ONE SMALL SUITCASE ENOUGH.

Landing by seaplane on the lagoon near Labasa was like whooshing down a water-chute at Butlin's, Skegness. Spray blotted out the view until we taxied slowly to a halt. Coral reefs, which from the air had looked like thin white ribbons, disappeared seawards. Land loomed up, a shoreline mangrove-fuzzed, with green hills rising above and beyond coconut-palms. But oh! the climate: sticky heat, so damp that it might at any moment become liquid, then drenching rain, sweeping down, clearing up, sweeping down again. Here was 'the real' South Seas.

Whilst waiting for a Captain Stokes to take me in his launch to Dr Verrier's village, I put up at the mosquito-haunted only hotel, happening to come in for a formal evening of the local European sugar-field society: men in ties; women in long frocks; stilted conversation interspersed with awkward silences. We feasted on Brown Windsor soup and steak-and-kidney pudding from a tin, whilst in the lagoon outside, fish were plopping their heads off as if begging to be caught. Captain Stokes turned up towards the end of the evening, looking like an Ouida* hero: tall, broad-shouldered and weather-beaten. 'He was ten

---

* Ouida (pseudonym of Maria Louise Ramé) was a prolific Victorian novelist, with a bent for adventurous, daring plots in her early career.

years in the Persian Army,' someone told me, making him even more of a romantic figure. Apropos of the unsuitable steak-and-kidney pud, he said, 'No complaints, mind! In Taveuni,* they used to keep men in special fattening-huts to be eaten by the Chiefs. It was considered a great honour.'

Whilst waiting for him to load his stores I met Ratu (Chief) Penaia Ganilau, in training as a District Officer – a Fijian for a change. Ratu Penaia was huge and with a grin to match. He'd been at Oxford, at Wadham. All the ingredients were in place for eventual stardom. At that time there was only one other contender for a paramount role in Fijian affairs, Ratu Mara, who'd been the first to be sent to England to complete his education. And who had sent him there? My doctor, Lindsay Verrier.

The launch owned by Captain Stokes had seats made out of sugar-crates. Reeking of copra, it chugged through mangrove swamps to the accompaniment of rain sweeping down, wetting us to the bone. On arrival at the Naduri jetty I was met by a young Fijian, barefoot, in under-vest and *sulu*, who conducted me along a raised track of red mud, past a store, until we reached a native hut with a roof of corrugated-iron. At the entrance there was a loose-box door, bottom half closed, top half open, in front of a faded chintz curtain. Inside, I saw a Coleman lamp and paraffin cooker, and beyond them a primitive bed swathed in mosquito-netting. To the right, two more beds forming a dog-leg piled with books and files overflowing on to a desk, behind which sat Dr Lindsay Verrier, a fortyish, balding, bespectacled man in singlet and khaki shorts.

He spoke: 'Welcome to the Witheringtons' friend! I see your eye is caught by what may look to you like a parrot's cage. Here we need to keep our sugars and other perishables well hung, for fear of the ants. Indeed, such daring foods have been known to make off on their own accord. In all other respects, you will find this a great place for spiritual catharsis!'

'I'm sure I shall,' I said. And I was sure I would, from the word go.

For the rest of that day and on succeeding days I accompanied Lindsay on his rounds, which gave me an unparalleled insight into the ills afflicting the island's inhabitants, TB, rickets and anaemia being almost as prevalent as the only-to-be-expected worms and dysentery.

---

* The third largest island in Fiji.

Much of my time was spent squatting on floors of coconut-matting laid over compacted coral, drinking the milky, peppery liquid called *yagona*. The word was written like that but pronounced 'yangona', with an extra 'n'. Similarly, something spelt with a 'b' was pronounced 'mb', and a 'c' was a 'th' sound. Just why the missionaries who had first reduced Fijian to writing had introduced such an unnecessary complication, I failed to understand. It was no more 'traditional' than the Mother Hubbard.

We were seldom comfortable; it was too damp for that. And we were always muddy, even after an evening dip in a stream, which Dr Verrier referred to (in his own kind of inverted commas) as 'the kiddies' bath-time'. It was his idiosyncrasy to describe everything we did as if we were still in England: a group of girls giggling outside were 'the Women's Institute'; a sundowner of whisky was 'sherry before dinner', though the dinner itself was invariably a kedgeree of rice and tinned Pacific salmon.

The good doctor was a truly remarkable man. At intervals he would play a recorder, at which he was expert. He was also an expert statistician, keeping his results (in spite of the way his papers were heaped all over the place) in an instantly accessible form devised by himself. It was the work of no more than a minute to track down whatever fact he might require. The ends to which he put such statistics were astonishing; he was particularly interested in the effect of this or that religious belief upon public health. He had compiled tables of ailments suffered by Roman Catholics, Protestants (sub-divided into C of E and Methodists) and Others, and had already discovered that the least healthy were the Roman Catholics, partly due to the greater number of children which they were likely to produce. Such findings were too controversial to be generally released, but they fascinated me – though not for nearly long enough. He had to attend a conference in Suva, so all too soon we were preparing to leave.

Lindsay took with him a tie which was no more than a piece of string dyed black: 'A real tie would scarcely suit the climate, and no tie at all would scarcely be respectable. This tie is just right!' [Reproducing his actual words can give only a slight idea of how odd they sometimes sounded. Accompanied by high-pitched squeaks of pleasure, they were uniquely arresting.]

Once again, Captain Stokes' battered launch chugged through intermittent rain-storms to Labasa ('Lambasa'). We were kept waiting whilst mechanics crawled over the seaplane, tinkering. 'The creature has moored its nose to a piece of water and has no wish to move,' observed Lindsay. 'A lump of sugar might induce it to reconsider. Dare we suggest it?'

Suddenly he added: 'Would you have any great objection to staying here with me for the rest of your life? I would have a hut built at the end of the garden – any garden above whose ground I happened, for a few fleeting moments, to be. We would meet only by appointment [here he sniffed the air, holding up a finger] ... except if you happened to hear the recorder tootling, when any audience would be better than none. Does that answer all your questions?'

The roar of the seaplane revving its engines would have made a reply inaudible, had I thought of one in time. As it was, I managed a noncommittal grin; and so the moment passed, unanswered. Of course, since then I have often wondered what might have happened had I taken him up.

When I got back to the Garrick I found I'd been put in a room off – and all but in – the bar downstairs. I feared for the safety of my few belongings. I needn't have worried; they were safer than I was, so readily accessible. A Panamanian ship was in harbour. Its crew were roaring drunk and affectionately maudlin. The 2nd Engineer put his arms round my neck; then, on second thoughts, undid his trousers and started peeing against the bar. That was too much for his mates, who threw him out on to the street before renewing their own chaotic carousing. Meanwhile, I chatted to a part-Fijian called Frankie, who seemed to be a general favourite, though he drank very little.

Somebody had lent me a book entitled *At Home in Fiji*, by Miss Gordon-Cuming, a spirited account of a Victorian lady's sojourn in the islands during the 1880s. It occurred to me, how different were my own experiences. No lady could have dreamt of associating with such undesirables, let alone considered mentioning them in print, and in her day ship's crews had doubtless been even coarser and more drunken. She would have missed what I definitely gained: adventures of a delightful and instructive kind, the sort of haphazard consequences which I was often lucky enough to encounter in life.

Frankie said he would take me to a party given by friends in Robertson Road. We found a taxi and drove to a wooden house amongst similar wooden houses, the difference being the terrific noise coming from it. The room into which I was led had a lino-covered floor, a piano overlaid by a long lace doily and shelves loaded down with china ornaments. Under an orange-shaded central light everything looked a bright orange, particularly the people prancing about whilst a woman banged away on the piano. There were men in *sulus*, a huge blond sailor from the *Hifofua* called Karl, a girl, Lil, tightly encased in a shiny green satin blouse, and a willowy young man who came forward in welcome. Others formed a blurred background of noise and movement.

Frankie shouted little snippets of gossip about some of them: the men in *sulus* were Tongans; Karl was recovering from a dose of the clap; Lil was 'no good'; the willowy young man was her brother, Sidney. Of greater interest to me was the identity of the woman bashing away at the piano; the Mother Hubbard she wore gave her a look of extreme primness. 'This is Voka,' said Frankie. 'Adi Gavoka. She like a sister.' I knew enough to realise that Adi (pronounced 'Andy') was the feminine equivalent of Ratu. But what was an Adi doing here? Enquiring further, I was told that she was the estranged wife of Ratu George Cacobau ('Thakombau'); so that really was extraordinary. King Cacobau had ceded the Fijian islands to Queen Victoria, handing over his war-club and swearing never again to eat human flesh. In return, the Queen had promised to protect his people for ever. Some promise! Ratu George, senior descendant, might have been King himself had it not been for that. So what did that make Voka? Clearly, a Somebody. When eight more Tongan sailors came in, they showed her considerable deference.

A tough-looking Australian in ultra-short khaki shorts fell to the floor and passed out. Sidney dragged his inert body through a hanging chintz curtain into a back room. Lil then briefly took charge of the piano, playing a cowboy song new to me that I liked, 'Teardrops in my Eyes', before letting someone else take over the piano so she could jive with three soldiers. She kept beckoning to me to join in. But Voka was doing her dance, in rhythmic island style, and that seemed more in my line, so I cavorted opposite her, inexpertly but enthusiastically. People might have laughed, but I noticed that nobody did. Voka chased away the over-zealous Lil by saying firmly, 'He's not for you, Lil, not now, not ever!' Then to me: 'I think I'll call you Ratu Roderic. You'd like that, wouldn't you?'

So began an extended flirtation – nothing too serious, yet persisting enough to be publicly acknowledged. I fell for Voka in a way which I hadn't done for anyone else for some time.

That didn't imply that I wouldn't try to indulge in other directions. I arranged to go bathing with an amiable policeman to whom I chatted sixteen to the dozen whilst he held up the traffic; and I became very friendly with the Australian who'd passed out on the Robertson Road floor. He told me that he was having one hell of a time fighting off the advances of the young man who'd held his head in the back room. Meanwhile Sidney, meeting me by chance in the Garrick, begged me to put in a word on his behalf with the Australian. All very complicated, in its trivial way.

———

36

Voka said, 'You want to get to know the real Fiji? I'll speak to Ratu Jope, the Buli of Bau. Maybe you can stay with him?'

She spoke, and since her request was tantamount to an order, what could Jope do but comply? My next outing was smoothly arranged.

Ratu Jope was a tall, rugged man, curt of speech, abrupt of manner. As Buli (Local Executive Head) he lived on Bau ('Mbau'), a small island which had once been King Cacobau's stronghold. It had been the setting for grisly occasions when men had been spread-eagled to act as rollers for the launching of massive war-canoes.

The Bau bus in which we travelled could go no further than a rocky causeway, submerged at high tide like the track leading to St Michael's Mount, connecting the island to the mainland. To get into a waiting punt, we had first to wade out to its moorings. I had to pretend not to mind wetting my legs, though actually I found it most uncomfortable. We were preceded by a man who'd been sitting in front of us on the bus – tall, powerfully built, bullet-headed. In the boat he spoke gruffly to Jope, pointing at me. Jope barked back an answer, waited a moment, then continued speaking in a gentler tone of voice. I wondered who the man could be.

As we pulled slowly towards Bau, loud and clear over the water came the song of innumerable birds. The island itself seemed like a little green crown floating on its own reflection in the lagoon. *Bures* (Fijian huts), dark brown, some with roofs of red corrugated-iron, were dotted here and there amongst trees and bushes. Everything glowed against a background of a blue-green evening sky, a sky shot with thin black layers of sunset cloud outlined against vermilion-edged puffs of distant cumulus. The punt wobbled and grounded on some sand-bagging, where there was neither jetty nor beach, but an apron of grass overshadowed by trees.

Jope lived in a *bure* with a traditional thatched roof. Its floor was of coral, covered in matting with finer mats laid on top. The huge high space contained two tables, one of them supporting a vase of red, white and blue paper flowers. Across one end of the hut a frilly lace curtain swayed in the breeze, concealing a double-bed covered in a mosquito-net. Against part of the lace curtaining hung an expanse of *tapa* cloth to which were pinned pictures of English royalty cut from illustrated magazines. The *tapa* was an agreeable brown cloth of mulberry bark, beaten out and decorated with simple, darker brown or black linear designs.

Jope offered me the double-bed he shared with Mrs Jope. When, somewhat to her relief, I declined the honour, he took me to the 'visiting magistrate's' hut. Much to my surprise, with the hut came Jope. It wasn't etiquette to allow a stranger to sleep alone, for fear of ghostly presences. But any idea I might have had of making something out of the situation was dampened by my host's extreme modesty, clearly a hangover from missionary influences. Out of sight of anyone else, we bathed in the lagoon in the fading evening light. I stripped completely; Jope kept on his underpants. That night we both put on *sulus* and he lay down near me on a mound of *tapa* mats.

I asked him about the bullet-headed man. 'That was Ratu George,' he said, 'Adi Gavoka's husband. That was why he wanted to know about you.'

'He didn't look too pleased.'

'He wasn't. But don't worry!'

'Won't it make things difficult for you?'

'What does that matter? I, too, am a man!'

Next day Jope took me to part of Bau where the Cacobaus had once ruled as absolute Chiefs, with powers of life and death over lesser people, not just over prisoners taken in battle. As we walked along I heard a percussive, thudding sound, taking place at intervals during the day. 'The *lali*,' explained Jope. 'A man beats a hollow trunk with a stick to tell us when to start and when to stop.'

'Start and stop what?'

'Work, of course! The Roku decides what work has to be done, then the Buli sees that it is done. Men obey me because I am Buli.'

We reached a grassy knoll, on top of which the body of the last inde-pendent Cacobau Chief lay entombed. At its foot was Ratu George's European-style house, which we ignored in favour of going on to where his mother lived. Politeness demanded that I pay that particular visit. Politeness also demanded that Jope crawl humbly before her on the floor.

The island was charming everywhere, never more so than on and around the Cacobau hill. Why then should my flesh creep? Probably because it was impossible to banish thoughts of cannibal feasts recorded by those few shipwrecked mariners who, from some whim of their cap-tors, had lived to tell the tale. One of those lucky ones had survived for years, having caught the fancy of a man whose head wobbled and shook from a disease for which there was no cure; a disease which had come, had he but known it, from eating human brains insufficiently cooked . . . scrapie, in fact – Mad Cow Disease in one of its forms.

I'd been pining for native food after so much bully-beef and I was soon to have my fill, and more. A diet of *dalo* root (like breadfruit, only coarser) and *dalo* leaves (like spinach) quickly palled. The fish remained delicious, though I soon grew tired of the way coconut smoke pervaded everything cooked in a native oven – food wrapped in leaves and left for hours on heated stones.

Jope took me on his rounds, visiting the villages for which he was responsible. Every day we would call in at a different village, eat a feast prepared in our honour, sit for hours ceremonially drinking *yagona*, walk round inspecting, eat again and finally sleep where we ate, in the best available *bure*. When we went through swamp after swamp my tennis-shoes kept squelching off my feet, until I found it simpler to go barefoot.

Sometimes there would be what Lindsay would have called 'a concert in the Village Hall', when girls, primly bodiced and wearing garlands of flowers, sat in a line, doing a *meke* (a seated dance, using every part of the body except the legs). Such *meke*s were mixtures of legend and prophecy, based on a minimum of fact. One of the best was about a German lord sailing through the islands in his warship – presumably a reference to Count Felix von Luckner in *Sea Raider* during the First World War,*

---

* Presumably Roddy meant *Sea Eagle* (*Seeadler* in German) rather than *Sea Raider*. The Sea Eagle was a commerce ship, but from it Luckner captured fourteen enemy ships, often through trickery – the stories read almost like pirate misadventures.

My function was simply to be present, any audience (as Lindsay would have said) being better than none.

There could be variations from village to village. In one, an ancient called Kalamedi offered to give me a massage; gnarled fingers rubbed coconut oil into tired muscles whilst he spoke of calling turtles in from the sea by tapping on the surface of the water. To illustrate, he tapped my stomach, inducing a warmly sexual sensation.

In another village the men mounted a fish-drive, forming a huge circle in the sea with a boom made of plaited palm-fronds. Shouting happy shouts, they dragged the circle smaller and smaller, then rushed in to spear hundreds of fish threshing about, trapped in the centre. I was handed a spear but time after time made thrusts and speared nothing, refraction giving a false reading as to the exact position of even the slowest puffer-fish. They tried to teach by example, youths standing behind me, holding my body, directing my arm down. I consoled myself with the thought that they were naturally better than I could ever be at that particular pursuit, whereas they didn't have a history of the DAF and a detective novel to their names. Seldom could I have had a clearer example of the value inherent in the diversity of human attributes.

Going from village to village through the lagoons, gliding through glassy water, it seemed to me that here, at last, was the Paradise of the Senses, a Paradise of sun and cooling rain and sun once more. Lying on the main structure of the outrigger – for I wasn't expected to take a paddle or handle a sail – I became as inert as a lizard, utterly under the influence of the moment. Layer by layer the past was stripped away. First to go, everything taught in books; then the opinions of others; leaving experience only, until it, too, faded into nothing but a NOW. The whole skin of my body seemed super-sensitive to that NOW, absorbing sight, sound, taste, touch and smell. Had heavenly choirs been singing, I could have joined in their jubilation. That was how I felt; not just glad to be alive, but alive for all time, immortal in mortality.

That night, as on other nights, mosquitos in their hundreds whined through the holes in whatever net was provided, to gorge on my fresh blood. A lumpy, itching skin made Paradise rather more realistic: experience was teaching me that there could never be such a thing as unalloyed pleasure, there were bound to be drawbacks, to be accepted gratefully as being part of a many-faceted whole. Perhaps that was the most significant lesson to be learnt from being at home in Fiji.

*

Fijians have an earthy sense of humour. One of the villages on Vanua Levu was called Vatani – 'On the Shelf'. Another, Dromuna, literally 'Strained Arse'. Their enjoyment of life could be just as basic. A party at Robertson Road was something to remember for ever, for its atmosphere of abandon, sheer joie de vivre. I was invited to another one just before leaving Fiji, when I was given a demonstration of a decorous *tara-la-la*, the only dance considered proper for Christian converts by the missionaries. Round in a circle, side by side, trotted the participants to a bumpy tune, eight to a bar, with splendidly unsuitable words:

> *The higher up the mountain, the cooler the breeze,*
> *The younger the couple, the tighter they squeeze.*
> *Ai-o-wey! Don't hesitate!*
> *I'm a-comin' very slow-ly!*

Samoan dancing was the exact opposite of the *tara-la-la*: wild, whooping and unrestrained. Tongans were more sinuous, Tahitians faster. A part-Tahitian who might have demonstrated a *heiva* said that she needed more room, so swayed to a slow Hawaiian hula-hula instead. Only Lil and the willowy Sidney jived in the American manner.

Our hostess, 'Auntie Jean', shouted above the din, 'You'll always be happy, Rod-rig, that's a promise!' Voka, from whom I'd been inseparable, put a wreath of ferns and frangipani round my neck, repeating, 'Everything is for you, Ratu Roderic,' until I really came to believe it.

They all came to the quayside to see me off when SS *Matua* sailed. My obliging Australian had helped me pack, ruefully admitting, 'With you gone, I reckon that leaves the door wide open for Sid.'

37

Towards the end of February 1949, I boarded a boat in Tonga called *Wairuna*, which was coloured a dull orange-brown. Not much to look at, but wonderful to me, possibly because I felt so revitalised – I had just spent three weeks exceptionally ill with dysentery and how incredible it was now to be over it. The ship's doctor poured sulfonamide powder into the sores on my feet, whilst the friendliness of all on board helped cure any remains of low self-esteem. I glowed with health and happiness, so contented still from my time in Fiji. What more could a young rascal want?

We glided over a gently rolling, opalescent Pacific – Paris-grey clouds always on the horizon – towards Tahiti. My voyage was costing £22. I could reflect that travelling all the way from England had been achieved for no more than £101. Renting my flat in London was bringing in as much as that; in fact, I might be showing a small profit. So much for logistics. All the same, I would have to bend my mind towards earning something soon.

Monsieur Poroi, Mayor of Papeete on Tahiti, happened to be on board, returning from a holiday in Sydney, his first for twenty years. We got on brilliantly by agreeing on one thing straight away: Tonga was a drab, dreary, pointless place. Poor Tonga! It wasn't necessarily any of those things, only for me it was now a place of bad memories.

M. Poroi discoursed slightingly of those whom he called 'banana tourists', who came to the islands hoping to 'go native' and live beneath a coconut-palm on whatever bountiful nature chose to provide. 'They don't last long in Tahiti – we deport them!' he said scathingly.

I arranged my face so he could not see that this was rather what I was half hoping for myself. It brought home to me that most reasonable people would agree with him. A man should earn his own living and pay his way. But wasn't there room for others, earning a less regular living by showing the daily-breaders that there was more to life? In sum, ought I to regard myself as a despicable cadger or as a shining example of the romance of beachcombing? Insofar as I could work out an answer on the spot, it was that it all depended upon age: a young man couldn't be expected to abide by 'the rules', whereas an older man could; it was senseless to apply one hard-and-fast rule equally to both. I was twenty-seven, soon to be twenty-eight, so this is what I told myself.

The aromas greeting us at Papeete were varied and enticing: the reef, smelling of coral; frangipani mixed with patisserie from the quayside; and an all-pervading reek of Gauloise cigarettes. France, unmistakably, but a France in a South Seas setting of lagoon and sharply rising hills, green all the way up to the jagged black crown of rock called La Diadème.

Beyond the quay Papeete looked welcoming. Some buildings (of wood and corrugated-iron) came right down to the lagoon, where boats

of all shapes and sizes nudged a tree-lined road. Instead of Indians, as at
Suva, there were a few Chinese – really very few compared with numerous Tahitians, men idling about, women walking in a manner which
was half provocative, half waddle. Such an entirely different *ambiance*
compared with any other port in the Pacific.

To enter, I needed a local passport from the Commissaire de Justice,
which involved having a special photograph taken; thumb-prints, too.
Since sugar was still on the ration, I was issued with a *carte individuelle
d'alimentation*. Everything happened rather slowly, helped by a letter from
the British Council in Sydney (wangled by an old school friend, Peter
Hiley) which guaranteed a degree of respectability to which, ordinar-
ily, I wouldn't have dared lay claim. Once in possession of the requisite
documents, I was let loose upon the town.

I went to the hotel recommended to me by M. Poroi, the Stuart.
So few tourists had been allowed to enter Tahiti since the war that
hotels were few and far between, mostly used by the more prosperous
locals for one-night stands. The Stuart had, in effect, taken over from
Lovaina's, famed throughout the French Pacific for its joyfully scandalous goings-on. My arrival was therefore something of an exception
to the rule; so much so that at the *vin d'honneur* to welcome home
their returning Mayor I was a guest of honour. They even pinned a
Union Jack flag over the entrance. M. Poroi's speech commented on
the rise in the price of copra (to 7 francs a kilo) and the possibility of
encouraging tourism, for a change, now that people from all over the
world were free to travel. Some of those present sighed at the thought,
disagreeing profoundly; others nodded. There were two sides to that
proposition.

My first mission was to find somewhere cheap to live, and after that
to latch on to someone to 'show me the ropes' – a quest reminiscent of
early days in the RAF. An invitation came along, on cue: a jolly party
of *fonctionnaires* keen on whooping it up at Papeete's two night-clubs, the
Lido and the Col Bleu. Both were simple places, far from chic, where
dancing was a *mélange* of decorous French and indecorous Tahitian.
Music whanged out, on this my first experience of Tahiti by night; feet
stamped, and glasses, even tables, crashed to the wooden floor. I had no
recollection of getting back to the Stuart but I must have managed it
all right, since I woke next morning to find a Chinese-Tahitian *vahine*
giggling as she plucked at a faded wisp of flapping pink curtain. With
the slightest encouragement I was sure that she would have joined me

on a bed smelling of vanilla, but coffee and aspirins were what I wanted at that moment.

Once recovered, I knew exactly what had to be done, and how. Dressing up in a coat and old school tie packed for just such an occasion, I went to call upon the British Consul, Charles Henderson. He lived next to his job in a white-framed bungalow where a huge vine had been trained over the whole width of the house and up over a porch and back again, as if treading on its own tail.

In order to tread carefully, I played the author's card, exaggerating the importance of *Desert Air Force* and mentioning, almost in passing, the prospect of Tedder's 'Life'. Charles was a small man with an intimate way of leaning forward and peering into my face at close range. As soon as he stopped putting his fingers together in a Gothic arch, I knew that I'd cleared the first hurdle. He asked me back to his house for a frosted beer.

From then on, everything went swimmingly. The Consul suggested that I might board with a Johnny Snow, living alone; he'd put me in touch. Then there was the famous author James Norman Hall, co-author of *Mutiny on the Bounty*;* he would be sure to want to meet an English writer. And would I like to be introduced to the Governor?

'Yes, yes and yes!' I agreed. 'Anyone and everyone, please!'

He took me to lunch at Chez Rivnac (a place which M. Poroi had described as 'little more than a *bordel*'). Sunshine seemed to be lighting up the entire day. But then came blow number one, he was about to go on leave, and blow number two, he'd already handed over temporary consulship to a couple named Hunt. 'They only sailed in on a yacht from Manahiki just before you,' he explained. 'I needed someone to take over and couldn't find anyone else. Only wish you'd arrived in time!'

He could hardly have wished it more than me. In a flash I could see

---

* HMS *Bounty* was the eighteenth-century British ship that docked in Tahiti for five months, during which time some of the crew formed relationships with locals. The captain of the *Bounty*, William Bligh, employed harsh methods to try to re-establish discipline which angered the crew. When the *Bounty* set sail again, some of the crew started a mutiny and cast Bligh and those loyal to him off in an open launch, so those left on board the *Bounty* could stay in the Pacific. This was an offence punishable by death and the Admiralty sent another ship in pursuit of the mutineers. Those who had returned to Tahiti were captured, but the rest, who travelled on to Pitcairn Island, were never found, the location of the island being unknown to the British for another twenty years. Descendants of the mutineers still live on Pitcairn today. The James Norman Hall book was the basis of the 1935 MGM film starring Clark Gable; today the most famous adaptation of the story is probably the 1984 film *The Bounty*, starring Mel Gibson and Anthony Hopkins.

what I'd so narrowly missed, the title of the book that might have been: *Consul in Paradise.*

'The 'unts are from Peckham,' said Charles. 'Solid but common. They've already blotted their copybook by becoming too thick with one of our local wrong-uns, Oscar Nordman – barratry and all that, y'know!' (Actually, until I asked someone, I didn't know what barratry – fraudulent behaviour on board a ship at the expense of its proprietors – was.)

On second thoughts, perhaps I had no need to repine. As acting Consul I would have been constrained to behave with official rectitude, which mightn't have suited me at all.

38

M. Poroi's son kindly lent me a bicycle, so I could ride off on the one road round the island, the Broome Road, in search of some people called Krainère who lived out at Pirae – friends of a friend of cousin Aelwyn's.

Skirting the Parc du Sport I pedalled along a dusty track, past a notice announcing LAITERIES HIRSHON, and on through a gate marked TABU towards a group of thatched palm-frond huts on a shore of black sand. A Tahitian woman shredding a coconut declared that m'sieur had gone into town and madame had yet to rise. Three naked, golden children ran up some wooden steps to the main hut, shouting in no tongue known to me.

I wondered what to do; and whilst wondering, was hailed by a thin, bony man enquiring, in a superior Anglo-American voice, whether I were a Pole or a German.

'English,' I answered, faintly annoyed. 'Isn't it obvious?'

'Oh I don't know about that. You English are in short supply hereabouts. I'm Otu Duryea and I'm from the States and I've been here sixteen years. An *otu* is a bird which pecks about on the shore. They think I look like one; and perhaps I do, just as you look like a Pole or a German. There now!' His introduction of himself was a warning that he was a talkative man, a thing to be welcomed.

Whilst taking me for a bathe, he filled me in about the Krainères: 'Marcel is splendid! Madame is fun, but – well, you'll see. I come here to teach English to their children, who don't actually have any one language they can call their own. They speak broken everything, including Chinese. It's a bit weird.'

Our bathe over (Otu having wound one of his *pareus*, a Polynesian sort of sarong, round me), we returned to the huts via a low, wide-topped wall. Otu said: 'This is the local lovers' lane; they lie there on the wall in the evenings, copulating. One has to shout quite loudly to get them to bugger off!'

At that, a man on a motorbike roaring like a threshing-machine came bumping over the track towards us: Marcel at last, indeed a splendid man, not in the least put out to see me.

'Pussy!' he shouted. 'PUSSY, where are you? We've got a VISITOR!'

A woman in a two-piece bathing dress appeared in the doorway, looking band-box fresh, as if from a Miss World contest. 'I'm his wife,' said the vision. 'Of course you'll stay to lunch?'

We retreated to the main hut, to drink the strongest rum-punches I'd ever tasted.

My head was whirling round. I began to feel that I'd known this enchanting couple all my life. What could Otu have meant by 'Madame is fun, but . . .'? However, that was soon solved. Pussy was downing her drinks at an alarming rate, her eyes losing their sparkle. Just in time, it seemed, we were served lunch by their Tahitian woman, chatting to us as we ate. Pussy revived after a helping of *boudin*, but her bolt was shot. A slurred goodbye was the best I could get out of her when it was time to go. For someone so lovely, it seemed outrageously unsuitable, but it was not up to me to comment.

I wondered where Otu had got to, then saw him hovering about, outside. 'He won't eat with us,' said Marcel. 'He says he doesn't like food. Actually, it's a kind of pride. He lives on practically nothing and he means to keep his independence.'

When I wobbled back to Papeete, he bicycled alongside, still talking sixteen to the dozen. 'You need somewhere to live free?' were his parting words. 'Ask your Consul about the Maison Edwards!'

As it happened I was meeting Charles Henderson the next day, to be taken out to see James Norman Hall, who lived in some state in a house beyond Pirae with his Tahitian wife, Lala. A maroon convertible stood outside. Almost the first thing Hall said was an apology for the existence of such a showy American car: 'It's useful, because it's open and I can see where I am all the time. You don't think it's – well – too much?' An endearing way of making me feel at home, I thought, making me all the more appreciative. He looked rather like a pastor from the American backwoods, silvery-haired and benign.

At some point during the day I felt it appropriate to ask, 'What's this I hear about the Maison Edwards?'

'It's a pretty rum sort of place,' said Charles doubtfully. 'Of course, it does need a caretaker, until such time as someone can be found to take it on lease.'

'Well, here's your man, then!' said Hall.

He didn't exactly wink at me, yet his eyes danced and glittered in sudden sympathy. I could see that my presence, linked to the sort of life I was proposing to lead, had released a spring inside him.

He spoke dreamily of his past: 'I came here in my twenties and wandered round the islands on a shoe-string, obsessed with the idea that a man should be completely independent of possessions. But I'm getting on, now.'

So will I be, one day, I thought, saying nothing. It was his reverie, not mine.

'Then that's settled, isn't it, Charles?'

'If you say so, James. Yes, that's settled!'

They began talking somewhat disparagingly about Mr Edwards and his Maison.

'You remember what an old miser he was? Where did the money come from?'

'South Africa – Edwards was a Boer,' said Charles, fingertips together. 'It was quite a respectable fortune.'

'He didn't seem to derive a great deal of pleasure from it. Could he have been crossed in love?'

'No, he simply liked to keep himself to himself,' said Charles, as if slightly annoyed by the suggestion. 'He didn't want to be bothered with other people. He could hardly be bothered with himself, in the end.'

'The sonofabitch!' said Hall. 'The poor sonofabitch!'

'I'll take young Roderic out there tomorrow. We've just got time to fit it in before I leave Tahiti,' Charles went on. 'That and dinner with Bunny and co. Wonder what she'll make of him?'

'He's really looking after you beautifully, young fella!' said Hall, smiling benignly.

In point of fact, I felt as if I'd been caught up in a mysterious cyclone, a whirl of destiny. So many odd things were happening, one after the other, such undeserved kindnesses from strangers. The very air of Tahiti seemed to be prompting me towards something, I couldn't tell what.

39

Bunny Gilmore was part-Tahitian, sister of Louie Phillips, who'd enriched himself by marrying a Miss Gump (of the Gump department store in San Francisco). There was a substantial Phillips property in Moorea, the island to be seen across the water from Tahiti. Bunny, like her brother, was young-middle-aged, intensely sociable, still very much 'available'. She enjoyed snapping up what few visitors came her way, hence her welcome to me. I was rather more engrossed with an exceptionally lively, plumpish woman called Turia Salmon, who was creating gales of laughter whenever she opened her mouth. I was told that, though very light-skinned, she was almost pure Tahitian, and a Princess. Except that the idea of such a title was French, not Tahitian. Turia was a descendant of the old ruling Chiefly family the Pomares, and of Alexander Salmon, a Jewish merchant who'd come for trade and stayed to marry. I wondered if I would ever see her again.

Bunny kindly offered to drive me and my things in a *camionette* to Maison Edwards, calling in at our Consulate to collect the key. 'You could stay with me while you're waiting to move in,' she said invitingly. However, I was already pledged to the Johnny Snow Charles had originally set me up with when I'd arrived, so back I went to his house for my one and only night with him.

Maison Edwards was at 'Km 12', Tahitian villages being customarily identified by their distance from Papeete rather than by their names. As Charles had said, it was a pretty rum sort of place, built in Spanish style round an internal courtyard. It was too small for such grand treatment; the inner yard was dark and dank. Coconut trees grew too near the yellow-ochre walls, casting gloom. Wind rushing through their green mop-heads created a low sighing, and by night the air was alive with the ever-changing roar of sea pounding against a reef and spilling over into the lagoon. It was never quiet for a moment. The house itself was dusty, wooden shutters (*auvents*) disintegrating. The only tap which worked was in the kitchen, the bathroom producing no more than a rusty trickle; but of course I had to count myself lucky that there was any *eau courant* at all. No electricity, so lighting was by paraffin lamp. And no kitchen stove.

Gloomy on the outside, eerie inside, gloomy by day, eerie by night ... I could quite understand why the house had failed to find great favour. When a rending crash was followed by a thump on the corrugated-iron roof, I jumped in fright. It was only a coconut falling, one of many – never a pleasant sound, particularly at night. I had to admit that I was scared stiff as I walked round my new domain, carrying a paraffin lamp as the sole talisman against the powers of darkness, dripping with sweat, eaten alive by mosquitos.

An ancient winding gramophone in the back room was still working. Putting on the first record which came to hand, I was soon listening to a scratchy 'Whistler and his Dog'. Out into the warm night air floated a tinny piping, the whistling effect unbearably sinister.

Otu soon came by, delighted to find that his suggestion had been so quickly taken up. He had a word of caution: 'You mustn't mind about the *tupaupaus*, the spirits of the dead supposed to haunt this place. That's just Tahitian superstition. They think there must have been something wrong with a man to make him build a house shaped like this one; and they may be right on that point. But no, you can be positive that the *tupaupaus* are perfectly content with their own traditional stamping-ground across the road. You've had a look at your local *marae* already, I take it?'

I hadn't, but with Otu I did. The *marae* almost opposite was a stepped mound made of largish slabs, overgrown with grass and shrubs. It had once been a place of high importance for Chiefs, who both belonged to it and served it, and in so doing shared in its prestige, its *mana*, which derived from their ancestors. All that seemed to have been forgotten. Nobody was even keeping it tidy. 'Quite so,' said Otu. 'Here, nothing matters but the moment. If they care one jot about the past, it's because they're afraid of it rising up at night and putting them off their stroke. I guess that's the unromantic truth.'

Off he went on his bike to give the Krainère children their daily lesson, and I spent happy hours going through old Mr Edwards' things, which were as he'd left them, in drawers and cupboards in every room.

Just as I was getting used to my new lodgings, a French couple called Vaissière – he with nervous hand movements, she would-be elegant in unsuitable shoes – drove up to view the house. They seemed to think that it might 'respond' if enough trouble were to be taken to clear away the coconut-palms. My days were numbered. I would have to find another nest.

I asked Marcel Krainère if he knew of anywhere else. 'We've been made acting agents for a place beyond Punaavia, until it's sold. It's a ruin, right on the beach. The last people to have it were doing Filaria* research, but they weren't living there. Maybe nobody can; some of it hasn't even got a roof.'

Then Pussy had her say: 'The good point is, you'd have Mr Robson next door. For years and years he was the uncrowned King of Easter Island.'

'Half a roof is better than none!' I said, thankfully accepting the offer.

Papeete was small enough to make it easy to run into familiar faces; it was even easier to make new friends. At Quinn's, a bamboo-lined bar, I came across a wealthy American honeymoon couple, Anne and Lou Werner, who already knew Otu. They were a tonic, intelligent and amusing. It was nice to feel that they liked me as much as I liked them. They asked me back for lunch. When we were talking in the street outside Quinn's before getting into their (hired) car, Anne said, 'Oh look, there's Turia! We must get Turia!'

So she, too, was invited back; and in that way I met Bunny's animated Tahitian princess for a second time. What a day!

The Werners had taken an elaborate hut on stilts with thatched coconut-frond walls and 'all mod cons'. 'Simple, but terribly chic!' I commented.

'I know it,' said Lou. 'And terribly expensive, too, for what it is!'

I mentioned the tumble-down place I'd been offered in Paea, next door to Mr Robson. Turia lit up at the mention of him. 'In the old days, one of my *fetii* [family] had the *concession* for Easter Island – J. G. Brander; *Roi des Moutons*, they called him, because of the sheep. Easter Island has nothing but sheep ... *mais oui*, the great J.G. he ruined himself by giving

---

* A parasitic worm transmitted by mosquitos and other biting insects, mostly found in the tropics and sub-tropics around the world. It causes filariasis which induces rashes and sometimes disfigurement (elephantiasis), among other symptoms.

the biggest feast Tahiti ever saw. *C'etait magnifique!*' Her eyes glowed with pride. Clearly that occasion represented the acme of princely behaviour.

'But were the *fetii* quite so pleased to think of all that good money going down the drain?' I asked.

'Of course! He was a great man. Everyone admired him!'

Lesson number one, I thought.

Bit by bit I learned a little more about that man. In the 1870s J. G. Brander, in association with Captain Dutroux-Bornier, had shifted most of the remaining Easter Islanders to Tahiti and set them to work on his copra plantations. There hadn't been all that many of them, because previously the fittest islanders had been carted off by Peruvian slavers to dig guano and die. Dutroux-Bornier married one of the few surviving females and declared her to be Queen. Both were promptly murdered by their outraged 'subjects', whereupon Brander's new representative, called Salmon, repatriated some of the islanders back to their lonely outpost. That Salmon was another descendant of the Alexander Salmon who'd married into the Tahitian 'royal family'. As far as I was ever able to make out, Turia was Brander's great-niece.

Turia said, 'I, too, shall be nearby when you move into your *château courant d'air*. Just ask for Maison Crane, Km 19, and you can't go wrong.' Her eyes sparkled with an intensity which was almost comic. 'No, you can't go wrong, that I can promise, Roger!'

She pronounced it 'Rojeay', which made a name which wasn't in fact mine sound exotic and unfamiliar. We were talking in a mixture of English and (in my case) dog-French, so that added to the feeling of alienation, as if I were being taken over by another person. Indeed, I could almost feel the process starting to happen . . .

———

40

The house which Turia called Château Courant d'Air was exactly that. Draughts could be only partly excluded by shutting such *auvents* as remained, three in all. It was constructed of boarding, formerly painted Pompeian red, and was roofed with the usual corrugated-iron (which had given way in places, either due to rust or to freakish gusts of wind). The wooden stilts on which it had been built were collapsing, and the front steps had collapsed already. On the other hand, an inside tap still worked and so did a seat-less lavatory (blocked with unmentionables when first encountered).

Through a large hole in the sloping floorboards of the front room I spotted a noticeboard to which the Filaria team had pinned their reports. Down below there lurked a rocking-chair, painted blue, which I hauled out for immediate use; and the same mine yielded a broken table over which I draped a Union Flag borrowed from Maison Edwards, for which the French Vaissières would surely have no use. When Mr Robson from next door kindly sent over a slatted wooden double-bed, I could regard myself as being fully furnished on a beachcomber level of living.

The first night revealed a number of drawbacks, but I was determined not to let them mar my newly found bliss. The room to seaward – my bed-sitter, because it was the only one with a roof intact – had been used for drying copra. Chunks of coconut spread over the floor had exuded rancid oil, which in turn had attracted copra-bugs. The hard little black insects banged against me in search of vanished food. They were marginally less disturbing than earlier visitors – wood-hornets, appearing at 2.30 in the afternoon and retreating to individual mud-holes under the tin roof at about 5 p.m. There were also a few smaller black wasps whose home was in a pile of palm-fronds. I left both hornets and wasps undisturbed and was never stung.

During the night, the reef roared, the copra-oil reeked, and the female mosquitos (some of them carrying deadly Filaria) whined and bit. I lay on my back on wooden slats without a mattress, looking up at rafters which – I was almost sure – seemed to be shuddering, though there was no wind. What was happening? Were the dreaded *tupaupaus* coming for me this early? Not so. Up there, bunched in a queue, a line of furry animals shuffled and squeaked, eyes glinting red – rats, going about their business. Next morning, the sole traces of their existence were oval droppings on the filthy floor. Whether by luck or by intent, they seemed to have missed the bed entirely.

The lagoon lapping against my beach was shallow, obstructed with lumps of coral too small to attract brightly coloured fish but large enough to stub a toe. A small headland formed a scoop, which gathered up and held a floating debris of palm-fronds. It looked attractive, but was really not an ideal place for swimming. That didn't matter as on my bicycle I could go where I chose. After a second night, slightly better than the first but still not too wonderful, I chose to pedal towards Papeete and was soon passing an elaborate series of huts set in a neatly manicured garden. Surely it belonged to an American?

''Allo, Rojeay!' someone called out. *'Iorana!'* The Tahitian word of greeting was superfluous. I recognised Turia, digging away at a bed of immense flapping cannas.

'Hello! This isn't at all the sort of place I imagined you living in!' I shouted back.

'Oh, it doesn't belong to me,' she said. *'Suis femme du ménage.* I guard it for Cornelius Crane, the plumbing-man, the *millionaire.'* Her Tahitian accent made the word sound the same as when used by Mistinguett,* but rather more respectful. Apparently Monsieur Crane was not only very rich but very charitable. The Crane Foundation was helping pay for Filaria research. Turia told me more about the man. He was *'un peu affligé'* – he suffered from an allergy which made his skin erupt at the merest touch of an insect. For that reason his Maison was a series of huts totally surrounded by a narrow concrete moat kept filled with running water over which no crawler could cross, except when a palm-frond, blown by the wind, created a bridge for a column of ants.

Tahitian-style to outward appearances as a result of using pandanus-thatching, great care had been taken inside to insert a layer of corrugated-iron, then another layer of pandanus, carefully lacquered. The effect was of extreme chic, yet extreme practicality. The only boon it lacked was air-conditioning – which in 1949 was all but unknown throughout the South Seas – but there were the usual overhead fans everywhere.

'Haere mai!' said Turia. It would have been odd had she not done so, for that was the standard invitation to come in and have a bite, which always, by custom, had to follow talking to anyone outside their hut. I could have declined politely, but of course I didn't. A bite of something tasty was just the ticket for someone living mainly on tinned fish, bully-beef and biscuits.

During the rest of the afternoon I pottered about after her in the well-kept Crane garden. Towards six o'clock Turia suggested a shower, when I was surprised (yet not all that surprised) by the show of modesty.

---

* A very famous French actress and singer of the time.

Throughout the Pacific, missionaries had made such a point of finding nudity disgraceful that even when their influence had waned the pro-hibition remained in place. To wrap me round, I was lent a *pareu* of the floral pattern much favoured in Tahiti at that time; then, in comfortable undress, I was treated to glasses of rum-punch, as strong if not stronger than anything produced by Pussy in Pirae. I watched the making of it: a tablespoonful of sugar at the bottom of a tumbler; squeezes of two limes for each; white rum (very cheap, from Martinique); finally a dash of Perrier water. The effect was to blow first the mind, then the body. I was soon floating free, coming down to earth in order to tuck into *pota* – chicken embedded in *taro*-top leaves tasting like coarse spinach.

We went through into Crane's own bedroom, where Turia kept a bottle of *monoi*, coconut oil scented with things such as *tiaré Tahiti*, fran-gipani and the unpronounceable ylang-ylang. She rubbed it gently over me, discreetly taking care not to disturb the folds of my *pareu*; until I loosened the knot myself and lay there erect and pulsating. Rubbing oil on her own body, she loosened her *pareu* (more elaborate than mine, as it had to cover both top and bottom halves), before rolling over on top of me, gliding and sliding this way and that.

The only light came from an oil lamp, which chose that moment to send out clouds of black smoke; not that it made the slightest difference. I was in a frenzy of sex, aware of everything yet selective in ignoring what didn't suit. What had begun by being dry and cracky became warm and glutinous, like lips; the knowledge excited me further, because I realised that I'd never known anything to compare with this before. So intense was the feeling that I imagined myself experiencing some of Turia's enjoyment as well. The saying 'made for each other' went through my mind. Was this what it truly meant?

'Ah, Rojeay!' sighed Turia eventually. Then, with a chuckle: 'Ah, ROJEAY!'

It hardly seemed as if she could be referring to me; and as if to main-tain the idea of having been transformed into another self I replied in French, which made the moment seem even stranger and more com-pelling: '*Ah, Turia, mon amour!*'

'*Ta belle sauvage!*' she said, laughing. '*Ta belle sauvage, Rojeay . . .*'

———

41

To make our continuing affair publicly acceptable, we announced our forthcoming marriage, which involved neither a French ceremony nor a church service. It sufficed to give a feast to celebrate the mutual bond; that was all. There were no reasons for Tahitians to bother with any convention other than their own as regards marriage or any other important event in their lives. Gone were the days when foreign missionaries, with a foreign system of morality, could dictate to Polynesians what should or shouldn't be done. It didn't make Tahitians less Christian in other respects – an important lesson for their Colonial masters to learn.

Our wedding-feast couldn't be on a Brander scale. Turia had tremendous *mana* but little money except what she earned from Cornelius Crane; and as for myself, we could hardly pretend to her super-materialistic people that I was much of a catch when my registered address was a semi-ruin. None of that seemed to matter. My own *mana* was more powerful than I deserved, for because of my connections a lack of money could be treated more as a misfortune than as a crime. Turia's *fetii* therefore scraped together the makings of a banquet: from somewhere a sucking-pig; from the lagoon, fish; from the streams Tahiti's greatest luxury, a kind of crayfish called *varo*; plus the inevitable foundation of breadfruit, *taro* and all the other ingredients of a proper South Seas shindig. The feast took place, of course, out-of-doors, separated only from a small knot of strangers by a palm-frond fence. The strangers were there to finish up the remains. They had rather a lean time of it that day.

I was far from sober whilst it was all going on; Turia, too. The rum-punches had begun earlier for us than for others and we had no chance of tailing-off. I had to get up and dance, having learnt in Fiji how to gyrate and quiver in the overtly masculine manner required of men. Turia didn't fancy herself as a dancer so she egged me on whilst seeing to it that no one remotely personable got an opportunity to try their luck opposite me. The result was, I capered in front of the oldest and fattest,

Turia's sister Melanie being one of them. She'd brought along her boy-friend, a minor French *fonctionnaire* whom she referred to as '*mon crabbe*'. With some justification: he was as squat as a man could be, moving sideways with crustacean gait, yet Melanie declared that she adored him.

The evening ended when the drinks ran out. Turia and I lurched back to Maison Crane considerably the worse for wear. I was overcome by sleep too quickly to be more than a perfunctory lover. Even in a South Seas Paradise a bridal night could have its longueurs, complete with splitting headache in the morning. Once our wedding was over and done with, we could settle down to a period of connubial bliss.

I adored her, but as many must have found before me, the fact of marriage can alter a relationship; time may be needed to adjust to the element of compulsion involved. We had tiffs where blame lay in this direction, then in that. No one, however expert, could have assessed exactly where the responsibility lay, but I was probably most to blame. Turia was sunny and jolly when not overcome by '*honte*', a kind of embarrassment which might lead to her being '*fiu*', or fed up. She knew that all men were fickle, myself included; but just how unmanly, she surely couldn't have guessed. Like her, I was expected to live only for the day – her day, when not overcome by moods. In short, I was supposed to be a Tahitian, a tall order indeed. When I told her that I couldn't be monopolised by anyone without causing sparks to fly, she took it hard, with the equivalent of 'We'll see about that!'

On one occasion things reached such a pitch that I rode off on my bicycle back to Château Courant d'Air, vowing never to return. But the next morning Turia suddenly arrived with a basketful of goodies described as 'a marketing'. Further resistance on my part was pointless. We ate a meal *chez moi*, really for the sake of it; then I returned with her to *chez* Crane. Our serious quarrel did have one good outcome: she made up her mind to help me repair the Château, which meant learning how to slash and plait coconut-fronds and tie them together to make a passable roof. I would never have attempted such a task myself. Finding how interested I was in things Tahitian, she took me out in her pirogue, across the lagoon to the roaring reef, till then heard but never seen at close quarters.

The reef was like a bombarded causeway, pock-marked with as many holes as a solidified sponge. On the seaward side it was a fortress-wall against foaming waves, descending steeply into unknown depths, whilst on the lagoon side it was gently lapped by clear and much shallower water. Fascinating! But equally fascinating to me, as we drew near, was a Tahitian lobster-catcher, a bronzed giant in thin white cotton shorts which revealed everything about him when he plunged in to pluck his prey from where it hung, greeny-black and quivering, against the outside of the reef. I had to pretend that his skills alone were what I found attractive. Doubtless confused by the strong interest he must have felt me expressing in him rather than in his lobsters, he bought me off, as it were, by giving me the largest of them. (Next day Turia went to thank him, without me being there, offering a present of rum to even things up.) I never saw him again, which was perhaps just as well for the sake of harmony.

Our expedition was marred by a potentially more disastrous episode. The lagoon was full of clumps of coral, some of them so large that when they bumped against the pirogue we had to get out and pull it round and over. I grazed my legs, but thought little of it, except that the grazes burned more than the usual kind. When under water, coral was decorative, brushed by swaying seaweed and attended by shoals of brightly coloured fish, so it was difficult to understand that it was a living entity, not dead rock. By the time we'd hauled the pirogue out of the water I felt as if a corrosive acid had entered my bloodstream, setting my whole body ablaze. Turia knew what to do, though it meant sacrificing the makings of a good rum-punch. She squeezed limes over the abrasions, paying no attention to my roars of pain. Next morning and the next, she repeated the treatment. As though cauterised (which in a sense they were), the wounds shrank and healed within days. As a cure, it was a miracle of simplicity.

As a married couple, we were expected to 'receive'. Callers duly came. One was Purea Reasin, a Tahitienne who'd married American Johnny; black hair floating to her waist, twanging away on a guitar. (One day she would sue Thor Heyerdahl, the *Kon-Tiki* captain,* for filming her without permission doing an abandoned hula. For us she performed freely – a real sight for sore eyes.) James Norman Hall and Lala drove up in their huge convertible – and that was (I think) how I first met Dale

---

* The 1947 *Kon-Tiki* expedition, led by Thor Heyerdahl, intended to prove that South Americans from the sixth century could have been the original Polynesian islanders (widely rebuked today). The six-man crew sailed across the Pacific in a raft made from traditional materials to demonstrate that it could be done. Heyerdahl's resulting book was a bestseller.

McClanahan, a shy and highly intelligent oil heiress who was staying with them.

Bengt Danielsson, from the *Kon-Tiki*, red-bearded and earnest, was another new friend; as were Dr Edgar of the Filaria team and William Robinson (Cornelius Crane's brother-in-law, also a supporter of Filaria research), living nearby. So Turia and I were very much in with the cosmopolitan society of the moment, which pleased me, because it was nothing like being a tourist.

Otu often dropped in, and we saw more of Anne and Lou Werner than of any other pair – so friendly (and so conveniently mobile in their hired car). Anne had a gift for coming out with remarks which at first sounded mad but which were actually quite sensible, such as: 'Has anybody really discovered any way of judging whether a picture is good or bad? I mean, does anyone ever know?' We happened to be on our way to that haunt of artists, Loti's Pool, a well-maintained pleasure-park with a statue of the famous Pierre near the ventilator-tunnel of Papeete's water supply. She and Lou had chosen to pinch each other intermittently that day – a strange domestic habit which apparently caused neither of them any ill-feeling.

Next thing I knew, Turia declared: 'It's time we went to Moorea, to Opunohu, *chez moi.*' My luggage was minimal, but Turia had all sorts of bundles tied with coconut-cord. There was no telling how long we might be away, except that we were bound to return to Papeete for Quatorze Juillet, to celebrate the storming of the Bastille. A date which could have had little meaning for French Colonials had somehow become their most treasured anniversary.

The ferry was a smelly little boat with a thin funnel, frayed at the top. To help haul the bundles on board I attracted the attention of a sturdy young Tahitian with bulging arm-muscles, a sailor from the *Orowhena* on strike (against his will) after a voyage from New Zealand. Turia took one look at him and said, in a matter-of-fact way, 'He has a *béguin* for you, Rojeay. Maybe he'll help fix our house.' When we reached Opunohu some four and a half hours later, he showed off by wading through the water, carrying our things for us. 'He'll be round tomorrow, you'll see!' she said, but not crossly. I didn't know quite what to think.

It had taken so long because of the leisurely way the boat had edged round Moorea, dropping off goods and passengers. Mercifully, a girl who'd sicked up a bright green ice-cream had disembarked at Cook's Bay. After the bustle of Papeete, the whole of the island, and in particular Opunohu Bay, looked dramatic but desolate, with no more than a scattering of huts near the water and only a sandy track for a road. Hills rose to jagged peaks, sweeping dizzily upwards, then tumbling almost vertically towards green foothills, feathery with innumerable trees. Opunohu was itself an exaggeration and epitome of all Moorea: more deserted, the still waters of its lagoon reflecting hills greener and steeper. The bay diffused such sheer, staggering beauty that it caught at the throat.

Turia's house (three thatched huts on an apron of golden sand) looked out across the bay to Mt Rotui, the strangest and steepest of all Moorea's fantastic peaks. The huts were sadly in need of repair, pandanus walls bulging, bamboo *auvents* sagging. Furniture looked as if it had been left higgledy-piggledy for ages under dust-sheets, which hadn't stopped the dust from getting in. But what did such minor details matter? I only had to gaze out from those dilapidated rooms, across the lagoon to the cloud-crowned hills, to recognise pure enchantment: the dream of a wanderer down the ages, the Earthly Paradise.

Turia was running in and out of each woven-walled hut, exclaiming like a child. 'I've been away so long, I thought I might never return, yet nothing is missing. *Rien, tu sais, rien … et maintenant, je t'ai trouvé … toi, Rojeay!*'*

'*Et moi, TOI, Turia!*'† was my lame reply, in poor French. The moment couldn't be allowed to pass without linking it to some foreign words, however trite.

Was it really me talking, when some part of me felt like crying? As once in Sorrento, looking out on a different sea, the sadness of unfulfilled yearnings threatened to take me over, but only for an instant. Instead, I laughed; and then we both laughed. What else was there to do, in a place so lovely and so overflowing with natural riches that even the poor could be happy? I had no wish to delve into the shadows beneath the substance on an island where all that counted was now, the glorious present. Tinged with melancholy, yet still glorious.

––––––––––

* 'Nothing, you know, nothing … and now, I have found you … you, Rojeay!'

† 'And me, YOU, Turia!'

42

Turia had three treasures in her house in Moorea: a hammer with a stone head lashed to a wooden shaft carved in a linear design of whorls and wedges; a two-handled wooden bowl incised on either side; and a signed photograph of a European woman in full evening dress. The hammer was a symbol of Chiefly authority; the bowl depicted a man and a woman up to two different versions of the precise behaviour which early missionaries had found so reprehensible; and the photograph was of Edwina Mountbatten.

I was told that Edwina, temporarily abandoning her husband Lord Louis, Admiral of the Fleet, in New Zealand, had arrived on a yacht and had been entertained by Turia in Opunohu. By then, my princess had made her debut on the international scene by capturing the body, if not the heart, of Theodore ('Tito') Wessel, whilst acting as a hostess at Bill Wainwright's hotel. Tito was rich and foreign and owned a luxurious yacht, the *White Shadow.* The relationship ended dramatically due to Tito being married, and after Turia's house in Moorea burned down, she was turned off the land it stood on. She married a Frenchman and went with him to Huahine, *Îles sous-le-Vent*, the companion island to Raiatea and Bora Bora, before returning, disconsolate, to Papeete for some steady drinking at Quinn's. The war sent her another man in the shape of Sergeant 'Woody' Wilson, a wrestler and body-builder from California. In spite of his splendid physique, he was a fearful let-down, I was told. 'All Woody wanted was to play *millionaire,*' said Turia. 'He spent our money on *rien, rien* . . . I tell you, I was *fiu*, yet he said he considered we were still married unless I chose to pay him to go. *Pfufff! Imbecile!*'

In the nick of time, Turia had been rescued and set on her feet by Medford Kellum, an American who'd settled at the far end of Opunohu. He allowed her to rebuild her house on a patch of what had become his land. Med and his family were her nearest neighbours – great friends, always very nice to her (and to me). We used to stroll along the bay track to pick limes from his tree, whenever we wanted.

On the other side of *chez* Turia lived her brother, Minou, in a cluster
of huts with sand floors. Minou had served in the French Army and
had a shirt with a swastika to prove it. He was a fisherman. With his
square, agricultural face, he looked like a typical *poilu*, a sun-burned
country boy; and his wife, Rozi, was a pinched little madam who might
have been mistaken for someone a cut above him. It was extraordinary,
the difference between Turia and her brother, not just in looks but
in outlook.

'Often, you cannot tell brothers and sisters in Tahiti,' Turia explained.
'None of us were brought up together. *Tu sais*, it was a disgrace for a
family to be looking after all the children. You had to be given away, to a
friend or to a relation, as a favour. *Quelle honte*, if nobody asked for you!'

My sailor-friend from the ferry duly turned up. Turia tried to get him
to help us clear rubbish, but after an hour or two he tired and simply
sat there, drinking beer. His indolence was thoroughly Tahitian, as was
the fact that though young he was already running to fat. Gratifyingly,
it was me he'd come for, so after an interval, off we went together for a
bathe in a freshwater pool high in the jungly hills.

If I'd hoped that the expedition might lead to water-fun, I was
quickly disillusioned. A group of young girls drew near, jumping in
with shrieks and screams – which meant that convention required
him to behave in a macho, jokey manner, whilst the girls bridled and
pouted according to their convention. On our way back, he invited me
to watch next day's football match in Papetoai; Turia decided to come
too. It took us about half an hour to walk to the village, where the only
level space for a football field had been created by running it across both
sides of the sandy main track. On the lagoon side there was a kind of
stand, anything but 'grand', where there was a bar and a booth selling
maa Tinito, Chinese food.

Turia's appearance with her new husband caused a minor sensation.
We were mobbed by a crowd 500 strong, many of whom were *fetii*.
There was much comment, most of it lewd, she said, unwilling to
translate remarks which would sound 'too shaming' in Anglo-French.
Their import was clear: looking me up and down, the *fetii* were debating
my attributes and possible performance in bed; and perhaps this time
she might manage to have the child which so far had eluded her? I felt
mentally – and all but physically – groped. Not that I minded.

The sailor had stayed in the background, but when the game started he came and perched like a bird on a stepped-up bench immediately behind us, putting his arms round my neck to keep his balance. In that position he took part in all our conversation; at one point he nuzzled, and I thought tried to bite, my ear. In other circumstances I wouldn't have taken it amiss, but preferably not in public and certainly not when Turia was entitled to enjoy what triumph was going. When I pretended to notice nothing, after a while he jumped down and made off, without even saying goodbye – a victim of '*honte*'. The whole episode made me realise that I would have to live up to my new position as married man, or quit. There could be no halfway stage.

Papetoai had been important in Tahiti's past as the stronghold of King Pomare. In the hills were several *maraes*, in which no one seemed to take much interest. The glory had departed; and who cared, provided that the *tupaupaus* chose to haunt those monuments rather than the huts of the living? All that mattered was the moment. I was being impelled by everyone and everything around me to follow suit and live only in the present, especially when the present was so idyllic: Moorea so stunningly lovely; the people so playful; the air so warm and enervating, even when it rained (as it often did).

Were there no serpents in this Eden? Yes indeed there were: those tiny torturers mosquitos, and *nohu*, stonefish. 'Opunohu' meant 'place of the *nohu*'; to tread on one was to risk an agonisingly poisoned foot. Against mosquitos I had the latest weapon, di-methyl toluamide, which smelt like burning gramophone records. Against a stonefish, nothing; so it was just as well that we never encountered one.

Turia taught me how to fish using a gigantic throw-net. Our catch was small, but enough for a meal after perhaps four or five throws. Also, how to 'marry' the male and female parts of vanilla which (unlike us) could only propagate with assistance from outside. Much of the time we did nothing but exist, all the senses of the body open to unceasing stimulation, delight without end. Yet, just as the mountains above Opunohu Bay kept part of it in shadow, so the melancholy overhanging my thoughts would not be completely dispelled. Partly, it stemmed from a realisation that we were at best temporary residents, sojourners; not just Turia and me but all the easy-going men and women of Moorea. In Opunohu the years would roll on. Others would know what we had known, perhaps in a slightly different form: in a bay ringed with smart modern houses, in greater comfort, yet still with those dark-pinnacled green hills reflected in the water. It wasn't the sort of idea to occur – and certainly not to appeal – to Turia, so I spared her the trouble of hearing it. I didn't bother too much myself, during those indolent days and velvety nights, in spite of being aware, in the back of my mind, that they couldn't last for ever.

One thing which our successors were not so likely to have was a tiny thatched hut perched over the lagoon, a *fare iti* – the 'little room'. Our *fare iti* had a distant view of Mt Rotui, and enjoyed the immediate spectacle of brightly coloured fish tussling over morsels of excrement the moment they fell into the water. Lavatory paper couldn't be used in those conditions, so water had to suffice. When Minou caught fish outside his hut and we feasted on them, we were playing our part in a food-chain unlikely to appeal to the squeamish.

————

43

At first, the golden days seemed to go on for ever, extended indefinitely by novelty. Then, as usual, habit caused the hours to gather speed until they were racing by. Soon Quatorze Juillet was beckoning my princess back to Papeete. I had never enjoyed carnivals or nights of public frolicking; and besides, we had no francs to spare. However, Turia was set upon going. What would we use for money?

A solution offered itself, arising from our practice of sitting, drinking rum-punches, gazing across the bay as darkness fell. Turia would have to light a lamp in order to do the cooking, and I would light another, to see to read. One evening, as I fondled the base of my lamp, I recognised that it was not so different from a fortune-teller's crystal. Then I thought of 'Willie-the-Witch' down amongst the dustbins in Queen's Gate, reading hands. I'd often watched him at it. What if I were to try a bit of crystal-gazing? Turia's sister Melanie had developed a useful sideline in Papeete, reading Tarot cards for a clientèle made up entirely of Chinese who, hard-headed in business, were apparently softies in all else.

'My *belle-soeur* isn't the only one who can tell fortunes,' I said on an impulse. 'I can, *tu sais*, as well; but I prefer to keep my gift to myself, you understand ...'

'*TIENS, Rojeay!* You must tell me mine at once!'

'I'd rather not.'

'*Mais, j'insiste!*'

As I should have guessed, the slight delaying tactic had merely made her keener. 'All right then. Here goes!'

To my amazement, the improvised crystal didn't, in fortune-teller's jargon, 'cloud over' so much as give rise to far too many conflicting scenes, of which I could truthfully make neither head nor tail. On peering into the glass base of the lamp filled with paraffin, tiny things undoubtedly appeared. Not only appeared, but swelled and diminished, quite without reason. The things might resemble people, or houses, rooms, streets, trees – anything. Were they eyeball spots, travelling towards the edge of vision, as such spots do? If so, they changed and changed again when reflected from a smoothly rounded, opalescent surface. How to interpret what I saw? That was the greatest problem.

And then of course the question was: why should those funny little moving scenes have anything to do with the life of the person sitting opposite me? It was a tall order, to assume that every vision had to refer solely to a designated customer. If I were to set myself up as a fortune-teller, I would have to let paying clients assume that my readings applied to them only and to no one else. Otherwise, why should they be prepared to pay for my soothing (or disturbing) words?

With the bit between her teeth, Turia pestered me for further readings, which I kept on refusing. But it gave me a further idea: I would declare that my 'sightings' (if that was what they were) referred only to a few days ahead; for longer-term divination, clients would need to consult Melanie and her Tarot pack. That would kill several birds with one stone, because customers would have to come back to me for return sessions and Melanie would be gainfully involved. As a quid pro quo, I could reasonably ask for Melanie's list of the credulous, keeping the business in the family. Preparations for our return to Tahiti were enlivened by considering all manner of ins and outs of my new career.

At that stage I wasn't worried about the degree of fraud, for I was undeniably seeing vignettes, appearing and disappearing. But I found the prospect of confronting a customer face to face disquieting. Would I have the nerve to persuade even the most trusting to part with cash for such amateur efforts as mine were bound to be? I kept such qualms to myself as Turia got on with her packing.

When we were ready to go, Turia insisted on my choosing one of her three treasures. I demurred, but the insistence was real. I couldn't take a signed photograph of a woman, and the hammer was loaded with too much symbolic significance, important to her, meaningless to me. I picked the bowl, made by Marquesan islanders, as being a gloriously accurate example of Polynesian rudery.

Then we waited and waited for the boat to come, but it was loading a cargo of pigs somewhere else and didn't put in an appearance until late in the afternoon, by which time rain was pouring down with tropical violence, clattering on our far-from-leakproof pandanus roof. A wind arose, making the waters of the bay rough with waves. Coconut-palms swayed and whistled and the upper reaches of Mt Rotui were wreathed in cloud, revealed momentarily then wreathed again.

'*Beaucoup de gens* will be sick,' said Turia thoughtfully.

'*Beaucoup malade*, I should say!' I echoed, which made her smile. She found some of my most ordinary remarks amusing, I never knew how or why. When the mood was on her, she laughed easily; at other times (like other Tahitians) she would brood without apparent reason, never for long. In the simple complications of her nature, she was like Moorea itself.

As the ferry-boat chugged, hooting, into sight, Opunohu chose that moment to put on a show of such splendour that we were stunned into silence. The curtains of rain sweeping down across the bay lifted. A hot sun made the green hills steam whilst we were boarding the boat and stowing the luggage; then down came the rain again, in swipes and lashes, as if engaged in a fight to the finish against the brilliance fitfully projected from the sky. Suddenly a rainbow shone over towards Rotui, then split, all four fuzzy ends quivering in translucent colours for five, perhaps six minutes. Silence was the only proper response, but the other passengers were pointing and exclaiming in French-Tahitian. Tears blurred my eyes. As by then we were sopping wet I assumed that no one would notice me crying; and in any case, goodbyes in Tahiti were always tearful.

Turia said, 'Ah, Rojeay! Opunohu's *vin d'honneur* for a Chief!' Was she simply being Celtic, saying the sort of thing a listener wanted to hear?

I asked: 'Did Edwina rate a double rainbow?'

'Certainly not! But the *White Shadow*, yes, more than once. You don't mind that, do you?'

'Mind? Why should I mind?' Yet to tell the truth, I did rather resent the fact, as Turia knew I would. What right had Opunohu to stage its double miracle for anyone except us? We were unique, weren't we?

———————

44

When we reached the neatly manicured garden of Maison Crane, it seemed coldly inadequate. Even my Château Courant d'Air seemed less charming when compared with Opunohu. When we sat, as we sat most evenings, gazing at the jagged peaks of distant Moorea, waiting for a green flash from the sea as the sun sank beneath the waves, it was easy to understand why Tahitians had once believed that the souls of the dead took off from nearby Tahaa Point en route for Mt Rotui. Some souls of the living would gladly have flown in formation with them, I thought.

In preparation for Quatorze Juillet, Papeete was *en fête*. Stalls called *barraques*, made from palm-fronds and roofed with corrugated-iron, were opening for business. Some were classed as *concessions*, such as the one where a rabbit waited for a customer to bet on which tray of food it would choose for its feed. The public showed little inclination to lay out francs on something so obviously open to manipulation by the management.

Most of the stalls were drinking-booths, their *réclame* depending entirely upon the personality of those running them. We favoured a dark little booth owned by Edna, who'd returned from Honolulu to manage a small smart hotel, Les Trôpiques, at Faaa. Those able to afford it had often fed Turia and me there.

Edna's star entertainer was a thin man with rolling eyes who strummed a guitar and sang in a high-pitched voice. One of his songs, to the tune of 'Ta-ra-ra boom de-ay!', sounded like '*Tuyau, Tuyau, Ma-hu-hu Aita iti pu-nu-ru*', which was followed by a crashing chorus, in which we all joined, of '*Ta – ra – ra – BOOM de-ay!*' When I asked for a translation, Turia didn't want to interpret, but Edna would, after her fashion: 'Tuyau was a famous *mahu*, like my guitarist,' she said. 'A what-d'you-call-it? A *pédé*.'

'Oh, you mean a pansy,' I said, with what casualness I could muster.

'Yes, that's it. They're saying he doesn't know how to use his you-know-what; and then it gets worse, far worse, when they go into details about what he does use. *Imaginez ça!*' Indeed, I could. 'As for me, I like all sorts. All are clientèle, like the rest of us, *n'est-ce pas?*'

'Yes of course!' I replied, glad that her booth was dark enough to hide incipient blushes.

Before further talk could impale me on that particular theme, my *belle-soeur* Melanie arrived, gasping for breath, with an urgent message: 'Rojeay, *cheri*, I have a *Tinito* coming to our house, coming only for you to tell his fortune. Let us go quickly!' Off I went with Melanie, leaving Turia with Edna.

The Salmon town house included a verandah on wooden stilts, a concrete surround over which hens stalked and clucked, and an outside WC. Somehow, all *fetii* had to be fitted in, when necessary, by Turia's Tante Manan, the head of the family. Melanie exercised jurisdiction over a plain room with table and three chairs, a chest-of-drawers, a cupboard and a wooden double-bed scattered with cushions upholstered in the cloth used for *pareu*s. On the walls hung a picture of a younger, but still small and fat, Melanie; also a Joan Crawford cut from an illustrated magazine, below the Duke of Windsor when Prince of Wales. As in Fiji, reverence for royalty demanded, *faute-de-mieux*, the only royalty available: ours. To accommodate Turia and myself, Melanie had turned out of her own bed and was sleeping with her aunt.*

In those homely surroundings I set about preparing a suitable lamp for my test-case Chinese man, by filling the glass reservoir three quarters full. Then I waited . . . and waited . . . until at last the *Tinito* appeared, an old-young creature, as wrinkled as a lizard. The first thing he did was to grumble because I hadn't been immediately available. A soft answer turned away his wrath, putting us on a proper footing of caterer and customer. After some moments of concentrated gazing, I allowed myself a sharp intake of breath, at which he trembled, in the right frame of mind to drink in every word.

'You are going to have a fight, over a matter of business, with a senior,' I said, seeing little dots clashing in what looked like a shop selling dress-lengths. 'You will be arguing about your stock of clothing.'

His eyes brightened. 'Yes, yes, it has already started.'

---

* Roddy doesn't explain why they're staying with Melanie as opposed to staying at Maison Crane's. Possibly it was because it was closer to the action on the night of Bastille day; possibly because Crane himself was at home for the festivities. We can assume they didn't go to the Chateau because it was uncomfortable!

'It will clear the air. You will come away in a much stronger position to call the shots. What you stock in future will be much more what you choose. Congratulations!'

Next, he wanted to know about his family, so I asked him how many children he had. He couldn't wait to supply enough information for me to be able to pass remarks about each by interpreting more moving dots. Emboldened by success, I looked up, rubbed a fist over my forehead as if exhausted, and curtly announced: '*Ça suffit!*'

'*Merci m'sieur*, I will send my partner to consult you,' was my reward. I was given the equivalent of £1 (worth enough for those days) and a small *pourboire* (tip) on top of that.

Dizzy with relief, I returned to Edna's with Melanie, at last able to pay my share of expenses. But genuine nervous tension had taken its toll: I wanted only to sleep, which was the one thing absolutely *tabu*. Enjoyment must go on and on – an iron rule for all *citoyens* commemorating the storming of the Bastille.

On and on went the festivities. Blurred with drink, dropping with fatigue, I met, as if in a dream, a Miss Bunkley, horse-faced and vampish. She hauled me on to a raised platform where, to the strains of 'The Eton Boating Song', European couples were decorously twirling. I succeeded in bringing Miss B crashing to the floor before staggering towards a bench where I would have dropped off to sleep had not Marcel Krainère appeared. He was spreading his hands out with worry. 'Pussy's GONE!' he declared. 'One minute she was there, and the next … *pfff!* …' Apparently, she'd picked up a *copain* of the evening, previously unknown, and insisted on him hiring a speedboat.

Whilst we waited for the runaways to return, Marcel told me that he'd just been authorised to offer Château Courant d'Air for sale at £500; I could have first refusal. 'Not a hope!' I said, knowing that such a possibility was completely removed from reality. 'I couldn't raise even a tenth of that, however much I wanted to.'

'A pity. It's a real bargain,' he said sadly.

Pussy loped back, minus her friend, and had to be plied with black coffee. We went to the covered market, where we ran into Med Kellum, buying meat, of all things. It was the last thing I remembered, but we must have returned in one piece to Maison Salmon, for the next thing I was aware of was a cock crowing vigorously beneath the *auvent* of Melanie's room.

Once able to move, we went to see the *Otea* dancing competition, which was genuinely exciting. Teams of dancers in grass skirts advanced towards a stand holding the Governor and assorted *fonctionnaires*. As if to prove that their garb was not traditional so much as 'missionary-traditional', loin-cloths and bodices were worn beneath the skirts, doing away with any suggestion of abandon. Each team had its own contingent of drummers, with a repertoire of rolls, taps and clicks in sequences as complicated as changes rung by bell-ringers. To such an extent did the drum-rhythms control the dancing that men and women, shaking and *hfff*-ing, seemed like puppets. How could they remember when to alter their bumps and grinds in unison?

'They talk all the time,' said Turia. 'The drums are drumming words, you see, our lovely Tahitian words. The dancers are being told each step, as it comes. So they cannot forget what they have to do next.'

'Do they never improvise?'

'Of course the famous ones, the stars, improvise all the time, and the others have to catch up with them. It's really something!'

Indeed, it was.

'What fun they must be having!' I said, to no one in particular.

A French woman standing near me shouted, 'Not nearly such fun as they used to have!' (She had to shout, to be heard.) 'When I was here thirty years ago they really went to town! You've never seen such costumes as they had then; nor such feasts! It's all changed so much, and for the worse ... I tell you one thing: never, NEVER come back! Because you won't like what you find, I promise.'

'But what you find so disappointing is what I call having the time of my life!' I argued.

'*Exactement*, you know no better. Once, I knew no better, and *la vie en rose* seemed as if it would go on for ever. Now look at me! I warn you, things can never be the same a second time. Remember my words: NEVER COME BACK!'

A crescendo of drumming prevented Turia from hearing what she was saying. In a way, I wished that I hadn't heard myself. I'd always known that the time would come when I would have to leave the South Seas and pick up the threads of 'real' life and Tedder's 'Life'. Was it true that there could be no going back? If so, Their Benevolences, the Fates, had chosen an odd medium through which to convey a warning.

Recovered enough to attend to a second Chinese client, I drifted, with another £1 in pocket, along to the Post Office to collect any *poste restante* letters. I wasn't entirely happy. Apart from drinking too much and staying up too late, the strain of telling fortunes was proving cumulative. In theory, I was content to exploit the easy source of income, but in practice I felt a bit of a low dog.

The first letter I opened was an amusing card from Kit the Purser on *Clan Urquhart*, signed by some of the lads still crossing and re-crossing the line between England and Australia. Kind of them to bother. Next, there were long letters from home. Would they have been any less loving had they known one tenth of what I'd been up to, I wondered? Disapproval rather than acceptance by the family had been my lot thus far.

I left to the last an official-looking letter, typewritten, with the address of an unknown firm of lawyers on its back, which I opened with a certain foreboding, thinking that it might contain unwelcome news about my sub-tenants in Queen's Gate. But no, not at all. It was to let me know that my dear old pussy of a godfather Alister Davidson had died, remembering me in his will.

He had left me £500 – exactly the sum required to buy Château Courant d'Air.

———

45

Coincidence may be stranger than fiction, truth stranger than both. I could have felt in that moment that I was being instructed from On High to settle for ever in *Océanie Française*. Instead it brought to the surface thoughts that had been swimming beneath. Were I to seize the chance, I would be letting myself in for a lifetime of achieving nothing, eked out by bamboozling not just one or two but hundreds of Chinese people, forever haunted by larger-than-life *tupaupaus* of moral inferiority.

Reality had been hard at work, shattering the fantasy of being a beachcomber in the South Seas. Having proved that I could live on my wits in Paradise, if I had to, I was forced to admit that I would rather not; at least, not for too long. It was the end of a dream, and like all such conclusions, hard to stomach. I had to recognise the truth: now that the purchase of Château Courant d'Air had been made possible, the option was unacceptable.

From Mataiea, a mere forty-six years earlier, the disillusioned poet Rupert Brooke wrote to his friend: 'The Game is Up, Eddie. If I've gained facts by knocking about with Conrad characters in a Gauguin entourage – I've lost a dream or two.' As far as I was concerned, I hadn't just been knocking about with such characters, I'd been one myself. But unlike Joseph Conrad's tortured ne'er-do-wells, trapped in surroundings at odds with their better selves, I was being offered an escape route. Wouldn't I be an idiot not to take it?

Papeete in holiday mood was no place for prolonged introspection, so I didn't introspect much. However, the situation obviously required some thought. Strolling along past the curving line of yachts to where pirogues were moored, I came to a public bench where I could be alone with my musings. The proper Tahitian thing to do would be to rush back to Maison Salmon, waving the lawyer's letter. There would follow all the excitements of winning the Pools: the drinks; the hired cars; the all-important feast on a J. G. Brander scale. Within a few weeks – months at most – the money would have evaporated, leaving nothing but *mana* behind. Nothing but *mana*? What could be more of a 'something' for Turia's prestige-loving *fetii*? If ever I needed an illustration that Tahitian ways were not my ways – and never could be – this was it. My aims in life were entirely different; not half as nice but twice as sensible.

The way I'd been living (even with board and lodging practically free) I'd wondered how on earth I would manage to scrape together the fare for a passage out of Tahiti. Till I earned enough to take the cheapest copra-boat to France, I'd been committed (or rather, condemned) to a future of crystal-gazing, whatever my qualms. All that had changed. Now, if I wished, I could hurl my paraffin lamp into the lagoon and with a song in my heart watch it sink.

As a first move, without telling anyone, I sauntered along to the offices of Messageries Maritimes to ask which ships were going where, and when. I was told that in September *Sagittaire* would be slowly ploughing its way from New Caledonia to Marseilles via the Panama Canal, Curaçao, Martinique and Guadaloupe, lingering at each port of call as long as it took to load and unload cargo. No dates, even for departure from Tahiti, were fixed; all were subject to alteration without notice.

That didn't matter to me. More to the point, the cheapest passage (described as 'Quatrième Classe') would cost £45, for which I would be carried in the hold and stand in a queue for food doled out into a billy-can. For a few pounds more, I could have the same accommodation but eat at a real table (with cloth) with the grandees of the Third Class. That was what I booked provisionally, breathing thanks to my godfather Alister as I did so; feeling like a millionaire because, for once, I didn't have to put up with the cheapest and worst. One thing spoilt the joy of the moment: the need to keep it all to myself. On no account must anyone know the true extent of my good fortune, not even Turia – especially not Turia. The decision burdened me with guilt. It wasn't kind, it wasn't fair; but then, I didn't dare be kind or fair when my whole future, as I saw it, was at stake.

When I told her some days later, I gave her half the truth and made it sound temporary: 'I promised I would go back to England, to write about our great airman, Tedder. Some money to pay for a ticket has arrived, with a little bit over for us now.'

It made me ashamed when Turia took the news very well: *'Au-ey, Rojeay!* I always knew that we were only together *pour les vacances*. But if you come back when your book is finished, maybe it will be for ever?'

What could I reply? I meant it, in a way, when I said, 'Oh I hope so, yes, I hope so!' But the words sounded as hollow to me as they were in fact. 'What about one of your rum-punches?' I asked, in an attempt to disguise the awkwardness of the moment.

'*Bien sûr, Rojeay, tout à coup!*'

Then, in August, Turia came dancing in with some news: 'Rojeay, I can hardly believe our luck, but two months have come and gone without me feeling unwell, even for a day! What would you say to a child?'

'I'd sing *ta-ra-ra BOOM de-ay!*' I said; and I really meant it. In Tahiti, children were no problem. Every family took them in or gave them away freely; no child would ever know what it was like to be unwanted. If it turned out that I'd managed to give satisfaction in that one direction at least, then nothing could be more gratifying.

It was a strange, limbo period of time: the hope the thought of a baby would bring and the pervading sadness of my upcoming departure.

'*Tu sais*, we are used to saying goodbye,' said Turia sadly. 'Life here is one long *adieu*.'

I began to dread the passing of the hours, the element of farewell which each hour contained, especially when *Sagittaire* duly docked on time and Messageries Maritimes were even then unable to say exactly when their ship would leave.

For what might be a final feast, Melanie arrived with a marketing which included *varo*. '*Hélas, Rojeay, comme je suis cafardeuse!*'* she wailed. Turia prepared a pot-roast of pork and vegetables, laying it out on leaves, having previously made *couronnes* for us to wear round our necks. As we ate, sad at heart, we were surrounded by the powerful aromas of food and fragrance combined, whilst Melanie sang her own version of 'Daisy, Daisy!' to cheer us up:

> *You'll look sweet*
> *Between the sheets*
> *Of a double-bed made for two!*

As usual, the sisters were making light of everything; and as usual, the sun shone, the palm trees glistened and rustled in the wind, the reef roared and sighed, roared and sighed. In some ways our lives seemed as settled as they had been since we met six months earlier; yet the threat of change overhung everything.

The blow, when it came, was crushing. *Sagittaire* overstayed by two days and during that time Turia miscarried. I knew it as soon as she did, for as we were lying in bed together it was impossible to disguise what was happening. We shuddered in sorrow, and I hugged her whilst she cried silently in the warm and muggy night.

She said: 'If only the ship had left on time, you would have had a month or two of happiness, Rojeay, thinking that all was well!'

So then I was crying too; not for the child which would never be born, but because Turia minded so much.

At 7 a.m. on the day of my departure, Turia and I went to Quinn's for a farewell drink. Even at that hour Eddy Quinn was up and about, his bamboo bar packed. The departure of a big ship was a big event in the days before the advent of anything except an occasional seaplane. Eddy kindly wanted me to sing what was known as 'my' song, taught me by Adi Gavoka: 'Teardrops in my Eyes'. It brought back memories of easy-going Lil, sheathed in shiny green satin, and of the piano being

---

* This translates as 'Alas, Rojeay, how cocky I am!' Quite possible that Roddy recorded this word wrongly because of his 'dog-French', as he would have put it.

pounded in Robertson Road. Of course, I was no more of a lonely cowboy betrayed by a saloon-bar tart than I'd been in Suva, but banal as the song was, I'd become identified with it. That morning in Quinn's, I was unable to sing without a sob in my voice.

It was the worst goodbye of my life. At the dockside, Turia produced a handkerchief to dry my eyes, but it was soon wet through. I was sweating profusely from the *couronnes* hung round my neck, moving in a cloud of frangipani and *tiaré Tahiti*, hugging and kissing everyone in sight, wet cheeks against wet cheeks, howling helplessly, face set in an archaic smile.

The moment came for the last, lingering farewells, followed by a rush to the ship's rail and all the paraphernalia of parting, including, finally, flinging the *couronnes* into the sea and watching them bob away in a relentless wake. I thought: *Never again will I make fun of people saying goodbye. Never, never again!*

The sword twisting inside me might have been made of living coral, its thrust left such a fierce burn; but without Turia to squeeze limes on the wound, how could my heart be healed?

As La Diadême, crown of Tahiti's mountain peaks, slowly vanished from the horizon, I stayed by the ship's rail, recovering from an emotional upheaval the like of which I'd never known before. Soon, however, a mischievous idea began to form. In those days, few cinema programmes were complete without a treacly American travelogue. I couldn't help thinking of how one might end: 'And so we say FAREWELL to Tahiti, Perle du Pacifique, to the sound of the happy children of nature dancing their *heiva* beneath the sun-kissed palms . . .' It made me smile in spite of myself, it was so utterly meretricious. I was already foraging, like a rat, amongst the refuse of discarded dreams, nosing out something comic; I'd become as irrepressible, even in grief, as any South Seas islander. It was Tahiti's parting gift. I could place it alongside one of Turia's great contributions: the idea that every circumstance, however grim, had a certain 'chic' attached, if only it could be viewed in that light. How grateful I was for such jewels of commonsense! Both were outlooks to be treasured for ever.

part five

new worlds, old worlds

1950-6

46

Dumped in the high-ceilinged communal entrance-passage of 94 Queen's Gate, my luggage looked like the sorry effects of a refugee: a battered suitcase; a seldom-opened trunk; coconuts in their green outer casing; and a crate of clam-shells taken at the last minute from the beach outside Château Courant d'Air. Those shells, I thought, would do splendidly as presents, original ashtrays as soon as I could rid them of their original smell.

Back once more in my 'real life', I turned my mind increasingly towards my proper business of writing, that time-hallowed refuge from the buffetings of 'real life'.

'So you're back from the South Seas,' Tedder said when I went to see him in his office, eyes twinkling in a familiar 'pixie' manner. 'Did you tire of being a beachcomber?'

'Oh I don't know . . .'

'Well, did you find a dusky princess? Did they lay on a cannibal feast? When I was a District Officer in Fiji, I sometimes used to wonder what that would have been like.'

I replied: 'Any human flesh on offer certainly wasn't for eating. But I did marry a Princess of Moorea!' Even as I spoke, I was swamped by the unreality of talking like that in a soberly furnished office in Air Ministry, in the grey-gloom of a winter's day. We were not just remote, but light-years away from Great Tahiti the Golden. 'We gave a feast to let everyone know we were married,' I tried to continue.

'No church? Not even a Registry Office?'

'You don't have a French civil ceremony in Tahiti unless you're a French civil servant.'

'Hmmm . . . well, what have you done with her?'

'We parted when I left. It's what happens out there.'

'How convenient! And now, you mean to start on my Life?'

'Yes, sir, I do.'

'Well, I suppose if you must, you must!'

At that time my literary agent was Ludo Ludovici, whom I'd met in Air Historical Branch. He wanted to wrest me away from Hutchinson's in favour of placing me with Collins, whom he described as being 'teak and mahogany'. I duly met William Collins, who showed considerable interest and said that naturally he'd have to check with Tedder that I had his full approval before drawing up a contract. I was dumbfounded when Tedder rang me to ask: 'What do you mean by putting your publishers on to me? They've been urging me to write my own Life. How does that strike you?'

'Teak and mahogany, forsooth!' I exploded to Ludo. 'The bugger's using my introduction to try and cut the ground away from under my feet. So much for your teak and mahogany!' All the same, I allowed myself to be soothed. What else could a nearly unknown author do, even one with a property as valuable as 'Tedder' up his sleeve? We signed the contract on 9 March 1950, the advance being £500, payable in three instalments – moderately good for those days.

As a vital preliminary, I had to get my subject to issue the sort of TO WHOM IT MAY CONCERN letter which I'd extracted from a compliant Air Marshal Medhurst in Cairo. Then I had to get to know my subject as he was: highly elusive and highly mischievous, as if he were putting me continually to the test.

So it was that my South Seas past began misting over: Tahiti no longer so clear in my mind; the rustle of coconut-palms, the roaring of the reef, fading from memory. Tantalisingly, the smell of *monoi* oil still hung about my clothes, because the bottle had spilled in my case. It took a long time and much washing and dry-cleaning before it disappeared; if indeed it ever did, wholly.

In gratitude for the gift of her rude (and much-admired) Marquesan bowl, I sent Turia one of the pieces of jewellery that had come to me through my parents' divorce settlement, a diamond brooch in the shape of a spider with ruby eyes. I had to tell her that being an heirloom it could only technically be on loan, but that I had no intention of ever asking for it back.

Writing in French, a language which was neither hers nor mine, Turia sent me a letter which was all the more heart-rending for looking so scrawly and naive upon the page: 'I live in your shirt and in your Kimono and I put monoi on my head according to your habits. I'm happy to think that your friends have admired our bowl. When I think that it is near you I know you will not quickly forget Turia who ADORES you, my beautiful Roger.'

Central heating would eventually dry and twist the wooden bowl, but Turia was right to assume that its blatant sexuality would never fail to remind me of her; it would always do so, with a smile. A little time later I heard that there was a new plan being drawn up for Air France to fly from Fiji to Bora Bora, then on to Papeete. I could assume that it therefore wouldn't be long before Tahiti experienced the full force of international airborne tourism – a thought to make anyone who loved the old Tahiti shudder. At least until the money came rolling in.

All of it together made me so homesick, it was an effort to bend my mind to the purpose for which I'd struggled so successfully. I had to remember that from now on Tedder's Life was my objective and that my address was no longer the Bay of Opunohu, but South Kensington.

As if to rub it in, a warning voice repeated: *'NEVER GO BACK!'* But I wasn't ready to listen, not just yet. Perhaps not ever.

47

When Tedder told me that he had been posted to 'a NATO job at the Pentagon', my congratulations were muted. He'd been elusive enough on this side of the herring-pond.

'I suppose you'll expect me to put up with you in the States?' he asked wryly.

'Well, it might be convenient to interview some of your American colleagues in Washington ... yes, it would be very useful – essential really!'

'I'll have to clear it with Toppy,' he said. 'If she says yes, then yes it is.' Yes it was.

Toppy was his second wife; his first, Rosalinde, had died in an air crash in Cairo, not far from Great-Aunt Bonté's Villa Beata. Toppy, sister of the actor Bruce Seton, had formerly been Mrs Black, the not-exactly-sedate wife of a rip-roaring racing driver. She was much criticised by those in the higher echelons of Service life who thought

her 'unsuitable'. In fact she was kind and highly amusing, doing much
to enliven her husband's life. Being as sharp as a razor himself he needed
someone sophisticated to blunt his witticisms, or he might have been
in danger of giving too much offence when dealing with more stolid
commanders.

I then had to consider how best to get myself to America. I didn't
want to go begging to Tedder; and in any case, it mightn't have got me
anywhere. After making a number of enquiries I found that an Israeli
agency in Soho could put me on what was described as 'an immigrant
boat', the SS *Washington*, very cheaply. *Washington* was one-class – in
other words, Third Class – a converted troop-ship with accommodation (for those, like me, paying the least) in large cabins with bunk-beds
in tiers, painted battleship-grey. In November 1950, I duly booked
and boarded.

Entry into the States at that time was an unpleasant experience.
Immigration Officers were rude and suspicious beyond belief, in spite
of the difficulties which most of us had experienced in obtaining a visa.
However, once I'd convinced my inquisitor that I would leave the country as unsullied as I found it, an Irish Customs Officer seemed impressed
by the subject of my book-to-be. 'Marshal of the Royal Air Force Lord
Tedder!' he repeated, in awestruck tones, as if the title were the thing
of most importance.

Once through, I wouldn't have known where to turn had I not been
befriended by a young American from the Far West who led me to the
Beekman Tower hotel, overlooking a rectangular new United Nations
building. Our room was on the fortieth floor, which in itself was an
experience, for never before had I perched so high. At nightfall, I knew
the authentic thrill – rare in life – of utter novelty when I stood at the
window, looking out at thousands of little lights shining in regular
dots all the way up from street-level to skyline. The towering heights
of New York coalesced to form one colossal palace, too immense to
be compared with any other palace on earth, beautiful in its glittering
impersonality, but frightening. It was good to have the reassurance of
a new friend at hand.

Next morning he took me to Penn Station to catch a train to
Washington. Penn was like nothing I'd ever seen before, not a station
so much as a concourse, as high and elegant as a cathedral but twice as
warm, with trains running from subterranean tunnels.

My destination outside Washington was exaggeratedly English, a Tudoresque house in ample grounds. It looked like the coaching-inn on an Xmas card, the ground being covered in thick snow. In the baronial fireplace burned logs sawn daily by Tedder himself by way of exercise: 'Like the Kaiser at Apeldoorn,' he liked to explain. Eager as I was to stay in his good books, I thought that offering to chop alongside him would be going too far. His other daily task, feeding the birds, was much more my style. The suburb was called Maclean, pronounced, half the time, 'Macleen'.

I wouldn't have seen enough of Tedder to justify my presence but for daily car-rides to and from the Pentagon. He had been allocated an Austin limousine, with extra bucket-seats in the back and what looked like an ordinary electric fire mounted on the partition instead of a fan-heater. It kept us as warm, en route, as we were indoors, in home and office. Each journey became a quiz-time, with me subjecting him to a barrage of questions from which there was no escape. He must have grown sick of the twice-daily inquisition, but he bore it cheerfully provided that I switched to Fiji whenever the going got sticky. The South Seas worked a spell too potent for the years to diminish. Our shared love made me less nervous about tackling a profession so full of technical detail as his. Another writer, ignorant of life in a Pacific Paradise, might not have been able to lull his subject as effectively as I could.

When back in the house, I saw a lot of Toppy. She didn't really have enough to do and had a loyal helper, Joyce, to do it with. To my amazement and exceeding gratitude they washed my socks daily, hanging them out on wire stretchers to dry in the bathroom which I had all to myself. They initiated me into the joys of nylon shirts which could also be washed daily and drip-dried – a process previously as unknown to me as the shirts themselves. Each morning, a Black woman drove up in a smart Cadillac to do the charring, which again was a surprise.*

To me at that time the really extraordinary phenomenon was a seventeen-inch TV with a wide choice of channels day and night.

---

* Roddy used the term 'coloured' here; as it is now pejorative it's been changed to Black. Why Roddy was surprised isn't altogether clear. Was it because he hadn't seen any Black house cleaners before back in the UK? Was it because Joyce already had everything under control to such an extent Toppy didn't have anything to do, and therefore having a third person to clean was excessive? I would propose the most likely reason is because she was driving a smart Cadillac, something charladies in the UK would likely not have been able to afford in the fifties, and so here was another reason to be impressed with America; but readers can decide for themselves.

Television hadn't caught on in England; Londoners owning a set were getting poor value for money. Our tiny screens, rounded at the edges, kept featuring waves breaking on a beach (or something equally banal) until it were time for a short programme of unbelievable amateurishness. We'd invented the thing, but we certainly hadn't developed its potential. It did just cross my mind that I ought to invest in anything to do with 'the Box', but I was using my godfather Alister's legacy to further my life then and there, not to lay up treasure for an uncertain future.

As there was only the one TV set, there could be differences of opinion over which programme to watch. The mainstay of Tedder's working life was 'the Cardinal', a stately English assistant responsible for seeing that his office ran smoothly. He often clashed with Toppy over the intellectual content of this or that and had been known to reach out, without asking, and turn the set off when something particularly second-rate was being shown. The Cardinal was always very helpful to me, the more so since he wasn't collecting material for a book of his own. I was glad to have such a competent friend in the River Room, Tedder's NATO office in the Pentagon.

The ground-plan of the Pentagon followed some internal logic all its own, which defeated me till, one day, I actually managed to get from the River Room to the Cafeteria (where a good meal cost less than a dollar) without once asking the way. Usually I seemed to be walking miles in pursuit of my quarry, the brass hats who had helped Tedder's career. Unfortunately, they were busier than they'd been for ages, on account of the Korean war.

Crisis followed crisis on the international scene, one issue coming to the forefront with irritating insistence: should we, 'the West', be prepared to use the atom bomb? 'No,' said Tedder. 'Absolutely definitely NOT!' I heard him coming out forcefully with that opinion whenever the subject cropped up. General (or perhaps by then he was Field Marshal) Slim swept in on a flash-flood of big-wigs and wasn't so convinced. General Lauris Norstad (almost too boyishly good-looking in a Scandinavian way to be taken seriously) supported the Tedder line. I oughtn't really to have been privy to their discussions, but it was impossible to prevent me.

I was able to strike two of my targets fairly quickly: the Generals Marshall and 'Tooey' Spaatz. Marshall had added to his wartime fame with the Marshall Plan for rescuing Europe from financial collapse. He was dry ('spinsterish', according to my notes) and gave away nothing about anything, sitting in an office hung with American flags. Spaatz was cruder in manner, but equally adept at saying nothing at interminable length. Both made frequent use of that dead-end phrase 'No comment!' which left me rudderless because I hadn't encountered it before. They tended to deal in long-winded platitudes such as: 'Your Marshal Tedder made a major contribution to the Allied cause by reason of his insight into methods whereby the enemy would sustain defeat.' But to the question 'What methods, precisely?' nothing but more flannel would be forthcoming. It may have appeared to Tedder that I was getting somewhere. I was the only one who knew that I wasn't.

Being Washington, parties were in progress, night after night. I attended very few, observing that at those functions where food and drink was choicest, fun was at its least joyous. I said as much to Tedder, who commented: 'It's always astonished me, the way people confuse fun with formality. The two are like oil and water: they never mix unless they're shaken together in a bottle. And why bother?'

'Yet here you are, being formal all day and most evenings as well.'

'Only when I have to. As you may have noticed, Toppy and I go out as little as we can; less, I should think, than anyone in Washington. And even that is too often for my liking!' I was grateful to him for helping me understand the dullness at the heart of the outwardly glittering – a lesson which, once absorbed, would never be forgotten.

By this point some weeks had passed and I had squeezed all I was likely to by taking limo trips to the Pentagon. The person I was keenest to meet was sitting in New York, having taken on the job of overseeing Columbia University whilst waiting for a far more important Presidency to fall into his lap: General Eisenhower,* Tedder's Chief during the most important part of his career, the Normandy landings. A few well-placed telephone calls produced a brief appointment, fifteen minutes at most. It wasn't much, but I was glad of an excuse to return to the electrifying city of New York where I wanted to stay on for a while afterwards – literally electrifying, my fingers giving off sparks when I stepped out of a car on to a sidewalk.

'Ike' was still very much a somebody. I wasn't permitted to walk in casually but had to be checked and re-checked before being allowed to whizz up in an elevator, on the very minute. The punctuality of our

---

* Eisenhower would be elected President of the United States two years later; he was inaugurated in January 1953.

interview provided my opening gambit. I said: 'I particularly appreciate your thoughtfulness, because I can't afford to waste a single second of our talk!'

The result was all I could have asked for: 'I gotta be downtown in a half-hour. You better ride with me, if that suits your schedule.'

Suits, indeed, I thought. *Oh boy, oh BOY!*

By the time we climbed into his waiting limousine, flanked by two hard-faced men whose function needed no explaining, he was nicely relaxed. What sort of man was I sitting next to? Well, he was sucking a scented cachou as he leaned back at an angle which drew attention to an incipient double-chin.

I was encouraged straight away by Ike's assessment of Field Marshal Montgomery: 'A tendency to advance without proper consolidation'; 'too many military adventures out on a limb', etc. He had never favoured Monty's attempt at establishing 'a Bridge too Far' of brave but expendable paratroopers. No, he 'surely hadn't favored that program!' He added: 'A thing which has always puzzled me. Was your distinguished Monty truly the idol of his men?'

I was so flattered to have been asked my opinion that I let loose a flood of garrulity: 'No, sir, I think he was too much of a puritan to be idolised by the licentious soldiery ...' Even as I spoke, I realised that 'puritan' was hardly the most tactful epithet of disapproval to use when talking to an American. However, on I went explaining my review.

'Not your hero, then?'

'Certainly not my hero! Auchinleck was that, for being the General who actually stopped Rommel at el-Alamein.' If I'd hoped that my opinion would spur him, I was to be disappointed. It passed with no more comment than a nod. So I continued: 'To my mind, Rommel was the pick of the bunch, although we aren't supposed to say so, even now.'

'We aren't supposed to say a lot of things!' said Ike feelingly. Then, as if regretting his candour, he clammed up.

Aware that I was doing too much of the talking when I was meant to be listening, but too far gone to stop, I embarked on the story of how Uncle Dick had reacted when a parachute detachment had been stationed at Well Vale during the war, which General Eisenhower seemed to find entertaining, if bewildering. It must have been quite a change from his usual type of interview. Obligingly, he said, 'Hey, that's good!', but he remained clammed up, too shrewd an operator to have his lips prised open to any greater extent. I was unable to extract any more opinions, abrasive or otherwise, from anodyne words about Allied cooperation, coupled with praise for Tedder's outstanding abilities. When he graciously dropped me off, my fingers sparked against the door-handle of his limousine (of course), but I felt as insulated as if I'd been wrapped in cotton-wool.

I wasn't all that pleased with him later, when I wrote to ask whether he would consider doing a foreword for my book about his cherished Deputy Supreme Commander. He wouldn't.

———

48

'New York! New York!' I hummed as the limousine containing General Eisenhower and his bodyguard glided away, leaving me stranded, on foot, in unknown parts of the great United States.

From the Tedders' house in McLean I'd been prudent enough to telephone Alphonso Ossorio (whose father worked for the Ossorio sugar-kings in the Philippines), friend of Hubert Fox from my days at Oxford in the University Ambulance Unit. I'd rung just in time; Alphonso was on the point of leaving for Europe, so would miss me, but I was welcome to stay in his house in McDougall Alley, a mews off Washington Square. I could sleep in the downstairs room and use the kitchen. I'd be let in and be given a spare key by Jackson something-or-other. All I had to do was turn up on the doorstep. So that is what I did, around lunchtime one cold day in December 1950.

The Alley was evidently something special by New York standards. A chain had been hooked across the cobbles at its entrance and the houselets were smart with paint, nothing like the shabby premises over garages (former stables) which were to be found in a London mews. A brisk tap upon a gleaming door produced no result at first; so I waited, sitting on a suitcase, getting rather cold. At last the door was dragged open by an untidy woman in a night-gown, looking uncannily like a younger version of Eleanor Roosevelt. She poked her head out and surveyed the street crossly, before starting to close the door, at which I gave a shout of 'OY! It's ME!'

'The heck it is!' she said, unperturbed. 'Come on in, then!'

I followed her indoors, whilst she explained: 'Alphonso had difficulty in getting hold of us and the Dragon only wanted me about an hour ago.'

'The dragon?'

'Yeah, that's right! I must have dozed off. Anyway, here you are . . . and Jack's still asleep. D'you need coffee?' I was shown the sofa downstairs which pulled out like a Z to make a double-bed; very convenient.

I got some information out of her whilst she fussed about in a narrow kitchen, doing some overdue washing-up. 'The Dragon' was Alphonso's determined but in other ways far from monstrous boyfriend, who wasn't living there; 'Jack' was 'Jackson' and she was 'Lee', the surnames being 'Pollock', which at that moment meant nothing to me.

The Pollocks were living upstairs in a studio with half-finished canvases stacked against the walls. When Jack awoke, he did so with panache, bellowing for coffee and looking like a balding backwoodsman recovering from an early morning's bout of tree-felling. I took to him instantly, and they equally took to me. We were all disposed to be amicable and we liked our drink, so during the next couple of hours we knocked back goodness knows how much, sitting about on the floor. Then, as I felt hungry (and they didn't), I relieved them of a spare key and went to see what I could rustle up in the nearest 'deli'.

In England at that time we were *still* enduring the rigours of rationing. It was almost impossible to explain our obsession with food, lovely food, to Americans; for after all, we had won a war, hadn't we? The sheer variety of savoury things in the deli was what registered most: the salamis; the sausages of every shape, size and texture; the huge limbs of cooked turkey; the cheeses . . . a dazzling display. I soon realised that the only thing holding me back was a shortage of cash – quite a jolt in its way.

In the studio, Alphonso's paintings were instantly distinguishable from Jackson's, being based on variations of red and orange, swirling as restlessly as fireworks trapped in a whirlpool. Jackson's were like segments of an old wall, often with what looked like traces of the original earth still clinging, sometimes even with pebbles added. I had never seen anything remotely like them before on canvas, and said so. My one concession to politeness was, when giving an opinion, to speak slowly and portentously, as if bowled over. It was far from true, for privately I thought that actual sections of an old wall might have proved a great deal more interesting. One day, it would seem the height of folly to make such an admission. By way of an excuse, I would eventually have to plead that my mind was on air power rather than art. But even so . . .

My mind was on lots of other things as well. I wanted to make the most of my opportunities and felt so much on top of the world in that magical city that nothing tired me. I set out on foot for Central Park, dawdling along to take in the novel sights and sounds. My slow pace attracted curious glances. Most people were walking purposefully and seemed almost to resent my lack of speed, as if at any moment I might stop them in the street and whine: 'Buddy, won't you spare me a dime?'

Passing the Savoy Plaza hotel, I was making for Harlem. At that time there was no reason to exercise caution. Harlem mightn't be the safest district in the world, but it wasn't specially noted for danger. My goal was the Mount Morris Baths, where (I'd heard) anybody could meet any other body in clouds of steam. Mount Morris lacked the prestige of the Everard Baths, being smaller and mostly for Black men. It cost very little, as such things did in those days.

Lack of confidence led to a ridiculous situation: I became the prey of an old Indian man who stalked me with relentless zeal, no doubt to compensate for a distinct lack of charm. I turned his persistence to good account by questioning him closely about where to go in the Big Apple. When it was obvious that the only role I saw him in was that of guide, he left abruptly, to pester others. I was then free to look around, and the most attractive person in sight was a Black young man with the kind of panther eyes which I always found appealing. His movements were tough but graceful, demonstrating a controlled strength. When we chatted, I was surprised to hear that he was a warehouseman, then not at all surprised to learn that he was also a pupil at the Martha Graham School of Dancing. He was called 'Hart', a surname so pleasant that I preferred to call him that, by-passing his Christian name. Within half an hour we were on our way to an apartment belonging to an artist friend of his, Paul England.

Paul's studio was completely un-English, being warm throughout and with a huge refrigerator humming away in the kitchen. In England we were living in the 'make do and mend' manner which inspired George Orwell's *1984*. English artists, being at the bottom of the prole-heap, froze in winter and wrapped themselves in smelly wool; their food, necessarily bought in small portions, had to be eaten quickly before it went 'off' in a larder. Once he'd got over the surprise of seeing what Hart had dragged in, Paul produced copious and delicious food. If there were a moment when the New World burst like a wave over my head, that was it.

Events moved with astonishing rapidity. We ate, we drank, we lay on an enormous bed with the lights on. A threesome was not my style ('too many cooks') but I was determined not to be a spoilsport – perhaps why I was urged to stay on for a party being held that very night, for which elaborate preparations had to be made. The guest of honour was to be Mrs McKinley, sister of the immensely rich Peggy Guggenheim.* Her other name was breathed with such a mixture of jokiness and awe that I didn't quite catch on: was it 'Heather' or 'Helen'? Whichever, I thought of her from then on as 'H'.†

'She takes an air-cushion about with her wherever she goes,' I was told.

'She broke her back, falling from a balcony at the Plaza.'

'Good heavens, poor thing! When was that?'

'Not so long ago. At least, that's *one* version. Her children weren't so lucky – she chucked them off first. Well, as the song goes: "My sister and I, we don't talk about that!" She might go for you, though. You're something new around here.'‡

I didn't allow the shock of such news to ruffle me; truthfully it didn't, much, in those off-beat circumstances. I was mainly pleased to think that I could be new for them when they were so absolutely new for me. I was used to my accent causing delight (and occasional mockery) but to be a novelty, in person, was something else. No one could accuse me of false modesty, yet even so it seemed to be an undeserved helping of bliss.

Guests arrived, finding me in a blur of exhaustion yet still lively,

---

* The Guggenheims had been a well-known family for decades and their influence can still be seen today (the Guggenheim Museum was named after Peggy and Mrs McKinley's uncle, Solomon). When Roddy says Peggy – who was also a famous art collector and exhibitor – was immensely rich, he meant it: some thirty years earlier she'd inherited \$2.5 million, which is the equivalent of over \$37 million today. An interesting aside: their father, Benjamin, died on board the *Titanic*.

† Her name was Hazel.

‡ The official ruling was that the fall was an accident, but rumours seem to have abounded. She was an interesting character; a prolific artist herself she lived in Paris during the bohemian twenties, as well as in London and all over the US, marrying six times.

thanks to the electric atmosphere of New York. To myself I was sounding hectic, my face distorted into a grinning mask; but to them I must
have appeared passable, for roars of laughter greeted my feeblest jokes.
Then, in came H. McKinley – and it was true, she was carrying a
doughnut-shaped rubber air-cushion covered in chintz. She was larger
than I'd imagined, and heavier, and when she sat, she spread. Paul
encouraged her to look around, and her eye lit on me. If I felt like a
rabbit mesmerised by a snake, I kept the thought to myself. Over she
came, patting the seat next to her, whilst I grinned hectically on.

Under a protective cover of aggression, she was rather nice. In the
usual run of things she might have been accustomed to getting too
much of her own way, but by choosing the company of artists she'd
made absolutely sure of coming up against stiff competition from egos
more inflated than her own. Presumably that was what she enjoyed,
because that was precisely what she got. Our chit-chat was interspersed
with routine Greenwich Village behaviour: plenty of sitting-about on
the floor, sometimes bursting into song with tunes like 'Greensleeves'
or 'The Foggy, Foggy Dew', surprisingly English and traditional. Most
of them knew the words better than I did.

Hart disappeared to attend one of his dancing classes, but not before
he'd agreed to come to McDougall on the stroke of midnight; which
meant that I had to extricate myself from Paul's party and walk back
to the Alley, savouring the crispness of the air, amazed by the clouds of
steam escaping from venting-grilles in the sidewalks. It was no more
than a short stroll, and from habit I was on time. But where was Hart?
Had he let me down? No, there he was, discreetly lurking in a distant
doorway, equally charmed by our mutual regard for punctuality. I let
him in, shushing to indicate the presence of Lee and Jackson upstairs.

All tiredness vanquished, I was as hyperactive as he was, threshing
about, totally unable to sleep when there were other and better things to
do and go on doing. What an extraordinary day and night. Where but
in New York could twenty-four hours be packed with so much without
bursting at the seams?

———

49

Next morning – or rather, later that same morning – the telephone rang. It was Paul, brushing aside my thanks with a show of impatience: 'Oh, the party . . . yes, OK, thanks, but that's not it. Say, how did you manage to make such an impression on our guest of honour? She kept asking where you'd gone.'

'Did you tell her?'

'Tell her what?'

'That I'd gone off to meet Hart?'

'Yes, of course. It simply made her keener! She's mad about you. I've been instructed to date you on her behalf, tomorrow. So, well now, when can you?'

I was exceedingly flattered, but it was disappointing to be told that our rendezvous wouldn't be in some massive brownstone house: 'No, she's going to be in a friend's apartment – it's her usual thing.' He then admitted that he'd spent half an hour tracking me down, having finally obtained the apartment telephone number from the Betty Parson's Gallery. Jackson had told me that he was having an exhibition at the Betty Parson's, but it hadn't registered. 'Won't you take me to the gallery?' I asked. 'I ought to know what Jack considers are his best pictures.'

Paul was more than willing, and from that alone I ought to have got an inkling of how well regarded Jackson was. Betty Parson's was avant-garde, a perfect setting for the thoroughly modern Pollocks. They didn't alarm me, because I'd seen so many in various stages of undress in Alphonso's studio; but there was one absolute masterpiece, a concoction of pebbles and other natural objects through which a light shone to cast a shadow on a white surface. Highly original, demanding a room all to itself to give of its best, so hardly a toy for the poor if I'd cared to give it any thought.

When I got back to McDougall Alley, I found a changed mood. Lee had taken offence at a passing remark of Jack's about one of *her* works. He welcomed me with extra enthusiasm, doubtless in order to add fuel to the flames. 'Why don't you take one or two of my paintings back to England with you?' he offered expansively.

'Love to, but there's the business of packing them properly and carting them about,' I replied, trying not to make it sound too ungracious. 'So I think I'd better not.'

Lee looked as relieved as I felt. Jackson's spirits revived, possibly because he'd had all the fun of making a generous offer without having it taken up.

Drinks, then; and more drinks. Lee abandoned us, then returned and decided to join in. Jack growled at her and I was afraid that their dispute might flare up again, but it didn't. She went off to cook a meal – in my honour, I was told. What with one thing and another, it took us up to the time when Hart was due to reappear, eager to demonstrate some of the steps he'd been taught that day.

I went downstairs with him, the better to learn. When I fell off-balance, he had to hold me up, nonchalantly taking my entire weight, but ending up happily on the floor. It was all most enjoyable, till off he had to go, back to his warehousing.

Next day was H-day. The 'friend's apartment' turned out to be no more than a few blocks away, so as usual I decided to walk. When I arrived, I wasn't sure that I'd got the right place: the battered building looked too shabby to house an affluent H, even on a temporary basis.

But there she was, rising unsteadily from a rickety chair, clutching her air-cushion, holding out both arms in greeting. I noticed that she was richly (but not smartly) dressed, so was out of keeping with her surroundings. The room was both bitty and untidy, echoing with poverty unrelieved by style. A thinly stocked bar in one corner provided little more than a slug of Bourbon, in which we both hastily indulged. Apparently no time was to be lost. After the fewest possible preliminaries she went on the offensive, a broken-down bed being pressed into service with practised skill, the light extinguished at the right moment, and so on. She was an expert cosseter, so I wasn't likely to object. On the contrary, she knew her stuff so well that I found it all most enjoyable, and said so.

Then the fun began, pure Hollywood. She told me that she was about to fly to Colorado, it didn't much matter when, as she had her own aeroplane. I was urged to come and stay indefinitely. Would I? Well, that was a teaser. My passage back to England was already booked and paid for; I didn't see myself affording another. And what if her pleasure in me quickly waned? I could see myself flying out grandly to Palm Springs then grinding slowly back to New York by Greyhound bus – not much of a prospect. So I made my excuses, leaving out that I wanted time for two tourist trips: an ascent of the Empire State tower and a boat-ride to the Statue of Liberty. When I left that shoddy apartment, the arrangement was that I would ring her up when I had a moment to spare.

The Empire State fell into my lap, as it were. Some people to whom I had an introduction took me there. It didn't remind me of laboriously climbing my previous highpoint, the spire of the *münster* in Ulm, because we whizzed up by lift and debouched on to a wired-in surround, secure enough to put paid to any temptation of visitors to throw themselves off. The same friends took me to dinner at the Savoy Plaza – a delightful mixture of the Hyde Park and Connaught hotels in London. I noted the splendid canopy which presumably broke H's fall, and thought that it might be better not to mention that part of my outing when next we met.

A visit to the Statue of Liberty was illuminating in a rather different way. In 1950 the battered old railway known as 'the El' was still running, as if on steel trestles, high across the city. Along Third Avenue the clutter of overhead rails helped create its own special atmosphere, a compound of noise, drunkenness and blatant poverty which attracted (or at any rate, didn't repel) artists, writers, actors and the like. Every journey on the El, long or short, cost a dime. I joined from Fifth Avenue, then waited on an extremely dirty platform for a train which, in spite of rattling along like an express, actually went at half the speed of carriages on the London Underground.

After the smooth luxury of Fifth Avenue, even after the down-to-earth shabbiness of Third Avenue, where I'd been beforehand, the places through which the El poked and quested seemed sordid. Decomposing brickwork supported grimy windows giving subdued light to people living lives – as seen from directly opposite – in stroboscopic flashes. It put me in mind of *The Crowd*, an early King Vidor film showing what it was like to have strangers intruding uncontrollably on private intimacies, the roar of passing trains punctuating quarrels and lovemaking impartially. No one would willingly put up with such conditions, except those who had no alternative: the poor. All districts traversed by the El were poor, the poverty differentiated according to race: Chinese; Hispanics; Blacks. Always in the background reared the skyscrapers, smooth cliffs of masonry – nothing ragged about those. They proclaimed that they were what New York wished its visitors to see.

At South Ferry, the station for Battery Point from which the Liberty steamers sailed, men with pushcarts were selling hot dogs: 10 cents for a Vienna sausage nestling on a bed of sauerkraut, protruding from small sweetish rolls, a bargain for which drugstores charged 15 cents. In the sharp wind whistling down the canyons of Wall Street, ferry passengers were waiting and shivering, dwarfed by the immensity of the financial quarter. It was obvious that we were all foreigners; even the native New Yorkers seeming like Displaced Persons. Those fitting in best were two schoolgirls chattering and barging into each other in universal schoolgirl fashion. I caught a snatch of their conversation: 'An' I said, "Aw-right, if you got more 'an two bits we can have a chocolate malted" . . . an' guess what he said? He said, "Geez, you don't want much!" . . . an' I said . . .' Giggles drowned the rest. Such wholesome liveliness provided a touch of reality to counteract the theatrical solemnity with which the rest of us piled on to the ferry. We might almost have been on our way to Lourdes.

Liberty looming ever closer was enough to dumbfound. Even her pedestal was like one of the seven wonders of the Old World, a Mausoleum of Halicarnassus reconstructed on an island off the New World. We landed on a well-kept lawn and in the biting wind we scuttled as rapidly as we could to the entrance where a wall-panel proclaimed: THE STATUE OF LIBERTY: ENLIGHTENING THE WORLD, THE SYMBOL OF FREE AMERICA. Hot air? Real gusts of warmth from an air-conditioning plant were already bearing witness to American technical inventiveness. If this were what liberty, unfettered, could achieve, then long live Liberty!

Deep inside, a spiral staircase painted battleship-grey coiled steeply upwards, so steeply and with so little space between each coil that it was impossible to stay standing upright. The thing to do was to crawl, almost in a sitting position, then flump down on to grey bucket-seats thoughtfully placed at two-step intervals. At the end of a crouching hop from perch to perch we found a circular room where perhaps as many as thirty could be squeezed in.

Round we walked, peering through the tiny windows which made up the jewels in Liberty's crown. In the distance lay Ellis Island, Liberty's antithesis, sorting centre for would-be immigrants (until its abandonment, some years later). Though past its heyday, Ellis Island could still pack a punch, a *cause célèbre* being the refusal to allow entry to such an exotic bird of passage as Vera, Lady Cathcart, on grounds of 'moral turpitude' back in '26 when I was a boy. Her crime was that she was divorced.

It was ironic to think that rascals such as myself, duly passported and visa'd (after hanging about for hours in the American Embassy in Grosvenor Square), were OK, provided that we kept our individual versions of moral turpitude under wraps.

Speaking of which, I managed a visit to the infamous Everard Baths and was bewildered by the presence of men dressed as police, guns and all, walking up and down between the heaving beds muttering 'Break it up, boys! Break it up!' as if they meant it. I couldn't easily get used to such a parody of real danger in a London bath. Admittedly, it made sex dramatic; but that wasn't at all what I wanted.

The real drama at that moment in my life was that I should have bowled over a super-rich older woman at a time when everything else was coruscating. I could hardly spare a moment for her; but alas, she could spare all too many for me. She took to telephoning at any hour. I had to admit that she wasn't boring: she had an agreeable, buttonholing way of flitting from subject to subject and she had a good mind and was prepared to use it. I liked her more and more, at a distance.

The trouble was, the hours were passing, forever urging that there wasn't a moment to lose. Hours to be spent 'chewing the fat' with Jackson, when I grew to like him so much more than his works; Paul and friends, for sheer entertainment value – yet never sacrificing a minute when there was a chance of having Hart steer course towards McDougall Alley. It was like living inside a kaleidoscope: forces beyond my control forming patterns, now simple, now complicated, at the slightest job of chance; forming and re-forming, ever-changing. I loved it for all its infinite variety but dreaded putting a foot wrong and causing offence.

The night before I was due to leave for England was particularly hectic. I had finally and decisively turned down H's invitation to Palm Springs, but could hardly refuse a grandly theatrical farewell. Nor could I abandon Hart, when his School of Dancing was staging a ball for invited guests only, complete with cabaret. The solution was to ask H to come along too. Black and White mixing in the name of Art was becoming thoroughly acceptable in New York by the end of 1950; so, as expected, she accepted with alacrity. There we all were, drinking champagne (some of which I tried to pay for, from a sense of guilt), and ourselves taking the floor occasionally. However, after the cabaret there was no reason to stay on, by which time we were all very merry.

The McKinley car had been waiting outside for the whole evening, complete with chauffeur. It happened to be pouring with rain, so we were glad to be swept along to McDougall warm and dry. The long-suffering driver had to be the one, of course, to unhitch the chain across the entrance to the mews, getting himself thoroughly wet. I got out and was just starting to say 'Good night!' to H when I saw that she was clambering out too, Hart gallantly holding open the door and being soaked for his pains.

As we stumbled indoors, Jackson happened to be on the stairs. He hailed us and was hailed with glad cries, which woke Lee. A party started up and seemed to go on interminably until at last Lee and Jack sloped off upstairs. Both Hs then confronted me, both rather worse for wear.

There was only the one sofa-bed, so there could only be one out-come: all three of us started shedding clothes and climbed into it, me in the middle. Hart switched off the light. Once again, ironically, I was committed to a threesome – as unwanted as before, but this time in the sweeping darkness of semi-drunkenness. Torrid moments could hardly rouse me to activity in any shape or form. Sleep came as suddenly as if induced by an anaesthetic.

I was woken by a force stronger even than sleep – an intense desire to pee. I rose and barged about in the dark and on my return climbed back into bed, but no longer in the middle. A spirit of devilment took control as I shoved one body against the other before taking up a new position on the outer edge. Apart from grunts, they remained as inert as sacks of potatoes. Sleep once more swooped down, though not for long: H had suddenly realised that the chap she was nuzzling was no longer me, and rebelled. She wanted out.

When I reached the light, she clambered over a still somnolent Hart and dressed haphazardly and at speed, lunging against the street door with an imperious shout. Before I could say 'That won't get you far in this weather!' I heard the sound of a car engine starting, and headlights flickered through the downpour of rain which presumably had never let up, all the time we were indoors. Her chauffeur had been patiently waiting, shivering behind the wheel, for his mistress. In a flash I under-stood what money, lots and lots of it, could achieve; and what might have been in it for me, had I chosen to play my cards right.

No good repining! There was far too much to be done in the way of fond farewells to pay much attention to flights of fancy. Hart was to accompany me to the pier from which my ship, the *Liberté*, would be steaming in two hours' time. Then Jackson and Lee were delightful as always, not asking a single question, sleepily murmuring what fun it had been. What a lovely exit! How could I ask for more?

It took years, rather than months, for it to dawn on me that the only real opportunity missed during that kaleidoscopic time in New York had been my nonchalant refusal of the offer to take 'one or two' canvases back to England. One or two Jackson Pollocks! It hardly bears thinking about! As a makeweight, of a sort, I came across one of Hart's vests amongst my dirty clothes waiting to be washed. But however fondly I regarded it, I could hardly frame and hang it up, let alone shine a light through to project its shadow on an expanse of an otherwise blank white wall.

———

50

Luxurious the *Liberté* certainly was – a prestige ship, the former *Bremen*, seized by the French from the Germans after the war. Had an individual done such a thing it would have been called 'looting', but goods officially stolen by a victor from a beaten enemy came under the heading of 'reparations'. The French had done their booty over in fine style, concentrating on First Class – in which, of course, I was not. I didn't mind. First Class was full of older people. Elsewhere we were much younger, therefore more likely to generate those bizarre experiences which were what I chiefly looked for in life.

I found myself in a two-berth cabin without a port-hole somewhere in the bowels of the ship, but as nobody came to claim the other bunk I had the 'stateroom' all to myself. Taking a cue from Toppy Tedder, I washed a couple of pairs of socks and hung them on the wire stretchers which she'd let me have as a parting present. Then I strolled up stairs so wide that the word 'companionway' seemed, for once, descriptive, and began to take stock.

There was what might be described as a Legion of the Lost: young men with baffled expressions, new to the Old World towards which they were heaving. They wouldn't remain withdrawn for long; *Liberté* being a French ship, free bottles of wine were placed on every table for lunch and dinner. When alcohol began to take effect, tongues were loosened and friendships struck up.

I turned my attention to two North Americans who looked agreeably dotty, Sylvia Braverman and Kenny Scott. They weren't averse to me joining them after they made it clear that they weren't 'a couple', 'just good friends', and that I was to be awarded to Sylvia. Once those ins and outs had been disentangled, the three of us managed splendidly, laughing our way into First Class (which we were politely asked to leave) and carrying-on generally.

Sylvia was a dress-designer, which called to mind high jinks with Peryl in 'Once Upon a Time'; but she was nothing like that instructress in the Cleopatran arts of love. Somewhere along the line, she'd married. 'For money!' said Kenny when he wanted to tease her. 'He was a complete drip and he had one of those Jewish hang-ups about domesticity and raising a family.'

'Anyway, it didn't work out!' was Sylvia's reply. 'So we're separated, at least for now. He keeps saying he wants to start us all up again, that's the trouble.'

'What? That bore? Not on your life, Syl!'

They soon switched to talking about the Princess of Berar* who had taken them up as unconventional companions for night-club junketings. 'The Princess was beautiful, but she was lonely,' they agreed. 'Fun while it lasted, but such a waste of time!'

When I showed Sylvia my cabin her reaction to the cubby-hole was an endearing 'OOhh!' What intrigued her most were the socks drying on their stretchers. 'You really are house-trained,' she said. 'How lov-erly!'

I had never seen myself in that light before, but greedy, as ever, for a compliment, I squeezed her nearest arm. It led to 'trying out the bunk' – and where that was leading soon became obvious.

However, she wished to observe some niceties. 'The light's too

---

* Dürrüşehvar Sultan, the only daughter of Abdulmejid II (the Caliph of the Ottoman Dynasty), and the last heir apparent to the Ottoman Imperial throne until it was dismantled in 1924.

bright!' she said after the shortest interval. Economical French elegance had evidently baulked at tackling the lowliest of cabins, for there was only the one main light in the ceiling and another, unsubtle, bed-light for reading by. Sylvia took off a kind of Indian shawl she happened to be wearing (India being her current theme) and draped it over the ceiling-light, switching off the other. By it we cavorted, absorbed in what we were doing . . .

For perhaps twenty minutes only, because of an unwelcome inter-ruption: fists beating a tattoo on the door, shouts of '*OUVREZ! OUVREZ!*' and other words in excited French.

'What can they want?' I whispered. 'Perhaps, if we don't make a sound, they'll go away?'

But there was no hope of that. Shoulders thudded against the door, which we had prudently locked. It shuddered, and there were more shouts of '*OUVREZ!*' There was only one thing to do.

Shouting '*Un moment!*' I climbed over Sylvia, clutching some piece of her clothing to cover my nakedness. Meanwhile, she scrambled under the bedclothes which, being on board ship, were folded in such a way that they didn't seem to have an 'under'. Mystified, I opened the door an inch or two. It was flung open to admit an inrush of stewards storming our love-nest, then stopping in their tracks with expressions of utmost delicacy – '*Mais Madame . . . je vous en prie!*' and so on – before gazing wildly about and spotting the ceiling-light draped in its shawl. Dramatically, the thing was yanked down, scrunched between fingers, and waved in my face. All was suddenly clear: close contact with the heat of the light had made the shawl smoulder; it had already charred in the middle. Smoke must have curled round the ceiling and escaped through a grille above the door, alerting a watchful steward.

'Oh dear!' sighed Sylvia.

It was indeed 'Oh dear!'

Passengers blocked the passage outside, none of them half as tactful as the steward. Loud American voices harangued and badgered, one woman repeating an unlovely 'I wanna know pree-cisely!' and elbowing her way in. The sight of Sylvia made her open and shut her mouth in silent disapproval till I felt like letting go of the blouse I was clutching round my waist and really giving her something to mull over.

At last they all cleared off, leaving an officer to give us a reproachful lecture on the dangers of fire down below. We apologised profusely, of course, fearing that we hadn't heard the last of it.

Nor had we. Spread by bush-telegraph, the story was soon all over the ship. Next morning we were being given strange sideways glances. Kenny declared that we'd be clapped in irons. It was not long before the Captain sent for us, via an officer discreetly murmuring in Sylvia's ear whilst we sat with Kenny in the lounge, brazening it out. We followed the man nervously to the bridge, hearts thumping.

What we found was a Captain frowning theatrically, then suddenly wreathed in smiles, taking us down to his private quarters and welcoming us to his domain with kisses on both cheeks and an *apéritif*. 'I am very concerned about you two,' said this lovely man, gravely. 'You must promise me never to do such a foolish thing again!' We promised. 'In that case, I would be charmed to offer you the freedom of my ship,' he went on. 'You may go where you please. First Class, any time you wish – anywhere – the freedom of my ship!' And with that he pressed another drink upon us and chatted away with utmost geniality, patting both of us impartially whenever he felt so inclined. We walked on air back down to my cabin, to celebrate in the manner so rudely interrupted, with the ceiling-light switched off.

On seeing us skipping into the lounge later, Kenny pretended surprise: 'Out on bail?'

'We thought of offering you a drink some place else, if you'd care to come along with us?'

'Somewhere less public, you mean? I don't blame you.'

We took him boldly through to First Class, where the bar-steward put up a hand and whispered to his assistant. A few hours earlier it would have been a signal to ask us to leave, but now it was because he wanted to serve us drinks on the house. It was the stuff of dreams. All the same, we didn't want to linger long in such a rarefied atmosphere.

All too soon the voyage ended, just two days before Christmas 1950. A few months later, Sylvia wrote from France, saying that I must come and stay with her in Paris. I replied swiftly and was soon making my way to the garret in Montmartre where she had found a perch, *sous les toits de Paris*, the clever girl.

It was like straying on to a film-set for simultaneous productions of *La Bohème* and *Seventh Heaven*. A rickety lift shuddered up to the floor below hers in a rickety house reeking (amongst other things) of artistic charm. Then there were the uneven stairs to her studio, which consisted of one enormous room in which the whole of life had to take place.

Accessible through a window, an unstable arrangement of wooden planks and iron railings provided space for pot-plants and came in handy for Sylvia's poodle at times when it would have been inconvenient to take it into the street for 'walkies'.

On first acquaintance, the studio froze the marrow, but that was before lighting a pot-bellied stove and feeding it with packages of fuel wrapped in brown paper, when it warmed up amazingly quickly. The stove was in the habit of giving a sudden cough, causing the cinder-door, embossed and shaped like a tortoise, to fly open with a *whooosh* and a tinkle. At such times it probably released clouds of carbon monoxide, but we were seldom there long enough to be seriously affected.

We went to the Café Flore and the Deux Magots, as was the duty of anyone with pretensions to be avant-garde, but we saw no obvious existentialists. At my special request, we squeezed inside the tiny Grand Guignol theatre for the scene where a thief, locked in a cell with a madman, has his face held down and fried on top of a stove not unlike Sylvia's. The screams, the burns and blisters were fearfully realistic. For years I'd heard of this famous 'Theatre of Cruelty', but when acted out on a stage, 'fanciful' seemed a more descriptive word than 'terrifying' for such goings-on. Each playlet was so dramatic in its frightfulness that at times the audience giggled. It brought home to me once again that I was not myself a sadist; nor, for that matter, a masochist. I could see no point in inflicting pain; and as for having it inflicted, why court discomfort?

Our *vie de Bohème* came to an end when I ran out of excuses for not buckling down again to Tedder's Life. Next thing, Sylvia soon discovered that her career might be furthered by coming to London with a portfolio of fashion-drawings, press-cuttings and so forth, when she would be very welcome to stay with me. She arrived, and obtained plenty of interviews, but nothing much beyond promises.

To cheer her up, I took her down to Langney – a risky business. I should have known that my mother would view her with deep suspicion, supposing her to be in the running for my fame and fortune (both at that time non-existent). Sylvia was uncomplaining, so at least that couldn't be held against her. Her lack of money wasn't the important factor either, because she was obviously talented enough to earn plenty; but my mother may have thought that she wouldn't have time to spare to look after me. All in all, the visit was not a success, and I continued looking after myself without too much trouble, as before. Where would it all lead me? There were more New Worlds to be explored, if and when the stars would align to show me the way.

51

When Sylvia returned to Paris, I knuckled down to Tedder's Life. Milton Waldman, my editor at Collins the publishers, went off to East Africa, instructing Peter Wyld to carry on the battle – against me, as it so happened: 'Chapter One is extremely remote from your subject and a cause of distress to the reader'. And when he'd handed the type-script to some other literary 'expert', the result had been discouraging in the extreme: 'He went so far as to say that it was out of the question to publish it with the first chapter, but then he did not know that we had already signed the contract.' Well, that was a blow. I didn't know quite how to reply to such a broadside. Obviously, he disagreed with the whole style of the book. I had to assume that they knew their busi-ness, which meant that I must be wrong. I cast out all the entertaining embellishments, jettisoning this, jettisoning that, finally producing a truncated version, shorn of oddity.

It worried me that much of my life, let alone my writing, would be considered undesirable by the majority of people in England, perhaps everywhere. There was this dichotomy; I was only considered 'respect-able' by those who knew next to nothing about me. If I were to portray my real outlook, my own private version of the truth, it might be pub-lished by some daring entrepreneur; or again, it might not. Failure to get published would be to remain safely unknown, but success might mean public disgrace. Which did I prefer?

When *Tedder* came out, the reviews were uniformly good. We were still near enough to the war to prevent critics from 'knocking' what purported to be the true story of a principal architect of victory. No critic was prepared to say that the book was uninspiring; perhaps none of them were expecting it to be anything else. (Incidentally, from the moment that the biography was approved, Tedder became as distant as an Olympian. I attended his installation as Chancellor of Cambridge

University, and he sent me a photograph of Toppy in answer to my con-
dolences on her death; and that was the sum total of our future contacts.)

What next to write? As I couldn't think of any other contemporary
character to write about, my thoughts reverted to the South Seas. A
travel book – yes. A novel or two, lushly set in a mosquito-haunted
Paradise – yes. I decided to split myself into three: a prim Quaker
governess, an amoral beachcomber, and an observant onlooker. Our
destinies would fictionally intertwine, in order to present a factual
account on three planes of perception. I even toyed with the thought
of getting 'us' all into bed (separately, not as a threesome, which might
have stretched things too far). All three were aspects of myself – a
revelation for the closing words of the final chapter. Alas, hardly had I
completed the synopsis before being told, in no uncertain terms, that
such a fantasy would be rejected out of hand by any publisher. I was
obliged to fall back on a conventional, personalised travelogue, 'acceptable' overall - i.e. with most of the amorous adventures changed.

It was thwarting, because I knew that with very few exceptions
every young man's world revolved around sex: the thought of it; the
procurement of it, whenever – not as something incidental, but as the
great driving-force in life. I understood that love could be an even
greater force, but in a different way. So, when sex and love chanced to
coincide, it was a wonderful bonus rather than a foregone conclusion.
It seemed so obvious to me that I would hardly have thought it worth
mentioning but for the extraordinary delusion which I kept encountering: namely, that sex and love were only legitimate when they sprang
out of each other. Utter nonsense! Possible, yes. Probable, maybe. But
no more than that.

However, I was forced to admit that what I wanted, above all else,
was to be published, for which I would sacrifice any number of 'unprint-
able' ideas. Not to mention the fact that in those days frankness might
provoke not only publicity but trouble with the Law – factors genuinely
to be feared, until such time as the law changed. How was I to guess
that the day would come when nothing, literally nothing, would be
considered too shocking to appear in print? I ought to have looked for
another crystal to consult, for by that time my minor peccadillos would
seem tame indeed.

And so I settled down to write *Where the Poor are Happy* as a travelogue shorn of fantasy, followed by *Green Heart of Heaven* and *Worse than
Wanton*, two novels set on the imaginary island of Manahoa. There was

to have been a third, to complete a trilogy, but I never got round to it, being heartily sick of my main characters.

Where the Poor are Happy came out in spring '54, attracting good reviews. I considered the title one of my best; it was what people yearned to believe about the South Seas. Truncated as it was, with imaginative parts deleted, the book nevertheless gave me small reminiscent thrills of pleasure (insofar as any of his works can satisfy a writer). Contracts were being drawn up for future books with a South Seas setting, so my literary life could be said to be progressing satisfactorily, if not exactly prospering. I was learning that writing was unlikely to be highly profitable except for the author of a bestseller, and I didn't think that I had much chance of becoming such a *rara avis*.

I did receive a big royalty cheque from Collins for *Tedder*, though. The amount was larger than expected, possibly because the uninspiring but accurate book became required reading for all students of air power. In those days, new cars were hard to come by. Whilst Morvyne was always happy to kindly lend me her baby Ford, I wanted a car of my own. Hearing of a garage in the East End where a Morris Minor could be obtained without months on a waiting list, I decided to splurge my whole royalty – a lovely way of making the money memorable.

Hardly had I acquired my Little Wonder before hearing that a great-aunt of mine – Evie* – had died. My presence was urgently required, so the first 'running in' trip in the new car was to Lincolnshire, in order to hold my grandmother's hand.

It was a freezing December day when we drove from Claxby Hall to Skegness, to the horrible little house where Evie had spent her last days. Seen through the eyes of grown-ups, she had been a comically mournful character, ever on the look-out for a likely man, advancing years being no bar to her appetite or its fulfilment. I found myself in sympathy with her.

A little while afterwards, it turned out that she had left her estate to my sisters and me – an absolute shock, and one that turned out whoops for joy from all three of us. The exception was that Aunt Susan was to have first choice of furniture, whereupon my awful aunt tried to 'rescue' – as she put it – all the best bits, until we shamed her into disgorging them in favour of Genissa. Well Vale was overstocked already, whereas Genissa, who'd settled with her husband Michael Harding of

---

* Evie was Roddy's maternal grandmother's sister.

the Birling Gap family in Sussex, was shortly to give birth to a son, Charles, and needed furniture to help fill empty spaces.

Incidentally, the wedding had taken place at Well Vale by the reluctant courtesy of Uncle Dick, who (once again and infallibly, it seemed) showed his wicked side when he discovered, to his horror, that I was the one who'd been asked to give the bride away. On the day, as we were leaving the house for the church perched high and away at the head of the Vale, my uncle came up to me, smiling and pretending to be diffident but actually very determined.

'I hear you are going to make a speech,' he said.

'Oh yes, Genissa has asked me to,' I replied.

'I don't think that will be necessary.'

'Oh don't you? Well, I DO!'

It was anyone's guess how that confrontation might have ended. Bishop Harland, Bishop of Lincoln, who was about to conduct the ceremony, swung round and simply interposed himself between us, smiling earnestly. My uncle turned away, shrugging his shoulders, still managing a shy, sly grin.

I was white and shaking, too shaken even to produce one of my all-pervading blushes. His malice had shattered me so much that as soon as the ceremony ended I retired to a corner to make a brief note on the back of a wedding-invitation. In a hand squiggly with outrage I wrote: 'It was as if I'd been an interloper. Alas, to him, that was just what I was. I was poor. He was rich. I was young. He was old. What sort of victory could victory over me be to him? I still can't understand.'

I never did understand, either. It was such an amateur effort at putting me down; so silly. Yet he wasn't a silly man, though at times pathologically mean. How I wished that he might sometimes behave decently towards me! But he hardly ever did.

My grandmother and I went to view Evie's corpse in the local undertaker's 'chapel'. It looked dreadful: sunken face with orange cheeks and a velvet bow to its neck. Worse, it was the face of an old man. The 'rat' which she always wore had been removed, leaving only her own hair, teased in white wisps over an otherwise bald head. How she would have hated ending up so unseductively presented by the undertaker's men!

Her blessing had provided something in the region of £7000 for each of us children.

'I fear you won't be getting yourself a proper job now,' said my grandmother severely.

'On the contrary,' I answered pompously, 'my proper job can now properly begin!'

The reply was a snort. To her, writing was something to be done in one's spare time, when the weather was too bad for such serious pursuits as hunting and shooting; even then it needed to compete with Public Service.

And so there I was: for the time being not in need of the money writing would bring, yet wanting to write something that wasn't stuck in the fictional South Seas I'd so reluctantly and yet gratefully created. Perhaps what I needed was new inspiration? Asking that question, and having the means to do so, was perhaps the first star to align.

———

52

Following those idyllic days in the South Seas, my travels had led to a plethora of confusing experiences in the way of sex. After swinging like a pendulum between the two inherent sides of my nature, I was coming to rest mainly amongst the men. Male, not female, romantic connections would be providing the networks for my future. It was a profound change, however much I'd seen it coming. I knew myself well enough to foresee that sex alone wouldn't do for long. Love, I trusted, was bound to crop up at some point; not a quiet love, but adoration to the sound of trumpets, if the past were anything to go by.

While I hunted for it, there were plenty of other distractions to soothe the most savage of breasts, the Vic Wells Ball being one of them. The ball was remarkable for those days. Men could go dressed as men, as women, or as intermediates; nobody cared, nobody objected. The takings went to a theatrical charity, which served to cast a mantle of respectability over some pretty rum goings-on. It took place in the Lyceum, where parties could book tables up on the balcony. I attended it two years running, Peter Hiley – the school friend who'd helped me secure paperwork to get into Tahiti – once again doing the honours.

On my best occasion I went as a beachcomber, in patched blue denim trousers and a floral shirt which Anne and Lou Werner had given to Turia (who'd passed it on to me). It felt lovely to be in such gear again. My spirit was dancing long before we reached the Lyceum. Once there, I leaped into action with both women and men dressed as women, impartially. There were the inevitable parodies of Mae West and Carmen Miranda,* even a Phyllis Dixey, an icon-of-the-day on account of looking like a suburban housewife whilst stripping to the buff on stage. There, too, were those dressed to resemble characters they hoped to attract. As, for instance, Basil Clavering, the notoriously maso-chistic proprietor of the Cameo chain of cinemas, swaggering about in the khaki uniform and red beret of a paratrooper.

In the early hours of the morning, I spotted a pirate, dancing clum-sily. What did that matter? He was very good-looking in a swarthy, piratical way, with broad shoulders owing nothing to padding. On seeing him retreat by himself to a corner, I hurried over before anyone else could step in, to ask for the pleasure of the next waltz. He smiled back boldly, yet shyly, as though not too sure of himself, before saying in a Scottish accent, 'I can only dance as a man, you know.'

'Oh, that's my line too!' I said. 'We'll just trot around the floor. We'll manage!'

Off we went, stumbling a little – mostly my fault – until beckoned over by one of the attendants. 'Excuse me, gents,' he said, 'but we don't allow two gentlemen to dance together.'

'Not allow?' I repeated. 'But what else d'you see all around you? I mean – just look!'

'Oh, those are gentlemen with gentlemen dressed as ladies. That's quite in order! It's two gentlemen dancing together dressed as gentlemen that's forbidden.'

'HEAVENS!!'

'We have to observe some rules, sir!'

'Well, we'd better drown our sorrows,' I said to my un-partner, who had begun looking cross and embarrassed. As it happened, I found the episode not wholly unproductive, because anger loosened his tongue. He told me that his name was 'Shone', which I supposed was his way of pronouncing 'John', and that he'd come to the big city hoping to find a job in the theatre. It seemed rather an unlikely aspiration for someone looking like a garage-hand, but what a splendid garage-hand! Good

---

* The Portuguese-born Brazilian singer well known for wearing fruit hats in films.

physique, doggy eyes and an attractive brogue, even if it were a dash too strong for professional purposes.

When the ball ended, I asked him back home. He said he had nothing better to do. Back I drove him to Queen's Gate where without further ado we hopped into the double-bed.

'I don't mind a bit of sky-larking, Rod,' he said. 'But I'd be happier with the lights out.'

A pity. He was hairy in all the right places and muscular, with another attraction, a soft/hard manner uniquely his own, effectively extinguished by darkness. However, my policy was never to argue about such things. It would be nice to claim that this was one of the best nights ever, but that wouldn't be true. As indicated, he didn't mind mild goings-on, but wasn't enthusiastic, merely tolerant – an unexceptional King Log.

Next morning – as ever, it was really later on that same morning – I drove him back to where he was staying in Manchester Square, to a flat owned by 'Vince', a clothes-merchant rapidly gaining fame by marketing figure-gripping men's underwear exhibited by imagination-seizing male models. My pirate chum apparently slept on a kind of day-bed in Vince's sitting-room. His host wasn't about, so there was no one to create a scene. I made a tentative date for the future, but it was cancelled by a friendly telephone call next day. I thought: *Oh well, that's that. Mustn't grumble!*

I ought to have brought one of those paraffin-lamp bases back with me from Tahiti, for this would have been the time to peer into its cloudy depths. At that moment, the name of that actor come south to seek his fortune meant nothing to anyone. Who could have guessed that he would shoot up as spectacularly as he did, showering an admiring world with thunderclaps? One of the great heart-throbs of our times, even voted 'the sexiest man alive'.*

A less obvious stage for 'rum goings-on' was the Coronation of Queen Elizabeth, on 2 June 1953. The world seemed to descend upon London to witness it. My day began with Harry Nuttall† at Patricia Denny's. Both were good friends of mine. I'd met Harry in the Fitzroy, a brainy

---

* All the clues point to this being Sean Connery, who would have been in his early twenties at the time, seeking to become an actor after an early career as a body-builder.

† No known connection with Sir Harry Nuttall of motorsport fame.

sparkler from Bolton who was a type new to me because, though a down-to-earth Northerner, he was also, as the saying went, 'as camp as Chloe'. I met Patricia through Harry. She was divorced from Denny's Pork Sausages, living in Upper Addison Gardens and sheltering Gina Edwards, who'd fled from those classics of melodrama, a drunken, spendthrift father and a costive *malade-imaginaire* of a mother. However unlikely it sounded, Gina had become pregnant as the result of taking a bath immediately after her boyfriend, a drip called George, who admitted that he'd tossed himself off in it.

Patricia had a distinguished lodger, HRH Prince Alexander of Yugoslavia,* working as a pilot for BEA, who lost no time in becoming more than a lodger. The first time I met him he appeared in his dark blue pilot's uniform, exhausted from flying.

'And who's this bod?' he'd asked.

'This bod's Rod,' I'd replied.

'This bod's Rod? Good God!' he said, rolling his eyeballs. The way in which he said it made it endearing and delightful, coming from such a bear-like man. I wanted to hug him; and in fact, whenever we met from then on, that's what we innocently did. On the day of the Coronation, Alex was, of course, elsewhere with the 'greats and grands' – in this case his relations, the Kents.

To view the Coronation carriages to best advantage, Harry and I walked across Hyde Park. When the procession was over, the ensuing *mêlée* allowed me to get hold of Ali Akhbar Khan, a Black Sergeant from one of the Empire contingents, skin shining as if buffed with boot-polish, who couldn't wait to be made a fuss of. His desire was granted and we parted with mutual regard. For once, enthusiasm was allowed to run riot. Whatever went on during that day, the police stood by with tolerant smiles.

My Coronation goings-on were no worse than they'd been for some time, only it was easier to misbehave during the atmosphere of festive relaxation. I had no regrets, though I had plenty of qualms about laying myself open to the Law.

There was a significant shift in the 1950s towards 'cracking down' on male homosexuality, and fear of being caught was very real. The

---

* This refers to the prince born in 1924 – who died in 2016, the 'globe-trotting playboy prince' according to his *Daily Telegraph* Obituary – not to be confused with Alexander, Crown Prince of Yugoslavia, born in 1945.

'Montagu Case'* brought the anomalous situation more into the public mind than anything since the trials of Oscar Wilde. The worst horror was what befell the least guilty, Michael Pitt-Rivers, who was given a longer sentence than Edward Montagu himself. I had a personal connection with Michael Pitt-Rivers. Not long ago I'd been sailing with him and a couple of friends down the Seine on a boat called *Barracuda*; he'd been the navigator and a very lovely man he was. It seemed too unfair, and also personally disquieting for me, should anyone care to do any digging . . .

It was some small consolation that the RAF men were booed by many of those waiting outside the court. The trial of Alan Turing (the hero who had helped crack the Enigma code and thus significantly shortened the war) hadn't made nearly such an impact on the public as this, involving a real live Lord. It was an interesting side-light on English snobbery that the whole episode did more to change an intolerably unjust law than anything else in years.†

Before, during and after the Montagu trial I had to contend with the certainty that however good, or kind, or highly moral (in all other directions) I might be, I could be hauled before a magistrate at the drop of a hat, if the hat were dropped in the wrong place. To understand this was a cause of deep disquiet, pervading every aspect of life; yet in the company of others I had to ignore such feelings as though they didn't exist – as indeed, for those others, they didn't.

I happened to survive unscathed, but with far too many near-misses for comfort. For those who came a cropper, usually by sheer mischance, I always felt the greatest sympathy. *There but for the Grace of God* . . .

It will perhaps come as no surprise that all this resulted in an urge to 'flee'. I'd gone swimming in the open-air pool at Roehampton and got into conversation with a young man called Abdul-Nabi al-Sharif; I didn't know quite *how* young until he told me that he'd just finished at Millfield, the public school much favoured by Gulf parents. He was engaging, in spite of a raw American accent and a trans-oceanic hankering after 'a good time' without knowing precisely what he meant by that. Though not exactly at the carpet-slipper stage, my Nuthouse

---

* In 1954, Lord Montagu, his cousin Michael Pitt-Rivers and his friend Peter Wildeblood were accused by two men from the RAF of encouraging them in homosexual behaviour. All three men were convicted, Montagu receiving twelve months in prison while Pitt-Rivers and Wildeblood received eighteen.

† Lord Montagu's trial is credited with prompting the 1957 Wolfenden Report which recommended the decriminalisation of homosexuality, which would take place in 1967.

days were long past, so I could be of no help there, but he was happy enough to play a game of squash instead. I took him to 55 Park Lane, not letting on that I'd originally been taken there myself by the junior pro, with whom I'd subsequently spent the night. I was relieved to find that my pro chum was no longer employed in that rather swish place.

'How come you don't write about Bahrain?' Abdul-Nabi asked accusingly, whilst we stood together under a shower. 'My family would make you welcome. *Betna betek*, our house is yours!'

'What a splendid idea! I'd love to, but I'll have to give it some thought,' I said.

I went as far as asking about visas for the Persian Gulf, but was somewhat put off when told that foreigners weren't allowed to stay in Bahrain unless they had a firm or a person to stay with. I couldn't imagine that my welcome at the al-Sharif house could be stretched to weeks, let alone months.

So for the time being I fled for a short while to Cyprus (on an aircraft bearing the name of Sir John Franklin, my great-great-great-uncle, the Arctic explorer who'd died – so I'd been told – discovering the North-West Passage). On one side of me sat a Mr Forbes-Sempill and on the other Sir Paul Latham, whose subsidised but unpaid companion I was. Paul (very rich due to a £100,000 coming-of-age inheritance from his father) had suggested the flight as a means of getting away from it all for the same reasons I had. He had only one leg, having lost the other by falling between a platform and a departing train when in angry pursuit of a lover threatening to leave him for ever. His disability had prevented him from any really active kind of war service, leaving him free to take an interest in politics; also in young soldiers manning an anti-aircraft battery near Herstmonceux Castle, his home in Sussex. He'd been caught 'molesting' one of them (who'd only complained to save his own skin). A tolerant Commanding Officer happened to be absent at the time; his second-in-command, a self-righteous prig, whizzed a complaint through to Higher Authority. The resulting short prison sentence left Sir Paul as damaged in mind as he was in body.

The Forbes-Sempill sitting on the other side of me was something of a mystery. Was he, in fact, a fully fledged 'Mr' at all? That very day the papers were carrying reports about Robert Cowell, ex-Spitfire pilot, who'd become a blonde 'Roberta' after a series of painful operations. Stories were current of another sex-change in the opposite direction involving 'a Grosvenor heiress'.

'I bet you anything you like our Mr Forbes-Sempill is the one they're talking about!' declared Paul.

But apparently not: during the course of conversation he claimed to be no more than a moderately successful theatrical entrepreneur.

Paul wouldn't believe it: 'I'm positive he's that Westminster gal; it's written all over him!'

The trip was short, and back in London I was occasionally prey to melancholy. One old friend was a contributory cause: Bridget Chetwynd, who I still saw much of, was going downhill, as I reluctantly had to admit. Her face and what could be seen of her body (she liked wearing a wrap-around blouse) was covered in red blebs, joining up to form a roughened surface which, she said, itched continually. She thought that it might be a form of lupus, so she regularly plastered herself with a patent garlicky ointment which stank to high heaven. I was none the wiser to the real cause, but she was still as inventive as of old.

Thanks to her I re-met Meric Dobson, whom I'd known slightly when he took a room opposite Balliol. Meric was the brother of Wayland Dobson who, with Iona Knabenshue, had given the famous 'non-husband-and-un-wife' party during my time at Oxford. Meric had become a financial adviser in Kuwait, which he described as the biggest boom-Sheikhdom of all time. Next thing, he was inviting me to stay with him, using the same words as Abdul-Nabi: '*Betna betek!*' Remembering that invite, too, I asked, 'What period of time does that welcome usually extend to?'

'Three days, perhaps ten at most. But of course you could stay with *me* as long as you like, no strings attached.'

'Would a Bahraini who'd said the same turn a guest out into the street?'

'Not if the guest had *baraka*, the power to bless your host by simply being there. They have a saying: "The fate of every man is written on his forehead". It's not a thing you can guarantee in advance, so it's no good looking at yourself in a mirror. But you never know, you might strike lucky from the word go by being *thought* to possess *baraka*.'

And so the Persian Gulf, like a cloud no bigger than a man's hand, was looming larger day by day.

———

53

The final star shone brightest.

Other than writing for my living, quests for sex and the hiding of them, I found time to make some friends for life, most of whom had one thing in common – 'common' they were not. One of those was Geoffrey Prendergast, who had achieved a kind of immortality by featuring as Christian de Clavering's guest in old Cyril Connolly's brilliant 'Where Engels Fears to Tread'.* Prendy had a genuine thirst for 'amusing people'; but alas, that was not his only thirst. Drink soon became a problem ... but not when I first got to know him. At that propitious time, his *entrain* made him welcome almost anywhere. I was given a demonstration, one day, during a walk in Hyde Park when Prendy spotted Rita Essayan sitting alone on a bench. Accusing her of being a lizard, waiting for the sun to warm her up, he jollied her into joining us for a two-mile walk. She was the only daughter of Calouste Gulbenkian, the Armenian oil-mogul known as 'Mr 5 Per Cent' – witty and kind, in a coarsely saurian way.

Peter Hiley, that old school friend who had been so helpful with regard to Tahiti and then the Vic Wells Ball, had become business manager to the Oliviers† and was sharing a flat in Albert Hall Mansions with Sir Ralph Anstruther. Ralph was also an Old Etonian – though I hadn't known him then – and a great friend of Richard Neville, one of my oldest school friends; so I felt included in a cosy coterie even when I couldn't afford to keep up with them.

Another meeting was of quite another sort. Gordon, a Naval-looking type, dressed in a military-style mackintosh, standing behind me, coughing, at Speaker's Corner, was the features sub-editor on one of the Beaverbrook newspapers. He happened to be there to meet (by way of

---

* You'll remember that Cyril Connolly was the famous literary critic Roddy met through Bridget Chetwynd when he first moved to London. In 1945, he published *The Condemned Playground*, a collection of essays, one of which was the spoof 'Where Engels Fears to Tread'.

† As in Laurence Olivier and his wife Vivien Leigh.

a conventional introduction) an American Fulbright Foundation scholar at Oxford called Ernest Hofer, of whom he would become suffocatingly fond.

One day in January 1952, Ernest (on quarrelling with Gordon – not for the first time) had taken himself off to the Harrow Road Turkish Baths, where he encountered an Irishman, Nick Walsh, and arranged for another meeting another day. Meanwhile, he made it up with Gordon, so there could be no question of him keeping the assignation. Would I stand in for him? Ernest enthused over what he called the 'donkey rig' of his new chum, adding: 'He's no spring chicken and his face is a bit battered, but he's sure to suit!'

I accepted, and duly turned up at the Roebuck at the appointed hour and hung about, studying every face to see whether it might conceivably belong to my blind date. For nearly half an hour no one seemed to fit, until in came a powerfully built dark stranger who strode over to the bar and ordered himself a pint of Guinness before looking around with casual (but I thought studied) indifference. On catching my eye, he winked and gave an almost imperceptible nod. I drifted over, not knowing quite what to think. He tapped his foot and stared into his glass, then said, without looking at me, 'Come here often?'

'First time, as a matter of fact.'

'Hmmm!'

I decided on a bold leap: 'Is your name Nick, by any chance?'

The effect it had on the man could only be described as 'electric'. He jerked, turned pale and muttered 'JEE-sus, MAry!' apparently devoid of speech.

I realised that I might have managed things more tactfully. 'The American couldn't make it, so he asked me to come instead,' I explained. 'Now that we've met, what'll you have?'

'No, I spoke to you first. What will you be dthrinking?'*

'Whatever you're having!'

Some pints later we staggered back to Queen's Gate.

'I'm still shaking like a jelly!' said Nick.

'We'll soon cure that,' I said in eager anticipation, this time with my voice shaky.

*

---

* Here and in other lines of Nick's speech, readers will notice that Roddy has attempted to convey Nick's Irish accent.

Nick was a good deal older than me and not who I expected to fall in love with, which in a way made him especially my 'type'. He could be inconsequential – one of the more charming things about him. He might suddenly come out with a coarse and extraordinary statement, often in the form of a question, such as: 'How's your arse for blisters?' At first I'd be completely bewildered, until he taught me the required answer, which was: 'The same as your belly for spots!' They were catchphrases, as repetitive as the jokes accompanying numbers called at Bingo, but far more shocking.

At times, he would refer to his childhood in Kilkenny; here, too, there were shocks: 'Me and my brothers were put to sleeping in the one bed. There was high old times we had, playing wid each other – "keeping it in the family", you might say!'

I particularly liked the way he would never light a cigarette without passing it on to me before seeing to one for himself, which was what I'd do for him too. Such little moments were intimately amicable, but I had to be prepared for them to change rapidly, for very little reason – he could fall into the foulest of moods. I tried to be glad that I had to make constant adjustments to my own behaviour to suit his temperament – a novel process for me, certainly.

A few days after we met, I took Nick to see 'Willie-the-Witch', down amongst the dustbins. Aelwyn was perfectly succinct in his opinion: 'That one is the real thing, mark my words! Of course he's as wild as a hawk, as the Irish often are. You won't be in for an easy time, not for one moment!'

With both the encouragement and warning ringing in my ears, I took Nick on a camping holiday in Wales. Songs were bursting out all over from both of us as we drove through Salisbury Plain – sheer, bubbling happiness. Nick would sometimes grip my knee and I would squeeze the gripping hand and grip back, until oncoming traffic forced me to attend to my driving.

We stopped at Stonehenge, where there were no charabancs and scarcely a single other visitor. Stonehenge demonstrated an important difference between us. We had run out of smokes. I was so enthralled by the stone circle that I really didn't care, but Nick seemed to have no other thought in his head except to drive on to some pub where he could satisfy his craving. Stonehenge to him was just an old ruin; he would have preferred it roofed and with a shop handy. It made me realise that our expedition was likely to provide a source of friction about what sort of things to stop and see. Would that really matter, if every other aspect were so pleasing?

The first night out we were too tired to erect a tent so we stayed in a bed-and-breakfast place. The second evening found us deep in lush grass in a field near Rhayader. It rained during the night, and in the morning the tent shuddered to the sound of munching and mooing as cows came questing against the guy-ropes, curious to see what the two humans jammed inside were up to. I could have saved them the query: after a night of bliss we were mainly worried about getting soaked, from the tent leaking all along its ridge. Fortunately I was able to produce hot water both for shaving and for tea. When dealing with a Primus, my right hand hadn't lost its cunning.

Other nights, other sites. We could generally obtain butter and sliced white bread (never wholesome brown) from friendly farms after asking permission to camp in their field. Nick procured a chicken which he plucked and then boiled, a process that took him hours and made him so bad-tempered that it was hardly worth it. But even when he was cross I found his turn of phrase delightfully Irish.

Being by birth an 'Owen of Bettws', I wanted to visit the ancestral home in Montgomeryshire, if it still existed. It happened to be a day of disagreements, and as the search promised to produce more of the same, I reluctantly dropped the idea. Hoping to placate Nick by downgrading my family origins, I said, 'The place is probably no more than a glorified farmhouse,' but he remained moody and silent. I was learning that it took him a longish time to get over what he took as a slight – a thing which I much regretted, never believing in nursing minor grievances. Mulling over a wrong was best reserved for life's few really catastrophic back-handers, I considered.

Another paradox: Nick was unbelievably sensitive. For such a tough man, he was almost feminine, with a larger bump of intuition than anyone I'd ever met, which he put down to being the seventh son of a seventh son. That quality deserved to be (and was) highly prized by me. For his part, he may have liked being with someone who 'thought the world' of his rough/smoothness and didn't treat him just as a jolly drinking-companion (which was how most of his mates did). At least, I hoped that I was right; there was always the possibility that I was exaggerating my own importance in his life.

As we drove back to London, I was what might be called 'a prey to mixed feelings'. Our mutual enjoyment had risen above all the setbacks of what ended up being a very rainy trip, but it had been a close-run thing at times.

Back home, I kept out of Nick's way for the next few days – even though his leave was shortly coming to an end – until I could bear it no longer and begged him to come round, which he did. Everything went so swimmingly that when I ferried him to the airport for his flight to a renewed contract, which happened to be in the Middle East (he worked in diving and construction out there), we were both in tears. The difference was that whereas I was still dabbing my eyes as we approached the terminal, he had long since recovered and was concerned only with what an impression such unmanly behaviour might make on others, known or unknown. He had an absolute terror of 'anyone seeing us, Rod', which was in comic contrast to his normal disregard of criticism as regards anything else he chose to do.

Cousin Aelwyn had been spot on. I certainly wasn't having an easy time of things, yet I had to confess that life was all the more exciting for that reason. I longed – how I longed! – for Nick's return. Our Odyssey, which had so nearly threatened so much disaster, had for that very reason turned out to be a staggering success.

————

54

Things continued much the same over the next couple of years. During one of Nick's absences, he sent along another member of the clan, his son Paddy, having explained: 'I was married once, Rod, before I had time to see the world. Trapped for a while, and then she was killed in the Blitz, God resth her soul!'

It was unlikely to be the whole truth, but I didn't enquire further.

Paddy had been doing his National Service in Libya, where the British government had an agreement to continue maintaining a presence at aerodromes such as el-Adem, known to me from my Desert Air Force odyssey. He was a refreshingly shy and cuddly young man, longing to return to civilian life, though he had no idea what he wanted to do. I soon discovered that in spite of looking so dissimilar, he shared many of his father's tastes, so he fitted easily into my unorthodox life. He was staying in Paultons Square, in Chelsea, in a flat belonging to an Irish Mrs Mayhew, from whom his father had bought cigarettes and sweets, on and off the ration, during the war. She had a daughter, Peggy, a kind girl with a slight limp due to an early illness.

When Nick came back to London, it was always triumphant; he was a great one for turning everything into a celebration. It would have seemed a thoroughly Irish art had I not encountered something of the sort amongst Polynesians. I recalled in the moment Turia telling me how *fiu* she'd been with Woody the body-builder – 'all he wanted was to play *millionaire*'. Nick had points in common with her show-off American Sergeant, the difference being that after months of grinding work abroad he had plenty of money to spend on others, including me. He was far more lavish by nature than I was and he had the wherewithal, a combination guaranteed to endear him quickly to everyone he met.

On one return visit, he thought that he might like to drive with me to the South of France, taking a tent, sometime during summer. In view of our no-more-than-half-successful camping trip round Wales, the project threatened to be something of a risk, but I wasn't going to say no.

Weeks before we were due to go, Nick stayed a night at Queen's Gate. We were in bed (as usual), rather drunk (as usual), when he began singing a song, at that moment all the rage, about the Trevi fountain in Rome:

> *Three coins in a fountain,*
> *Each one seeking happiness . . .*
> *Just one wish will be granted,*
> *Which one will the fountain bless?*

It was the sort of thing he loved, half mockingly rather than seriously. So when he came out with a remark which seemed (at first) unrelated to the words of the song, I was taken by surprise: 'There's something I've been meaning to tell you, Rod. I'm getting married.'

I was stunned. Eventually when I managed to speak it was a 'Good Lord, Nick!' that came out of my mouth.

'Yes, it's my mother, see? She won't die happy till she sees me settled down.'

'You haven't yet told me who the girl is,' I stuttered.

'Peggy, see! Old Mrs M's Peggy. I know you like her.'

So I did; but all the same, it was a body-blow. Not just worse than a wet sponge, but something soaking me to the core with misery. Too stunned to be angry, I asked feebly, 'Couldn't you have let me know sooner?'

'Didn't know it meself till I popped the questhion! Anyway, 'twill make no difference to me an' you.'

'No *difference*? You'll be there and I'll be here. That'll be the difference!'

'I'll come and see you just as often, that's what I mean,' said Nick blithely, under cover of darkness. 'You don't have to worry!' He went back to singing more of that now very irritatingly relevant song:

> *Through the ripples how they shine!*
> *Just one wish will be granted . . .*
> *Make it MINE! Make it MINE! Make it—*

But I refused to let him get away with that as well. 'MINE!' I interrupted. 'Make it MINE!'

'All right, Rod, make it *yours*.'

After that he had the sense to shut up; but I caught him humming the wretched thing on other occasions.

The wedding was to take place on 10 July, at Holy Trinity, Sloane Street, with a reception afterwards at the King's Head.

'You'll be there, won't you, Rod? I shall need your shouldther to cry on.'

'What nonsense, Nick! You know you'll be loving every minute of it.'

I felt I was the person most seeking a shoulder to cry on, but I attended the wedding all the same. If he had to marry, then Peg was as good a choice as any; she seemed absolutely under his thumb, but perhaps she was only biding her time. I couldn't be entirely happy with my own role in the drama.

Nick said, 'When we get back from the honeymoon, me an' you will be off to France, won't we?' squeezing my shoulder as he spoke.

What was I supposed to make of that?

Exactly what he said, it seemed. Back they came, and round he came to discuss plans. It was breathtaking. I didn't object, wondering, rather, what Peg had had to say.

'I let her know before we wed,' was his reply to my question.

So that was how we came to be driving through France towards the end of July. Within three days there'd been three quarrels, but they'd been interspersed with moments of such intense pleasure that I was disinclined to dwell on them.

A few days before Nick was due to return to work, which happened at that time to be in Bahrain, he said, 'Why not write about the Persian Gulf, Rod? If you can get yourself there, I'll look afther you.'

All the signs seemed to be pointing me there! Although I could hardly see an average British construction company (overseas) welcoming a writer prying into its affairs, and what would I find to do when Nick was at work? Sit dripping with sweat in the cheapest available hotel?

Our manner of parting did much to overcome my objections. This Gaelic tough and I sat crying together in Queen's Gate, whilst an automatic gramophone dropped record after record on to its turntable.

I drove him to the airport, by which time, as usual, he had recovered and I had not. Off he went, and back I went to wait for a letter. Weeks later:

12/9/54.

I am sorry that I have not written to you sooner, but I could not put my mind to writing. Well Rod I never missed anyone so much in my life as I have missed you in the last few days, my heart is really broken. I cannot settle down. I miss you terribly. I never had an idea that I could get like this. I keep looking at my watch and thinking if we had been together now what would we be doing. I do love you Roderic and I mean that. I could kick myself for been so naughty at times during the first months but I knew you would forgive me. Thanks for your telegram which was very sweet, also your letter which I received today. I could not stop the tears running. I had a good journey over, and had a little party in my honour that same evening but I didn't enjoy it very much because my mind was not in Bahrain but at 94.

> *God bless you always*
> *My love for ever*
> *N.*

55

On the day in 1955 when I disembarked at Kuwait, the thermometer was registering 108°F in the shade. In the South Seas, in 1949, such a reading would have had everybody gasping for breath under whirling fans. In the Arabian Gulf only six years later, air-conditioning (from individual machines projecting from sealed windows) was the norm. At Kuwait Oil Co.'s cool HQ no reference was made to the unbearable heat outside. A Mr Jiggens who had so kindly met me off the ship talked of little else but sports fixtures. 'The company encourages us to work hard and play hard,' he said.

'To make sure none of you get into mischief?' I asked.

'Oh well, I wouldn't say that, exactly!'

'That's exactly what they mean – specifically "mischief with the natives", i.e. getting too friendly with the Kuwaitis!' murmured Meric – the Meric Dobson who'd promised me *Betna betek*. He'd come to collect me. 'It's different for me, I'm employed by the Government of Kuwait; I'm paid to be on their side.'

Driving through crowded streets, he drew my attention to places soon to change: older roads mud-paved and older houses constructed of hardened mud. 'The rare times it rained, everything would start to melt, like ice-cream. Beautiful but inconvenient! Whereas these [a row of tall, half-finished concrete blocks] signify the City of the Future!'

It got cooler around sunset; and then he took me for another drive in his smart green Dodge. When the guns boomed to announce the end of that day's Ramadan fasting, the town sprang to life. He pointed to the place in the square where the Ruler and his family had been accustomed to sleeping out on hot summer nights. The souks still formed the most important part of the town, looking haphazard, each stall apparently selling the same wares as its neighbours. An evil-smelling alley-way with urine running down the middle led to the fish-market, an open area where a group of men could be seen as if posing for a painting by Wright of Derby, lit from behind by a flaring kerosene lamp. Further on, men were playing cards on a carpet, sitting bunched closely together, as in a Greek Orthodox icon. 'The whole old town will disappear within the next few years, if not months,' said Meric regretfully. 'And there won't be a soul to mourn its passing – except for an old romantic like me. All they want is "New Lamps for Old!"'

A week or so later, Meric drove me to Kuwait's little airfield. In those days, the runway was a landing-strip, the lounge a shed with tables covered in brightly coloured plastic cloth of floral design, and the plane a Dakota taking one and a half hours to fly to Bahrain at a cost of £10. I wasn't yet sure who I was staying with, young Abdul-Nabi or Nick, so before leaving Kuwait I sent a telegram to each.

From the air, Bahrain looked surprisingly green, divided into two unequal parts: the island of Muharraq, where there was a recognisably mature aerodrome, and the main island of Bahrain, with a causeway connecting the two.

Abdul-Nabi had turned up to greet me in a mauve spun-nylon shirt and tight black trousers. No sign of Nick, nor any message. I was whisked away in a green Ford Country Sedan. Driving on the left (in Kuwait it had been on the right), we crossed the bumpy causeway into Manama, where he pointed out the many decorative towers to be seen here and there, mostly decaying, some with mats flapping from a lower storey. 'Old Persian wind-machines,' explained my young guide. 'In hot weather, they draw down a breeze to ventilate the ground floor.'

'Isn't the air just as hot, up or down?' I asked.

'Maybe yes, but at least it's moving. Before we had air-conditioning, that was better than nothing.'

I had to assume that what he would call hot weather was yet to come – an appalling thought. I baked and sweltered as we took the Awali Road, which would have landed us up at the oilfield had he not chosen to turn off to bump over a sandy track towards some little mounds. 'They're graves,' he said, 'burial-places of an ancient civilisation. This is where we all come to make love.' The penny dropped. From Cairo days I dredged up the word *ba'din* – 'later' – which was nicely imprecise. It was far too hot for any of that. Back we drove to Manama.

I was mystified by not being taken direct to the al-Sharif house, a huge, battered-looking place with a high doorway in front of which a gang of children were playing. It was pointed out to me as we swept past. 'Those weren't all ours!' said Abdul-Nabi, none too pleased.

'Aren't we going in?' I asked.

'No, I'm taking you to the Bahrain Hotel. Our house isn't ready.'

I had to take that unlikely excuse at its face value.

He went on to explain that since tourists were practically non-existent there was nowhere else to stay except Speedbird House, run by BOAC on the aerodrome in Muharraq. 'You wouldn't want to be there, among all the English businesspeople, would you? You'll find the Bahrain Hotel more interesting, I guess.' He was right. All the same, pleased as I was to be looked after in any shape or form, I could hardly stay as his guest in a hotel for many days. I would have to find somewhere of my own – pretty expensively, too, in view of the sky-high cost of living in Bahrain.

As we drove about, he kept stopping to talk to friends, all men, some in European dress but most in white robes. Few women were to be seen, mostly veiled in stifling black cotton. A tall girl buying a roll of cloth from a shop near the entrance to the souk was an exception, because she was wearing a silken head-scarf and dark glasses. Introduced as 'one of the ladies of our household', she moved aside the glasses to say a few polite words of greeting.

'You see, we aren't all living in the Middle Ages!' said my little friend, unaware that even this 'open' meeting seemed, to me, to belong to another era.

I was left alone in the hotel for a while, to prepare for the evening's entertainment: a meal with one of the al-Sharif brothers and a visit to the open-air cinema. In my room an air-conditioner rumbled away, doing its best to overcome blasts of heat from an adjoining, un-air-conditioned shower-closet. I tried telephoning Nick, to be told cheerfully that he wasn't back from work.

'You're to come round for a beer and we'll take it from there!'

'I can only just call in for a moment. I'm staying with a Bahraini,' I replied.

'Oh I see!' Some of the friendliness had gone out of the voice at the other end. 'Well, come round anyway!' A foretaste of things to come? Only too probable.

Abdul-Nabi duly took me to Holloway's yard, to a single-storey shed divided into rooms where some of their contract engineers, including Nick, were living. He went bouncing ahead of me and tapped at the door of one of the rooms, where I saw, through its window, Nick sitting with an older man, drinking beer. Both were in singlet and shorts, and the room reeked of socks and aftershave. The only one to look welcoming was the other man, introduced as 'Uncle'.

Nick was shouting 'Down, Satan!' at a black pi-dog which rose, growling and cringing, from under a table heavy with cans of export lager. 'I see you've brought your friend with you,' were his first ungracious words to me. 'Well, don't just stand there ... tell him to make himself at home!'

Unexpectedly, Abdul-Nabi said, 'I know you. You're the Mr Nick from the quarry, aren't you?'

Equally unexpectedly, Nick actually seemed to blush beneath his sun-tan.

'Your fame has spread!' said Uncle, giving a knowing sort of look.

I invited Nick to come with us to the cinema.

'Can't say I fancy it, much. Too noisy!' he said. 'But you go, Rod, and enjoy yourself!' Having thus guaranteed that I would feel uneasy about things, he cheered up, but remained distant.

The quarry where Nick was working was not far from the spot to which I'd been driven on the day of my arrival. I hopped on to a Holloway's truck, hoping to find him alone; which, thank goodness, he was, at last, sitting in a stuffy hut, naked but for khaki shorts stained with sweat. His job was to oversee a gang of local men shovelling stone into trucks from the pit below. This time, black Satan was fawningly friendly, but the heat was doubly devastating.

'I've found somewhere for you to live, Rod,' he said. 'It won't cost a fortune and it's not far from our yard. Doesn't do to overstay your welcome!'

My heart sank when he left me at the suggested place – a room above an Indian restaurant, reeking of curry. Its only window opened on to a corridor into which other windows of other rooms also opened, so there was no fresh air and no privacy, either. The slender young Indian proprietor stared at me in hostile disbelief. 'Oh, are you Mr Nick's friend?' he asked with a marked lack of warmth. 'I am Mr Nick's friend myself!' I was left in no doubt that it meant exactly what I took it to mean. I would have to find a new place to stay.

Next day, Abdul-Nabi took me to meet a man called Hussain Yateem, who was restlessly jiggling his feet, greeting visitor after visitor, motioning them to sit on one of many chairs round the wall of a large downstairs hall. After a most friendly greeting and a few rapid questions (where was I staying, for how long, and what was I hoping to do in Bahrain?), he broke off to fix up a deal for importing fruit juice from Cyprus, then started arranging the hire of a holiday villa. In

Arabic mid-sentence, he pushed his head-dress back at a rakish angle and greeted a new arrival with the customary formal words of welcome before switching to English: 'Your brother's house in Raiya is empty, isn't it? Why not let this Englishman have it?'

The man was Sheikh Ahmed, one of the junior members of the ruling al-Khalifa family. Hussain's query made him hum and ha before promising to raise the matter with his brother, Sheikh Salman, that evening.* 'Raiya is very secluded,' he explained, as if that ruled it out.

'Yes, yes!' said Hussain, impatiently. 'We know that!' Then, to me: 'You'll need a car. Maybe one of the Sheikhs will give you one of their old ones. We'll see!'

When Ahmed had gone, he said, 'Anyway, come and sit here whenever you're passing, and let me know how you get on!'

Expressing thanks (which were brushed aside with a show of impatience), we left.

Once we were outside in the souk, Abdul-Nabi said, 'He means it! He's a powerful man. He owns the water-distillation plant and has an English wife. Perhaps that's why he's taken to you.'

Even so, I had a residual worry: 'If Raiya is all that secluded, hadn't I better get a bicycle?'

'Of course not! I'll be coming round every day.'

A very kind suggestion, if he meant to keep to it. However, it raised a further worry: how would Nick react? Not at all favourably, if their visits happened to coincide.

———

56

My kind of travelling had taught me exactly what to do on an official level when arriving in a fresh country. I went to the grand old

———

* Salman bin Hamad Al Khalifa I (1894–1961) was the ruler of Bahrain from 1942 until his death. Roddy spelt Salman as Sulman, but Salman is the standard spelling. He also spelt Ahmed as Hamed; Salman didn't have a brother called Hamed, and Ahmed was a junior member of the al-Khalifa family, so it seems most likely that this was another spelling error rather than a different person.

Adviserate to call on the Adviser, Charles Belgrave. Sir Charles was said to be out bathing, but I didn't wholly believe it because his car, a black Humber, was standing in the drive. However, I duly 'signed the book' before going on to Bernard Burrows, 'Political Resident, Persian Gulf'. Our Resident lived in a building which was the last word in Festival of Britain modernity, inside and out. He received me courteously and explained fairly early on that he and the Adviser could not always see eye to eye. 'He represents the interests of the Ruler, not HMG' was the way he put it. When offering me a drink he commented: 'Alcohol is one of our problems when we mix with Bahrainis. We are allowed it and they are not, which makes for a certain awkwardness; or rather, it would do if we hadn't hit on a way round it. At our parties, we are careful to have a man coming round with a trayful of drinks all looking alike, but in fact on one side the glasses are with, on the other, without. It's up to them which they choose. And if they get too – how shall we put it? – "carried away", they can always claim it was a mistake!'

I asked about an alcohol permit for myself. Had I been staying like any normal English visitor with a business firm or person – had I even been in Speedbird House – I would have been entitled to a ration. But as a guest of a Bahraini in the Bahrain Hotel, I wasn't eligible. 'You will be, as soon as you get your own place to live,' he assured me.

Later, Nick took me on to the Speedbird House about which I kept hearing. The place was all that it should have been: the men in wholesome white short-sleeved shirts; the women in cocktail dresses; tables laid with a full complement of knives, forks, spoons and glasses on a snowy table-cloth; Bristol Cream sherry before, Drambuie after dinner. It was the standard 'Brits Abroad' set-up; agreeable enough on its own terms, but it served to strengthen the resolve which had been forming in my mind: in essence, this was not what I'd come all this way to see and do. Obsessed with the yearning to follow Nick into his lair, I hadn't given enough thought to what entering into his foreign life might mean. In pursuit of that aim, I had agreed with my publishers to write a book, and entering into such an agreement had inevitably altered my outlook. Nick and his life couldn't loom as large when I would have to study every aspect of Arabian Gulf affairs. However, that was something better kept concealed, when with him.

In the bar of Speedbird House I was pleasantly amazed by the scope of Nick's acquaintance. He suddenly said: 'Oh, there's James, the Adviser's son. Best meet him!' I was taken over to be introduced to a tall, baby-faced man with a friendly look to him.

'Are you Owen?' was his opening remark. 'I've just sent a message to the al-Sharif house to tell Abdul-Nabi to bring you round to my office, any time. Oh, and incidentally, my father wants to apologise for being out when you called at the Adviserate. He was busy cutting wood!' Of course, I had made no secret of being a writer, though careful to say that I was not a journalist (journalists being held in low esteem in those parts). Possibly my profession had been in my favour.

I was soon telling James details of my life-story since arriving in Bahrain: al-Sharif guest; under the wing of Hussain Yateem; meeting Sheikh Ahmed; about to meet Sheikh Salman. 'Goodness,' he said, 'that's fast work,' adding, slightly mysteriously, 'I don't think I need warn you against anything; you'll find out for yourself soon enough!' I saw that he didn't want to be drawn into explanations, so I left it at that.

Sheikh Salman lived in a modern block of a house beyond the aerodrome in Muharraq. I was shown into a lofty room on the first floor, furnished with easy chairs in pale green-sheen. In one corner, a substantial radiogram; in the other, an even more substantial standing fan.

After we'd drunk several tiny cups of cardamom-flavoured coffee from a beaked Damascene-silver pot, he suggested we drive out to Raiya in his Cadillac, straight away. 'The house was constrrructed by us as a *majlis*,' he said, meaning reception-room, with a fine roll to his 'r's. 'It is in a rrre-grettable state of rrrepair!' I asked him where he'd learned such excellent English. 'The American University in Beirut' was the answer.

We were driven by his servant, Sultan, along a track of hardened mud through gardens of date-palms, past a tall sand-coloured house with ornate tracery which had been built by a pearl-merchant in the old days when pearls had been the mainstay of local commerce. Further on, we reached a rocky coast where the sea was shallow. On a flattened shore-site stood the *majlis*, arched windows extending on both sides and round one end. From the stony, coralline shore there wafted a smell of seaweed and sulphur. Wavelets lapped and retreated, lapped and retreated.

I knew at once what it reminded me of: my Château Courant d'Air in Tahiti. Sheikh Salman's pavilion was lovelier than the copra-strewn ruin where I'd lived before moving into Maison Crane with Turia, and the palms were date, not coconut, therefore less feathery and more squat. But there *were* mud-nests for hornets near the roof, though thankfully no rafters for scurrying rats.

Sheikh Salman pointed out a cubby-hole of a kitchen and another cubby-hole of a lavatory which (as in the Château) was blocked solid with unmentionables. Another small downstairs room could be slept in, or there was the flat roof, easily accessible, cooled by every breeze. However, one drawback instantly occurred to me: there seemed to be no facilities for washing of any kind, even the most primitive.

Salman said: 'You have something much better, Rrroderic, your own *hammam*, on the doorstep!' Some fifty yards away under the date-palms there was a little white building, its upper parts trellised with faded bluey-green wooden slats so that those inside could see what was going on outside without themselves being seen. The building housed an octagonal bath, tiled mauve, brown and green, large enough for several bathers to stand about in water coming up to their shoulders, or to lie prone on the tiled ledges above. It could be filled very simply by inserting a chog of palm-fibres into an upper hole, and could be emptied as simply by pulling out another chog near the floor. The water came from a deep basin on the far side (concealed by that part of the *meshrabiya* trellis). It looked the epitome of ancient luxury-and-practicality combined.

'I suppose this has been here for centuries?' I asked.

'No my dear Rrroderic, the *hammam* was built by my family in 1938,' said Salman, clearly none too pleased by the idea that the bath wasn't considered completely up-to-date. 'Sometimes, on hot days, we still come here to bathe.'

'It's wonderful,' I enthused, 'really wonderful – a Xanadu, a pleasure-dome. Would you really let me stay here?'

'You will restore the WC to working order?' he asked quickly.

'Of course. As soon as possible!'

'Then you are welcome, my dear frrriend. The place is yours!'

57

One evening there was a Staff Dance at Cable and Wireless, where an Indian Master of Ceremonies chanted, 'Ladies and gentlemen, you need not fear that undesirables will be familiar!' – whatever that meant. The announcement was made that Mr al-Sharif was prepared to dance an exhibition mambo, if the public so desired. There was sporadic clapping as Abdul-Nabi bounced on to the floor, alone, waiting for a partner daring enough to join him. When there were no takers, he leaped and jerked all by himself, sitting down at last to thunderous applause.

Our table could supply no one to partner him because, like nearly every table in the room, we were all men. In other ways we were varied: the thoughtful Ibrahim, of Middle East Traders; Rasac, a Persian-Bahraini of much goodwill who ran an import business; and Jusuf, dark-complexioned, pan-Arabian fanatic, red-hot against the West yet so friendly that his words seemed utterly at variance with his true feelings. Jusuf spoke more than warmly of a body known as the 'High Executive Committee', an alternative 'government-in-waiting' demanding the right to vote and scornful of the ruling al-Khalifa family – including those who supported it, such as Charles Belgrave and the entire British business community.

It might have been supposed that Jusuf would wish to have nothing to do with me. On the contrary, he responded warmly to my overtures, for I liked and trusted him straight away. My faith was justified almost at once by the way he reacted when asked whether he could arrange for a plumber to fix the *majlis* WC. Unlike all the others (who said they would, but did nothing), he turned up the next day with a man ready to start plumbing immediately. Then, on our way back to Muharraq, he ACTUALLY INVITED ME INTO HIS HOUSE. I had been perfectly prepared to stay outside in the street, but he merely asked me to wait whilst his assorted ladies 'covered up'. When I was allowed in, three veiled figures were squatting on a mat in the small courtyard, eyes presumably trained on their visitor – which was more than their visitor could do as regards them.

Though not my usual practice, I decided to make the effort to go to church on Sunday, for reasons which weren't wholly pure. I was partly motivated by nostalgia for something English to the core in contrast to my odd style of living, and I hoped that I might meet some of the 'heavies' of our expatriate society as well. The vicar of St Christopher's – which was very near Holloway's yard – was a bearded Alun Morris; he greeted me warmly and introduced me to Sir Charles and Lady Belgrave, whom I'd seen genuflecting during the Creed from seats out in front. They expressed the hope that I'd come to dinner with them soon, and in fact a written invitation followed within a couple of days. Seldom could a church service have yielded more beneficial results; and when Alun and his wife Edith invited me back to a full English breakfast at the vicarage I was even more content. From then on I determined to go to church every Sunday, not just for self-advantage (important as that was) but because I felt the stirrings of a need to show gratitude to an agency outside myself.

The Adviserate where the Belgraves lived was as charming inside as out. The high, old-fashioned rooms managed to keep cool without air-conditioning and eyes were soothed by the sight of fully grown trees in the surrounding garden. At dinner I was slightly surprised to meet Brooks Richards, No. 2 to Bernard Burrows, obviously on the best of terms with his hosts, particularly with their only son, James. I had to conclude that what united the two British 'sides' was more important than what separated them. Lady Belgrave was said to be fearsome. I didn't find her that at all: she was kindness itself in what seemed to me to be a shy rather than curt way.

'I can't think why you've come all this distance simply to study Arabs,' said Sir Charles. 'The tribal customs of the Oilies might be much more rewarding!' I couldn't agree with him there, even though I did find Brits Abroad interesting. But since it would be difficult to write about their prejudices without laying myself open to libel actions, I decided to invent a character (called 'Amanda') as a whipping-girl for the purposes of my book. If someone were to ask me who she really was, I'd give a Gioconda smile and refuse to be drawn. (Needless to say, as soon as he heard, Nick would sometimes refer to himself by that name.) Amanda could safely be shown as a prejudiced silly, alternating between cocktail parties and 'do's at the Gymkhana Club, seldom accepting an invitation from a Bahraini – in which way she was unfortunately typical of many.

Dinner with the Belgraves was closely followed by another with Sir Bernard Burrows. At one bound, I had moved into the top echelons, much to Nick's amazement – and to my own amazement as well.

I spent a good deal of time with the 'Oilies' too. 'Uncle' took me out to the Bapco (Bahrain Petroleum) camp at Awali for the evening. We should have had Nick with us, as it was his idea, but at the last moment he cried off, pleading that he had 'things to do'. *Such as trotting round to that Indian restaurant for TLC*, I wanted to say, but didn't.

I passed out on Nick's floor once the evening was over, lying directly under the air-conditioner, to be woken next morning by the sound of a champagne cork popping. 'I won 450 rupees playing roulette at the Gymkhana Club last night,' he explained. 'That would be about thirty quid – not bad going. Here's the celebrathing of it!' So those were the 'things to do' which had prevented him from coming to Awali? He was in such a good mood that he suggested coming back with me to Raiya.

'How are you fixed for money, Rod?' he asked.

I told him that at the moment, I could manage. All the same, it was very good of him, for not only had I caused embarrassment by turning up on his patch, but I was already friendly with too many of those who were no friends of his.

He must sometimes wonder what's hit him! I thought.

'Well, just let me know if you're running short, and put your hand in my pocket when yiz feeling like it.'

'Thanks, Nick, thanks a lot. I may have to!'

He bent over and suddenly half bit, half sucked the back of my neck. I was not startled so much as pleasantly perturbed, afraid that it might raise a red weal, which it did.

'What's this in aid of, Nick?'

His answer was to give a wicked grin. 'You are the one I care for, Rod. Nobody else. But you know that, don't you?'

One day, Sheikh Salman suggested a picnic, which he would provide. He duly arrived in his Cadillac together with the indispensable Sultan. We were to use the *hammam* whilst Sultan prepared a meal. At first he appeared shocked when I took off all my clothes, total nudity (unless absolutely necessary) being considered unseemly amongst Bahraini men, even in the presence of other males only. Then he said: 'Like you, Rrroderic, I too will undress completely' – indeed a concession. After a few drinks in the *majlis*, we enjoyed a long and woozy bathe. By the time we got back, Sultan had arranged canvas chairs and a folding table on the terrace, where we tucked into a mountain of rice on which sprawled most of a lamb, with a caramel custard to follow. The Sheikh insisted on tearing off strips of meat with his right hand, pushing them over to me. He demonstrated how to roll a nugget of rice between thumb and two fingers so as to produce a ball solid enough to be flicked into the mouth. He seldom used his left hand, considered 'unclean' from its role in bottom-wiping (with the help of water, lavatory-paper being thought superfluous).

That feast was my first 'mutton grab' in Arabia, therefore memorable, the very stuff of romance. I was in a mood to be grateful.

'I used to have an English frrriend, called Patrrrick, now gone,' said Salman. 'He was so good at intrrroducing me to English girls. Perrrhaps you, too, would like to ask one or two English girls for an evening at my house?' I looked dubious. 'You need have no worries,' he went on, 'I would arrrange the food and the music.'

I was hesitant because of feeling considerable unease. I recognised that social intercourse all over the world depended on introducing one person to another, yet there was something distasteful about the way (I felt) that the Sheikh was asking me to procure for him. How to explain the wide gap between being a good host and becoming a procurer, when the distinction relied on so many nuances? So I was distant, putting him off with vague phrases. He wasn't pleased, but remained beautifully polite.

That night I lay awake in bed, worrying, worrying. This wasn't the only time the Sheikh had asked something of me I wasn't prepared to give. He was a great lover of whisky and kept asking me to bring it to him. If I had and been discovered, I would have been in a lot of trouble. I kept therefore finding myself in tight spots, which made me feel uneasy. I couldn't afford to quarrel with my benefactor; indeed, it would be difficult to face Hussain Yateem or his influential friends if I did. Clearly I needed to move out so I was no longer a dependent.

Jusuf was my saviour, having heard of a house in Muharraq above a garage. He drove with me through the narrow streets of the old town until we came to a mosque, opposite which there was just room for two cars to park without blocking the road. A heavy wooden door opened to reveal steps leading upwards to two flats on the first (and only) floor.

The one to the left was the one we'd come to inspect. Once through its door, a small courtyard led to two interconnecting rooms with wooden balconies overlooking the mosque and a small side-room. Another little cubby-hole on the far side was a lavatory, a simple hole in the concrete floor covered with a square of wood the size of a book. From the courtyard, open-air steps led up to a roof, L-shaped, with fretted walls, from which there was a remarkable view of the minaret of the mosque, no more than ten aerial yards away in the foreground, with the harbour of Muharraq in the middle distance and the Manama causeway forming a background. As we stood there, an old man appeared beneath the cupola of the minaret, raised his hands to his face and began a Call to Prayer: *'ALLAHHHH . . . 'KBAR . . . ALLAHHHH!'* It seemed too good to be true, so wonderfully evocative of everything about my new and foreign life.

The flat had electricity, to the extent of two naked dangling wires and two sockets. It didn't have water, which had to be bought from a water-seller, coming round daily, shouting his wares. 'A bread-man will come too,' said Jusuf. The rent would be 155 rupees a month (about £15). I took it on the spot from its owner, a thin, harassed-looking Ali Zayani, who asked me to be careful not to block the entrance to the garage below, where a lady-doctor – an almost unheard-of rarity at that time – kept her car.

Jusuf was delighted. 'It will be easier for us to look after you here,' he said. 'In Muharraq, the High Executive Committee is boss.' It sounded slightly ominous, but hardly a matter for great concern.

58

Sheikh Salman was most generous even when I was turning my back on his generosity: he lent me a Cadillac to help me move my things. I asked if I could hire or even buy it from him for the foreseeable, but he wouldn't hear of it.

'If you would have a use for it, then let me lend it to you!' he said.

'*El hamdu l'Illah!*'* was my only possible reply. Praise God indeed!

What with the Cadillac, Nick's pick-up truck and Abdul-Nabi's capacious green station-wagon, I was transferred with a minimum of fuss to my new home, together with the carpet, chairs, table, bed and all the other things accumulated by magpie borrowings from anyone going. Now that I was in a small town with shops I could consider cooking again, in modest style. Up till then, if not eating out I'd been living on unleavened bread baked to a crisp by being stuck to the sides of a primitive oven, and a fleshy kind of cress which kept for days without wilting in spite of the heat.

To add to the general atmosphere of felicity, Nick insisted on

----

* Usually written as 'Alhamdulillah'.

spending the first night in Muharraq with me – the endearing sort of thing so typical of him. We were coming closer together, with past difficulties forgiven and forgotten. In some ways they'd acted as a cement – a situation comprehensible only to those who have been through a similar mill.

The little house did its best to oblige. As we climbed to the roof, a muezzin was climbing the minaret of the mosque across the narrow street. The Call to Prayer seemed to be directed specially at us, it was so loud and clear. Men in djellabas were thronging outside, their long white gowns and black-corded white head-scarves looking marvellously right for the time and the place. Even at sundown the air was still bakingly hot, intensifying an aroma of spices and dried fish wafting up from the street; joined, as the tide receded, by other smells of glue and shark-oil from the hulls of sailing-dhows in harbour. 'Those dhows aren't much to write home about,' said Nick knowingly. 'They's always full of cockroaches!'

I had some water in a jerrican supplied by Nick, which could be replenished daily at a cost of 1 rupee. For 35 rupees I procured a twenty-gallon drum which, when perched on a ledge in the courtyard, made a reservoir for a shower *en plein air*, the run-off being carried down a pipe into the street. By then we had visited the little cell beneath the steps leading up to the roof and learned the worst: the lavatory was no more than a long drop which no sanitary engineer could have passed. Its contents fell into a pit and from them arose an indescribable stink, kept in check only by ensuring that the small covering-board was always left tightly in position. No septic tank, much less a main drain. 'Good old Oirland couldn't improve on this bog!' said Nick. 'It makes me feel quite at home in the country.' Not that I cared. The lack of mod cons was the very thing which had put the place within my range, so I could hardly complain.

Discomforts notwithstanding, I soon found that the smartest of my new friends were bending over backwards to be invited for drinks. It was clearly a chic thing to venture into the narrow streets of Muharraq in search of an eccentric Old Etonian living in such romantic squalor. On such occasions I took care to dress reassuringly in 'Persian Gulf Rig': short-sleeved, open-necked white shirt, dark trousers and cummerbund. The muezzin, of course, held centre-stage. Seldom had any of them found themselves so near a Call to Prayer.

As for myself, the Call, echoing and re-echoing over loudspeakers near and far, began to have a hypnotic effect, as if a message were being beamed at me personally. Five times a day I was reminded of a world outside my world, repetition progressively stripping me of defences. How was I to remain unmoved?

After a little while of being installed in my new quarters, Abdul-Nabi and Rasac came by in a state of high dudgeon. A Mr Brown had asked them to a Bapco dance at Awali, where Abdul-Nabi had done his exhibition mambo. Mr Brown had apparently been sent for later and told not to invite one of those friends again. When he had protested 'But our rules specifically state that we are allowed to bring Bahraini guests', the Superintendent was reported to have replied: 'Yes, it says so in the rules, but we always hope that people won't take advantage!'

That had been bad enough, but what particularly irked Abdul-Nabi was the fact that he alone was the friend referred to; Rasac wasn't included in the ban. He begged me to compose a letter of complaint to Bapco, which I did; but then his brothers wouldn't let him send it, for fear of jeopardising their business dealings with the company.

It happened that Hussain Yateem, that live wire, had already introduced me to Bapco's chief, Mr Skinner, at one of his daily sittings. The following Sunday I encountered him in church, so was able to lay the facts before him in informal fashion. He, of course, promised to take immediate action to rescind the order. Mr Skinner was the sort of American I remembered meeting in England before the war: very little trace of an American accent and a manner both drily polite and slightly amused. Would there ever be an end to the advantages of my newly adopted practice of regular church-going?

It seemed not, for another benefit simultaneously cropped up. I saw a fattish man with a red face seated in front, near the Belgraves. When we got outside he took my arm, saying, 'M'dear fellow! I do believe you don't know who I am.'

Just in time, prompted by that opener, I remembered him as a friend of Mary Stanley-Smith, the Oxford hostess who had taught me never to turn anyone away. Tim Hillyard, that was the name. He'd become a successful businessman, a BP local manager, and was in Bahrain only for a couple of days before returning to a place sounding like 'Aberdovey'.

'Aberdovey?' I repeated. 'Isn't that rather a long way off? I mean, all the way from Wales just for two days!'

'Not Aberdovey. Spelt ABU DHABI, pronounced ABUTHUBBI. It's by far the largest Sheikhdom on the Trucial Coast, and the least known,' said Tim reprovingly.

'Oh, I see . . .' But I didn't.

'Before we drew its teeth, the Trucial was called the Pirate Coast,' he explained. 'We are still quite wild and woolly in our ways. Why not come and see for yourself?'

'Why not indeed? I really can't think!'

'Then you can start thinking, m'dear fellow, as from now! The BP dhow will be leaving Bahrain within the next few days, with you aboard, if you like. Once you reach Abu Dhabi, *Betna betekum!*' I noticed his use of the plural 'our' and asked if it meant anything special. 'Oh yes, I got married, y'know, but Susan is away with the brat, Deborah, the apple of our combined eyes. It will be nice to have someone with whom to share a noggin or two, of an evening.'

59

For the BP dhow *Faares* to set sail, it needed a strong wind known as a *shamal* to help propel it. There was no commanding it, so we simply had to wait. Whilst waiting, I held a party on my roof which didn't end until midnight, and saw much more of Nick, always at his best when living from day to day.

During the period of uncertainty a crew assembled: the *Nakuda* (captain), thin and grave; two older men (one of whom was known to Tim as 'Oh-my-Uncle', that being the literal translation of his name); a youth, Abood, supposed to be looking after me; two small boys to act as dogsbodies (but amongst Muslims such a description would be unpropitious, dogs being considered 'unclean'); and lastly a Muscati man, self-evidently tubercular.

The dhow was brown and blistered, railed aft with slanting wooden 'banisters', as if from an ancient galleon. Amenities were primitive. The galley was on deck forrard, with a cut-down oil-drum for a stove, minimal food stores being kept in a nearby box. The lavatory was on a crossed plank aft, with a direct drop into the sea. A dinghy was lashed to one side of the engine-hatch, but otherwise very little was carried on deck, the supplies we were carrying to Abu Dhabi being stowed below, along with a wireless transmitter/receiver. It would be curious, one day, to recall that once a line of dhows had bobbed at anchor off Manama jetty. Before long, most of them would be gone for ever.

At last we cast off, heaving to and fro because the *shamal*, before blowing itself out, had left behind a swell which would take days to subside. Making notes was difficult when spray was flying, but I managed a few rudimentary jottings.

That night, sheltered by a reef, some of us composed ourselves for sleep. In the stifling cabin below, rats could be heard scuffling. Across a deck tilting now this way now that, cockroaches warily stalked, whiskers quivering, occasionally putting on bursts of speed. Seen in close-up as they quested near my mattress they were like tiny lobsters, newly emerged from the sea. They were said to like nibbling a sleeper's toes, but fortunately they didn't seem to fancy mine.

We reached Abu Dhabi at 8 p.m. the following evening. There was no such thing as a road, but an ADMA (Abu Dhabi Marine Areas) Land Rover came roaring over the sand in four-wheel-drive. It picked me up and away we went, lurching through sand-ruts, mounting hillocks of rubbish where broken bottles glinted in the headlights, swerving round *barasti* huts, pursued by hysterically barking mongrel dogs, until at length we arrived at a concrete house painted a light blue. The building was distinguished by having two storeys, also an electricity generator, whose stuttering roar was the only sound to be heard when the Land Rover's engine was switched off.

Tim was waiting, waving an airmail edition of *The Times*. 'M'dear fellow, welcome to Abu Dhabi from the only other Englishman!' he said. 'Have you dined?'

Dinner was a feast of turtle soup and lobster, washed down with chilled white wine. Besides the lights and a refrigerator, the invaluable generator also ran the only air-conditioner, which was in Tim's bedroom; so that was where I would be sleeping. I couldn't fail to notice that he was suffering extensively from 'prickly heat' and wondered how long it would be before I succumbed. (In fact, I was already starting, tell-tale red patches spreading over the inner surface of each thigh.)

Next day the Land Rover took us to BP HQ, an old Persian-style building near the shore, outstanding amongst the *barasti*s everywhere else because it had a top storey of rooms surrounded by a covered verandah. From it there was a fine view of a sand-mud fort, which, I was told, was the palace of the Ruler, Sheikh Shakhbut, as well as being both prison and seat of government.

Fifty yards out to sea, *Faares* bobbed at anchor. The sloping shore in front of the BP office seemed the obvious place for landing stores, but that wasn't in fact the case, because that part of the sand was reserved for other functions. Below the high-water mark, the shore was a public lavatory; men to the right, women to the left. By common convention, all eyes had to be averted whenever a figure wandered along to crouch, clothes hitched, leaving behind evidence for the waves to wash away – a sensible solution to an inevitably recurrent problem.

'Shakhbut will expect me to bring you along when I call on him this morning,' said Tim. 'Do you happen to have an ode handy?'

He'd decided to introduce me as '*es-Sha'ir*', the Poet, because, not being a journalist, there was no other category into which I could conveniently be fitted in the Abu Dhabi world. The title was not wholly unjustified: I'd written plenty of poetry in my time, just not lately. It faced me with a quandary: what if the Ruler should ask me to write something specifically for him?

'I shall have to rely on guidance for inspiration,' I said, with a Quakerly assurance which I was far from feeling.

'That ought to do the trick!' said Tim, encouragingly.

When we arrived at the fort, some half-dozen soldiers with leather belts chased with silver and silver-mounted knives were leaning against wooden benches arranged outside an enormous iron-spiked wooden door. 'The Sheikh's open-air *majlis*,' explained Tim. 'Anyone who feels so inclined waits here for the Ruler to put in an appearance. If necessary, they are prepared to wait all day.' After some minutes of shouting by the guards to others within we were motioned towards the gigantic door, which remained closed, but were then taken through a smaller door let into it, and along a passageway between high walls of hardened mud. A need for defence explained the absence of a hall. The palace was a fort within a fort.

Sheikh Shakhbut happened to be sitting in his mother's *majlis*, surrounded by gilded mirrors, many of them tarnished. His mother, the powerful Sheikha Salama, was away in el-Ain oasis (known to us at that time as Buraimi), otherwise she might have been keeping watch from behind a screen. He himself was a small man, simply dressed, without

'Lawrence of Arabia' finery except for the gold-sheathed dagger at his waist; no golden *agal* around his head, but an ordinary black double-cord laid over a plain white head-scarf. Narrow face with small, dark, twinkling eyes, an aquiline nose, a beard startlingly black, and thin, claw-like hands ... my first impression was of a bird, strongly resembling King Charles. But which bird and which Charles? Hard to decide. One thing was abundantly clear: he meant to treat me extraordinarily well. A conventional *'Kef halek* ente?'* – How are you? – were his first words of greeting. To my stock answer of *'El hamdu l'Illah!'* he repeated the question over and over again, in correct formal fashion, all the time gripping my hand. Then a man with a gammy eye was motioned forward to be introduced – his brother, Sheikh Khaled.

Whilst that was going on, the BP interpreter was standing close at hand – Abdullah, known by the courtesy title of 'Sheikh' Abdullah. He was a moon-faced Palestinian with tiny darting eyes expressing such extremes of deviousness that the effect was almost comic. Tim had already warned me: 'I can absolutely rely on the man not just to double-cross but treble-cross anyone whose interests he's supposed, for the moment, to be serving. Once you decide what he thinks will be best for Number One, you know exactly where you are with him!'

The Ruler motioned me to sit on the carpeted floor to his right, then shouted *'GAWA!'* and a servant appeared with one of those beaked Damascene coffee-pots and three small china coffee-cups without handles. Coffee was poured from on high in a visible stream, culminating in an audible clink of jug against cup. The first was offered to Shakhbut, who waved it away, indicating that it should go to me. I waved it back to him, whereupon he waved it back to me again. Taking that as a sign that I was to proceed, I tossed down three cups running – what I understood to be the correct formal helping. Tim also took three cups of the bitter, cardamom-flavoured liquid before the Ruler allowed himself to be served. After that, coffee was taken round to everyone else. Reflected in the many mirrors, the ceremony took on a special meaning of its own, enhanced by the presence of soldiers crouching, rifles between their knees. And all the time, the heat was stifling.

Demands of etiquette having been met, silence fell – a silence lasting for a full minute. It would normally have been my cue to speak up, for the sake of *entrain*. Fortunately, I decided to do nothing (which, as Tim

---

* Usually spelled 'Kaif Halak'.

told me later, was the correct thing). Silence was finally broken when Shakhbut stroked his beard and asked: 'Oh Poet, have you been to the North Pole?'

'Not yet,' I answered.

'What makes the Eskimos wish to live in such a place?' he continued. 'How can they enjoy being so cold all the time?'

'They might say the same of you, only it would be the heat they'd be wondering about.'

'Hmmmm ...' said the Sheikh. 'Of course we go when we can to el-Ain, which isn't ever really cold, but cold enough for us Bedu. Do the Eskimos believe in God?'

As we were leaving, our visit having been cut short from business necessity, Tim said, 'Shakhbut has an endlessly enquiring mind. Some people can't understand what makes him tick.'

'I think I understand him very well,' I said, which I was convinced was the truth.

'Just as well, because he does expect you to write an ode for him, only he was too polite to say so, openly. Whilst you were hard at it, explaining how to build an igloo, Sheikh Abdullah was whispering the glad tidings behind the back of his hand. So, m'dear fellow, what about it?'

'I'll try not to let you down.'

'And by the way, he must have taken to you no end! Next time, we've been ordered to stay for lunch. How does that strike you?'

How Tim's niceness was unimpaired since the days of Oxford! It filled me with optimism as I paced the shore outside his house, grappling with the need to write sensitive verses against a background of the generator stuttering away.

I didn't go for a dip, because so greeny-grey with grit and overheated was the sea that swimming in it was actually unpleasant, the temperature in the shallows being 101°. Might there be oil beneath such an uncompromising exterior? The Ruler was patiently awaiting news of golden bubbles which were already enriching the more fortunate Sheikhdoms higher up the Trucial Coast. *Nobody will be able to say that I'm grovelling to riches by becoming Shakhbut's poet*, I determined. *He may never be blessed by Allah in that particular direction, but he'll have me to console him, for what that's worth!* I wondered what the Ruler really thought of me. An oddity? Probably; but at any rate an oddity who (unlike most Westerners he met) wasn't trying to get money or concessions out of him.

*

My time in Abu Dhabi was limited because, having established myself in Muharraq, I'd asked Meric Dobson to come from Kuwait and put in a few days with me, not thinking that he would accept. I'd underrated his sense of curiosity; the thought of discomfort didn't put him off in the slightest. So I had to get back to Bahrain to welcome him. *Faares* was soon due to leave, with me once more on board.

Meanwhile I sat daily with Shakhbut, talking about everything under the sun. I delivered poems, as had been requested of me on the second visit, but after that I promised but produced no more: poetry, especially poetry that would then be translated into Arabic, was not my strong suit, I decided. His reply was invariably '*In sh'Allah!*', eyes rolling heavenwards. At one time I might have considered such repetition exaggerated, but I was coming to see it as a reminder of the frailty of human hopes and found myself not just using the words, but thinking along those lines. When I told him that I had every intention of returning to Abu Dhabi, I acknowledged that it would be entirely dependent on the will of God; and I meant it.

To my astonishment, Tim told me that the Ruler hadn't been treated with much courtesy by our government, having not been considered important enough to be invited to the Coronation. Shakhbut had come to England off his own bat and retreated with a tiny entourage to Great Fosters, outside London, waiting; then after receiving a last-minute invitation, he had taken himself off to Paris. To be by far the largest of the Trucial Sheikhdoms apparently counted for less than being minus oil, which had obviously been why the protocol importance due to him had been withheld. To me, that was a lamentable state of affairs, an example of disastrous (and typically short-sighted) British foreign policy in need of an overhaul. I conceived that it would be one of my tasks, as Court Poet, to do what I could. At that stage, I wasn't sure how to set about it.

Abu Dhabi was in the news because of the way Saudi Arabia was fomenting trouble in Buraimi Oasis. (The actual village bearing the name 'Buraimi' was controlled by the Sultan of Muscat, who shared with Abu Dhabi, subject to their own disputes, the whole complex of oasis villages.) The Saudi claims were tenuous, but, rich in oil, they were able to bribe support on a large scale for their claims, whereas Shakhbut's brother Zayed had little but his outstanding personality to use for ammunition on behalf of Abu Dhabi; that and the protection of the British military (represented by the 'Trucial Oman Levies', to be renamed 'Trucial Oman Scouts'). Our presence in that area stemmed from the original treaty obligations which had been instrumental in changing the name of the coast from 'Pirate' to 'Trucial'. There was a snag to our treaty liability: ARAMCO, the oil company operating in Saudi Arabia, was American, and bent on acquiring fresh concessions around Buraimi; their ruthless commercial imperialism was something to which neither BP nor the other *concessionaire*, a French oil company, could be expected to submit tamely.*

On *Faares* once more, I had time to digest that information and think about what I ought to do. Bill McLean, the friend who had helped propel me to the South Seas, came to mind. He was only a junior MP†, but he knew a lot of people, so a word in his ear might do some good.

60

Meric's stay was a great success. Being eminently presentable, he was duly asked out by both Belgrave and Burrows. He was as effective with my Bahraini friends, too (driving out on an al-Sharif picnic he started quoting Persian poetry). Strolling about with him in Muharraq, I was able at last to hold conversations with those on the other side of the language barrier, to whom, before, I'd been able to do no more than nod.

The advantage was immediate: we found a carpenter, Mohammed, prepared to carry out a number of minor improvements in the house, cheaply. What made young Mohammed so acceptable was his randy personality. He lived with a pet parakeet called Bibi (short for *habibi*, my darling) in a shop cluttered with the tools of his trade. The bird would hop on to his arm to peck at strangers, in which way it differed

------

* The dispute over the Buraimi Oasis was complicated, and continued to be so for decades. Those interested should read more around the subject and make up their own minds as to who was 'in the right' – which is not to say Roddy was wrong for siding with Abu Dhabi and the British, only that it's perhaps unsurprising that that's where his loyalties lay.

† Bill was elected as a Unionist Party MP for Inverness-shire in 1954.

entirely from its master, who welcomed any diversion. On entering his workshop I might find him bending over a vice screwed to his massive carpenter's table, whereupon he would straighten up, white cotton shorts dripping with sweat and sawdust, grinning and shaking my hand for just that little bit longer than politeness required. Through Meric, I understood that he was currently saving money to buy a bride for which he'd have to pay 5000 rupees. Apparently a cut-price girl was on offer at 1000 rupees, but he didn't fancy her.

From then on I spent many happy hours with Mohammed, teaching him English, amongst other things. The pleasure of his company was mine at any time for a couple of whiskies. I had to insist upon the greatest discretion on his part, because what we got up to was technically forbidden; but Mohammed was very discreet, coming silently upstairs to scratch on the door of an evening and going silently away if he heard sounds of others being there.

After Meric left, I was at something of a loose end. Matters weren't helped by Nick's increasing condemnation of 'new friends' which weren't (and weren't ever likely to be) his. I knew that I was the one to blame for insisting on having my cake and eating it, but I couldn't bear to sit twiddling my thumbs in Muharraq, waiting for him to turn up – or rather, all too often, not turn up – when there was so much to do and to learn. When we met, he would usually suggest yet another visit to the Sergeants' Mess where, entertaining as it was, I had to exercise caution. I didn't dare let him feel that I might be getting on too well with someone other than himself. I was getting sicker too: my heat-rash was getting out of control, the soles of my feet were erupting with sores and, though not nearly as badly as I'd had it in Tonga, I was suffering bouts of dysentery. The vicar's wife, Edith, took me to the Manama hospital to be treated by a doctor who was himself covered in heat-rash.

Nick grew crosser with me, daily; I could do nothing right, and suddenly seemed to be in a downward spiral of illness. *I've got to get away from it all!* I decided. *Where better than Meric's cool house?* As a feeble sort of revenge for his lack of concern, I would leave for Kuwait without telling Nick.

The drama of sudden exit was counterpointed by an incredible chance: Nick happened that day to be working on the airfield and caught me leaving. 'I'm not your enemy, Rod!' he said, scowling like a mandrill. 'You can dthrop us a postcard if away for long.'

The truth is, he couldn't care less! I thought, as the aircraft soared away from blistering heat into a wondrous coolth. *He couldn't care less!*

Meric's air-conditioning continued a process of alleviation started on the aeroplane; but then my patches of red began spreading again. He took me to a doctor whose first question was 'Have you been under any particular stress lately?', which was shrewd of him. But very shortly my feet developed so many sores that I had to go to Kuwait's splendid new hospital for treatment. There they promised to keep me in bed – free – 'for as long as it takes'. Unloved (I thought) and unwanted save by strangers, I'd reached the nadir of wretchedness.

'Kuwait General' hospital had an excellent library, from which I borrowed extensively, chancing upon some verses by Gregorio Martínez Sierra which hit exactly on the chief cause of my disenchantment:

> I asked a sick man the complaint
> Of which he was to die.
> 'Of loving you, of loving you,'
> The sick man made reply.

In a delirium of fever caused by the inflamed skin of my body, I repeated the lines over and over, with Nick in mind; they seemed to sum up my deteriorating state. But then a change set in – typical of me, I had to admit. That sentiment might come in useful; it could provide the theme of another poem for Shakhbut. Hackneyed but evergreen, nevertheless true, the message was: *LOVE IS EVERYTHING!*

I ended up staying in hospital for nearly six weeks, lying in an air-conditioned room, my feet shielded even from the touch of a sheet. It wasn't until a Palestinian doctor remembered an ancient remedy that I began to respond. He suggested we try the resin exuded from an incense tree. Within three days the sores dried up beneath their coating of gum, and within a week I could be discharged.

A long-suffering Meric had visited me daily, until such time as he went on leave to climb in the Himalayas. Without a close friend, there was nothing to detain me in this richest of all boom-towns, where the only things in short supply were the indigenous people themselves. I let Nick know that I'd be arriving on 4 October, happy because I had successfully avoided the hottest part of an Arabian Gulf summer, but he wasn't there to collect me. Eventually I cracked and went to find him.

He was off-handedly polite with me until broken down by a few beers, when he was off-handedly rude.

On evenings alone I looked with freshly appreciative eyes upon the glorious view from my roof. At sunset, a greenish light glowed over the battered walls of the houses near the mosque from a technicolour sky. I would take drink after drink up to the roof, to perch on a west-facing parapet. There was so much that was endlessly fascinating to be studied: the *barastis* of neighbours immediately below; the square, colonnaded on one side; an old café, Persian-style, source of raucous broadcasting; the plain black cabin of a water-point, a squat water-boat out beyond; and other boats churning slowly over green-silvery water towards dhows at anchor. The whole quaint scene was brought up-to-date by cars travelling over the causeway, headlights rocking as they bumped over its uneven surface towards Manama. Astonishing, truly staggering, yet one observer was far from finding it enough. I was still not so different from that young Flying Control Officer who'd lurked inconsolably in a garden in Sorrento on a night heavy with the scent of orange blossom. What use was beauty if it couldn't be shared with the right person?

I had to snap out of it, and soon.

I was all set to return to Abu Dhabi in mid-November. Till then, I was determined to see as much as possible of what Great-Aunt Evie would have called 'greats and grands'. Drinks at the Adviserate led to break-fast next morning at the Residency. There I met Edward Henderson, who I found most interesting, as he was in from Buraimi and shortly to return to that disputed oasis. My comment about him was: 'thinning hair turning slightly grey, amusing slightly catty manner and a general fed-upness with oil company governess-cheer'. By which I meant the prevailing manners and customs of the Oilies, their determination to have their employees conform – or else. When he heard that I was due to call at Das Island on the way to Abu Dhabi on *Faares*, he said, 'That should be an education in itself!'

Tim had told me a certain amount about Das, namely that it lay some 170 miles from Abu Dhabi and had been uninhabited throughout his-tory … till recently. Now there was a newly established population of hundreds of Bedu men from Abu Dhabi complete with their own Imam and Emir; also a few clerks and technicians from India and Pakistan, all under the control of an English boss from BP referred to as the 'King of Das'. Edward Henderson filled in a few more details: 'The Bedu are there because Das would be a convenient terminal, should oil eventually be found in Abu Dhabi. The important thing is to have men already on the island, in case anyone else tries to claim it.'

According to Bapco's chief, Mr Skinner, there might be a good chance of striking oil in Abu Dhabi, but it was by no means sure. The 'shelf' which was currently enriching so much of the western side of the Arabian Gulf perhaps petered out beyond Qatar. It might reappear around Buraimi, or it might not. 'Oil is a mighty queer commodity,' he said. 'It forms, over millions of years, in one place, then it moves along some place else. Until we drill, we never know where it will fetch up.'

His words reinforced the views which I already held about Buraimi. To visit such a potential flash-point became one of my principal aims – one which I thought it best to keep quiet about for the time being. Now that it was no longer so infernally hot, I was quite looking forward to another voyage on *Faares*. And Das sounded fun.

61

I stepped ashore on to an island where Robinson Crusoe would have had no chance of survival: rocky, without trace of grass or tree and a flat brown sandiness with a range of reddish, craggy hills. Overhead, sea birds were wheeling and shrieking, whilst on and around our heads buzzed myriads of small black flies. Das flies didn't just buzz; they formed a thick mat on one's back as one walked along, leaving a once-white shirt speckled with the imprint of their unhygienic feet. What they really craved, of course, was sweat – salty, delicious sweat. They got it in bucketfuls from everyone who set foot on the island, and a nice change it must have been from a staple diet of bird-guano, which had brought them there in the first place.

From tents and a pre-fabricated hut a motley crowd emerged to greet us consisting of Bedu, one or two Indians and an Englishman, Ian Cuthbert, who welcomed me warmly but wanly with the words: 'I'm afraid I'm feeling dreadfully off-colour, old man. Must get back to Bahrain as soon as possible.'

'Of course you must. Anything I can do?'

'Well yes, there is! Would you mind staying on as King of Das in my place?'

Would I mind! How should I mind, if it would be a way of helping Tim, who had helped me so much? Tim had mentioned the possibility of constructing a landing-strip on Das, should there be room for one. If I were to be staying for a day or two, I could give the matter serious attention, as befitted an ex-Flying Control Officer. Although there were no roads, there was already a jeep which had been used by a surveyor; it was said to be 'broken', but might be repairable. But my priority would not be that so much as to get the Indian fitter to unpack a generator and have it working straight away, otherwise there would be no electricity to produce refrigeration, lack of which had clearly contributed to Ian's state of health.

Once sorted, I composed an informal report of the island – the state of the ground and where one might lay a runway – for Tim, hoping that it would prove to be of some value, and, having reached official conclusions, I was careful to reiterate that nothing about them could possibly comply with any conceivable Civil Aviation standards. It didn't worry me as much as no doubt it should have done. In wartime, when I'd learnt my trade, we hadn't been in a position to attend to more than a minimum of aircraft safety requirements.

The final ploy was to pretend to be an aeroplane coming in to land. Accordingly, I roared up and down in the jeep, shifting my run sideways a few feet each time, until I'd covered the whole area of the presumed runway, avoiding nothing in the way of soft patches or hard bumps. By the end of the day I was a bruised and nervous wreck and so was the jeep, its power of recuperation, without spare parts, being less than mine.

Whilst all that was going on I had to attend to details of kingly administration, which involved paying a courtesy call on the ancient Imam as well as on the Emir, both snugly installed in a *barasti* at the far end of the island. Also, there was a dispute to be settled about that most important of men, the labourers' cook. The Bedu chef employed by BP hadn't learnt how to make unleavened bread of the simplest sort, and everyone wanted him sacked. But then what? No cook! My solution was to send one of the resourceful Indian clerks to show the man how.

The Asian staff formed a splendid backbone, willing to do anything within reason without 'demarcation' objections. After the sunset Call to Prayer, when the flies were starting to settle down for the night, I asked a Pakistani called Gulzaman [literally, 'Rose of Time'] to help me take a shower by standing above and behind, pouring water from a jerrican. The man looked to be ten years younger than me, very thin, not very brown, with an urgent manner, a Pathan from Abbotabad who had wandered into the Gulf to seek his fortune but found, like so many others, little more than sand, flies and tough taskmasters. A lingering regard for the departed British Raj had led him to seek out a British company, which had led to more sand and flies – though less hard tasks – on Das.

Even with the benefit of a shower to cool me down, it could not thwart my dysentery. I'd kept it in check with Entero-Vioform or Spasmo-Cibalgin (a mixture of Trasentin and Dial, first gumming-up then sending the gut to sleep). But on Das, neither of those specifics did much good. Gulzaman declared that massaging my stomach would help, which it did a little. I was sad to say goodbye to him. As the dhow cast off, I saw him loping along the crooked jetty until he reached the end. There he stood, waving continuously, like a child at a departing train, until he was nothing but a speck in the distance. My reign as King of Das was over; and so, presumably, was any chance of seeing Gulzaman again.

Whilst we sailed slowly to the mainland, no amount of stomach trouble could stop me noticing an extraordinary outpouring of marine magnificence. The sea was so smooth that it looked positively oily and birds were floating on the faintest of faint swells as though nesting, like the Halcyon of legend, on the waves. At sunset, a gauzy mauve mist hung low over water which was itself mauve, flecked with orange. The dhow was not sailing so much as gently rolling over brocaded shot-silk, towards a dark grey mass on the horizon. Even the boat itself turned golden, with the crew in their dirty white robes golden too, like figures from an illustrated Bible. As if to maintain the Biblical atmosphere a fish was caught and cooked in the open for our supper. One of the men poured me a hot ginger drink, directly from a kettle. I mixed it with tinned milk and whisky, to make a nectar both enlivening and soporific; after which, undisturbed by the soft padding of bare feet on the restricted deck, I fell into a profound slumber.

Early next morning, we approached Abu Dhabi in time to see a desert sun rise over Sheikh Shakhbut's honey-coloured fort. Once more, I wetted my feet by wading the last few yards and was picked up by Tim's

Land Rover. Not the most comfortable place in the world, but lovely to be back again . . . if only my tummy would agree to halt its protests, even for ten minutes.

———

62

'Come, Poet!' said Sheikh Shakhbut, whilst we waited for a mutton grab to arrive on a huge circular aluminium tray. I rose from the place of honour on his right and retreated, as usual, to a corner, to declaim verses which had first seen daylight in hospital in Kuwait:

> *Love is not the sudden desire*
> *That looks on lust and finds it good.*
> *Love is not a leaping fire*
> *That flares when light is set to wood.*
> *Love is not a coloured plume*
> *Down-drifted from a jewelled wing;*
> *Nor yet a silence in the room –*
> *But, simply, LOVE IS EVERYTHING!*

Next, some counterbalancing abstractions which I knew would require a lot of explaining, if indeed they could be explained at all:

> *Give me your golden wings, your voice*
> *To wrap my music in a cloud.*
> *I cannot see, I have no choice*
> *But what you sing and sing aloud.*
> *Perhaps a part may penetrate*
> *My poor, defeated, blinded brain.*
> *But that small part will compensate*
> *For all my part-imagined pain.*

I then repeated the first stanza, to drive the message home.

There followed a lengthy discussion between Shakhbut and Abdullah

Moon-face, none of which I understood; except, that neither had the nerve to challenge the supremacy of love over all earthly things, however complicated the possible result. Trite as it was, my work had given pleasure, and that, after all, was its intent.

Talking of love made me realise how little I knew about that side of life in the sheikhly establishment. At the end of a meal, Shakhbut would suddenly rise and sweep out of the room, presumably to visit his harem, or his formidable mother – I thought it would be rude to enquire which. As soon as Shakhbut had gone, I could leave too, knowing that I was to return on the morrow. Once back in Tim's house, a lengthy siesta was all that I required. I seldom managed such a thing, due to the increasing demands of dysentery.

Unfortunately, my standard of health continued to deteriorate, to a point where I became almost as ill as I'd been in Tonga – which was very sick indeed. 'We'd better send you to Dubai, to see the quack,' said Tim, there being no doctor in Abu Dhabi. Sheikh Shakhbut happened to pick that day to say how happy he would be should I decide to pitch my tent in Abu Dhabi for as long as I saw fit. The listlessness of my response wouldn't necessarily have surprised him, because it was not de rigueur to express appreciation for a favour, nor even gratitude for a gift. However, he then asked more than once how I was feeling, to which I replied with the usual '*El hamdu l'Illah!*', but with an exaggerated whine, betraying weakness, which paved the way for telling him that I was in urgent need of medical attention.

'In that case, you shall go to Dubai in my car, Roodoo,' he said. 'My driver will come and fetch you tomorrow.' I was gratified by the way he'd dropped the use of the word *Sha'ir* in favour of calling me 'Roodoo', the nearest he ever got to my name.

Next day, after a meal in the fort which I could well have done without, the Ruler's blue Buick set out for Dubai, with me clutching my stomach and making moans as we bumped along. By the time we reached Dubai night had fallen; and it looked enchanting, this 'Venice of the Gulf', with us on the wrong side of a navigable creek winding towards the sea. In order to cross the *canale grande* we had to embark on a boat with a quasi-Venetian prow and chug past some thirty or forty wind-towers, each hung with mats at the base like those few remaining in Bahrain.

The BP Marine Areas office was a Persian fantasy in its own right: upstairs, a pillared balcony with fretted walls from which sprouted emblems such as a crescent moon, a pineapple and a coffee-pot; within, stained-glass partitions portraying flowers and geese.

More importantly, a Dr McAulley was to be found practising in a clinic supported by a consortium of Trucial Sheikhdoms, Abu Dhabi included. The doc was a gruff man with an Indian manservant, to whom he spoke only in fluent Hindustani. He at once prescribed Emetine, that old-fangled remedy which, taken in drops on a lump of sugar, had proved so efficacious in Tonga when all else had failed.

Optimistic that the Emetine was at work, I set out to call upon our Political Agent, Peter Tripp, who inhabited a thoroughly modern building, dependent on air-conditioning, a feature I welcomed in my parlous condition.

Tripp, at that moment, was being frank and informative. He had plenty to tell me about Dubai: gold was the foundation of its prosperity, gold smuggled in from the Indian sub-continent – that and the fact that there was only a 4 per cent import duty. With its navigable creek the Sheikhdom had become a centre of free trade, challenged only by Ras-el-Khaimah further down the coast, whose creek was smaller and less useful. Not so long in the past, the Ruler of Dubai had been notorious for treating his enemies to a particularly gruesome form of 'persuasion', a red-hot iron brought nearer and nearer a victim's eyes until they burst and shrivelled in their sockets.

I also heard something about Sharjah, the adjoining Sheikhdom; their ancestors had been even more successful pirates than the men of Ras-el-Khaimah. One of them had slain an ancestor of Shakhbut's in single combat. Till recently there'd been little love lost between those warring fiefdoms. 'But now oil is at work, lubricating past differences,' said the Political Agent. 'Plans are afoot to create a federation under the name of "United Arab Emirates" – that is, if it ever comes off!' I didn't have to be told the reason for the new creation: its purpose was obviously to give the small states a better chance of resisting pressure from mighty Saudi Arabia.

I went with Tripp to Sharjah, unable to resist the outing, despite being below par. On being dropped back at the florid BP office I was astonished beyond measure to see a familiar figure hovering in the doorway: Gulzaman, greeting me with fervour, head cocked to one side, transferred by Tim from Das to tend me until I got better. As soon as I emerged from yet another obligatory visit to the lavatory the Indian clerk couldn't wait to fill in a few gaps. After attacking one of the Bedu with a knife, Gulzaman had been sentenced by the old Emir on Das to a flogging, something which Tim couldn't permit, because his Asian employees were, by the terms of their contract, subject only to British jurisdiction. His easiest course had been to remove the fierce Pathan forthwith, before the incident could develop into a test of authority, and instead send him to work for me as a nurse.

So without asking, I had acquired a possibly dangerous attendant – a thoroughly quirkish manifestation of Providence. Nothing, as I was learning, was beyond the power of Providence, whether going by the name of God or of Allah. It was up to me to make the best of the situation and be grateful, whatever the outcome.

To be removed from Das and sent into my service might have seemed much odder to Gulzaman, but he declared that he'd always known that we were destined to meet again. As if to set the tone for a future of misconceptions, he claimed to be a cook, overlooking the fact that he didn't know the first thing about cookery: anything boiled was 'curry', anything fried a 'chop'. However, he could make a cup of strong green tea, which was all that an upset stomach required.

Coinciding with his seemingly magical reappearance, my dysentery threw in the sponge. Within a couple of days I could eat without having to leave the room immediately afterwards and could contemplate without dismay the lavish extremes of Gulf hospitality, Gulzaman's attempts at breakfast, uncooked marmalade pudding (which he called 'a cake') tastefully set alongside two fried eggs with microscopic yolks (produce of the local hens), being one of them.

———

63

I began thinking about how to get to Buraimi without much luck. The political routes – Edward Henderson, whom I'd met back in Bahrain, and Peter Tripp – had several excuses as to why it wouldn't be possible, usually revolving around what they considered adequate transport for me. Meanwhile I did learn a number of curious things from an Indian lady-doctor who assisted McAulley and seemed to enjoy retelling horrific tales about traditional feminine practices. The burka worn by all respectable women was bad enough (being stiff with indigo, it came off blue wherever it touched skin on the nose and round the eyes, a disfigurement favoured by the ladies because it gave them a fashionable pallor); I also learned that after a baby was born, a respectable wife was required to pack her womb with salt, so as to shrink her vagina quickly enough to pleasure her husband within a day of giving birth. Puerperal fever, from which many died, was apparently the rule rather than the exception.

Christmas was drawing near, and I'd been invited to spend it in Abu Dhabi with Tim (who'd been joined by his wife, Susan, and their ewe-lamb, Deborah), so back I went in a BP jeep. On Christmas Eve, what should I hear but news that Shakhbut would be leaving for a hawking-trip in and around Buraimi which might take several weeks. Over I went to the fort, returning to Tim with the outcome I'd desired: I would accompany Shakhbut on his trip, and he was also going to pop over for Christmas.

If Tim had been the sort of man to whistle with surprise, that's what he would have done. 'M'dear fellow, I'm overwhelmed, absolutely over-whelmed! You don't yet know it, but you've brought off a coup which may cause consternation in official quarters. Our people will get one helluva shock when they see you with Shakkers in Buraimi. I can tell you now – I couldn't before – he's to meet the Sultan of Muscat and Oman in the oasis on 28 December, finally to decide who owns what, the idea being to present a united front against the Saudis. It's all very hush-hush. Then there's another thing: if he calls on us on Christmas Day, he'll be pushed to reach Buraimi on time, the way he travels. It could cause an international incident!'

Oh dear.

Yet the Ruler had no intention of going back on his word. A cav-alcade consisting of him in his new car (a cream Cadillac convertible with a blue hood), his brother Khaled in a maroon Buick and soldiers in a red Chevrolet 15cwt truck duly negotiated the sandy, rubbishy track leading to Tim's concrete house-by-the-sea. Over tea, coffee, biscuits and tiny cakes Shakhbut showed great interest in 'our Eid', wanting to know exactly what we did to celebrate it. When Susan mentioned carols, he asked her to lead us in singing one, so we obliged with 'Once in Royal David's City', a reminder of Israel which he might not have been expected entirely to relish.

However: 'You *Nazrenis* ought to have a church in Abu Dhabi,' he said, stroking his beard. 'It might help to make you better behaved, which would be a blessing for us all!'

In order to appreciate just how remarkable Sheikh Shakhbut was, it is only necessary to take a leap forward to 1993, when, according to a report in the *Daily Telegraph* (14 September): 'Saudi Arabian police have arrested 329 people over the past three years for taking part in Christian acts of worship, which are banned in the Kingdom, Amnesty International said yesterday.' It was not much of a consolation to read that Saudi intolerance went further, embracing not even the other main, non-Sunni, Muslim sect: 'Shia Muslims and Christians are forced to worship in secret, in terror of religious police, who are given free rein to raid private houses and arrest those caught praying or in possession of rosaries, pictures of Jesus Christ or Shia or Christian religious literature.'

Shakhbut was indeed outstanding, for his day and age.

On Boxing Day the red Chevrolet 15cwt came round to pick up Gulzaman and me. We joined the Ruler's cavalcade, with Khaled's car and several three-tonners for the stores, soldiers and falconers. Ostensibly this was a hunting expedition, so hawks were its main feature. We got no further than the fort at the end of the mudflat, where we stopped for sweetly-sticky *halwa** with Shakhbut's son Sayed.

When we moved on, Shakhbut asked me to join him in the Cadillac, a signal honour. We sat together in the back, squashed between soldiers, the Sheikh smelling strongly of rose-water. Three more soldiers sat in the front, their hawks on their arms, the birds digging their claws into armlets of carpet-material to keep their balance as we bumped along a sandy track, their eyes hooded.

The honour of being at such close quarters was a stuffy one: Shakhbut preferred to keep all windows tightly closed. His conversation alone transcended the atmosphere: 'How long is the *Queen Mary*?' he asked. 'Would the ship fit into Abu Dhabi, if we made the sea deep enough?' When the car stuck in the sand and the engine conked out, he sighed: 'Now I'm left with only half a Cadillac!'

Shortly afterwards – for the first and last time, ever – he started asking the sort of questions an American might have raised during the first five minutes of acquaintance: What did I do for a living? Was I connected

---

* A type of confection.

with any business, or political party? He sought the truth, and it was easy for me to be truthful because I was no more and no less than what I claimed to be: a writer who could, if necessary, turn his mind to verse; certainly no journalist. A writer, and a moderately unsuccessful one at that.

We managed to get moving again, a gang of soldiers manhandling the Cadillac on to sections of pierced steel plating, such as I remembered using for landing-strips during the war. Then Shakhbut ordered a halt, so that the hawks could be released from cramped perches and flown for exercise.

'Would you like to be a hawk, Roodoo?' asked Shakhbut.

'I'd rather be here with you, right now,' I said. I didn't add that to be a captive with sewn-up eyelids was hardly my idea of fun.

I didn't have to pursue the subject, because one of Khaled's birds chose that moment to make a bid for freedom. Off it flew, and no amount of shouting or whirling of a line baited with meat could lure it back to its handler. On top of the general frustration, I detected an underswell of a rumour that the Poet must be a bringer of bad luck.

They hadn't reckoned with a Gulzaman. At the height of the hullabaloo he set off on his own, a thin figure with a long, loping stride. Half an hour later, back he came, the hero of the hour. Long-sighted, not unlike a bird of prey himself, he'd kept the bird in view right up to the moment of seizing it, and he'd never handled a hawk before. Khaled offered a 30-rupee reward, which Gulzaman wouldn't accept, thereby adding to his prestige – and mine, also. Nothing further was breathed about the *Sha'ir* being a Jonah.

The day we were to arrive in Buraimi, we awoke in tents on the sand to sunrise, with the usual stirrings and coughings in the cold morning air. Also as usual, they all knelt humbly on the sand to pray, whilst I, in my prayerless state, remained isolated. I felt the urge to join in, but was too shy to make a public profession of it, which might have caused annoyance. All the same, I was burdened with unease.

'When do you pray?' asked Shakhbut – assuming, as a matter of course, that I did.

'When alone in my tent,' I replied, aware that this was at best a half truth. If I'd had the Christian God more in mind lately, it was mainly due to the example set by Muslims.

They started applying kohl, a black antimony powder, to the insides of each eyelid, until their eyes looked enormous. This was something that I could do also, I thought, so I borrowed a little silver flask and dipper from one of the men and got Gulzaman to use the black powder on me – not easy, since it involved drawing a line touching, without damaging, the eyeball. I was left weeping blackened tears but otherwise looking like the rest, a result which gave enough pleasure and amusement to make it worthwhile.

Long before we were all ready, the heavy lorries left. Shakhbut's notable brother, Zayed, came out to meet us with his own retinue. He laughed when he saw a truck bogged down and lent a hand to help, like a good Boy Scout. Unlike his bird-like elder brother, Zayed was a competent tough, yet he was careful always to defer to Shakhbut, whilst behaving as a first amongst equals with everyone else. I was most impressed.

Without warning, Shakhbut held out a claw-like hand and presented me with 1000 rupees (about £75), saying that there was a souk in el-Ain where I could buy the sort of food I might perhaps be missing. Taken by surprise, I tried to hand it back, but no, he wouldn't have it. So here was the 'purse of gold' which Tim had prophesied might be mine. I couldn't pretend not to welcome it, but so as to reduce the feeling of one-sidedness I told Gulzaman to buy a small prayer-rug for 100 rupees when he went shopping for water-biscuits. I called on Shakhbut and put it down in front of him. He looked bored, but at least he accepted it. So then what must he do but send two larger, silken carpets round to my tent. Once again, I had to recognise polite defeat.

We rolled and bumped slowly in the Cadillac towards a three-storeyed, honey-coloured fort, evidently a centre of British military occupation: curtains hanging in front of each doorway; camp-beds with neatly rolled-up bedding; plain, bare rooms lived in by British officers wearing khaki but with chequered red head-scarves. We were greeted with deference and some relief. Soon, who should appear but Peter Tripp, followed by Edward Henderson, both of them looking startled, not to say guilty, after they'd made so many excuses about why I couldn't get to Buraimi.

Sensing what was going on, Shakhbut was highly amused, positively crowing. As we were leaving the fort, I asked Edward, 'Do tell me the programme. What happens next?'

'There's coffee with the Sheikhs, but I don't know if you'll be going to it.'

It needed Shakhbut to come over and take my arm – a thing which he normally never did – and lead me back to the car before the penny dropped and they were made to realise beyond doubt that I was part of the party. Even so, as we were driving off I noticed one of the officers nodding towards me and pointing to his eyes, mouthing: 'It's just not done!' Was he referring to the kohl or to the fact that I was there at all? Probably the kohl. The done thing amongst the Levies was to wear male head-dress but not male make-up. I could understand the nuances of that convention, but refused to apply them to myself. They weren't to know that I'd spent a lifetime circumventing sartorial (or any other) rules whenever I didn't wish to conform to such.

At the meeting itself there ensued one of the longest silences I was ever to encounter in the Arab world, one that lasted for nearly five minutes, indicating enormous mutual respect. Neither of the two principals found it embarrassing.

The Sultan was flanked by civil and military advisers, one of them being his Foreign Minister, an Englishman, Neil Innes. He, too, stared in alarm at my kohl-transfigured eyes but didn't comment. Someone else, a trim little man with an engaging smile, actually dared voice his approval, thereby gaining mine.

'Who can you be?' I asked.

'I'm James Morris, *Times* correspondent,' was the answer. He told me how he'd been travelling with the Sultan round his domains after the defeat of a powerful Imam. He was so far from being a typical journalist that when I said, 'Oh yes, that's the man the press keeps calling "the so-called Imam", isn't it?' he replied that the 'so-called' bit had been inserted by a propagandist censor, not by him. I was even more delighted when it transpired that he had known and liked my honorary great-aunt Bonté in Cairo. We both agreed what a shame it was that Shakhbut, ruler of the major part of the oasis, should have been left on his own to hold his end up against a Sultan with a whole flock of advisers. 'But at least he now has a court poet on his side,' said James mischievously. 'Our lot can't beat that!'

As a writer who'd taken to journalism, James Morris to me was an honorary *Sha'ir*. Just then, his claim to fame had been his reporting of the recent Everest expedition,* but it was as a writer that he would

---

* Edmund Hillary and Tenzing Norgay had made it to the top of Everest for the first time in May 1953.

become famous. That, and for something else, very different: he would soon be undergoing an operation to change sex from male to female. Unaltered powers of readability would ensure a poetic rather than pedestrian description of the whole experience, which would give hope and encouragement to others less articulate.

It would be nice to be able to say that I noticed this compulsion about him at the time, but I didn't. He was sensitive and witty and much the most entertaining man there. The irony would be that by being willing to undergo a drastic transformation from 'James' to 'Jan', she had displayed a single-minded determination commonly held to be a masculine rather than a feminine characteristic.*

That evening I was invited to the fort for some very British drinks. Cold-shouldering the Poet was at an end, having outlived its usefulness. On the contrary, I found myself sought after, to give a first-hand account of life with Shakhbut. Everyone, even an expert like Edward Henderson, wanted fresh examples of the Ruler's quirky remarks to add to the general repertoire. I sensed that what I said was having the effect of changing the prevailing, slightly superior way of looking at him to one of appreciation, so I rubbed it in with a heartfelt 'And high time, too!'

Next day, Sheikh and Sultan were to set the seal on their agreement about who owned which villages in Buraimi, Shakhbut as the major proprietor being the host. For a final time, the Tripp eyebrows nearly disappeared into the Tripp hair when the Sheikh beckoned me to his side as we sat in front of a full fifty yards of food laid out on the ground – a longer feast than anything I'd seen in the South Seas. Shakhbut gave me his permission to take photographs. The Sultan didn't much care for that and might normally have uttered a wrathful 'No!', but as a guest he couldn't do anything about it, merely asking me to refrain from snapping him whilst in the act of chewing.

Shakhbut mischievously (I thought) pushed two testicles of an unknown animal over to me, but as I'd previously learnt how to deal with that situation I murmured 'The honour is too great!' and passed them on to an English Major in the Muscati Infantry who mistook them for hard-boiled eggs, discovering his error too late to do anything about it.

---

* James Morris's 1957 book *Sultan in Oman* makes a reference to Roddy, describing him as the Court Poet who was clearly thoroughly enjoying himself.

Innumerable goats and chickens and at least three camels had been slaughtered. Flanking a huge variety of meats were all kinds of tinned fruits and sticky puddings, which, like the underlying mounds of rice, were lukewarm. A houbara* supplied by Zayed was in the place of honour, on top of a mountain of rice, but its exalted position put it out of reach of the Sultan and no one else dared grab it until after the departure of the official guests, when, as in Tahiti, there was a free-for-all for selected onlookers.

The meal over, the Sultan rose and left abruptly, as was the custom. He looked a fierce old thing. Luckily I'd been warned in advance that he didn't share Shakhbut's liberal attitude towards smoking, so I didn't try and light up. Off he sped in a red Ford truck, escorted by his host (and me) in the cream-coloured Cadillac with its blue hood. We must have made a wonderful moving tableau against the sands and date-palms of the oasis; I wondered what the crowds of onlookers, on the outside, really thought of it. Inside the car, rose-water sprinkled at the end of the feast competed with incense from tiny earthenware braziers that puffed at us as we left, creating an aroma which seemed the very essence of ancient Arabia. I was thinking: *Can this be real?* Then: *If it is real, how utterly unreal that I should be a part of it!* My own unaided will could never in a million years have thrust me into such a sequence of events. I suddenly realised that every illness, disappointment and setback of recent days had led inexorably to this moment of glory. I could never have devised the mechanism of such an elaborate plan, nor carried it through, by myself.

Beside me, Sheikh Shakhbut yawned, and to cover it up, as usual, muttered, '*La Illaha il-Allah!*' – there is no God but Allah. If there were a moment when I was aware of a flash of enlightenment, then that was it. The pace of understanding quickened till I realised that for the first time in my life I was actively hoping to be a fit servant of God, regardless of what else I might choose to be. I didn't go so far as to imagine that such a miracle could be brought about by the workings of Grace, because that idea was unfamiliar. Yet even at that moment I remained naggingly suspicious of my own motives, fearful of succumbing too easily to pious double-talk instead of subjecting it to criticism in a reasoned, analytical fashion.

---

* The houbara bustard was a prized bird in areas across the Middle East and Pakistan because it was considered an aphrodisiac; the intensity of the hunts mean conservationists now say the bird is endangered. Pakistan has banned the hunting of the bird in response, though still grants a handful of hunting permits each year to wealthy Sheikhs.

Shakhbut tugged at my sleeve, saying something which I couldn't follow. All I had to do in reply was to smile. I was in a state of utter exaltation; not just happy, but deeply contented.

––––––––––

64

On New Year's Day 1956, Sheikh Shakhbut sent his driver round to my tent with a superb Kashmiri wool head-scarf, off-white and embroidered with occasional 'Paisley' plumes in red and blue. The formidable Sheikh Zayed wore one, so did the falconers and some others; it seemed to be a matter for individual choice. The scarf kept the head beautifully warm, and didn't need an *agal* to moor it in position because it wrapped round the chin. When I made my first appearance thus garbed, the men shouted '*Mabrouk!* [Hooray!]', to which I replied (phonetically) with their own phrase '*Allah yibar ichefeek!*', presuming it to mean something like 'It's Allah's doing!' I was told that only at a formal *majlis* was there a 'right' way of winding and tying the thing, and that even then it hardly mattered; it had to be prevented from unwinding, that was all.

The coming of the new year made me think of the pranks which I might have got up to in London: first-footing; drinks and revelry at party after party; and a final obligatory descent upon Piccadilly Circus just before midnight, to embrace a policeman and solicit a stranger to the strains of 'Auld Lang Syne'. Did my increasingly more moral attitude to life make me feel that it had all been rather tawdry? Not at all. I saw no reason to disapprove of indulgences well suited to my nature. Long ago I'd decided that individual sexual practices had little to do with the scale of Good and Evil; for why should we have been given such strong urges by our Maker only to be told by His self-appointed interpreters that they were 'sinful'? It didn't make sense, when there was so much real wrong-doing to try and avoid. I was quite clear that the hope of having my will coincide with God's needn't preclude sex, except in some of its more distasteful forms, such as when it involved exploitation of the young or the feeble-minded.

The influence of Islam had ostensibly made me reassess my aims; yet I only had to reflect upon the past to see that the Church of England had been interwoven with my life from the very beginning: born on Easter Sunday; country vicars for ancestors (on both sides of the family); actual church buildings always close at hand – the decorative temple at the top of Well Vale, the church adjoining Claxby's garden, the church below Kingston House in Dorset, St Augustine's opposite 94 Queen's Gate, and finally our own twelfth-century Langney Priory. When had I ever not been surrounded by portents of Faith? The wonder was, perhaps, that so many Christian influences, so diverse and so continually present, hadn't opened my mind to religion much earlier. Yet it had needed the many Calls to Prayer from the mosque in Muharraq and the daily prayers of Shakhbut and his followers to stir me to re-examine my beliefs.

In Zayed's presence, the Ruler repeated his question: 'When do you pray, Roodoo?'

Again I answered, 'When alone at night,' which was truer than it had been before.

'You see, Zayed, they must have their own church in Abu Dhabi!' said his brother. I understood why he was making such a point of it: he wanted to make the idea as official as possible.

Another time, whilst we were talking, his portable wireless was broadcasting a quiz programme from Radio Cyprus, where a man and a woman were jokily 'chai-aiking' each other.

'How long will it be before you allow a *bint* [girl] from Abu Dhabi on the air?' I asked.

'As soon as Abu Dhabi has its own broadcasting station,' he said. 'If we have oil, we'll change even the way our *bint*s behave. If we have none, we needn't!'

Moments as significant as that were like currants in a cake, welcome because so much of my time was spent in silence, straining to catch the meaning of what was being said and done. My Arabic had come on leaps and bounds, but when an interpreter wasn't around, which was often the case, I could struggle to follow the conversation.

The new year was memorable for another reason, a request which was suddenly sprung on me. A cut between my toes was turning septic, so Gulzaman fetched a bowl of water and started washing the offending foot; and whilst engaged in that Biblical pursuit, he begged me to take him back to London. It wasn't altogether a surprise; in a sense, I'd felt it coming on. Without giving the matter a second thought, I agreed, and only later during the night started seriously wondering what I'd let myself in for. There was precedent for rich families to 'import' Indian bearers, but if I were to do so with Gulzaman he would have to be fitted into a flat with nowhere to sleep except in a cubby-hole between floors.

I tried to warn him: 'You see me here, travelling about as if on a magic carpet, and you are bound to get wrong ideas. In London I'm neither rich nor important. Even to provide your food will be a struggle!'

But the language barrier nullified my efforts. He neither believed me, nor did he care. 'No, no, you are lucky, very lucky for Gulzaman! If I do not come with you my life is finish!'

Obviously, I couldn't let that happen. I warned him that the dizzy project would depend on many factors: getting him signed on as crew in an oil-tanker and securing a permit for him to enter England, when he didn't even possess a passport.

'I think you can do this thing, *In sh'Allah!*' Gulzaman said, eyes flashing with a quality new to me – devotion.

This strong character ran through him from top to toe. One day I found Gulzaman playing with a scorpion in our tent, declaring 'He not sting Gulzaman!' and flicking it with a show of contempt. The scorpion arched its tail and dug into the aggressive finger, only to be seized and put into an empty match-box. 'He friend of Gulzaman,' I was told. Certainly the sting seemed to have no effect on him.

I understood why he wanted to keep the scorpion when I saw what use it was put to. He'd borne the taunts of the soldiery for being a foreigner long enough. (As the Sheikh's companion I was mercifully exempt.) Now, he had a weapon. All he needed to do to make them retreat was to open the box a crack and wave it in their faces. From then on I was often to hear a shout of '*Agrab!*', until the little pet escaped – and in our tent, what's more. Even after that, for a while the match-box on its own was enough to strike terror into a Bedu heart.

Gulzaman's antics could be a source of entertainment to others, not just to me. But I alone had to suffer the downside, when he would clutch his head and lie groaning on the ground, a caricature of misery. A kind word was usually enough to affect a rapid recovery, so I was hard put to determine whether those pains were wholly, or partly, imaginary.

When we were on our way back to Abu Dhabi, Shakhbut gloomily contemplated the after-effects of an atomic explosion. 'Aren't Western scientists clever enough to invent an injection against radiation?' he asked.

I told him I thought that unlikely.

'All the same, it would surely be possible!' he said anxiously. Then: 'How far away is the nearest star, Roodoo?'

We stopped at the fort guarding the *sabkha** where, for a change, we lunched off fish cooked in hot embers. My continuing interest in Arab food amused the Sheikh; he couldn't understand why I set so little store on the stodgy, gooey sweetmeats beloved by the toughest of the tough on the Trucial Coast. 'If you didn't drink or smoke, you'd find our *halwa* tastier,' he said, criticising me (for the first and last time) for indulging in those two bad habits. He had never before so much as hinted at finding gin-fumes breathed all over him nauseating, or cigarette smoke in the back of the Cadillac – with all windows closed – as distasteful as it must in fact have been.

We arrived at his honey-coloured palace/fort without drama, no more than a handful of his subjects realising that their Ruler was back in their midst until he was safely inside. When the news spread, men began arriving to greet him formally, with a great deal of urgent whispering, to which Shakhbut reacted by stroking his beard. We sat down on a sofa in his roof-corner *majlis*, a perch which seemed almost sinfully luxurious after the sands of the desert. All the falconers crouched nearby, their hawks on their wooden stands, the favourite, Tallal, on his keeper's sleeve. Then in came Tim Hillyard, beaming, followed by Abdullah Moon-face, also beaming. We rose to our feet.

There followed the usual exchange of '*Kef halek?*' and '*El hamdu l'Illah!*', repeated over and over again before getting down to any other business. Tim and the interpreter took up positions on either side of Shakhbut, earnestly talking nineteen to the dozen. Later, when others arrived, I asked Tim what they'd been discussing so excitedly. 'M'dear fellow, great news. The best!' he replied. 'Our Marine Areas are going to town. BP will be spending millions on sample-taking and so on, with Das the centre of operations!'

I glanced at Shakhbut. He was giving not the slightest sign of having heard anything so momentously to his advantage.

Tim said: 'He's convinced that your *baraka* has influenced our decision to go ahead with drilling. What do you make of that?'

---

* *Sabkha* are areas of land which consist of mudflats or sandflats. The Abu Dhabi *sabkha* is an area of coastal, supratidal salt flats (*sabkha* in Arabic means a salt-crusted flat depression).

'He's being polite. *Baraka* comes from Allah alone; no one knows that better than he does. Still, it is rather a thing, to think of my having a hand in the blessings raining down on my dear patron!'

'You mean, blessings gushing up, don't you?'

'Yes, I suppose that's what I do mean.'

How their lives were bound to change! But did it mean that they would all live happily ever after?

———

65

Shakhbut renewed his invitation for me to stay on in Abu Dhabi indefinitely. No specific position was mentioned, nor money, but I knew that I would only have to ask to be given a full measure of either. I toyed with the idea, but always declined. If indeed, as the Arab saying went, 'The fate of a man is written on his forehead', then what was written on mine was that I must be moving on. I would settle down one day, but not just yet. Nevertheless, my heart was full of regret when I declined the magnificent offer on the grounds that, like a Bedu, I had to keep shifting my tent, something which Shakhbut, of all people, couldn't take amiss.

When he realised that nothing would persuade me to stay, he spoke of my future, taking me to task about my attitude towards the family elders. For almost as long as I could remember I'd thought of (and described) Uncle Dick as 'wicked'. It was a way of making a rueful joke out of his weak unpleasantness towards our family. But Aunt Susan's malice was too strong to be dispersed in humour; my label for her was, simply, 'cold'. That feeling had been entrenched shortly before I'd left for the Middle East.

Hubert Fox, that dear old friend from my days at Oxford in the ambulance unit, happened to come across Marjorie Scaretti, who had made so much of 'Cousin Roddy' at the time when Rome was being liberated. Since then, Aunt Susan's bosom friend had back-pedalled somewhat as regards me. She couldn't resist passing on a tit-bit of gossip: namely, that this same 'cousin' had been disinherited by his uncle in favour of John

Reeve, Susan's nephew. She told Hubert, 'Roddy has always been rather unsatisfactory, they say, and I suppose they know best.'

'Quite so, from Dirty Dick's point of view,' I commented. 'All the same, I never thought he'd go to *those* lengths!' I almost added *And I don't believe he can* but preferred to hold my peace until after I'd consulted Edgar Norman, of Larken and Co., the Rawnsley family lawyers.

My understanding was that my darling grandfather had left his estate through his widow and son and then, should there be no son's son, on to me. I only had doubts because of my grandmother's generosity in immediately handing over her half share in the Well Vale Estate Company to Dick, in spite of all that a medium could say to convince her that she was acting contrary to the wishes of her late Walter.

Mr Norman's reply to me was that I was correct in my assumption. Although Well Vale itself was irretrievable, nothing had changed as regards the money except that there was much less of it than my grandfather had envisaged; which was why my mother had apparently been left 'nothing', when in fact she'd been left half of what wasn't there. Because of the excellent way in which my grandfather's will had been drawn up, such money as Granny Rawnsley had handed over to Dick to enable him to live at Well could be income for life only. As things stood, nothing could disinherit me unless Dick produced 'issue' – impossible with a wife of Susan's age. There were of course some 'what ifs'. What if Susan died or Dick divorced her, and instead were to marry some fertile young hopeful? Then, at the snipping of an umbilical cord, I would truthfully stand to be disinherited.

But the 'what ifs' were not something I'd been brooding about. Hubert's news had merely confirmed that Well Vale would never be mine. I couldn't say that I minded too much: the lovely place would have been a great burden for a town-lover such as myself, though it would have been good for Genissa and her husband Michael. Claxby was another matter; it could have been a familiar dower-house for my mother in the evening of her life. I pondered and pondered, but couldn't decide what my true feelings were. Shattered rather than surprised by the spitefulness of it, I didn't know whether to feel anger or relief.

Whatever Granny Rawnsley's opinion, I had never doubted that my uncle continued to hold two early 'crimes' against me, disapproval festering for years: my refusal to go out hunting again after the first hateful experience of being 'blooded', and a famous 'Slaughter of the Innocents', an occasion when my grandmother, determined that I must impress her disbelieving son with my sporting prowess, had sent a reluctant me over to Well to shoot ducks, during which I'd brought down four birds as they were cumbrously gaining height from a lakeside thicket. On bearing my victims back in triumph, I'd been icily informed that they were tame Oriental creatures, purely ornamental, my aunt's pets. No apologies of mine could prevail against the verdict: '*He must have done it on purpose!*'

Anyhow, Shakhbut supposed that I meant 'wicked' with regard to Uncle Dick literally, so was very distressed. 'Perhaps he would be better disposed towards you if you gave him the opportunity,' he said. 'It is up to you as the younger man to defer to his judgement. You should sit with him in his *majlis* and beg his forgiveness!'

'All right, I will,' I said. But what I meant was: *I'll try!*

The day came for me to leave. No particular ceremony, I simply got up and went, as I'd seen them do. In fact, I struggled to hold back tears. On passing for the last time through the great door leading to the sand outside I wanted to yowl uncontrollably, but I couldn't because a bunch of soldiers had to be greeted, then bidden farewell with a prolonged '*Fi'am'Ullah!*' (short for *Fi aman Illah* – in Allah's keeping). Tugging at their cartridge-belts, they shouted the words back, two of them seizing my right arm and kissing it – very gratifying. When leaving Tahiti, so heaped with *couronnes* that I could hardly breathe through flowers, we had all been wildly crying. Turia and myself, of course, but all the *fetii* as well, as custom demanded. How feminine Tahiti seemed, compared with masculine Abu Dhabi, where I had no woman to say goodbye to, except for Susan Hillyard!

As a BP jeep was going to Dubai, my few things were loaded on to it and we set off along that bumpy bulldozed bobsleigh run, our progress advertised by a roar from a broken silencer. I wasn't leaving on *Faares*, but in the comparative luxury of a BI (British India) boat, SS *Dara*, which was circling the Gulf on its way to Bahrain. I could afford the passage for Gulzaman and myself without qualms, because of the money given me by Shakhbut at Buraimi. But first there was a little business to transact at the Political Agency in Dubai. I had to persuade Peter Tripp to let me have a document certifying that Gulzaman was in possession of a work permit attaching himself to me, like a limpet, for as long as

I chose to employ him. With it (so I'd heard) Gulzaman could travel anywhere with me, for a year. Anywhere? Yes, incredible as it seemed, anywhere, including England. And that pearl beyond price cost no more than 9 rupees.

———

66

Back in Bahrain, I was aware of a new (and not very nice) atmosphere in my adopted home-town. An Iraqi from Baghdad with five children, who was friendly but apprehensive, told me that the High Executive Committee were stirring things up against foreigners, himself included. I tackled my friend Jusuf, because he was a cousin of the committee's No. 2 man, Abdul-Aziz Shamlan, who I knew and liked, and was met with an irritating mixture of logic and skewed propaganda. 'We demand democratic rights,' he said. 'Belgrave [he pronounced it 'Bell-er-grave'] is preventing His Highness from granting us our democratic rights. BELL-ER-GRAVE MUST GO!' Argument was useless. For good measure, Jusuf continued his harangue with disparaging remarks about Bapco: 'They're stealing our oil!'

'But the company is paying for it, Jusuf.'

'Exactly! Stealing Arab resources sent by Allah and giving us worthless pounds and dollars in exchange!'

Annoying as that reasoning was, Jusuf was too handsome and helpful to cause me more than faint irritation.

In my absence, Nick had been given the run of the house. His time in Bahrain had already come to an end, but he had left me stocked with drinks of all sorts; which was just as well, because Abdul-Aziz Shamlan was not averse to a drop of forbidden alcohol, nor, of course, was my earlier benefactor, Sheikh Salman. Those two opposites never happened to come calling at the same time, though there were one or two narrow shaves. One of Shamlan's visits coincided with a Call to Prayer, when Muharraqis were milling about in the street below, pointing up at my balcony, waving greetings.

'You see how popular I am?' he said. 'If His Highness refuses to come to terms with our committee, his days are numbered.'

Oh really? I thought.

I had occasion to be saying 'Oh really?' quite a lot during the next few days. As stated in their manifesto, one of the HEC complaints was that there were too few Bahrainis in the police force. When I met Colonel Hammersley, their English Chief, at dinner, I tackled him with that. He said: 'We keep appealing for more Bahrainis to come forward; it's been on the radio, the last three days. What we usually get are ex-Levies, Omanis, Yemenis and Baluchis, good trained men with character. But suddenly yesterday a whole gang of Bahrainis turned up, an awful lot of fellows. It was a plot, of course!'

'So what did you do?'

'Welcomed the lot of 'em, which wasn't what they were expecting. Interviewed 'em and told 'em to come back next Wednesday, when I'd have their eyes examined (or something), and get them to come back the week after that, to have their teeth looked at, and so on.'

On 2 March, Selwyn Lloyd, the British Foreign Secretary, turned up on a visit of goodwill to Bahrain. It was a Friday, the Muslim Sabbath, when few would be working. The Ruler went to meet his distinguished guest at the airport, to bring him back to Manama in a cavalcade. It was too good an opportunity for the HEC to miss. At a signal given near the causeway the crowd began chanting '*BELL-ER-GRAVE MUST GO!*', switching to '*DOWN WITH IMPERIALISM!*' when the car containing Selwyn Lloyd was forced to a standstill, kicked and rocked.

I happened to be standing near enough to see the expression on the victim's face, so couldn't fail to observe that our archetypal civil servant looked as outraged as a broody hen about to be chased off her nest. Had he tried to speak, he might have got no further than a squawk. I had every sympathy with him.

On sighting the Ruler's Rolls-Royce the chanting reverted to '*BELL-ER-GRAVE MUST GO!*' Men slapped his car and one threw a stone, smashing a window. I then saw what I obviously wasn't meant to see: precisely how the riot came to an end, when a blue car containing members of the HEC drove up – proof that the demonstration, later described as 'spontaneous', had in fact been orchestrated.

I strolled about to see what damage had been done and met Colonel Hammersley advancing on foot, spearheading a small force of police pushing their way through the hostile crowd.

He was none too pleased to see me. 'Ought one to arrest you, eh, Roderic?'

'Well, not exactly,' was my reply, 'or there'll be no one to do the drinks tomorrow, when you're supposed to be coming to my roof.'

'So I am! I'll try and turn up at 6.30, if this lot will let me.'

For the next few days I spent time and energy picking up the threads amongst the British greats and grands – Burrows, Brooks Richards, and especially Belgrave himself – a process made easier by the fact that all of them were church-goers. On Sunday we sang 'Onward, Christian Soldiers!'

Over a full English breakfast with the ever-accommodating vicar and his wife, I spoke warmly of Sheikh Shakhbut's enlightened views about establishing a church in Abu Dhabi, but I didn't expatiate on my own change of heart being due to my time spent with Muslims. I couldn't be sure that my conversion mightn't turn out to be a mere flash in the pan, and I didn't want to let on how shaky the reasons for my attending his services had previously been.

The atmosphere in Muharraq was worsening, but quite unrelated to the HEC, on the night of 11 March an unknown Bahraini banged on my door, swaying and demanding drink, declaring his readiness to pay for it. My deepest suspicions aroused, I told Gulzaman to get rid of him. A fight looked like starting. Gulzaman rushed off and rushed back with a knife, which I had some difficulty in taking away from him. When the man finally backed down, I delivered a sharp lecture on the use of knives, but I doubted whether it had sunk in.

After he came back from the souk next morning he had an alarming tale to tell: 'Mr Nick' had acquired a reputation for supplying drink to far too many eager clients, which had caused rumbles of indignation amongst the more respectable of our neighbours, the very ones on whom I might have to depend should 'the troubles' get worse. It made me particularly angry, because Nick himself was safely out of the way of the possibly lethal consequences of his thoughtless behaviour.

Things were indeed getting worse. Rumour had it that five protesters had been killed. An angry crowd forced two policemen to take refuge in the equivalent of a town hall, from which other policemen had been unable, for hours, to rescue them. The man whom I'd relieved as King of Das, Ian Cuthbert, was greatly concerned for my safety. He offered to put me up for the duration, but James and Enid Belgrave had already got in first with their offer, should I be forced to flee. James had married

Enid, a Bapco nurse at Awali, and settled down in a bungalow on the well-protected road to the Naval HQ at Dufair.

Events took their course as follows:

Monday, 12 March: To commemorate the killings, the High Executive Committee called a General Strike. However, Gulzaman managed to procure some unleavened bread from the local baker and the water-carrier came round as usual. Bahrainis meeting me in the street went out of their way to be extra polite. I set out in Sheikh Salman's Cadillac, but before I'd driven 200 yards saw trucks pulled up by the side of the road; so I stopped, too. A small boy ran up and shouted: 'Don't go on, Sahib, there's trouble!' I backed the car all the way up the one-way street till I reached my house. There I found the landlord moaning that wicked men were threatening to set fire to any moving vehicle.

Disregarding the risk, Abdul-Nabi and Rasac turned up, having managed to run the blockade. They were in a prickly mood. 'Burrows ought to have intervened with troops, and would have, if Belgrave hadn't stopped him!' they declared.

'Would you have welcomed an intervention?' I asked.

'Yes,' said one.

'No,' said the other.

That evening, Gulzaman prepared a meal, and after washing up, asked whether I had a son. 'Not as far as I know,' I replied.

'Then I am your son,' he said, as if the matter were beyond argument. 'I am your son!'

13 March: Ian Cuthbert sent along Jaafar (who'd been fifteen years with the Belgraves) with a six-volt accumulator because the Cadillac wouldn't start. He arrived in a delivery-brake belonging to Moon Stores and stayed long enough to switch batteries with the help of two men from the local bicycle-repair shop. When the car still wouldn't start, we pushed it a few yards; but before it could give a cough of life, it attracted unwelcome attention. There'd been a Call to Prayer. Men entering and leaving the mosque were milling about and some of them took it into their heads to give the Cadillac a thump. By the time that we pushed it back in front of the house, a riot was flaring up. From all round, men were pouring into the street.

I called out 'Ana Muharraqi! [I'm a Muharraqi!]' and was pleased to see some of them nodding. Back inside the house I could hear an argument developing on religious grounds: 'Why did you leave your prayers to help the Unbeliever?' 'It is our duty to help our neighbour!' etc, etc.

All the time, the mob was increasing in number, the shouting growing louder by the minute.

Suddenly I missed Gulzaman. Then I realised that he'd rushed downstairs and was standing, alone, outside in the street, a knife (actually our bread-knife) in one hand whilst with the other he patted the Cadillac. 'The first man to touch this car will die!' he was shouting. With a final flourish, he came back inside and stood by the door, ready to pounce upon anyone trying to force a way through. My heart pounded in anxiety when I saw the expression in his eyes, something quite new and frightening. Those eyes were fierce beyond belief, yet as blank and shining as pebbles wet from the sea. His was the naked face of loyalty, a quality likely to be underrated until the moment when it and it alone is what counts.

To our considerable relief, we heard a new kind of shouting. I hoped that the police had arrived to disperse the crowd, but no policeman could have ventured into those narrow alleyways at such a moment. From the balcony I saw a number of Bahrainis with armbands, making shooing motions, and the mob wavering uncertainly, then backing away, cheering. Their extraordinary reaction was due to the timely arrival of HEC stewards sent by Abdul-Aziz Shamlan in person. '*El hamdu l'Illah!*' we said fervently. '*El hamdu l'Illah!*'

It was a moment or two before I remembered to add: 'And thank God!'

Inflammatory speeches from Radio Cairo were a daily norm. Since everyone with a wireless seemed to be tuned in, the raucous sound of accusatory voices regularly echoed from street to street in Muharraq. I couldn't follow what they were shouting, so I asked James Belgrave for a translation of a typical one. He obliged with an excerpt from *The Voice of the Arabs*, broadcast at 8.10 a.m. on 5 March, therefore well in advance of the riots themselves:

> Oh Arabs, oh toilers, oh workmen, receive your smiling day with the golden beams of the sun which are shining to pierce the darkness! Be like those beams and dispel the darkness of Imperialism in every place . . . Oh you, the toilers of Muharraq, struggle and strive to fight the nightmare known as the English, these are the ones who dominate your interests, who batten on your produce, who control your country's wealth . . .

It was nice to know that Muharraq had been deemed worthy of special mention, but not so nice to realise that such overblown rhetoric was being swallowed in daily doses by my neighbours. I was further alarmed by warnings from the Indian proprietor of a café who slipped into the house under cover of darkness to tell Gulzaman that a plot was afoot to break in, that night or the next. I was forced to agree that our only sensible course was to move.

Moon Stores were to send their van to fetch us. I started packing a few things: my all-important diary and whatever came under the heading of that awful word 'toiletries', plus assorted clothes, including formal wear in case of some ultra-British evening occasion. The arrangement was that my bag should be taken – not by me – into the Moon Stores brake, then Jaafar would get in, then Gulzaman and finally myself, all as quickly and smoothly as we could. And off we'd go.

But what actually happened? Gulzaman flitted about, attempting at the last moment to tie his tie in some complicated knot. He fiddled with the lid of the bread-tin, and lastly fumbled and fumbled with the lock on the street door, loudly proclaiming: 'He stuck!'

Conspiratorial seconds ticked by, stretching to minutes, whilst I remained on the stairs, neither properly in house or car. As much from excitement as from sinful alcohol, the Moon Stores chaps were jollily intoxicated.

We moved forward with a jerk and were about to go the wrong way up the one-way alley when a watchman from the mosque, till then invisible, loudly informed us that it was a one-way street. The irony was that at this lawless moment it never occurred to us to break that particular injunction. On we careered into, rather than out of, Muharraq, whilst I sat upright enough to prevent my face from being seen by anyone outside, the van windows being unusually low.

We got lost in a maze of Muharraqi cul-de-sacs and a back tyre had nothing better to do than to puncture, making the vehicle flop along, which apparently disconcerted nobody but me. Eventually we emerged on to the sea-road, scene of Selwyn Lloyd's discomfiture, where cordons of revolutionaries, faces partly hidden by head-scarves, made some attempts to stop us until reassured by our cries of '*Mabrouk!* [Victory!]'.*
Soon we were flumping across the causeway, where things were much

---

* Mabrouk means 'blessed' but it can be used interchangeably as a word of congratulation, hence why Roddy is using it as 'Victory' here, but earlier used it as 'Hooray'.

quieter, though the road was scattered with tacks hammered into Pepsi-Cola bottle-tops, none of which led to further punctures. Without incident, we reached the open stretch of the Dufair Road, the centre of the British world, and were delivered, like merchandise, to the door of the BP bungalow where Ian Cuthbert was staying. That night I slept on a vi-spring mattress, in blissful calm.

14 March: That afternoon I saw James and Enid Belgrave, who told me that they were running short of food and paraffin, both of which Ian could and did arrange to have delivered to them, just as he also arranged for a fresh supply of flour for the Residency. James's car had already been stoned and so had his father's. All the same, he insisted on driving his deputy, Shirawi, round to the Adviserate. Sir Charles Belgrave, the principal target of the moment, even wandered, by himself, into the souk, so as to be seen chatting to the merchants as if all things were normal. The Belgrave family certainly lacked for nothing in the way of courage.

Hearing that the revolutionary leaders were at that very hour being received by Bernard Burrows, I asked whether the committee had yet been recognised. I was told that it was in the process of so being, but under the less provocative name of the Committee of National Union. In which case, had it been received by His Highness?

'No, not yet; but it will!'

The Bapco camp at Awali had been sealed off. No European was supposed to leave the environs of Dufair without special permission. The Englishmen employed by Kanoo, the Niarchos shipping company, were confined to their quarters, as were most others. The situation continued to be tense, all round.

It was very useful to be near a telephone for a change. I took advantage of it to ring Jusuf for a chat and was disconcerted by his insistence that I should return immediately to Muharraq: 'It was rumoured yesterday that you were dead, my dearest friend. Allah be praised that this is not so! If you go back to your house I will guarantee your safety and the People's Police will be on your side.' Gulzaman was bitterly against doing anything of the sort, but I realised that the HEC couldn't afford to have harm come to me. On the contrary, it would be a feather in their cap if they could claim that they, and not the government police, had been my real protectors. Having been specifically invited back, I couldn't very well refuse without slighting Jusuf. I didn't regret the precipitate flight from danger; it had been useful for keeping me in touch with what was going on, but it had been prompted by cowardice disguised as caution – as I knew, if no one else did. So I left my precious diary in the church safe, just in case, whilst Gulzaman repacked our things.

Duly, along came Jusuf in a Red Crescent car with four Bahrainis wearing streamers dangling from their lapels to show that they were committee men. We drove, untroubled, through cordons lounging at ease, scarcely bothering to give us a second glance, and were soon back in Muharraq, being greeted effusively by the neighbours and even more effusively by Hateem, the Iraqi with five children.

15 March: I got up and had breakfast as usual, then strolled about and said good morning to my landlord. A small crowd gathered, so back I went indoors. My friend Ibrahim, of Middle East Traders, sent a message advising me not to make a reappearance, which meant being mewed up for the rest of the day. Gulzaman could move about freely. He went marketing, duly procuring some liver (at 3 rupees, 8 annas), unleavened bread and fleshy cress. The water-seller came by, beaming all over his face to see his customer back in place.

I had nothing to do but reflect; and reflection led to action. Pen in hand, I composed a letter to my uncle, using Sheikh Shakhbut's words as an excuse: 'The Sheikh was extremely distressed to think that there should have been any coolness between you and I, and lectured me quite often about it to a point where I really have begun to feel that I may often have been guilty of disrespect towards you. In which case I am sorry, but I have gone through many lives rather quickly and always more or less off my own bat. I expect that that will continue, but I hope that you do not think that I forget for long that you are my uncle.'

On re-reading that badly expressed draft, I thought: *No! Apart from the fact that it's not the absolute truth, I simply can't give such feebly boastful hypocrisy an airing!* Anyway, it wasn't likely to do much good, beyond making Dick distrust me more than ever – and with better reason. One result of having plenty of time on my hands was that I could think twice about sending it, before deciding not to.

My next ploy was to turn enforced idleness into time well spent by trying to instruct Gulzaman. He could neither read nor write English and was barely literate in his own tongue, Urdu, so it was an uphill task. The first of all lessons was to try and make him understand the meaning of the word 'meaning', a proposition almost as surely doomed to failure as asking him to 'think of nothing'. When he finally managed to write a few simple words, he clung tenaciously to one selected pronunciation, however inaccurate it had been originally. Thus 'cat' was 'kite' and remained 'kite' for ever, though 'mat', which began as 'mat', stayed as 'mat'. The result was 'The kite sat on the mat', for all eternity. Some people are born teachers. I certainly was not, being far too impatient.

16 March: Another day of boredom and frustration. Having no radio and of course no telephone, I began to feel out of touch. My neighbour's wireless kept going full blast. Being a Friday, that meant hours of chanting excerpts from the Holy Koran, clear male tones only interrupted by the famous Egyptian singer Umm Khaltoun sobbing out her love-songs for the love-lorn.

Ali from the bicycle-repair shop called in to say that Belgrave had agreed to go in three months' time and that the duties of Adviser would be taken over by an Advisory Council. He had two other bits of news: the al-Sharif car had twice tried to reach me but had been stopped at the Muharraq Police Station and turned back, and there was unwelcome confirmation of the earlier story that some people, confusing me with Nick, were saying that I'd been selling crates of beer to the locals. I regarded it as another nail in the coffin, one more reason for leaving Bahrain. I was awaiting an answer from Norman Gregory, to whom I'd written about a possible voyage back home in a Niarchos tanker from Kuwait, incidentally asking if I might bring Gulzaman with me.

17 March: The day dawned bright and clear (there had previously been a *shamal* which had now blown itself out). Fed up with being trapped indoors I wandered into the street to test the atmosphere and was amazed at the change which had come over everybody and everything. Shops and booths were open. Taxis (gleaming from hours of polishing during enforced idleness) were charging about. To save it from possible damage, Sheikh Salman had sent Sultan to remove his Cadillac, so I went by taxi into Manama, where the news was that the strike had been brought to a sudden end by the threat of sending in British troops. Al-Bakr,* the Secretary of the nationalist movement, had addressed a mutinous meeting when Shamlan had been told to order the workers back to work, and both revolutionary leaders had been invited to dinner

---

* This is the spelling Roddy used; spelling more commonly used is al Bakir, first name Abdulrahman.

at the palace. 'It was just in time,' I was told. 'The rioters were about to set fire to the causeway and attack the power-house' – the fact that such actions would have made life extremely uncomfortable for their own selves being conveniently overlooked. By no means were all happy about the way that the newly named 'Committee of National Union' was hobnobbing with royalty. Jusuf had no doubts at all on that score. 'They're no better than prostitutes!' he snorted.

Of course, I went to call on Hussain Yateem in his office in the souk. There I found him, relatively unconcerned, together with my other benefactors, Sheikh Ahmed and his brother Salman, both of them pretending not to have been affected by the troubles. 'I could have moved frrreely, all the time!' Salman claimed. But I noticed that he wasn't saying precisely when or how. In general, there was an air of anti-climax and a tendency to play down the events of the last few days, which made it all the more bizarre that two British newspapers had despatched reporters eager to scoop a good disaster story: Stephen Harper of the *Daily Express* and Eileen Travis of the *Daily Mail*. Both were hoping for some dramatic denouement. Entirely in vain! It was all over; yet there they were, stuck for the next day or so.

Lean and hungry Harper had filed his copy about the arrival of a British cruiser to the rescue: OIL MOBS RIOT! provided a banner headline for a front-page story of gunboat diplomacy still with a part to play in our foreign affairs – the sort of thing his readers wanted to hear. As it happened, there'd been no trouble for Bapco at Awali and the cruiser had been scheduled for a courtesy visit from some time past. Eileen Travis, an American purringly larger than life, displayed more balance in her reports, going for the human angle, as instanced by a swoon article on the Belgraves.

Although they were rivals, the pair went everywhere together, even coming to see me together. By then they were hardly on speaking terms because Travis, having agreed with Harper not to file that day, had promptly done so. She had cleverly obtained a translation of a *Voice of the Arabs* broadcast guaranteed to send a chill down the spine of anyone back in England ignorant of its customary over-the-top ranting.

I told Harper what I thought of his story: 'It was absurd! Much too patronising towards the Bahrainis.' He wasn't in the least repentant. 'A threat to the standard of living of fifty million of our folk is more important than kow-towing to a handful of Arabs,' was his line.

'Even if untrue?' I objected.

'Doesn't much matter. It'll be true some time, somewhere, you bet!'

Miffed by my criticism, he took himself off with Travis; but she soon returned, on her own, wanting, as she put it, 'to get the important bits straight from the horse's mouth'.

I was highly flattered and willingly pontificated to the top of my bent, whilst she rolled about on my hard iron cot, trying to make herself comfortable. In that she succeeded; my monologue almost sent her off to sleep. Jerking awake, she said, 'I do believe, three months in this house would restore my sanity!' Once talking, she couldn't stop, saying how much she distrusted women who said they didn't like other women, which was what her son's girlfriend had said, the first time they met. It became clear that the one thing she needed to talk about was herself. As I couldn't help liking her, I adjusted accordingly. We had plenty of time and plenty to drink, and partook lavishly of both.

67

The reply from Norman Gregory was kind but firm: 'There shouldn't be any difficulty in accommodating you any time between mid April and May and I suggest you let me have a closer idea later on as to when you will actually be in Kuwait ... but I don't think we could go along with the addition of the Pathan for various reasons which I will explain to you when you arrive.' Welcome as his letter was, the reference to Gulzaman was profoundly disappointing. In fact I was stunned. It was a body-blow. Had we come all this way together, only to be parted now?

I felt that the classical Fates simply couldn't allow it to happen. I imagined Clotho and Lachesis disputing the toss. Had all their spinning and cutting of the thread been in vain, if their sister, Atropos, were to remain unyielding? Judging by the speed with which the Benevolent Ones customarily enforced their verdicts, we mightn't have to wait long to find out.

When I told Gulzaman the bad news, he smiled the archaic smile of Greek tragedy and shook his head. 'No, father!' The mulish expression which I'd come to know so well took over. 'No, not possible! We find another boat!' Not wanting to dash his hopes, I didn't tell him how difficult that might be, knowing from experience that crew were normally signed on for an out-and-back voyage only. And how could Gulzaman, with inadequate documentation, enter the country by doing a 'pier-head jump'? My brain whirred and clicked in despair until a friend suggested they could get Gulzaman on to a Swedish tanker, and there the matter rested. With no great feeling of certainty, I prepared a TO WHOM IT MAY CONCERN letter, asking the world to give every assistance to the bearer. Also, I gave Gulzaman a visiting card engraved with my name, address and telephone number in London, in the hope that one day soon, he would arrive.

My last few days in Bahrain were spent in a whirl. James took me out to see Hussain Yateem in his country house, then on to the island on which the Ruler had allowed his Adviser to build a holiday home. The island doubled as a prison; men could be seen walking round in chains. 'When we need anything done, the murderers are the most reliable types – decent fellows on the whole,' said James.

A flourish of farewell parties didn't stop me from an energetic goodbye to Mohammed the carpenter amidst the planks and sawdust of his workshop, with the pet bird, Bibi, squawking jealously.

The actual day of leaving (8 April) produced a hotch-potch of farewells. People who had little in common except knowing me briefly appeared and disappeared, as if stage-managed to prevent clashes of opposites. Jusuf and Ibrahim insisted on taking me to lunch with Shemlan, in his house with green shutters and a hen-coop on its roof. There I was told that al-Bakr had been 'sent to the Lebanon for his health', which sounded as if his had been the first committee head to roll. We went on to the airport, where I was greeted by Sheikh Salman and Abdul-Nabi, waiting in separate corners, before James and Edith turned up.*

In such a way, I was never alone with Gulzaman for long enough to

---

* Some months later, in October 1956, the situation in Bahrain again grew tense as the National Union Committee, as they were now called, organised protests against the Israeli-Anglo-French invasion of Egypt because of the Suez Crisis (the invasion's aim being to regain Anglo-French control of the Suez Canal, which the Egyptian president Nasser had nationalised). Violence in the streets ensued. Roddy's friend Sheikh Salman ordered the arrest of Roddy's other friend Abdul-Aziz Shamlan – Jusuf's cousin and the No. 2. of the National Union Committee – along with the other two leaders. All three were found guilty and were sentenced to fourteen years in prison; they were released in 1961 and given compensation by the British government for wrongful imprisonment.

feel the true impact of our parting. Relegated to the sidelines by circumstance, his only defence was that same archaic smile, fixed as if soldered to the bones of his sweating face. Would I ever find such loyalty again, this side of Paradise?

––––––––

68

After a year away, I arrived back in England on 8 May 1956, first into Liverpool before making my way to London. In the railway carriage I suffered a mixture of emotions: nostalgia, apprehension, dread of the future and excitement for it too.

When I arrived at Euston there was plenty of luggage to be collected: not the single bag of an air-traveller, but the paraphernalia of the sea-borne. I was so busy hauling things on to the platform that I missed spotting the two men approaching until they were within yards. And then I got the shock of my life.

ONE OF THEM WAS GULZAMAN!

We talk of hearts 'leaping for joy', or 'missing a beat'. It isn't something which happens often in life, but when it does, there can be nothing in the world to compete with it.

I was stunned and incredulous to hear him say 'Hallo, father!' and to have my right arm clasped all the way up to the shoulder, whilst Mike King-Smith, my lodger at 94 Queen's Gate, stood, hands in his pockets, waiting to get a word in edgeways.

'He arrived on the doorstep yesterday,' said Mike. 'Lucky I happened to be there to let him in.'

The whole sequence of events was unbelievable, but true. A letter dated 17 April from the friend back in Bahrain awaited me at Queen's Gate, explaining some of the facts. He'd secured passage for Gulzaman by getting him a work permit on board the M/T *Pan Gothia* until the vessel arrived in Avonmouth. Arriving in England on 7 May – the day before me – Gulzaman had then somehow managed to persuade James and Hodder, Ship Brokers, to help him – without a passport, and with no more than the work permit issued to me personally in Dubai, my visiting card and the TO WHOM IT MAY CONCERN note. Had his appalling English made them take pity on him? Or had they thought that anyone so ill-equipped to enter our strict country must have some influential hand behind him? Whatever it was, with Certificate of Identity No. 228/56 he'd contrived to get through Immigration and on to a train to London, then to make his way to Queen's Gate where, by what must have seemed another extraordinary dispensation of Allah, Mike met him on the stairs as he was about to leave for his office.

Once I'd absorbed the wonder and delight of the new situation, I was faced with some serious thinking. What on earth would I do with a semi-literate Pathan; and equally, what would he do with me? How would he occupy his time? Would he find friends easily, amongst compatriots, perhaps? I would soon have to start writing my Gulf book, *The Golden Bubble*, for which a contract had already been signed with Collins. That would involve me going down to Langney Priory and squeezing page after page of manuscript out of a resistant brain, up in the Monks' Dormitory and alone, always alone, during which time Gulzaman would be functionless. Ought I to impose him on my unwilling mother, or should he stay in London and attend English classes? It was not just one problem, but a whole compendium. *There'll be an answer*, I thought, *even if I don't know what it is, at the moment. There has to be an answer!*

I could never have guessed the form which that answer was to take, nor through whom it would come. Lindsay Verrier, unique doctor from Fiji, was visiting London, struggling to maintain his eccentricity unimpaired. He didn't find it in the least odd that I'd imported a Pathan. He said that he might have done so himself, in a similar situation.

'But you should send him to be tested for TB,' he added, as soon as they met. 'He's had a hard life and he's a shade too thin. Take him to UCH and tell them that he has an intermittent but persistent cough, with an abundance of sputum, otherwise they may affect to take no notice. Make sure that they agree to subject him to an attack by X-rays. Then fasten your seat-belt!'

We did what he ordered, taking him to University College Hospital, where I'd once been a confidential number-only patient.* The upshot was rapid and frantic, for he did indeed have TB. Hearing that there

---

* Roddy was, perhaps unsurprisingly, treated for syphilis in 1952. Before arriving in Fiji some years earlier, he'd also had crabs.

was a superb TB hospital in Eastbourne, I managed by dint of special pleading to get him transferred there, still on the National Health. The Eastbourne hospital had wards which were two-bedded rooms, chalets opening on to sheltered verandahs – a holiday camp on a small scale.*

The swings of mood to which Gulzaman had been subject when we were with Sheikh Shakhbut were explained. I felt guilty, but how could I have known? Now it might be too late. Literature was awash with stories ending in a gallant, hopeless 'Let's pretend!' prelude to the inevitable death-bed scene. Yet I was the only one to be anxious; he was unconcerned, having a blind faith in my ability to pull a cure out of a hat. Since I couldn't bear to disillusion him, I had to put on an act, as if tuberculosis were no more than a simple inconvenience.

The amazing, the staggering aspect was that this had become nearly true, very recently. Only for the last three or four years had Streptomycin been combined with Izoniazid PAS to make a magic cocktail, offering, for the first time in history, a genuine chance of a cure for the disease feared by generations under the name of 'The White Plague'. Gulzaman's *baraka* was meeting the challenge of a lifetime. There was no way of explaining why this should be, only how. I felt awed by the sheer coincidence of his luck. But we were by no means out of the wood. Had they caught him in time?

He shared his chalet/ward with one other, John Shaw, member of the Magic Circle, whose conjuring tricks were enough to lift anyone's spirits. The staff were exceptionally nice, so Gulzaman found himself in clover. It was almost as if he were in a state of reincarnation, being rewarded for a former life of extra hardship by extra kindness. Exhausted after a daily stint of authorship, I would visit him, when finished for the day, if only for ten minutes, seeing him gradually transformed. Until one terrible afternoon I found him coughing into a blood-stained tissue. In a panic of misery, close to tears, I approached Matron and was told that he was merely suffering from a severe nose-bleed.

Matron was quick to prick my resultant euphoria: 'Yes, he's doing very well. But he will keep smoking!'

'I thought it was allowed?'

'So it is, but we discourage it. What's more, I've seen you smoking, when you're visiting him. We don't try too hard to stop the patients,

---

* Readers might be interested in the quasi-*Carry On* film *Twice Round the Daffodils,* which was made a few years after this event and set in a similar-sounding TB ward.

because although it does them harm, they say it's their greatest joy in life. But visitors, now ... how can we expect our patients to do what's best for them if their friends continually set a bad example?'

I assured her that I would abstain during my daily visits, which from then on I did. But it made me think (again) about giving cigarettes up altogether. I'd toyed with the idea years before and had almost succeeded after a bout of flu, but had succumbed when a friend poured scorn, saying that it was pointless to deny oneself a major pleasure when life held so few.

This time, Ralph Anstruther returned from Army duties in France and presented me with a carton of duty-free Benson and Hedges – completely out of character. 'I don't need them any more,' he said smugly. 'I've taken the plunge!' Had he said 'I've taken the Pledge' I couldn't have been more astonished, for like me, he was – or rather had been – a three-packets-a-day man.

It made me think much more seriously: if Ralph, well able to afford any quantity of tobacco and with no one else's welfare to consider, could give up the habit so easily, then surely I, low in funds, who had been specifically asked not to encourage Gulzaman, could do likewise?

In 1956 there was no general awareness of the health-risks of smoking, so that consideration didn't count for much. But there was one conclusion which I reached on my own, without prompting: unlike alcohol, nicotine could do nothing positive to transform a mood, create a carefree attitude or build confidence; the most it did was to appease a craving produced by it alone. Drink could make the humdrum seem fantastic; smoking couldn't. It was as simple as that. So began the weary hours of abstinence, familiar only to those who have tried breaking any strongly entrenched habit. The world became the Vale of Tears which pessimists had always insisted that it was. I resorted to everything I could think of, including prayer, the strongest deterrent to my backsliding being the patient lying in bed for week after week, slowly but surely recovering. He had intervened to save my life in Muharraq, so the least I could do was to intervene to help preserve his in Eastbourne.

With Ralph's carton half untouched I stopped lighting up and took to snuff instead, the strongest and cheapest, made by Wilson, obtainable in tiny tins for a sum so small that it hardly registered. Snuff, sniffed not in pinches but in ever-increasing dollops from the back of a hand, could produce an explosion of the mind – a fair substitute for inhaling. The downside was the mess it made, staining handkerchiefs a nasty diarrhoea-brown; but I didn't care, so long as it did its job of weaning me off cigarettes.

To add to the irony, after all my efforts Gulzaman himself seemed unable to stop. At first, when I came to see him he kept up a pretence, but his stained fingers were the giveaway. Nevertheless, I knew that the worst thing in the world would be for me to revert, so much was at stake.

How I missed the familiar mechanisms: pulling a packet, or a case, out of a trouser-pocket; offering it round to others; lighting up; even the simple intimacy of a cigarette lit by or for a special friend! Did anything in my past suggest that I would forgo, for ever, something so well liked? I scarcely dared think so. But then, that past was reassuringly behind me; and might remain so, if only I could be granted the strength to persevere.

part six

good fortune

1956-9

69

No one going away for a whole year can expect to find people and things exactly as they were before. The good news was that various friends had married and were blissfully in love, or had married and were blissfully pursuing extra-marital activities.

But there was bad news too. During my absence abroad, a terrible fate had befallen my university friend Hubert Fox. Bicycling along a country lane, he'd hit a pot-hole, fallen off, cracked his skull and died. I mourned him greatly. We'd been together as 'conchies' in Hawkspur, striving to do our duty as we saw it, though he had no real need, being unfit for military service. It was he who'd passed on the vital information from Marjorie Scaretti that I'd been cut out of my wicked uncle's will. Thanks to him I'd stayed in Alphonso Ossorio's mews-house in New York and caroused with the Jackson Pollocks. In years to come, how I would miss his drawly friendship!

And it was sad for me to witness the continuing deterioration in Bridget Chetwynd, physically and mentally, though she remained a superb party-giver. In the autumn of 1956 I found myself sitting on her stained sofa next to a woman in her late forties, introduced only as 'Mavis' – blonde, with a heavy face, over which flitted a succession of delightful expressions of knowingness and naivety; one moment an elder sister, the next a courtesan, yet without a hint of malice. Whilst she talked animatedly, she touched; it was obviously her style.

I was entranced. 'Who is she?' I asked.

'Mavis Mortimer Wheeler, the one who shot Tony Vivian in the balls when both were plastered!' Bridget said. 'You know . . . or perhaps you don't? She must have come out of jug whilst you were having fun with your Sheikhs. It was frightfully bad luck. She wouldn't hurt a fly, intentionally – I mean, look at her!'

It was unfortunate that at that moment Mavis heaved about, spilling her drink on the carpet.

I recalled some of the details of the famous shooting affray and the even more famous trial which followed. An emergency court had been convened in hospital, to enable a wounded Lord Vivian to give evidence from his bed against Mavis, his lover.

'Of course she always has too much, but can you blame her?' was Bridget's only reproach. It was difficult to imagine anyone wanting to be unkind to that fallible, charming woman; but clearly, someone had been.

I was instantly allured, and she seemed equally keen on me. I had proof of that when her friend Stuart Wilson showed me one of her letters, written on 29 October:

> There is an interesting chap now on my 'visiting list' who writes books (!). Some quite good – shhh. He goes off to the Sahara and Tahiti and places remote for his material – dressing and living as the natives. His name is Roderic Owen, very pleasant to talk to and gives one delicious luncheons cooked by his Parthian [she meant Pathan, of course] . . . he is kind and considerate – has kissed me on the right cheek once and offered to run me anywhere in his tiny motor.

Mavis was one more introduction owed to Bridget, role-model of my early years in the Big City. But I was 'growing out' of her, that was the trouble. Fascinating as she remained, I was beginning to feel that she was over the top in her sophistication. Her sitting-room was a louche work of art in itself. On a sill beyond the sofa where I'd sat with Mavis, avocado stones were ranged in jam-pots, dangling their roots into water, and the curtain above them was multi-coloured, sewn with pieces of mirror-glass the size of halfpennies. An old grey nursery-cord carpet was full of holes, partly concealed by a table with an aquarium leaking on to it. There were three decrepit armchairs and a glass dome covering a clutch of brightly plumaged stuffed birds. Another table was littered with papers, pot-plants, china pigs and china shoes, the latter overflowing with stubbed-out cigarette-ends.

Above one fireplace (the room had two) hung a mirror round which she had stuck paintings, done by herself, with rhymes written underneath. The oddest thing was that the paintings bore a curious resemblance to the artist, even when they were of men. My favourite, which might have been a child's attempt at drawing a character from *Struwwelpeter*, had been given the wistful sub-verse:

This person's sad
Because it's mad
And doesn't know where it's going
And can't explain
Or face the strain
Of endlessly not knowing.

'I feel just like that!' she said. 'I don't know why everybody doesn't. They jolly well ought to!'

The sitting-room, being two rooms thrown into one, extended to the back of the house, overlooking a garden deliberately left to run wild. Over years of total neglect trees and bushes had formed an impenetrable thicket, where sexually active cats prowled in competition with Bridget's own Siamese.

To reach the window, a visitor had to get round a clutter of objects, including an oil-stove, and past a table from which food (stale bread, butter, the remains of some nameless meat and chocolate biscuits) was seldom wholly cleared away. Somehow she managed to fit in a small portable typewriter, together with piles of typescript. But recently I'd noticed something which sent cold shivers down my back: a used hypodermic syringe. She was drugging, and had ceased to mind who knew it. She even tried to persuade me to 'have a go', as if it were the most natural thing in the world.

I most certainly would not. My experience with drugs had never included heroin or cocaine and I didn't intend to start. My past attempts had been modest. At Eton, we had experimented with benzedrine, which had just appeared in the form of a metal tube of inhalant. Levering open the container and steeping the impregnated cotton-wool in a glass of water, we made a draught which kept us super-awake, capable of boning up all night on the subjects for next day's 'Trials'. The tube could be bought, without prescription, at any chemist. Tablets of benzedrine which were soon on sale didn't have nearly the same effect.

My second experiment was with ether, removed from the operating theatre at Guy's Hospital, Orpington, during pacifist days of chronic overwork. Guiltily unstoppering a stolen bottle, I would sniff away, thrilled by the great wave of semi-unconsciousness which would nearly (but not quite) overwhelm me. When it began to produce nothing but headaches, I gave it up.

Thirdly, there was 'kif', offered by my friend, the sculptor Leonard

Byng, at that time living in The Salutation, a superb Lutyens house in Sandwich. Leonard broke off a piece of what looked (and tasted) like compressed grass. The effect it had was to make me sweat, hot and cold, whilst my voice seemed to be coming from the other side of the room – an experience far too unnerving to be worth repeating.

Even before drugging, Bridget had started a habit of railing against Randolph, her nice but boring Guards Officer husband who did his best to accommodate her every mood, and in so doing, infuriated her all the more. Her irritation increased to a point where she begged me to let her have a key to my flat, so that she'd have somewhere to go 'when maddened beyond endurance'. Of course, that was hardly a conventional thing; I couldn't expect Randolph to welcome the move. But by then he was sufficiently inured to her vagaries to say nothing. Whilst I was away writing my book in Langney, she was probably there quite a lot.

I was in for a shock on one of my rare London visits, when I found the flat-door standing open. My first thought was *Burglars!*, but going through into the sitting-room I saw nothing odd. Everything seemed to be in place. I quested about. The kitchen, window open, was in a mess: a broken plate lay on the floor in front of the ancient gas cooker, and the cooker-door had been left carelessly ajar. Going on up the stairs I reached the bathroom, to be greeted, as always, by the little Indonesian puppet Djongelan, given to me by my lovely lady Emilie in Anacapri, fixed so as to raise an arm whenever the plug was pulled. Today Djongelan was gazing at a message on the bathroom mirror, scrawled in lipstick in huge undisciplined capitals – unmistakably Bridget's:

SORRY ABOUT THIS. WAS FED UP AND CAN'T THINK OF ANYTHING ELSE TO DO – B.

What did it mean? I raced round the flat again, without discovering anything else in the way of a clue. Perhaps the word 'WAS' carried a hidden meaning? I decided to ring 10 Selwood Terrace. The telephone was answered by Randolph.

'Is everything all right?' I asked.

'Very far from being all right,' he said guardedly. 'Yes, Bridget's here, but she isn't seeing anyone for the moment.'

I took the leap: 'Did she try doing herself in?'

'She may have done . . . we don't want to talk about it . . .'

So with that I had to be content until the next day, when Randolph would be at work. This time I managed to speak to Bridget. 'Of course I did!' she said in a sleepy voice. 'That was the whole object of the exercise. Come round and I'll tell you all about it!'

Round I went. Her sitting-room stank of the garlic ointment which she rubbed over her neck to help alleviate her angry skin-rash (which was looking angrier than ever).

'Oh, you poor thing!' I said on seeing her. 'The rash, I mean!'

'Yes, it is pretty fiendish! I'm not sure it isn't what they call "St Anthony's Fire" in one of those awful home medicine books.' Then, with a quick turn of the head, presenting me with her face in profile: 'I suppose you're dying to know why I did it?'

'*How*, would be my first question.'

'Oh, I thought you must have twigged. You didn't? Well ... I went to your place. I was fed up. I put my head in the gas-oven, turned it on and waited. So far, so good. I felt iller and iller, until I passed out. But then I came to! I mean, it was shattering! I pushed off and staggered back here, feeling jolly dizzy, I can tell you. And dying to have another go, but lacking the energy.'

I thought it better to ignore that last remark. Also, I felt that this was not the moment to reprove her for leaving my flat-door open. But there was one question which certainly did require an immediate answer: 'Did it never occur to you that you'd be dropping me thoroughly in the shit?'

'Oh it occurred to me, all right, but it simply didn't matter. At that moment nothing mattered, absolutely nothing. Of course I'm most dreadfully sorry now, but then I couldn't have cared less!' As always, she was being as honest as she knew how; but in that very honesty I could see danger. Without a doubt, she'd try it again. As if reading my thoughts, she said, 'I expect I'll have to give it another go. As you're such an old friend, I do want to make it clear: from now on I'm not to be trusted!'

It was then that I revealed the ironic fact about my cooker, bought second-hand in Tottenham Court Road to go with the furniture which she herself had kindly lent me for the bug-ridden rooms in Cleveland Street. Blue-enamelled and as old as I was, the oven had a 'Regulo' knob which had long ceased functioning. For years it had been incapable of producing a flow of gas beyond setting 3, taking three and a half hours to roast a small shoulder of lamb.

'Just my luck!' she said ruefully.

When Bridget did as I feared, she did it in her own home, and no more successfully than before. But there was publicity, and she was sent briefly to prison. She was outraged: 'This horrible wardress person seized me and pulled my legs apart and jammed a thing up me, saying it was what they did to everyone. Testing for VD, I suppose; but she did it so roughly it hurt like hell. Sadist! I told her so and she simply prodded all the harder . . . I don't think I want to go through all that again!'

Good news from bad? It might have been, had she not become such a bosom friend of Daniel Sykes, himself a heroin addict but without Bridget's originality or charm. Heroin was a slower method of committing suicide, that was all. She continued giving her parties and I was still on her list, but she was taking against me for being so reproving, of which I had proof when she issued a rather grudging invitation to a birthday celebration for her younger son, Tom. She said, 'There'll be a roulette wheel and I know you're too pi for words about gambling. If it won't bore you too much, do come, as long as you won't give one of your pep-talks. You've shown a tendency to do that once or twice, lately.'

I couldn't feel too happy about being accused of priggishness, when to my mind I was simply trying to be more responsible, more conscious of a need to distinguish right from wrong. 'And high time, too!' as some would have said.

Another female friend, of more recent vintage than Bridget, was also showing signs of deterioration. Patricia Denny had parted company with Prince Alexander, who had left her and married Princess Maria-Pia, daughter of Umberto, ex-King of Italy. The parting had not been easy. Then she took up with a Nigel Hope, who dropped her for being 'too tense', marrying my beautiful cousin, the heiress Iris, instead (about whom he was not particularly nice).

Patricia's next was Andrew Faulds, the actor. When he became an MP on the outer fringes of 'the loony left', nobody could have been more surprised than me. He was pleasant and unfanatical in those days, and I daresay found Patricia educational. Be that as it may, their affair didn't last long. Clearly, she was meeting no one to match her Prince.

Gina Edwards, the friend who'd been impregnated from the bathwater, continued living with her in Upper Addison Gardens, through thick and thin. When Patricia wrote a suicide note, then crashed the Bristol into the Queen Mother's cavalcade outside Peterborough, Gina was the one to see her into an asylum, from which she was extracted after a fortnight's detention. So good a turn proved unforgiveable, and Patricia took violently against her dearest friend. Gina rushed off in tears to a bed-sit in Cumberland Place and found a job as an office receptionist. I did what I could to make her feel less abandoned and we remained friends for life.

―――――――

70

With Nick away on another contract overseas, there was nothing to hold me in check. I ranged freely, picking up likely prospects, finding it exciting. However disappointing an occasion might turn out to be, such contacts were valuable for the insight which they gave me, if only briefly, into the manners and mores of anyone, regardless of class or colour. In no other way could I have learnt so much, so quickly, about strangers.

An important watershed was the publication of the Wolfenden Report in 1957, when I was thirty-six, even though its implementation was to be delayed for another ten years. 'Wolfenden' was an appropriate name. His report signalled an ending to the eternal presence of wolves ravening to tear the careless or the merely unlucky to pieces. Life after his report promised to be – and was – just that little bit better for adventures and much, much better for misadventures. Eventually, we fervently hoped, life without a cloud hanging over it would be better still.

People then and people now might be shocked to learn how frequently experiences materialised out of the blue for one avowedly open to such. For instance:

At the end of an evening in the Fitzroy I invited two territorial part-time paratroopers back for the night. They were in fact brothers-in-law, Fred, a bus conductor, having married the sister of Mick, a builder. They were both all for 'a bit of the other' and uncommercially minded. A few days later I was invited in my turn to their place, a flat belonging to Fred and his wife Lizzy in a council block off the Old Kent Road. Mick, by then, was away on a job, I was sorry to hear, so we obviously weren't going to have the repeat performance to which I'd been looking forward.

I arrived at one of the most under-furnished flats I'd ever seen anywhere (Islington included): bare floorboards except in the kitchen, where there was a bit of lino; a sitting-room with a broken-down sofa, a deeply scored sideboard and a table; a bedroom for their three small children sharing one cot-bed and a wardrobe; and in the main bedroom a double-bed which wobbled when touched. I particularly noted that there were no pictures (with the exception of photographs) and not a single book to be seen. *I needn't feel so bloody superior!* I thought. *It's their life, not mine.*

This being a Saturday evening, the three of us went to the local pubs, all of them lively with customers singing and pianos thumping. At one pub a famous character called Elsie, in tight black chiffon sewn with jet, belted out an old favourite:

> *I love my Muvver-in-law.*
> *Gor Blimey! Don't she snore . . .*
> *I wish she'd break 'er back,*
> *Cos I'd look smashin' in black!*

We all joined in the chorus:

> *'Ow I love 'er!*
> *'Ow I love 'er!*
> *'Ow I love my Muvver-in-law!*

'Mine's an old cow,' said Fred.

'No she int, she's been real good to you!' said Lizzy indignantly.

'She's going to be a grandmother-in-law again soon,' said Fred, patting a protuberance I hadn't noticed until then.

'You would bring that up out of turn,' bridled Lizzy.

'Well, mind you don't!'

'OOOOH!'

On such lines the evening proceeded, smoothly except for times when we ran out of anything to say, to the accompaniment of much humming and jiggling. My function, I realised, was twofold: I could carry them from pub to pub in my car – this being in pre-breathalyser days – and I could pay for the drinks at a ratio of about six to one.

Only when we got back to the flat was I informed of a third require-ment: I was to stay the night and that was that. I made some sort of gesture towards the sitting-room sofa, but when they turned surly, I had to pretend that I'd been joking. No children appeared; apparently they could sleep through almost anything.

We piled together into the rickety double-bed. Turning off the light was the signal for Fred to push me firmly up against his missus. Taking my head, he rubbed it against a tum more pregnant than I'd supposed, indicating that I was expected to lick and suck – not at all what I would have chosen, even with Fred bucketing about behind. It proved that I was expected to be there mainly for her benefit, with Fred aiding and abetting; so I did my stint, trying not to think about what I was doing, until a series of heaves and groans indicated that some satisfaction had at last been achieved. Fred then rolled over me into the place next to Lizzy; and as he did so, the bed, which had been lurching about as if we were at sea, collapsed, leaving us heaped at an angle against the wall. Fred wrenched it off its hinges and we spent the rest of the night on its leg-less frame on the floor.

Early in the morning we were roused by one of the children totter-ing in to be cuddled. He (or she, it wasn't immediately obvious which) stared solemnly at the heap of humanity, then clambered purposefully over us to reach his mother, showing no trace of surprise or shyness. Clearly I wasn't the first stranger to appear out of the blue on a Sunday morning. When we were all thoroughly awake, Lizzy produced mugs of tea thickened with sweetened condensed milk, of a turgidity equal to any wartime desert brew-up. No reference was made to the previous evening's activities. As soon as I could, I left, in time to catch, and stop, youngsters kicking a ball against my car. Luckily they hadn't got round to letting air out of the tyres.

A few days later I was surprised by another telephone call from Fred, suggesting a second helping of that unsatisfactory night. My reply was that I'd love to, provided that it would be just with himself and brother-in-law Mick. 'No offence, mind,' I quickly added, 'but it's best we don't include Lizzy.'

There was a pause. Then: 'Oh, I see, Rod. Yes, I understand. Well, that's that, then. Cheers!'

We didn't meet again.

Enough to turn hair white overnight was another experience. In the Victoria Dive I chatted up a dark-haired young man claiming to be a Lithuanian refugee whose family had been wiped out by the Russians. I trotted out the story of my time with the Russkis in Vienna, which he enjoyed hearing because it was so much to the discredit of the Red Army.

'He would like to come back with you and you will tell him many fine things,' he said, using the third person. 'We will stay like that till the dawn, perhaps?'

'Perhaps!'

We retired to Queen's Gate, whilst I kept on talking; but for lack of obvious encouragement in any other direction, I dropped any plan I might have had. And anyhow, I was gradually being overcome by sleep. Drowsily I noticed that he kept shaking his left wrist, causing his wrist-watch to make an odd sort of clicking sound. I asked what he was doing.

'This!' he said, thrusting his watch against my face. 'This is how he protects himself when the Russians come!' Tugging at the bracelet he pulled out a small knife on a chain, the blade perhaps two inches long – a real oddity. After putting it back in its sheath, he suddenly pulled it out again.

'What a clever idea!' I said.

'Not clever. Dangerous!' was the reply. 'Dangerous, like he is, very dangerous!' Replacing it, he pulled it out again, replaced it, and pulled it out again, stroking the little knife lovingly, first against his neck, then against mine.

I was absolutely terrified. The bedside light being still on, I could see a fine glint of madness in his eyes. 'Oh, I'm sure it is,' I said with what casualness I could muster. 'But you're not in any danger here, so let's get to sleep.'

'He's not tired.'

'Isn't he just? Well, he may not be, but I AM!'

And with that I reached out a quivering arm, fumbled for the switch – it seemed to take ages – and plunged us into darkness. My heart was thumping so loudly that I was afraid he'd be bound to hear as well as feel it. As I lay there, breathing deeply but as silently as I could, I heard the dreadful clicking sound of him continuing to play with his lethal toy.

On and on it went. I didn't stir. Then I turned away with a grunt, as though already asleep. Again I heard the clicking. I could imagine myself telling friends: *Oh yes, of course I was scared stiff, but the chap was bound to fall asleep in the end.* Was he? (And would I live through it to find out?) Even with the amount of drink in him, sleep was by no means certain. And that habit of using 'he' instead of 'I' suggested that he saw himself as more than one person. I remained on guard, awake and terrified.

We reached a watershed when I couldn't put off going to the loo for a minute longer. I simply had to get up and go. Cold with sweat, I levered myself out of bed. Nothing happened on his side: he genuinely was asleep. Once up in the bathroom, I debated whether to lock the door and stay put. *No,* I thought, *he's mad enough to try breaking the door down. Better go through with it!* In an even colder sweat I crept back into bed and managed to keep awake all night long, jolted into fresh awareness each time he stirred and clicked.

Morning came at last. I waited until the reasonable hour of 8.30, then gently nudged. The first words he spoke were the classic 'Where am I?', followed by: 'I don't like you. Why am I here?'

In the circumstances, this was encouraging, for they indicated that I was no longer dealing with more than one character. 'You're here because you wanted to be here,' I said brightly. 'I'll make us some coffee.'

He shook his head at the suggestion, but when it came drank it down eagerly enough. I chatted hectically away about the weather, that standard English ploy. Then came the moment when I offered to run him home. He took his time about moving downstairs and out to my car, but once sitting next to me hardly stopped talking about his murdered family and the iniquities of the Red Army, adding that it was a hard life for a foreigner on his own in a strange city. It occurred to me that this might be his way of asking for money, so in spite of the horrors of the night I pressed a note into his hand.

He took it unsmilingly. 'Yes, this will help!' With that, to my enormous relief, he got quietly out of the car and out of my life.

Another chance encounter was much more positive: Ward Fleming, the primo ballerino from the New York Negro Ballet. Their English manager, Theo Hancock, had been at school with Mike, my lodger, and in 1957 he asked me if Theo and Ward could take the divan in the hallway; the rest of the company had to find the cheapest digs they could. I helped ferry them in my Morris Minor on their arrival in England, roping in Bridget's car (unfortunately driven by druggy Daniel Sykes) to help too.

Poor Bridget. Early that year she went alone on a cargo-boat to the

Canaries, the idea being to put the recent past behind her. She was unlucky. An uncharitable fellow passenger, having read a tabloid account of the attempted suicide, took against her and was overheard haranguing another passenger: 'That dreadful woman! Did you see, she has green eyelashes and dyed hair – you know what that means? She's a sodomite, that's what she is! If we'd known, nothing would have induced us to come on this ship.'

Normally Bridget would have found such a denunciation so deliciously incongruous that she would have noted it in detail, for later use in a book; but as it was, she was distraught. She jumped ship at Tenerife and Randolph had to fly out to rescue her. The good deed was one more nail in his coffin, as far as she was concerned. She took against him more and more.

Whereas she was *seeing* more and more of ghastly Daniel, and she was growing more dangerous than ever to her friends. One of the things she did was to buy the said car: an enormous black saloon, not quite old enough to be considered 'vintage' but with nearly every old-fashioned drawback in the book. Steering it required not just strength but a knack of turning the wheel only when the car itself was already moving. To change into a lower gear, she had to 'double declutch', a complicated manoeuvre which most of us had thankfully forgotten about since the introduction of synchro-mesh. She called her car 'Proud Pussy'. One day she took me for a hair-raising ride, missing two other cars by inches. Before coming to a halt a yard out from the kerb she had waved at a woman, dressed to the nines for a wedding. 'That's the sort of awful old bitch who took against me on the boat!' she said bitterly. 'I'd point Puss straight at her, if only I had the nerve!' I didn't comment, in case she meant what she said literally.

Ward and Theo wanted the New York Negro Ballet to be taken on by Peter Daubeny,* or failing him by some other impresario. They were, they proudly proclaimed, the only classical all-Black ballet in the world. Apparently, that wasn't enough. Negotiations were protracted. I tried my best by asking Willie-the-Witch to see what he could do, as he worked on and off in the theatre; and Aelwyn did in fact manage to introduce some of their set-designs and photographs into Peter Daubeny's office via Leon Heppner, without much result.

---

* Daubeny was an impresario who had been responsible for the Berliner Ensemble and Moscow Art Theatre's recent visits to London.

On the plus side, I got Ward to demonstrate his dancing-gear. Under black nylon tights he would be wearing a black brief, and under that a white jock-strap.

'In the States, male dancers are two a penny,' he told me. 'Whereas over here, it's girls, girls everywhere and hardly a man in sight! It might pay for me to move to London for good.'

Besides his ordinary gear, Ward obligingly demonstrated an intimate pouch, super-tight, which pulled private parts between and under his legs. 'It's for when I want to do drag,' he explained. 'You can't see even the smallest bump.'

'Isn't that somewhat extreme?' I said.

'Wa–al, a'course you want a peek at what's there. But I tell you, some men can be taken in completely. They think it's a vaggy up to and including climax, the suckers!'

It was a shame that the New York Negro Ballet wasn't a success. But at any rate, they enjoyed the trip over.

71

After cutting a dash in the Gulf, I'd been shielded from having to face up to insignificance by being wholly occupied in writing *The Golden Bubble*. Now that the book was finished and revised and had gone through the stages of galley and page proofs, there was nothing further to be done – except await publication. Without that cushion of work I was forced to consider and reconsider the incongruity of Gulzaman's position. He was attending daily classes in English under the supervision of a Colonel Giffey, but was proving too obstinate to be a good pupil. For the record, I made an exact transcription of his answer to my question 'What did you do today?':

> I did do see Natural History Museum. Natural History
> very big hall, my idea that is the nicest house in world.
> Many bone I don't know what is calling, Daddy. Many
> student with me and I looking too many picture and

bone and taking photograph with Mr Colonel Giffey
and Mrs Williams. Well, 2-30 to 5-30 and some
picture have 700 years ago and 1,700 years ago some
picture, too long time. One she's in college in school
and one boys he's come with me to my house he's see
my picture. I am go out and be in a coffee-bar I'm
drinking coffee and talking to some friend and one
girl and she's say I'm not tomorrow working and next
time I meet with you.

By then, I could disentangle almost anything he said. He was learning that it was easy for a personable young foreigner to pick up girls
in London. It was an unfamiliar art for him, previous experience in a
Muslim world having limited him and his male friends to the undesirable or professional. Since he had no way of judging the background
of those he met, I had to be on the look-out in case he got himself
into trouble.

He was not getting on well with Mike, and for a good reason.
Gulzaman distrusted intrusions into my part of the flat and he didn't
take kindly to being ordered about by someone whom he considered
to be in no position to do so. Mike was baffled by the sudden flare-
ups, ruefully admitting: 'The man's an Elemental. He doesn't go by
any of the rules in the book!' An accurate assessment, I thought, for
even to me Gulzaman had always been something of an enigma;
just what that something was remained a conundrum to most of my
friends.

Publication of *The Golden Bubble* failed to create the stir for which I
was hoping, though an old friend from Cairo days, Patrick Kinross,
gave it a brilliant review in the *Sunday Times* which helped it become
a Book Society recommendation. But in the first three days it sold no
more than 2000 copies, hardly what might be called 'getting off to a
racing start'.* On the other hand, I was suddenly in demand, the editor

---

*   Whether 2000 copies of a hardback non-fiction book within the first three days of
    publication is considered a success today depends on expectations, size of publishing
    campaign, existing precedents, platform of author, advance level etc. But the reader
    might like to note that from January to August in most calendar years, a book achieving
    those sales would today have a very high chance of entering the *Sunday Times* best-
    seller charts.

of *News Chronicle* on the line asking me to lunch in his club; likewise Eldon Griffiths, foreign editor of *Newsweek*.

A letter from Lord Geddes, President of the Institute of Petroleum, read: 'I am planning to visit Iraq, Kuwait, Bahrein and Iran during December. I feel sure that a talk with you before I go would help me to understand better what I find when I get there.' To such a flattering request I hastened to reply: 'Most authors love pontificating and I am no exception ... I will expect a letter or telephone call from you ...'

I ought to have been gratified by the amount of attention I was attracting, however small; but I wasn't. I felt under-appreciated, in which way I was like every author that ever lived. One development, however, shone out like a beacon through the twilight of dashed hopes: Bill McLean had been in touch with a fellow MP, John Biggs-Davidson, of the Suez Group, who came to see me. He in turn contacted the Pakistani High Commissioner, who sat down on 10 May 1957 and personally issued Gulzaman with the first passport he'd ever possessed. At last this wandering Pathan became, officially, a citizen of his own country, as well as a legitimate resident in England.

Anyone recalling the impact of Gian-Carlo Menotti's opera *The Consul* will understand what a tremendous leap forward that was. A passport was the Holy Grail for which millions of displaced persons longed in vain; the foundation of existence – let alone prosperity – without which an individual had no pigeon-hole in a bureaucratic world. My heart sang in joyful recognition of the workings of Providence behind the sequence of events which had led to such an outcome. That such a conviction was irrational didn't bother me. To Gulzaman, with eyes alight with gratitude, I said sternly, taught by Arab example: 'Don't thank me, thank Allah!'

Just then, as if on cue, I was brought face to face with the very opposite of good news. There had been a change in the law, which I'd ignored until it was brought to my attention by a solicitor's letter: my landlady, at last in a position to rid herself of an unsatisfactory, rent-controlled tenant (as so many of us were after the war), served me with a Notice to Quit.

———

72

I was in the strange position of agreeing with something greatly to my disadvantage, as I thought that changes to the Rent Act were long overdue. The situation was that thousands of tenants were occupying flats and houses at rents which had remained almost static since before the war. Not only were the rents frozen, but so were the tenancies. Those fortunate enough to be already in occupation had acquired a right for life, including the perquisite, at death, of passing the enforced lease on to any member of the family living with them. It was monstrously unfair to the actual owners, who found themselves locked into subsidising housing for those often better off than themselves. But who had cared about who owned what when the Blitz was blowing everything to bits?

Now, due to the new Act, not only could our rents be increased, but – more importantly – we lost our everlasting security of tenure and could be evicted. Of course my landlady wanted me out. She could let the flat, furnished, for three or four times what I was paying her. The new law provided for delaying tactics. Plenty of notice had to be given and a Court Order finally obtained. Meanwhile the controlled tenant could serve a Schedule of Dilapidations. So before my little household would find itself out in the street, there was a little time.

What remained of Evie's Blessing could cover the cash needed for a deposit on a new flat or house. The rest of the purchase price would have to be borrowed; and in so doing, I would run counter to every vestige of natural caution. Long before I'd understood the meaning of the phrase 'paying off the mortgage' I'd learnt from nursery-story after nursery-story that a mortgage could mean ruin for families burdening themselves with such a thing. In which case, the sole remaining recourse would be to approach my uncle and ask him for an advance. He needn't be the loser, since I would offer to pay him interest.

I could never have contemplated such an extreme course of action had it not been for Sheikh Shakhbut's words of wisdom: 'Perhaps he would be better disposed towards you if you gave him the opportunity. It is up to you as the younger man to defer to his judgement.'

As it happened, I'd already made overtures. Hoping to impress them, I'd let Dick and Susan read a couple of chapters of *The Golden Bubble* before publication. It hadn't achieved the desired effect. My grandmother reported Susan as saying in a cool, amused voice: 'What a nuisance he seems to have made of himself out there!' Dick had simply given no opinion. I knew that he still thought I must be a coward for refusing to go out hunting; in which case, what would he have made of the way I'd spent weeks hawking?

Towards the end of May I was down to Claxby, a plan of action fermenting in my mind. I would grasp the nettle. I would shake the begging-bowl in humble supplication. Privately, I didn't think that it would work, but it wouldn't be for want of trying.

'It must have been a great disappointment to Dick when I joined the RAF,' I said to my grandmother. 'It deprived him of his best excuse for disapproving of me, aside from the famous "Slaughter of the Innocents"!'

'Oh, I'm sure he's forgotten all about that,' said my grandmother.

But I knew, and she knew, that he most certainly hadn't.

I arranged to go and see him by appointment, saying that we had 'something to discuss'. No doubt it put him on his guard. The weather was perfect, that day. The Lincolnshire Wolds looked romantic and charming. Well's two lakes reflected a deep blue sky, dazzling to the eye as I walked slowly down the hill from the church towards the great wrought-iron gates. On an impulse, I tried to open them, but when they wouldn't move I looked furtively over my shoulder to see whether my boldness had been spotted from the house. No sign of life. The house itself had been drained of animation ever since Susan had stripped the Virginia-creeper from its walls. Following the dictates of Elwes the decorator, she'd had the lines of Georgian sash-windows painted stone-grey instead of white, a conceit which had merely given the gloriously proportioned building an air of drabness.

Through the side gate I went. I crunched over the wide expanse of gravel to the semi-circular steps leading up to the pillared porch. To avoid giving offence, I rang the bell, though it was a tradition (tolerated by Dick, who'd known it since childhood; loathed by Susan, who hadn't) that any of the family simply walked in and shouted. A chorus of yaps heralded the arrival of my aunt's white miniature poodles, pattering, red-eyed and red-arsed, into the flagstoned hall from the poodle-parlour. The little dogs were unresponsive to any show of affection and had none to offer; in which way, I felt, they were fitting representatives of the new regime at Well since my grandfather's death.

Much had been changed. The hall had been remodelled in order to provide, on coming through the front door, a 'see-through' view of the lower lake – an admittedly splendid new vista. That alteration had been achieved at the expense of the old dining-room, which had suffered further by being chopped up to make the poodle-parlour. Since my grandfather's day, there'd been none of the large-scale entertaining for which Well had once been renowned. My aunt and uncle ate at one end of the drawing-room and congratulated themselves on saving on heating.

The enlarged hall was neither as homely nor as welcoming as it had been in former days. It tended to be cold, even in May; and in winter, icy, because a log fire no longer blazed in the massive grate behind a leather-padded club fender. I was shivering when my aunt appeared, hands dripping, having been in the middle of washing one of her pets. Momentarily I took to her for that, thinking that she mightn't really be as awful as I usually found her. I was in a mood to compromise, to make every allowance and admit that I'd been wrong; anything, anything to ease an awkward situation, even at the cost of sincerity.

At lunch, I did my best to sing for my supper, and they in turn were affable, as if they too had begun to discover that perhaps I wasn't really such a fiend in human form after all. Dolly, adenoidal, dished up the food: three kinds of vegetables, tiny blobs of meat, mouse-trap cheese and biscuits. Lunch over, my aunt left the room and my uncle turned to me and said, 'I believe you wanted to see me about something?'

The moment had come. My heart was thumping, my mouth dry.

'Yes, it's about somewhere for me to live. I'm about to be turned out of my present place.'

A silence.

'I was wondering whether you might consider using some of the money from the Rawnsley Trust to invest in a house in London? I'd live in one part and let the rest. I could pay you interest from the proceeds, so you wouldn't be the loser. And I could do it in cash, if that would help.'

Silence still. He squirmed in his special chair, put his fingers together and grinned. *Foolishly and shyly*, I thought, though 'slyly' seemed nearer the mark. I feared the worst. The worst came.

'I'm afraid I can't even consider investing in a London property. It's out of the question, quite the wrong thing to do. No, I'm afraid not!'

I felt sick and turned away; not, for once, to hide a blush, but to conceal the fact that I'd gone white with disappointment, which I had no intention of letting him see.

He continued: 'Why not ask Gilbert Estates for a flat? I believe they go in for London.' (Gilbert Estates was run by Genissa's Eastbourne in-laws.)

Shattered as I was, I managed somehow to blurt out that I understood his point of view. I wasn't going to let him feel that his sanctimonious refusal had affected me in the slightest. We chatted away, apparently parting on friendly terms.

But I was seething with fury as I walked back to Claxby. Never having asked my uncle for anything in my whole life, why should this be my reward? To help me would have meant nothing to him. I was seething all right, from trying and failing, but I was damned if I was going to admit it to anyone.

'Did you have a friendly talk with Dickie this time?' asked my grandmother.

'You could call it that!'

'I'm so relieved. As they may have told you, Dick hasn't been feeling up to much lately, and they're off to Portmeirion next week. You went there once, didn't you?'

'Yes, with a friend,' I said, unable to enlarge on the details of my tour with Nick. I couldn't talk truthfully about such matters with the family, and had long accepted that this would always be so. That night, as I tossed and turned, I wondered whether perhaps *that sort of thing* was the real reason for Dick and Susan's disapproval of me. But I didn't think so, they couldn't have known about it.

Back in Queen's Gate, I told Gulzaman that no one was going to help us. There'd been a vague, double-barrelled plan in my mind to make Pakistan the subject for my next book so Gulzaman could find a wife. That would have to be shelved.

'Wife come later. We buy a shop, father!' was his instant reaction. It wasn't such a bad idea. He could run it and we could live over it, possibly letting one or two rooms as well. Really quite feasible. Something fairly modest – in Fulham, say – could be bought for £4000. Well, at least it was a thought. We might do worse.

So matters stood when on 7 June, lovely Rita Essayan gave a party in her son's flat near South Kensington station. Geoffrey Prendergast (Prendy) was also there, getting drunk and being annoying, as usual, but Rita continued to invite him. She was steadfast in her old friendships, in the back of her mind the idea that it might be bad luck to drop anyone she'd once liked. There was plenty to drink and plenty to eat, including a memorable *saucisson* stuffed with pistachio nuts, brought from France.

I could only just manage the short walk back to my flat, so dramatically was my head going round and round in circles. Before going to bed I downed a pint of water, to diminish the likelihood of a rampant hangover.

I was abruptly woken, at some unearthly hour, by the telephone ringing. Thinking that it was probably a mistake, I very nearly didn't answer; but when it went on and on ringing, I reached out a shaky hand and heard an unfamiliar man using what could only be called 'a voice'.

'Bill Reeve speaking,' he said. (Colonel Reeve, my aunt's brother, who lived at Leadenham.) 'I have some bad news for you. Are you ready for it? I have to tell you, your uncle died last night at Well.'

I sat up. 'Died, did you say? Uncle Dick DIED?'

'Yes, in the early hours, this morning. Of a heart attack. Susan got him back from Portmeirion and he was on his way up to bed. Everything possible was done for him, but it was no use. He went a short time ago.'

'I see. How terrible it must have been for her! I don't know what else to say.'

'Yes, terrible. There are a lot of people to be told, so I'll have to say goodbye.' And with that he rang off.

In those days I hadn't learnt to say, automatically, 'God rest his (or her) soul!' to indicate a complete acceptance of the finality of the change brought about by death. The truth was, mine was the life which, in the twinkling of an eye, had been transformed. I was stunned into speechlessness. How could the sad news be sad for me, when the last I'd seen of my uncle was a man grinning slyly, refusing to be of any assistance whatsoever in my time of need? What sort of memory was that?

A wave of nausea almost overwhelmed me. Then and there I vowed that I would never behave to anyone, above all to anyone in my power, as he had behaved towards me. I had made that sort of promise to myself in other circumstances, when poor; this time, I would be in a position to carry it out. The family fortune had been greatly diminished since my grandfather's day, but enough remained to guarantee independence for life. At the same time, my heart leaped and sank as I realised some of the implications of the unexpected turnaround: marvellous good fortune, certainly, but with warnings, too. If I weren't careful, it could wreck the rest of my days by removing, at a stroke, almost every incentive by which I'd lived in the past.

My thoughts turned to Gulzaman, asleep between-floors, in discomfort because we'd been unable to afford anything better.

'You were right to stick with me, you loyal thing,' I said, as I prodded his sleepy form. 'Allah be praised, I have some money at last! We can go to Pakistan and find you a Mrs Gulzaman. How would you like that?'

'Yes SIR!'

———

73

As can often happen with invalids, my Uncle Dick's death had been hastened by the ignorance of those most eager to tend him. An early chest pain had been put down to indigestion, so when it recurred at Portmeirion it was thought to be 'something he'd eaten'. They cut short their holiday, but continued to drive; and when they reached Well Vale, Dick wasn't bedded down in the hall. On the contrary, he was going upstairs when he collapsed.

Aunt Susan was said to be shattered, which I felt required a leap of the imagination to think of her thus, even after she'd written to my mother recalling a lifetime of happiness: 'I know that I am neither beautiful nor witty, but Dick thought I was, and never found out his mistake'. It sounded so humble and sincere that I tried giving her the benefit of the doubt, but the effort stuck in my gizzard. Surely those were sentiments stolen from some other brave widow – how she wanted to be seen, not as she really was? An uncharitable judgement, but perhaps not so far from the truth. In case I were wrong, I would try and forgive the past and behave well towards her in future – a mammoth task, indeed.

As for me, I was not to be immediately enriched. Nearly ninety-one, my grandmother Maud had become the sole beneficiary, for her lifetime only, of most of the income of the Rawnsley Trust. As for Well Vale, as I already knew thanks to Hubert Fox, Maud's gift to Dick of her interest in the Well Vale Estate Company had been absolute and Dick in his will had left the estate entirely to his wife, who would see to it that her own nephew, John, would inherit.

I drove down to Lincolnshire for the funeral, my head buzzing with new considerations, but determined to behave soberly and properly. At the burial service in the elegant Palladian church I found myself the object of intense scrutiny, followed by half-hesitant questioning from the old retainers: Mulford the chauffeur, Kirkham the groom, Dixon the gamekeeper. What was going to happen to Well? Did I intend to keep things going as before?

'It's not up to me, I'm afraid,' I had to answer, with a sad shake of my head. 'I believe that young Reeve will be the heir, after Mrs Richard of course.'

'Oh, aye!' they said, far from pleased.

I thought to myself: *What an old-fashioned drama this is! I couldn't be more miscast in the role of dispossessed young master. Thank God, I'm out of the running!* But I was sorry for those ageing men, at the mercy of my chilly aunt after a lifetime of service. I could almost hear her sacking the least useful of them, claiming that she was 'doing her best for Well'. Would I be proved right?

'What are you going to do with the money?' asked my grandmother. 'Play ducks and drakes with it?'

My answer was to grin. 'Is that all you think of me?'

'No, but I shouldn't blame you for wanting to make a bit of a splash!'

The moment seemed right for me to suggest being made a trustee. She agreed at once. Then she announced that she intended giving my mother some of the money which had come back to her as the result of Dick's death. Finally, she said: 'I suppose I should continue to let Susan have something. Will £500 a year be enough, d'you think?'

'More than enough, I'd say, when you think what she's done to Well,' I said. It was no use pretending that there'd been any love lost between the two. As part of her changes to the house and garden she had deliberately downgraded her mother-in-law's old bedroom, finest in the house, by using it as a glory-hole to store junk. Of course, not all changes had been for the worse: some of the rooms had been given their own bathrooms and the kitchen had been moved from a steamy cave near the back door to what had been an upstairs pantry. 'Civilising the place', she would explain when showing people round, accurately, perhaps, but not kindly.

'Two wrongs don't make a right and never have!' reproved my grandmother. 'Susan will be quite hard up, now, and through no fault of her own.'

I felt chastened as I said, 'All it means is she has become what she's pretended to be for years – and what I've always been!' I was rueful rather than resentful.

With my grandmother's support, I could start re-directing the flow of trust money as soon as we obtained probate. She was beginning to forget that I'd been regarded as the family ne'er-do-well – a grey, if not a black, sheep. I was perfectly happy not to get my hands on a lot of money for myself immediately: it saved me from any 'ducks and drakes' temptation. And because she was so accommodating, I can truthfully say that I never, for one moment, hoped for her death. In case of personal need I could simply dip into Evie's Blessing, knowing that it had become no more than a stop-gap. Good fortune was already at work, smoothing away some of my rough edges, making past 'poverty' seem interesting rather than burdensome.

I tried to do as much as I could for my grandmother, such as order-ing trust capital to be spent on installing a Hammond home-lift at Claxby. 'Dickie never got around to doing it, however much I asked; I can't think why!' she said, slowly but thankfully zooming between floors. And I could start making life easier for my mother at Langney with some small but significant modifications, such as modernising the heating system.

In due course, I was invited to Well to 'talk things over' with Granny, Aunt Susan and Sir David Hawley, Susan's new agent. I was a little sus-picious, but as it turned out the meeting was no more than an exercise in diplomacy. Susan wanted to continue the mortgage (of £8000) held over the Well Vale Estate Co. by the Rawnsley Trust, which I was quite prepared to do, if it would help her. At the same time she announced that she intended to 'rationalise' her management of the estate. *Here it comes!* I thought. She declared herself very much against submitting animals to the torture of intensive rearing, called 'factory farming', for which I was bound to congratulate her whole-heartedly. But, yes, she did also mean to sack the old faithfuls.

74

Plans took shape for Gulzaman and I to head off on our trip to Pakistan in December 1957, ostensibly so I could write another travel book, *Away to Eden*, that Hutchinson's had agreed to publish, yet really in order to look for a nice young lady for Gulzaman to marry. Wanting to be prepared, on 19 November I dropped by the House of Commons to see Bill McLean. In those trusting days a visitor could be admitted without fuss by using the St Stephen's entrance and muttering to the policeman standing behind the push-doors, 'Appointment with a Member!'

At a desk along a corridor I was asked to fill in a 'green card' in order to see Bill, whereupon I met John Biggs-Davidson, of the Suez Group (though this was over a year after the Suez crisis which signalled the end of British Colonial influence in the Middle East, to be replaced by American financial influence), who swept me off down beige-carpeted stairs to the bar, where, most conveniently, I was introduced to Nassim Ahmad, correspondent of the Pakistani paper *Dawn*. Then and there, Biggs-D. wrote out a letter of introduction to Feroz Khan Noon, Pakistan's Foreign Minister, and told me to be sure to contact a Mr Bull, Pakistani Press Attaché, about getting a lift by air to Gilgit. Only then was I released in order to find Bill.

With him I returned to the bar, in time to meet two other Members: Eden* and Orr-Ewing.† Eden (ex-Gilgit Scouts) promised to write about me to the Mir of Hunza, the ruler of a small mountainous corner of Pakistan. An afternoon well spent.

Next day I gave a small lunch for Mavis Mortimer Wheeler, with Gerald de Gaury (sometime Political Agent in Kuwait) as keen as ever on the prospect of a free meal. Mavis got well and truly oiled, and on some pretext or other started to undress in the kitchen. She stopped when

---

* This refers to John Eden, MP for Bournemouth West, not Anthony Eden, who had stepped down as Prime Minister earlier that year.

† Orr-Ewing was the MP for Hendon North, and would be until he retired in 1970.

Gulzaman declared that he had one of his headaches coming on, which she chose to believe could only be cured if he put his head in her lap. The party ended with Gulzaman taking her back home to Cadogan Lane, leaving me free to indulge in a siesta and bath before going to see Bridget, who by then had left Randolph in favour of running off to live with druggy Daniel Sykes in a studio at Gunter Grove at 8 guineas a week.

Farewells, including with family, achieved, Gulzaman and I set off. We couldn't go so far east without first calling on dear friends; so it was that we spent Christmas at Tim Hillyard's in Abu Dhabi, with the Sheikh in attendance. Shakhbut was on fine form, as ever, and invited Gulzaman and I to Das to watch the inauguration of the oil rig there. What would happen next for my dear friend, I wondered?

Afterwards, Gulzaman and I were to catch a BI boat from Dubai, which would finally land us, by way of Muscat and Gwadur, at our destination of Karachi on 8 January 1958. My first sight upon arrival were blocks of brown sheds and a clock-tower, flocks of tiny terns wheeling and dipping in unison overhead, glittering like a shawl sewn with sequins.

I asked the taxi-driver who collected us if he could take us to an inexpensive hotel, not wanting to be stuck in tourist land. Gulzaman then elected to argue instead of interpret. It only occurred to me later that they were speaking different languages, which didn't augur well for the future. As nobody could understand what made the driver prefer one place rather than another we ended up at the Palm Grove. FISH SUPPERS OUR SPECIALITY stated a notice pinned on the wall outside, contrasting oddly with another: OUR SPECIALITY EVERYTHING YOUR DESIRE. On a smaller board, a 'Jam Session' was promised, at some date unspecified.

The establishment was agreeable, low-built, with rooms giving on to a tattered garden. Simple rooms: stone floors and wooden beds with blue bed-spreads doubling as sheets. In a dark recess lurked a bathroom (cold water only) with grimy bath, filthy loo, and a ledge papered with old copies of *Dawn* carrying the story of the Sputnik.*

Mavis's friend Gerald de Gaury had provided me with an introduction to Desmond Reynolds, an ex-Indian Army Colonel who'd become a travelling salesman for Reckitt and Colman† and lived at Sycamore Lodge

---

* The Soviet Union's successful launch of the first man-made satellite had taken place a few months earlier, on 4 October 1957.

† Manufacturer of household products.

in Clifton, a smart suburb of Karachi. A telephone call established that he was usually to be found at the Sind Club. So I hired a motorised tricycle-taxi and chugged along to present myself at its imposing brown-sandstone entrance-hall. I thought I knew what I might be letting myself in for. Of his time (in August 1920) at 'this temple of Sahibdom', the author Robert Byron wrote to his mother: 'The terror is worse than one's first day at Eton. I have done the one unforgivable thing by not bringing a dinner-jacket and am obliged to have dinner in my room as a result. It is really too awful to arrive in India and find the outskirts of Balham.'

I looked around me. The Sind Club was enormous, occupying several acres of prime city space, but showing signs of dilapidation. Polished brass tables were scattered forlornly amongst pillars with dados of brown lin-crusta. Discreetly dressed hordes of Anglo-Indians were notably absent. I wandered through half-deserted rooms to the bar, where I found a slim, youngish Irishman with a regulation drawly voice, and with him three others, all obvious bachelors: Peter Knox, an old pussy; his friend Bobby Cochrane, an ex-chorus boy subsequently employed in circumstances of greater pomp and unwilling to acknowledge his own past; and Dick Garrard, a middle-aged Burmah-Shell executive with a rugged *Boy's Own Paper* face. To meet with them, along with my original prey Desmond, was an instant tonic.

Desmond's first question was: 'Where are you staying?'

'The Palm Grove,' I said.

'The Palm GROVE? You can't possibly stay there! You'd better come and live with me!'

Politely I declined, wishing to retain my independence, but I pumped him for information about possible other hotels. It seemed that the Central was the one, cheaper than the Palace, which in turn was cheaper than the air-conditioned Metropole.

'You simply have to have a proper address,' said Desmond, reminding me that we were in a country which had been for a very long time under the British Raj, where engrained native ideas of caste had been honed by generations of British Colonial administrators. I saw his point. If I wished to go my own way in other respects, I would do well to conform where conforming was relatively easy.

For 26 rupees a day all in, including food, the Central represented a bargain. My room was, in effect, a suite: a large bedroom, and off it a sitting-space, and beyond the bedroom a bathroom with an immense old-fashioned bath which looked as if it had been moulded from a single slab of porphyry. As the whole place was dark, it was also cool. I could have had Gulzaman in with me on a truckle bed, but he preferred the ultra-informal Khyber hotel where, for 5 rupees, he crouched with the other Pathans in a portioned-off space, the partitions extending no more than halfway up to the ceiling. 'I might try living like that in time, just for the experience,' I decided. 'But not just now, when "face" is apparently so all-important.'

Gulzaman immediately set about getting his own affairs going – his 'affair', rather. Having found and spoken with his sister, shortly afterwards he told me that she knew of a possible wife for him. Gratifying as that was, he was brought up short with problems caused by custom and religion. He wasn't allowed to see her face; she had to remain veiled until after they were married. I felt that I really ought to know more about her, considering that she would be living in my house in London. Was she healthy? Was she honest and, above all, good-tempered? Without listing desirable qualities in an order of precedence, they were each in turn too important to remain concealed behind a veil of anonymity. Yet how to proceed, without giving offence?

I said that custom or no custom, I must interview the girl – fully chaperoned, of course. Round came Gulzaman's sister's husband to the Central, afire with indignation. Confronted with my terrible demands of common-sense, the girls' father had accused Gulzaman of conniving with me in regarding her as a dog; a pariah, unclean.

'What sort of education has she had?' I asked. Neither of them knew. 'Well, where did she go to school?' Didn't know. I said: 'I'm asking because I could go to that school and have a word with the headmistress.' But no, even to think of such a thing was improper. 'Then please may I talk to your sister?' I begged Gulzaman.

'Talk to my sister? Oh no, father. Her husband – this man here – would object!'

During these exchanges I was constantly aware that Gulzaman suffered from a defect that I'd often encountered before. He was incapable of interpreting my words; instead, he kept interposing his own ideas. At first irritating, it became progressively more maddening, finally reducing me to incoherent splutters of rage. At that moment the floor-servant came in, without knocking, hovering about till shouted at to go away. It had been ages since I'd lost my temper so completely. I exploded. 'Oh, get out of the fucking room, the lot of you! And as for you, Gulzaman, from now on you're ON YOUR OWN!'

They fled my swearing presence and I collapsed on the bed, burying my face in the pillows and drumming my feet – behaviour better suited to a B-movie than to real life.

My head was a-whirl with conflicting thoughts, I tried to imagine life without Gulzaman. Bliss, in some ways; but short-lived bliss. Gulzaman and I had shared such memorable moments already, quite beyond an ordinary process of valuation. Round and round swirled my thoughts, always reverting to the same conclusion: though no one else could be so maddening, there could never be another Gulzaman – an Elemental, uniquely himself. Had I really, in an uncontrollable access of anger, chased him away for good and all?

Time went by ... then, there he was at the door, staring silently at me, uncertain whether to come or go. Recognising defeat, I told him to fetch a glass of water.

'You mustn't mind my outbursts,' I said. 'Not now, not ever.'

'No, father, but I want to run away when you crossing with me!'

So, for the moment, that was that. Nothing had been solved. To whom should I turn for help?

Desmond to the rescue. He knew a Mrs Bailey, a shrewd old woman, going blind, who ran the boutique Estelle from her suite in the Palace Hotel. Estelle sought the company of English bachelors in Karachi because she liked to think of herself as an honorary one of them. They reciprocated by taking more trouble with her than many of the expatriate colony were prepared to do. She was eager to be enlisted as my go-between and enthusiastically agreed to interview Gulzaman's intended bride, woman to woman, unveiled. My role was to take her to the poorish district in Lalukhet and wait outside in a taxi.

Gulzaman's sister's house looked superior to many and I was in fact invited in, via Estelle, my actual hostess ducking about in the yard because it was hardly proper for her to meet me, even in her own house, unveiled. The room in which I found myself was plainly furnished with a couple of chairs and a bed. There were shelves (out of reach of the various children wandering in and out) supporting a display of crockery arranged on stripes of newspaper tinted red and cut into 'teeth', like home-made Xmas decorations.

When she went out to fetch Manzoora, the girl she had in mind for her long-lost brother, she hung a kind of white tent sewn with a special panel over her head, so as to see without being seen.

I withdrew to sit, steaming and dripping with sweat, in the waiting taxi; and eventually I saw a small figure in a black veil approaching, presumably Manzoora. There was a long wait, with more steaming and dripping, until Estelle emerged and beckoned me in to meet a little black-veiled bundle from which protruded a good, sturdy pair of hands. I was told to ask no searching questions, but simply to make a few remarks indicating goodwill, which I did. After a short interval, we left. I could hardly wait for the verdict.

'A nice little girl,' she said. 'I don't think she can be more than fourteen and she doesn't seem to have had much of an education, but she was so shy, I couldn't tell. If I were you, I'd proceed with the utmost caution!'

'Has she at least been to school?'

'Yes, but I don't know whether you and I would call it school. She says she can use a sewing-machine.'

'Well, that's something.'

'I gave her a necklace,' said Estelle, peering into her bag as if to make sure that it had really gone. 'So she won't feel that her time has been wasted, whatever the outcome.'

I was most grateful. Had I been a woman, I might have shown it in a practical form by buying one of her frilliest frocks; as it was, I could at least take her out to dinner.

A worried Gulzaman came to me. 'What do you think. Father. Old woman give Manzoora necklace, to show you happy with her. She wearing it now.'

'That wasn't the idea.'

He shook his head. 'She take the present. The matter is finish!'

'Oh, lordy, lordy!' I muttered, recognising another impasse. Even at that stage there might be some way out, but I didn't know what it was. Countdown to nuptials had begun, without any of the conditions on which I had tried to insist being met.

75

As for my book, I was prepared to harry a Mr Deen (Government Public Relations) into arranging for me to make the sort of visits I deemed necessary. It was tricky not to be attached to a newspaper. 'We might have sent you to get to grips with female education,' said Mr Deen, wagging a finger, 'or village aid, or something of that nature, had you been properly accredited.'

I waved my publisher's letter, I waved *Tedder*. 'Here's the proof that I am a serious seeker after truth!'

Mr Deen let me have a ticket for a top perk of the moment, the ceremonial enthronement of the Aga Khan.* I took a tricycle-rickshaw, pedalled by a doleful man who told me that he was being driven out of business by do-gooders concerned with the welfare of such as he. It was beginning to be considered 'beneath human dignity' to employ anything except a motorised tricycle. 'How then am I expected to feed my family?' he asked rhetorically. 'My mouths are many!'

'How many, in fact?' I asked.

'Sahib, there are nine. Ten including an old granny.'

My letter of introduction from John Biggs-Davidson to Malik Feroz Khan Noon (who'd become Prime Minister) worked a treat. Being written on House of Commons headed paper, it looked just sufficiently official to get me past the guards and into his presence on 20 January. I was conducted through a hall and into a room formally furnished with beige-gold chairs and sofas ranged round the walls, some specially set under a showy crystal chandelier. Then I was led out into the garden, where the PM sat with his Parliamentary Secretary, breaking off their business, whatever it was, at my approach. He was a biggish man with a wide face, aged perhaps sixty,† dressed in a dark brown suit. He took me towards a circle of chairs where we could talk in solitary splendour over a whisky and soda. I felt as if *he* felt that I might have something highly confidential to impart.

Perhaps, in a sense, I did, for to my surprise Noon started sounding off about Buraimi Oasis: why didn't we let Ibn Saud have the place, so long as we (the British) controlled the oil – if there was oil, which, he'd heard, was doubtful. Out of the blue, an opportunity had come for me to do my stuff. I launched into a (by then) well-rehearsed diatribe about

---

* The Aga Khan is the title given to the Imam of the Nizari segment of the Ismaili subsect of Shia Muslims; they claim to be direct descendants of the Prophet Muhammad. Aga Khan IV, whom Roddy was to see inaugurated (and who is still in the position at the time of this book's publication), was born Prince Shah Karim al-Husayni, inheriting the title from his grandfather, Sir Sultan Muhammad Shah Aga Khan III.

† Feroz Khan Noon was sixty-four in January 1958.

the falsity of the Saudi claim, 'which is based on the Saudis historically keeping merchants there to deal in slaves ... and for NO OTHER REASON!' I said with as much dramatic indignation as I could muster.

'Well, why not let the Sheikh of Buraimi have it, then?' the Prime Minister said.

'Sheikh?' I repeated. 'There's not just one Sheikh, there's one for each of the villages which go to make up the oasis. If you have to choose *one*, then it would have to be Sheikh Zayed of el-Ain, brother of Sheikh Shakhbut, Ruler of Abu Dhabi. All the tribes in the area owe him allegiance, apart from those belonging to Muscat and Oman. Not one is Saudi, not *one*.'

'My goodness!' said a startled Prime Minister. 'You seem to feel most strongly on the whole subject! Can this mean that you are, equally strongly, right?'

'Yes, I think so, sir ... if you don't mind.'

'Mind? Of course not! It is most refreshing to hear views expressed so passionately. Would you describe them as official?'

'I expect so, by now.'

'Very well, then! We will take another *chota peg* and I will tell you how I became Prime Minister.'

I was amazed and delighted to be thought suitable for confidences.

'You see, I was the leader of the moderates of the Muslim League, the compromise between Suhrawadhy, who represents Bengali interests, and the extreme right wing of the League. So now I find myself teamed with Iftikaruddin.' It was all Greek to me, but I listened attentively. My reward was to be invited to stay in his country house, some time in the future. *Oh BOY!* I thought. *This is really getting somewhere!*

Flushed with triumph, I boldly imposed myself on the Mir of Hunza, who was in Karachi on account of the Aga Khan: the people of Hunza belonged to the Ismaili sect of which the Aga Khan was spiritual head. The Mir, though still titular Ruler, had been stripped of most powers by the new state of Pakistan – to which, of course, we didn't refer. A letter of introduction from John Eden had arrived that very morning, so I was made welcome and invited to visit Hunza whenever I chose. Sadly, I wasn't ever destined to reach that smiling valley of apricots, even when separated from it by no more than a mountain range.

Away to Eden went into the sort of details to be expected of a travel book, so they need not be repeated here. My book as it stood left a record needing to be put straight, for all too often I 'covered up' in order not to give what (at the time of the book's publication in 1959) might have been considered gratuitous offence. The truth, formerly unmentionable, was that I would never have got within a mile of many important and interesting people had I not been introduced to them by those who would have been castigated as 'queers' had their hidden natures been generally known. Not only were such contacts vital to the pursuit of my profession, but I also had to recognise, with gratitude, that a stranger in the night would often, as I put it, lead to 'unscheduled toe-holds in the cliff-face of the unknown'. On the evening of the Aga Khan's enthronement, all those factors combined to provide a thoroughly entertaining time.

At a stiff party at our High Commission, to which I'd been invited thanks to a judicious shuffling of introductions, I met Norman Todd, Naval Attaché. His formal manner soon succumbed to my determined attacks, and he ended up asking me out to dinner. After that, he promised to take me to a place which I was sure to find fascinating, but which he didn't dare be seen in himself. I didn't press him on the point; he'd been rash enough as it was without being forced into making more compromising admissions.

Duly he dropped me off in a garishly lit area of booths and huts reminiscent of Papeete on Quatorze Juillet, except that everyone within sight was male. On the other side of a crumbling wall I could see a courtyard some eighty feet across, hung with hissing Tilley lamps and jam-packed with men squatting around a couple of empty spaces. Up and down those spaces cavorted women in bright garments glittering with gold, singing – tunelessly to my Western ear – as they pranced. A simple outdoor cabaret, perhaps.

My head was whirling from a little too much to drink, so I had no inhibitions about picking a table with three or four young men loosely dressed in *longhois* of faded cloth, obviously very poor. They asked for chai, for which I willingly paid. I noticed that when the tea was brought, theirs was poured out, already milked and sugared, from a large container, whereas mine was served on a tray with milk and sugar in separate pots (which cost a fraction more). I sent mine away, in favour of having the same as them, and I pressed 10 rupees into the hand of the handsomest of my little coterie, telling him to spend it on anything else he thought fit.

Meanwhile, on the dancing-floor prancing and singing continued unabated to music provided by guitarists, thrumming away for one girl to stop and another to start up. Their songs sounded peculiarly hoarse, and there was something slightly overdone about their gestures. I asked if they were gypsies. 'No gypsies!' laughed the young man sitting next to me, giving my thigh a squeeze. 'These are all men!' On hearing the glad news, I squeezed back. They loosened up, pretending to be as drunk as I was – which of course they weren't. They'd simply been waiting for a definite sign from me.

A dancer sidled up, twisting rhythmically in front of us. I was instructed to hold out a rupee note, which was plucked from my grasp with swift elegance before being stuffed down a corsage. I might have been in Algeria, in a Casbah café with a group of *légionnaires*. My new friends grew excited, relishing the prospect of being with someone providing largesse. In pretended (though not wholly pretended) jest they indulged in mutual horse-play, including me in their frolicking. In spite of badly wanting to pee, I was having a whale of a time when a man came up shouting, 'Oh-ho! It is the Sahib from the Hotel Central, is it not?' I twisted round, to confront the rickshaw-wallah who'd taken me to the Aga Khan's shindig.

His disclosure cast an immediate blight: I was clearly too grand to be played around with. I couldn't shake him off; and in fact he turned out to be useful. He didn't have his own man-powered rickshaw with him, but he quickly found me a motorised one, to take us back to the Central. 'Us', alas, because he insisted on climbing in with me, 'to see the Sahib isn't cheated'. Very considerate, no doubt, but scarcely how I'd been hoping the evening would end.

I was amazed to discover, next day, that the louche dancing-place was near enough to be almost visible from Desmond's smart suburb. It was called Zenda Pir, being the site of a saint's entombment, a saint who'd refused to grow up, his name translating as St Evergreen. Nowhere was it claimed that this Peter Pan had sought a Wendy to share his boyish enthusiasms. In life and in death, his desire had been for disciples to enjoy themselves after his own peculiar fashion, the Holy Darling.

I was glad to have had Zenda Pir confirming that one moment I might be up in the clouds with the great and grands, the next, subterranean, alternating between extremes, equally happy with either.

Such was my nature and such were my opportunities, thank the Lord! My plain duty lay in making the best use of them.

———

76

On enquiring at the hotel reception about going to Mohenjo-daro in Sindh, I was questioned, somewhat abruptly, 'Why do you want to go there?'

'Doesn't everyone?' I asked mildly. When that seemed to cut no ice, I added, 'It must surely be one of the most famous archaeological sites in Pakistan.'*

'In that case, you should buy your train-ticket from Universal Express.'

So I went along to their office, where it took nearly half an hour for a clerk to fill out a form, in duplicate, in order to book me a coupé, whatever that was. Apparently, Sahibs were not expected to occupy an ordinary seat; no, they had to have a whole compartment to themselves.

After many slow, jolting and dusty hours (because this was only a branch line, served by inferior trains), Gulzaman and I arrived at Dokri station just before midnight. It hardly deserved the name of a station, being no more than a 'halt', without even a platform. Our luggage was hauled out and loaded on to a tray beneath the seat of a horse-drawn *tonga*, then we set off to pick up a policeman, that being necessary, we were told by a sleepy station-master, 'as a precaution against naughty men'. Away we drove to do just that, trotting through the night by the light of the moon over a road with a mainly sandy surface.

The policeman had gone to bed. Gulzaman had to get him out of it, when the man tried to make us dismount and stay the night in a cell. Only the sure knowledge that a tip would be forthcoming persuaded him to accompany us along the seven-odd miles of road, metalled in a thin strip down its centre, to Mohenjo-daro. All the while, the

———

* Mohenjo-daro is an example of one of the earliest cities on the planet, built by the Indus Valley Civilisation in 2500 BCE (the same time Ancient Egypt was flourishing). It was rediscovered in the 1920s.

driver clucked affectionately at his horse and greeted the few others we passed by rattling his whip against a wheel. Entering on to a further patch of soft sand we arrived at the drive of a bungalow, though called Circuit House, marked out by bricks, painted white and arranged in a saw-tooth pattern, the sign (as I was to learn) proclaiming 'Raj' throughout Pakistan.

The night was chill, a real change from the damp heat of Karachi. I woke to a breakfast arranged by Gulzaman and the senior *chokidar*, the young man of the night being merely a junior. Tepid fried eggs and warm chapattis were followed by something cloying and glutinous; not porridge so much as porridge's little sister, familiar throughout Arabia. Lunch was a matter of haggling. Catering at the bungalow was achieved by purchasing the raw materials and paying a cook. Gulzaman contracted for a small goat to be slaughtered.

That was my first lesson in how a seasoned traveller had to set about things in Pakistan. I was to learn that except in the larger towns there would never be anything more than the most rudimentary of hotels. A traveller needed to be self-contained as regards bedding, prepared, as it were, to camp, though without requiring a tent, there being some sort of shelter always available. I saw how absolutely necessary it was for me to have Gulzaman, for who else could act as go-between? I had better make the most of him and be thankful.

An Antiquities Clerk appeared, speaking good English, offering to show me round; Gulzaman preferred to remain in the rest-house, 'seeing to things'. The clerk was hyperactive, leaping, like one of the goats we were to have for lunch, from paved court to ruined wall to excavated sewer, eager to make the most of what, I had to admit, were fairly boring sights. In every direction lay those 'Mounds of the Dead',* set flatly down on flat country through which ran the mighty Indus river, intermittently changing its course throughout history. The most remarkable thing about the ruins was not just that they should be there at all, but that they'd been so well constructed thousands of years ago, with so many urban amenities. The municipal draining system boasted 'all mod cons' long pre-dating the achievements of ancient Egyptian sanitary engineers and the communal conveniences of Greece, not to mention the Roman contribution to grandeur through cleanliness. It seemed appropriate that the distinguished excavator

---

* The literal meaning of Mohenjo-daro is 'Mound of the Dead'.

before Mortimer Wheeler (incidentally, Mavis's second husband) had been a Mr Dikshit.

The most dramatic feature was a tower shaped like a Kentish oast; it was a Buddhist *stupa* superimposed thousands of years later. 'It doesn't count!' said the clerk scornfully. 'Are you by any chance acquainted with Sir Wheeler? It was that man who made this spot famous by his digging.'

'I know his second wife very well,' I was able to say, truthfully. But the picture of the lovely Mavis evoked by my words seemed utterly incongruous. Could I imagine her in khaki-coloured silk *tussore*, solar *topi* and shooting-stick, helping whiskery Sir Mortimer poke these ancient ruins? No, I could not.

'Very quick man, Sir Wheeler!' said the clerk. 'Never stopped walking, walking, walking . . .'

The clerk had obviously profited by having such an active mentor. We kept going mile after mile, all the way to the newest bed of the Indus and back – a peculiarly exhausting trudge without what I thought of as 'much to see'. But as we trotted back to Dokri halt, dust rose from unmetalled verges behind, gleaming gold in the sunlight, smelling of horse-manure. Cocks were crowing. The atmosphere was idyllic, almost the country atmosphere of childhood.

Later, Gulzaman told me that he'd asked the head of the local orphanage to appear at Circuit House in the morning. A breakfast of the inevitable tepid fried eggs and warm chapattis was hardly over before he came dancing in, to persuade me to go outside at once to meet him. There I found the entire orphanage, seventy-two strong, in neat blue serge, with caps. Two bigger boys carried a banner which read: WELCOME TO YOU FROM THE SHAUKAT UL ISLAM SCHOOL. At the sight of me they chanted in unison 'As-salaam alaykum!' to which I shouted back 'Wa alaykumu s-salaam!', giving rise to a ripple of respectful laughter. An old bearded man was in charge of them, standing to one side, his head bowed, hands clasped together, in loose-flowing cotton breeches, cotton shirt with long tails, and fur cap. This was the Principal. When he raised his head to look at me I encountered a gaze of such clear, shattering kindness that I felt I should be on my knees before him.

There was a story behind their group appearance. This was the orphanage and this had been the Head responsible for tending a young wanderer on the loose answering to the name of Gulzaman. They'd been unable to keep such a wild thing captive for long, but their care had given him a breathing-space of kindness in an unkind world and an idea of right and wrong. Now the wandering lad had returned, trailing clouds of glory in the shape of a Sahib important enough to rate the Barrage Circuit House, a spectacular gratification. An old gardener rose to the occasion by darting forward with a button-hole for me. I handed it gravely to the Principal, whereupon he produced a second button-hole from behind his back, to be pinned to my shirt.

I wondered what I ought to do next. *Inspect the troops!* I decided. So then we proceeded slowly up and down the lines of orphans, shaking each shyly proffered hand, pausing to ask fatuous questions such as 'How old is this boy?' and 'How long has this boy been with you?' All the while smiling and smiling. I thought, *Goodness, the Throne does earn its keep, if this is what it has to do every day!*

Unfortunately, Gulzaman's interpreting was no more than par for the course. I couldn't get him to ask the sort of questions I wanted answered, such as 'When was the orphanage founded?' and 'Whose idea had it been?' Silence, followed by more silence.

When one little boy wouldn't put out a hand and wouldn't look up, I asked why. 'He blind,' was the matter-of-fact reply, followed by a titter from the child next in line. All I could do was hug the poor lad, who started back in some alarm and was given a ticking-off, the poor thing – but me, too, trying so hard.

I arranged with the old Principal to visit his orphanage that afternoon, which seemed to please him greatly. To get there, I went with Gulzaman through parts of the town full of Partition refugees* (150,000 of them) where *barasti*-type huts had been planted on almost every square inch of urban land, leaving narrow 'streets' with open drains running down them. It was depressing, yet the inhabitants seemed cheerful enough; and children were, as usual, shrieking and playing unceasingly. At last we reached a crowded area, buzzing with flies, in front of a broken-down Tudoresque building. Attached to a kind of cage used for tethering horses was a blackboard. 'Outdoor teachings,' said Gulzaman.

Inside, the house was crammed with the boys' gear, overflowing from

---

* The Partition had happened a decade earlier, in 1947, when the British divided land away from India to form Pakistan (later Pakistan and Bangladesh) on the grounds of religious tensions within the country (the idea was Pakistan would then be a Muslim country, whilst India would be a Hindu country, after Britain granted independence). It displaced between 10 and 20 million people who found themselves on the 'wrong side' of the new border and hundreds of thousands, perhaps millions, died as a result.

wardrobe-presses in the corridor into a poky office piled with papers. High up in the roof of the entrance hall there was a ventilator grille, with another in the floor of a door-less room where seventy-two boys had somehow to pack themselves into half that number of beds, alongside a cooking space. Downstairs were two classrooms with a minimum of furniture and washrooms consisting of two dripping shower heads. There were loud cries of welcome as we entered, becoming even louder when I presented them, at Gulzaman's suggestion, with 40 rupees' worth of oranges, enough for more than one each.

The Principal had written a pamphlet, which he pressed upon me. It began: 'This institution has got an old history. It originated in the pre-Partition days at Ludhiana in Mustaw Ganj. At that time I was running a hosiery industry there, most of the earnings of which were spent over this institution.' The paper went on to describe how in 1947 it moved, twenty-seven strong, from Walton Camp to Nawabshah, but for twelve months couldn't find anywhere to settle.

What difficulties they must have suffered during that gypsy-like life can be imagined by the fact that this gang of thirty persons was packed in a small house like animals. Then they'd moved to Sukkhur, where 'also no accommodation could be provided for us for about eight months and we had to enjoy a poetic life of river banks until the end of 1949'. The pamphlet ended by thanking the Sukkhur authorities for putting what I was seeing at their disposal – though it also mentioned that the place was far too small for so many orphans.

What the old Principal wanted was permission to build on a site outside the town, for which he'd already obtained a grant from Central Government Welfare. But he was being obstructed by the local town planning department – a fate not entirely unheard of in England, I assured him. At my words, he smiled benignly and said that pukka Sahibs were able to achieve many things denied to ordinary mortals such as himself; if I were to seek out the head of Social Welfare, Hassan Mahmoud, and interest him personally in Shaukat-ul-Islam, all the rest would follow ...

Back at Circuit House, I asked if anybody knew where to find Hassan Mahmoud. 'Oh yes,' said someone. 'He's attending a conference in Bahawalpur, quite near here.' By a coincidence as strange as such things can often be, I already had an introduction from Desmond (by word of mouth only) to General Marden, Commander of the Amir of Bahawalpur's private army. Tenuous as that connection was, it gave me an excuse to ring him up – without result, as I couldn't get through. Nevertheless, by making full play of the letter extracted from Public Relations, Karachi, I talked the District Commissioner into agreeing that I was important enough, press-wise, to be fitted into the limited accommodation reserved for those attending the conference. My success convinced me that it was all 'meant to be', for who was I to make such a high-handed demand and expect to have it granted?

A day later and we were surrounded by a concourse of smart cars and smartly dressed non-entities. I was given to understand that the big fish I hoped to hook was somewhere about, but no one seemed to know precisely where. Eventually I bribed a Circuit servant to keep watch on the Minister's movements and tell me when he was alone. Armed with that information, I burst in on him when he was just finishing his lunch, finding a smallish, solid man, surprisingly good-looking for an official of such eminence.

'What have we here?' he asked, without a trace of resentment.

Instinctively, I knew that I could get somewhere with him. I began by apologising profusely for interrupting his sacred meal. He waved excuses aside: 'Everybody who comes to see me wants something. I wouldn't be sitting here if they didn't!'

I said: 'Yesterday I met a saint. I think you ought to know about him.'

'An English saint? How very curious!'

'No, one of yours. He has an orphanage at Sukkhur.'

'A suitable occupation for a saint. Does he have a grant?'

'Yes, but that's not what I've come about. He wants to be given a planning permit to build a proper institute. It's not money he needs.'

'Extraordinary! May I ask why you are so interested?'

I thought for a moment, then unblushingly turned Quaker: 'It has become my concern.'

We were interrupted by others, some no doubt with credentials better than mine. The Minister was affable and I left him to it, walking on air. Soon after, presumably owing to Hassan Mahmoud's intervention, the saintly Principal acquired his enlarged institute. I could assume that he would die revered, the thanks of thousands of poor orphans his reward on earth. To have been allowed to play a part, however small, in that charitable process was a rare privilege.

Many years later, my belief in his saintliness crumbled somewhat, for how often are things in life simple? Gulzaman was telling me about his brief stay there when he said of the Head: 'He like his boys *too* much!'

If he meant what I thought he meant, this was rather a facer. Speechless for a moment, I eventually said, 'Did the boys object?'

'Object no good. What they doing? Where they go?'

'Yes, but all the same . . . did they mind?'

'Not too much. Life was very hard and they very grateful to the old man.'

His words had the ring of truth; and as I was not dealing with an ideal solution, but with a real situation, I had a genuine conundrum to consider. Would it have been better if Shaukat-ul-Islam had never existed? In which case, during those dangerous days following the partition of India, many a ragged urchin would have died in misery after a short life of utmost degradation, rather than have lived and survived because of the orphanage. Who would fare worse on a Day of Judgement, I wondered, the old Principal or a moralising critic who did nothing to help the poorest of the poor when need was greatest?

———

77

Lahore, the capital of Punjab, was rightly called 'Queen of Punjab', with fine open spaces, monuments galore and the indefinable air, possessed by ancient cities throughout the world, of hiding secrets from better days behind closed doors. No less a guide than Rudyard Kipling had set a seal upon her qualities: 'Often at night I would wander till dawn in all manner of odd places – liquor shops, gambling-and-opium dens, which are not a bit mysterious, wayside entertainments such as puppet shows, native dances: or in and about the narrow gullies under the mosque of Wazir Khan for the sheer sake of looking.'

Kipling wasn't giving much away about himself and his predilections, but I thought that I could read between the lines. On occasions, hadn't he done more than just look?

A chance meeting in Zelin's, one of the rare coffee-rooms in Lahore, gave an extra push to my fascination with the grand and beautiful Wazir Khan Mosque. I passed by Zelin's daily on my way to the bank to collect my mail, so it was easy to call in there. I happened that day to have seen children playing a game in the street: a simplified version of cricket, boys whacking a small, diamond-shaped 'ball' with a wooden stick, to the peril of passers-by. As I was sitting at the same table as two middle-aged men discussing sport, it seemed an opportune moment to find out more.

'It's not cricket, it's called *gilli-danda*,' one of them said. 'I can't remember any Englishman asking about it before. What else would you like to know?'

'I find the Mosque of Wazir Khan very interesting. Who *was* Wazir Khan?'

I couldn't have asked a better question. My new acquaintance (called Mirza Jaffar Hussain) gave an astonishing answer: 'My family owns that place. We have the documents, in Persian, going back to the time of the original grant.' I was amazed to hear that a building of such public importance could be private property; to which was added the further surprising information that the mosque depended for its upkeep on rents from the booths surrounding it. 'The gentlemen of the Archaeological Department are always nagging at us to clear away the unsightly shops,' he said.

'I don't find them unsightly at all; to my mind they provide atmosphere,' I said.

'Thank you, my friend, you are one hundred per cent right! Would you care to mention this in the proper quarter?'

'Of course, if I get the chance!'

Next thing, he offered to take me on a guided tour. 'With me you may even climb the minaret, which not everyone is permitted to do – certainly not a Christian!' I was most intrigued. 'I trust that you are not a naughty man,' he said. 'Because from the minaret you will see many ladies going about their business.'

'I shan't look,' I promised. In fact when he took me clambering, shoeless, through substantial amounts of pigeon-droppings, such ladies as I couldn't help seeing out of the corner of an eye were distant figures, waddling about on roof-tops, hanging up or taking down washing – not exactly an activity to excite male lust.

'The Wazir Khan who had this mosque built in 1634 was Shah Jehan's Viceroy,' said Mirza. 'But I doubt if even he would have dared be seen resorting openly to this very spot.'

I was so indebted to him for the experience that, as promised, afterwards I called on the head of the Archaeological Department, Walliulah Khan, in order to subject him to a flow of opinion on the unwisdom of tidying up an ancient monument too zealously. He bore my stricture cheerfully, even accompanying me to Jehangir's Tomb on the outskirts of Lahore. We trotted there in my private *tonga*, which Gulzaman had arranged to hire for 10 rupees a day. Gulzaman had picked a splendid beast, in strapping good health, capable of doing fifteen miles or more without tiring. So, like a Kipling character, I could be seen spanking daily down the Mall, though without a dog pacing behind and between the wheels – sine qua non of smart young officers in Kipling's day.

Other trips followed, including a truly magical one to Chitral, which was tucked somewhere into the high Pamirs beyond Dir and was almost impossible to reach both physically and because of all the paperwork and nods needed from big guns. Another, to Peshawar, led me to meet Major Baro Ibrahim, who commanded the detachment of Khyber Rifles at Shagai – the fort in the middle of the Khyber, the pass which had historically been a bone of contention between the British, Afghans and Pathans, as they played what Kipling called 'The Great Game' against Russian expansionism under the Tsars during the nineteenth century. Desperate to see the Khyber, one thing led to another and Baro agreed to take me out there, arriving under cover of darkness at Shagai, a stubby fort, coral-pink, against a back-drop of rugged brown hills. It was gripping to have arrived and walked through the cool fort at midnight. Baro was in his late thirties; a fit, tough-looking man with a slightly podgy face, which I could study covertly when he invited me to sleep in his bed, then joined me. I could only hint at such things in *Away to Eden* of course. I gave a summing-up (reminiscent of Daphne du Maurier's *Rebecca,* I must confess):

> 'I have since returned to Shagai many times in dreams, and have again seemed to sleep in Baro's pyjamas, and woken to see through a loophole the hills of Khyber, solid in the sunlight, tumbling away from the fort into the barren distance.'

Whether anyone understood the true significance of such thoughts, or what they aroused, I'll never know.

Before that dreamy occasion, Desmond and I went exploring whilst Gulzaman went to Karachi to marry Manzoora, on 16 March 1958.

I learned this not from Gulzaman – on returning from my trip I had two telegrams from him enquiring about my health, but containing no actual news – but from a hotelier called Yasin Ghani, described by Gulzaman as his agent. Ghani also told me that a dowry of 4000 rupees had already been handed over, but to the bride and not to her family. So that was something. 'Manzoora is a lucky girl!' said Ghani. 'Not all brides have the good fortune to start married life with their own cash.'

The *fait accompli* forced me to consider what would have to be done before Manzoora came to London, if that were what she was prepared to do. I would have to leave Queen's Gate – I'd have to leave it anyhow, under the terms of the recent Rent Act – and move into something much larger, especially if Mike King-Smith wanted to move with us.

It was in this mindset that I returned to London in April. Towards the end of May, Granny Rawnsley came up to visit the Chelsea Flower Show, as she'd done for years. My role during that time had been to propel her round the show in a wheelchair whilst witnessing the 'tweedy ladies' thronging the marquees on Members Day and exhibiting amongst the rudest and most ruthless behaviour I'd seen on earth: pushing and shoving; banging against the chair; knocking her stiffened, outstretched leg without apology, causing her to 'Oof!' and 'Erf!' in pain. Yet they were supposed to be – and in most cases *were* – properly brought up. It was noticeable that the men, on the whole, had better manners, probably drilled into them by those same Gorgons, their avidly gardening wives and sisters.

Pushing the wheelchair was therefore a penance, involving glares (from aggressors) and apologies (from me).

Members Day 1958 was, as always, a Tuesday. I pushed as usual, pausing to let my happy Granny order single plants to be sent to her from this and that stall, whilst others waited, champing at the bit, to place far larger orders. Eventually she confessed to having had enough and I took her back to my cousin's (45 Pont Street, with the large ballroom, where my parents had held their wedding reception) where I collapsed on a hard sofa in the 'Persian Ceramics' room, utterly exhausted.

'Now you ought to set about looking for somewhere to live!' said my grandmother, revived by tea.

But that was quite beyond me. 'Oh, tomorrow,' I said. 'Not now, for goodness' sake!'

'In that case, I'll come with you,' said my mother, who happened to be there too.

'Why not try Harrods?' she asked next day. 'It's only just round the corner.'

'Harrods? Whoever heard of anyone getting a house through Harrods?'

'Merrie Rawlinson did. And all sorts of other people [her way of admitting that she couldn't think of anyone else].'

As there was no point in arguing, my mother and I set off for Harrods Estate Office, at one side of the huge store. There, a superior-looking man called Trotter instantly recommended a detached property in SW10 district, which aroused my suspicions.

'What's wrong with it?' I asked.

'War-damaged,' he admitted. 'But the owners have seen to the repairs the property required.' Apparently, besides being detached it had an unusually large garden, running between two roads, with street access at either end and a front and back door.

'Has it a separate basement entrance?' I asked, with the Gulzamans in mind.

Yes, it had that too. The asking price was £10,000.

'Rather far out,' said my mother, dubiously, which in her day it would have been. But I was of another era, during which time the motor-car had changed (or ought to have changed) people's ideas about what con-stituted 'far out-ness'. By thinking as I did, I was several jumps ahead of the smarter London house agents and their usual prey, prowling the select streets of Mayfair, Knightsbridge and Belgravia; not that I realised how valuable my theory – which to me was simply a matter of common-sense – would turn out to be.

We went by bus along the Fulham Road to a point beyond the Forum Cinema, then walked down Gilston Road. No. 22 was no ordinary London house, being a stucco'd Italianate villa with a tower. The front garden wall had been skimpily reconstructed, allowing passers-by freely to inspect what lay behind: two plots of badly cut grass surrounded by gravel paths; marigolds, marigolds everywhere, eked out by occasional overgrown rose bushes; twin banks of catnip leading towards the front steps; and a side-garden bed lapping up against the house. The overall effect was agreeably countrified, though somewhat dishevelled. Most importantly, huge old acacias along every wall were (as Hubert Fox would have said) 'proper trees, not stunted London things'.

The door was opened to us by a nervy little woman called Mrs MacNab with a roving eye and yellow blouse tightly stretched across her bosom. She was quite a card; a good amateur pianist, too, judging by the way her enormous concert grand blocked the end of the main drawing-room. She told me that she'd had the two downstairs rooms thrown into one so that a larger audience could benefit from the acoustics. The drawing-room(s) gave on to a passage perpetually kept in semi-darkness. 'It means nobody outside sees you walking about the house,' she said. 'You can go about without a stitch on, if you like!'

Having made a show of pointing out the separate bedrooms for her husband and herself, Mrs M wouldn't accompany us beyond the first floor because, as she told us, her son, her only son (by her first husband), had lived in 'the lid'. 'He died in a motor smash soon after his twenty-first,' she said sadly. 'Such a waste – just as we were starting to enjoy his company. We never go up there now.'

It showed her in a very different light, as a much more sympathetic character. My mother stayed behind to comfort her whilst I plunged on upstairs. There was nothing notable about the highest floor except for the tower, consisting of a top and a bottom room, about seven feet by eight, the upper part (accessible only by a ladder) containing an ancient laundry basket riddled with worm-holes. The room was lit by one tiny arched window, another five windows being 'blanks', unglazed.

When I got back downstairs, we shivered, because even though the day was warm the house felt damp. In the basement, walls were peeling. 'It's amazing how quickly it hots up with a gas fire,' said Mrs M brightly. 'You'd never guess that all the walls are outside ones. We don't come down here often, only to eat.'

We arranged to come back the next day.

Once we were out in the street I asked my mother, 'Well, what d'you think?'

'A gold-mine,' she said. 'An absolute gold-mine – that is, if it isn't riddled with dry-rot, which wouldn't surprise me after what you said about the wormy laundry basket.'

Next afternoon, my grandmother came with us to see the house. Having sat us down near the concert grand, Mrs M said to Granny, 'Do tell me – where are you from?'

'Lincolnshire,' said my grandmother. 'The wolds, you know.'

'OOhhh!' was the ecstatic response. 'Anywhere near Louth, by any chance?'

'Oh yes, very near. And of course as a young gal I knew Louth *very* well. We had Westgate House. Then later we took Thorpe Hall . . .'

'Thorpe HALL?'

'Yes, for a month or two, when we couldn't settle into Well Vale because there was too much to be done getting the house ready.'

'But I'm the NIECE, the St Vincent NIECE!' crowed Mrs MacNab. 'I was *born* in Thorpe. So you *must* be . . . Mrs Rawnsley?'

Unbelievable. Tea was quickly disposed of. Out came drinks, when she insisted on us downing not one, but – as she put it each time – 'the other half'.

I rang her up that evening to put in a bid of £9500, confirming it the next day with Harrods. 'Say "subject to contract"!' hissed my mother. 'You can't be too careful.' Sensible advice, but I had no choice in the matter – it was calling me! I knew it as surely as if it had appeared to me in a dream. It was a coincidence that it happened to be an Italianate villa, considering I'd returned from the war in Italy – to the great annoyance of my family – so pro all things Italian. It could have been rocked to its foundations by bombardment or been mouldering with rot of every sort and kind and I would still have been unable to resist its summons.

With a terrifying survey in hand and a warning from my solicitor not to proceed, I matched the £10,000 offer Mrs McNab already had and she promised the house was mine. I was sure she would be as good as her word; and so she was.

I went ahead and signed the contract the day before going to Eton for 4th of June celebrations. Strolling round with my mother and Morvyne, exchanging pleasantries with those met on that occasion – and on that occasion only as year succeeded year – I would casually mention that I'd acquired a house near The Boltons.* One or two asked: 'Where's that?'

'You see,' said my mother. 'I told you it was rather far out.'

I said nothing, but thought volumes. To me, it was already the centre of the universe.

Completion was due to take place in a month's time, yet I remained a bundle of apprehension, fearful that something could go wrong. To calm disquiet, I plunged, as usual, into sexual adventure, with surprising success. It seemed impossible to make a mistake. One new

---

* Gilston Road runs into The Boltons, which was (and is) a set of large, expensive houses arranged on two roads around an oval-shaped garden.

chum (a Jamaican) not only insisted on doing the washing-up but offered to clean the Queen's Gate flat (in which I was still living) from top to bottom, for the love of it. 'No thanks, it's not necessary,' I was able to say, wanting to leave that for the landlady who was getting meaner by the day. Even so, I looked around me with nostalgic affection at the shabby grandeur of the flat in which I'd been so poor and so happy.

At last came the day when the keys to Gilston Lodge were handed over. Friends came round to help me pop the champagne in front of the Anderson shelter in the garden. Once inside I dashed upstairs, to the top tower. From the lower tower window I looked down and liked what I saw, exceedingly. 'Boy, oh BOY!' I exulted.

78

Though approaching forty, there was to be no question of me settling down. 'In', yes; 'down', not for some time, I hoped.

Mike King-Smith came with me, as planned, taking the upper and lower tower; the oddity of such accommodation appealed to him. I had a trap-door fitted to the upper tower (where he would be sleeping), to which access was only by ladder. Eventually I meant to put in a narrow staircase with a hanging-cupboard built in underneath and have all five tiny blank windows glazed.

Other arrangements reflected what had gone on at Queen's Gate. Those who'd stayed on the divan in the hall, my good friends Richard Neville and Ralph Anstruther included, could look forward to a proper bedroom, for a change. Richard proved unexpectedly useful. A few years before, he had left banking in England to become a broadcaster in French Indo-China, where he created a minor sensation by ending one of the last telegrams to reach the besieged Dien-Bien-Phu with the word 'baisers' (kisses), the recipient being a légionnaire, Gerhardt, whom he'd met in Sidi bel Abbes, Saharan HQ of the Foreign Legion. To the sound of fireworks exploding on Quatorze Juillet the Bastille of love had been successfully stormed. Gerhardt, known as 'Goonie', would be given his own quarters in Slolely Hall by Richard's mother, Lady Neville. Their story appealed especially to me because almost alone amongst my old friends Richard believed in the paramountcy of love, and proved it by the way in which he chose to live.

When I moved into Gilston Lodge, he brought his ex-*légionnaire* with him and Goonie displayed carpentry skills of a high order. Together they fitted cupboards and constructed one or two bits of furniture in a style best described as 'Regency Napoleonic'. They were not so successful when let loose upon a dining-table of solid mahogany. They removed the many blemishes, but then re-tinted it with Ronuk cherry-red – a disaster which even leaving it out in the rain couldn't mitigate. I enjoyed having them there whilst the work was in progress. Left to myself, I would have been rattling round like a pea in a pod.

As for Ralph Anstruther, he needed a bed less at that particular moment. He might have been at a loose end when his time in the Army expired, until one day he told me that he'd been offered the job of Equerry to Queen Elizabeth the Queen Mother. 'Oh, take it!' I urged, ever ready to approve for someone else what I could never, in a month of Sundays, have contemplated for myself. His courtly manners fitted him admirably to be a superior servant to royalty. It gave him a splendid excuse to avoid returning to Balcaskie as resident laird – a fate perhaps worse for him than being saddled with Well Vale might have been for me.

Meanwhile Gulzaman and Manzoora were waiting in Karachi for their ship. I was glad that they weren't in the house whilst everything was in a state of chaos. My priority was to have a central-heating system, and luckily they arrived shortly after it had come on for the first time, when the whole house was purring approval. Upstairs, it was gloriously warm. In the basement, plaster, damp for years, turned to powder as it dried out, leaving the walls in a mess of exposed brickwork. What the poor little bride must have thought of her new home was better left unexpressed. Everything was topsy-turvy, painting and hammering going on all day, with barely more than a bed, a chair and a table for furniture. I couldn't say that I really minded the discomfort. It was all leading somewhere.

As can be imagined, my move to Gilston Lodge came as a great surprise to Nick. He had to suppose that I planned to let such a large house out in rooms, to make it pay. Of course, I'd told him that all the improvements as well as the house itself were due to trust funds and that I had become a trustee; but I didn't mention the extent of what I stood shortly to inherit. Fortune or no fortune in the offing, I refused to throw money around as he did when on leave.

I was still to some extent in his thrall, though relations between us remained complicated, as was evident whenever we went to a pub. If he caught me staring at a distant face he would growl: 'You'll be knowin' *him* again next time you meet, thath's for sure!' Yet when he felt like picking up a stranger he'd do so without the slightest compunction. My earlier feelings of despair when that happened had begun to evaporate. I no longer minded (too much) what he did, beyond being occasionally irked by his lack of discrimination. He spent nearly all his time with me, only going home to sleep. As he enjoyed cooking, I let him cook in spite of the mess he habitually made. There was no point criticising him for being untidy, for that was his nature.

I was grateful for the way in which he was forever pushing me into a world of popular-song sentimentality (which I'd dipped into in the South Seas, but which had since become remote). Having got over 'Three Coins in a Fountain', his latest obsession was a song called 'He'll Have to Go!', sung by 'Gentleman Jim' Reeves in a voice of deepest velvet.

We gradually drew together again to such an extent that we agreed to drive to Ireland, even though much trouble in the past had come from being cooped up in my car for mile after mile.

I had reservations about pubbing in Ireland, but they didn't survive the actual experience of meeting Irishmen on their own home ground – voluble and poetic chaps, with whom Nick was at his dominant, flashing best. But the amount of Guinness I was expected to down was a drawback. It produced wind, and because both of us were eating and drinking similar stuff in equal amounts, that gave rise to a peculiar – and unmentionable? – effect. Guinness passed through both of us and came out still dark and grainy, unaffected by stomach acids, whilst our farts, which were bound to be numerous, were undifferentiated: they might come from one, or from the other, they were so alike – impossible to tell which from which.

Prompted by all that, Nick started reciting doggerel verses entitled 'The Great Farting Contest' that I assumed must have originated anonymously in the Army or some such. It caught my fancy as being a genuine contribution to popular folklore. It began:

I'll tell you a ditty that's sure to please
Of a great farting contest held at Shitting-on-Peas,
Where all the best arses parade on the fields
To compete in the contests for the various shields.

He wasn't too sure of the next eleven verses, apart from:

First prize Mrs Shingle, pull up your drawers!

Our Irish trip was much more of a success than our previous South of France tour. So much so that in Dublin we were able to draw on experience to give advice to one John English (who was on the point of splitting from his long-standing friend) to think twice and then twice again. Years later he was still thanking us, for they stayed together right up to the day when John died of cancer.

But all the time, sadness hung over me. We went to where two streams joined at Avoca, the 'Meeting of the Waters', flowing together to form one river from then on. *Lucky for some!* I thought, slipping effortlessly into the trite jargon of Bingo. But what right had I to expect that kind of luck on top of so much good fortune in other directions? *Mustn't be greedy!* I said to myself, unconvincingly; for in fact I was greedier for love more than ever and even less satisfied by continued lack of fulfilment.

79

It was a great mystery to me as to why my fortunes were going up, whilst for others they were going down.

I had hoped that when Randolph's rich American mother died, Bridget would go back to her husband, but nothing would induce her to. 'He's such a bore!' she claimed. Yet that bore had seen her through horrendous times of drugging and attempted suicide; all to no avail, it seemed.

Bridget rang up to say that a Mrs Evelyn had offered her and druggy Daniel accommodation and pocket money in return for 'light duties', whatever that was supposed to mean. The prospective employer lived in a nice terraced house in Belgravia, near Gerald Row Police Station. 'So handy for all our friends, good *or* bad!' explained Bridget. She asked me to help transport themselves and their belongings, which of course I agreed to do.

We plodded up and down the basement steps, dragging this and that unwieldy bundle until, like a harvest of a few grains of wheat mixed with a substantial quantity of tares, all was safely gathered in. Suddenly the internal door at the top of the basement stairs shook to a knocking. Daniel rushed to unlock it. Mrs Evelyn followed him slowly to a point halfway down, taking in (I noted) the general air of mess and confusion. 'Oh!' she said, with a frozen smile. 'I didn't mean to interrupt. I'm sure you must be *very* busy, settling in. This is to be *your* domain completely, that's our understanding!' So saying, she turned smartly and left, pausing at the top of the stairs to add: 'I think *perhaps* we'd better keep this door unlocked? Not that I'll ever want to interfere, but still, perhaps ... you never know ...'

'Oh, Daniel would be very good with burglars,' said Bridget in her best drawly voice. 'He'd get round them in a trice!'

'I'm sure he would,' said Mrs Evelyn, disappearing but somehow contriving to leave her smile, like the grin on the face of Lewis Carroll's Cheshire Cat, frozen in the air.

'The hard old bitch had better watch out for her son, that's all I can say!' muttered Daniel. 'I bet he's a crook; she as good as said so at our interview.'

I couldn't help feeling sorry for the woman. She might be made of steel under that gracious exterior, yet little did she realise what hostages to fortune she had given by those few unfortunate words 'this is to be *your* domain'. Her newest treasures were about to take her literally.

Even so, in spite of my misgivings, the weeks went by without incident until one day a letter arrived in Bridget's huge, self-indulgent script, one long wail of indignation at Mrs Evelyn's 'awfulness'. She'd reneged on her promise, constantly haunting the basement, spurning with her foot such objects as lay, inevitably, all over the floor. 'And after she pretended to find it "interesting", the way we chose to live,' complained Bridget. 'The real trouble is, her wretched weak son keeps playing her up and she pretends he doesn't, so she takes it out on *us*!'

I lost track of them for a while, but eventually they came to

roost in Dolphin Square, in a flat on the seventh floor paid for by
Randolph, who was careful not to give them cash to manage the rent
for themselves. He himself left Selwood Terrace and moved to a more
stately house in Lamont Road, where he lived in the orderly manner
which he must always have preferred but had never known since
marriage.

From time to time Daniel was to be seen walking unsteadily, looking haggard and appalling. I ran into him near the ticket office in South
Kensington Underground and seldom had I met such a wreck: body
twisted to one side, stick in gnarled hand sliding at an angle across the
floor. He didn't see me, because his whole being was concentrated on
fumbling in a pocket for his fare. It came as no surprise when Bridget
rang me up to say that he had died; and would I mind coming to visit her?

Would I 'mind'? Unusually humble for her, not at all what I'd been
accustomed to – and in its way, intimidating. Naturally I dropped
everything in order to hasten round to Dolphin Square, bringing one
of my books with me, to have something to talk about. I had no idea
what I might find; at least, not in detail. I knew that she would be living
in a mess.

A mess? Much worse. Utter confusion, on a scale far exceeding the
norm in Selwood Terrace: dust and dirt everywhere, a sink choked with
greasy dishes, a bin overflowing . . . and in the midst of it all, threading
her way through furniture arranged as if to trap the unwary, a frail
Bridget, so thin that her bones protruded from a black dress, over which
she'd cast a fringed shawl. The greatest change of all was in her face: no
longer cat-like but shrunken and pointed – how a child might suppose
a witch would look. Her drawly voice was wistful, although still with
the overtones of the super-sophistication which I'd always found so
attractive. She offered cider and a thimbleful of Cointreau, saying that
she had nothing else handy.

She invited me to admire a pet white rat, which had emerged from
under a far-from-clean cushion, whiskers quivering. 'He's livelier than
those fish I used to have, but not nearly so restful,' she said. '*Much* easier
to feed, though. None of those awful tit-bits dropping madly through
cloudy water. Such a relief!' Taking a black wig from a dresser, she tried
it on, demanding to know if I thought it suited her. She twirled her
shawl, presenting me with her face in profile, as of old; but the effect
was grim rather than fascinating. Then suddenly she grew serious. 'You
won't believe this, but I'm lonely!'

'YOU?'

'Yes, and madly bored, too! I know I used to say that only the bores were bored. And you remember how I'd find *any* excuse to avoid meeting people. Well, that was all very well when the public was queueing up to see *one*, for the sake of getting their picture in the *Tatler* with some fatuous write-up to go with it. But now, when no one's interested, life can be jolly boring, I can tell you!'

'I think I see—'

'NO YOU DON'T! You can't, until it happens to you. Daniel wasn't a bore, whatever else he was. I know you couldn't bear him; nobody could. In the end he had to rely on me for everything. I mean, literally everything . . . and I was helpless and hopeful, I'd no idea what to do. I've never even *liked* people being ill – I mean, there are those who revel in it but not me – I should think I did *all* the wrong things!' She looked suddenly sharp. 'And now I'm boring *you*, I shouldn't wonder!'

I said: 'What would you like to do? Come round for lunch, or dinner, or something? You only have to say.'

'Oh I don't think so. I might get too tired, you see . . .'

As she spoke she fondled her white rat, putting it on her thin shoulders, where it crouched unsteadily, digging in tiny paws. She squeaked, and I could imagine that it squeaked back. There was one improvement, at least: she no longer had a red rash spreading upwards from her neck and there was no smell of garlic ointment, so to that extent she was better. But the expression in her flecked cat-eyes suggested deep trouble, even panic, as she repeated her plea about being 'too tired' to come and see me.

In fact, it was to be the last time I ever saw her. We had known one another for almost twenty years; she was perhaps the very first friend I made when I moved to London. I felt guilty for letting her down. I could have 'done a Prendy', who would go round, uninvited, to check up, disregarding the wilful dirt and confusion, the manner in which she was choosing to live. But considering what she had been like once, it was too disturbing to be a witness to her self-inflicted descent into degradation. Perhaps I ought not to have minded so much, or made a greater effort to ignore such qualms. I just couldn't. Perhaps I wasn't as nice as I'd been at one time. Perhaps that was the unpalatable truth.

———

80

Looking for furniture for Gilston Lodge, I went with Mike to a sale at Crabbett Park (the Blount house where Lord Byron had stayed for a while), hoping to pick up fragments of Byronic memorabilia. Wandering into the bedroom once graced by the scandalously amorous poet I noticed a large rectangular (and brighter) patch on the faded green wall. Propped in the passage outside I found a looking-glass in a plain gilded frame whose measurements fitted the patch. That lot came up right at the end of the sale when the dealer had left, so I secured my prize for £5. I set a value on the thing because it had to be the very glass in front of which Byron would have preened himself before, or even during, bouts of sexual athletics, including an over-fondness for his sister Augusta. I saw at once where it could be placed to best advantage: at the bottom of the Gilston stairs, from which it would reflect all those going up and down, incidentally doubling in size part of the house which could do with a little lightening.

I looked upon it as a great coup and was not at all averse to being reminded, several times daily, of historic behaviours more reprehensible than my own.

Sadly, however, my attachment to Nick went on diminishing; waxing at intervals, before continuing to wane. I knew it, yet what good did it do? Unlike many of my friends I wasn't looking for a one-night stand, grateful as I was for them. I had one consolation: all such yearnings for love were far more tolerable with, than without, money.

Though missing out on Crabbett Park, Bridget's friend Mavis Mortimer Wheeler enjoyed going to auctions with me. We went to several together, when she displayed good taste but less judgement. I was seeing more and more of her, and in September '58 Mavis asked me to drive her to Plymouth to meet her son Tristan, then stationed there in the Navy. I found him to be a tolerant young chap with a mind of his own, and I enjoyed getting to know him better, without feeling attracted to him in any other way.

On 28 September we drove back to London, stopping, at Mavis's suggestion, in Potterne, the village which had hit the headlines at the time of her trial. She insisted on revisiting the cottage she had shared with Lord Vivian, figuring inevitably in the papers as their 'Love Nest'.

I should have recognised the great importance of being at the scene of the crime with the chief protagonist in one of the most famous trials of the century and asked her more questions. But having been in Arabia at the time I had no idea then that Mavis had given several different versions of the affair to the police, and that this had weighed heavily against her.

'He did shoot himself. He knocked my hand down!' she said, close to tears as we stood inside Pilgrim Cottage, near the very window from which the fatal shots had been fired.

'How silly of him,' I said weakly. 'He ought to have known better.'

'They tried to make me say I was standing back in the room, shooting to kill,' she said. 'Now you can see I couldn't have, which proves it was an accident!' The height of the window-sill in question gave point to her claim: it was waist-high. She couldn't have shot her lover in the balls, unless she had been leaning out; in which case he certainly might have tried to grab the gun from her.

I could have asked her to go into much greater detail, but I didn't. *What a wasted opportunity!* I was to think later.

Meanwhile, Granny Rawnsley, who had unwisely declared after a hunting accident 'I won't let my body get the better of me!', was having to capitulate, little by little, to old age. As she started the run-up to ninety-four her health was visibly failing.

She was, however, well enough in July 1959 to attend my first ever garden party, to celebrate a year in Gilston Lodge. I invited a wide variety of guests, even those not seen for years such as the great Dove-friend of yore, Hallam Tennyson.* He seemed stuck fast in a bygone era: still deliberately scruffy and under-dressed, still pretending to be the oik which in reality he was not. The star was Mavis who, finding herself alone with my grandmother, kissed her enthusiastically and stayed by

---

* This is Roddy's last mention of Hallam. Roddy wrote his memoirs in the 1990s; had he continued, I'm sure he would have mentioned that in 2005 Hallam was murdered in his bed, the culprit never caught. He definitely knew about it: a newspaper clipping from *The Times*, dated 23 December 2005 with the headline 'Tennyson's gay great-grandson stabbed to death in bed', was inside one of the volumes of his memoirs. What a way for him to have found out.

her, patting an arm. 'Touching' was something which Mavis always did, particularly after a drink or two. Most people found it endearing. Not so old Maud.

Everyone said – as everyone naturally would – that the party was a success. Back went my grandmother to Lincolnshire, to be cared for by jolly Nurse Teesdale, with 'Auntie' Herrington still in the kitchen, grumbly and stone-deaf but unable to complain too much about her increasing age when her employer was fully ten years older. It was a relief for us to know that she was being well looked after; but even so, it wasn't altogether a surprise when an urgent summons came for us to rush down to Claxby. She had suffered a stroke, not as disabling as her first which had occurred some years earlier, because she still had (limited) powers of speech. I abandoned everything else to take my mother and Morvyne to be with the patient.

We were in time to find her coherent, but one look at the shrunken figure on the bed confirmed that she was going rapidly downhill. There wasn't much for us to do except take turns sitting with her, nodding and smiling whenever she uttered slurred words. Of great comfort to her was Rufus, her aged brown-and-white cocker spaniel, a staid old boy of twelve with smelly ears. 'Lovey!' she would call out, at intervals, reaching down for him. It was therefore something of an emergency when 'Rufie' chose to run away.

I drove out to look for him, thinking that he might have gone across the park to Well. He hadn't. So then I turned on to the Alford/Spilsby road and arrived at the top of the Vale. I thought, *It's years since I've driven the length of the Vale.* In a mood of intense nostalgia I started along the overgrown track, once intended to be the main drive to the house. It was very quiet. Near the area cleared of woodland known as 'Grassy Hill' I saw a pheasant, which put me in mind of the brightly plumaged dead jays which Dixon the gamekeeper used to string along conspicuous branches – jays being objects of hatred because of the way their hoarse screams warned the rabbits that a man with a gun was out after them.

So many things came surging into my mind: Rye, the fat pony which I was always given to ride, even after the 'shameful' confession that I only preferred to go on horseback 'to save the faff of walking'; the Vale shoots, the noise of gunfire echoing through wooded slopes to the addictive smell of used cartridges; the heaps of shot bird – even a dead owl, my mournful contribution when I'd known no better.

Muddier and muddier grew the track, deeper and deeper the ruts. Soon I had passed the hut near which someone (we'd been told, as children) had lost a wedding-ring, for which there remained a reward, as yet unclaimed, of £5. Eventually I steered the car towards the Sherwood Oak, in whose hollow trunk gallant paratroopers stationed at Well during the war had started a fire, the day before being dropped to their death on Arnhem on the order of an over-ambitious Monty. How could I forget that this was where I'd seen a manikin in colourful garments, bowing and doffing a plumed hat, making the pony shy, whilst a disbelieving groom, who'd seen nothing, scratched his head in bewilderment?* So many memories, the pleasant predominating, the unpleasant fading . . .

I didn't find Rufie, but he eventually turned up near Willoughby Station – as if hoping, faithful dog that he was, to catch a train to Happier Hunting Grounds one jump ahead of his mistress.

Though dying, my grandmother was still delighted to hear a carefully edited version of my drive through the Vale. It occurred to me that it might give her pleasure to think that the Queen Mother was taking a special interest in her well-being; so I asked Ralph, at that moment with his employer in Balmoral, if he would be good enough to send grouse purporting to come from a royal source. He promptly did so, explaining (for my ears only) that Balmoral wasn't exactly at the heart of grouse-shooting country, so he'd actually bought the birds. By the time that they arrived, a decent interval after 12 August, my grandmother was almost too far gone to understand. However, she managed to murmur: 'Most kind!' By then, since she could only swallow with difficulty, we were peeling and pipping grapes and popping the squashy remains into her mouth, which was about as much as she could manage to get down.

She fell into a state of unconsciousness and started 'Cheyne-Stokes' breathing: a sound as spasmodic as waves against a rocky cliff. Loud, groaning breaths echoed from her bedroom, along the corridor, down the stairs and into the hall. Then everything would go quiet, as her breathing faded to absolute silence, before restarting and swelling.

'How long can we expect this to continue?' I asked the doctor.

'Oh, for someone as strong as Mrs Rawnsley, several days!' was his reply.

She became deeply unconscious, her lips blackened, throat hard and

---

* This story doesn't appear elsewhere in the memoirs to provide more explanation. In the context, I think this must have been a young Roddy seeing a 'ghost' of a small man dressed colourfully – rather than a misspelling of mannequin, or a manakin (bird).

dry. It would have been criminally unkind to have countenanced 'bringing her round'; indeed it was never seriously suggested. Anxiously we awaited the inevitable end.

Meanwhile the house was resounding with another noise, as if in competition: the *thump-thump-swish* of a machine being turned by hand to extract honey from combs stacked in the room next to the downstairs lavatory, the very room where Budi and I had changed clothes after playing tennis all those years ago. As had happened then, honey had spilt over the floor. The honey drop had been unusually bounteous and old Archer, who kept the bees, had left honey pouring out of the extractor and into the ripening tank until it overflowed. The accident made its own unique contribution to the atmosphere of those last days. A strong smell of honey penetrating to where the invalid lay in bed upstairs may well have given her a tingle of reminiscent delight, a reminder of the continuity of country life at a time when her own was ebbing away. 'There is something very wonderful about honey-bees!' I realised, as if I'd been granted a sudden insight.

Next day, whilst we were in the dining-room about to start eating, Nurse rushed down to say that we must come upstairs at once, which we did, with glasses of sherry still in our hands. The Cheyne-Stokes breathing had stopped, but the thin figure on the bed was faintly gasping. As we watched, her mouth opened, then closed ... and opened again and firmly closed. Each time, her whole face underwent a change, from a faint quivering to a marble stillness. We were witnessing what, for all my hospital experience, I hadn't seen before: the breath of life, half failing, half reviving. Death was happening repeatedly, over and over again, to the accompaniment of death-rattle after death-rattle.

Within a few minutes it was all over. The great, stern woman who, so luckily for me, had survived her son, had passed on. Claxby would revert to the Well Vale Estate, breaking our last family link with Lincolnshire; for how could we count Susan as 'family' when that had never been how she saw herself?

In a daze, I wandered round the house, as if seeing it properly for the first time. 'Homely grandeur' was the main impression, the family portraits being vital to the atmosphere: the pastels by Russell of Charles and Charlotte Chaplin; the Wright of Derby of Charlotte's mother in French hunting dress; the portrait of the Reverend William Chaplin in his country house (not Thorpe) with his dog; and of a young Richard Chaplin by Reinagle, with an even larger dog. They looked down on good Persian carpets, log-burning grates, Blanc-de-Chine figures of Kwan-yin and 'export' China plates decorated with flowers and exotic insects in an eighteenth-century escritoire/display cabinet, above which hung a circular picture of Maud's father and his sister Carrie, as exceedingly pretty children.

More than ever I admired one special feature running all round the downstairs rooms – a wooden 'chair-rail', waist-high, painted gloss-white. On it my grandmother had stood all sorts of small things, cards, plates, even pictures, creating an impression of pleasing fussiness, bearing witness to real life rather than to a decorator's whim. I remembered the day when I'd taken down those bits and bobs, saying that I thought the room looked better without them cluttering it up ... and was then astonished by the vehemence with which she had insisted on them being replaced at once. She'd been absolutely right. Out of homage, I decided to repeat that feature at Gilston Lodge.

My mother knew precisely how her mother would like to be buried. She arranged for the coffin to be placed in an old-fashioned farm waggon and pulled by a carthorse across the park from Claxby to Well churchyard. It delighted the local people, particularly the older ones, who could remember when that had been the ordinary way for a country woman to go to her long rest.

In the graveyard, near the memorial to a luckless stranger who'd been 'hurried into the presence of his Maker' by a highwayman, the shrunken corpse of Maud Rawnsley was interred by the side of her beloved – and my beloved – Walter. I could imagine her body, free of human ills yet still partly earthbound, levitating the better to survey a scene familiar to her since the turn of the century – the Vale of Well, enchanting in a sparkling August sun. From the Georgian church the view was striking as always: the downward sweep of the upper and lower lakes to either side of the great and grand faded-redbrick house and the humbler outbuildings. The magnificent ensemble still hadn't entirely relinquished its grip on me.

But now I had to recognise that Gilston Lodge had become my Well. The stern grandmother who'd unwittingly done me out of her adored estate had been chiefly responsible for me securing a property even more desirable – to me – in London. The irony was extreme.

RIP you splendid old Thing! I thought. *You'll be happy to know at last that it was all for the best.*

part seven

for love

1960-7

81

1960. The coming young were swinging in a direction of their own and nobody was going to stop them. But for now, the loosening-up process was taking its time. Whilst the Wolfenden Report had appeared in 1957, the reforms to which it would give rise were delayed a further ten years. To feel free, someone like myself still had to go to 'The Continong', which I could easily afford to do. So could Nick when home on leave, pockets bulging with money which he couldn't spend in the places where he'd earned it. We decided to go to Amsterdam and to Zurich, both of them noted for laws complaisant where sex was concerned. We were travelling as good companions only, every hint of jealousy ostensibly abandoned.

Via the grapevine it was common knowledge that there were two clubs in Amsterdam of the sort we were seeking: 'The Cock' and 'The Dock' – in actual fact the 'C.O.C.' and the 'D.O.K.'. The Cock had pretensions to be intellectual, the Dock prided itself on being rougher. Both were male *agapemones* after their own fashion and both would enrol foreign members at the door. We were to stay in what was familiarly known as 'a safe house', i.e. one to which anyone of either sex could be brought back for the night without question.

At the Cock, an immense woman sang 'He's got de WHOLE WORRULD in his HANDS, he's got de WHOLE WIDE worruld RIGHT in his HANDS!' as I watched a slim Dutchman sidle up to Nick and proposition him instantly. Boldness met with success. Nobody chose to lay a finger on me so back I went to bed alone.

Next morning I was still alone. Midday came and there was no Nick. Rather than pace the floor in a quandary, I decided to go to the museum containing Rembrandt's masterpiece *The Night Watch*. I couldn't avoid feeling slighted, but my attitude was given a fillip at the sight of a young man earnestly studying pictures with the help of an illustrated guide. Within a second or two I was at his side and about to embark on an opening gambit when he said, disarmingly, 'I can't follow this. Can you read German?'

His accent was North American, actually Canadian, but I tended to confuse the two.

'I'll have a try,' I said.

In fact a try was about as much as I could manage, so far in the past were my days as an au pair* in Ulm. My new chum put me in mind of Werner, the freckled, auburn-haired hero who'd rescued me from the swirling waters of the Danube. He was of similar build, with the same squared-off face.

I leaped in like a Samurai, sword flashing, prodding my victim around the gallery, swamping him with information. If he were startled by the vehemence of my behaviour, he didn't show it. In a leisurely drawl he said that his name was Bob and that he worked in a Canadian Consulate in West Africa; I think he said Lagos. He asked what I had planned for the following day.

'Nothing much,' I said.

'It's my last full day of freedom,' he said. (*What did he mean by that?* I wondered.) 'And I haven't yet seen Leyden and Vollendam. What say I hire us a machine and we go visit?'

When I got back to our safe house there was still no sign of Nick, but there'd been a telephone call to say that he was going on being out and that I wasn't to worry, he'd be back in time for our train to Zurich late the following evening. I didn't worry; I was intent only on meeting Bob, with whom I went to a hire-shop for motorised bicycles of all sorts. So far so good.

The machine which was trustingly handed over to him was of the kind seen everywhere in Holland, travelling along special lanes to keep them out of the way of other traffic. Bob had never ridden one. His first solo attempt ended in him falling off; but after a few more turns he contrived to master it, after a fashion. What was not so certain was how he would manage with me as pillion. I felt *most* unsafe, clinging on behind him; I'd seldom felt so exposed to ridiculous danger. The passenger-seat was so small that I was jammed up against him, as if welded to his solid bottom. We phut-phutted along streets incised with tram-lines, and when we had to stop I would put my feet to the ground too. Dangerously, but not lethally, we emerged without incident on to a smooth flat road leading

---

* You'll remember that an au pair in Roddy's day simply meant being a foreign house-guest, rather than somebody who worked for the family they stayed with, as a nanny etc.

out of Amsterdam, soon switching on to a cobbled bicycles-only track, speeding along at perhaps twenty miles an hour.

RRRAWWWPP! went the wheels over the cobbles – a soothing sound, in its way. At the same time, the machine rhythmically shuddered, as though I were riding pillion to a pneumatic drill. I was wearing an overcoat – those were pre-anorak days – which splayed out on either side in the wind. The result was, in my thin trousers I was pressed up against an equally thin-trousered Bob, holding on to his bomber-jacket, vibrating against him in a way which gradually became intensely pleasurable. After a while I realised that a little more of the same and I would blow my top. I tried holding back but then came the inevitable, followed by an even more inevitable *tristesse*, when I had to think what on earth to do. When we stopped for a few cupfuls of petrol, which was all that the economical machine used, I fled to the lavatory to mop myself down, which left me wringing wet in a place and in a manner difficult to explain away. Buttoning up my overcoat, I hoped that it would soon dry.

Our visit to land-locked Vollendam passed off boringly. Vollendam was an early example of a 'heritage' tourist-trap, the pretence being that hefty Dutch women in pinafores and dirndls were still living like their ancestors in Hansel-and-Gretel cottages, bright as new pins. Only one man, whey-faced and wearing the obligatory clogs, gave the game away: 'We were fishermen before they reclaimed the land. Now that they've stolen our livelihood, there's nothing left for us except this nonsense!'

We retreated to a restaurant. As with all Dutch interiors, it was heated to American standards. Bob took off his jacket and mopped his brow. 'PHEW! It's as hot as the Gold Coast in here. Aren't you going to take yours off?'

That was a distinct poser. My trousers still hadn't dried sufficiently, so I pretended that I preferred to get really warm first. Eventually, remaining seated, I slipped out of my heavy overcoat, but at the end of the meal had to slip back into it, still sitting, grinning hectically, sweat pouring down my face. I must have been quite a sight, but not nearly the sight I would have been minus the covering coat. By the time we reached Leyden to see men rushing about, rolling cheeses, whilst a carillon chimed continuously overhead, I was drying; and by Amsterdam, completely dry at last. Bob must have been fairly bewildered, but if so, he was too polite to show it before we parted.

*

I was late. I was told that Nick, having settled both our bills, had gone on to the station. I followed swiftly, to find him rampaging up and down. 'I t'ought you wuz lost!' he said, grinning. 'I knew you had your passport, so I t'ought I'd best pay up and look big and go on to Miss Swiss by meself. PWM?'

In our common short-hand, PWM meant 'pleased with me'.

'Oh, PWM, I suppose!' I said, rather impatiently as I was as eager to question him about his escapade as he was about mine, but we both pretended otherwise.

We had heard that there was a hotel in Zurich, the See-Quai, which might have been specially designed to cater for the likes of us. A lift at street level could be sent straight through to upper floors, by-passing the desk. For an evening's entertainment there was the Fleischmarkt (literally, 'flesh-market'), famed for casual encounters. As usual, Nick effortlessly exercised a unique magnetism combined with a lack of discrimination. Those approaching him could be sure of success, pro- vided that he wasn't already in pursuit of someone else. As for myself, so impenetrable was my disguise, necessarily employed as a protective device, that also as usual I invariably attracted the wrong type. However, I struck lucky a few times, so we had a whale of a time; starting off together, soon going our different ways, perhaps meeting up again at the Bar Füsser, perhaps not.

By the time we returned to England we were on good terms, on a level playing-field. It wasn't precisely what I would have chosen, but it was better than nothing.

———

82

Away to Eden wasn't a success, yet I didn't much mind. Publication was all-important, maintaining me as an author. All I needed now was a new project to work on.

It was with this in mind that I went to see Ralph at Clarence House. He didn't impart any wisdom on what my next subject could be as he was too occupied. The wedding of HRH Princess Margaret to the young fellow popularly known as 'Mr Jones' had taken place on 6 May and there were innumerable letters from well-wishers to be answered. Ralph had to see to some of these, though they were all supposed to emanate from Iris Peake.* Sitting in Ralph's office, I was handed a pile of them to deal with, which at best prayed to God to help P. Margaret, and at worst were semi-literate. The replies were already typed out in a formal 'bids me state' manner but I had to insert the mostly 'Dear Mrs –', sometimes 'Dear Miss –', seldom 'Dear Mr –', and then the 'Whatsername'.

Having finished my stint, Ralph gave me a tour of the place. I remember being impressed by the main drawing-room upstairs, which ran above the two (one big, one small) dining-rooms downstairs. Its great feature, a portrait by Annigoni of Princess Margaret, was flanked by two graceful mirrors and there was a bracket light in the shape of a Prince of Wales feather that I liked, with candle-holders at its base. However, the chairs were upholstered in what to my mind was the wrong colour of pink silk candy-stripe (such a pity) and all in all it felt too tidy. I liked a little mess myself, to make a place feel lived in, which is exactly what was to be found in Gilston Lodge.

Life in that capacity rumbled on. Gina Edwards (that long-suffering once friend of Patricia Denny) became my lodger, occupying the two connecting rooms next to Ralph, who at this point was staying in the upstairs. Gulzaman was supporting Manzoora through being a market trader, so in between looking for subjects for my book I managed to create a company (to be called G. K. Sales (London) Ltd) which would promote him into what he wanted to be most in the world – a company director.

The new company's transport was a blue Ford Zephyr, obtained very cheaply by Gulzaman second-hand. I thought it a bargain until discovering that a line had been deeply (and irremovably) etched into its windscreen by a defective wiper. With the car to give him mobility, Gulzaman began selling shirts and ties in the East End. Next, he took a stall in Basildon New Town, at £3 10s a week, three days a week, then sub-let half of his stall for £1 15s. We worked out that it took 10 shillings' worth of petrol to get him to Basildon and back, so he had to sell at least £13 worth of goods to break even. That didn't stop him from talking wildly of a turnover of hundreds of pounds, which, alas, never materialised; but it kept him happy – for the moment.

---

* A lady-in-waiting to Princess Margaret.

I, on the other hand, *still* hadn't found a subject for my next book. Stuck for ideas, I looked to my family. There was my great great-uncle on my mother's side, Canon Hardwicke Rawnsley, co-creator of the National Trust. Also on my mother's side was Sir John Franklin, the Arctic explorer who had frozen to death on a final expedition in the nineteenth century. Both were prospects to be considered, yet my eye was continually drawn to my great-uncle on my father's side, Major Roddy Owen. Roddy Owen had been my grandmother Maya's brother. Maya herself was notable for having had three husbands and numerous affairs. She was considered to be such a harlot in Edwardian society that the Irish author Sir Shane Leslie described her as 'the most notorious old beldame in Europe'. Leslie even spun a story that my father, George, was not a Fenwick Owen at all but a Frewen, son of the incompetent businessman, writer and sometime MP Moreton Frewen. Apparently, George once happened to be staying in a house where Clare Sheridan, the well-known sculptress, was also a guest. Clare was Moreton's legitimate daughter. In the early hours of the morning, doors were heard softly opening and closing, in true Edwardian country-house fashion. Shane took it upon himself to rush on to the landing, intercepting an amorous George, hand on Clare's door-knob, with a melodramatic: 'Stop! Stop! She may be your half-sister!'

I knew far less about the love life of Maya's brother Roddy, whom she had worshipped, though of course I did know he had won the Grand National on Father O'Flynn, which, coupled with an impish sense of humour, endeared him to everyone, including that accomplished huntswoman the Empress Elizabeth of Austria. I also knew that all the while he'd been in the Army: a man-about-town stationed in India who had then died at Ambigol, on the Sudan Nile, having caught cholera from his goat-boy. An 1897 biography about him filled in some gaps but not many. It was for that reason that Africa, in the shape of Great-Uncle Roddy's exploits, began tugging at my sleeve. Through Dick and my grandmother Maud's deaths I'd also inherited a holding in Rhodesia – a 'ranch' according to her – that was proving complicated, so I thought I'd better see to it in person.

Everywhere I looked, more reasons to go on an African adventure seemed to call to me. Through someone I met in the YMCA off Tottenham Court Road I was introduced to His Excellency

Endalkachew Makonnen,* which led to an invitation to the Ethiopian Embassy where Ambassador Makonnen stationed himself at the head of a long buffet, personally helping his guests to *wat*, the hottest stew in the world. 'There will be dreadful consequences should you leave anything on your plates!' he warned, heaping up a mound of the mouth-scarifying meat.

My return bout was to invite Endalkachew and his wife, 'Inky', to a dinner with Bill and Daška McLean. Whereupon Bill asked me to meet Asrate Kassa, one of the most powerful princes of Ethiopia. Asrate was a heavily built brute, devoid of charm. Bill told me that he actually liked the old toad, but I didn't believe him. What he fancied, as far as I could see, was being asked out shooting in almost medieval splendour. Bill also produced the Governor of Khordofan, with whom I got on very well – in fact inviting me to stay 'for a few weeks', should I find myself in his Sudanese province (which, I gathered, was rather larger than England).

The Sudan beckoned from another quarter. Through another friend I was sent a tall, well-built Colonel Mohammed el-Baghir Ahmed† looking for a place to stay whilst attending a Staff College course at Camberley. I liked him so much that I invited him to stay a few nights at the end of his course, which he did. 'I shall soon be returning to Khartoum,' said this shiningly able officer, in excellent English. 'Should you ever come my way, my house will be yours.'

So it was that, either in reality or in hindsight, I began to see stars aligning once more, and by the end of the year my mind was almost made up. I saw 1960 out at 8 Lincoln Street, near Sloane Square, as a gatecrasher at a party with a friend called Bud Farmiloe. The party took place mostly in the upstairs drawing-room, where a gramophone was kept going for those who wanted to dance. I knew nobody, but that didn't stop me from chatting to a slim, fair-haired Italian, hazel-eyed, looking more like an Austrian, whose name I didn't catch. He'd come to England in May the previous year with a group of friends in order to take up the sort of hotel jobs spurned by the English. He had travelled up from somewhere out of town for the party, though how he'd come

---

* Makonnen was very much part of the Ethiopian elite. His father had been the first Prime Minister of Ethiopia (from 1943 to 1957), and Makonnen himself would be Prime Minister for a brief time in 1974. He was also a stepson of Princess Yeshashework Yilma, the niece of Emperor Haile Selassie.

† Mohammed el-Baghir Ahmed became First Vice President of Sudan in the seventies.

to be invited wasn't explained. His English was shaky, but as he didn't have much to say for himself it hardly mattered.

For want of anything better to do I asked him to take the floor with me; but after a round of treading on one another's toes established that we could both only dance as men we gave it up. I abandoned my short-term partner in order to chat with a more forthcoming pair, the choreographer Kenneth Macmillan and Robert Auguste, from St Lucia. The famous Kenneth was in such demand that others soon swept him off, leaving me free to get Robert's telephone number before I left for Piccadilly Circus, alone.

The streets were jammed with revellers. I arrived in the Circus too late for seeing in the New Year and too late for 'Auld Lang Syne', let alone embracing a policeman. Still alone, I drove home. Chagrin was short-lived because after a couple of telephone calls Robert Auguste became a friend, and remained one for years.

With any luck, 1961 would be different from 1960. After a year of treading water, I was ready to swim in a direction.

83

Not unsurprisingly, Nick and Peg divorced. When he returned from overseas he would stay at Gilston Lodge and we would slip back into old routines, habits and mischief. One day I received a letter from him out in Pakistan which described a fancy dress party where he'd gone as Lady Chatterley and his friend as the gamekeeper. He was clearly pleased with the effect, yet he concluded the story: 'My only wish was for you to be with me. I think I will be with you by the end of the year ... yes R I wish I was at home with you now. You may not have known it but I loved messing around in the garden especially when we were not on speaking terms.' His letter, of course, was signed 'IWALU'. The merest glimpse of that easily decoded message, so remote in form (and content) from anything written by anyone else, gave rise to a pang of nostalgic delight.

It only needed another letter from Nick announcing that his contract was ending early, in July, and that he was thinking of another contract in Tanganyika,* for me to write suggesting: 'Let's go there together in a Land Rover!'

Equally rapidly came back his reply: 'Very excited!' Out of the window went our mutual resolve never to attempt long journeys in a car again. I began a serious search for information about how to go and when.

I had cause to be immensely grateful to Sir Charles Belgrave. I had stayed in touch with the family after Bahrain – James and his wife had even asked me to be godfather to their daughter, Soraya – and Charles had sponsored me to join the Royal Central Asian Society and to secure a fellowship at the Royal Geographical Society. The latter instantly proved its worth. They supplied a Trans-African Highways book published by the Automobile Association of South Africa in 1956, which, in spite of being out-of-date, did at least give *some* clues as to the likely state of what roads there were. I was encouraged by coming across, in their library, a book by Mary Hall, published in 1907: *A Woman's Trek from the Cape to Cairo*. If a long-skirted Edwardian Mary had been able to contemplate such a journey on foot in those days, then surely two modern men, however inexpert, could manage to propel a four-wheel-drive Land Rover on a similar trip, but the other way round. From my reading, November seemed to be the best month if we were to avoid getting stuck in a monsoon downpour. Since this happened to tie in with Nick's new contract – an obligation to present himself at Hale, beyond Tanga, by 15 December – the omens were propitious.

By convenient chance Gina's current lover dealt in motor-cars and was able to recommend Gethin Bradley at the Rover works in Solihull as the man to consult about making modifications for a car that would fit our needs. Gethin advised a 'Martin-Walter' conversion of a long-wheel-based model, providing sleeping accommodation for two: the front seats slid forward and turned into a double-bed. There was a stove, a sink, a water-reservoir and a fridge, a hanging wardrobe, cupboard space and plenty of drawers; in fact it was a caravan of an unusually tough breed, with heavy-duty tyres.

With Gethin at hand, I also devised a number of improvements, including a system of fine-meshed sliding windows, to my own design, behind the ordinary windows, so that we could sleep in fresh air when

---

* Modern-day Tanzania (Tanganyika ceased to exist in 1964).

surrounded by deadly disease-carrying flies and mosquitos. Over and over again those mesh-windows were to make a vital contribution to our well-being. The whole Land Rover, plus all conversions, cost £1158, which seemed at that time a fortune.

Next, the question of permits. With my contacts, a visa for Ethiopia was a foregone conclusion; and I should have been equally well provided for in the Sudan. But difficulties arose over our intention to motor through that vast country, permission being subject to lengthy form-filling and a last-minute demand for a certificate of roadworthiness – even for a *new* Land Rover. In spite of all my expert string-pulling, that particular permit hadn't come through by the time we left England. However, I went ahead with bookings for ourselves and the Land Rover on a ship leaving Piraeus for Alexandria on 25 October. Getting to Athens presented no real problems. We were to drive through France, Switzerland and Italy, then be ferried from Brindisi across to Itea, on the Greek mainland.

As soon as I had a positive plan to promote, others were eager to assist. Bill's colleague, Douglas Dodds-Parker MP, wrote for me a sort of 'Old Boy Network' memo: 'Khartoum: Call on Frank Brenchley, Chargé until another Ambassador is posted. He will put you in touch with our friends ... Addis: I have a number of friends there but you, and they, must be careful as my name was blackened by my attempts to get the Haud for the Somalis ... In Cairo, go and sign the book. Harold Beeley is a knowledgeable chap. One must be careful in Egypt, though many are still all out to help.' I looked at it and couldn't help thinking it might have come from the pen of Evelyn Waugh.

Once committed to the drive, we could consider in detail what and what not to do en route to Northern Rhodesia. I used my great-uncle's movements as a guide: Ambigol, where Roddy's corpse had been provided (at enormous cost) with a memorial by his sorrowing sister; the Owen Falls, named after him, were obviously a must; and Wadelai down the Nile, where Roddy had signed a treaty on behalf of our country. I hadn't arranged a publishing contract in advance, only a helpful TO WHOM IT MAY CONCERN letter from my publisher, but I didn't care at the time. I was determined I could show them why they should be interested when I returned.

Horace Walpole once wrote scathingly about 'Old fools who have gone abroad at 40 to see the world'. Well, I would never see forty again, and Nick was over eight years older. Our combined age was nearing ninety, but neither he nor I felt as ancient as that at the time we left England. How we'd feel eventually was anyone's guess.

———————

84

No amount of preparation could mollify the nature of mine and Nick's relationship. The arguments started early.

A shingly beach at Portonuovo, outside Ancona in Italy, provided the setting for the inevitable flashpoint. When a thunderstorm was at its height, we actually came to blows, in spite of which Nick rushed out into the wet and windy night to fix the flapping concertina-roof of the Land Rover and stop it from tearing loose. For the first time, whilst appreciating his foresight, I was actually afraid of him; he was so much the stronger and his temper seemed ungovernable. What if he were to explode?

At a point of near-desperation on my part, the pilgrimage site of Loreto came to the rescue. The Holy House with its Black Virgin and Child, the fervour of worshippers crawling from afar on their knees, worked on me – and even more on Nick – to make disgruntlement evaporate. But it occurred to me that we might soon run out of spiritual remedies; and then what? It was like being on an endless emotional switchback.

A few miles short of Bari I stopped to talk to a farmer's boy, who obligingly nipped off to get a present of grapes. Nick glowered at what he considered was 'showing off', me speaking Italian when he couldn't, though I did my best to interpret. That night he had his revenge, by refusing to stop at all sorts of good camping sites, finally approving of an unsuitable olive-grove near an aerodrome. On grounds that 'people might be watching' he refused to have the concertina-roof raised when I suggested it. 'You don't call the shots round here. Y'not with y'mother and sister and y'not with Gulzaman, y'with Nick!' he proclaimed. 'I only come along as a favour and I'm ready to leave, any minute.'

My heart seemed to miss a beat, then to thud faster. The unfairness of it was like a plunge into cold water. I mulled over chapter and verse of our semi-continuous disagreements. The trouble was (as I'd discovered on our original trip, round Wales) that he was inclined to sulk after the slightest reverse and maintain his grievance instead of quickly forgiving and trying to make the best of things. When he woke up next morning, still sulky, my determination was confirmed. After twenty miles of grim silence he asked how much driving I thought we'd be doing in Greece. That was my cue: '*You* won't be going there, will you? From what you said, we'll be parting company in Brindisi.'

The effect of that thrust was not at all as expected. After a longish time of glum acceptance he started to cry, dabbing his eyes and snuffling. But he'd been so exceptionally rough with me that at first I pretended not to notice, unwilling to allow myself the slightest concession to kindness, in case I wavered in my resolve. We drove on in silence.

Just before Brindisi he said: 'I'll most likely be hearing from B.B. in Athens. Would you mind if I come wid you that far?' It was all I could do not to choke as I said: 'OK by me!' Anything which would postpone our parting was a gleam of sunshine in the all-pervading gloom.

Following on that hopeful sign, things took a turn for the better. We boarded the ferry (total cost for both of us £35) by night and were shown into a Pullman with four bunks. A married couple, sent to the same Pullman, indignantly protested and shuffled off elsewhere. It put Nick in high good humour: 'Let's have a sangwidge in the bar, Rod! I don't feel like a dinner.' Then, after a drink or two: 'You don't suppose you get rid of me as easy as that, do you? I promised your mother I'd look after you.'

I could think of nothing to say to that but 'Oh, did you?' which apparently sufficed. He made a grab for my knuckles and cracked them – a sure sign that we'd got over the latest and worst of our rows. That night he continued to be most agreeable. Next morning, too, as though nothing had happened. Risking all, I said, 'I can't stand being bullied, Nick. I'd break up with almost anyone rather than put up with more of it.'

'You's the one always wantin' your own way,' he said.

'Yes, that's because I usually know what has to be done and how to do it – which you don't!'

For some reason, no offence was taken. It was a great relief to have brought things out into the open. But what a narrow shave!

Pre-booked in London, our passage from Piraeus to Alexandria in *Achilleus* presented no problem. We occupied a First Class cabin and were put at the Staff Captain's table with an addled poet from Beirut and a naive American schoolmistress called Jane, all set to join her brother, a parasitologist, in Cairo. Clearly, we were the *crème de la crème* of the moment.

It was unlikely that our disembarking would proceed as smoothly as our embarking; nor did it. *Baksheesh* of £5 doled out to the port representative worked wonders; some tiny part of it, redistributed, preserved us from any kind of inspection. Amoral, no doubt, but worth it in conditions as they were. An unlovely Colonel Nasser had taken over from charismatic General Naguib.* Egypt was in the grip of such nationalistic fervour that foreigners were being persecuted. My honorary great-aunt Bonté, notwithstanding all her years as a pro-Egyptian resident, had been given twenty-four hours to leave the country, twelve more hours than most. Yet unofficially the Egyptians seemed remarkably unchanged. Whatever their rulers ordained, they knew how many beans made five and that the bean of beans was a tourist with money to spend. Hence, though all the street signs in English had been removed in favour of signs in Arabic script only, anyone asked the way was hyper-eager to be friendly and informative.

We drove to Cairo and were to stay at the Pension Select, on the eighth floor of a block of flats in Adly Pasha Street. As soon as I could, I rushed round to the British Embassy to 'sign the book', which indicated my familiarity with the correct diplomatic drill. I left Sir Harold Beeley a note in which I pulled out all the stops: recommendations from Dodds-Parker; writing Tedder's biography; casual references to Belgrave and the Gulf. No one could accuse me of not knowing my business.

On Sunday I resumed what had become my normal practice of going to church – a redbrick building on the Nile Corniche. There I was rewarded by meeting a War Graves Commission man who, to my astonishment, was able to give me the latest news about the Roddy Owen memorial. I was told that his bones had been removed from Ambigol the previous winter and re-interred in the New Military Cemetery in

---

* Gamal Abdel Nasser had become president in 1954; he'd been responsible for overthrowing the monarchy and the nationalisation of the Suez Canal. General Naguib had also been responsible for the overthrow of the monarchy so it wasn't any royalist/pro-British fervour that meant Roddy disliked Nasser. Whilst he is generally considered to have been popular in Egypt (an estimated five million people went to Cairo for his funeral), Nasser is often criticised for his dictatorial policies (for example, his re-election in 1965 was a shoo-in because he banned other political opponents from running) and human rights violations. He was also a socialist, which, as you might have inferred already, Roddy mistrusted.

Khartoum. Apparently it was official War Office policy for all graves in the Sudan to be centralised, because otherwise they couldn't be properly maintained.

'What about the red granite tombstone, sent out at vast expense by Roddy's sister?' I asked.

'Oh, it would have been left behind. Too difficult to shift a heavy thing like that!'

Which made up my mind that Nick and I should seek it out.

Back at the Pension Select I contemplated having a bath, then thought better of so bold a move. Like practically the whole of Cairo at that moment, the gleaming bathroom only functioned intermittently, if at all. The lift was subject to repeated breakdowns; no small matter for those marooned on an eighth floor, though it was possible to walk across roof after roof to find one still working. The telephone system similarly suffered: it hiccuped or lost its dialling tone whenever I tried to ring Desmond Stewart, the only person I somewhat knew in a no longer familiar Cairo.

Desmond, like me, had been in the Friends' Ambulance Unit, though we'd only met once, so I probably wouldn't be able to recognise him. I finally tracked him down to a tiny flat in a battered beige block off Liberation (Tahrir) Square – very central and convenient. I'd been warned to expect a number of quirky facets stemming from an outrageous admiration for Sir Oswald Mosley, which must have combined oddly with pacifism. Post-war, he'd been working in the Middle East and had learnt to speak fluent Arabic.

Desmond's 'aide', Sayed, was lent to me as escort (and guard) for a visit to the *hammam* of Saida Zeinab. 'It will be an eye-opener!' said Desmond. 'And the experience will be all the better if you're sozzled.' Duly, towards the end of an evening of too many glasses of Egyptian so-called 'rum', I left wallet and watch behind and set off with Sayed for the narrow alley-way near the university, home to the most notorious bath in Cairo. Nick's fear of being 'seen' prevented him from accompanying us; probably just as well.

'Please sir, hide your money in your sock!' said Sayed.

'I'll do better than that, I'll let you have it,' I said, keeping back one Egyptian pound.

He paid some tiny sum the equivalent of pennies at the entrance: the *hammam* was affordable for the poorest of the poor. In we went to a gloomy atmosphere not helped by a partial power-failure. Our clothes were taken away, ostensibly to be locked up. 'It means nothing,' said Sayed, wrapping a loin-cloth decorously round his middle. 'Anyone can get at them!'

We walked through semi-darkness into a standard hot-tiled room with a heated central slab. Part of the floor was awash with dirty-looking yellowish water, as if a drain were blocked. The most original feature was a room up some stone steps leading to a hot plunge-pool – too hot for comfort, the water being almost scalding. It was so dark that I could hardly make out the features of the various men sprawling at the pool's edge. They, however, could apparently see that I was a foreign tourist, because – as I quickly realised – I immediately became 'the cynosure of all eyes'. It might have caused consternation. It didn't, because they were just as quick to guess what I was there for. First one, then another, slid across the tiled floor towards me to squeeze and pat, smiling directly into my face, stimulated rather than put off by an unavoidable blast of rum-breath: it must have indicated that I was drunk enough to have cast off all inhibitions. There they were right.

Beneath an outward decorum of loin-cloths still wrapped round bodies, everyone – as far as I could see, which wasn't very far – was fumbling and playing about. I was rolled this way and that like a doll, doing whatever was required of me, disregarding pain, unable properly to see faces or bodies, aware mainly of larger or smaller invaders, of grunts and sighs and sudden gasps reeking of garlic. When I had time, or even the drunken ability, to think, I was thinking: *How fantastic this is! No one will ever believe it!*

Unbelievable? Not really. Many, in the past, had done what I was doing and many more would, if they dared, in the future – a future without the necessity of having to be as prissy about it as Lawrence of Arabia. But I was also thinking, *This once and this once only! Degradation may be fascinating, but it just isn't my cup of tea.* I couldn't have found that out in any other way. I lost count of the number of what might loosely be called my admirers. *A Royal Salute,** I wondered, *or more?* I had no wish either to diminish or exaggerate.

Too far gone to be sensitive to anything else, after encountering someone much larger than normal I was aware of acute bladder discomfort. I was afraid that they mightn't let me go, but after I'd repeated the international word 'toilet' often enough I was escorted – no other

---

* A Royal Salute is a twenty-one-gun salute.

word for it – down the stone steps and into a small cubby-hole off the main hot-room where the floor was nearly ankle-deep in swirling yellow sludge.

'*Halas?* [Finished?]' asked Sayed primly after I'd done my business.

I had the idea that his '*Halas?*' had been referring to my pranks rather than my bladder, but the word suited both. Not only was I finished, but it was almost as if I would never, ever again want to begin; yet I wouldn't have missed the experience for worlds. That even applied to the scene attendant on our leaving, for in spite of having hidden an Egyptian pound in my sock, it had been found and pinched. I didn't mind nearly as much as Sayed, who felt that it was a reflection upon his guardianship. I had the greatest difficulty in preventing him from threatening the clothes-man with nameless penalties. *His* money was intact, so we could leave to the accompaniment of numerous small tips, whilst Sayed pursed his lips and looked disapproving.

On reaching the Pension Select, I ran a bath. For once it didn't matter that the water was tepid. It cleansed well enough; at least, externally.

It would take me quite some time to recover.

We didn't have long to wait for a reaction to my signing the book at our Embassy. The Beeleys invited Nick and me to dinner, and it was only then that I realised that I'd been entertained by them before, as a brash young RAF officer staying with Bonté when I argued with one of their guests who I felt was being beastly to the Germans. They'd never forgotten. They were very friendly, and Nick was charmed; he had to admit that the dinner was not as intimidating as many a formal function in Bahrain. On hearing that I'd pestered every Sudanese Consulate within reach for the permit that still hadn't arrived, Sir Harold promised to put pressure on Khartoum. 'A special telegram should do the trick,' he said. It worked. Within three days the permit so vainly pursued for four months arrived and Nick and I were ready to move on.

On our way to Ambigol, the site of Roddy's last moments, we passed through places I had visited at the end of the war. At that moment, tourists in Egypt were few so it was hardly surprising that at midday I should find myself alone in the courts of the imposing sandstone structures of the Temple of Karnak, mooning about and baking in the sun whilst pigeons wheeled overhead or landed in groups near me. The wondrous Luxor Temple, with its many pillars and statues to be explored, was as deserted, even in daytime, as it had been on that moonlit night when Ali the guide had pointed to the figure of Min incised on an inner wall in order to engage the attention of a newly moustachioed young Flying Control Officer. Nobody could say that I'd been wanting in respect for ithyphallic Min since then; indeed, if anything, the opposite. On this my second visit I noticed that the niche behind the gigantic statue of Rameses the Second was piled with rubbish. I wondered what had become of Ali. Ought I to have gone with him down the Nile in a *felucca*? Had a feverish cold really been my salvation in disguise? Impossible to tell.

It was frustrating to realise that, though I was more experienced, I was as dissatisfied when it came to love as I'd been in those Service days. If only Nick had been more constant! Yet what right had I to make such a claim on him when I was forever straying myself? Momentarily, my verdict was: *I wouldn't have, if he hadn't!* Until I recognised that it probably wasn't the whole truth.

85

It was of Roddy Owen's own making that he ended up in a position where he would die at forty – he wasn't supposed to be in Africa at all. Hearing in Bombay that there might be 'a spot of bother' in the Sudan, he applied for home leave, then sent a wire to Sir Herbert Kitchener, Sirdar of the Egyptian Army, begging for employment in any capacity. The Sirdar ordered him to the front in April 1896. Roddy went up-river from Cairo to Aswan, to see to the purchase of two camels. 'Goodness knows how I'm going to ride them, uncomfortable brutes,' he wrote. 'But nevertheless, if all goes well, I could after this campaign leave the service before my forty-first birthday, having accomplished the dream of my life, to take an active part and be in at the death in securing the Nile to England.'

Next day: 'We are on the river with four barges attached, each carrying about 20 or 30 tons, on the way to Wady Halfa.' Then, in a statement most uncharacteristic of him: 'I'm afraid I don't feel quite the same man physically I used to. Africa has been too much for me.' He was suffering from 'gippy tummy', the dreaded dysentery to which Egypt had lent its name.

Before he had time to recover – if indeed he ever did – he was attached as 'Special Service Officer' (which meant they couldn't think what else to do with him) to the Camel Corps, with the job of conducting convoys from Ambigol up to Akasheh. The idea was to cover the flanks of the Egyptian advance. 'We have to fear a Dervish force getting round and attacking the line of communications or the convoys moving on it; and it is our business to prevent this.'

Then he was placed in command of a detachment of Alighat Arabs, and by June he was happily contemplating the taking of Dongola, so soon as the Nile should flood and the gunboats could be brought upstream. 'From Dongola, after sowing crops and making friends with enemies between Dongola and Abu Hamed, we ought to creep up to Berber. Once there, we can dominate the Soudan, and by control over the waters of the Nile hold the keys of Lower Egypt.'

He added: 'If the Dervishes really pluck up courage and defend Dongola in force, we shall have our hands full, and I personally am inclined to think the news of the cholera will imbue them with spirit and vivify them afresh . . . On the other hand, they may elect to sit tight at Omdurman, but I don't think so . . . It is possible the cholera continuing might stop any further advance now.'

When writing his opinions of Kitchener's tactics, he was within an hour of collapse, himself the victim of what he'd feared for others.

His sorrowing sister in England recorded the reaction of shock, nationwide: 'Great posters throughout London and leaded type at the head of newspaper columns throughout the United Kingdom, almost throughout the Empire, and also in many continental papers, announced at the beginning of the busy day the death of "Roddy" Owen.' She didn't exaggerate. Many of those who mourned would be wearing a 'Roddy Owen' collar, even though it was uncomfortably high and starchy for the average neck. The praises and plaudits nowadays heaped on sportsmen, actors and pop-stars were his in even greater measure, because in days when communications were slower, such idols as were available were apt to be known only to a smaller public. His fame was the reason why he'd been able to twist the military authorities round his fingers so easily. In all his campaigns – in Uganda, in India, finally in the Sudan – he'd carried on as if he were a Prince, albeit one who was borrowing far too much money he could never repay.

I have often wished that I found his aspirations more digestible. The main goal of his life, when not in the saddle, was to further the interests of Empire. For someone like myself for whom riding was a last resort, and around whom an Empire had crumbled in clouds of recrimination, Roddy's aims were none too sympathetic. Nevertheless, I wasn't going to let that interfere with my appreciation of a man who was such a hero of his day, the quirky amateur par excellence, effortlessly – or so it seemed – surpassing the expert in all he chose to do.

He died not only in debt, but still a bachelor, a condition which may have helped him remain a figure adored by men as much as women. Was he really, as his sister claimed, 'too busy for affairs of the heart'? I had to confess that, bereft of clues, I didn't know what to make of him in sexual terms; which was doubtless as he intended.

We reached Ambigol, the site of Roddy's death, on 26 November 1961.

It had been an uncomfortable drive, sliding on and off a cindery causeway which had once been the bed of a long-defunct railway built by the Turks. The occasional massive truck which we met had left deep ruts, into which we, with our narrower wheel-base, slipped and bumped. The 'Belly of the Rock' was a series of outcrops, imprisoning the Nile, out of sight somewhere off to our left.

But for sighting a tiny mud-shack with an awning of palm-fronds, we mightn't have known that we'd reached Ambigol. The unlikely hovel turned out to be a coffee-booth, to which the proprietor could be seen running to greet us from another shack a hundred yards further on. He was most impressed when told why we'd come. 'Yes, yes, the tomb is there!' he shouted, waving dramatically towards a distant slope. 'But you gentlemens have come too late. They have stolen him away!'

'I know,' I said, putting his mind at rest. 'They didn't want his bones to be covered by the waters of the new dam.'

'Yes, that is so, but they were wrong to disturb him. Every British soldier passing this way would pay respects to this great soldier!'

'Were there many?' I asked.

'Not so many, recently,' was the tactful reply.

We followed the man through the sand towards a kind of pen, a square of stones, nine feet by nine, which seemed to be enclosing nothing but more sand. The barrier had been broken down at one corner, and over it our guide scrambled, then started burrowing with his bare hands.

'What's he doing?' I asked.

'He wishes to show you something,' said our interpreter.

We watched and waited, not knowing quite what to expect.

Suddenly, from beneath those questing fingers emerged a block of smooth red granite. It seemed purest fantasy when clear black lettering began to appear, obscured by sand trickling back across the sloping stone for every handful that was brushed away, but nevertheless more and more lettering emerging:

> IN EVER LOVING MEMORY OF 'RODDY' . . .
> RODERIC OWEN, MAJOR, LANCASHIRE
> FUSILIERS . . . DIED . . . CHOLERA . . .
> AGED 40 YEARS.
> 'Under . . . Sword . . . adise'

Slowly, slowly, in spite of the way the sand kept trickling back, the whole text was revealed, the last line a quotation from the Holy Koran:

> 'Under the shadow of the Sword is Paradise'

It was certainly not the most obvious valediction for a Christian grave.

We were amazed and dumbfounded, quite overcome by the solemnity of the moment. Tears came into my eyes, whilst Nick went as white as a sheet. The coffee-booth proprietor, whose strong dark hands had conjured the monument out of a brown waste, grinned and rubbed the sweat off his face with parts of his robe, pleased beyond measure at the success of his demonstration.

Finally I asked: 'From now on, until the new dam covers it for ever, will you promise to keep this memorial clear of sand?'

'Ai-wah, ai-wah! Always clear, effendi, for when you come back this way!'

I left him a substantial tip, of course, but it was probably unnecessary. There seemed very little else for him to do.

I sat on a knoll intentionally alone and read the letter Roddy wrote, early in the morning of 11 July 1896: 'I am seated on a rock surrounded with desert, the only European here, with seven cases of Cholera on the 5th, 6th and 7th inst., but I think we've tackled it. The quarantine

has so upset arrangements that it is within the bounds we do not pros-
ecute our journey to Dongola as yet. But we must stick to Khartoum
as an objective, and, bar European complications, the dream of Cecil
Rhodes* looks likely of accomplishment . . .' At which point he collapsed, retching, and was dead by 9.30 that same evening. It was an
extraordinary and uncanny feeling to be alive in such a place of death,
when the site itself had remained unaltered over the years – you could
still see the circles on the ground where the bell-tents had stood, neat
pathways marking out military areas.

We passed by again next day on our way to Dongola and points south
and found the whole enclosure swept clear, without one grain of sand.
Had I thought to bring roses from the Nile Hotel's garden (as my mother
would have done) my flowers would not have been for a brave soldier
whose bleached bones had already been removed to the New Military
Cemetery in Khartoum, but as a belated tribute to the fierce sisterly
love which had caused the slab of granite to be brought from afar and
set amongst those dark, satanic hills. It must have been a tremendous
undertaking for my grandmother, for which she deserved her grandson's
respect. As it was, I may have been the last to weep over the memorial
to Major Roddy Owen, who'd been no more than a few months older
than me when he died.

And here was I, alive and on my way to the town of Dongola mentioned in the last letter that he ever wrote. How strange it seemed!

———

86

Roddy's first visit to Akasheh, on up the Nile, was hindered by his
dysentery, for which the Medical Officer advised immediate rest.
His advice went unheeded because his patient was too busy learning
how to control an animal other than a horse: 'As it was my first long

———

* Cecil Rhodes was an ardent Victorian imperialist, who had wanted to connect
  South Africa and Egypt by one railway line. Rhodesia (which is now Zimbabwe and
  Zambia) was named after him; he established it along with his own British South
  Africa Company.

camel ride, it tried me very highly. We were very nearly shot at as we advanced on Akasheh. They had actually laid the guns. We spent a most uncomfortable night in shoals of black sand, with a mackintosh sheet and no pillow.'

Now we ourselves had passed Akasheh, along a road hemmed in by barren rock-outcrops doomed soon to disappear under the rising waters of the new Lake Nasser, and were heading on to Dongola, which entailed crossing the Nile at some point only vaguely marked on our map. We suffered many a false alarm from seeing mirages in the distance, lines of 'trees' above and below the horizon, separated by gaps of blue 'water'. They quivered too much to be mistaken for the real thing, but they were disturbing, particularly when multiple tracks were apparently taking us away from the river. We were glad to see something at last which was definitely what it seemed to be: Shell and Caltex storage-tanks glistening in the sun, for they could only be sited on the Nile, and only at some crucial point. In fact a mobile pontoon was moored nearby, waiting to take men and donkeys – and us – over to Dongola before sunset at a cost of 15 shillings.

We made a courtesy call on the District Commissioner. He was asleep but he rose at once to take us personally to the Rest-House, an astonishing place – a palace, no less, which had once belonged to Stack Pasha, British Governor.* We were told that the Governor had found Dongola so attractive that he'd stayed on, with a harem of fifty women, vowing never to leave – a vow which he'd been forced to break on being summoned to Khartoum to greet the Prince of Wales. The Residency wasn't going to last much longer, that much was obvious. Wooden floors lurched this way and that, wooden walls were splitting and decaying; I soon fell into a pit housing a disused pump and bruised my nose.

Dongola accomplished, our next target was Khartoum, the new resting place of Roddy's bones. To get there we had to head for Omdurman, and the drive was eventful. We struck soft sand and it was truly appalling: great waves of sand, crests facing this way and that, twisting the poor Land Rover sideways. At times we would race forward as fast as our wheels could spin, crashing in and out of four-wheel-drive, with

---

* Major-General Sir Lee Stack was both Sirdar of the Egyptian Army and Governor-General of the Sudan. In November 1924 he was assassinated by Egyptian students while being driven from the Egyptian War Office in Cairo to his official residence.

the clutch roaring and smoking. I couldn't speak for concentrating on the awful moments when we would nearly grind to a halt, somehow moving on, in any direction, so long as we didn't stop. If we stopped, it was a sure thing that we'd never be able to start again.

After about half an hour the loose sand seemed to be hardening a little, so when I saw a man on a donkey I dared pull up to ask: 'Are we over the worst?' Apparently, we were. We made a pitstop at Debba to calm our nerves, where the post-master, who spoke fluent English, gave us coffee poured from a clay pot shaped like a wine-flask with a spout, straining the cardamom-flavoured liquid through a chog of palm-fibre. He offered to fix us up with an Ancient, who for a fee of £7 would conduct us 250 miles across the desert to Omdurman.

'I wouldn't touch the auld rogue with a barge-pole, Rod,' argued Nick. 'Two quid's enough!' But what was £7, or even £70, as the price of safety? The desert was notorious for swallowing the foolhardy. However much Nick objected, I had to ignore him: the issue was too vital to be sabotaged by politeness.

Nick might have admitted – but of course did nothing of the sort – that the Ancient was a treasure, a proper guide, able to distinguish the best track from any number of others, forewarning when the going would be rough. That night the old thing slept contentedly enough on the sand, leaving us to our own devices in the Land Rover's convertible double-bed. As I was driving, Nick was in charge of the catering. He had decreed that the old man's mug had to be kept apart from ours, and in the morning he brewed tea and gave him some. The guide handed the empty mug back to me.

'Where d'you want it put?' I asked Nick pointedly.

'Oh, put it *there*!' he said, jabbing with his finger at the box where we kept our own mugs.

I said: 'You haven't answered the question. I asked you where you *wanted* it kept.'

I was answered by volley after volley of expletives (so bizarre that asterisks and capital letters hardly do them justice): 'I said PUT it THERE, you f***ing c*nt! Why d'you always have to f***ing argue? F***ing MAD, that's what you are, f***ing useless C*NT!'

So extreme were his reactions that I half expected a repetition of previous threats of 'getting out and walking'. But the desert was hardly the place to make such threats stick. Instead he finished his rant with, 'I'm driving from now on. It's safer!'

Since there was no good reason not to, I handed the wheel over to him. He grabbed it; and within an hour he'd all but overturned us, coming to a halt by swinging violently across a sand-rut, breaking off an underside flange which he spent the next half-hour repairing. He then handed the old man *my* mug and tried forcing our food on him, which the old thing had already politely refused – and again refused.

I said nothing . . .

A truck came heaving towards us, the only one we'd seen all day long. Nick slowed down and pulled off to one side to let it pass, but not quickly enough. 'Look out! You're going to hit it!' I shouted. And the next moment, hit it he did, all along one side, damaging us slightly and the truck not at all.

'It's all your fault, for being a Jonah!' he muttered. 'If tings *can* go wrong, they do, with you around!'

It made him so cross that when thorn-bushes began hemming us in, he hardly made any effort to avoid them. Branches smacked against our sides, deeply scratching them. My thoughts were dark and grew darker as he drove grimly on, sometimes over a hard desert floor, sometimes into drifts of sand stuck with shrubs and small trees, before getting back to a reasonably hard surface again. Then I noticed his head nod . . . and jerk, and nod again . . . Sheepishly, he had to admit that he was falling asleep at the wheel, so I was allowed to take over for the last fifty miles to Omdurman.

Unlike neighbouring Khartoum, where there were city blocks complete with metalled roads, street-lighting and telegraph poles, Omdurman was a town of reddish mud-brick with minimal amenities. We would drop our Ancient off there and go ourselves to Khartoum, where I was looking forward to one thing only: to the luxury of lying down in a dark room with a wet cloth over my eyes, alone. Once again, I had made up my mind to ditch my deeply loved, deeply loathed companion.

But what in fact happened? Determination came to a dead end at the *poste restante*, where we found no letter from his contract employers to tell him what to do. He was plunged into gloom. 'What am I to do, Rod? They was to let me know for sure, here, they said.'

'Looks like you'll have to put up with me till we get to Addis,' I said, not quite as glad as I'd been in Greece.

'Hmmmm,' was the reply, also not entirely happy.

As we both knew, the glue keeping us together couldn't be easily unstuck, but I for one was no longer prepared to be as accommodating as before; so to that extent things had changed. For him, too? Possibly. I really had no idea.

Khartoum's New Military Cemetery, adjoining a civil burial-ground, was dusty and depressing. Soldiers dying on active service had a continuation of uniformity to look forward to; the graves were set in well-aligned rows, as if waiting for a word of command before being stood down. Search how I might, I couldn't find Roddy's grave. A Sudanese warden was sitting in a nearby tent with an exercise book containing a list of the interred, but Roddy's name wasn't on it. I left Nick chatting to the warden and wandered slowly up and down the lines, without finding what I was looking for.

On my return to the tent I heard a scuffle; then Nick poked his head out asking, 'Why couldn't you have been five minutes longer?'

I was both astonished and in no mood to go complaisantly away. 'There are some questions I need to ask him, that's why!'

The warden, though flushed, was not too out of breath to inform me that there was a heap of containers and blank crosses stacked at the edge of the cemetery. 'Perhaps one of those containers might contain all that is left of the one you seek,' he said, patting his hair and avoiding looking at Nick.

I found out later from a Foreign Office official anxious to be of assistance that the bones of my elusive great-uncle had been re-interred in Plot 12, Row C, No. 8, on 31 May 1960. But the Commonwealth War Graves Commission had been dilatory, doubtless never dreaming that they'd be found out. All things considered, I was glad to have missed seeing an undistinguished cross with an undistinguished new inscription to mark the spot where those cholera-ridden bones had been re-interred. The red granite block at Ambigol would shortly be inundated by the Nasser Dam, yet as far as I was concerned it would remain Roddy's true memorial, broadcasting to the water instead of to the desert air that strange, ringing announcement:

'Under the shadow of the Sword is Paradise'

87

In Addis Ababa, the capital of Ethiopia, Nick had confirmation of his job and booked his flights, so we set about extracting his things from the general mess inside the Land Rover. The confusion was even worse than we'd imagined. Sugar had tipped into a pool of paraffin, spilt when we'd bumped over some of our rougher tracks, then penetrating to the pots-and-pans cupboard. The problem was too dispiriting to be tackled at that moment, at that altitude – we were both having to adapt to being at 8000 feet. Alas, fresh quarrels were a foregone conclusion, and all too soon they started. *Thank God he'll be gone by tomorrow!* I thought.

With that in mind, I started at once trying to locate Endalkachew Makonnen, the ambassador I'd met through my YMCA friend, who'd returned to his country as Minister of Science and Commerce. Reaction was immediate. 'I'll come by this evening and take you home with me,' he promised.

'You go, Rod. Best I don't meet him!' said Nick, putting on his 'mandrill' face. 'I'll take Miss L-R out and give her a good clean.'

I left him doing just that, and off I went to Endalkachew's smart suburban house where I was entertained by him and his chic Inky. With them I downed much whisky – too much, inevitably; I had to stagger back to the hotel as tight as an owl, trying not to wake Nick (who was probably awake anyway, but pretending not to be).

Next day I was greatly touched on seeing the results of Nick's work. The Land Rover was looking clean for the first time since leaving England. It served to emphasise the scrape-marks for which he'd been entirely to blame, but it made it impossible for me to mention them. Praising him and apparently blind to anything but the Land Rover's new sparkle, I dropped him off at Haile Selassie Airport to wait for a much-delayed flight.

I drove back to the hotel, loudly humming a tune which changed, without conscious intention, into 'Put your sweet lips a little closer to the phone . . . !' My bravado was premature: soon I could hardly see for blinding tears, trickling uncontrollably. Intent on luxuriating in being miserable, I lay stretched out on a bed which creaked at the slightest movement, as if in sympathy.

I remembered other moments of feeling utterly, utterly alone: when pushed, motherless, through a green baize door at Summer Fields into an unfamiliar world of shouting boys; after hitching a ride back to the Officers' Club in Foggia, knowing that I would never see Sgt Joe Birmingham again; and when casting garlands of *tiaré Tahiti* and frangipani into the sea, waving to Turia until she became a dot too small to be recognisable. All of them were occasions of anguish, readily dredged from the depths of memory to be nostalgically mulled over.

But flashes of consolation seemed to spark from the lumpy pillow wet with my maudlin tears. *I'm far from being as soft as I'm making out,* I mused. *Not nearly so soft!* It was a comforting idea, and might even be the truth. But I had no intention of pulling myself together before wringing the last drop of self-pity out of the situation.

Since I couldn't very well appear in public looking so woebegone, I helped myself lavishly to whisky and opened one of our cans of bully-beef, eating the pink stodge straight from the tin with a spoon. After which, feeling slightly sick – and no wonder – I took to studying a large-scale map of Ethiopia, as intently as see-sawing vision would allow. One track only ran south into Kenya and it wasn't depicted as a proper road. Finally overcome by exhaustion as much as by drink, I undressed and reached for my pyjama jacket. Something crackled in its breast pocket. A note:

> *My dear Rod,*
> *I hate leaving you here, but what can I do? In spite of all our ups and downs I don't think that there is anybody on earth like you. Look after yourself Rod and I will pray for you always.*
> *All my love to U.*
> *Nick.*
> *I.W.A.L.U.*

I jumped as though shot; then bit my fingers. I had no wish to admit to being touched to the heart. Grabbing a pen, I wrote in my diary: 'Well, if that's not melting, I don't know what is.' Then, more savagely: 'It's all very well, he was most awfully tiresome and cross too often – this whole trip so far has made circles round him and through him.

It's unimaginable, the dance we have danced – and he is 48 – perhaps that's why.'

No sooner had I put my scorcher down in writing than I wanted to scratch it out. I didn't, because I didn't ever want to forget the confusion of thought, the numbness, the conflict of sadness and relief produced by that loving, homely note at journey's end.

————

88

Over the coming months I travelled around Ethiopia, Kenya and Zanzibar before reaching Northern Rhodesia, now Zambia, and setting foot on the so-called ranch I'd inherited. As I'd suspected before heading out there, it was a money pit, and so my final act in Africa was to identify the correct people who could help me to sell. Or I should say, it was my penultimate act. My final one being to sell the Land Rover.

Now that we were so near parting for ever, I looked fondly, but dispassionately, at my jungle-green nest-on-wheels. Those wheels had been splendid, taking me everywhere I'd needed to go. But the 'nest' part of the deal had been slightly disappointing, not only because of the way the steering wheel hindered most forms of nocturnal activity, but because so little had been on offer. With a few exceptions, I might have had a far more riotous time had I never left London. All the same, I had to be profoundly grateful for the fact that it had seen me through difficulty and danger unscathed. (Such scars as I bore were mental, caused by the sad diminution of love. Love, always love, perhaps never again to come within reach.)

I had always been afraid of something going wrong, of incurable mechanical breakdown or of some dreadful accident. Nothing of the sort had happened. Instead, a complete amateur like me had got away with it. I only had to recollect moments of near-disaster to realise that very little had been due to my own powers. To thank God was not just advisable, but mandatory.

*

I returned to England to find that the Berlin Wall, started by the East Germans in 1961 under orders from their Russian overlords, had become a monstrous barrier disguised as an 'Anti-Fascist Defence Line', fervently welcomed (they claimed) by those effectively cut off from the rest of a thriving Europe. George Orwell's *1984* seemed to be coming true, with official 'double-speak' triumphant over common-sense.

The Soviet Union had scored a public relations hit with their space programme. Yuri Gagarin, the pioneer astronaut, was not only handsome but looked thoroughly nice. Could he really be a typical Russki? Before falling into a swoon over Soviet space-ascendancy it was as well to reflect upon one aspect of what had preceded it. The dog Laika had been the first sentient passenger, wired up and sent into space by the Russians without a chance of returning to earth; whereas NASA had sent the chimpanzee Ham roaring off in a Redstone rocket (two months before Gagarin) and brought the animal back to live to a ripe old age in a North Carolina zoo. There could have been no sharper illustration of the difference in outlook between the two superpowers.

Such out-of-this-world activities were bound to interest a wider public more than *Roddy Owen's Africa*, I thought. However, I started writing up in the Monks' Dormitory at Langney. I asked my father for the letters, newspaper-clippings, reports and documents that I believed to have been at Brantham, but he replied that they'd been misplaced when he'd moved out at the end of the war. A great pity, and it left me with the conundrum of what Roddy was really like. More sensitive than he cared to admit and with more secrets to hide? Nothing, not even a diary, was said to survive. I advertised in *The Times* for information, and an item came in from a fellow officer called Tim Bishop, who'd served with him in India.

'Roddy was a most amusing asset to the Mess and used to make a point of wearing, both in khaki and plain clothes, something different from everyone else,' Bishop wrote. 'He had a small khaki helmet that he insisted on wearing until it mysteriously disappeared, when he had to get the same pattern as everyone else's. In plain clothes he affected a yachting cap.' He told me why he thought Roddy exerted such a fascination on his contemporaries: 'For me, it was because he was the first of many regular officers who, when it came to the push, turned out infinitely better soldiers than their more serious and law-abiding brothers, but who, when the bullets were not in the wind, insisted on

leading their own lives, caring nothing for red tape and authority ...
He was also the first amateur [jockey] to take on the pros and prove as
good as they, which was a dashing, skilful and colourful thing to do ...
I still have the Spy cartoon of Roddy, with bowler hat, umbrella and
suede shoes, on my dressing-room wall.'

On reading this, my first thought was: *Suede shoes, with a City man's
bowler, forsooth!** Had someone else been doing it, people might have
concluded: 'The fellow doesn't know how to behave!' But when it was
Roddy they were dealing with, the suede was on another foot. He was
clearly determined to make the point that he, the great I AM, could do
anything he chose and get away with it – for which I applauded him
heartily. He still seemed a remote figure, but I was discovering more
sympathetic qualities in him. I hadn't expected to admire him so much.
I might have asked his adoring fellow officer about more intimate affairs.
But as nothing had been volunteered, I feared that the question would
be considered too impertinent to be answered truthfully; in which case,
better not ask at all.

For the first time ever, the act of writing proved unexpectedly difficult, probably because so many things stood in the way of telling the
truth. Nick *should* have played a large part in the narrative, but how
could I contrive to present him as he was without endangering his
career? A series of flimsy fibs would be no substitute for the real thing.
Discontented with a story so emasculated, I tried to drop hints, but
they were arch and unsatisfactory. Hence 'writer's block'; hence an
increased intake of alcohol with resultant hangovers and more writer's
block to follow.

When I eventually submitted the first few chapters, I was unsur-
prised – yet still taken aback – that they were rejected. I tried to pretend
that rejection of the book didn't matter. (Indeed it didn't, in some ways,
since I didn't need the money.) But it was as if I'd been jilted. The setback prevented me from undertaking my usual painstaking revision. As
always, every word had been written in long-hand, because I imagined
that something mystical flowed from direct contact of pen with paper.
I even had a special, solidly nibbed pen for the purpose. Switching off

---

* The Spy cartoon can be found in the National Portrait Gallery, titled 'Men of the
  Day. No. 525', and was featured in *Vanity Fair* on 28 November 1891. It is unlikely
  that Roddy had seen the picture in question. He might have been happier if he had:
  the shoes appear to be brown cap toe Oxfords, but it's not altogether clear that they
  are suede!

the lights in the Monks' Dormitory I left everything in an untidy clutter and went back to Gilston Lodge to recover by plunging into other forms of life.

———

89

On the rebound from writing, I started taking a greater interest in Gulzaman's efforts to make a life for himself and Manzoora. When she miscarried twice, it provided an added spur: we wanted to take her mind off procreation, if that was to be denied her. Gulzaman and I had formed G. K. Sales (London) Ltd, a limited company to start him on a clothes-selling venture with a Sikh partner. The venture had folded but the company survived, with me as an inactive co-director. Gulzaman took a stall in Portobello Road market, operating on Saturdays only, by which he cleared £2 to £3 a week for one day's work – hardly a handsome return, but (in those days) better than nothing. I soon realised that what we needed was some foolproof scheme whereby, no matter what mistakes he made, he couldn't lose; which was how we came to be involved in property. Although stubborn on most issues, he was easily convinced, because so many of his friends were doing well by buying houses cheaply and doing them up to rent.

Gulzaman unearthed Ismail Khan, who offered to sell us his house in Battersea. Ismail was so attractive in a melancholy way that for that reason alone I was inclined to do business with him, though the house in Wycliffe Road (No. 3, one of a late-Victorian terrace ascending an outcrop of Lavender Hill) was no match for its owner. Its three floors were fully let: to three Jamaicans paying £3 10s 0d each on the ground floor, and five Pakistanis in the basement at £4 4s 0d. Ismail and his wife wanted to continue occupying the top floor at 5 guineas a week – useful, because Mrs Ismail was prepared to do the cleaning for 15 shillings per week. All of it could be ours for an investment of £2950, of which £400 was for fixtures and fittings of a very basic nature. Gulzaman was content.

As for me, enforced idleness prompted less edifying activities; more dangerous, too. The scars from one episode made such a lasting impression that they may have saved me from much worse.

Each year, Earls Court became the centre for the Royal Tournament* (known as 'The Royal Torment'). Some of us liked to wander round outside the arena, to meet, talk to and possibly pick up performers whose acts had finished. Years earlier, Hubert Fox and I had been interrogated by a gingery plain-clothes detective who'd sent us ignominiously back to our seats. I wasn't going to risk a repetition, so confined my activities to pubs nearby where hundreds of servicemen were on the look-out for anyone, of either sex, prepared to show them a good time, in return for which they were ready for almost anything. The most sought-after were those from the Naval gun-teams. I was once privileged to be present at a complete 'Sod's Opera' lasting nearly an hour, put on by three 'Oggi-Oggi' gun-team sailors, i.e. those from Plymouth, an oggi being a Cornish pasty. Their repertoire was a true example of folk art in lower-deck British style; in its way, wonderful.

On another occasion, when my old school friend Richard Neville was staying with me, we were driving back home late at night, flown with wine, making a detour through Green Park in order to see what Guardsmen were 'working the Mall'. There seemed to be none about, but even so we thought that we'd stroll by the lake and sit on one of the benches. Within minutes a Marine Commando in uniform, together with a friend in civvies, approached. On spotting us, the Marine put his thumbs into his belt and grinned. We only had to nod back to find ourselves with company – apparently good, jokey company. Pretending to pick up a newspaper, the one in uniform read out: 'Wanted, a friend for two lonely Marines. Will do anything required to make the party go. Apply within!' Boldly he was unbuttoning his trousers when the other saw a policeman coming, so they hummed a tune until the bobby had gone on his way, suspecting nothing. Then: 'What about you kind gentlemen taking us back to your place for a beer? You do have a place, don't you?'

'He might have,' said Richard cautiously. 'I'm just a guest.' (It was his way of giving me time to decide yes or no.)

They said that they were both from the same unit, up in London to take part in the tournament; but from subsequent remarks it seemed that

---

* A military tattoo where soldiers took part in competitions and pageants, which ran from 1880 to 1999.

this only applied to the one in uniform, called 'Robbie', his mate being 'Clancy'. I didn't much take to Clancy, his eyes were set too closely together; in fact I doubted whether he were a Marine at all. Not that I cared: Robbie was for me, Clancy for Richard. They came back with us. Beer was produced, but they seemed disinclined to linger over it or to want more – most unusual. In view of a strenuous day ahead in the arena, they were eager for 'a bit of a kip'. We led them upstairs.

I had just taken off my coat when something hit me a tremendous crack on the back of the head, followed by a blow to the side of my face. That was all I could remember till I came to on the floor, to find Robbie pulling Great-Aunt Evie's gold signet-ring off my finger. 'Be quiet and stay quiet if you know what's good for you,' he growled, throwing a coverlet over me. In blank terror I remained motionless, utterly unlike a Hollywood hero.

Dimly in the distance I could hear thumping noises, so I assumed that Richard was being similarly attacked. Still I lay motionless. Then came the sound of booted feet pounding upstairs and a girl's scream, followed by something entirely unexpected: both of them were running down-stairs, and shortly afterwards the front door slammed, then the garden gate clanged. Still I lay there with the coverlet over my head until my confused brain decided that the fiends had gone. At which point I heard Gina calling. She had been on her own up in 'the lid', Mike being away and Ralph having moved into a house he'd bought in Lambeth. I raced downstairs, to check that the birds of ill-omen really had flown, then ran back up to Gina's room. By which time she had prudently locked her door, but she opened it for me, with a breathless account of what had happened: 'A thin dark man [Clancy; Robbie was fair and stocky] burst into the room and switched on the light. When he saw me he tipped his hat, said, "Sorry, madam!" and tip-toed out, carefully pulling the door to. That was when I screamed!'

'Thank God you did!' I said. 'You frightened them off better than any guard dog.'

I must have been a sight. My lip was bleeding profusely. I pressed a handkerchief against it and went into Richard's room, finding him kneeling against the bed, moaning. His face was already swelling omi-nously and there was a cut near his eye, dripping blood. There was a disgusting smell in the room. I saw why when I picked him up and sat him on a chair: on top of everything else, he'd suffered a distressing attack of diarrhoea. I had never given first-aid to a victim of violent assault before, but I'd heard of that kind of thing happening, so wasn't surprised. I helped him to the bathroom and into the bath, then put his trousers to soak in the basin. I bandaged his head with an antibiotic dressing near his eye and helped him back on to his bed.

'Oughtn't we to call the police?' he asked.

To which I was inspired to reply: 'Good heavens, no! We've had the injury. Why suffer the insult as well?' It required little imagination to visualise the possible headlines in an exultant press should such an incident, in those pre-a-change-in-the-law days, become public knowledge.

We rested for a few hours, then at 6 a.m. called the doctor. By then Richard's face was so swollen that its shape had changed; his chin looked wider than his forehead. My own jaw had swollen, but not to the extent of his. Our injuries were nothing like those to be seen in every film featuring a bar-room brawl. Apart from misshapen lumps and bumps, our bruises were far from decorative, the colour of raw beef. The doctor sent us off to be X-rayed, when Richard was found to have a bone broken, whilst I merely needed a few stitches. The trouble was, Richard had fought back, whereas I had been as quiveringly inert as a jelly, hence he'd come in for far greater punishment.

When I came to check what things were missing – other than the money we'd had on us and my ring – I was amazed to find how little had been taken. No time, presumably, thanks to Gina's scream. A Victorian carriage-clock, a portable wireless and a monster bottle of champagne, a gift from Ernest Hofer (the friend who had gifted me his first date with Nick all those years ago), made up the total. Margaret, the char, would instantly have noticed had other things been missing. As it was, we were more concerned with the problem of how to explain our wounds.

'I know, a motor accident!' said Richard.

The fact that Gulzaman had slept through it all downstairs removed any suspicion that our 'motor accident' might have taken place on the premises. Truth to tell, I was relieved that Gulzaman hadn't come upstairs. He would have been bound to intervene, possibly laying into them with a knife, thereby magnifying the scandal ten-fold. Damaged as we were, neither Richard nor I would have welcomed that publicity.

The episode proved that there could be distinct drawbacks to a life of affluence and idleness. A private station was not all roses. It put me in a quandary: could I sincerely thank God for a timely warning? I tried hard to see it in that light and (in the end) partly succeeded. The harsh lesson, after all, might have been even more harshly driven in, with far uglier results. I doubted whether Richard could be easily induced to agree; his injuries were more serious than mine.

He remained one of my closest friends, all the closer for that horrific shared experience. The letter which he sent me afterwards was a treasure: 'To sum up as best I can, all I can say is that if I have to be nearly murdered, I couldn't have anyone better than you to be nearly murdered with! Just another link in the chain that binds us together ...'

90

London continued to do well by Gulzaman and Manzoora. They'd settled down nicely and Manzoora's brother, Manzoor, had seized the opportunity to emigrate to England. During 1963 the one cloud continued to be the miscarriages. My char, Margaret, declared that it had to be Gulzaman's fault, then was forced to recant when a Fertility Clinic said that his sperm was normal. The fault was nobody's. Margaret was short-tempered from being in the throes of a change of life, and an attack of shingles made her understandably yet more irritable. She was treating herself all round the middle with a thick layer of Savlon.

Hoping that a return (for a while) to her own country might facilitate the birth of a child, Manzoora went back to Karachi. No sooner had she left than Gulzaman pined for her, so had to be sent to Pakistan too. When they returned, in much the same condition as when they'd left, we agreed to invest in another house in Battersea, next door to the one we already had. On completion in January 1964, Gulzaman was fast becoming a man of property.

Increasing property meant increased freedom. Next thing, Gulzaman decided to drive overland to Pakistan, carrying Manzoora and a full cargo of things to sell at high profit, perhaps enough to break even. One of my fears was that they might find paperwork at the various frontiers too tricky, but that wasn't my only concern. If I'd understood him rightly, his cousins had been involved in a shooting affray, when two brothers had been killed: might Gulzaman feel that it was up to him to pursue a family vendetta? Some serious words with Manzoora put that worry to rest. She said that she had no intention of letting him.

Some months passed during which I played rent collector, until Gulzaman returned minus Manzoora – who wanted to stay on until the following April – but plus a boy of twelve called Kamran, son of a Pakistani diplomat. They arrived at Gilston Lodge utterly exhausted, having slept in the car and eaten as little as possible in order to make their money last.

Kamran was an unusually polite and grown-up boy. Gulzaman had no difficulty in getting him into the superior Bousfield school at the end of the road – interviewed the Head, bought him clothes and so on. However, I felt that it would be better to have a woman looking after him, so I wrote to Manzoora asking her to come back sooner rather than later: 'You are needed here and Gulzaman is missing you very much,' I urged. 'In other respects, things seem to be all right.'

'Seem' was the operative word. There was unease in the garden flat; I couldn't quite lay my finger on the reasons for it. After a short absence staying with my old school friend Peter Hiley and his family, I returned on 10 December to find Gulzaman as much altered as if a switch had been turned off. At four in the afternoon he was still unshaven – some sort of warning, but of what? He began complaining that Manzoora had never treated him as he deserved and had refused to prepare his food. 'Father, I have kept these things hidden, before, but now I want you know everything. My heart is broken. She is seeing other men!'

'I don't believe it!' I said, because I didn't.

'And she ought to have returned with me, yes, why she not? I never want to see her again!'

It was obvious that he was talking nonsense. I found it very disturbing and put my arm round his shoulders, but it failed to have the usual calming effect; he remained distraught.

That night, the cat which he'd looked after since it had been a tiny kitten rushed out of the house and never came back. 'Everything gone!' he intoned. 'Wife gone! Cat gone! [As usual, he pronounced the word 'cat' as 'kite'.] Money stolen!'

'Money *stolen*?' I asked sharply. 'First I've heard of it. When did that happen?'

'ALL THE TIME!' came the desperate answer.

Could a backlash of exhaustion be responsible? Something had to be wrong . . .

When Kamran got back from school I warned him that 'Uncle' was very sad, but that he mustn't worry.

'I know that, father,' said the boy in his sensible way.

Next morning, when I buzzed on the intercom, Gulzaman sleepily croaked that he wouldn't be getting up because Kamran was capable of getting his own breakfast, which was true. All the same, I felt uneasy. At 9.45 I was on the telephone when Gulzaman came rushing upstairs and flung himself on the floor, crying: 'He want to kill me!' At which point I realised that we had a full-scale crisis on our hands. We went to the doctor and she accordingly made an appointment for him with Dr Parker at St George's Hospital in Tooting for Monday the 14th.

Fortunately he was still sane enough to arrange for a friend to come in and keep an eye on Kamran; but when the man arrived, Gulzaman cowered back into a corner, saying, 'He want killing me!' and repeating over and over again, 'Wife gone! Kite gone! Money stolen!', adding suddenly, 'Car gone, too!' In fact, the car was still in the garage.

On the 14th, we managed to get to the hospital by car, Gulzaman like an automaton, barely making sense, muttering and moping. Up a staircase, and we were in paint-peeling premises which looked as though they'd just been released from requisition by the Army.

Dr Parker, when he appeared, could hardly have been more charming, young and good-looking. He took enormous pains with Gulzaman, starting off by asking him which year, which month, which day it was, then going on to more personal questions. At first, Gulzaman wouldn't answer until prompted by me, when he grudgingly admitted that he knew the day of the month. As soon as Dr Parker flagged, Gulzaman turned to me and said: 'Now we go home, father?' I took him home and put him to bed.

The next day, Dr Parker rang up, early morning, to say that he'd arranged for Gulzaman to be admitted to Banstead, the asylum which served the area. Getting Gulzaman out of bed was a frightful business. He wept when I told him I was taking him to hospital. It was such a drizzly, sad day. In the car, I didn't dare look at him, until he stretched out an arm, as before, and asked anxiously: 'We go home, father? We go home?' I wanted to burst into tears, but of course couldn't.

At last, through the misty drizzle, remote at the end of a drive as if in the country, loomed a vast building in the Victorian-Italianate style, commanded by a domed tower – Banstead. A giant tree on the lawn outside the main entrance was already being decked with lights to suggest a Christmas tree; and just inside, all was starting to look Christmassy, paper favours and coloured streamers proliferating. It reminded me sharply that this was the start of the festive season, even (perhaps especially) for those who had little to celebrate.

To get to the ward we had to walk for five or six minutes along wide corridors reeking of unwashed socks, through doors made of bendable, translucent talc, which whooshed as they were pushed open. Old and far from smart men and women shuffled by on slippers (hence the smell of feet, of course), turning to stare in an utterly unemotional way.

'I don't like this place,' said Gulzaman. 'People very bad.'

In truth, the ward wasn't very nice, more like a barrack-room. Paper streamers were being hung up by nurses (all male) and one or two inmates. Whilst Gulzaman started to undress, his particulars were slowly and meticulously taken. He was issued with ward-pyjamas, ill-fitting, the top not matching the bottom; when I protested, he was allowed to wear his own. There was no doctor to be seen, just the charge nurse, to whom I tried to give a tip; but he wouldn't take it, saying that it wasn't allowed. I tried to get across to him, without sounding too pompous, that Gulzaman was used to better things than this, whilst Gulzaman again repeated: 'We go home now, father? We go home?' I thought my heart would break as I turned away, leaving him there, but I waited until I got outside and back into the car before completely giving way to uncontrollable tears.

I went back to see him the next day and was glad that the place didn't look so forbidding as before, though it was pretty terrifying seeing people wandering slowly, slowly down the wide corridors whilst those sinister semi-transparent talc doors whooshed shut behind them. When I reached the ward I found Gulzaman lying listlessly on a bed which was almost *in* a passage with inmates shuffling by continually. Less than a couple of yards away a poor creature gibbered from behind the open panel let into the door of a locked room – a padded cell. When I asked him what he wanted, he let out a wail and launched into a diatribe about his wife leaving him – almost a parody of Gulzaman's obsession.

I turned my attention to Gulzaman. His fantasies were not significantly altered, but he was calmer, even indulging in a little humour – such as saying 'Fine five pennies!', a favourite remark of his when he wished to tick me off without being offensive. However, he was soon embarking on a rambling story about running a man down in Germany and handing the body over to a petrol-pump attendant to bury. That was why, I was given to understand, 'they' were after him.

By Thursday, Gulzaman still hadn't been seen by a doctor, try as I might to get hold of the one he'd been referred to. On visiting him I was pleased to find he'd been given a better bed, no longer directly on the passageway. However, a thin young man with excrement smeared on his face was pestering him, Gulzaman waving him away. On seeing me, Gulzaman recognised me, sat up smiling, and began talking the first common-sense I'd heard for days. Putting on his dressing-gown he hopped out of bed and walked with me to the 'lounge', with its formica tables. Treatment had begun, he said. A nurse rolled up a pyjama sleeve to show a bruise round a vein on the inside of his elbow. I didn't ask what the treatment had been. Clearly it had had a dramatic effect, for the disturbed person I was talking to was recognisably Gulzaman, not some strange Thing. Unprepared for such a change, I was thoroughly grateful for it.

Gulzaman continued to improve so on Saturday I took his brother-in-law, Manzoor, and his cousin Bashir to see him. Manzoor brought letters from Manzoora which enquired anxiously after Gulzaman's health. There was no question of any discord between them. But she also said, 'I am not well myself. I have got smallpox.'

SMALLPOX? On hearing that, I metaphorically hit the roof. Smallpox? How could it be smallpox, in this day and age? And why so little concern, in a jaunty letter?

'She must mean chicken-pox,' said Bashir.

But Gulzaman was mournfully seizing on the worst interpretation, and I noticed his hands trembling again.

I spent the Sunday at Langney and called in at Banstead the next day on my way home, only to be told that Gulzaman had been sent suddenly to London to see a dentist. I couldn't think why he hadn't warned me about this. It sounded very odd. As I was already in the ward, the charge nurse asked me to talk to one or two of the other patients: 'They enjoy it so much and it does them so much good!' So of course I did. The one who'd smeared his face with excrement was undergoing temporary confinement, so I wasn't able to chat to him. Instead, I listened to a long, reasoned complaint from a man who seemed perfectly sane about how unfair it was that nobody came to visit him. 'Obviously, they don't know who I am,' he explained. 'I'm God, of course, as I'm sure *you* understand. I could *make* them come, if I chose, but I prefer not to interfere with the workings of free will.' He said he'd be going home for Xmas, then coming back again. He wished it wasn't such a business, catching first one, then another bus, on his own.

The next day, the mystery regarding the dentist was solved. The treatment Gulzaman had received had loosened his teeth, breaking one of them. This meant that they couldn't continue the treatment (six sessions planned) until his jaw had recovered, which might not be for six weeks. It was only then that I realised he'd been given ECT [electroconvulsive therapy]. He had literally been shocked back into sanity. I recoiled in some horror from the idea, but on reflection had to admit that it had achieved a minor miracle.*

At last I managed to see a Dr Purser and was told I could take Gulzaman home for an experimental day and night. It proved a success, which meant I could also take him to Langney with me for Christmas. After Christmas, when Gulzaman had to return to Banstead, he did so under protest, saying that if they kept him there much longer he was sure to be driven mad. I wrote a worried letter to Dr Purser to that effect and they grudgingly agreed to let him leave with me. The objections were that the standard amount of shock treatments hadn't yet been given. I said, 'But they've already had their effect. Surely more of the same might damage his jaw still more, without doing the slightest good?'

'I still advise against letting him go,' said the doctor. 'If he'd been sent to us under restraint, we'd keep him here for the full six treatments. But as he's a voluntary patient, we can't stop you removing him, if that's what he wants. Unwisely, in my view.'

Gulzaman a voluntary patient? That was a good one! On our drive to Banstead, he'd hardly known what was going on. He'd never wanted, for one moment, to be taken there, let alone stay there. The responsibility was mine. But because of that technicality, I could spring the trap, and no one could prevent me. It occurred to me that doctors at an asylum can grow so used to the place that they simply forget how horrifying it is for *anyone*, normal or abnormal.

---

* The use of ECT on Gulzaman suggests that his doctors thought he was suffering from severe depression. ECT is still viewed with mistrust, possibly because of its portrayal in popular culture; the fact it doesn't look at the underlying causes of depression; the way it was administered in the past (sometimes without anaesthesia); and because of the possible nasty side effects, especially at this time when the electricity levels used could be higher (as in Gulzaman's case, who suffered a damaged jaw). Yet recent reviews of ECT show it can have a positive impact on depression and mania. For this reason it is still used today, though a lot less frequently than during the sixties.

That night I wrote another begging letter to Manzoora: 'Gulzaman needs you more urgently than ever. You MUST come back immediately!' Then, as an afterthought: 'I mean, as soon as your spots are better.' They soon were, and back she flew. With her there, Gulzaman made a rapid recovery.

Years later, I would discern what at the time I only saw in a glass darkly: that all the strife Gulzaman and I sometimes experienced with each other could be excused by the simple fact that we stayed together through thick and thin. No matter how incompatible we seemed to be (and were), the bond remained unbreakable. It said much about relationships in general and devotion in particular, for ours was an enduring devotion, overriding common-sense. I wondered then as I wonder now: how can anyone ignore the power of love in all its shapes and forms, likely and unlikely?

91

In the mid-sixties, I set about looking for a house in Malta. A friend of mine, Jack Ripley, had bought himself a flat out there in a place called Floriana, then gone on to acquire other properties with a view to doing them up and selling them. Knowing Jack, I assumed that they would be grotty. He had a great nose for a bargain, provided that it was going cheap; anything expensive was anathema.

When I arrived I was met by Guido Busuttil, a young man working for Cable and Wireless, who turned up dressed in sober black, like a City gent. Although shy, he had a gentle sense of humour which attracted me; and I was still more impressed when he talked knowledgeably about the many churches we passed. By the time we reached Floriana, the stately suburb outside the walls of the capital, Valletta, I was starting to appreciate that side of Malta. It chimed so well with a similar side – for all my faults – of myself. We pulled up in front of a high stone building called Verdala Flats.

A gusty wind was whipping up clouds of dust (which attacked my eyes) and rubbish (which nagged my legs). As we came through the street door, a dog was doing its business on the stairs. 'I'm afraid this is Malta!' said Guido nervously.

'I don't mind a bit,' I said; and it was true, I didn't.

Up we went to the third floor, where Guido let himself into a flat unmistakably Jack's: over-full of spindly furniture, and hung with pictures in various states of disrepair, surprising in that most of them were of religious subjects which I'd never before associated with him. My host himself was still abed, but he rose to prepare an elaborate breakfast – always his best meal.

Afterwards we were to go on a round of his properties and call on the agent through whom he'd bought some of them. The idea was that I could enquire about something for myself at the same time.

The agent, Mary Caruana, was thick-set and hoarse-voiced. Jack had already told me that she wanted to marry him, or for him to find her a husband. In confirmation, she greeted Jack with a 'DARLING!' and pushed a bowl of nauseating cockles in vinegar at him. Then she sat us down and tried to sell me a block of flats in Gzira, the area between Msida and Sliema.

'That's where the tarts hang out,' said Jack flatly.

'Oh Mr Ripley, it's not right you put Mr Owen off!' was the hurt reply. Meanwhile, I was turning the pages of her agency book, stopping at one describing 5 St John Baptist Street, near at hand, priced at £2600. Miss Caruana interrupted: 'I have an offer for it at £2500, the people they haggle and haggle for months over the missing £100!' As it wasn't yet sold, I arranged to be shown over it next day.

Next morning we were sent walking up from the Strand, turning left and then right at a magnificent stone gateway (which apparently led nowhere). The second house up was No. 5 – actually Nos 5 and 6 combined – externally in a poor shape, its peeling beige door surrounded by a facing of muddy matt-green composition-marble. As with all other houses in the street, a wooden *galleria* hung as though stuck on over the front first-floor window, projecting enough to let an inmate see up and down the street without being seen. Inside the house, a passageway of surprising grandeur led to green marble-composition stairs, supported by an Ionic column decorated with a plaster dolphin. The downstairs passage ended in a room giving on to a small yard, from which steps led up to a long, narrow garden, stocked with orange and lemon trees.

Leaving Jack finding fault with the crumbling ground floor, I rushed upstairs to the roof – multiple roofs, really. Turning this way and that, I gasped at the totally unexpected panorama: in front and to one side, Sliema Yacht Harbour, Manoel Island and beyond it a great unknown town, as striking as the view from my house in Muharraq; to the back, an outlook over the garden, ending at an angled wall; and beyond it the extensive, but unkempt, grounds of a magnificent *palazzo* in the Italian style, built of Malta's finest golden stone. The Villa Bonnici – as the *palazzo* was called – was the epitome of elegance, with inset *tondos* of paler stone and urns, urns everywhere. An extraordinary feature was a yard-wide stone ledge, about a hundred yards long, positioned high up along its walls and protected by wrought-iron railings.

Downstairs I flew. 'It's just right for me!' I told Jack.

And that was that, house acquired.

There were many things to be done to it: it had no proper bath, nor even basin, just a kitchen sink; nor did it have a proper kitchen, because cooking had been done on a paraffin stove mounted on a stone block. However, I couldn't begin spending until completion, which wouldn't be for another month. In the meantime I tagged along with Jack, gradually learning why he found the very British – yet utterly *un*-British – group of Mediterranean islands so fascinating. He took me to Senglea, above the dockyard, an obviously poverty-stricken area. Washing flapped in our faces as we walked along narrow streets – not actually 'washing' so much as clothes hung out to air, unwashed. From the houses drifted a hot smell of paraffin stoves, as characteristic as the stink of cabbage which used to greet those visiting poorer dwellings in England.

Once the sale of the house was completed, I set about renovations. A carpenter higher up St John Baptist Street had made a firm double-divan, and in summer I needed no blankets, sheets being enough. In the downstairs sitting-room I already had a sofa, two armchairs and two padded pouffes, bought for £12. And though their springs had seen better days and the faded orange covers were far from smart, they were good enough for a holiday home.

Next I wanted to fix up the kitchen and bathroom, helped no end by Indri Ellul who'd actually come to install mains gas. Guido supplied me with a char, 'Guse' (short for Giuseppina) Azzopardi; tiny, with fingernails worn nearly down to the quick – by biting, by scrubbing, who could tell? She set to work with unbelievable enthusiasm, starting from the roof downwards, even removing the orange covers from the

Zammit suite and bringing them back, washed, next day. She seldom spoke without shouting, so I had to get used to it. I also had to get used to her habit of standing, hands on hips, skirt hitched up to her waist, staring at Indri. She looked as if at any moment she might reach out and stroke his hairy thighs, amply displayed by his brief khaki shorts. Who was I to blame her for that? But I did wish that she would show a little of the restraint voluntarily enforced on everyone else.

Guse had a husband, an ex-sailor who'd 'hung up his hat', lateish in life, content to let her do the work and earn the money. To our astonishment, he was lured from idleness by the prospect of painting my house. Taking brushes in hand he worked for week after week, slowly and carefully. He wanted a traditional result and knew how to achieve it, so I let him have his head whilst the *genius loci* clucked approval. 'Traditional' meant a barrier of high-gloss paint two feet high at the bottom of each wall – practical, because when water was sluiced over tiled floors it left splashes which would have shown up on a matt surface. The barrier was brightly coloured – cerise, brilliant green, clear yellow – the effect being not nearly as *outré* as it sounded, especially when ceiling beams were painted to match. Even clashing colours contrived to co-exist amicably in strong sunlight, contributing to the pleasing overall effect. Finally he painted the front door and all the shutters beige, a colour which I *would* have said I loathed; but again, the Spirit stared contentedly on. The house greeted the visitor, from the moment of stepping up and over the threshold, with a message fifty years behind the times, and all the warmer for that.

A thing which I hadn't taken into account was the humid heat generated inside a house made of porous limestone on an island surrounded by a warm sea. Malta was near enough to the mainland of Africa to be occasionally affected by a *sirocco*, stickily damp, thick with almost invisible sand, apparently immovable for days on end; or, if not a *sirocco*, then a *gregale* coming, as its name implied, from Greece and the north – sticky too, but chill, and with a propensity to blow hard enough to stir the sea into a frenzy. The heat of course brought the pests so a mosquito screen in the bedroom was a must-have, as was a fan.

In fitting out the house I went to many auctions, and at one found a whole set of engravings of the Grand Masters of the Order of St John, which I secured for 15s 6d for each picture. The Grand Masters, arranged in the shape of a huge Maltese Cross, would admirably line the entrance-corridor of 5 St John Baptist Street.

That particular coup spurred on my mother to come out, which delighted me because it was partly for her that I'd wanted to buy a house in a warm climate. I reckoned that her life might be prolonged by a yearly escape from the worst of an English winter. The longer she lived, the more I could congratulate myself. To underline the intent, I arranged for a small marble plaque bearing the name BETTINA to be inset into the street-wall, an idea which gave immense pleasure: 'I never thought to have a house named after me!'

Now established, I got on with creating a social life. Going to church led to drinks with a Rev. Davis where the only interesting thing I learnt was that Malta came within the jurisdiction of the Diocese of Gibraltar, stretching from Tangier to Ankara. He was soon slurring his words, having obviously started the evening's indulgence long before I arrived. I didn't feel too censorious, as I was to meet Jack later for a saunter down Valletta's street of shame, 'The Gut', likely to be lively because the USN *Springfield* was in port. The street hummed with activity, with hundreds of American sailors drifting about in their tropical 'whites', many of them ready for anything.

The bars we went to included the Cairo, whose proprietress was outstandingly friendly, and Dirty Dick's, basically an 'English' pub, run by 'Mrs Dick', built like a tank, and with a coarse, cheerful voice. Downstairs one lavatory bowl, always full to overflowing, stood in a corner; but it hardly mattered, because every wall was in use as a urinal and any corner was for being sick into. I was told that at the end of each evening the whole caboodle would be hosed down, ready for fresh fouling by generation after generation of seamen. The whole place might have strayed not just from the nineteenth but from the eighteenth century, or earlier. The Gut wore the air of a bygone era, incongruously extended into the present, an anachronism too dated sadly to last.

I attended all the 'proper' social gatherings too. At a party given by a Roger and Melita Strickland I met Borg Olivier, the Prime Minister. I was socially hyperactive, not so much because I enjoyed that sort of thing, but because I was determined to 'crack' Malta. Once I knew enough people, I wouldn't bother; but until then I was assiduous in following up introductions. Jack thought me mad, but I knew what I was doing, having done much the same sort of thing elsewhere in the world when gathering material for a book.

My main target was Mabel Strickland, known as 'Queen of Malta'.* Roger and Melita weren't much help in that direction, as they didn't really get on with her. I owed my original introduction to Basil and Audrey Lindsay-Fynn, who were promoting, largely for their own purposes, an organisation called 'The Friends of Malta', of which I became a member. Seeing the L-Fs floating round the floor of the Phoenicia Hotel in Valletta to the strains of a waltz, I was inspired to go over and tell Audrey that she danced better than any other woman in the restaurant. My sycophancy – which happened to be true – bore immediate fruit: I was invited next evening to a Friends of Malta party at which Miss Strickland was guest of honour, sitting majestically on a sofa whilst people were brought up to meet her. Most survived no longer than a minute. I clocked up nearly ten, by displaying an interest in her newspaper, *The Times of Malta*, instead of airing my own concerns.

'I must see more of you!' said the formidable Mabel, grabbing my knee.

I was in.

Once started, the ball kept rolling almost of its own accord. A friend recommended me to the English cricketer Eric Harben, warning me that he was keen on being the Old Etonian. Eric had leased a Gothic fantasy, Castel Bertrand, on the heights of San Martin. Donning my OE tie I called on him, and after the briefest of glares (as if he weren't seeing right) was asked in and shown round with ever-increasing friendliness. He was living with Peggy, an elderly girl to whom he happened not to be married – a situation more shocking to the Maltese than to the English. Eric imagined that by fitting automatic insecticide dispensers in every room, he wouldn't need mosquito-screens. What he achieved was the near-poisoning of himself and his live-in partner. His cachet was that they'd arrived by small private aeroplane, complete with dog. His downfall was drink: on swerving back to Castel Bertrand one night from a party, his Rolls-Royce struck a tree – and that, regrettably, was how he met his end.

The sum of all this was that by the time my mother and Morvyne

---

* Mabel Strickland was an interesting character. The daughter of the fourth Prime Minister, she was better known for being the editor of *The Times of Malta* in 1935, later becoming the Managing Director of the Group in 1940 and keeping the show running through the war, even during the Siege of Malta, despite the offices being bombed more than once.

came to visit, I could introduce them to an assortment of 'suitable'
people as well as ferrying them round all the sites.

Though glad that such matters were going so swimmingly, I had to
confess that I still wasn't content. For many years I'd been aware of a
great gap in my life: no one really, really to love or be loved by, at least
not in the sense that I meant. The more unlikely it seemed that I would
ever find what I was searching for, the more I'd tried pretending that
it wasn't all that important. Good health, money, lots of friends, occasional sex and the blessing of a critical eye – what more did I expect, at
my age? Surely I was lucky to have what I had, without complaining
that it wasn't enough? Yet I did complain, sitting nightly on the roof
of Bettina, downing glass after glass of wine till falling asleep, then
waking with a start, bitten by mosquitos, too much alone . . .
    If only there were someone to share this with! I'd boozily reflect. *If only I
could find what others seemed to have found so easily!*
    Nobody could pretend that the local wine was wonderful, but at least
it didn't take much to be sent spinning into oblivion, when to remain
fully conscious was so unrewarding.

———

92

In autumn 1966, Ernest Hofer was staying in Gilston Lodge when he
happened to mention a little Spanish restaurant in Park Walk. 'You're
sure to love it,' he said. 'It's special!' His enthusiasm didn't always
chime with mine, so I took that particular manifestation with a pinch
of salt. However, since he was doing the paying, I agreed to go there.
    In those days my friends and I were often out to meals; in fact it
was only rarely that we ate dinner at home. We were able to walk to
the Bodegon – as pleasant, in a simple, predominantly brown fashion,
as he'd indicated, if nothing out of the ordinary.
    Hardly had we sat down before Ernest said, 'Look, there's Giuseppe!
Let's go talk to him.'
    I saw a small Italian sitting alone with a half bottle of wine on

the table in front of him. *So sophisticated*, I thought. *Eating out, all by himself, drinking only moderately . . . very Latin!* Naturally, I also took in the fact that he was good-looking, even distinguished-looking in a pug-faced sort of way. In excellent English he invited us to join him. He was working for the Banco di Roma, he said. A chance remark about my African safari led to his mentioning early years in Egypt, surrounded by servants, which possibly accounted for his air of superiority.

Allowing for a decent interval, I invited him round and heard that he was mourning the collapse of an affair with an oh-so-correct, bowler-hatted City type. He was ready for any consolation on offer, and I was ready to supply it. We became intimates.

I soon discovered that he had a peculiarity of a highly original kind, a foible never met with before. Instead of going to bed, he preferred to get up to whatever pranks we chose anywhere else in the house – drawing-room, bathroom, tower, corridors, or indeed in the garden, in the tool shed, formerly the air-raid shelter where Paris the gardener and I had demolished a concrete curtain-wall with hired pneumatic drills. I found all that as entertaining as it was bizarre, and when in London, frequently asked for more.

However, I wasn't in London all that much. Malta dominated my life. I brought Harry Nuttall, my 'camp as Chloe' Northerner chum, with me in November, aware that he would behave with an absolute lack of discretion, but deciding that his sparkling if occasionally drunken company was worth it. He bore out my worst fears by making a dead set at Indri, who treated it with amused tolerance. He wasn't very nice about Guido, the mainstay of all my times in Malta, saying, 'I can't see the point in him.'

'He may not see much in you!' I said sharply.

He was ever restless, urging a quick visit to Libya, just across the water. With memories of Benghazi and Tripoli at the end of the war, I too was keen on seeing Cyrene from the ground, having only overflown it during my 'swan' through the Western Desert in an Anson.

Those were pre-Gaddafi days, before alcohol was banned, enough passable Italian wine to keep us happy being easily obtainable in hotels and restaurants. Tourists were few, but visitors were many, mostly Americans out to turn a fast buck. The airport bus dropped us at the Grand Hotel in Tripoli where we were told at the desk that all the rooms were taken.

'Nonsense, dear!' said Harry, rolling his eyes at the reception clerk. 'Don't give me that! Surely you can fit us in *somewhere*?'

To my astonishment, it worked. Far from objecting, the man bridled and flashed several bold smiles, admitting that one of the staff rooms at the top might be available.

'You see, dolling, all he needed was a *leetle* encouragement,' said Harry, pursing his lips.

I soon saw that wherever we went, his outrageous manner was like a magnet. We flew on to Cyrene, then drove the few kilometres to Susa, on the coast, to stay in a hotel with no pretensions to grandeur. Soon after we arrived Harry announced that he was going to wander off 'to spy out the land' – meaning the local talent. He returned flushed with triumph. 'I had to fight them off!' he claimed, obviously truthfully, as he never lied about such things.

After dinner we strolled out together, along a promontory where there was a rock-pool known as 'Cleopatra's Bath'. Within minutes we were approached by several youths, one of whom Harry had already met earlier – hence their friendly audacity and readiness to play. When we got back to the small hotel, some of them came streaming in, asking for 'the English visitors' – either, or both of us – to come for fresh walks with them. It was fun to be behaving disgracefully again, after a long lapse into apparent respectability.

When it was time to return to London, I decided to do something with a Harry Nuttall-style flourish: I commissioned an elderly painter, Robert Swan, to do a group portrait. The idea was that Gulzaman and Manzoora, together with Manzoora's little sister Nasreen, who had travelled over not long ago, would sit in the drawing-room at Gilston Lodge, drinking tea with me after dinner. I duly donned a dinner-jacket and Manzoora wore an opulent blue sari to pour from Great-Aunt Evie's silver teapot, whilst Nasreen squatted on the floor by a double-headed Kalash Kafir horse from Chitral. I had asked for a 'conversation piece' which wouldn't clash with ancestors already on the walls. The result was recognisably a likeness of all of us – just what we wanted.

93

In the summer of 1967, at the tender age of forty-six, I met Giuseppe for a game of squash at Kensington Close Club, where I'd long been a member. He had become and remained more of a delightful friend than a grand passion. It was too familiar a situation to cause me great concern; I was so inured to disappointment that one more setback was of minor consequence. That was how things stood when we picked up our racquets. Giuseppe had assured me that he knew how to play, but that he might be a little rusty. 'No matter,' I said. 'At least we can have a swim in the pool afterwards.'

When we entered the court and began knocking up it was obvious that he couldn't return even the simplest serve. He missed, or mishit, every ball patted in his direction. We soon called a halt, though I continued knocking up by myself till exhausted. We went for a swim before resorting to the bar, which was empty.

The barman, greeted by Giuseppe as 'Gian Carlo', lapsed into rapid Italian, too rapid for me to follow, until I was introduced, with apologies, in English. We ordered drinks and withdrew to a corner whilst other customers came in. 'I've known that boy for years,' said Giuseppe. 'He's broken up with the friend he had and moved into Chelsea Cloisters.' Soon after that we left.

My mind was made up. I would return for a swim the following evening, my real motive being a desire to see Gian Carlo again. I found him again in an empty bar, polishing glasses. We chatted. I asked him what time he finished work. 'Difficult to say,' he said. 'Sometimes eleven, sometimes eleven thirty or later. Depends how busy we are.'

'I can wait for you tonight and give you a lift in my car, if you like,' I said, as casually as I could. 'I've nothing better to do.'

I went to dinner with a friend and made a point of leaving early; and in the appointed place I waited ... and waited. The night was warm, and it was true, I had nothing better to do. Whilst waiting I tingled from head to toe, wondering why I should be so anxious. Experience coupled with cynicism warned me not to expect too much, yet I was in a rare lather of anticipation.

At last I saw, in the driver's mirror, the long-awaited figure trotting down the street.

'I didn't think you'd still be here,' were his first words.

'I try never to miss an appointment,' I said, aware of how flat and pompous it sounded.

'I'm the same,' he said. 'That's often been my trouble!'

A multi-stage rocket of gladness seemed to be exploding inside me as I suggested going back to my place first. Gian Carlo didn't reach his own bed until eleven o'clock in the morning.

My mind and body went into a spin of excited desire such as I'd not known for years. Yet as a counter-blast to complete contentment I had to take into account the existence of a 'Timothy', described as being a hopeless drunk. It posed a problem: all my life I'd been careful not to poach someone else's friend, except on a once-only basis; but good resolutions faltered when challenged by new facts. I found it impossible to live up to noble past intentions. Signalling 'FULL STEAM AHEAD!' I went into action, guns blazing; ashamed of myself, of course, yet unabashed.

In the weeks that followed I behaved like a bat, wheeling and jinking, squeaking suggestion after suggestion, terrified in case I might be found wanting – or worse still, boring. I kept thinking up things that we might do: drives in the car, theatres, restaurants and so on. Drives were fine, Gian Carlo enjoyed those, but not theatres. As for restaurants, they were invariably the setting for disagreements, sometimes amounting to minor quarrels.

I was dense, ignoring what was staring me in the face because it lay outside my experience to be dealing with someone who didn't want to go out. He was a home-body, who preferred pottering about to doing anything expensively public. Most in my favour was the fact that Gilston Lodge had a large garden, where he could potter to his heart's content. In Chelsea Cloisters, his flat was a one-room 'studio', with tiny bathroom and a kitchenette in a cupboard.

My final enlightenment came during a visit to Hampton Court, which promised to be a success. He knew little about antique furniture or old pictures, but he wanted to learn; and in an inexpert way, I could teach him to avoid some obvious pitfalls. He adored the famous maze: getting lost; recovering his bearings; taking a quarter of an hour to find the central tree where I stood smugly waiting (having known since childhood how to solve the puzzle). But following those idyllic hours, I made the mistake of taking him to lunch at the Mitre, the ancient and expensive hotel just outside the gates. 'Waste of money!' was his crushing verdict, after a meal accompanied by silence after silence. 'We ought to have tried the cafeteria.'

The penny dropped at last. Working, as he did, in an hotel, surrounded by strangers, 'going out' was merely an extension of his working life, whereas 'staying in' meant true relaxation. It irked me, because I myself was an 'outer', able to maintain such a style by the happy accident of having the wherewithal to pay for it. So when my newest and dearest friend spurned what I was accustomed to offer, I was baffled. Hopefully, not for long.

I seemed to be living in a fairy-tale which reminded me of Hans Andersen's *The Snow Queen*. (The only one which I'd ever really fancied, as a child. Most of his others had been too whimsical for my liking.) The lump of ice in my own heart was melting, without the help of tears and in spite of a young man's indifference to much of what I had to offer. A 'young' man? Not all that young, as distant in age from me as I had been from Turia, but seeming younger due to an odd combination of naivety combined with shrewdness. As for his looks, they were open, devoid of guile. Such doubts as I had at first soon dissolved in feverish happiness. When not at work, he began going everywhere with me.

I brought him to stay with the Nevilles at Slolely Hall. Richard took us to see Audrey Something-or-other, said to be both rich and eager to marry him. She kept otters in the stream running through her garden. I couldn't help noticing that one of her animals looked very like my Italian: questing, fierce in a flash, yet timid. It didn't please him at all to be told so. 'Otters are too greedy!' he said. 'I only want what I want.' I glowed with pleasure, taking it, rightly or wrongly, as a reference to myself.

'Great love can never be wrong' remained a favourite dictum of 'Bobbie' Neville, Richard's mother. But the times were still too repressive to allow me to unburden myself to her, even though she'd had plenty of opportunity of finding her opinion freely interpreted by both of her sons.

I reflected that other than Turia and Nick, my loves had been few, though contacts many. Turia would always be in a category of her own; and as for Nick, fond as I still was of him, our drive to Africa had finally extinguished a flame which had been guttering for some time past. He continued to go his own way as extravagantly as when he was supposed to be attached solely to me; the difference being that I no longer minded.

With Gian Carlo a new version of something old and cherished entered my life; his too, I hoped. So many things contributed to the difference: he drank almost as much as I did, but I could hardly blame him for that; he smoked, yet lying next to him I never found his breath unpleasant. No one since Turia had so well exemplified my beloved grandfather's Latin tag, translating as 'No smell is the best smell!' His feet alone let him down; but they, at my insistence, responded to determined treatment.

I found our lovely situation difficult to take in, even when it became clear that ours was no passing fancy. An early step was asking him to move in; there seemed no point in him maintaining a separate establishment when Gilston Lodge was large enough for the two of us to be together without being too much on top of each other.

There remained – or might have remained – the problem of Timothy. Everything Gian Carlo told me about him encouraged me to feel free to act, for not only was he a heavy drinker, but sexually inadequate. His mother, he said, would lie abed late in the mornings, sipping Bucks Fizz and exchanging tearful camp remarks with her hungover son. It sounded meretricious and awful, so on I went, trying to impress him, stifling scruples for the first time ever, regretting nothing. Soon, Timothy was a friend belonging to Gian Carlo's past.

Did I realise that this was to be the love of my life? Perhaps not all at once. Engrained habits from years of easy liaisons were hard to shake off. The sheer unlikelihood of a middle-aged man such as myself forming so lasting an attachment didn't bother me. If it was bizarre, then at least I could appreciate that the unusual had always been my destiny, perhaps always would be. The idea of settling down was finally one to be welcomed with open arms, so long had it been in the coming.

Shortly after Gian Carlo moved in with me, we were faced with an important decision. My mother and Morvyne came to stay and there was only one spare room. At which point the easy pretence would have been that he was politely vacating his room in order to accommodate them and temporarily retreating to the lower tower until they left. But suddenly I rebelled. We had a life to lead according to our own, not other people's, rules. We were sharing a bedroom and would go on sharing a bedroom, neither pretending that it had not been so in the past, nor apologising for it continuing to be so in the future. I had to overcome my own nervousness at having to make so bold a statement of intent, as well as his, and his was harder to tackle. Nevertheless, somehow we managed it.

The result was all that we could have hoped for. No comment was ever made by either of my two girls; at any rate, never in my presence. By taking such a definite stand, right from the start, we avoided many occasions for deceit and embarrassment.

For those days, it was a real inspiration. All our lives, *that sort of thing* had been a criminal offence, but on 27 July 1967, an 'Enabling Bill' had received the Royal Assent and we were criminals no longer. It may be hard to remember how things had been before a trio of Members of Parliament – 'Boofy', 'Humph' and 'Leo'* – got going so effectively on the Wolfenden Report of the previous decade. Variously described at the time as 'A first step on the road to ruin' or as 'The dawn of a new era', the passing of the bill earned the warmest of welcomes in thousands of homes throughout the land, not least in Gilston Lodge. It made a tremendous difference, to be law-abiding citizens for the first time ever. With the threat of prosecution out of the way, we could live our lives without fear and without reproach.

It went without saying that I had done as little to deserve achieving Heart's Desire as anyone else. All the more reason for gratitude, not just to Lord Wolfenden but to God, for the deep and joyous contentment which was to be ours, through thick and thin, in sickness and in health.

A strange postscript remained concealed for years and years, as if choked by the undergrowth of memory, until a chance remark about different New Year's Eves brought it to light. I happened to mention the party

---

* 'Boofy' was Lord Arran; 'Humph' was Humphry Berkeley; and 'Leo' was Leo Abse. There were eleven people on the Wolfenden committee (four women, eight men) who wrote the report – these three weren't on it but they were the ones to act on the report's findings. Berkeley introduced a Private Members' Bill in 1965 which tried to legalise homosexuality (it failed). Arran then introduced the Sexual Offences Bill into the House of Lords in 1966; as soon as it passed Abse introduced it to the House of Commons. Its passing (after intense debate) meant homosexuality would be decriminalised in law in 1967 (although only for men over the age of 21, and it imposed harsher penalties on those who publicly engaged in homosexual acts).

in 1960 that I had gatecrashed in Lincoln Street: 'There was an Italian chap – whose name I didn't catch – up from the country. We tried taking the floor, but as I couldn't dance backwards and neither could he, we had to stop after a few seconds, so that was that!'

With recognition dawning, Gian Carlo stared at me, till I got the message: 'You know who that was, lovey?'

Perhaps it hadn't been love at first sight, but it was to prove no less enduring on that account.

part eight

goodbyes and hellos

1968-79

94

All the best fairy-tales end with 'And so they lived happily ever after'. One compelling reason may be that no further adventures can hope to compete with whatever the leading characters have already been made to undergo. Love requited leaves little more to be said; the unrequited provides the material to make the pages hum.

I certainly found that nothing banished incentives to action so effectively as desire fulfilled, especially now I had my own spot in the sun: why bother to go anywhere else? A second visit to Malta by my mother and Morvyne increased contentment. They were looking on the house as 'theirs', which was as intended. Maltese attitudes, too, gave pleasure. 'How lucky you are to have a mother still living!' people would often say, whereas in England, as like as not, a man expressing fondness for his mum risked the accusation of being 'a mother's boy'. We all particularly liked another Maltese usage, the statement 'How well you're looking!' quickly followed by 'God bless you!' To be old in that society was to be cherished, not merely tolerated.

Second only to my mother and sister, Ernest Hofer established himself as my most frequent guest, being as fond of Malta as I had become. My brother-in-law Michael Harding, on the other hand, loathed the heat and the dust and never came back for a second helping. His and Genissa's three children only returned when they were grown-ups, Charles by himself, David with his wife Marian for their honeymoon. It proved that the world divided itself into two groups: those who found the island nostalgically endearing, and those who were irritated by – well, by almost everything about it.

Nick (whom I could not dislodge as a friend even if I'd wanted to, so intertwined had we come to be) was in the former category: 'This place will suit for when I retire, Rod. See if you can get me something on the Strand!' His idea was that he would run a small bar and live over it; which, at that time, English people were allowed to do. I made every effort, but failed, to secure a suitable property near the Manoel Island bridge. During long-drawn-out negotiations, the Socialist party won the election, and to its leader, Dom Mintoff, we became unwelcome 'foreigners'. In spite of which, Nick asked me to go ahead with another property, a house on the main road leading out of Paceville, an area reputed to be up and coming. The reputation was soon to be deserved, when the arrival of a Sheraton hotel, with the Dragonara Casino nearby and the building of a brand-new Hilton, established Paceville as the main tourist centre. Nick found himself near all the tourist pubs, though new laws were quickly passed to prevent him from running a bar of his own. One of the first things he did was insert a stone tablet outside his front door inscribed: ROD. I was as pleased with him as my mother had been with me.

During frequent visits I searched for Malta's best bathing-place, finding several that were excellent, such as Peter's Pool (rocky) and Selmyn Bay (sandy). My nearest was at Bahar-iç-Çahag, beyond the British barracks; but because of being near for me it was also near for others from Sliema. I preferred solitude, if it could be found. My quest ended when a friendly Regimental Sergeant-Major I met in the Museum of Militaria at Fort St Elmo told me of a cove so difficult to reach it had been virtually monopolised by boat-parties of Naval ratings on 'official exercises'. It was called Ras-el-Fenech, literally 'Rabbit's Head', otherwise known as 'Island Bay', because a tiny slab of rock stuck up, off-shore, inviting a short swim and a landing. As soon as I could, I followed his careful directions in the car and parked up. I found a path leading to a structure built into the cliff, presumably a wartime look-out post, with a locked door. A few yards away, a series of foot-and-hand holds led steeply down to a sheltered bay from which it was possible to walk directly into the sea, or else dive from a flat-topped outcrop of natural rock. There were even two strategically placed ledges making it easy to clamber out again.

Not a soul was about. Having looked carefully round I judged it safe to strip off completely and dive in, to experience the rare luxury of swimming naked in buoyant salt water. Clambering back, I sunbathed, decent in trunks, thinking, *This is IT!* All the same, I wondered what lay behind the locked door of the look-out.

It didn't remain a mystery for long. On returning the next day, I found the door unlocked and a youth in his late teens rummaging about in a sizeable room equipped with fishing gear, a table, chairs and shelves. The youth was a pocket Hercules, blond, muscular, yet so shy that he could hardly manage to utter a word. I persisted in my questioning, and he opened up to the extent of admitting that his family rented the post from the government.

A sudden idea came to me: 'Would your father let me borrow the key and spend a night here?'

'Maybe,' he said doubtfully. 'Family in Zejtun.'

Having come on foot, he was glad of a lift back to the alley where they lived. His mother looked me over, then agreed, trustingly handing me a key, simply asking me to make sure to lock up again before leaving.

Late afternoon the next day, I returned to Ras-el-Fenech with an elongated tubular deckchair, sandwiches, a Thermos of coffee, water and a couple of bottles of Maltese wine. Somewhat to my surprise, Hercules was there, sitting on the curtain wall in front of the post, nervously jiggling his feet. Apparently hospitality demanded that he should welcome me with a hug. I began to hope that he might consider staying all night, but that wasn't on the agenda. Off he loped and I was left alone, listening to the soughing of the wind and the gentle sound of the waves lapping the rocks far below.

The night was not just warm, but baking hot. I hand-held my way down the cliff and plunged naked into the star-reflecting water, relishing every minute; then clambered slowly back to my eyrie to eat and drink, savouring each mouthful before lying back, wrapped in a towel, staring at the moon travelling into the dome of the sky as rapidly as a gas-filled balloon. 'Ah, Paradise, Paradise!' I sighed, already aware of a serpent ready to strike – mosquitos. *Well, there may not be too many,* I thought, as I dropped off to sleep.

I woke to a tinny trumpeting, louder, ever louder, until a moment when – like the engine of a flying bomb during the war – it cut out, to allow a mosquito to target a tender spot. More and more were trumpeting around my face, which was already blotchy from their onslaughts whilst I'd been asleep. One eyelid had half closed. Ankles had been bitten and my tummy seemed on fire, extraordinarily tricky as it must have been for a mosquito to reach beneath an enveloping towel and emerge unscathed.

Admitting defeat, I packed up and fled in the middle of the night, regretfully abandoning the gentle lapping of the waves under a moon that was both bright and high-riding, turning the whole bay into something so throbbingly beautiful that my eyes filled with tears. But my skin was itching too unmercifully for me to think of staying.

Later, I told the story of that uncomfortable time to Gian Carlo. He

fastened only on to my description of young Hercules, demanding to
meet him when he came with me to Malta and being rude when he did.
'That's all you wanted the key for, to have him to yourself!' he claimed.
Against his jealousy, protestations were useless. I simply hadn't realised,
before, how powerful the Green-eyed Monster could be, once aroused.
Nothing I could say made the slightest difference; I wasn't believed. It
came as a terrible shock. I didn't know what to do about it and was never
to learn – a side-effect of 'true love' I had to presume.

———

95

During 1968, Gulzaman had the idea that we should buy a grocery, which he would manage with the help of Manzoora's brother,
Manzoor. The ambitious project would be a substitute for running
our two Battersea boarding-houses in Wycliffe Road, which were
about to be the subject of a Compulsory Purchase Order served by
Wandsworth Council.

For the grocery, Gulzaman came up with a sixteen-and-a-half-year
lease (at £1 a week) of 56 West Hill, on the borders of Wandsworth
and Putney. We bargained the price down to £5500. He was supposed
to provide £1000, but of course couldn't. I asked him: 'How is it you
talk of having money in Pakistan, one day, then the next day say that
you've nothing?'

'I like to talk, to make myself happy!' was his answer.

£500 was also supposed to come from Manzoor; and in fact he did
produce £400. I approved of the deal because the place fulfilled my
criteria for avoiding loss. Should we have to sell up, with property prices
increasing yearly by leaps and bounds we could hardly fail to make a
profit, even with a diminishing lease; and meanwhile it would provide a
home above the shop for Manzoor and his newly acquired wife, Brenda.

The premises were on a main road, with a subsidiary entrance for
goods from a side-road at the back, including direct entry into a large
storage-entrance. It was a solid Victorian building with high-ceilinged
rooms – an asset which would remain an asset in the future. The business

was to be called Gulburg Stores and would form part of G. K. Sales (London) Ltd. We took over from a Mr Ohler, who had run it in a traditional, old-fashioned manner. Miss Ohler kindly stayed on for a week, helping price what stock they were leaving behind. The 'fixtures and fittings' ought really to have been preserved for posterity – they included a 'village shop' cash register which displayed pop-up price labels when struck. But we needed to refurbish radically with 'gondolas' in which foodstuffs could be temptingly arranged. The major purchase was to be a cold-store capable of hanging whole carcasses for halal Islamic butchery. Manzoor thought that it was an extravagance, and said so. I thought he was probably right, but I supported Gulzaman in order to bolster his authority. Gulzaman was to see to the meat himself; I lived in terror in case he cut himself to the bone. Considering how shaky his hands had been since ECT it was a dispensation of Allah that this never occurred.

It wasn't the best of times to be starting a small grocery business. Supermarkets were everywhere expanding and local shops were going to the wall – a process clearly set to accelerate. So much was obvious, but we hoped to fill a gap in the market by being 'ethnic'. In the event of failure, we might have to fall back on more cheap boarding-houses, though I hoped not.

We were to open on 24 August 1968, St Bartholomew's Day. To start off on the right foot, I attended Early Service at 7.15, being one of only three communicants, then went to the shop at 10.30, to find some of Gulzaman's colleagues already there. Manzoora and her women friends were dispensing tea and samosas. Quite a few people came in for bread, which had been under-ordered, and also for the meat, which couldn't be served as there wasn't yet a chopping-block. Overall, it did give a feeling of being a going concern, which was more than that garment shop in the East End ever did.

Gulzaman's venture into halal butchery threw up some exceptionally tough meat. He knew nothing about hanging carcasses, supposing that, as in a hot climate, freshness was all. I had to hope that he'd learn quickly from customers' outraged comments. As seller and buyer I suffered like the others when I proudly fed Aunt Susan and her friend Dorothea Russell on a joint of 'our own' lamb, so tough and uncertain in taste that they thought it was stewing beef. Our takings, the first week, were a minuscule £23, the second week proving better because the meat, having hung for a week longer, found more favour. Takings went up each week from then, to sighs of relief all round.

I was intrigued to find how my ideas were undergoing a sea-change. I was obliged to regard everyone in a new light, as customers: rich, poor, ugly, handsome, pleasant or unpleasant – all were potential clients to be served politely and persuasively. It was a salutary lesson in how to treat other people, not just in Gulburg Stores, but out in the wider world.

———

96

Though I was content with goings-on in Malta and London, I was roused to action by my two girls: my mother and Morvyne. We travelled widely together, including to Italy where the warning from Tahiti rang in my ears: 'Things can never be the same a second time. NEVER COME BACK!' I found it to be half true. In Rome, whilst we stayed in the delightful lodgings of the Ambassador to the Holy See (the husband of Michael Harding's sister), I couldn't be as impressed as I had been during the war; but it was rewarding to go back to the house in Anacapri that I'd saved from the tender mercies of American troops. As we walked up to the garden of Dil Aram I saw a gardener, white-haired, wispy-balding, poking a stick into the earth – it was Domenico! The same Domenico who had looked after me all those years ago.

At the beginning of 1969 we headed to Asia. I was only recently recovered from pneumonia, but I was too keen to see the Khmer remains at Angkor to stop me from going. Ever since my voyage out to Tahiti on *Clan Urquhart*, when I'd read and re-read that copy of *Wide World*, I'd wanted to go to the hard-to-reach places of Tibet, Easter Island and Angkor, and now finally channels were opening up that made such visits possible. Angkor Wat, Angkor Thom and many other Khmer ruins had been stumbled on only during the last century by a French naturalist, Henri Mouhot, who'd found a city submerged in greenery, strangled by the roots of surrounding trees. As I flew over it, peering out through the plane's old-fashioned small windows, I was rewarded with a spectacle of a complex of grey buildings laid out in plan below, sprawling, more immense than Luxor, with a cluster of sheds and macadamed roads nearby.

The sheds turned out to be the Auberge Royale des Temples, where we were to stay. There we were handed cold towels to wipe away traces of travel and shown to rooms well adapted to the climate: air-conditioned hutches imbued with French comfort. Above all we were no more than a few yards from the entrance to a temple rivalling any of the seven wonders of the world. Day and night, the mighty Angkor Wat would be on our doorstep.

That evening we had our first Cambodian meal. It was delicious: for starters, puffed rice and prawn crackers with a tiny saucerful of curried mince pork; to follow a fish omelette with bits of bacon in it; then a mild chicken curry; and to end, tiny sweet cubes and little rubbery cakes. Beer, however, was 6s 6d a bottle, which made me note in my diary 'it doesn't look as if I'll be having it again'.

The next morning produced the usual problem I faced when travelling with my two girls: they could never be ready on time. But we made it round all the sites and were well rewarded for the trouble. Angkor Thom's main entrance was an arch, with stone faces glancing in all four directions. The Khmer kings seemed to have been obsessed with massive architectural heads – the Bayon Temple was essentially composed of nothing but huge faces of King Jayavarman VII. Another temple had been left in the state it had been found in, with tree-roots wrapped around ruined walls, like huge snakes, writhing for fifty yards or more. It was called the cheese tree, because it reminded someone of the way camembert cheese dripped down. By virtue of such a devastating embrace, the whole ruin had acquired a sort of chic. Cicadas shirred and shrilled all the time, as loudly as an electric bell, but without drowning out the almost liquid bubbling of birds flying through the high branches overhead.

Angkor Wat was enormous and, unlike other temples, it faced west, not east, which we were told may have been to remind worshippers of death, always connected all over the world to the setting of the sun. Then as now, corpses were burnt during the afternoon, before sunset, and their ashes washed in coconut water (thought to be the purest of all natural liquids) and put into a container. The King's remains were placed in a golden pot in the central shrine.

The builders had understood how to manipulate perspective, by grouping each mass to create a diminishing vista. Rising levels of pyramidal stonework, brought to life by quantities of carved panels, led upwards to the grand version of an imaginary Mount Meru, a peak where four shrines faced in all four directions, each complete with its own Lord Buddha. Traces of paint, brown and green, proved that the stone panels had once been brightly coloured, as I had seen in Greece, Egypt, Mexico – indeed everywhere.

Down below, we discovered a working shrine crammed with Buddhas in gilded wood, together with what purported to be the secret footprints – evidence that worship in the form of prostration and meditation was still going on. There was even a great bell, or gong, waiting to be struck with a wooden wedge – the gift of a man who had won a lottery as the result, he thought, of prayer.

One thing was abundantly clear. Whatever else they'd done, the kings and priests conducting the Khmer system of beliefs had been infinitely more humane than the Aztecs of Mexico. Aztecs had gone in for cutting the hearts out of living victims because they had been led to believe that nothing but such institutionalised cruelty could guarantee that the sun would continue to rise and set. To have arrived at and clung to such a grotesque theory proved, to me, they must have been exceptionally bloodthirsty in the first place. History indicates that literally nothing is beyond human ingenuity where weird forms of religious theory (and even weirder practices) are concerned. In Mexico some years earlier, I had been told, as if in extenuation, 'the Aztecs, lacking scientific data about the way the world worked, couldn't be expected to know better'. The Khmers, several centuries earlier, were technically just as ignorant about natural phenomena and how to influence them, but they didn't feel required to sacrifice all their prisoners of war in order to maintain a plentiful supply of fish. They constructed ingenious fish traps to take advantage of the rise and fall in the Mekong River instead.

I could never have guessed the extent to which modern Cambodians would let down their ancestors. As the years went by, the bloodthirsty excesses of the Khmer Rouge,* their gleeful adherence to extreme Communist dogma, demonstrated that kings and priests were no longer necessary for the propagation of truly awful ideas. What horrors might the future hold, anywhere in the world, if the masses are to be so easily manipulated by the opinionated strong? Nobody can pretend that it's not a daunting prospect.

———

* The Khmer Rouge came to power six years after Roddy's trip to Cambodia, ruling from 1975 to 1979 and killing an estimated two million people during that time.

97

Before returning home we went to India with a National Trust tour, on our travels visiting the Taj Mahal where our spirits rose to new heights. No amount of foreknowledge had prepared us for its perfection. Water was the key: the larger long rectangle mirroring the whole; the smaller rectangular pool reflecting only a part, compelling admirers to bend in order to receive the reflection in its entirety. Had that been the designer's aim? It was difficult to remember that the Taj was not a jewel in a princely pleasure-garden but a memorial to a much-loved wife.

It led me into a maze of thoughts about official monuments to the dead and their significance. Their main function seemed to be to assert and go on asserting the might of those authorities still surviving; the more extravagant the tomb, the more honour to the constructors. I remembered the soldiers' epitaph at Thermopylae (which I'd had to construe for an exam paper):

> Go tell the Spartans, passer-by
> That here, obeying their command, we lie!

Rebelliously, I wondered how to put that into contemporary language, closer to the jargon of the soldiers themselves. Perhaps:

> Go, tell our bl**dy Generals, passer-by
> That thanks to obeying orders, here we lie!

The twenty-seventh of January was Morvyne's birthday. A 'birthday girl' was traditionally allowed to do what she liked (within limits). Her Jaipur day promised to be good; and in fact turned out to be as good as any in her life. We were to go to the Amber, the fort/palace on which the Golestan in Tehran had been modelled. Amber rode high on the crest of a hill, and the standard tourist way of getting up there was by elephant. The huge beasts were hung with what looked like faded bedspreads, and their trunks and hindquarters had been painted with crude stars. The docile creatures turned this way and that in order to let the tourists mount (four to each one, two on either side of a kind of padded cradle in front of which sat the mahout, practically on the animal's head). It wasn't comfortable, and one had to be penned in by an iron rail, back to back with the opposite number on the other side. The slow rolling motion gave me a headache, not helped, I'm sorry to say, by the cries of a beggar hopping on one leg all the way up with us, to music provided by a musician sawing away at a kind of primitive steel violin hung with bells.

We disembarked – no other word for it – in a courtyard, just in time for a celebration in the Temple of Kali. Attending service meant taking off not only shoes, but socks as well. Our middle-aged women didn't hesitate to hitch skirts and pull stockings, even tights, which were less easily removed.

The temples consisted of a small open courtyard arcaded all round. There were two pictures of Kali: one with a necklace of many heads, as Kali the Destroyer, the other portraying the goddess sitting on a lotus leaf, giving a blessing with all eighteen of her arms, as Kali the Universal Mother. A man continuously rang a silver bell; two others beat upon drums. The altar, which was railed off, contained the slab of Shila Devi, had been found in the Bay of Bengal. A small black face was visible with large pendant circular gold earrings and gold hat, the rest smothered under material. Flowers were garlanded in front of the idol and a multi-light was brought out and waved in front of her, then passed along the front row of 'worshippers' who put their hands into the flame very briefly. Then a man came and dabbed those who came up to the rail with something red, making a red spot on each forehead. We were told that to achieve the maximum benefit we must let the red spot remain until it wore off of its own accord.

The great glory of Amber was its 'Shish-Mahal', a room made up of tiny fragments of mirror-glass, glowing *eau-de-nil* from the reflection of itself and the sky outside. One candle alone was enough to create a fairy bower flecked with stars.

As if spurred on by our *oohs* and *ahs*, the guide suddenly decided to lecture us on aspects of modern India, mixing deference with criticism. The Maharajahs, he said, had come from Gwalior a thousand years ago, conquering the local tribes and building such fortresses that they'd lasted ever since. He praised the present one for keeping alive the traditions of craftsmanship, employing at least 60,000 people in Jaipur. Then he turned to the question of religious tolerance: 'Here we absolutely accept the right to be Muslim, whereas in Pakistan we Hindus are not allowed to practise our rites at all. But many things hold us back. For instance, that miserable man with one leg who followed your elephants up hill. I myself have offered to supply him with an artificial limb, but he refuses to accept my gift, saying that his disability is his only means of gaining a livelihood. I ask you! What can we do with this sort of man today?'

We were shown something truly remarkable that afternoon: one of the former Maharajah's three observatories in monumental stone, giving the time all over the world, together with the movements of the planets and the signs of the zodiac – essential to both astronomers and astrologers, yet all done at a time when few except for navigators and savants chose to admit that the world was round.

The prospect of shopping, of course, called us away from these marvels; perhaps fortunately, because I was able to buy a garnet (for 30 rupees) as a birthday present for Morvyne and a metal dancing Krishna (20 rupees) for Gian Carlo. For myself I wanted to taste a *pan* and asked the guide where to find one. 'In all my fifteen years as a guide, no tourist has asked me that question,' he said. 'One will cost ten, perhaps twenty paisas, and it will be my pleasure to make you a present of it, milord!' The tiny bundle of betel-nut, lime and areca-leaf was bought for me with a flourish. I began chewing it on the spot, heedless of staining my mouth and the harm *pan* was supposed to do to the teeth.

That evening we were to be favoured by a visit from the Maharajah in person. He was to meet us all in the Polo Bar, hung with photographs of the royal sportsman and his various teams. As soon as he heard it was Morvyne's birthday he suggested a birthday drink. What would she like? 'Oh, champagne, of course!' said Morvyne; so champagne it was.

For the rest of that evening we played a short 'gamey' of quarrelsome three-handed bridge, then walked on to the terrace to listen to the harsh screams of the peacocks, sweeping across the lawn in the moonlight. How wild and splendid they sounded – and how princely and Indian! All in all, it had been a thoroughly gratifying day for a birthday girl and memorable for her closest relations as well.

———

98

It was always marvellous to come home from anywhere in the world and find Gian Carlo in Gilston Lodge without having to explain him away. Copying Nick's habit of using initials, I thought of him as 'LM' or the Little Man. The diminutive wasn't patronising, simply a recognition of the fact he was relatively short. LM knew nothing about my business concerns and wanted to know nothing. He resented Gulzaman, at one moment declaring 'Either he goes or I do!', which was what Nick had threatened some years earlier. To first one, then the other, I had to say that those silly alternatives were something of *their* choosing, not mine, and that I could have no control over what they might decide to do. In both cases I was mightily relieved when that was as far as it went.

The 'Swinging Sixties' were over. Had they swung convincingly for me? Yes, because the honesty of their permissiveness, after years of restrictive hypocrisy, pervaded all parts of our lives from then on – great cause for gratitude. Most of us weren't less, but *more* moral – more open, less censorious, and above all no longer so apologetic, praise the Lord!

My major business concern was not going well. Slowly, slowly in 1970 I was being forced to realise that Gulburg Stores would never be profitable – one more disappointing venture for Gulzaman. Quarrels between him and his brother-in-law Manzoor were coming to a head. At first Gulzaman said that he was prepared to carry on, then that he wasn't. Of chief concern was an illness which struck Manzoor suddenly. From being mysteriously 'tired', he turned yellow. At St James' Hospital, Tooting, he was told that he had liver trouble that might either be caused by, or lead to, cancer. Meanwhile Brenda and their child were living above the shop, and if there were to be any question of it closing, what was to happen to them? If, if, if . . . I had to tread with the utmost care through the tangle of circumstances because, in the end, those other lives depended on me.

On my birthday, I recorded: 'The shop is about to be sold. It was a potential gold-mine for Gulzaman and brother-in-law, a consideration which I thought would solve itself because it was to everyone's interest to solve it. But nothing was solved. They quarrelled on and on, and Gulzaman was probably right – when Manzoor went to hospital, huge debts piled up, and these G. is gradually reducing. Manzoor wasn't overworked, as he liked to say. He was, as we now know, ill and unable to cope.'

A month later, the shop was sold to a Pakistani family forcibly uprooted from East Africa, a real businessman. We got a good price for it, because of the number of years to run on the lease and the prospect of the buyer having the right to acquire, as a sitting tenant, the valuable freehold. My insistence on buying something which would be saleable in the event of a collapse was fully vindicated. In fact, because of that we made a profit out of the whole affair, and I lent Manzoor £500, interest-free, enough to make the mortgage down-payment towards buying his own house in E15. He would have liked more from me. I had to remind him, bluntly, that I had adopted Gulzaman alone, not anyone else.

It made me realise – as if I needed reminding – that nothing Gulzaman could do would separate him from me. When people were talking about so-and-so being lucky, I would remember what I used to say, to cheer him up when in the depths of depression: 'They may think they are lucky but THEY HAVEN'T GOT A GULZAMAN!' It remained true, but how could I expect people to understand? From saving my life, he'd turned me into a shop-keeper, looking upon everyone in the world, however tiresome, as a 'customer'. I had to acknowledge the lasting benefits of our intertwined lives.

Around this time I took up bee-keeping. In a way, I'd begun three years earlier at the Chelsea Flower Show, when I'd chatted to a weather-beaten old thing demonstrating the workings of a 'WBC' hive. She rather lost interest when I said that I only wanted a hive if I could find someone to look after it, for that apparently wasn't at all the right attitude for a person genuinely keen on 'The Craft'. I *should* be doing all that sort of thing myself.

Then, when I'd mentioned it to Harry Nuttall in 1969, he'd said (rather surprisingly) that he, too, would like to keep bees. Having left his cave in Thurloe, he'd bought one of Ralph Anstruther's houses in Pratt Walk, Lambeth. Ralph had taken away part of the garden running up to the railway lines in order to build garages to let, but there would still be space for a hive outside his back door. 'After all, dear, it isn't as if the bees mind what they come back to. It's what they go out and find that counts; rather like us!' However, we got no further that year, so in 1970 I mentioned it again. He said that one of the civil servants in his office (Ministry of National Insurance, he having ceased to be a Public Prosecutor) knew all about bees. Further pestering produced a meeting with the self-declared expert. I noted at the time that he was 'a rum cove, owl-eyed, tubby, with a high-pitched giggle. He'd once been a magistrate in Fiji, though one could hardly imagine how.'

Duly the three of us journeyed out to Robert Lee and Co. of Uxbridge, where Harry and I each bought a WBC hive made of aromatic red wood. They were so bulky that we could hardly manage to stow the bits and pieces in the back and boot of a single car. Our equipment didn't end there: we required a 'smoker' for controlling the poor tinies by filling their home with panic-inducing fumes; gloves to absorb their defensive stings; and a semi-rigid bee-veil to attach to a hat – all of which cost £30 or more. Finally, of course, we had to order a 'nucleus', one for myself and one for Harry: two attenuated colonies each with a young queen, freshly reared and rarin' to go into a world within a three-mile radius to collect honey for themselves. The surplus brought in by those busy creatures would be for us.

On a sultry 3 June I drove to Uxbridge to collect the nuclei. Each nuclear box contained four frames of bees, loosely wrapped in cardboard. I put them in the back of my open car; but then it occurred to me that they mightn't like the sound of flapping, besides resenting the unshaded heat, so I put the roof up. On reaching Gilston Lodge, I set the two nuclei down on the front lawn and waited for the expert to arrive to put them to bed, which duly he did.

From then on I was bee mad. I wrote to the Bee Research Institute about where to find the local bee-keeping officer, and from the Ministry of Agriculture I got a number of pamphlets and took the trouble to contact a Pole called Mr Jennings at Norwood Hall, luring him into Gilston's garden and watching as he enlarged the brood–chamber with more frames and talked of doing 'an increase' (whatever that might be) the following April. Jennings found the queen at once: something like a wasp, long, thin, curved and rather blacker than her sisters. It was all most exciting. I bought a bee-keeper's hat, kept a bee-keeper's diary, and learnt everything I could about eggs, pupae, sealed brood, etc. and the difference between worker bees, drones and the queen. I would never have dreamed bees could be so interesting.

They settled in good-temperedly, flumping on to the landing-board with full loads of pollen, for all the world like old-fashioned aircraft with fixed undercarriages. Harry's were doing all right too. Once properly set up, they'd been quick to discover the joys of the Lambeth Palace garden and were losing no time in bringing in the bounty.

We then both joined the Twickenham and Thames Valley Bee Keepers' Association (the T&TVBKA), where old Bernard Prichard reigned, eventually to be superseded by Robina Clark, who ended up becoming queen bee of all the bee-keepers in Britain. Better instructors it would have been impossible to find, and a hobby most becoming of a man not far short of turning fifty.

———————

99

On 21 October 1970, a notice appeared in the paper:

> Mortimer Wheeler. On 16th October at 22 D'Oyley St S.W.1. Mavis Mortimer Wheeler, beautiful and beloved. Cremation private. No mourning or service by her special request. A gathering at 10, Gypsy Lane S.W.15. Wednesday 28th October, 2 p.m. No flowers, but donations, please, to the Hon Treasurer, Cameron Group, Registered Charity, Assisting Women Prisoners, 1 Heath Close, N.W.11.

I was shocked by the news. The death of someone known for years must always come as a shock, particularly someone well liked but not seen much of lately. The notice of Mavis's death reminded me why.

Alarm bells had first started ringing when she'd called me out of bed at 4 a.m. one morning on the pretext of being frightened by 'noises downstairs'. 'I think they may be burglars though I can't imagine what they hope to find *here*!' she whispered down the telephone. 'They haven't reached my bedroom yet, as perhaps you've already guessed. They won't know I'm ringing you up; but if they *do* find out ...'

I shot out of bed at furious speed through the slush of a recent fall of sleet to D'Oyley Street, off Sloane Square. When I reached the pebble-dashed cottage which had whimsically (not by her) been named 'The Little House', I rushed to the door, which opened at a push, and raced upstairs. On my way up I had time for a quick look round. I'd been expecting the fearful mess traditionally left by burglars, but everything looked normal – in other words, cluttered and none-too-clean, but normal, all the same. I tried bursting in without knocking, but the bedroom door had been barricaded with a table and chair. Mavis had to scuttle over, naked, to let me through before dawdling back to her double-bed, pretending to cover up but actually giving a fine display of her charms.

The room was boiling hot. As there was no central heating, an electric fire had obviously been going for a considerable length of time. I could smell that she'd been drinking, which may partly have accounted for her being so fey.

'It was a test,' she said, 'a test to see whether you'd come. I wanted to find out who my real friends are.'

'That's all very well!' I said angrily. 'I can't pretend to be best pleased. On top of everything else, in the rush to get here I believe I've left my back door open. Test, indeed!'

'You needn't be so cross!'

'I *am* cross!'

'Oh, dear Roddy, do come and sit on the bed, but first put the kettle on for a cuppa!' Her chic was to give one of the throaty chuckles for which she was famous – unique, invitational; alive with complicity and understanding. There was no limit to the meanings which could be read into her chuckle, and I was fortunate enough to know most of them by heart. I did as bid.

She was clearly awaiting an amorous approach, but I had no intention of taking advantage of the situation. Mavis had a curious naivety where some men were concerned; she didn't always 'cotton on'. She didn't seem to realise that my days of fancying women were well in the past – she *really* didn't seem to realise. What I was rejecting so cavalierly was something for which duels might once have been fought, but it had to be rejected, all the same.

'I'll drink up and push off,' I said, trying not to sound too ungracious.

'Just check downstairs, won't you? I mean, in case there *is* someone there, after all.'

'Yes, of course.'

It wasn't our last meeting, but it was definitive in that I realised that she was a nuisance and would inevitably become more of one. I didn't want the burden of acting as a buffer. A cause for regret? Now that it was too late – yes.

At the inquest, the pathologist opined that death had been due to a combination of drink and drugs, actually whisky and sleeping pills. Said the coroner: 'This is a well-known dangerous combination. It was incautious self-dosage.' On hearing the manner of her death, I felt convinced she hadn't done it on purpose; and was even more sure when told that her little dog, Jolly, had been shut in the room with her. The Mavis I'd known would have put food and water out for him.

In order to attend the advertised 'gathering' I drove out to Putney Bridge, then took a road across Barnes Common to Gypsy Lane. I'd known Mavis's son, Tristan de Vere Cole, ever since his days as a Naval cadet. His metamorphosis into TV director* presented me with a new Tristan, married to an artistic Diana. The change in him was almost as remarkable as their house: detached, with a large garden and rugs on polished floors. Countrified in the nicest way. So where had the money come from?

Why aren't we all TV directors? I wondered.

It was a very mixed, not to say ill-assorted, gathering. In the corner I saw Admiral Sir Caspar John and Mary John, both of whom I'd met before. (Caspar could have been considered Tristan's half-brother, had Augustus John been officially recognised as his father.)†

I asked Diana how she'd hit upon the words 'beautiful and beloved' for the obituary notice; they had such a wonderful ring to them. She said: 'Mavis kept every single thing she could, in cardboard boxes and old trunks. I came across letters from you there, too; nice ones. Well, Horace – Horace de Vere Cole – began many of his letters to her with the words "Beautiful and Beloved", so I simply took over his description as perfectly fitting the occasion.'

'It surely does!' I said. 'Everyone who knew Mavis would agree.'

---

* Tristan directed episodes of *Doctor Who*, *Emmerdale* and *Bergerac*, among other series.

† Augustus John was a famous Welsh artist, especially in Edwardian times, perhaps *the* most famous artist in Britain at the outbreak of the First World War. He was arguably even more famous as a philanderer; wild rumours estimated he'd fathered up to a hundred children. Mavis had sat for a portrait by him, which was how she'd come to be his mistress.

After a time, we heard a crunching of gravel on the drive outside. Tristan called out: 'Come on, all of you, to say goodbye to her!' So we trooped outside and stood around, holding our glasses of champagne. The undertakers opened the door of the hearse, revealing a closed coffin. I edged forward to see if the coffin had a glass top. I don't quite know why I thought it might, but it certainly hadn't. The idea flashed across my mind that an embalmed figure might suddenly thrust open the lid and sit up, waving her own glass in response to our mumbled, 'TO MAVIS!'

Shortly afterwards I took my leave. I'd been determined to attend, in spite of not being addicted to funerals. I sent a small donation to the Cameron Group in Mavis's memory – not a thing that I would have done normally. But I was in the grip of feeling a pre-destination; why or to what end I didn't quite know, yet strong enough to be acted upon.

I mulled over Mavis memories, a rag-bag of incidents. I'd once driven her to Woking for an auction of my (distant) Tennyson d'Eyncourt cousin's effects. Prompted by her, I'd bought (for £4) the first refrigerator I'd ever owned (she having established that it was in working order), and for £9 a splendid silver salver. Meanwhile she'd only acquired two pairs of curtains and several strips of old carpet, including old lino from the kitchen floor.

'What *can* you want with all that stuff?' I asked her.

'Oh it's sure to come in useful!' she said, treating me to a chuckle.

Other memories: once, Mavis brought 'Sir Arthur' along to Gilston Lodge, one of her elderly admirers whose end would be bizarre but at that time was just a randy old buffer. To meet them I also invited Angela Geere, the lady-doctor Manzoora went to. Sir Arthur sat beaming as if slightly bemused on the sofa, whilst Mavis took it into her head that Angela was a lesbian – which, as far as I knew, she wasn't – and started flirting outrageously, out of devilment.

Then there was the time when Randolph Chetwynd (who'd finally taken himself off to live in Lamont Road) asked us to come back to his neat house to continue a party started in Gilston Lodge. Mavis was by then muttering unintelligibly, claiming to be speaking Romany – a favourite conceit, based on her connection with Augustus John.* Just as I was saying to Randolph 'You see before you a completely innocent

---

* John was fascinated with Romany culture after meeting Irish tinkers on a walking trip as a young man, and often indulged thereafter, such as by travelling in horse-drawn caravans.

person!', Mavis gulped and was sick all over his highly polished floor. He cleaned things up without a murmur, saying: 'Yes, of course, she has no malice in her whatsoever!' – for which I awarded him full marks, though on Bridget's account I seldom felt entirely easy with him.

I remembered how generous Mavis could be, provided that she didn't, disconcertingly, demand her presents back, which I'd been warned she was liable to do on occasions. (She never did it to me.) Her presents were always nice, her taste being excellent. 'I often had to teach Rick (Mortimer Wheeler) what was what,' she boasted, which I was sure was true. I wondered how she'd contrived to learn so much, considering she'd started from so little (she'd come from a humble background, starting work at the age of fourteen in a mill). It wasn't as if anyone could have accused her of being brainy.

My bee-keeping class that evening dealt in all manner of abstruse bee-subjects. I found it difficult to concentrate on pupae, imagos and 'the June gap', but I dutifully scribbled down everything for later study.

MAVIS – RIP. Could it really be the end of that beautiful and beloved woman? If so, why the nagging feeling that it was nothing of the sort?

100

As I told Tristan, truthfully, it was only slightly surprising when he asked me if I'd consider writing a 'Life' of his mother, with his help. My premonition was taking shape, and there was something poetic in turning a 'goodbye' to a dear friend into a 'hello': by the end of the process I was to know her better than I did when she was alive. Tristan assured me that there was plenty of material, stored haphazardly, dating from his mother's earliest days. I took a brief look at it and was thrilled by what I saw. Plenty of letters and notes from her first husband, Horace de Vere Cole – who she'd met whilst working in an Indian restaurant in Piccadilly Circus called Veeraswamy's.* This was important because

---

* You can still go to Veeraswamy's today; it's the oldest surviving Indian restaurant in Britain, having been established in 1926.

so little had been written about him in spite of his fame – notoriety, rather – in the twenties. He'd been the greatest practical joker of all time, a position from which he was unlikely to be dislodged by posterity because many of his 'jests' had depended upon lavish spending to achieve a declared aim of 'taking the self-important down a peg'.

One of those jokes had become famous because Virginia Woolf and her brother, Adrian Stephen, had taken part with Horace in 'The Emperor of Abyssinia Reviewing the British Fleet' hoax;* sensibly they'd recorded the startling facts for private circulation. Fame had already been his, from arranging for workmen to take up the road in Piccadilly; also from when he'd chased a prominent MP shouting 'STOP THIEF!', pretending that the man had stolen his watch. There were plenty of other 'haves', equally memorable, as when he'd given one end of a tape to a man in one street and the other to another man round the corner and asked them to do nothing until instructed to let go – which they never were. So little had been known about his private as opposed to his all-too-public life that no one had been able to make a proper study of the man. Yet there, in front of me, were letters and verses, all the evidence I needed, gathering dust amongst Mavis's effects.

There were a few matters to be ironed out before I could give a definite 'yes'. I wanted Tristan's name to appear as a participating writer for obvious reasons: the name itself guaranteed authenticity; and in return, it would be useful for him to reap the benefit of being recognised as a serious author. As I was actually going to do most of the writing of the book, with a few contributions from him, my name would come first. All was speedily settled and ready for a start when we encountered an unexpected snag. Curtis Brown, the literary agent to whom the placing of the book was first offered, turned the idea down.

We'd only gone to Curtis Brown because the firm had been Mavis's agent for the autobiography which she'd signally failed to write. They kept my synopsis for two months before rejecting it – much to my amazement. Didn't they realise what a fantastic life this mistress of Augustus John had led, before and after her liaison with Horace de

---

* More commonly referred to as the Dreadnought hoax, when Cole and Stephen organised a fake delegation of Abyssinian royals and persuaded the Royal Navy to show the fraudsters around the fleet's flagship battleship, HMS *Dreadnought*. The prank was so notable because the British Navy was perceived as being all-powerful at the time, and the *Dreadnought*'s technological capabilities were supposed to be second-to-none – hence why the pair identified it as a subject deserving of being taken down a peg or two.

Vere Cole, a man well above her allotted 'station'? Were they blind to the fact that she had not just attracted but married the world-famous archaeologist Sir Mortimer Wheeler (voted This Year's Outstanding TV Personality for his appearance on *Animal, Vegetable and Mineral*)? Her dealings with Lord Vivian, which had resulted in her incarceration, had been described in the newspapers as 'the Love Court Drama of the Century'.

I sent the synopsis to my own agents, Pearn Pollinger and Higham (later David Higham Associates), and Hutchinson and Co., my former publishers, duly offered a contract.

I had no shadow of a doubt about our title: it had to be *Beautiful and Beloved*. Its cadence took everyone by storm. The joy of it cast a golden glow on Horace, its begetter, and made me more sympathetic towards him, for I hadn't found much to admire in his perpetual efforts to wrong-foot everyone except himself.

Curiously enough, my father was able to shine a side-light on Horace, known to him as 'Molar' when they'd both been well-off young men-about-town. George Fenwick Owen had only filled that role when not busy organising expeditions to faraway places, but he'd known Molar well enough to go on a walking-tour with him, which, like all Horace's walks, had been well planned. The man would tirelessly stride along all day, but would never put up with discomfort at night, unless forced. He would send his car and chauffeur on ahead to book rooms in the best inn, so that by the time he and whoever he was with reached their destination – any destination – everything would be ready, even down to the ordering of the meal.

My father said (as recorded in *Beautiful and Beloved*): 'Molar had a roar like a lion which he'd use on people. He was quick to pick a fight but couldn't last long because of his lung ... I remember getting him up against a wall in the old Empire and holding him off until he tired, when I managed to send him flying. What was the fight about? I forget now; probably some remark he passed about a woman. He would go making up to girls he didn't know, and being deaf he caused no end of a stir. But he was really a very kind and generous man, always to the fore.' So Horace had been deaf, had he, as well as having a weak chest? Those were important factors in helping us understand him better.

'The old Empire was a great place for what we called, in mixed company, "Ladies of the Town",' said my father. 'Among the fellows, we had other names for 'em.' I was amazed at the way his reminiscences were making him unbend; it was a side I'd never seen before, as a small boy. 'Molar knew everybody and everybody wanted to know Molar – as long as they weren't victims, which many of his best friends were!'

'Were you, ever?' I asked him.

'No, the fellow steered clear of me after that. He had plenty of common-sense, when he cared to use it.'

Having thought of Horace as a rich man, it was staggering to discover that he'd died in penury, as a remittance-man, on a pittance of £3 a week from his brother Jim and his sister Annie – who happened to have become Mrs Neville Chamberlain. It was one more strange fact about him, suggesting either incompetence or extreme unworldliness, coming on top of the bravado which had enabled him to marry a girl like Mavis, born east of the East End of London.

The more I discovered, the more excited I grew. Mavis had been an enchantress, or an adventuress – or a bit of both – for whom things had gone swimmingly till the terrible moment when she had shot Lord Vivian and been sent to prison for 'malicious wounding'. Yet, from what I'd known of her, she'd never intended to hurt anyone, least of all wound, or try to kill, a lover. 'An innocent, if not innocent in law' was how I thought of her. I didn't forget her taking me (on the way back from seeing Tristan in his aircraft-carrier) to the cottage in Potterne which had been the scene of the shooting. For someone hoping to write a true account of her life, nothing could have been more important.

I said to Tristan: 'We *must* tell the truth, even though she was your mother. Otherwise the book will be valueless.'

He agreed. 'De Vere Cole may not have been my father,' he said. 'Mavis always used to claim it was Augustus, which "Gussus" certainly believed to his dying day. But once or twice she said it wasn't him, even. We may manage to find out; or we may not.'

'As long as you won't object?'

'No, I won't mind. I'd like to know myself.'

I knew then that we were in business. What I didn't fully appreciate was that I was sentencing myself to three years' hard labour. Worth it in every way, but hard labour all the same: the resurrecting of an actual Mavis, beautiful and beloved, from the ashes of past scandals.

———

101

Work on beautiful and beloved Mavis continued in full stride over the following year, with hardly a day going by when I didn't discover something that would elate or shock. But on Monday, 22 November 1971 I was to receive a shock from different quarters. I looked, as usual, at the Deaths columns of the *Daily Telegraph* only to find:

> Fenwick Owen. On Nov. 21st, at his home at Melton, Suffolk, George Fenwick Owen, M.C. Cremation private, No letters or flowers, please.

I rang my mother, in time to save her from experiencing a similar shock. Then I rang my father's wife Beni, only to discover that they'd moved within the last few months to a different address. Tracking her down at last, I was told that there would be a cremation at 11.30 a.m. on Thursday at Ipswich Crematorium. My mother, clinging to a grievance so ancient that she was the only one for whom it retained any meaning, preferred not to meet the third Mrs Fenwick Owen, sending violets in her stead and asking for them to be placed on the coffin – violets, because those were the first flowers my father had bought her, from a flower-woman at Piccadilly Circus, when they'd just got engaged.

But Morvyne and Genissa, though they'd refused to have anything to do with their father whilst he was alive, were determined not to be done out of sniffing the air on so unique an occasion. I, on the other hand, genuinely mourned him and thanked God that I'd gone to talk to him about Horace de Vere Cole so recently. It seemed like a bonus for having agreed to do Mavis's 'Life'.

Another strange thing had happened on the 22nd: in the early hours of that Monday morning, Gian Carlo, much to my astonishment, wet the bed, which he'd never done before. I simply didn't know what to make of it; and reading the announcement of my father's death a few hours later I got the idea that the two things might be somehow connected.

As I lay having a siesta after lunch, the telephone rang. It was Beni, to say she would send 'her' taxi from Melton to meet us. She asked what flowers we'd like; I said roses with the message 'in loving remembrance'.

'Wouldn't you rather have "with love from"?'

'No, I'd rather put "in loving remembrance" because that's how I feel about it.'

'Oh well, perhaps it would be rather awkward!'

I could hardly pretend to be pleased. Nor did I find it too convincing when Beni protested that she *meant* to contact George Whateley, the solicitor my father and I both used, to ring round to all of us, his first family. The point was: *she hadn't actually done so.* I had learnt of my father's death from a newspaper. No, I was not pleased at all.

Morvyne, Genissa and I trained together to Ipswich, where we had to wait in a waiting-room so hot that it was positively claustrophobic. At last Beni's taxi arrived and we reached the crematorium with only five minutes to spare. The only other mourner there, besides Morvyne, Genissa, Beni and me, was a Mrs Martin to whom Morvyne had been bridesmaid a long time ago. Perhaps the lack of other friends was because all his old ones had already died.

The service was dull: there was no music, and the coffin didn't go forward and disappear from sight, though the arrangements were devised for such. Afterwards, Beni briefly talked to Genissa and Morvyne, and I gave her a modest peck on the cheek. George had been ill for some weeks. He was said to have been 'tired' and to have 'slipped gently away'.

Why weren't we told? I kept thinking.

Mrs Martin insisted on lunching with us, and took us to the White Horse (which she kept calling the White Hart), to its grill room (which she kept calling 'The Buffet'). Her incessant chatter was disquieting, but we were trapped. She did finally drive us to the station, as a recompense of kind.

In London, my sisters went back to Sussex and I returned alone to Gilston Lodge, whereupon the phone rang – it was Bill McLean,* asking

---

* This is the final mention of Bill in this abridged version of Roddy's memoirs (he appeared again in the original version). He died in November 1986; Roddy remembered him very fondly for having enabled so many parts of his life, including his trip to the South Seas, Gulzaman's entry to the UK, and his travels through Africa. His memorial was a 'terrifically grand affair' with plenty of Lords, Dukes and ambassadors from other countries.

would I come with him to see the Dervishes whirling at Friends' House, with dinner afterwards.

The meeting hall – or auditorium – of Friends' House was properly Quaker in its plainness. We were allotted seats in the gallery, uncomfortable benches from which it was impossible to see what was going on without standing up. We were then treated to a service with much grave bowing of head by head, and a long chant (solo) from the Koran. After some banging and fluting, the Dervishes removed their cloaks and swirled slowly out, like formation dancers, only they only ever perform the one act: they rotated, white habits undulating out as gracefully as white poppies caught by a breeze. A Senior, with a beard and white (not brown like the rest) and high tarboosh, moved slowly about amongst them, and another Senior in a slightly more elaborate brown tarboosh in the end teetered slowly in the centre of the dancers (about twelve of them). This was symbolising the movement of the Earth and stars and indeed the atom and its nucleus and electrons, too. Arms outstretched, parallel with the ground, the right-hand palm upwards, the left palm downwards. Twirling, twirling, with the music changing to quick waltz time.

The Whirling Dervishes took my mind off what had happened earlier in the day. In bed, I reverted to the funeral, turning away from Gian Carlo to brood and ponder in isolation. My father had shown some faith but very faint interest in my doings. He'd visited me at school, taking me for rides in the car. Having moved on to Beni, he lent me furniture for 22 Nassau Street and had met that first girlfriend Jacqui Lowder-Downing (of whom he neither approved nor disapproved, simply thinking of her as my 'bit of the right sort'). More significantly, on hearing that I was about to go beachcombing, he'd produced a tip and muttered something about being 'prepared to help you out of a jam if you get into trouble'. Decent of him.

As regards the rest of the family, he'd come to hear Morvyne sing at Wigmore Hall and he'd attended Genissa's wedding. On the other hand, he'd shown no interest in Charles, David and Mary, his grandchildren; never actually saw them and never tried to meet them. Genissa had made no effort to get them together, either. (The three children were to tell me later that they wished they'd known more about him.)

Afterwards, Beni let us have a few of George's things, which was very nice of her: the picture with multiple quarterings of the Owen descent from Rhodri Mawr;* *Views of Shropshire* by Archdeacon Owen; sundry pieces of silver to the probate value of £80; a book of Japanese sketches bought on my father's first honeymoon; a box with drawers containing coins and cameos; but chiefly (and to me, most impressively) Roddy Owen's gold repeater watch on a heavy gold chain, a beautiful thing.

102

They say everything comes in threes. Where was the last goodbye to come from?

By August 1971, following the collapse of Gulburg Stores, all the properties belonging to G. K. Sales (London) Ltd in Battersea and Wandsworth had been sold. In case it might be needed later, I kept the company going, investing the proceeds into stocks and shares.

Gulzaman announced his intention of going back yet again to Pakistan, this time with Manzoora and her by then not-so-small sister Nasreen. There was a tearful farewell in the street outside the back garden door of Gilston Lodge, and about an hour later Nasreen rang up from a call-box to say an extra goodbye. I was pleased, but it made me wonder what was in the wind.

Some weeks after that, I went downstairs into the basement in search of their sewing-machine, but couldn't find it. Evidently Manzoora had taken it with her. 'That proves they've gone for good!' said Gian Carlo, in triumph. But I felt a lump coming into my throat and went off quickly by myself to avoid him seeing me break down.

In fact, Gulzaman was scheduled to return to London, by himself, in March 1972. Hearing that Manzoora was staying on in Karachi, Gian Carlo was sceptical: 'He wants to milk you for more, that's all!' Against remarks of that kind I'd learnt never to argue. How could I explain that I didn't mind *some* people getting anything they wanted out of me – a Little Man first and foremost.

----

* Rhodri Mawr – or Rhodri the Great – is sometimes referred to as King of the Britons or King of Wales. He ruled over a significant chunk of Wales in the ninth century.

Once reunited, Gulzaman complained that he felt ill and unloved. It emerged that he'd quarrelled with Manzoora and was thinking of leaving her and staying on with me. I was not at all in favour of such a move, foreseeing that it would send him spinning into fresh depths of depression.

A key conversation took place in June, during which it was agreed that he had better go back to Pakistan for good this time. I could then set about determining his share of the 'muckle roup' of our company properties – about £5320, or 150,000 rupees. It didn't sound much, but for those days it was a tidy sum. Unfortunately the pound sterling started floating downwards and I had to fork out another £400 to keep its head above water in terms of equivalent rupees.

Gulzaman really was going and he had indeed got something out of me, but no more than his share of the reward stemming from my insistence on dealing in property, over and above shop-keeping. I was content to have been proven right. Having been blessed with so much unexpected luck, I was glad of the opportunity to give something back, for a change.

Soon after Gulzaman had gone, I rushed to make private notes:

> 8th July 1972: Oh, how heavy I feel. For the last few days I've cried at intervals. After 18 years it isn't easy to be severed from Gulzaman, I have always had to do so much for him. I can never ever be grateful enough for being continuously given the chance. And how interesting (and maddening) it has been, the whole saga of GK Sales and Gulburg Stores and knowing about Pakistanis and all. And always feeling that a Gulzaman was there. Expensive, too, a constant drain and getting more expensive each time. I foresaw it right back in Bahrain, when he used to cost shillings: later, pounds: later, hundreds of pounds. He was just on the brink of thousands and tens of thousands. Goodness knows where it would have ended.

The dear Loyal thing. There can never be anything like that again. I can't stop crying and he kept on crying. Gian Carlo says it's all a fake and that Mr G. is excited by going and that I'm relieved he's going. There's some truth in that, of course, but it's far too narrow a view. It's infinitely more complex.

At that point, I was doubtless refilling a glass, struggling vainly to explain the inexplicable. I knew that there was so much more to add, when trying to sum up the special relationship between us truthfully and accurately:

> I've always been able to believe Gulzaman even though he has often lied. He's lied about certain specific things. It hadn't affected the fact that his heart has always been clear. I've often thought him saintly, even though I've seen him do harm. It's difficult to explain this paradox. I can't wholly explain it myself, but I *feel* it. I know that the sort of feeling between Gulzaman and myself can never come again and that it was of great value, possibly *is* still. In spite of being able to communicate with words, I find it hard to communicate this. Tears are as good as anything; when I forget other things, will I forget the tears as well? I ought not to.

And that was that. A tumultuous, strange and love-filled eighteen years came to a close.

———

103

On getting back from one of many visits to Malta, I went down into the basement and found, in the kitchen, a ball of living fluff sprawling on a piece of old blanket. 'That's Marco,' said Gian Carlo, when called upon to explain the puppy's presence. 'Please don't be cross!' How could I be cross? Marvellous Marco was tiny, appealing, with long silk-sandy hair, captivating all who saw him. He was so young (having been rescued by Battersea Dogs Home) that he could hardly have been weaned and hadn't even begun to be house-trained. We put an alarm-clock with the alarm switched permanently off near his little basket, because someone had told us that the ticking of a clock was a good substitute for a mother's heart-beat.

How we grew to adore that lovely mongrel! When he grew up, he looked like a snub-nosed, sandy-haired collie, but with shorter legs. If anyone asked what kind of dog he was, we would answer: 'An MOB!'

Those who still insisted would be told: 'A My Own Breed, of course!' What a joy he was!

That year, my mother was to be admitted to the Esperance Nursing Home in Eastbourne, run by a Nursing Order of nuns, to be provided with a vanadium-toughened stainless-steel ball-on-a-post as a hip replacement. The operation was not then the routine affair which it would later become. It was serious for a girl of her age, and I wanted to go to Langney in order to be with her. But the Sunday before that I was still in London and happened to hear Marco barking, upstairs, above the strains of *Songs of Praise*. At that moment, the congregation was singing 'Praise, my soul, the King of Hea-yea-ven'.

When I went upstairs to see what was the matter, I expected to find Gian Carlo lying down, he having previously complained of feeling unwell. Marco might be frisking about, trying to get him to play. That wasn't what I found. I saw the dearest friend of my heart twitching on the spare-room bed, frothing at the mouth as 'PRAISE HIM! PRAISE HIM!' came pouring out of the TV set in the corner. He couldn't speak properly and made no sort of sense when he did. Marco was licking at his face. I felt as though my whole life was streaming away.

I knew that it was a fit. At first I thought it might be a one-off, till calling to mind some disquieting things. A few weeks earlier he'd come home from the restaurant he was working in at Kensington Close with one tooth broken and others loosened, having, he said, slipped on a piece of tomato, for which he blamed the kitchen staff. Then there'd been that strange wetting of the bed, the night before I'd learnt that my father had died. And Sukhan, the Turk living temporarily in the basement, had told me that on one occasion he'd found Gian Carlo sitting staring into space, not answering when spoken to. I'd thought nothing of it, but little signs and portents suddenly took on a new meaning, frightening to contemplate.

He came round but I couldn't stay with him because I *had* to go down and see my mother; which, reluctantly, I did. Rightly as it turned out: immediately post-op she'd been running a temperature due to a suspected blood-clot and we were genuinely worried for a night and a day.

All the time, a different major personal anxiety was rumbling away. Had the Little Man become an epileptic? And if so, how best could I help him? If it were possible to discern a new purpose in life, then this was it, of that I felt absolutely sure.

Before a month was out I found him lying helpless on the floor again, eyes bulging; and he had another seizure two months later, in the kitchen.

On that occasion he mentioned he was aching all over. When he sat down at the table he suddenly stopped speaking and went very white. He smiled twice, apparently with a great effort – which reminded me of the changes of expression on my grandmother's face, the last few breaths before she died – then gave a loud cry and went rigid. Foam trickled out of his mouth and down his chin. There was a very noticeable, almost antiseptic, smell. 'Oh God, dear God, please help us!' I was muttering, over and over again, whilst laying him quietly back against cushions and covering him with a rug to keep him warm.

It didn't take him long to recover from each fit, when what he wanted more than anything was a strong drink of neat vodka. I was in no mood to refuse him anything.

In between those frightening moments, we tried to inject some happiness by looking for a small restaurant he could run given that his gig at Kensington Close was up. His mother was prepared to come from Lake Garda to help him start up. 'Mamma Cesira' was not only an excellent plain cook, but she had run a *cantina* in Sicily during the war from necessity (for German troops, though we kept quiet about that), so knew something about the business side of catering.

Mamma Cesira had already stayed one whole winter with us in London. I found her *molto simpatica*, both for her kindness and for looking after us and for her earthy sense of humour. She learned a few words of English, but she wasn't about to use them in a hurry; my Italian improved by leaps and bounds.

Gian Carlo and I came very close to buying a suitable place on the Bayswater side of the park, but then it came to light that the Italian restaurant next door was in possession of a restricted covenant that prevented any nearby competitor serving Italian food. Perhaps just as well: instead I invested a portion of the money in Bernard Matthews and made an absolute fortune.*

A few months later, assured by Gian Carlo that he was well enough, Morvyne, my mother and I headed off to the Holy Land for an eye-opening trip. Wondrous in so many ways, I couldn't get past the fact all the sites were authenticated by nothing more than historical guesswork, a thought I couldn't shake when staring at the stable where Christ was said

---

* Bernard Matthews being the Norfolk turkey farmer, who achieved success through large-scale farming and a well-known TV advert.

to have been born. I did my best to content myself with the idea that it was what they represented that mattered.

We then went to Jordan in October 1972 for my mother's eightieth, spending her birthday at Petra, where I tried not to give the girls a cold I'd picked up on the plane, knowing I'd never hear the end of it if I did, by practically drinking a vat of honey. Thus encouraged, I felt shiveringly ready for a ride on a horse through the Siq, the time-honoured way of seeing Petra.* To be mounted, our steeds had to be approached down a rocky slope, slippery with sand and loose pebbles, where my mother all but lost her balance. We were not given reins, but had to cling on to the neck end of a saddle fitted with an iron hoop. Our 'ride' was a matter of being led by a groom in Arab dress along the bed of a wadi, till cliffs began closing in on either side for the Siq proper, historically the only way into the Nabataean capital. After another twenty minutes, the gorge narrowed and the red rocks almost met overhead. The narrow, beetling Siq became a valley, in which the main city had been built. The ravine through which we had ridden had been, and was, a veritable wadi, subject to sudden flash floods in which, over the years, parties of people had been caught by surprise and drowned, tourists included . . .

Yet safely I returned home to London to my two loves: Gian Carlo and the bees. Gian Carlo had joined me in my obsession, but his hive was not too healthy. Was that the reason for his sometime mood swings? He was sometimes unaccountably bad-tempered for no reason that I could fathom, for there were no more fits. Whatever the problems were, we'd surely get over them together, wouldn't we?

———

104

Mavis, Mavis, Mavis . . . each word I wrote about her was in long-hand. Multiple typing errors and early clashes with a Dictable wire-recorder

---

* Petra being the 'Lost City' (or 'Rose City', given the hue of the stone from which its architecture is carved) in southern Jordan; a major trading hub for the Nabataeans of second century BC, and probably even earlier.

had continued to convince me that composing directly on to a machine was for others, not for me. I'd been heard to say: 'There's something mystical about the contact between pen and paper.' All rot: I simply hadn't found the right medium, and wouldn't until word processors were invented.

While alive, Mavis had often thought of writing her story herself but had lacked the mental stamina to set about it. Had she overcome inertia, she would have fetched up against the tricky problems facing me: how to describe, accurately, dealings with people still living, when many of those dealings would cause shock and/or resentment. I might be prevented from stating how often this person or that had been to bed with her. Would I even be allowed to reveal amatory facts amusing rather than damaging, such as, for instance, that my old friend Ian Askew, no fancier of girls, had enjoyed (or, at any rate, achieved) a 'knee-trembler' with her just inside her front door? That sort of problem hadn't arisen with Tedder, for the man was too respectable to have caused eyebrows to be raised except over the minor matter of his choice of Toppy as second wife.

That was only one aspect, amongst many. As serious, from my point of view, was the censorious attitude of Romilly, Augustus John's son and literary executor. Romilly had literary pretensions of his own and was determined to protect his lecherous old father's reputation by preventing us from including the really juicy bits of John's verse in celebration of Mavis's feats in bed. But since the old man's reputation in that direction was non-existent already, it was a lost cause if ever there was one.

Then there was the question of Lord Vivian, the wet peer Mavis shot – still alive, and with a wronged wife still alive. I had to exercise the utmost discretion there, even though it tipped the truth off-balance.

I also had to understand how difficult some parts of the book were for Tristan, because we were writing about his mother. She'd *revelled* in sex; and though by the seventies it was becoming acceptable to say so in print, it still wasn't wholly accepted by much of the prurient public unless the details were presented in puritanical tones of shock/horror. Nothing was going to persuade me to be so hypocritical, and Tristan went along with that to a greater extent than I had dared hope.

With the passing of years – and of people – some of the omissions could be remedied. A former 'unmentionable' came from Joy, sister of Robert Newton, the actor with whom Mavis enjoyed many a fling. She contributed an item which startled even me. 'My brother Bob was the best sex any girl could wish for,' she declared (over a lunch where wine had been flowing freely). 'I'm telling you – and I should know, from experience!' Mavis and she had often compared notes, she claimed, enlivened by many a fruity chuckle; and I had no reason to doubt her.

Mavis herself revealed another startler: she'd (innocently) helped do in 'Sir Arthur', the old fellow she'd brought round to my house to meet Angela Geere. He'd been accustomed to call on her, at intervals, for what she'd been best at (I called it 'tease and sympathy', because tea played no part in their frolics). He was generous with his money at a time when only whisky could make her feel even half the woman she'd once been. One disconcerting day in 'The Little House', Sir Arthur suffered a seizure, from over-exertion *in flagrante*. She managed to rally him sufficiently to bundle him into a taxi and send him back to his club, where the hall-porter found him to be dead on arrival. 'Lots of people told me he couldn't have asked for more,' she said ruefully. 'But it was a very great blow to me when he wasn't any longer there. He was always *such* a help.'

When, after endless revision, discussions with libel lawyers, etc., *Beautiful and Beloved* finally reached print, in 1974, it did quite well. What a way to become a published author once more.

105

One night Gian Carlo got out of bed and started peeing. I heard him, and switched on the light – he was simply peeing on the carpet, having dreamed he was in the loo. The penny finally dropped: he was an alcoholic. This was the effect of drink. Another night he got up and I crept downstairs after him and caught him in the kitchen pouring out an enormous vodka and tonic from a hidden bottle.

I soon realised that he hid drink cunningly – in the boiler room, in amongst the rabbits' hay (we kept quite a few), in cupboards.

I wondered what to do for the best, for there could be no question of him running a restaurant, which would merely allow him unlimited access to alcohol. So then – what? We would have to fall back on the one thing in which I had never been known to fail – property. If I could find a nice small house we could own it jointly and the Little Man could run it and take all proceeds. That would keep him going, whilst giving me half a house in return; all that I would be losing was the income from the capital employed in buying it. I resolved to start a search for something suitable.

Judging from past experience, it shouldn't be difficult: my property record was one of unbroken good luck. It was simply a question of waiting for Fate to steer me to the right place. Duly, that was exactly what Fate did, using the dog, Marco, as a pilot. I'd been taking Marco to Battersea for his daily walk, because that park was easily reached and parking the car was easy; but in summer the place became Bedlam. At length it occurred to me to try Chiswick. Years earlier, when we'd been looking for a suitable home for his mother, I'd taken Geoffrey Prendergast to what he called 'Burlington Villa'. Unless they'd changed a lot since then, the fifty-five acres of Chiswick House grounds were surely ideal for canine sniffs and poos.

We started going to Chiswick daily, dog and I, sometimes with, sometimes without Gian Carlo. Then came the reward: one day, after skirting Paxton's conservatory (where regulations forced us to bond together on a lead), Marco chose a new direction. Lead removed, we were walking parallel with a high wall, partly concealing a row of cottages with only their tops visible. Each cottage obviously had a small garden of its own on the other side of the wall and an unrestricted outlook over acres and acres of countrified greenery. I resolved to look further and left via the massive wrought-iron gates leading on to the busy airport road, turned right and shortly right again, reaching Paxton Road, a narrow tree-lined avenue.

As Marco and I walked on, the street got quieter and quieter, until no sound of traffic from the main arterial road could be heard. There was just the one central area of tranquillity, for walk another twenty yards and a roar began coming from the Richmond road at the other end. As if by magic, one of those little middle cottages was for sale: No. 36, its bricks tinted red, the interstices lined white, like a gingerbread house. As a crowning touch, Paxton Road was without parking-meters, free of all restrictions.

I loved that house at once, knowing that it would do splendidly; and so did the Little Man.

I agreed with the owner, a woman who looked pleasingly like Beatrix

Potter's Mrs Tiggywinkle, to pay £15,500, a sum which practically guaranteed our getting it because £15,000 was the 'cut-off' for stamp duty, which most buyers did their utmost to avoid paying. When we started bargaining, house prices were rising steeply. They'd begun to falter towards December 1973, because the stock market was falling and was to continue falling, to a point where it threatened to become a 'crash' – the worst, some thought, since 1929.

In spite of the harsh financial climate, we – my little circle and myself – seemed moderately well set after that: Gian Carlo with the security of a small letting-income; Gulzaman having bought a house in Islamabad (cheaper than he'd thought possible because of hostilities between Pakistan and India over Kashmir) with the proceeds from his share in G. K. Sales; and my family all with property I'd partly assisted helping them to acquire.

All in all, as I looked around me, I hoped that I could claim to have been acting according to the Will of God, not putting my own interests forward as a priority, but trying to do the best for those for whom I had some responsibility. I hoped, desperately hoped, for mercy on us all, particularly on the least guilty and most suffering, my Little Man.

'Please God, let him be cured! Please, please God!' I would mutter, lying in bed next to him on a sheet which, for obvious reasons, had to be spread over a rubber undersheet. But he only seemed to get worse.

106

In the summer of 1974, Aunt Susan died. I could not honestly claim to mourn her passing, but I did do the right thing by going down to Well Vale for the funeral service. It was nothing like the traditional, country way in which we'd buried my grandmother, but I had a friendly chat with her nephew, John Reeve, who had inherited the stately house and land. I invited him to dinner, should he ever find himself in London; and in due course he came. It was nice to know that there was no feud between us – he with the property, me with the money.

The night of 2 June was the first Gian Carlo and I spent together in our Chiswick 'Villa Marco'. We slept on a sofa-bed in the downstairs back room which led directly into the garden, where bees from a WBC hive were already busy producing honey. In spite of the house being between two main roads, all the noise we heard was the occasional raucous scream of a peacock from the grounds of Chiswick House; and in the early morning, the dawn chorus of a thousand birds claiming their territorial rights – just as we were doing. No. 36 might have been a cottage in the country.

Luck for the Little Man was what I most desired and prayed for, yet grounds for hope continued diminishing. There'd been a short period when he was drinking less, with fewer fits, possibly because of being absorbed with playing with his new toy, the house. But optimism had been short-lived; he was simply growing more adept at hiding his bottles of vodka, brazenly denying that a glass full of neat spirits contained anything but hot water, even when I took it from him and sniffed the contents.

I knew that alcoholics couldn't be cured against their will, only when they themselves decided that they'd had enough, so my aim was to keep temptation to a minimum. The obvious thing was to lock up the drinks, which I didn't enjoy doing because increasingly I wanted – 'needed', was the way I put it – drinks myself. Nothing that I did had the desired effect and sometimes we had really dreadful rows – drink-inspired, of course, but understanding their cause didn't help reduce their intensity. Despair brooded over our life together, briefly folding its wings when we went to the Villa Marco, but cawing triumphantly when, even there, I would catch the Little Man going to a corner behind the bee-hive or to some other secret place to unearth his fatal tipple.

So matters stood one day when we were driving back from Chiswick, with him reeking of vodka. He suddenly interrupted whatever it was we'd been talking about, gripped my sleeve and said, in a choking voice, 'Help me, Lovey, help me!' It was such a total surprise that I nearly ran into the car in front. Having spoken, he didn't explain himself further, and I had more sense than to ask immediately what he meant. I knew that this was the signal for which a good friend of mine (and fellow bee-keeper) Dr Tom Damant and I had been waiting, waiting. 'Of course!' I said breezily. 'As soon as we get in.'

Tom was coming to lunch that day, which made things easier. For a change, now that he'd made the vital first move, we could discuss ways and means in front of Gian Carlo.

'There's a Dr Glatt,' Tom suggested, 'very well known. We might get hold of him privately and ask if he'll admit Gian Carlo to his clinic on the National Health. Otherwise, treatment could be *rather* expensive.' Then, turning to my Little Man: 'He won't take you unless he thinks there's a good chance you'll forswear the Demon for good. So it will be up to you to convince him – and I warn you, he's no fool!'

When Tom was gone, Gian Carlo turned quite savagely on me. 'You didn't try nearly hard enough, before, to get me into hospital! That's your trouble. You only do for me what I don't really need and *don't* do what I do need!' I was appalled by his unfairness, but bit back a pro-test, content to absorb any amount of blame, however unreasoning, if it would get him into the right mood to be interviewed by Dr Glatt. I even started coaching him in what he ought to say and how to say it, risking his anger at my interference. All that counted was that he should remain willing to undergo the humiliation of continuing to ask for help.

He was trembling (and so was I) with a mixture of elation and appre-hension when the day for the appointment came: 3 July, one of the most important days in his life and in mine, too. Dr Glatt was German or Austrian and almost certainly Jewish, his manner well adapted to instil confidence in a problem patient. He sat with his back to the light in the drawing-room of Gilston Lodge and was both sharp and kind in his behaviour and in what he had to say. Welcome indeed was his verdict: he would accept my poor broken friend for treatment within a week. Such treatment would last for at least two months, possibly more. 'It would be best if you could manage to come "dry" into my care,' he said to an unusually humble Gian Carlo. I doubted whether there'd be much chance of that.

With the dog Marco in the back, I drove the Little Man out to St Bernard's, Southall, a part of London previously unknown to me. It looked very far away on the map but was easy to reach, out to the right beyond the Hoover factory on the Great West Road. Our first glimpse of the hospital inspired terror rather than confidence: buildings of black-ened, yet liverish, brick; a gateway massively arched and barred, as if to guard a fortress. 'Abandon hope all ye who enter here!' that gateway seemed to be saying. We hadn't realised that St Bernard's was a mental hospital. When I asked the way to 'Male 18 and 20' we were taken in hand by a harmless simpleton, padding slowly along in a manner instantly recognisable as the Banstead shuffle.

At length we reached a detached building overlooking broad playing fields, acres and acres of them. The building contained 'Arnold' and 'Addison' wards – another way of referring to 'Male 18 and 20' – which were reassuringly unlike the rest of the asylum. TV was quacking away in a general atmosphere of relaxed bustle. I signed Gian Carlo in with the minimum of formality. It wasn't at all like the time when I'd shepherded Gulzaman for treatment to that other madhouse; more like being a parent taking a child to his first school. I was the happier to help Gian Carlo go through the motions of signed consent for knowing that it would make him feel that he had to stay put till such time as they were prepared to release him, for a 'trial visit', after six weeks. He was told that he'd be 'more or less in bed' for the first week, under sedation to ease painful symptoms of withdrawal.

While such matters were being seriously discussed, I came nearer and nearer to breaking-point, but couldn't actually break down, being too busy attending to what I was expected to do and how. For instance, I had a long talk with the Area Health Authority social worker, Ann Friend – appropriately, her real name – who, even down to a Canadian accent, uncannily resembled my literary agent, Anne McDermid of David Higham Associates. To her I unburdened myself of every possible relevant fact which came to mind, holding back nothing about our relationship, the money I gave him when he asked for it, our rows over his drinking. It felt peculiar to be pouring all that out to a complete stranger when I wouldn't have confided in her look-alike (who was far better known to me), but it seemed of paramount importance to 'come clean'.

Ann's aim was to urge me to attend a group session for the relations of both drug and alcohol abusers, which took place each Tuesday. 'Everyone connected with those who are in here have their part to play,' she said. Somewhat to my surprise, she chided me for having been too lenient with Gian Carlo: 'He may have wanted firmer handling, particularly as regards money.' I didn't tell her that experience had taught me never to let money give me a hold over anyone, particularly not over anyone loved or respected. She ended by remarking on his fits: 'They may be entirely alcoholic in origin. When drink goes, the fits may go too.'

'My God!' I said. 'D'you really think so? I have been thinking it was the other way round!' That one remark lifted a great weight off my shoulders, one of the most crushing burdens of all, a load of pity.

But it was proving all too much, for as soon as I'd driven back through the massive security gateway and was in the outside world again I finally broke down, howling so uncontrollably that I thought it best to pull in to the side of the road. I simply couldn't afford to risk an accident at such a crucial juncture in our lives.

Echoing with emptiness – like the house itself – I went round looking for bottles of booze. I found them amongst logs of wood piled outside; in the former air-raid shelter; behind a loose panel under the bath; hidden by clothes or shoes in the bottom of more than one cupboard; even under a pillow in the spare room. There'd been no limit to his ingenuity. The more I found, the grimmer I grew. Could he ever be trusted to give up an addiction so firmly rooted?

On 13 July I visited him for the first time, bringing Marco with me, though it meant leaving him in the field outside the ward. Gian Carlo was in pyjamas and dressing-gown and wanted above all to see his dog, who reacted by jumping up rapturously, exactly as he was meant to do. Then he returned with me into the ward. I said, 'Which is your bed?', thinking that he probably had the one in the corner out in front. He didn't reply, so I repeated the question. I saw him look bewildered and start to sway, so then I quickly guessed that he was about to have a fit and caught him. He gave a shout just as I did so and went rigid. It wasn't too difficult to drag him over to the corner bed where he went purple and foamed at the mouth. Meanwhile the assistants came, including one with spectacles, who said, 'Keep him on his side.'

I said, 'I'm quite used to this. Are you?'

He said, 'Oh yes, we have plenty.'

LM came slowly round, and gave his usual start of horror – the shock of returning consciousness, as if he'd been up till then blind.

The next day I found him in a sweet mood, none of the vituperation I'd grown to dread during the last year. I noted that most of the other patients were young men, barely more than teenagers, a few of them thin or sad-looking, mostly solid if not slightly fat. LM told me that after three weeks everyone was allowed home for a weekend, but that nearly all of them came back drunk.

Duly I attended the 'family' session, conducted by Ann Friend and her agreeable colleague Bob Hendra. Earlier, I'd seen Ann sitting in a yoga position on the grass, doing exercises. Now she lay back in an armchair, heels digging into the carpet. Once I got over the 'Oxford Group-ish' atmosphere, I copied her air of nonchalance.

The ones who spoke first were, (a) a woman married to a drug addict. She said she had to do everything for him, he was in and out of jobs all the time, he only wanted a job near the chemist where he could get his fix in the morning. Then there was (b) an older woman with frizzy black hair who brought her friend, a younger platinum blonde woman, along. Her son sold his things, not hers, to get drugs, and went and lived rough as a hippy. And (c) someone with an alcoholic son, who said how anxiously he'd be watching to see whether the boy would succumb to drinking again. 'Treading on eggshells,' said Bob Hendra, who then added that it was wrong for relations to be reacting all the time – this was giving too much importance to the addict and allowing him or her to influence their lives too much. In fact, both he and Ann were determined to get across the message that addicts were experts at making their 'keepers' feel guilty and responsible. The clinic's advice was: DON'T feel either the one or the other. DO the minimum to look after your 'charges', and leave it at that.

'Alcoholics are responsible for their condition, not you. The sooner you get that into their heads – and yours – the better!' I was taught.

It was a real revelation, not just to me, but to everyone present, obvious as it seemed in retrospect. All of us were being torn apart by a mixture of anxiety and guilt. We needed absolution, and those chill blasts of realism did the job beautifully.

After less than a month, I was allowed to take LM away at 4 p.m. on a Saturday and return him by Sunday night. As far as I knew, he didn't have a drink during that time, but there was a moment of doubt when I'd given him £5 to go and get cigarettes. The pubs were shut but then I suddenly remembered the cigarette shop sold drink and went racing to intercept him. I looked at the bag he had (eggs, cigarettes only) but didn't make him turn out his pockets – it is just possible he had a half or quarter bottle there. He looked rather sheepish just before going out. His face was a little red and his eyes enlarged, but at the same time his tooth had made the left-hand side of his face swell, as it had before, so it was difficult to tell. Incidentally he wasn't cross when I intercepted him. I told him that it was what he'd said he, or rather anyone alcoholic on a weekend leave, would need.

On another of LM's 'days out', I thought I detected the smell of drink on his breath and he suddenly reverted to being cross. I thought it best to let St Bernard's know, and they asked me to ensure that he took his tablets of Antabuse in my presence. Antabuse was a compound supposed to make it impossible for alcoholics to touch the stuff without making them sick.

To his dismay, the Little Man was called upon to become an author, to write his own account of his life and of how he came to be an alcoholic. He had to stand up from what was known as 'the hot seat' and deliver it in front of the others, that being considered an essential part of the cure. St Bernard's didn't like discharging patients until they'd complied. The trouble was, he had great difficulty putting words on paper, even in Italian, in barely legible handwriting. In English he was hopeless. I encouraged him by saying that perhaps no one had to *see* what he wrote, only to *hear* it, and in any case I would type it out for him.

On 17 September, he called me to say he was about to be in the hot seat. I said I'd be thinking about him and that he must tell the truth. 'You can say anything you like about me. Say I'm silly or dreadful or anything, I shan't mind.'

He replied, 'How can I, when I have to tell the truth?'

At which tears came into my eyes. He then asked about the dog and I said he sent a great big wuff to him. *'Augurie, tante belle cose, augurie,'* I went on. 'We're both thinking about you, we're all thinking about you.'

I was booked to go away on a trip to Poland on 29 September, not just with my two girls, as usual, but with Genissa and Michael. Ought I to go? I asked the experts. 'Yes,' they said. 'You *must not* change your plans to suit your friend's weakness! If we've managed to teach you anything, then that's one of the most important lessons.' Fortified, I went ahead with the arrangements, even though on his latest visit Gian Carlo had reeked of eau de vetiver, which I thought might be a stratagem to mask the smell of alcohol.

Then came the shock: on 23 September he rang up to say that his last urine test had indicated traces of barbiturate. I was puzzled, and he was indignant. Barbiturate? How could it be? As he told the slip committee, he didn't even know what a barbiturate was, although I had to realise that as in a prison, no inmate would ever admit to being guilty, however strong the presumption. They decided to 'gate' him. There could be no appeal against the decision. The upshot of it was that he discharged himself.

He didn't want me to come into the ward to fetch him, because of the emotional goodbyes which he knew he would have to face. Instead,

I waited at the gate until he approached, his face wet with tears. 'They all say they're going to miss me!' he snuffled. 'But I don't think I shall miss them, much.'

I said to him: 'I do hope you don't blame the hospital. You are simply caught up in its machinery.'

He agreed. 'I don't blame them at all. The doctor was at the party. I said, "I'm not talking to you this evening."'

'But did you?'

'Oh yes, of course I did, he was very nice to me.'

So that was the manner of his homecoming.

The day before I left for Poland, I happened to be counting jars of honey stored in the lower tower when I came across a bottle of vodka and a bottle of tonic water, both half empty. Potentially I had missed them in my search before. I asked him if they were recent and he of course denied it. I asked him, 'If you'd come across the stuff, would you have had the sense to pour it down the sink?'

He said, 'No, I couldn't waste it like that, but I wouldn't drink it.'

He would, of course.

107

Ironically, whilst all this was happening, my career was taking a turn for the better: as the result of writing about Mavis I was actually in demand once more; and not only that, I could choose my own subject.

Just as Mavis's 'goodbye' had caused a 'hello', so Aunt Susan's closing of a door opened a window – all the more surprising for being so unlikely from that quarter. Not unsurprising was that this guiding hand hadn't been intentional. I discovered that she had expressed a wish that 'her' collection of books about Sir John Franklin (the Arctic explorer, who was the uncle of Catherine Franklin, my great-grandmother) should go to the County Library in Lincoln to join some which she'd already presented. It really was too much to be borne. They weren't her books at all. They'd descended to my grandfather, Walter Rawnsley, then to his relict, Maud, thence to my mother, without ever being removed from Well Vale. I set about extracting them from a county librarian who, to give him his due, was embarrassed by what had happened rather than unwilling to let them go.

Having got hold of them, I started reading. They were absolutely fascinating. I ripped through them at tremendous speed (an art acquired when doing research for *Desert Air Force*), excited by the unfolding of an unremittingly dramatic story. I spotted a promising bone of contention, in that Dr Richard King, for whom no one seemed to have a good word, had been more correct than any other 'Arctic' in his assumption as to the whereabouts of the lost hero. Why had he been so underrated? Because he'd been too bumptious for British stomachs and poor, to boot – hence, thoroughly disapproved of by what might be described as the 'North-West Passage Establishment'. I took him straight to my heart and thought: *Why don't I do Franklin next, and possibly rehabilitate King, amongst other things?*

'John Franklin?' queried my agent, Anne McDermid. 'You mean *Benjamin* Franklin, don't you?'

'No, John. Sir John of the Frozen North!'

'Oh, that one ... we know a lot about him in Canada, of course. Well, I can always put it to Hutchinson's.'

She sounded less than keen; but then, few people seemed to know much about the man, famous as he'd been in the mid-nineteenth century. He'd died in the attempt to discover a North-West Passage through Arctic ice; sought in vain by ship after ship, his fate had at last been revealed by Leopold McClintock, due to John's unremitting wife, Jane. Had it not been for the books which I'd been devouring, I wouldn't have known much about him myself.

'I'm a direct descendant of his brother, Sir Willingham Franklin,' I added. 'Access to family papers ought to give me a head start.'

From then on, my passage was as smooth as Franklin's North-West Passage had been rough. Once the idea had been fleshed out, Hutchinson's (in the person of Tony Whittome, who'd handled the Mavis book) showed considerable keenness about *The Fate of Franklin*. It helped that thanks to Sir Charles Belgrave I was a fellow of the Royal Geographical Society, which would give me access to any number of documents, not easy for others to consult. 'It could make an exciting story,' was the verdict.

'More than that,' I said, 'a very important one!'

I was preaching to the converted; and to say that I went on my way rejoicing would be an understatement. I was as cock-a-hoop as when I'd talked Tedder into letting me do his 'Life', possibly more so because of being a Franklin myself, with Franklin as my middle name. The Franklin contract was soon drawn up, and I was committed to years of work ahead.

When I got back to LM I wondered how on earth I'd be able to write a closely considered book and look after him as well. At that point, a friend, Barbara Spencer, mentioned that she knew of a hypnotherapist who specialised in curing people of addictions: Geoffrey Glasboro, with a practice in Park Street. I decided for good measure to try him out myself, first: part of the exercise was that I'd give up too, so as to give LM no excuse. After all those visits to St Bernard's, I was prepared to take the crucial step of standing up in front of anyone, admitting: 'I am an alcoholic!' Because, according to their teaching, I *was* one, though so far unrumbled and apparently able to cope. It was vital that I should first blaze the trail by forswearing alcohol for ever, then set to work, hammer and tongs, on my prospective convert.

On 10 June 1975, I lay me down on a narrow, high couch and was told softly but insistently to relax all my muscles. 'Now you are very relaxed,' Glasboro announced, 'the envy of all who know you, I should think.' He pressed his fingers on my forehead ... and I dropped off to sleep, waking after a split second. Luckily, I'd been very sleepy, so by that happy accident the cure had been given the best chance of working on my subconscious mind. The hypnotist went on and on about how much better I would feel, how my writing would approve – all stand-ard guff, not at all convincing. Subsequent interviews, at £10 a throw, were repeat versions of the first, except that in all those weeks I hadn't touched a drop, much as I'd wanted to. But with Gian Carlo always in mind, I didn't dare. The combination of motives seemed to have worked extraordinarily well, given that one vital moment of unconsciousness within the first five minutes of the cure.

In spite of all my efforts, my treatment was a success, Gian Carlo's a failure. By the end of 1975 I couldn't trust him even to look after our beloved Marco.

108

Day and night, the North-West Passage haunted me – an obsession historically shared by many others. Franklin's lost expedition in 1845 had merely been one in a sequence dating back over a hundred years when an Act of Parliament had established the huge reward of £20,000 'to the owner or owners of any ship or vessel which should first find out and navigate the North-West Passage through Hudson Strait to the western and southern oceans of America'. The successful conclusion of the Napoleonic wars left the British Navy with scores of wooden vessels afloat; some rotting, some still in prime condition, all without any obvious purpose. Hence, with the will and the means conveniently to hand, why not try seriously for the elusive Arctic waterway?

There was one disturbing drawback: no telling, for sure, whether such a passage through ice round the top of the world really existed. It should be there, certainly, but was it? Should such a passage eventually be discovered, would a ship be able to sail through it? Mightn't a vessel become beset by the ice, possibly for ever? The thought sent shivers down some spines, thrills down others. During the first quarter of the nineteenth century, the question appealed as much to the authorities as to the general public. Of all the names connected with the venture, John Franklin's was foremost in view of his many attempts at it. When, finally, it sank in that his latest expedition was irretrievably lost, his fame increased. A prolonged search by ship after ship for the two at his command, HMS *Erebus* and HMS *Terror*, guaranteed that his name as a tragic hero would live on. The more I read about his fate, the more I wondered why I'd not had the sense to take him on board much earlier.

Just think, I used to say to myself, *if it hadn't been for naughty Mavis, publishers would never have given me the chance to make an exhaustive study of deeply religious Franklin.* I often used to wonder what John would have made of her. She would have shocked him to the core; but she might have found him rather attractive, till he grew too fat, in later years, as if to compensate for nearly dying of starvation on his first Arctic expedition.

When I started, I already knew Franklin had been remembered as 'the man who ate his boots' for attempting to resort to scraps of leather when the food ran out on his first trip, and that he had been Governor of Tasmania, but much else had been a mystery. As the months went by, the whole of his career took shape in my mind. I began by finding him worthy but dull; but I kept coming across enlivening episodes which indicated that a sense of fun could often break through to endear him to most of those with whom he came into contact. My book was to go into considerable detail promoting that particular point, in order to try and alter the public perception of him.

Several times I thought I ought to visit the Arctic if I was going to write about it properly. All very well, but apart from the expense (enormous) there was the problem of how to be sure of finding many of the places reached by my heroes so long ago. I happened to mention my predicament to that brother-in-law by marriage, the former ambassador to the Holy See in whose house in Rome we had once stayed. No amateur when it came to worldly wisdom, he suggested: 'Why not get someone to send you there? It shouldn't be beyond your ingenuity!'

His prod came at the right moment. It had already occurred to me that August 1976 would see the 150th anniversary of Franklin's discovery on his second expedition to Prudhoe Bay, which had subsequently become the largest oilfield in the USA. The probability was that BP, one of the gigantic oil companies working Prudhoe, would be interested to hear that a Franklin family descendant was writing a Franklin book and that they might think it worth their while to assist. I got in touch by tentative letter and their reactions were all that could be desired. They were indeed interested, had already cottoned on to the anniversary and wanted to do something about it. My own background of cooperation with BP as 'King of Das' was known about, which also made things easier. All expenses paid, I accumulated duties: a public service broadcast on TV, a speech to the local Chamber of Commerce, and finally a lecture to the combined learned societies of Anchorage. I wasn't by nature a lecturer. I knew nothing of the tricks of the trade. One talk about the Gulf Sheikhdoms at Oxford and the same at the Royal Central Asian Society was the limit of my experience – yet I would have done anything if it were to get me to the Land of the Midnight Sun.

Having boarded an aircraft at Hamburg, I was to look down on the

North Pole from above. Whereas the South Pole was a point on land which at least stayed where it was, ice which once marked the pole beneath me was forever floating in blocks on a perpetual journey in all directions save to the north. The teasing aspect of my flight was that by crossing the international dateline, we arrived in Alaska an hour before taking off from Germany.

Another small aircraft would fly me, via Fairbanks, into the Arctic Circle. Once in the air I felt it was my duty to record my first sighting of Franklin's Furthest. We might have been over the Western Desert: flat stretches the colour of mud, cracks into polygonal shapes; dark brown gravel and dark brown rocks jutting into an unfrozen sea. Otherwise, Prudhoe reminded me of Saltfleet, the desolate Lincolnshire resort renowned for nothing but mud and samphire – where Franklin was supposed to have seen the sea for the first time in his life.

Icebergs still floated on a partly frozen sea, so it was cold outside when we landed. I was lent a woolly parka and wool-lined over-boots to zip over my unsuitable shoes, then taken to the pilot's room on the helicopter pad. I wanted to compare Captain Back's rough sketch map with their accurate charts (Captain Back having served on several of Franklin's oversea and overland expeditions). My aim was to identify 'Return Reef', the furthest point reached by Franklin's expedition of 1826. I was determined to land on the reef so as to be able to claim that a journey which had taken him a year and a half had taken his descendant only one day. We couldn't quite manage that as it seemed likely that the reef had washed away, but we landed on nearby Stump Island instead. Mission gratifyingly accomplished.

One of the many places I wanted to go was Fort Enterprise on Winter Lake, Franklin's advanced headquarters on his first journey, the scene of death for some and utter misery for all. A man called Alex Gordon was contacted and offered to fly me in his floatplane up to Fort Enterprise the very next day.

Alex was a good-looking, solidly built man in his late thirties. He turned up in an enormous mobile home, capable of sleeping six – just what he needed for his four children, one of whom, Sandy, aged about seven, was coming with us. We drove down to the water airport where a young man called Colin was to be our pilot. We loaded fishing gear and finally ourselves into a small aeroplane on floats, which skimmed along the water before rising into the air over a landscape pockmarked with lakes, pools, streams and patches of water of all shapes and sizes.

We were overflying the course of the Yellowknife River, but there was so much water – in channels, turned into rapids, zigzagging into other lakes – that following it wasn't always easy.

The further north we flew the fewer the pine trees sticking up. Fort Enterprise had been constructed, logically for an advance headquarters, at the far edge of the tree line, after which came the barren lands of the Arctic Circle, lands of low scrub and shrub which in turn would end in tundra and permafrost. The sun sparkled; visibility was near perfect. We passed low over Green Stockings Lake (named after the indigenous Canadian* belle for whose favours two lieutenants, Back and Hood, both of them then only twenty-two years old, had come to blows) and landed on Winter Lake, skimming across boulders grouped by the water's edge. Reaching dry land was complicated by having to leap from boulder to boulder; even then 'dry' hardly described the lakeside areas, where soggy grass was interspersed with low willow and birch, more impenetrable than their like in Scotland. Narrow tracks through the wilderness were explained by the presence of what looked like black seeds scattered along every trail – caribou droppings, no larger than rabbit pellets.

The ground was intensely uneven and bouldery, the hazards half hidden in tufts of springy grass. To move at speed was a perpetual strug-gle. Even for the shortest of journeys we had to walk warily, minding each step; which cast new light on Franklin's frantic footslogging during his first expedition, repeated less fatally on his second.

Even when sitting on the site of Fort Enterprise I found it impossible to reconstruct the Franklin party's experiences realistically. Nothing fitted my preconceptions. Things as I thought they would be had to be replaced by things as they were. Yet what extraordinary days that site had known! Young men from the other side of the world plotting out from it, weighed down by stores, hoping to trace the shores of an uncharted sea. Then, young men forced by the onset of winter to turn and plot back to it, freezing and dying. Young men prepared to quar-rel over comely Green Stockings, yet unwilling to enlist the services of tougher natives in keeping them fed and in good health – a tactic which might just have preserved their lives. Akaitcho, the Chief of the Yellowknives Tribe, had finally rescued some of the party at point of

---

* Roddy used the term 'Red Indian'; as it is now considered pejorative this has been amended.

death, having gladly boiled and eaten not only their boots but rotting caribou hides thrown into a midden months earlier.

Something else that perhaps seems obvious to note was the cold. Even when warm inside with food I was as cold outside as I've ever been in my life, and this was high summer, when the sun shone practically all day. What would the winter be like, lived in perpetual darkness? Franklin's sailors had known nothing of padded parkas. They had worn wool and flannel. They must have felt the cold most terribly.

Yet the sparkle of sunshine on an Arctic summer morning helped me understand what drew men back to the uncompromising realms of the Snow Queen. It was not too fanciful to find it akin to the lure of the barren but scorchingly hot desert. Apparently complete opposites, actually both places had points in common, both exerting a strong magnetic pull in spite – or because – of their obvious disadvantages.

Back in England, a lot of hunting down of material was still required, something my hands were not happy about. When it came to typing I found that the fingers of my right hand grew quickly tired, sometimes so tired that they could hardly press the keys. Nevertheless, I spent a lot of time at the Royal Geographical Society, then at Greenwich, then at the Naval Library at Earls Court. At the library of the Victoria and Albert Museum I was left on my own to leaf through dozens and dozens of copies of *Illustrated London News*, dating back to an era of line-drawings before photography took over. My research led me down many rabbit holes: for example, I learned that scurvy, which all of Franklin's crew suffered from, was said to mimic the worst symptoms of every other disease, including the dreaded syphilis. Once the research was done, all that was left was to write the thing.

My conclusion was that by dying, beset in ice halfway through his cherished North-West Passage, Franklin was doing what he most wanted to do, to his very end. I didn't need to feel regret for his fate. It was the means whereby he escaped the penalty historically awaiting those who have achieved their highest ambition: ennui engendered by finding, like Alexander the Great, no further worlds to conquer.

In Westminster Abbey, his memorial – a panel of a ship beset in mountains of ice and a marble bust (for which, of course, he had been unable to sit) – is hidden away in the Nightingale Chapel, opened only on special request. His famous relation, Alfred, Lord Tennyson, composed a ringing

> *Not here! The white North has thy bones; and thou*
> *Heroic sailor-soul*
> *Art passing on thine happier voyage now,*
> *Towards no Earthly Pole.*

It was erected by Franklin's wife, Jane, who had spent so much of her life since he'd departed arranging for searches to bring him home.*

109

Gian Carlo relapsed and recovered, relapsed and recovered. One terrifying occasion of three fits in as few hours saw him taken to hospital where he had to stay for weeks. At last it seemed to do the trick.

When Nick returned from one of his overseas contracts it threatened to make the situation trickier, but he was under oath never to take the Little Man out on a pub-crawl or encourage him in any way to drink (which for someone like Nick was pretty difficult). 'It's a matter of life or death, it's that important!' I told him. For once he listened to me.

On coming out of hospital, LM's liver was apparently on the point of sustaining irreversible damage, but might still – just – be all right. I was heartened by the news but in dread of the future; hoping for the best, fearing the worst. There were still slips to come, but by September 1977 something seemed to have truly stuck. He came back from a two-week holiday in Italy with his mother where he'd spent three days surrounded by parties and temptation. He said that, when at a low ebb, he thought of Timothy – the man he'd been with when we first met. Timothy had died horribly after trying to kill himself when drunk. LM had thought: *My life is finished if I have a drink.* So he didn't.

*

---

* Roddy would have been excited to note the discovery of the wrecks of HMS *Erebus* and HMS *Terror* in 2014 and 2016 respectively. Readers interested to hear more about Franklin's voyage and the recent discoveries can seek out Michael Palin's book *Erebus*, or for a fictionalised account they can read Dan Simmons's *The Terror* or watch the series by the same name.

One and a half years went by, and Villa Marco had been transformed: what had been a dining-room became a tiled kitchen, the old lean-to kitchen having been pulled down to form a new glass-walled dining-room extended by a conservatory; the garden could be floodlit at the turn of a knob; and a substantial balcony had been created, overlooking Chiswick House grounds. Gian Carlo's sister-in-law called it 'Casa di Bambola', a Doll's House, which was not wide of the mark. A transformed Little Man occupied himself with every detail of its resurgence, keeping it tidy and seeing to the garden. Whenever we quarrelled (which was bound to happen occasionally) it became his bolt-hole, where he could hoist a banner of independence, soberly and responsibly. At length, in case I died before him, I presented him with my half share of the house, whilst his bank-balance, like his investments, surged ever upwards to make him a man of substance.

The Chiswick bees continued to be highly productive, from so much nectar-bearing blossom in their immediate vicinity. The neighbourhood was as idyllic for them as it was for us. That dear little house put out more and more flags, providing much happiness for us both.

So much had happened that I thought I was ready for anything, until what actually happened threw me off guard: a profound shock administered by a telephone call from my nephew, Charles, in the early hours of 26 February 1979. 'I'm afraid I have some very bad news for you,' he said. His parents had been in a car accident up in Scotland. His father, Michael, was killed, and his mother, my sister Genissa, was critically ill in Bridge of Earn Hospital, Ward 15.

The accident had been the result of sheer misadventure, in no way their fault. They'd been staying with Ralph Anstruther at Balcaskie in order to visit their daughter Mary (who was Ralph's god-daughter) at St Andrew's University. Leaving Balcaskie in the evening, they were on their way to Edinburgh to catch the Motorail back to London when a lorry, thundering along in the sleet, ran into them just as they were emerging on to a main road. Michael was killed almost instantly, his aorta ruptured, Genissa severely damaged, with bones broken above and below the knee, amongst other injuries.

My first anxious question was: 'Is her head all right?'

'Yes, apparently. A bang but not a break.'

'Oh, thank God for that!'

I suggested that no one should tell my mother till morning, so as to let her have at least a few more hours' rest. If told, I knew that like me she would be tossing and turning for the remainder of the night, desperately afraid that Genissa was dying. As soon as I judged that there might be some point in ringing the ward sister, I got through to Bridge of Earn and was greatly encouraged by the news: 'She's better! Hardly any longer in critical condition, but still in danger to some degree.' So then I could let Bettina know and calm her fears, all in one.

Fortunately, Genissa had been wearing a seat-belt, which had saved her life. Up till then, I'd been fairly sniffy about seat-belts. Not any longer.

Our family descended on Balcaskie *en masse*. Hospitable Ralph bore the invasion very well, proving, as always, to be such a good friend. He had to put up with us at intervals, because Genissa had to lie in hospital for several weeks, slowly recovering but suffering a mental black-out, unable to remember a thing about the accident either then or in the future. What I most remember from that time was that in the evenings, Ralph's man Gumley, dressed in a kilt, white shirt and black bow-tie, marched up and down playing the bagpipes – his own idea, for in fact he was English.

One paramount factor helped Genissa's recovery: she was determined to attend Charles's wedding in Cornwall at the end of April. He was marrying Margaret, daughter of Sir Leonard Allinson, formerly 'our man in Zambia', subsequently High Commissioner in Kenya.

Having only just learnt how to clamber up steps with her leg in a calliper, she managed the flight to Gatwick with it sticking out on a board. I was able to supply my Ford Granada to pick her up, the fully reclining front seat coming in handy in an emergency. (It wouldn't go flat enough for really comfortable amorous activities, though that had been its (unmentioned) selling point.)

The wedding day drew near. An unhelpful booking-office in London took no notice of my plea to help an invalid. For the outward journey to Cornwall I could arrange nothing better than a Second Class sleeper for two. It involved rolling poor Genissa on to a bottom bunk whilst my mother – at the age of eighty-nine – had to scramble up the ladder to the top. Morvyne took nearly an hour to settle them down with a bed-pan apiece, then joined me in a carriage where a prong sticking out of the seat actually worked a hole in my trousers. But it was no matter; despite all that had happened, we were all there to witness the marriage. It was both a tragic and uplifting reminder that life always went on.

part nine

at the eleventh hour

1980-9

110

1980 swung around. How had that happened, I wondered? I would soon be sixty and, according to my medical notes, was already considered elderly.

The weakness in my right hand had grown dramatically worse. My fingers had lost almost all power of resistance; they might have been made of cloth. I couldn't turn a key in a lock. I could hardly write my signature on a cheque. Useful bee-keeper Dr Tom sent me to see Dr Henson at Maida Vale Hospital, who referred me to the neurosurgeon. They wanted a myelogram of my spine, which would entail a lumbar puncture. The resultant phrases used were 'intervertebral part of the cervix', 'obstruction of the main nerve of the spinal column' and such like, the recommendation being a 'Clowerd's Process' operation, the sooner the better.

Mr Crockard, the neurosurgeon, was an Irishman who'd honed his skills in Belfast amongst those damaged by the IRA. At the end of April he performed on me the operation perfected by Mr Clowerd, an innovative American surgeon who'd come to the fore during the war in Vietnam. The process entailed chopping a piece of bone the size of a cork off my hip and transferring it to the back of my neck to hold the cervical vertebrae apart. It sounded horrendous; but what choice had I got?

Tom came back from a holiday in time to be present in the theatre for the actual scene. 'Quite frightening,' he said afterwards. 'Your *dura mater* took such a hammering I couldn't think it would ever recover. The whole operation was an extraordinary combination of delicacy and sheer brute force. Most impressive!'

I came to, to find myself like an octopus: a drip-feed in my left wrist, a drain from my right hip, and an unexpected drain from the front of my neck. But such success! Within a day I was on my feet, and within a couple of days I was scrambling slowly up and down the ward, trailing my drip and drain lines. I knew how lucky I'd been when I talked to two patients who'd been given 'laminectomies' – discs cut from their lower backs – in Ipswich. Both were still unable to move without assistance, even from bed to chair; neither could walk. I was able to leave hospital after just nine days because Tom could remove the stitches from my hip (which would take much longer to heal than my neck), at which point I was delivered into the arms of Nurse Gian Carlo. He played the part well enough to make me feel that he'd missed his vocation; and meanwhile, there was absolutely no question of him turning to alcohol. He didn't stay on downstairs at night, nor did he come to bed reeking of toothpaste. He was never unreasonably cross; in fact he was marvellous. I was gladder than Pollyanna to find that *my* physical misfortune seemed to have shored up *his* cure more effectively than anything else had ever done. The success of the hour: providing him with someone who needed to be looked after. It was a lovely reversal of roles.

That was not the only effect. From then on, sex took a back seat, a situation made worse after an operation on my prostate some years later.* After that occasion, it took two months and several packets of sanitary towels before incontinence ceased. Then I experimented with masturbation, to find out what would happen before risking any other form of indulgence. The result was hardly encouraging: greatly reduced pleasure, some discomfort, and nothing, nothing else. Lack of sex made me wistful at times. I would once have found it intolerable, but in fact Gian Carlo and I were happier than ever before.

Perhaps I really was 'this elderly patient', as my medical report divulged. It jolted me until I realised how true it was. I *was* now elderly; these niggles were just what was to be expected of an Old Thing tottering on its last-but-one lap towards the grave. Why not admit it? My fingers could wield a pen again, but wouldn't get all that much stronger; so I had to conclude that enough was enough, that I ought to thank God and be content with what could be done rather than worry about what couldn't. But perhaps, with some luck, there were still one or two more adventures to be had in one's sixties, surely?

―――――――

* Before having this operation, Roddy froze his sperm. Having children 'wasn't something I cared greatly about', he wrote. 'Continuing the family line – yes, but not necessarily from *my* loins, when a gaggle of Knights-move children through Genissa already existed. Tom couldn't imagine why I concerned myself with such a thing.' He did it because he 'didn't like to contemplate a forced finality'.

111

The Falklands war in 1982 hardly impinged, so engrossed was I in other affairs. It never occurred to me that our country might be in a position to re-take such remote islands from those who'd stolen them from us. My involvement came through knowing a volunteer officer on the cruise-liner *Canberra*, Nick's son Paddy. The huge ship had been turned round at breakneck speed, ready to leave Southampton on 9 April. The risk to a liner like *Canberra* was great; yet an even more prestigious ship, the *QE2*, was also dispatched to the scene of battle. *Canberra* was sent into the hottest of spots to do the job of standing by for the wounded; *QE2* couldn't be allowed so near danger; but both were at considerable risk. Surprisingly, the gamble was crowned with success; the resultant British achievement astounded our own people almost more than the rest of the world.

When *Canberra* steamed slowly back into Southampton on 11 July, the whole port went mad with joy and relief. Men on board had rigged up banners, messages of encouragement for those waving and cheering on the dockside. Paddy was the originator of a challenging CANBERRA CRUISES WHERE QE2 REFUSES, which made people smile. From another ship, the sight of HRH Prince Andrew, helicopter pilot, stepping down the gangway with a rose between his teeth delighted all onlookers. They felt proud to be British, possibly for the first time since the Second World War.

A closer brush with the Navy came a few years later when I was invited to take the starring role in a Franklin bicentenary service at the Royal Naval College, Greenwich. They wanted me to give a dissertation, which of course I willingly agreed to do rather than have 'my' Sir John fall into other hands. I began boning up on my hero, having already forgotten most of what I'd learned about him in the intervening years since *The Fate of Franklin* was published. I would deliver my address at the Royal Naval Chapel, having preceded this with a trip around the back of the altar to lay a wreath on the Franklin memorial.

The day came and we were all set. With the transporting of my mother in mind, I'd bought a Renault, in 1983, with a boot large enough to take the wheelchair in which I pushed her at innumerable functions. Other parts of the family were making their own way, including Cousin Conrad, grandson of the National Trust Canon and therefore the senior Rawnsley.

Armed with a special permit to allow us to drive through the gates of the Naval College, we set off from little Chelsea at ten o'clock – the 'we' consisting of me, my mother, Morvyne and Gian Carlo, who wouldn't allow me to take a stick, which had been necessary ever since another operation on my spine to relieve pain in my left leg. 'You don't need to look like an old croc!' he said firmly. Nobody argued: his opinions had long been accepted as being as valid as those of any other member of the family, sometimes perhaps more so. He was very smart in a herringbone grey coat and was burnt brown from a holiday in Kenya, where the highlight had been a trip in a balloon over the Masai Mara. Just looking at him, miraculously transformed as he had been for years now, was a tonic to fill my heart with gladness at a time when I was bound to be a bag of nerves.

The address went well, and it prompted me to think about writing once more. I thought of tackling the 'Life' of Canon Hardwicke Rawnsley, to mark the centenary of the National Trust. Hutchinson's were keen on the idea, and so was I, for Hardie had really been the most significant of all the recent ancestors; he deserved a special place in history for his contribution to the welfare of our whole country, ripples of his inspiration spreading out worldwide. However, it turned out there wasn't much to go on, only a slim hagiography from his wife, my great-aunt Eleanor. I also learned that there was a clergyman already engaged in preparing a slim volume about all three founders of the National Trust, and there was a formidable expert, Harry Ruckley, who had been at work on the Canon for over ten years, so far without producing a publishable result.

The more I went into things, the more I turned against the idea. There were no intimate letters from Beatrix Potter to her mentor, though family hearsay suggested that she had had a crush on him as a young girl, and my sympathies towards him were somewhat dashed on learning of his ridiculous persecution of shop-keepers displaying comic-vulgar postcards.

Whilst I waited for new inspiration to hit, I instead began to persuade

Ernest Hofer to come with me to Tibet. For years, Tibet had been a *'Belle Dame sans merci'* holding me in thrall, and not the only one to do so: her past competitor (with Tahiti out of the running) being Angkor, her rival, Easter Island. Famous Austrian mountaineer Heinrich Harrer had made Tibet sound utterly fascinating, whilst humbly presenting himself as an engineer too ordinary to inspire enthusiasm. His book describing seven years in Lhasa as a wartime refugee had provided a unique insight into the workings of the young Dalai Lama's mind and the problems he'd been up against in a monastic theocracy almost unmodified (except by invaders) throughout history.

Even so, Harrer left me wondering why the British Army officer and explorer Francis Younghusband (with whom Roddy Owen had ridden to lift the 'minor siege' of Chitral during his time in India) had been changed for ever as the result of his successful expedition to Lhasa in 1904. Tibet had got under his skin and stayed there, undeniably redirecting his life. Amongst others, there were the writings of Alexandra David-Neel, going into minute detail about Lamas sitting lightly clad in the snow, magicians transporting themselves over vast distances, and mystics exerting hidden influence behind the scenes. If this were all literally true, then Tibet had to be a spiritual powerhouse. Yet it had failed to prevail against the brute force of Chinese invaders – a perplexing paradox. I was keen to learn more.

Ernest persuaded, the only reason for stalling was my mother. She was getting weaker, month by month, but she was holding her own, hoping to live to be 102 like her great-gran, even with some prospect of beating that record. There seemed to be no reason why she shouldn't when, as usual, she put on her long red velvet dress, her 'Boyar' seed-pearl earrings and her 'Egyptian mummy' gold necklace for the traditional family Christmas dinner at Langney Priory.

But then, come the new year of 1987, she was rushed to Eastbourne hospital, having contrived to bang the lid of a commode down on to her leg. The wound, streaming with blood, was dressed and she was sent back home, but the shock had greatly affected her. She developed a pain which moved round her tummy without warning; she had difficulty in breathing and sounded distressed when she did, and was soon rushed to hospital again. We feared the worst at one point when she was coughing and bubbling, yet still she managed to rail at me for not coming to tea, of all things: 'I'm disgusted with you, absolutely disgusted!' And for our next visit a transformation had taken place and she was soon feeling a little better.

A month later and I could seriously consider going to Tibet once more. Following transatlantic consultations with Ernest, the dream at last looked like coming true. Our booking with a tour company called Bales was confirmed for May.

'I don't suppose I'll be here when you get back,' said my mother near the end of March, to which I could only reply: 'Oh, surely you wouldn't do anything so inconvenient?' I made her laugh as I helped her on to the commode, and I noted: 'She's walking round the bed now, helping herself with her hands. She's taking her food herself from a bowl. She's maffling* solids such as pork and bread and butter.'

Yet soon she was asking Dr Boyd: 'Why am I taking so long to recover?'

'Age, my dear,' he answered.

'*Very* tiresome of him!' said Bettina, roused to fury. 'As if I didn't know I'm not getting any younger!' She was looking at me steadily, challenging me to argue, but of course I wasn't about to do any such thing. 'Which reminds me,' she went on, in a voice growing fainter, 'I do want you to go to Tibet. You *must* go! Such a shame, the Dalai Lama won't be there. I only hope I still will be, by the time you get back.'

'I know you will!' I said.

A sigh was her answer.

———

112

A 'Free Tibet' exhibition was to be held in Westminster, by the cathedral: stalls would be selling Tibetan artefacts; there'd be the opportunity to taste Tibetan food; and a talk would be given about the iniquities of the Chinese usurpers. I went expecting a sad experience and got it in full measure. The talk disclosed, had I not already learnt it from Harrer's follow-up *Return to Tibet*, that the Chinese had not only suppressed and destroyed the Buddhist monasteries but had swamped the place with

---

* This is the word Roddy used, though 'to maffle' means 'to mumble' so it isn't correct in this context.

their own nationals, so that the Tibetans were fast becoming a minority in their own country. Nothing that I heard was encouraging, except perhaps that the more people from outside visited Tibet, the greater chance there might be of the world learning about the true horrors of Chinese Communist 'liberation'.

As a result of that dreary evening I learnt where to find the Tibet Agency in London, occupying an unlikely office alongside the railway lines at Olympia. In their wooden hut I was told that the most acceptable present throughout Tibet was a photograph of the Dalai Lama. I therefore bought fifty for Ernest and myself. I was warned to keep quiet and show them to nobody in China, otherwise they'd be confiscated. Not 'might be' but 'would be', with a great fuss being made as well. Accordingly, I put each into a separate buff envelope with cardboard backing, to preserve them intact. I intended to slip them to those whom I considered deserving, whenever feasible.

On 2 May 1987, members of the tour gathered in Heathrow Terminal 4, some nine of us in all. Ernest was searched thoroughly before being let through to the departure lounge, but I was not. In case this were a foretaste of what might happen elsewhere, it made us decide to keep all the Dalai Lama photographs in one of my pieces of baggage.

On our first morning in China we were to go to the Great Wall, or rather, a small 'showcase' part of it, restored and rebuilt to within an inch of its life – a tourist trap if ever there was one. The talking-point about the Great Wall was its length, significant enough to be seen from the moon; but the splendid originality of that feature could hardly be inferred from the tiny section over which we (and thousands of others) were being encouraged to clamber. Five minutes would have been enough for a visitor to reach that conclusion.

Eventually, after lunch, we were allowed to go on to see something really interesting, the Ming Tombs, which burst upon us as a complete surprise – a huge pagoda-pavilion with large high red cedarwood pillars and an ornate 'Chinese' tiled roof, brilliantly coloured. In the large pavilion there were exhibits in cases, one being an elaborate jewel set with crystals and cat's-eyes. I noted later: 'Tara instantly said she felt the power coming out of it through the glass.'

Tara was one of two bulky vegans on the tour with us. They were not just what might be called 'New Age Believers', they actually ran an institute with the Buddhist name of 'Shambhala', suitably sited outside

Glastonbury, that English centre of alternative spirituality. 'Tara' and 'Orion' were the names by which they wished to be known, so of course that was how we always addressed them. They dealt in esoteric remarks combined with utmost seriousness. Once one got used to that, their ideas could be seen to follow a pattern – whether logical or not, it was up to the listener to decide. They were certainly fuelled by their convictions, which made them interesting regardless of whether the remarks they came out with could be taken as literal truth or purest baloney. We were lucky to have them on the tour, because they saw most things in a completely different light from the rest of us – which could be very entertaining, if not always in the way they might have chosen.

Next day, the Forbidden City, so called because formerly no uninvited stranger had been allowed so much as to set eyes on it. Thousands of Chinese were thronging the once-sacred pavilions, their presence a testimony to a determination to dissociate themselves from Red Guard excesses.

In the vast Tiananmen Square we joined a queue of dark-blue-coated Chinese shuffling towards the tomb of Chairman Mao. As 'Honoured Foreign Guests' we were ushered towards the head of the queue, near the mausoleum steps, saving at least another hour of shuffling. There we were shushed, and so contagious is that sort of discipline that some of us even began acting like prefects and shushing others.

Up the outer steps and past a bank of trees and shrubs we were confronted by the strange spectacle of a more than lifesize stone man sitting in a stone armchair of thirties design – it might have been made of uncut moquette with a loose cover over it. Behind that enlarged effigy of the deceased there was a painted backdrop of a vague and cloudy landscape. Beyond and to either side, the queue-line split before entering a dimly lit area leading into the high hall where a Thing lay, draped in a dark red piece of cloth, in a glass case; a Thing treated with preservatives in order to sustain an illusion that it was merely in a state of suspended animation: the puffy, yellowing corpse of Chairman Mao. The face protruding at one end looked rather large and as if made of rubber, pale yellow eyes open, pinched and wrinkled.

Just what *were* the Chinese people thinking as they filed past that profoundly shocking monument to human vanity? Power was still throbbing out on to the hall, the power being generated by the very powerlessness of the little creatures in dark blue who were doing the filing-past.

*

We were soon on our way – our unbelievable way – to magical Tibet. The fact that we would be flying in proved how much things must have changed, for when an American aircraft had force-landed outside Lhasa during the war, the crew had narrowly escaped a lynching by Tibetans outraged that anything other than a bird should dare skim the sky above the Potala, a zone of heaven sacred to their Dalai Lama. We would merely be a few out of the many descending, uninvited, through the air on a people robbed by Chinese conquerors of their power to protest. Our presence might only be considered worth tolerating if we could say or do some small thing to alleviate the lot of people facing dilution or even dispossession in their own country.

All the same, and with all that in mind, I couldn't help thinking, as we boarded the Boeing 707 which was to take us to the heartland of a God-King in exile: *shame on us, oh shame!*

———

113

'LAdies and gentlemen, MAY I have your attention for ONE MOment, please!' said our tour guide Patricia Hallett in her clear voice, standing very erect and waving a paper – her standard method of calling for silence, which worked as efficiently in Tibet as elsewhere. She was announcing that Customs could be very thorough in their search for subversive – i.e. pro-Tibetan – material. Duly I queued behind Ernest, whose luggage again underwent scrupulous examination, whilst mine was simply nodded on. The first hurdle had been surmounted. Now it would be up to us to distribute pictures of the Dalai Lama as discreetly as possible.

I myself presented a woebegone appearance. Our plane landed at 10 a.m., and on stepping down from gangway to ground, I burst into tears. Nowhere else on earth had I ever done such a thing. Perhaps it was because of some special quality of sparkle in the air at an altitude of 12,000 feet; or perhaps I was being affected by the 'Younghusband Syndrome'. Tara and Orion noticed at once – noticed and approved. I went several rungs higher in their estimation, presumably because my behaviour could be interpreted as a recognition that I was returning to a land familiar from a previous incarnation, rather than visiting it for a first time. So strange was the emotion surging through me that the idea didn't seem as fantastic as it might have done earlier. I soon recovered, aided, as always, by an intense curiosity about new surroundings.

The first glimpse of Lhasa was bound to cause shock. The Chinese had succeeded in making the holy city resemble one of their own ugly modern towns, full of white concrete blocks of apartments, redeemed only by lines of trees planted along the roads. Nearly all the traffic seemed to consist of trucks and bicycles. Not until our minibus turned towards the Lhasa Hotel did we see, in the distance, the Dalai Lama's palace, riding high on its hill – unforgettable. When the Potala wasn't white, it was a curious very dark Chinese red, and its golden domes shone in the brilliant sunlight. It was partly like a stranded whale and partly like an acropolis, and whatever it was, at first sight it was marvellous.

Patricia discovered that there was a 'courtesy bus' going into the centre of Lhasa at four o'clock. I insisted on coming with her, even though it meant leaving a worn-out Ernest asleep. I, too, was tired, but also uplifted. I *had* to see the Potala without delay; the imperative was absolute. Over the years, I'd learnt better than to question such urges. Irrational as they had sometimes seemed to be, very often they'd turned out to contain something of great value, well concealed – one aspect of the 'Jewel within the Lotus', no less; a prompting of the Divine. I might be short of breath in the rarefied air, but that was no excuse for inaction in the face of clear instructions.

The bus dropped us outside the Potala and tootled off into the distance. We were left looking at the Dalai Lama's sacred stronghold towering above, protected from the main road by a fringe of small lodge-like buildings. We could do no more than look, because only then did we discover that the Potala was closed for the afternoon. The bus wouldn't be returning until after six. We were stranded.

I grabbed hold of two passing strangers who looked like Americans. In fact they were Austrian and didn't know when the Potala would be open. They said that they were on their way to a tiny monastery, close at hand, called Palalubu, which was built into the side of a cliff opposite the massive rock of the Potala. The gap between the two establishments had originally been filled by Lhasa's West Gate, shut each evening in the old days against anyone failing to reach it before closing-time. The Chinese had torn the barrier down to allow their trucks to roar through, night and day. The monastery formed part of 'Medicine King Hill', so called because there'd formerly been a School of Tibetan Medicine at its summit (also destroyed by the Chinese, who'd replaced it with a TV mast).

Palalubu, I read in my guidebook, had been founded in the seventh century by one of the wives of King Songsten Gampo ('Songzamgambu'). Another of his wives, the Chinese Princess Wen Cheng, was given credit for having founded the great Jokhang Temple nearby, whilst he himself had ordered the building of the earliest Potala. Palalubu was approached by a dusty, rocky path where children were playing. Dogs lay about peacefully, not bothering to bark, looking in fairly good condition, though unkempt. It was also a pleasant surprise to find any monastic property at all surviving. Above a first cave of shrines there was an antechamber where monks sat, smiling, on some of the filthiest rags imaginable, chanting as they formed *tsampa* (barley-meal) and yak butter into sculptured shapes. There were no more than a handful of monks when there should have been crowds, but there were also a few nuns in similar rough brown garb, barely distinguishable from the men.

We were taken through to where there was a central column of rock carved with four statues of the Lord Buddha, and round the walls, sculpture in relief, including a statue of Songsten Gampo. Yak butter lamps were burning, smoking as they did so. An ancient Tibetan came up with a jar of butter, and one of the monks spooned it into a pannikin, where it began melting into the liquid already there. The smell of yak butter wasn't too bad, but as the only light came from it (and heat), the floors were black and slippery with it, and so was every ledge on every wall – so it wasn't exactly easy going.

The whole little monastery was wonderful and bizarre, equipped with an enormous treasury of small objects. Huge drums inscribed with the Buddhist OM MANI PADME HUM could be twirled vigorously by anyone passing. I did it the wrong way round at first, until a wagging head (face still smiling) gently warned me to think again. Bizarre and wonderful; but, oh, how tired I was, and how my legs hurt! I felt guilty, too, because they *all* asked for pictures of the Dalai Lama and I hadn't thought of bringing any with me. It meant that I had to promise to come back better equipped, which committed me to returning – in itself an added blessing.

*

A day or so later we set off for Tashilumpo in Shigatse, seat of the Panchen Lama, who in former times had been considered to exercise greater spiritual – though not actual – power than the Dalai Lama. The Panchen had tried to come to an accommodation with the Chinese invaders, incurring the wrath of his followers, but had eventually surprised them all by turning out to be not quite the traitor to his country which most people had supposed.*

The monastery was huge, and spread out along the bottom of a hill, mounting upwards in browns and whites and golds, and its beams were a 'fairground' mass of colours. For a first time, we were confronted by monks actually monking. In one of the many chanting halls they were sitting in rows facing each other, brown-robed; whilst in the middle and to one side sat a supremo on a kind of wooden bed-throne covered in dark-coloured cloths. Suddenly some of them interrupted their chanting to pull out long horns and blow on them discordantly, whilst others beat drums or ting'd away on hand-bells – with enthusiasm, with widening grins. It was undeniably exciting.

The chanting-room walls were covered in paintings, in front of which were all sorts of statuettes of Buddhas or of Lamas and little objects like pagodas made of *tsampa* and yak butter, coloured like Daz roses. There was a big white Tara flanked by two green Taras. Such a lot of decoration made it impossible to find it vulgar. The goddess Tara was described in the guidebook as being 'the most beloved of all female deities. Special protectress and saviour of the Tibetan people.' Green Tara was associated with the night, White Tara with the day. Her special feature was to have seven eyes distributed here and there, on face, hands and feet; so *our* Tara had a lot to live up to.

Tashilumpo's largest statue was of the Maitreya Buddha, eighty-six feet high, sitting on a lotus throne in the 'teaching' position. One of Maitreya's fingers was four feet long. How such a glorious background

---

* Roddy is referring here to the 70,000 Character Petition. The Panchen Lama had publicly supported the Chinese government in 1959 (the year the Dalai Lama had fled to India), which was when the Chinese appointed him the chairman of the Preparatory Committee for the Tibet Autonomous Region. However, in 1962, after a tour through Tibet, the Panchen Lama authored a document detailing the abuses the People's Republic of China had enacted against the country. This eventually led to his imprisonment in 1964; at this point he was only twenty-six years old. He wasn't released for another thirteen years, and was under house arrest for a further five, when he was considered to have been re-educated and allowed to serve as Vice Chairman of the National People's Congress.

of religious clutter had survived the onslaught of the Red Guards was a mystery, for according to Heinrich Harrer's second book, there'd been wholesale destruction. If so, the monks must have been remarkably efficient at hiding their treasures until such time as they could safely be put on display again.

Monks could be met walking about, carrying scrolls with leather tops and bottoms, each bundle bound up in faded yellow cloth; but no novices were to be seen undergoing instruction. We assumed that the Chinese had wielded the big stick, restricting such teaching to a handful only, in order to claim that they were showing religious tolerance, when in reality . . .

There was a 'free market' in Shigatse – meaning, as far as I could make out, simply 'a market'. Without asking its age, I bought an amulet, a hollow box of thin silver pricked out with coloured symbols, the main one a *gdugs* (umbrella), an assurance of protection against an attack by eagles. Its usefulness didn't end there. By inference, 'protection' could be extended to include anything falling from the sky: a bolt of lightning, lava from an eruption, even a bomb. As I only discovered later, the amulet's symbols also included a Banner of Victory (over ignorance and death), a Dharma Wheel (for the unity of all things, represented by Sakyamuni himself), and an Endless Knot, symbolising the unity of the whole, hence the illusory character of time.

Since no eagle has yet swooped, and since time, for me, has retained the illusory character it will always possess, it must be assumed that the amulet has proved its efficacy. Well worth coming all the way to Tibet for that alone.

114

The fourteenth of May was Oracle day, when we were to visit Drepung Monastery, once the largest in the country, with four Tantric Colleges and 10,000 monks, now dwindled to a mere 600. At Drepung, the State Oracle used to occupy the small Nechung Temple, which had been sacked and looted by the Chinese as being a fountain-head of patriotic superstition.

The Oracle's main function, formerly, had been to go into a state of trance and advise how to find the next Dalai Lama, but it had served other purposes equally well. In the shape of an elaborately dressed doll, crown on head, open-mouthed, it could be seen (and consulted for 5 yuan – less than £1) in a chapel at the back of the Nuosele College's chanting hall.

I wondered what sort of questions some of our party would be putting to the Oracle. I half thought Tara and Orion might seek to turn the tables by telling the Oracle *its* future. My own past contacts with Oracles had been mixed. The most illumination had come from an encounter in Siwa Oasis, when, as a young Flying Control Officer, I'd asked the Oracle of Jupiter Ammon whether we would get back to Mersa Matruh in one piece. That pronouncement had been an uncompromising 'Wait and see!' During a lifetime of adventure all over the world I'd done exactly that, so could hardly complain.

The next day was at last the day we'd all been waiting for: a visit to the Potala. We had passed and re-passed it, gazing up at its towering, backward-leaning splendour, once known only to a privileged few in the Western world. We drove through a gate of ornate wood and debouched into an enclosed courtyard, once the Dalai Lama's stables. A small doorway to the right led through a high, narrow passage into wider halls which had the feeling of being the servants' entrance. We were led on through a bewildering warren, a small number of the rooms said to number more than a thousand.

I was afflicted by something more sinister than simple bewilderment: the atmosphere of everything seemed dead, compared with Tashilumpo or Drepung. There was nowhere we came across monks chanting, drums banging, bells tinkling or horns blowing. It was soul-less, as if the spirit had departed, leaving nothing but a Thing preserved as artificially as the corpse of Chairman Mao in Tiananmen Square. On entering a small chapel dominated by an image of the White Tara flanked by the Green Tara, I put half a yuan into a bowl and asked *our* Tara to take out a small handful of barley grains as a gesture to ward off the evil which seemed to have settled into the very structure of the desecrated place.

Up and up we climbed, further and further away from the prison at the lowest level, the 'Cave of Scorpions', hollowed out of the rock below the soot-blackened cells where monks and servants had formerly lived. Our way was never by means of stairs but by very, very steep steps like a stepladder with six-inch-wide rungs, bound with slippery brass and with wooden handrails on either side in the form of poles bound with more brass. It was surprising to think that everyone in every monastery, however infirm, had only been able to go up and down by such a precarious method; and normally, of course, the rungs would have been slippery with yak butter. My shooting-stick was in continuous use as a prop, yet even then I had great difficulty in keeping my balance, because it kept living up to its name by shooting sideways on smears of dairy fat.

Nearing the roof, the Potala changed in character, becoming airy, even luxurious, with courts and little gilded pagodas, upper roofs shining with gilded emblems. On the outside, a broad flight of paved steps confronted a great bare expanse of wall, the 'Thangka Wall' for displaying huge pictorial banners, messages to the faithful, sometimes simply teaching aids. From that point the Potala had been cleverly constructed to lean inward.

At the end of the tour I reflected that we had obtained some idea of how those rows of windows – outlined in faded blue, each with its over-lintel of carved brown wood – looked against walls of dazzling white, walls of terraces sloping up towards the dark brown mass of the upper Potala, and nothing could dilute the excitement of seeing such an extraordinary place from the outside. But woe, oh woe! Inside, it was as if a piston were continually hammering home the message of Chinese domination: 'We are the masters now!' With my hand on my heart, I would never wish to return to the Potala unless to see a Dalai Lama once more installed, breathing life into those cold rooms.

That evening, I was glad to be shaken out of despondency by being asked, along with everyone else, to the suite occupied by Tara and Orion. They had procured cakes and wine from the restaurant, but instead of being handed those at once, we were invited to sit down. Orion then began talking in an unusually low voice, and I wondered what was coming. In fact, we were being told what to do in order to go on a psychic journey. The first instruction was that we must all shut our eyes, then place the right hand on the heart. After that, we had to imagine a golden ball slowly descending from the head to the heart, culminating in a swelling of the heart and an expansion of love.

To be sitting alone in a room with eyes closed is one thing; doing it in a group, quite another. The pressure exerted by other people conforming creates an atmosphere of persuasion, even downright coercion. My critical sense went into overdrive as I waited for what was to come.

Orion began by asking questions; our answers had to be how we would rate ourselves on a scale of one to ten. I didn't want to give offence or spoil the group fun by not entering into the spirit of things, so I prepared myself to be honest, on the whole, as long as that wouldn't involve me in embarrassing disclosures; after all, it wasn't as though we were at a session of Al-Anon.

Tara then joined in with: 'Do you feel you are *really* here?' To which I awarded myself ten.

Next, we were asked to put ourselves into a bottle and answer where we thought we were. 'Outside the bottle, and still ten,' I said.

Finally, we were each asked to name the person in the group for whom we felt a particular affinity. Patricia's reply was a diplomatic 'All of you.' There was a slight surprise when a Scotsman cited Ernest; everyone had expected him to name his companion from Berwick-on-Tweed. When it came to my turn, an inspired flash of irreverence made me choose a timid middle-aged Eleanor, at which there was an audible gasp and just the suggestion of a titter – as I'd intended. Ernest silently opened and closed his mouth. I had evidently broken a spell; but also as intended, the effect was no more than temporary.

We were then switched to something more serious: Orion leant forward and began telling the Scotsman that his son, who'd died three weeks earlier, was still walking beside him; that the links binding them together had to be broken by a conscious effort of love. At which, the Scotsman started to cry. I was somewhat disconcerted, till realising that the man was actually lapping up every drop of the attention being directed on to him, as if he'd been given a licence to weep in front of us all.

When it came to my turn, I was asked to accept that my mother would be passing away within a month of our return to England and not to be too sad about her release at such a ripe old age. Although normally easily moved to tears, those words failed to make me feel like crying. Then and there I resolved that my mother would *not* die within the month, but would survive, if only to prove that my powers of divination were stronger than theirs, as I genuinely felt them to be.

I noted in my diary: 'E and I discussing it afterwards agreed that it had been a moving and (we had to believe) sincere performance, but that it also showed colossal cheek and was highly embarrassing.'

As a young boy, Ernest had been taken to a Revival Meeting and had even then distrusted the way in which certain people came, quivering, up in front of the congregation to announce that they were 'saved'. No wonder we were such firm friends.

However, by the end of the trip I was much moved, and some of my snap judgements had to be modified. I had to concede that both Tara and Orion had practised overflowing sympathy to a point where they had brought it to a fine art. The fact that I was more immune than most to that process didn't imply any fault in them; they were fulfilling a need felt desperately by those to whom the solaces of a conventional religion meant nothing.

What was it like for people who, having little regard for the Christian God, eagerly reached for the comfort offered by Tara and Orion? On departing from an attachment to the Society of Friends I myself had once been inclined to agnosticism, whilst yearning for consolation, so I could speak from experience. I could also claim to have some under-standing of the ins and outs of conversion, by casting my mind back and recalling a time in the desert with Sheikh Shakhbut. Those calls to prayer, answered five times a day, that frequent, fervent exposure to Islam, had paradoxically helped bring me into the Church of England fold – where, by the Grace of the Good Shepherd, I'd stayed.

———

115

I returned home to Gilston Lodge via Heathrow, to be greeted by a radi-ant Little Man on the stairs. As always, it was good to be back in such a loving home, completed by our new dog Silver delightedly leaping up at me. Our beloved little Marco had died of cancer aged eight. Gian Carlo had wanted another pet as soon as possible: not so that we could forget Marco – we never would – but because his going had created such a gap in our lives. A brown 'sable rough collie' had been his choice and the result was Silver (so called even though the pup was golden).

I was soon on the telephone to Langney to hear my mother telling me in a strong voice exactly how she was getting on – a good sign. Until then, all I had known was that things were going 'as well as could be expected for Mung', having spoken to Morvyne whilst away.

'As well as could be expected' – code-words for a gloomy prospect. She was having continued difficulty in swallowing solids, so was being fed on slush of all sorts, which kept her going, but little more. Even liquids were becoming a problem. I travelled up and down between

London and Langney in order to do my share of the nursing, though of course the brunt fell on Morvyne, there all the time.

The real day of reckoning wasn't to come until 15 October, when I happened to be in London. I rang up and was taken aback by a dreadful tone in Morvyne's voice. Mung had been very sick and might normally have been sent back to the hospital, but this time there was no question of that. I arrived at midday to find an emergency nurse in the room and another booked for the afternoon.

It was pouring with rain; the wind was getting up ever more strongly, till it was gusting at incredible speed. I read my mother one of her favourites from Tennyson's *The Princess*: 'Blow, bugle, blow, set the wild echoes flying'; then let my voice dwindle to a whisper at 'Answer, echoes, dying, dying, dying'. Eventually I retired to bed, all the windows tightly shut.

At some unearthly hour there came a great crash outside and the whole house shuddered. Drawing back the curtains, I saw that the mulberry tree which Bettina had planted shortly after we came to the Priory had heeled over immediately below my window. She'd been so proud of that tree, saying: 'It will be here long after I'm gone.'

Watery morning light revealed the extent of the devastation: two trees down across the drive; fallen branches everywhere; the poles carrying live electricity cables swinging precariously against the evergreens at the side of the barn, flashing whenever they made contact. Each flash was accompanied by a roar of frustration from the hot water/central heating boiler down in the kitchen, as it automatically switched the oil-fired system off and on, off and on. To have that happening just when our invalid was feeling the cold most was thoroughly unwelcome.

A poor day all round, though my mother seemed to know little about the storm until Genissa rang up to say that her giant pine had crashed, completely blocking the road from Hole Farm to the outside world. Her cellar had flooded, and Charles and David could do no milking because she had no electricity at all. It had been undoubtedly the worst storm in living memory.*

---

* This was the Great Storm of 1987, when hurricane-force winds battered south-east England and parts of northern France, killing twenty-two. The storm is also famous because the BBC's weatherman Michael Fish had said earlier in the day, 'Apparently a woman rang the BBC and said she heard there was a hurricane on the way. Well, if you're watching, don't worry, there isn't.'

We read her more poetry, her lips moving as she tried to join in with Tennyson's *Maud*. But next day, even poetry couldn't rouse her. Genissa came over, reproachful and in tears because the nurse when rung up had used that dread phrase 'as well as could be expected' after saying that Morvyne was asleep (she was) and that I was out (I wasn't). I wrote in my diary: 'Here we three are and we can't do anything.'

She died two days later. On television there was a programme about the Jews in concentration camps. It quite stopped my crying, when I thought how much love surrounded her end in contrast.

Up in the Monks' Dormitory, where so many of my books had been written, I set to work on the funeral eulogy, which I read out in the chapel downstairs to a crowd of family and friends. I ended with my right thigh black and blue from pinches which had helped prevent an unseemly breakdown, the sharp pain caused by each pinch keeping me on my toes. It seemed axiomatic to me – though clearly not to others – that excessive sorrow, like excessive joy, should not be inflicted on strangers in public. I had long disliked the way winners danced about, punching the air, shooting fountains of champagne over themselves and others. Equally, I distrusted the TV interviews where the bereaved wept uncontrollably before an audience of millions. Both ways of carrying on seemed to me to come under the heading of 'showing off', however genuinely inspired. I had written my eulogy as a conscious work of art, devised for Bettina, not in order to draw attention to my private woe. I gave it all I'd got for her sake.

116

My mother's illness had stimulated me to think of writing. She had urged me on, reverting to the subject at intervals, lamenting her own missed opportunities. After she died, a chance friendship encouraged me further.

In the past, Dr Tom had often spoken about his patient, 'Tops' Vestey, of the meat and shipping family, whose letters he referred to as examples of extreme felicity. Tom finally introduced us at Gilston Lodge. One look at her and I was at her feet. I found her delightful; intelligent, and with an instantly recognisable quirkish sense of humour. We talked of this and that, and then she happened to mention the 4th of June at Eton. 'No show on earth was ever as good as those fireworks following the procession of boats,' she said. It put the germ of an idea into my mind.

'She rather took to you,' Tom told me later.

'Not half as much as I took to *her*, I'll be bound!' I said.

Our meeting was followed by a particularly charming letter, in which I'd become 'Dear Roddy (May I?)'.

Danny Danziger had written a book about the old school: *Eton Voices*, published by Viking. As an Old Harrovian, he had persuaded a number of Old Etonians to talk frankly about their schooldays. When Tops thoroughly recommended it, I got hold of a copy and found that the actor Patrick Macnee – 'Brutus' to my 'Cinna, a Poet', at Summer Fields – was one of the contributors, boldly mentioning his mother's lesbian affair with 'the heir to Dewar's Whisky'. Another contributor was Sir Ranulph Twisleton-Wykeham-Fiennes, deploring his prettiness as a boy; and some forty assorted others. Each had a different point of view: some sad, some funny, some bolshie, all entertaining. But none came near saying what I would have said, had I been asked.

Why don't I write a chapter of my own? I wondered. *Just for interest, nothing more.* Which I did, finally breaking in the word-processor function of the Smith Corona.* And then I thought: *Tops might like to see my bit.* So I gave it to Tom for when he saw her next.

My reward was a letter on a par with those which she'd previously sent Tom: succinct; appreciative in no more than a mildly critical way; amusing; intelligent. She'd particularly liked the main excuse for sending her the article, a detailed description of the 4th of June fireworks. 'Do PLEASE send me some more, about other parts of your life!'

She had recently been diagnosed as suffering from cancer of the throat. She was too old to be operated on, but not too old for radiotherapy, by which it was hoped that her affliction could be at least slowed down. The least I could do was provide her with fresh pages of manuscript, which stimulated me to rack my brains to remember

---

* In the mid-eighties Smith Corona released a typewriter which had an electric spelling function, which is probably the machine Roddy is referring to here.

episodes which she might find entertaining. To follow the Eton fireworks I produced a blow-by-blow account of my first *affaire* with Peryl,
the Marchesa di Montagliari (complicated, as it was, by having to be
conducted from the unlikely *venue* of a camp for conchies).

She wrote: 'Thank you so much for the wicked little story, which
I enjoyed enormously. Haven't you got any more? Couldn't you make
a little collection of naughty little short stories and print them? I wish
you would. There is a real need of such a thing in these unlikely
times.'

We established right from the start that she enjoyed reading details,
however frank, of my behaviour, so long as they were true and unex-
aggerated – '*sans blague*', as she put it. Her particular outlook on such
aspects provided me with what I most needed – parameters; limits set
only by taste, not by injunctions to record what others might call 'proper
conduct'. When I sent her my next piece (about life with the von Machs
and the Siemers in Germany, pre-war) I was consciously writing for
her – not something I'd ever done in my life for anyone else, though of
course I'd always had to bear publishers in mind. She wrote back: 'You
have a very enviable way of making it feel as if it wasn't a récherche
perdue at all, but just the other day. I enjoyed it so much, do please go
on – more and more . . .'

She often came out with an amusing slant on the people I mentioned:
'I'm fascinated by the number of ladies you met who were apparently
impregnated by contact with their friends' or husbands' bath-water.
(Was it a habit of those times not to run a clean bath?)'

Then at my mention of the pianist Irene Scharrer, in whose Holland
Park flat I'd stayed with her son, Ian Lubbock: 'My mother had a very
warm attachment, well a love affair really with Irene, and she (Irene)
moved into our very large house almost personally with her own suite
of rooms for several years.'

Her random remarks were addictive enough to develop a craving
in any writer to whom they were addressed – balm to the soul. She
followed them up with an intense, uncensorious interest in my moral
development, which I was trying to reveal, step by step, in successive
chapters. Her letters were followed up by sessions of discussion, going
into minute detail, each letter being the excuse for a visit of literary
dissection, whilst she herself grew progressively weaker, propped up
in bed. As I wanted more chats, I had to write more – Tops offered no
alternative.

It was helpful beyond imagining; and the matter didn't end there. Very soon, my disjointed bits and pieces were demanding to be set in a larger pattern, like hexagons of random material carefully selected to make up a patchwork quilt. They had to be rewritten and placed in context, with a timescale in mind. It didn't happen all at once, by any means; but it did happen in the end, as ponderously as a ship edging towards a quayside. Tops had spurred me on, not just to write, but *how*: the style, and the manner in which I could deal with things normally extremely hard to say.

Tops was my Egeria. For the first time in a too-often half-truthful career, I was hunting for the truth, wherever it might lead. I thanked God for Tops.

Soon I was 'Darling Roddy', to which my response was to work the harder; till increasing weakness, then death, took her untimely away, leaving me, less than halfway through my labours, to continue on the lines which she had so perspicaciously laid down.

Even though she knew that I wasn't short of money, she left me £1000, having said that she intended doing so as a reward: 'For a new machine, perhaps, when you need one.'

————

117

Perhaps it was because I'd been writing down old stories for Tops, but at night I kept finding myself swooping back over the years, obsessed with Tahiti, wondering whether an octogenarian Turia could still be alive. I even telephoned my American friend Dale McClanahan (the heiress I'd met all that time ago through James Norman Hall) to see if she'd heard anything on return visits to Tahiti.

Then in early 1989, after a lapse of thirty-three years, another old flare lit up my horizon. On 15 February, I had written to His Highness Sheikh Zayed, Ruler of Abu Dhabi and President of United Arab Emirates, as follows:

Dear Zayed,
I am writing to sympathise with you at the death of your brother Shakhbut.

When I was his poet, back in 1955, I got to know him very well. Indeed, that was the time when I got to know you, too, at Buraimi. I have never forgotten those days, when I had so much to learn and when things were just starting to change. I was actually sitting with Shakhbut on the day when Tim Hillyard sent in a message to say that B.P. had decided to start sample-taking out in the sea beyond Das Island. I remember his gravity, his refusal to be overwhelmed with joy at the prospect; and I thought that he was entirely right to behave like that.

I have so many happy memories of him – seeing him in a London hotel, going with him to look at a boat; and finally a short visit, not so long ago, when he told me I'd put on too much weight. His sense of humour was always idiosyncratic and extraordinary (this remark will be difficult to translate into Arabic, but it is what I felt about him).

As it happens, my house in Gilston Road is only a few yards from your house in The Boltons. I would be delighted if you would call upon me when you are next in England. It would be such a pleasure to reminisce about those days, so long past, when I was with you and dear Shakhbut, hunting the Hubara in the desert beyond Buraimi.

Once again, let me repeat that my sympathies go out to you on this very sad occasion.

I had last seen dear old Shakhbut in 1984, when we'd met at the Churchill Hotel. He'd been deposed in favour of Zayed back in 1966, after Abu Dhabi had indeed come into money because of oil, as had been hoped – but then Shakhbut had refused to spend any of the income. When I saw him, he'd invited me back to Abu Dhabi where he was still allowed to live (a really odd state of affairs). I wished I'd taken him up on the offer, not realising that was the last time we would see one another.

The letter received in reply came from Khamis Bin Butti Al Rumaithy, Director of the President's Office, saying that His Highness the President was 'very touched'. It continued: 'H.H. instructed me to tell you that he looks forward to meeting you and to extend to you on his behalf an invitation to come to the Emirates to see him in Abu Dhabi.'

Hooray! Hooray! Through a friend, I was quickly reintroduced to that old acquaintance I'd met in Bahrain who had tried to put me off a trip to Buraimi, Edward Henderson. Edward had written a book with the title *This Strange, Eventful History* about his experiences with Sheikhs

and oil companies in the Middle East and he was working (as archivist)
for Sheikh Zayed in Abu Dhabi. I wrote congratulating him on his
book, asking if he'd be at his post during my stay as it would be lovely
to see him. Back came his reply: 'It will be nice to see you. You won't
recognise anything and I expect I look a bit different too.'

I also set about composing a few poems in case Zayed were to
expect celebratory verses from me. I remembered the hawking expeditions, deep into the desert, when I'd got to know the brothers so
well. Zayed might like to be reminded of those days of informality,
before oil utterly transformed his life. The trouble was, after so many
years the iron of my poetic streak had grown rusty with neglect; I'd
have to hope he didn't ask, but at least I had something in my back
pocket if he did.

Important matters concluded, I packed my green safari suit, last
worn at my niece Mary's wedding, and I even managed to lay hands
on an old black cummerbund, in case that still formed part of the 'Gulf
Rig' for formal evening wear. Otherwise, I required little beyond my
usual short-sleeved shirts of terylene and cotton, presents for Zayed
and Edward, and plenty of dollars to use as tips, because they came in
denominations more convenient than pounds. As I had space, I also took
a packet of All Bran, just in case.

My memory of Abu Dhabi's airport was of a flat surface of baked
mud, a wooden hut used by Gulf Aviation, a wind-sock and little else.
As for Abu Dhabi itself, it had been a scattering of *barasti* huts, a few
merchants' buildings including the BP office, Sheikh Shakhbut's fort –
and again, very little else. Arriving over that once semi-desolate spot I
was astonished by the sight of brilliant lights stretching out for miles in
every direction except into the sea; lines of yellow, red, blue and white
lights, suggesting the presence of a town as impressive as any in the
West. Edward Henderson's 'you won't recognise anything' had become
a statement of fact before we even touched down.

It was then 10.30 p.m. and I was tired, but not too tired to gasp at
the extraordinary airport buildings. I felt as if I were in another world,
as indeed I was, a world of the future; not exactly to my taste, but
fantastic.

I was collected from the airport by an Indian man in a red head-
dress, saying that he'd been sent by 'Foreign Affairs' to fetch me. We
drove along a wonderful four-lane highway, lit by thousands of coloured
bulbs, surviving evidence of Abu Dhabi's National Day (their eighteenth

anniversary of independence – from us). That was why it had looked so dazzling from the air. Cascades of lights all along the streets made everything look like Christmas. It made me think of Gian Carlo: he always went in for intensive decorations; not only looping coloured ruched paper and glass baubles over pictures, dressing a Christmas tree and so on, but on the front of the cottage in Chiswick he would create such an original outdoor display, supported by concealed wires, that complete strangers would ring the bell to comment and admire. Similarly, here there were lights everywhere, illuminating palm trees, ashoka trees and grass – an absolute transformation.

After some twenty minutes the driver, Rashid, pointed to an enormous modern hotel, set amidst greenery on a slight rise. 'The Intercontinental, very good!' he said.

'Is it the best hotel in Abu Dhabi?'

'Oh yes!'

To my surprise, he started driving up to it, and only then did I realise that I would be staying the night there. I would much rather have been in an Arab house, for preference in an old-fashioned one, but I knew that I was sighing for something gone with the wind. I was shown into a standard, comfortable room, with TV and air-conditioning, masculine mahogany furniture and modernistic abstract picture on one wall. From a huge window I had a panoramic view of the streets and lights of an all-new Abu Dhabi. It rather made me feel lost and disorientated.

I didn't know whether or not to unpack. Normally I'd have washed out a shirt, but thought that it might be embarrassing if I were to be moved on the morrow. After a night of fitful sleep I drifted downstairs in my green suit for a superb buffet breakfast in the hotel coffee-shop: sausages, bacon, eggs, fish in amazing variety; I needn't have bothered to pack All Bran – it was there alongside every conceivable other cereal.

Rashid came round to pick me up, as ordered, but I had no idea what to do next.

'Presidential Court?' he suggested.

'OK,' I said.

Swiftly and smoothly I was borne along one tree-lined boulevard after another and deposited at the bottom of marble steps (gleaming white and veined, like the front steps which Gian Carlo had made me install at Gilston Lodge). Mounting them, I was led through a fountain

court, then along a black-and-white chequered passageway with a reddish carpet down its middle, and into an office with English-speaking
Abdul Khaleq from the Hadramaut.

I asked if I'd be moving to Sheikh Zayed's guest-house.

'No, you will be staying at the Intercontinental, like all His Highness'
more important guests!' was the gratifying (but to me disappointing)
reply. (Edward's wife later told me that it really was most impressive to
be 'put up' there; that was where Zayed had not too long ago hosted
Charles and Diana.)

Abdul Khaleq telephoned Edward for me. When he arrived I noticed
he was now frail and a little slow on the uptake, but with the same merry
smile. Abdul Khaleq told us about some boat races that were to take
place that afternoon, and we agreed to go after Edward had finished a
lunch he had scheduled with the Italian Ambassador (who was tickled
pink when I greeted him in Italian, and produced some delicious ice-
cream as we sat by his swimming-pool).

For the boat races, we took a road which was in fact the top-surface
of a very long jetty thrust into the sea. There we were checked by
guards before getting out of the black Mercedes at a point a short walk
away from the viewing-stand proper, past a troop (almost a 'troupe') of
soldiers in bright scarlet uniforms tricked out with gold. We were led
into the grandstand, to seats at the back, where we sat drinking crushed
iced watermelon, waiting for President Zayed.

A fanfare from a band and there he was, with a retinue including
Yasser Arafat,* walking with immense dignity towards a line of white
overstuffed armchairs. Then the boat races began, unlike any races I'd
ever seen except in Tahiti, and not really much like those: long-boats
seating fifty, a hundred or even more oarsmen. Evidently a tradition
revived from a past, real or invented, long before my time.

Zayed looked very much the same, but grander, much grander,
scarcely looking older, what with kohl-enhanced eyes and beard dyed
black, as had been de rigueur thirty years before. Suddenly we were
sent for. A soldier barred our path and was duly brushed aside with nods
and instructions. I walked up in front of Zayed and was treated to a full
Arab greeting: side-kisses, prolonged handshake, a torrent of 'Kef halek?'
and 'El hamdu L'Illah!', so well remembered. Then it was indicated that
I should go through the same rigmarole with Yasser Arafat, which *did*

---

* Chairman of the Palestine Liberation Organisation from 1969 to his death in 2004.

come as a surprise; his lips were wet and slightly squashy. I noticed press photographers taking pictures of us all at it. *It will be the Israeli Secret Service files for me after this!* I thought.

Edward made a most useful interpreter; I couldn't have done without him. I was able to get across the message that I'd written a couple of poems for Zayed and we exchanged a few stilted sentences. He would see me again when he had more time, he said.

In scarlet and gold, the band struck up the national anthems of Abu Dhabi and Palestine (for which we had to stand to attention) and women began dancing, throwing manes of hair from side to side in gestures of abandonment.

Later, I dropped Edward at his office, which happened to be none other than Sheikh Shakhbut's old fort, still standing, but done up to within an inch of its life, gleaming white.* Once it had stood, honey-coloured, in the enveloping sand, separated only by a small mosque from a stinking shore. Now it squatted, dwarfed by ultra-modern surroundings, on grass fringed by metalled roads, in the midst of high-rise buildings. Once through the same old spiked entrance door and we were in the narrow passage – deliberately narrow, for defence – sharply turning before coming to a black marble fountain which had certainly never been there before. A veritable orchard of fruit and palm trees grew where once Shakhbut had hidden his iron trunkful of cash. The uneven steps up which I'd once walked (and stumbled) to the roof had been smartly marbled in black and white. But across that roof there was still the tower-*majlis* where I'd sat with Shakhbut when Tim Hillyard had arrived to announce the momentous decision that BP would start sample-taking.

Incidentally, I went to see Das – where I'd laid out the first runway it had known and met Gulzaman; Das, the formerly deserted, once the haunt of myriads of flies – whilst I was out there. As I flew over it, I couldn't help but think how it now resembled a suburb of Southampton.

I was given a tour – the place was so wholly transformed it was as if I'd never been there before – and then taken to lunch. Everyone wanted to talk about anything except their work, which suited me,

---

* The fort is Qasr al-Hosn, which readers are invited to Google (the building is visually very impressive). Travellers to Abu Dhabi might also be interested to learn that it is now partially open to visitors.

totally lacking technical knowledge. Within the last month – actually starting on 9 November – the Berlin Wall had been overrun by East Germans revolting effectively, at last, against the tyrants of their own flesh and blood who'd subjected them to years of Communist misrule. We couldn't foresee that one collapse would lead to another, until the very heartland of Socialism, the mighty Soviet Union itself, would disintegrate into history, as if to fulfil the prophecies of Fatima.*

At the time, cosmic questions were all the rage, much publicity being given to a possible 'solving' of the origin of the universe, the 'Big Bang' theory.† It soon transpired that none of us would admit to understanding it. One after another, we demanded an intelligible answer to the query 'WHAT HAPPENED BEFORE?' The statement that nothing preceded the Big Bang was, for each of us, a prime example of logical impossibility. All else could be easily understood – including the idea that the universe would expand and contract, expand and contract ad infinitum – but a *nothing* before the beginning of time itself, followed by a timed *something*, was, by definition, ungraspable by the ordinary human mind, however much scientists declared their belief in it as a working theory.

Whilst I was making enquiries about how to get to Das, I was indeed summoned to speak with Zayed once more. As Rashid drove us out towards Zayed's palace – one of his palaces – the heavens opened and rain came down in tropical strength, ending with an almighty rainbow hooped across the sky. I was told this was very good luck and taught to say '*Mubarak aleikum s'muttair*', meaning 'a blessing on your rain', embodying the suggestion that Zayed himself had brought it.

We reached a red-pillared hut in which we were to wait, sitting against a wall on a padded cloth laid over a carpet. When we were called for, we were driven up a steep incline to the Ruler's new *majlis*, a circular room, green as green: green arabesque arches all round; green walls; armchairs upholstered in green; even 'trees' of floral design

---

* The Three Secrets of Fatima were apocalyptic prophecies supposedly given to three shepherds by the Virgin Mary in 1917. These apparitions were investigated, and given ecclesiastical approval, by the Catholic Church.

† The theory had been around since the fifties and was widely accepted by scientists by this point in time. This is therefore probably a reference to Stephen Hawking's bestselling *A Brief History of Time: From the Big Bang to Black Holes* which had hit bookshops in 1988, prompting popular discussion. The Cosmic Background Explorer Satellite, created with the intention of gathering more evidence to support the theory, was also launched in 1989.

going upwards into a green dome from which hung one of those multi-coloured chandeliers. Each pair of armchairs was separated from the next pair by a small fixed table with fretted legs, convenient for holding the glasses and coffee-cups of ritual hospitality. In my green suit, which might have been specially bought to match the surroundings, I was waved to a seat on Zayed's right, but after the formal greetings (including the rain remark, which went down very well) I wasn't spoken to for some twenty minutes, because on his left sat the editor of a Kuwaiti newspaper who'd got in first.

When we did speak, H.H. wanted to talk about the improvements to Abu Dhabi since my time.

'Now I have money, by God's grace I can spend it on other people,' he said.

We reminisced about the hawking trip we'd been on together and I read him my poems and gave him the presents I'd brought, which included honey from my bees. This really made him animated and we almost argued about what makes the best honey; how far bees in our respective countries travelled; when the best time to collect the honey was, and so on. We were having such a cordial time, it was as though the bees had blessed us by their presence – a honeyed time, with Zayed as he used to be.

I telephoned Gian Carlo to hear how things were at home. He was suffering from a sore throat that made his voice so hoarse at first I thought that someone else was speaking.

'I'm gargling, but it doesn't seem to make much difference. But *you* sound OK. Are you having a wonderful time?'

'More than wonderful. Unbelievable! I saw the Sheikh today and I'm flying to Das tomorrow. What more could I ask?'

'Do you mean to stay on, then?'

The Sheikh had in fact offered me to stay on for another week if I chose to, but I chose not.

'No, I'm longing to get back to you,' I said.

That night I slept soundly for the first time since leaving London.

———

118

On arriving back in England, Little Man's sore throat hadn't gone, in fact the change in the timbre of his voice was actually rather alarming. The upshot was, he was booked into the Royal National Throat, Nose and Ear Hospital – his second appointment for the same complaint. He'd had a check-up earlier in the year for a similar thing which hadn't turned up any problems. But this time he came back looking glum. 'They say they want to operate immediately and send the results for biopsy. What does that mean, Lovey?'

The result of the biopsy was that it wasn't just the one tumour, there were two primaries, possibly more. It seemed that nothing in my whole life had struck home so forcibly. If ever I had failed to show sympathy towards the ills of others, I bitterly regretted such lack of comprehension and grasped at anything from the past capable of offering the smallest crumb of comfort. 'I suppose one must be joyful because at least he wasn't swept away by drink back in 1976 as he so easily might have been. And he's had a good deal of what he liked in life since then, even though he's had to put up with me as part of the package deal,' I wrote in my diary.

He'd have to be operated on quickly, probably to be followed up by radiotherapy. At the meeting with the surgeon, Gian Carlo asked, 'Will it mean taking away my voice?'

'I'm afraid so,' was the reply.

Terrible, terrible moment – poor darling Little Man, he was *so* brave, his eyes did no more than fill with tears. The doctor then said that the new voice-machines were very good and that one seventy-year-old had even managed to sing after having one fitted. But to add to the bad news, he would have to breathe through a hole in his neck; his nasal passages would be cut off and rendered useless for ever. Not only would he lose his voice, but his sense of smell, together with a marked diminution in his ability to taste. Should he have to have radiotherapy to follow, taste-buds would be weakened even further. For someone so

fond of cooking, it was another terrible blow, yet over lunch he told
me that he could accept the idea that he would never be normal again,
which meant I felt the pain even more on his behalf.

First he had to go to 115 Harley Street for an Immune Deficiency –
AIDS* – test. The result being negative, there was nothing to prevent
the operation from going ahead. A speech therapist, Joyce Cook, was
lined up; also the Middlesex Hospital oncologist, Dr Cassoni. Joyce
was a small optimist in spectacles who emphasised that 'speech with a
machine was a knack', and that 'the mastery of it would depend on the
patient'. Gian Carlo listened intently, even managing to smile. Since Dr
Cassoni – also a woman – spoke and was Italian, being dealt with by
her promised to be a sensible arrangement.

The operation went well, and we were pleased to hear that 'the surrounding tissues looked healthy and not threatening, which isn't always
the case'. Afterwards he had to undergo treatment after treatment, so I
spent a lot of time sitting outside his room in the passage, waiting. He
suffered severely from wind, but even so I was able to observe: 'Such a
good patient. Smiling sometimes.'

On 20 January 1990, the last drain (from the skin wound on his back)
was taken out by a nurse. The surgeon saw to the main drain from the neck
muscle connecting to his throat, a manoeuvre which evidently caused great
pain, though, having no voice any more, LM was incapable of crying out.
Much depended on the day when, after being X-rayed, he would have his
nose-tube removed, with the idea of taking liquid food orally from then

---

* This is one of three references to HIV or AIDS in Roddy's memoirs, although he
perhaps hints at it on two other occasions, the first with regard to the night when two
men attacked him and Richard Neville at Gilston Lodge (Chapter 89). Roddy said
it left such a 'lasting impression that [it] may have saved me from much worse', and
from then on has far less casual sex. The next occasion falls after this story in Chapter
125, which is similarly a reference to Roddy having avoided the dangers of casual sex
(reader advised not to skip ahead due to spoilers). The other two direct references aren't
in this abridged version but were in the original memoirs. After Gian Carlo recovers
from alcoholism and isn't as sexually inclined as before, Roddy writes that he 'would
go to Russell Square or the Strand Sauna where, more than once, I witnessed Rudolph
Nureyev [the famous ballet dancer] accommodating eager clients. (The hapless admirers may have had reason to regret their enthusiasm later, when poor Rudi died of an
Aids-related illness. I could, with luck, achieve my kind of relief less dangerously.)'
The final reference was in a story regarding Franklin. A writer had suggested to Roddy
that Franklin liked to sleep with prostitutes. Roddy disagreed on grounds of Franklin's
religion, adding: 'Would he really have sought the company of sailors' doxies at a time
when the Pox was as feared and as incurable as Aids is today?' We can assume that it
therefore did concern Roddy at the time, but that none of his immediate friends contracted it.

on. Should all go well, he might be able to come home two days later.

His X-rays would reveal what remained of his throat. 'If we are lucky, it will be all right,' said the medical orderly, 'but sometimes there's a hole and then it takes a few days longer before the patient can take food orally.' Fortunately, there was no hole. Next day, the remaining stitches were removed, and I could come and fetch my poor friend that very afternoon.

The night before my mother died, there'd been the 'Storm of the Century', bringing her mulberry tree crashing to the ground. The afternoon when I was allowed to fetch the sadly flickering light-of-my-life from the Princess Grace witnessed the staging of a virtual replay, a storm with the strength of a tornado littering the streets with branches, even snatching slates off roofs. As an emergency measure, Hyde Park was suddenly closed to cars, so traffic in the Marylebone Road soon became immoveable. In spite of starting out in very good time, I was five minutes late collecting my patient, who silently upbraided me, so keen was he to be off.

Happier than he'd been for weeks, Gian Carlo wouldn't go to bed till eleven that night. His hands constantly reached out to fondle the dog, who responded with utmost devotion, though clearly puzzled by hearing nothing but gurgles in place of his master's voice.

We were a quiet domestic trio once more; too quiet, for the moment. We dared hope that this condition might change, now that the first horrendous hurdles had been overcome. The future was a little brighter. I smiled, and he smiled back; but my heart was like a lump of lead. His heart must have been even heavier, but he never complained. Noble, noble Little Man!

———

119

On his first day home, the wounded warrior managed to swallow a small portion of scrambled egg; next day, a little pasta. Anything not too scratchy for his reconstructed throat was what he chose to send on down.

We procured some 'Buchanan Protectors' from John Bell and Croyden, netted patches like parts of the pierced white cotton veil worn by certain Muslim women. They discreetly covered the hole where the stoma went into his neck, just above the chest-bone. He was having physiotherapy to help get him back into shape and would soon be planning sessions with Joyce, the speech therapist, who said, encouragingly, that he'd already mastered the making of a noise, 'which is half the battle'.

On 13 February I took him to the Middlesex Hospital to be measured for a plastic masking device, an accurate description of the thing like the transparent head of a robot which would direct the killing/curative radiotherapy rays on to the exact spot required.

At first, I would sit waiting for Gian Carlo in the car on a double yellow line, often moved on by traffic-wardens before returning to the same spot – till they got to know me and my purpose in waiting and had the grace to let me be. When he said that he was perfectly capable of coming and going on his own, I let him, fearful as I was in case his gurgling led to a clash with someone hostile or jokey. To add to his distress, he lost all sense of taste after two weeks of irradiation, as we'd dreaded; and his throat went a dusky red, inside and out, hurting terribly.

We obtained large boiling-fowls, reserving the sediment-rich broth for him and the meat for me, for which he insisted on creating a salsa verde. He wanted to resume cooking, having earlier apologised for *not* doing it. Whatever he wanted he got, if it were in my power to give it him. His slightest word was law.

On 6 May, we received the first encouraging diagnosis of recovery. I took him to the Syon House Nursery to buy plants in celebration, sitting on a shooting-stick whilst he went up and down rows of seedlings, picking out whatever he wanted. My optimistic outlook remained unaffected: the monthly, then three-monthly, bulletins from the surgeon Mr Croft continued to state 'no further unwanted developments'. Meanwhile the Little Man was working every day in the garden, massing plants in pots on wooden ledges, making the house look more and more like a Roman villa. He enjoyed taking Silver for long, long walks; and he liked shopping, especially when there were bargains to be had.

Each sign of complete recovery was like a shower of blessings, far more significant than gold. Not that I underrated the power which money had conferred on us; I was well aware of the way in which it had enabled him to by-pass every queue. But I understood as never before that love was the great driving-force, for us as for all others lucky enough, or wise enough, to admit its supremacy. We were closer than ever, utterly intertwined. I didn't thrust my views and feelings on him, because we never talked about such matters, but I was sure that he felt the same. His adaptation to the way in which his life had been excoriated by cancer was truly admirable. He seldom complained. He simply got on with things; and one of those things was the job of looking after me. Gleams of contentment shone through the gloom for us, as autumn came.

———

120

Advancing years had come for all of us, of course, and if the eighties had spared one love of my life, it had swallowed up another.

At the beginning of the decade, Nick's back had been aching, though not enough to stop him signing on for a new contract in Northern Ireland. Then he complained of being slow to urinate and of it hurting when he did. His voracious appetite for sex diminished, he couldn't think why. However, he remained cheerful. 'When God shuths one door He opens another!' he quoted, as if that decided the matter.

Suddenly, his waterworks stopped functioning. At Dr Tom's direction he was rushed to St Thomas' Hospital, catheterised and operated on for a swollen prostate. When he came out, he looked puzzled. 'I have to report to the radio department, Rod. What would they want me to do thath for?'

'Oh, they just can't see enough of you!' I said. But a dreadful buzz ran through me, surging all the way down to my feet. Radiotherapy? It could only mean one thing, and Nick hadn't grasped what that one thing was.

I drove him to his first, crucial appointment. We happened to pass the Roebuck, the pub where we'd met so many years ago. He looked at me quickly, then looked away. He didn't have to say a word. *He does know, in a sort of way*, I realised, *but he thinks I don't*. I reached out to pat his knee and he put his hand on top of mine – a long time since we'd done that. Then we talked about other things, such as when he'd be well enough to return to his job.

Since I would have to be the nurse, Dr Tom felt it advisable to tell me a few confidential details. Nick's prostate had shown signs of malignancy; the cancer had possibly already spread elsewhere. (As indeed it had, to his bones.) In fear and dread I asked that awful question 'How long has he got?' and was given the standard reply: 'No one can be sure.' However, when probabilities were discussed, the tentative verdict was: 'Not much more than one year, perhaps two.'

Was he to be told?

'Not unless he asks.'

When by myself I cried uncontrollably, stopping only because I realised that it wasn't doing anyone any good. I didn't cry again. Nick took a long time before he officially asked what was the matter with him. He was feeling progressively worse, but unable to understand why he wasn't responding to treatment. During that 'nothing-much-seems-to-be-the-matter' period, I wondered how I might have felt in similar circumstances. I decided that I would *always* rather be told. There is something macabre in making false plans, even though this is our general human lot, for we none of us know for sure when we are going to die. On the other hand, none of this was happening to me. Would I be so brave and matter-of-fact if it came to the crunch?

I watched Nick having to give up the little things which had once meant such a lot to him. In my diary I noted: 'He is anyhow in a quandary as he grows older because he has so few mental resources – he doesn't read; he doesn't really much like watching Television. He liked going to the pub and all that camaraderie, but the prostate removal has changed much of the impetus for that.' In recompense, he tended to concentrate upon domestic details, such as buying food, particularly meat; but with his infirmity he could no longer bear the sight of blood. The same with cooking: he used to love it, but was starting to find it nauseating.

He took pleasure in the dog though, who bullied him by sitting down beside his chair and nudging him, even barking, to be taken out. Nick liked to do it but was soon to find even an easy walk difficult; once or twice, he told me, he'd fallen down in the street. He had always enjoyed a siesta; now he was spending hour after hour in bed. He was taking a prescribed liquid pain-killer which in fact contained heroin, though he may not have been aware of that. It tore at my heart to see the changes in him.

As summer wore on, he told me that his papers had been transferred to a hospital in Belfast. He said that it was St Thomas' doing, which I doubted. More likely, he'd requested it himself. I couldn't know whether it were being done to spare me, or whether he reckoned that my weak back would make me incapable of humping him about in bed. He still insisted on coming daily to Villa Marco, but once there, he would sit out on the balcony, waiting for me and the dog to appear. I would call up to him and wave, and he'd wave back and call down to us. I thought: *How infallibly he has hit upon a way of reducing Villa Marco to his own sentimental and human and endearing scale, just as he always has done with everything and every place all his life!* But that vibrant, confident life, I feared, hadn't got much longer for this world.

I drove Nick to Heathrow. We went via Chiswick, so he was able to sit as usual on the balcony, waiting for me to pass with the dog on the other side of the wall. As usual, he waved and called to us, and then we headed off to the airport. In the car, anxiety made the minutes fly without other thoughts interrupting, till Nick suddenly said: 'I'm leaving everything to you, Rod!' When we'd discussed the dreaded subject previously, I'd suggested Paddy as his heir.

I said: 'I don't need the money, Nick. I'd rather have you!' It sounded terribly ordinary, but its very triteness seemed to fit a moment so loaded with emotion.

'All right then, wouldth you be my executor, Rod? You've always been the one I care for!'

I felt sick and nervous, but in a voice as even as I could muster, I assured him that I would.

I took his bag in to the counter and said goodbye to him there, not giving him a kiss because it would have made him shy. The poor thing had a hollow look to him. His face was much thinner, and because they had filled him with stilbesterol, a female hormone, to prevent the prostate cancer I suppose, he had grown great baggy breasts. He had kept up with his hair-dye, though, as always. I don't think anything could have made him let go of that.

After I left him I recalled how he'd written (with difficulty, almost illegibly) in one of his rare letters from overseas: 'A lump comes into my throat when I think of you, Rod.' A lump was not just coming into my throat as I drove away, but staying there, almost choking me.

When I got back home, nobody else was in. I was alone in the house. Nick had left plenty of his things behind, including a handkerchief oozing snuff, thrust under his pillow and forgotten. He'd usually taken his hand-kerchiefs into the bathroom to wash them secretly himself, but as the brown stains wouldn't come out properly, all of us knew what he'd been up to and never referred to it. It was different when he'd used a dark dye on his hair. He couldn't hide the fact, because though lavishly blacking eyebrows and chest-hair, he'd been unable to reach a fuzz of white hairs on his back, prompting my comment: 'Madame Butterfly, I presume!' It might have made him cross, but fortunately he decided to adopt it as an acknowledged joke. To a cry of 'Where are you, Nick?' he would often answer: 'In the Madame Butterfly-ery!'

I didn't think *I might never hear him say that again*, because we would be in touch by telephone.

Towards the end of that month he wrote (from hospital): 'I am on drugs four times a day. Coming near mornings the worst when they are fading out . . . I don't know what I am going to do, I will have to stay in hospital another week and it is then back to the flat which costs about £27 per month and I think one month will do there, so God knows.'

I couldn't imagine that he could be really concerned about money, but I hastened to write back that he must have everything he wanted, without worrying, 'and that's a promise'. He rang me up when he got my letter but didn't refer to its contents. He was evidently going downhill fast; he sounded very confused and weak.

Peg, the wife who'd divorced him – he'd never treated her with much respect – and Paddy, his good son, went to Northern Ireland to stay close to him. Peg was absorbed in Nick's welfare, visiting him regularly, often two or three times a day, cooking up little easily digested dishes when he took against the hospital food. I sent her money to help pay for that.

Paddy brought the Gilston Lodge keys back with him after Christmas – a token of finality if ever there was one. Nick asked me not to visit him; he wanted me to think of him as he'd been, not as he had become.

I was told that he would sometimes say 'I'm getting out of here!' and start packing. Then he'd be sedated again, and by the time he woke up he would mercifully have forgotten his intention. He said crossly to one of the nurses: 'Have you ever met my friend Roderic? I tell you, he'd write a book about this if he knew what went on.' I was not surprised by his attitude; Nick, in Bahrain, had never made a good invalid. Even now that Death's door was the one which God was opening, he was unlikely to be acquiescent.

I waited anxiously for the inevitable news and, by and by, the telegram came:

DEAR NICK DIED AT QUARTER TO TEN THIS MORNING.

I mused miserably: *God rest the Irish soul of that darling man, for all that he could be a rascal, betimes!*

part ten

the end of the era

1990-5

121

Throughout 1990, Tahiti had been calling, calling. It had been over forty years since I had stepped foot on her shores. The warning of 'NEVER COME BACK!' rang in my ears, but the call was louder. If Paradise had changed, then so be it; I had changed too. In 1949 I had been a twenty-seven-year-old wannabe beachcomber; now I was an almost seventy-year-old truth seeker.

In October, Mr Croft the surgeon pronounced the words we had been dreaming of to Gian Carlo: 'There's no sign of a recurrence of your trouble. I can see you less often, in future.' Relief tangibly flooded through his consulting-room as I heard – actually heard – the Little Man gasp a rudimentary 'Thank you!'

The 'All Clear!' impelled me the very next day to telephone a Wimbledon firm called 'Best of the South Pacific' to enquire about ways and means of returning to the South Seas. I wanted to widen my scope to include Easter Island, the last of those three key faraway places to be visited which had haunted me since 1948, reading *Wide World* on *Clan Urquhart*. With the advantage of modern air travel, there was no reason not to take a passing peep at Bora Bora, said to be the most beautiful island in the whole Pacific. But that I doubted, for how could anything compare with Moorea?

I wrote off to Dale McClanahan in California once again, and Dale came up trumps, telephoning with a mass of information about Tahiti, and useful telephone numbers for Medford Kellum and Purea Reasin. Med and Purea were the ones I remembered: Med, who had let Turia build her hut in Opunohu Bay on land near his own house; Purea, the beautiful guitar-player, married to Johnny, the man whom I privately thought of as an American wide-boy.

'I've gone back to Tahiti at least fifteen times,' said Dale. 'But right now I'm a little disillusioned with the place.'

'Why's that?' I asked.

'Well, you might say it's been getting out of hand!' What she probably meant was: *Too popular with the wrong sort of people.*

There was only one way to find out.

I flew from Gatwick on 18 November via Los Angeles, landing at 4 a.m. in Papeete and being welcomed by a committee of two fat Tahitian *vahines* twanging guitars, one hanging a white *tiaré Tahiti* over my left ear. Jet-lagged and sweaty, I was then told my luggage had gone missing; most likely it had been sent to Auckland and I would have to wait for three days for it to find me. The wash things and socks in my hand luggage would have to do some heavy lifting.

Next day, the heat and humidity, fiercer and higher than I remembered, forced me to buy a pair of slightly too tight (rather than too floppy) shorts, an underslip in which I could also bathe, and a couple of ill-fitting short-sleeved shirts. Papeete had altered a lot: no longer an endearing rag-bag of French Colonial shops and shacks, dominated by an aroma of vanilla and Gauloises, but a modern town, thrusting and impersonal. Everywhere cars, cars, cars ... I could hardly visualise myself pedalling a bicycle through those crowded streets. The people, too, were not as enticing as they used to be; they looked unhealthily fat, particularly the men. I had to bear in mind that originally I'd come to Tahiti from Tonga, where obesity was a prized quality. Compared with the subjects of Queen Salote, Tahitians had appeared positively svelte, if somewhat fleshier than Londoners thinned down by wartime deprivation.

I rang Med Kellum in Moorea (who I thought must now be nearing ninety), having been told that he'd become something of a recluse. Recluse or no, he was very friendly on the telephone, promising to take me in hand all day, once I'd settled in to the Moorea Lagoon hotel, chosen because it was just up the road from the tiny shelf of sand where Turia and I had once been cocooned in contentment. So long ago; so long, long ago ... ah me!

I wandered down to the long curve of waterfront, where, of old, yachts tied up, their owners or crew on deck ever-ready to chat to passers-by. It used to be such fun, exchanging gossip with old friends, meeting new chums, generally being asked on board for a drink. Now there seemed to be no one about, though one of the larger boats had a dozen dogs barking away as I mooched casually by. Near it, a man with his arms covered in tattoos lay on his back on one of the stone slabs which did duty as a public bench. I noted in my diary: 'He was dark and rather bald and wore one gold earring and he had no top on but blue-jean trousers into which he thrust a hand and either rearranged himself or was playing with himself, it was difficult to tell which. A curious, erotic sight!'

With a sudden jolt, I recognised that slab as the one on which I'd sat in 1949, reading and re-reading the cable saying that my godfather had died; where I'd decided against telling anyone about the £500 which had come my way – selfish (or simply self-preserving) beast that I was. Without Alister's unexpected legacy I might have found it difficult to scrape together enough francs for the passage from Tahiti; might never have left, in fact, but grown old with Turia and become – what? A drunkard, perhaps, smoking sixty cigarettes a day, earning a precarious living (when neither too drunk nor too sober) by gazing into a *soi-disant* crystal on behalf of everyone except himself.

The main wharf was at the other end of the waterfront, memorable because from it *Sagittaire* had sailed with me on board – a tearful me, hung with *couronnes* of frangipani and *tiaré Tahiti*, waving to Turia and to such of the *fetii* as could manage to be present. That part of the docks was presently occupied by a gigantic liner, *Royal Viking*, from which hundreds of passengers were spreading out over Papeete like ants disturbed from their nest.

At eleven the next day, round came the Manureva Tours rep with a taxi to take me to the local-flight section of Faaa airport, to board an Islander light aircraft for Moorea. I'd chosen to go by air so as to get an overall impression of the whole island, which had formerly consisted, for me, of little more than Opunohu, Papetoai and Cook's Bay. The Islander would take six minutes only, which wouldn't give me much of an opportunity, though better than nothing.

Swiftly we wheeled over the sea and were coming in to land almost before I'd had time to distinguish Mt Rotui from its neighbours, leaving me with the expected impression of green, green greenery from shore and upwards to all save the sharpest pinnacles at the very top. Its beauty caught at my throat, but I said to myself: *I must not have false expectations. What's real would be enough for most people; and should be enough for me.*

But the problem was nothing new: nothing in this world was ever enough without love. And love, which had once been so near at hand in Opunohu, was now thousands of miles away in London, under threat. That was the reality separating the past from the present.

The tiny plane taxied to a halt. 'See you in three days' time, if you can bear to leave!' said the pilot cheerfully.

The *camionette* waiting to take me to the Moorea Lagoon picked up another passenger, an American from Hawaii who said that planes were full of Tahitians going to Honolulu to do their shopping, Honolulu being that much cheaper than Papeete. 'Tahiti today is what we used to be, forty years ago,' he said. In which case, what *must* Hawaii be like now?

Where once there'd been no more than a sandy track, we drove along a broad tarmac road, past a petrol station and a supermarket, dropped the Hawaiian off at the Bali Hai hotel and arrived at the Moorea Lagoon reception hall, a large thatched hut in what I would once have called 'Cornelius Crane' style (Cornelius being the millionaire Turia had worked for) – fake-folkloric, with an inner ceiling of varnished pandanus. But as I was soon to discover, it was what everywhere passed for 'traditional' Polynesian. *Traditional my foot!* I thought, whilst acknowledging that it made for more comfortable living. The bulky girl who'd been doing the driving became the receptionist, bridling as she booked me in, having already asked, en route, whether I were a bachelor. I said 'No', as I always did, because it avoided misunderstandings with the ladies.

I was led to my thatched hut – another example of Cornelius Cranery: polished wooden floor; huge cane double-bed with coverlet of red hibiscus design upon green; a cane table and its accompanying chair; and outside in front, an apron of verandah supporting two chairs and a table. At the back, a basin and shelves in sage green, through all that a loo, and through that a blue-tiled shower. I set an overhead fan on low speed to stir the still air, then realised that the hut was so dark and the light so dim that I would have to retreat to the basin-room to do any note-taking beneath a fluorescent strip.

There were twenty-five other guests staying in the hotel. All but one were couples, the odd man out having a nervous propensity to BO. After a few friendly words with this and that person I walked into the lagoon in the underslip bought in Papeete and found myself amongst clumps of coral, attended by brilliant blue, yellow and brown fish. Other bathers were using snorkels to get a close-up of them, but I was quite happy as I was. A few huts were set on stilts, sticking out into the lagoon – a thing unheard-of in my day, when only the *fare itis* were built like that to provide the fish with excrement to tussle over. Those huts were much more expensive, which was why they hadn't been included in my pre-booking.

After a bathe, I tucked into a lunch of *poisson crû* and a green salad (setting me back £9). Then I retreated to my hut to continue the process of catching up on sleep, mosquito-free. Something made me put out a hand, as if Turia were lying beside me, but of course she wasn't there.

On 21 November – luggage arrived and so properly attired – I met up with Medford. He was small, wiry and freckled, limping from a hip replacement done in Papeete at a cost, he said, of considerably more than he would have been charged even at the Princess Grace in London. He kept saying how much he missed his wife, Gladys, who'd just died. He drove me first to the Belvedere, a place with a superb outlook which had once formed part of his still-large estate. I'd never been up there before, my sole sally inland having been with the strong-armed sailor who'd developed what Turia called a *béguin* for me on the boat coming over to Moorea. I'd gone with him into the hills for a promising bathe in a Pierre Loti-esque pool, only to be interrupted by a bevy of schoolgirls – a frustrating memory. 'The Japanese are buying up whatever land they can, around here,' said Med. 'They want to construct a golf-course, of all things!'

We passed a spot on the metalled road beyond his house.

'Where's this, Roderic?' asked Med.

'I'm not absolutely sure, but I think it *may* be . . .'

'Yes, that's right. It IS!'

It was the place where Turia had built her three huts, not forgetting the *fare iti* directly over the water, each hut joined by a paved path, screened from the track by greenery. No traces remained, not even the sandy spit with its wooden landing-stage. Our abode of love might never have existed. Nor was there any sign of the hut where Turia's brother Minou had lived uncomfortably with his prim wife.

Med told me something about Turia herself. She had gone back to Tahiti to look after his other house in Punaavia, where she'd been joined by her sister Melanie. Arthritis had increasingly menaced both of them, till Melanie died and Turia, unable to manage on her own, was more or less forced to retire into an old folks' home in Taravao, where, some six or seven years previously, she had ended her days.

'Happily, I believe,' said Med cautiously.

He took me back to his house, which I only vaguely remembered. I hadn't described it in *Where the Poor are Happy*, because at that time (paying heed to a publisher with libel in mind) I couldn't afford to identify every character, even Turia going under the pseudonym of 'Maya'.

Med said shyly, 'I hope you don't mind a *couronne?*' and whipped out a lovely *lei* of red and white flowers. He hung it round my neck, the old dear. It transpired that he'd made it up himself earlier that morning. Every day, he said, he'd performed that chore for Gladys; the habit had become so ingrained that he missed it terribly. His wife had been ninety-two when claimed by Alzheimer's – 'a disease which seems to afflict too many in these parts'. His own memory was apt to wobble. I asked about the tree near the water's edge where Turia and I had been allowed to come and pick limes, whenever we wished.

'Lime tree? What lime tree?' he asked. 'Can't ever remember one growing where you say!'

I didn't argue.

We lunched at a smart converted boat, called Lina Reva, run by a nice Frenchman. I ate *mahi-mani*, rather like a dolphin – but not a dolphin, being fish, not mammal – whose penchant for closely following boats made it easy to spear. I asked where to find a *pareu* of what used to be considered 'traditional' floral design, for whenever we passed a shop displaying *pareus* nothing but the most lurid lengths were on show: sunrises melting into sunsets; Gauguinesque figures squatting under coconut-palms; even highly coloured maps of Tahiti and Moorea. 'These are the kind the tourists want nowadays,' said Med. 'The old ones used to come from England, but I don't know about this lot. Vulgar, aren't they, like the people who buy them?'

Med also took me to an orchard where *tiaré Tahiti* was being grown commercially. 'There's such a demand for *couronnes*, these days,' he said. 'It's a real paying proposition!'

We drove past the football ground in Papetoai, between the spectators' shed and the lagoon. I remembered how, careful to behave becomingly, I'd ignored the sailor in favour of meeting a crowd of *fetii*, my new relations. 'Papetoai was where Queen Pomare IV was induced to accept French protection in 1842,' said Med. 'What a woeful mistake!'

'If I remember rightly, Edwina Mountbatten and her lover first came to Opunohu on Bill Leeds' yacht,' said Med when I tried pumping him about days before my time. 'Opunohu was where Captain Cook first dropped anchor, not in Cook's Bay, as is generally supposed, but that's by the way. Edwina was really fascinated by Turia, and so was Tito Wessel. Wessel was a tall, good-looking chap in his thirties ...'

I said goodbye to the kind, slightly lost old man on the landing-strip. If it hadn't been for him, I would have had a thin, impersonal time in a Moorea already developed for tourists. He alone had ensured that my link with well-remembered times proved to be more of a reconnection than a *récherche*.

Largely because of Med's ample land holdings, Opunohu had remained relatively unspoiled, still as lovely and with the same undertones of sadness as it had formerly held for me. *Once upon a time*, I thought. *Once upon a time . . . the way all the best fairy stories begin.* That was the way in which my own idyll had begun, certainly: a young man at odds with a wicked uncle, going out into the world to seek his fortune, prepared to help an old woman gather sticks in the forest or be of service to any not-too-outrageously repulsive king. In so doing, my chance encounters had been the true stuff of fairy-tale, praise the Lord!, even to the point of winning the hand of a princess.

This time, however, no double-rainbow chose to loop across Opunohu; no salute to a Chief from Mt Rotui to send me back to the outside world, drenched to the skin but glowing with reflected radiance. Yet Moorea had lost none of its power to shatter a visitor's complacency with green fantastic images of a different past.

———

122

Much time was spent searching for my Château Courant d'Air, because the driver wouldn't slow down, however often he was asked. Finally I had to order him at least to stop and ask the way, fortunately choosing a house on the 'wrong' – i.e., non-coastal – side of the road. There was a pregnant girl there who said Robson had been her grandfather! Mr Robson, that uncrowned 'King of Easter Island' who'd kindly lent me a bed. The pregnant girl relished hearing about her grandfather.

Thanks to her I could identify my Château Courant d'Air – modernised, and at that moment empty. From its tiny beach I could see the jetty of Maison Crane, where Turia and I used to sit of an evening, waiting for the authentic green flash of sundown. I couldn't revisit Cornelius Crane's house, scene of so many argumentative but happy hours, because the tightly locked gates displayed a notice: CHIEN SAUVAGE!

My next stop should have been Taravao, to see where Turia had spent her last days in a home. But at that point I suddenly couldn't bring myself to do it. For once, I simply didn't want to know.

I was shortly to fly to Bora Bora, to the grandest of hotels, part of the Raphael chain which included the Du Rhône in Geneva. It was a one-hour flight in a twin-engined plane, and that was just for starters. Disembarking, we clambered aboard a launch for a half-hour journey across a shallow lagoon, then transferred into a 'Truck Bus' driving (it seemed) halfway round the island before landing us up at a fearfully superior collection of so-called 'traditional' thatched huts.

That night there should have been a Tahitian feast on the shore, but rain poured down at intervals and the feast was cancelled. There was instead a sunset cruise (£15 extra) alongside the islets forming mini-atolls on the edges of the lagoon. I could imagine doing that on a first evening out from London, marvelling at the silky-smooth water and typical Pacific sky of rounded, Paris-grey clouds: the infinite numbers of various greys were subtle, merging on to one another and laid across and into one another. Green and fertile, the atolls were uninhabited, being too little above the level of the lagoon to escape inundation from tidal waves when, like an outer bailey, they protected the main island. For which reason those waters had been selected as a suitable base for American submarines during the war.

After dinner, a troupe, booked to perform out of doors, had to do their act near the bar. It was immediately obvious that they were professionals, the girls writhing and jerking with all the abandon of a proper *Otea*. Their ecstasy was electric, characterised by the typical knee-tremor which I'd only mastered after much practice. Two of the male dancers were blond, doubtless of GI descent – not directly, but as *grandsons* of GIs of course, time had flown so fast since the war. They wore their *pareus* so very low on the waist – five inches below the navel – that at any moment, I thought, they might come undone in mid-wiggle; but alas, they never did.

I was determined to enjoy the best of the best, just the once, which meant a hut on stilts out in the lagoon, approached by a broad wooden gang-plank. It had a shaded verandah with a view of the *massif centrale* of Bora Bora: a tilted thick funnel of black rock, cloven and permanently plumed with cloud. I put on one of the two kimonos hanging in a cupboard and sat listening to water lapping against wooden stilts. The sole drawback was that the lagoon had suffered such pollution from the upmarket hotel that all the coral within reach had turned grey, and nearly all the brightly coloured fish had gone. I had imagined plunging straight from my hut, as from some Victorian bathing-machine, but certainly not into such dead and deadly water.

I put my name down for one of the hotel's scheduled entertainments, a (free) sail in a pirogue, the outrigger canoe of those parts. By a wonderful stroke of luck, I was the only taker. The crew consisted of two Bora Borans: one, in ragged khaki shorts, standing on the outrigger, the other seated at the back, his *pareu* bunched up to form a kind of pleated bathing-dress. Both men grinned and flexed their muscles, as if aware that I would find it attractive. They showed off. One of them did a series of press-ups; and when we passed a girl bathing in the shallows he adopted weight-lifter poses, laughing, jerking and gyrating his hips towards her.

It was clear from the outset that they were in a happy mood – by no means always to be reckoned on with Tahitians, but all the more exhilarating for being spontaneous. Hardly had we started out before the men began singing, at first shyly, but then when I got them to sing 'Vahine Annamite' and 'Il faut en dollars' they picked up no end and sang and sang so that there was no stopping them. They asked for a contribution from me, probably expecting something by Cole Porter. Instead, I launched into

> The higher up the mountain, the cooler the breeze,
> The younger the couple, the tighter they squeeze . . .

and so on, as taught by Adi Gavoka in Fiji, ending with:

> Ai-o-wey! Don't hesitate! I'm a-comin' very slow-ly!

which went down so well that I continued with other songs learned a lifetime ago.

They stopped the pirogue at an hotel further along the shore, saying that it was so that I could use the lavatory. I had the impression that had I gone in, one (or both) of them would have accompanied me; but that sort of thing simply didn't chime with my mood of the moment, so I declined with a polite 'Maruru!' This seemed to amuse them very much. '*Maruru!*' they shouted; and shouted it again as we sailed back to our hotel. '*Maruru!* Thank you, thank you, thank you!' But of course it was I who should have thanked *them*, for rolling back the years with such gusto.

On the beach I was hailed by two Americans: 'Whaddy'know? We could hear just about every word of your singing, echoing across the lagoon.'

'Hope you enjoyed it?'

'Sure, it was really nice and tuneful!'

I had forgotten how voices carried over calm water. Back I went to my super-pad over the lagoon with a spring in my step.

Housed in such splendour and after such a nostalgic interlude, I signed up for a demonstration of how to make a *couronne*. You had to take a piece of ribbon and make a thread of it by splitting it into two and two again, lengthwise. You take a long needle threaded with this 'thread'. You put it through the open-flower end of a frangipani or whatever, run the flower nearly down to the end, then thread again with another flower. When your thread-necklace has been filled up, there you have the *couronne* all ready. Simple, really, but like all simple things, the tech-nique had to be learnt first.

Draped in the management's kimono and liberally sprinkled with my own di-methyl-toluol, I sat on my sea-girt verandah watching a sunset reflected off a cloud still pluming upwards from Bora Bora's tilted *massif centrale* as if from a live volcano. Across the lagoon the atolls began to resemble the mirages which Nick and I had seen when chasing stories of Roddy Owen, flickering as if doubled by their own reflections. It was an effort to remember that the atolls were really there. In a technicolour light, the whole place looked luridly unreal, the only spoiler being a line of lamps along the gang-plank connecting us favoured few to the beach, without which survivors from a convivial evening would have found weaving a way back to their huts something of a problem.

I rose at 5.55 next morning and went out on the verandah to enjoy the sight of birds wheeling and diving on to the beach to pick up wisps of straw for their nests. Sunrise had already come and gone; gleams of blue were appearing in an overcast sky. And then, there it was, over the smaller island – a RAINBOW, an authentic rainbow. I could hardly believe my eyes at the sight: Opunohu's celebrated farewell, though on a smaller scale.

It seemed splendidly inapposite that the most luxurious time in the most expensive hotel in Polynesia should evoke such a cherished memory of a money-starved beachcombing past. But there it was; and I certainly wasn't about to grumble.

————

123

After a six-hour flight, I arrived at Easter Island – the third of the three quests I had promised myself back in 1948 to accomplish – to find a free-for-all at the baggage check-out, where Customs officers, for some reason best known to themselves, opened every single case of every passenger, then didn't examine the contents closely – a thoroughly mystifying performance.

On the other side of a glass partition, Easter Islanders could be seen beckoning, waving placards advertising accommodation in their own homes. Whenever a host was selected, the tourist was triumphantly claimed and bags removed. Already booked in advance at the Hotel Victoria, I wasn't affected, though when I saw how attractive some of the touts were, I felt I might have missed the bus. The hotel was run by a George Edmunds, the oldest tortoise in creation, who couldn't speak much English and collected me in a car with an even less English-speaking wife and a child who kept sneezing. But they were thoroughly nice, if not at all what I'd expected.

The hotel was just as surprising: a detached suburban bungalow, extended sideways, the rooms like military quarters. I was shown into a capacious but bare sitting-room where coffee, buns and jam were set down in front of me, without speaking, by Mrs Edmunds, who withdrew immediately, leaving me on my own. In silence I stared at the food, in silence I inspected the room; not a sound came from anywhere, except for a sneeze from the child following its mother wherever she went. Never in my life had I encountered such an eerie atmosphere of intense loneliness; so eerie that it was as tangible as a Presence. *Goodness, what must it have been like for the Polynesian voyageurs, making landfall after weeks of uncharted sea?* I wondered. *This awful, awe-full silence, after all their accustomed mirth and chatter!* I thought, too, of the obvious remedy: *Nothing but dancing to dispel it, dancing and keeping themselves so fully occupied that they had no time to let it affect their normal spirits . . .*

Was I right? Was there something unendurably sinister about Easter Island? I needed to learn more, and as quickly as possible, for there was no time to waste. The only plane back to Tahiti for a week would be leaving the following afternoon.

The hotelier had his own jeep and offered himself as a guide. He also had some local postcards, but not stamps, which his daughter (who worked in the post office) would supply. A slim guidebook could be bought for the huge sum of $35 at the Tourist Office – to which we drove first – where a young man speaking good English helped plan an itinerary to fill every moment of the available time. Without his assistance, I would have been in a flat spin. With it, the fact that my guide was not exactly fluent in English didn't matter so much.

We started by making for the quarry site of Rano Raraku, over the bumpiest tracks imaginable. The island had no 'proper' roads. The landscape was as rough as the roads, Hebridean, with black rocks jutting aggressively into a restless sea. Polynesian pioneers had christened the faraway and un-tropical island 'Rapa-nui' (Great Rapa), because it was more like the place already known to them as Rapa than any other island in their fertile group. [The original, smaller Rapa would have to be re-christened 'Rapa-iti'.] Rapa-nui was not lush, nor was it encircled by a coral reef. No reef meant no lagoon; no lagoon, no easy source of food. Above all, it was cold and dry – forbidding for those accustomed to heat and humidity.

Hanga Roa, the only modern settlement of any size, looked ramshackle, yet each cabin-like house had its garden of luxuriant flowers and vegetables. Evidently the soil was fertile when properly tended. Where there were trees, they were usually eucalyptus, few in number and looking recently planted. It was as if, at some time in the past, a giant rake had denuded the island of most growing things, leaving behind a harsh, barren environment. Treelessness was even more striking than the humpy landscape, shallow conical hills suggesting volcanic origins, but lacking the towering dagger-peaks of the Marquesas, from which the earliest settlers were thought to have come.

We took the southerly track towards Ahu Vaihu and Akahanga, driving past gigantic stone figures – *moai* – so long fallen that they were barely distinguishable from the rocky surfaces where they lay. The day was calm and almost windless, yet waves dashed continually against the broken black coastline, as though unable to fathom why they should suddenly be encountering an obstacle after thousands of miles of nothing but ocean.

Near the first *ahu* – platform site – a feral cat prowled, and in the air three hawks were questing, flying low over the broken ground, adding to a feeling of menace. It was not difficult to imagine how impressive those *ahus* must have been, each with its row of statues four or five times the height of the humans who'd so laboriously dragged them from a quarry and set them upright. The figures always faced inland, never out to sea, suggesting that they were not guardians so much as jailers, rows of Orwellian Big Brothers casting stern coralline eyes over the goings-on of the inmates of an island prison. To move them had been a gigantic task, taking up much time and energy; however, it had been done, somehow. Theories tumbled over themselves to prove that this or that method had been employed, from 'rolling' to 'walking', still without anyone knowing for sure.

Having seen where, and in what condition, some of the statues had ended up, it was all the more dramatic to find groups of them clustering on a grassy hillside, half an hour's drive away. They'd been moved a little way from the quarry of Rano Raraku (source of the only stone suited to the carver's needs) to make room for the construction of more and more of the same. As we bumped over uneven ground towards them, they were revealed, gradually, in their weird glory, not another soul to be seen.

Some fifty or sixty of the statues were immediately visible on the grassy slopes, with more beyond the curve of the hill. As we drew nearer you could see the strange angular faces and flat backs. Some had slightly toppled, so it was as if they were talking between themselves. The grassy slopes behind came to an abrupt end at the quarry, towards which I limped laboriously, stick in hand. One giant lay like an Egyptian obelisk, only partly formed, waiting for the final chiselling of a sculptor long dead. So these great stone idols were what I had come to see, at such trouble and expense? Certainly they were worth it, to such an extent I asked George to take me three times that day.

At first the *moai* had seemed depressingly alike, but then they became individuals, long stone ears and long stone noses just differing enough to give each its own chic. The dark, lichenous stone from which the statues had been carved perfectly contrasted with the green of the grass, and the downward sweep of their chins and noses was perfectly complemented by the angle of the slope against which they rested. Over the years, the level of the earth on which they'd been abandoned had risen, so no more than their heads, necks and perhaps shoulders protruded.

Moreover, whatever impression the statues had been intended to convey, it was certainly not benign: they looked as stern as Rottweilers. The islanders were said to be afraid of spending a night alone in Rano Raraku, but I inclined to the view that they'd learned that kind of fear from Western visitors. Ghostly *tupaupaus* were supposed to haunt the huts of the living, not congregate where formidable but lifeless stone guardians were on hand to protect against them.

'Now bird-men!' said George after I'd had my fill, referring to another aspect of the 'Mystery of Easter Island' so prized by tourists. The bird-man cult, begun in the 1700s, had left in its wake elongated carvings and carefully worked stone graffiti, the 'petroglyphs' – not as interesting to me as the giant *moai*, but of course they had to be seen. The real surprise was to find a huge volcanic crater nearby them, Rano Kau, with dark green pools and incipient vegetation. I felt dizzy on two counts: the high rim of the crater was separated only by a thin strip of grass from black cliffs which had been used for depicting the bird-man petroglyphs; whilst, far below, the sea shattered the silence with a continuous roaring. Huts (with tiny low entrances) of Cyclopean dark stones, expertly fitted together, would have been at home in the Orkney Islands, whatever might originally have been the reason for their construction.

A bird cult was supposed to have superseded the system of belief represented by the *moai*. What everybody really wanted to know was why the islanders had become disillusioned with their stone guardians and turned to the birds and the bird-men for help – a counsel of despair if ever there was one. Shortage of food was thought to have been at the bottom of it. But what could birds have done for a starving population, increasing unchecked, using up the only available timber, the trees, with careless prodigality, guaranteeing that they would never again be able to build boats either to fish or to escape from their remote island? Perhaps, by a process of sympathetic magic, it was hoped that birds, alone able to fly to warmer climes, could teach stranded humans to do the same.

What surely must have happened on Rapa-nui was a tragedy of Classic proportions, of mortals pitted against the inexorable laws of nature. One dilemma, above all, would have sharpened the tragedy of their downfall: moving the *moai* would have required wasting the last of the precious wood, whilst abandoning the *moai* where they stood on the grassy slopes would have been sacrilegious. Was disillusionment with the traditional guardians for failing to solve the dilemma the main reason for their (literal) downfall?

The tragedy struck home the more vividly to me because the past fate of the Easter Islanders on their small territory could be seen as no more than a step removed from our possible future: reckless disregard for finite planetary resources; an ever-increasing population, not only sanctioned but encouraged by religious beliefs; pollution on a worldwide scale from sheer weight of numbers. It took no great leap of the imagination to realise that the inhabitants of Easter Island, trapped in a place where, by their own folly, they'd either exhausted most of their natural resources or rendered them inaccessible, would gradually have become like maggots on a corpse, finally compelled to feed on each other before themselves expiring.

That grim scenario made me recall how, years before, Bridget Chetwynd had shown me an article illustrating a model (in concrete, the size of a small room) of a 'town' built to house rats and only rats, the idea being to study how they would react to increasing in unlimited numbers with a limited amount of food in a confined space. As their numbers had grown beyond tolerance, friendly contacts ceased, the weaker cowering in rat-tenements, starving to death, the stronger ambushing each other in the 'streets', till finally forced to cannibalise to prevent their own extinction. The experiment had been aptly named 'Rat City'.

Seen in that light, Easter Island had been a kind of Rat City, the microcosm of a macrocosm, their doom the precursor of our doom ... Wasn't the voice crying in the wilderness loud enough to hear? Could humans in positions of power and responsibility ever be persuaded to listen, instead of leaving such matters to an admittedly quirky Greenpeace? It seemed to me that we would do well to engrave Easter Island on our hearts, before it was too late.

124

At the Mandarin on Papeete I was installed in a *matrimoniale* with a view over the harbour and beyond to the pointed peaks of Moorea. After a sound sleep I woke refreshed. A previous lunch with Purea Reasin, whom I remembered from my trip but who hadn't remembered me, had produced a telephone number for Bengt Danielsson. Red-bearded Bengt had been one of the *Kon-Tiki* crew who came to call respectfully after Turia and I had been married, and we'd been friendly after that.

I telephoned, and duly we met, where I was treated to a fine round-up of information to help satisfy my curiosity about the differences between 'then' and 'now'. Bengt lived in a genuinely Tahitian-style shack by the lagoon, his study so lined with books that they might have been the main building-materials holding the house together. His huge beard was no longer flaming red, and incipient baldness was no longer just incipient, otherwise I would have known him from a mile off.

He showed me early photographs, picking out one of an elderly man, formally dressed, in a panama hat, saying: 'You know who this is?'

It stumped me. A familiar face, yes – but whose?

'Your Consul,' he said. 'Now do you remember?'

How could I have been so forgetful as to be unable to put a name to the face of Charles Henderson? It was he who'd taken me to see James Norman Hall, he who'd made me official caretaker of the Maison Edwards. He'd been the principal founder of my fortune in Tahiti.

I mentioned Otu Duryea. 'Oh, he only died quite recently. He kept on bicycling about everywhere, in spite of all the traffic you see now. That's what finally did him in.'

Speaking of traffic, Bengt told me that when he was in Tahiti in 1951, his car-plate read 702, meaning that there were only that number of cars on the island for the 500 Frenchmen – *fonctionnaires*, or others who'd mostly been absorbed into Tahitian families. But suddenly 30,000 French had arrived, a huge Army contingent, plus all those services dependent on them. 'Thirty thousand French meant at least that number of cars,' he said. 'Otu hadn't got much of a chance, really.'

Marie-Thérèse, Bengt's wife, came in. 'She will tell you about Turia,' Bengt said. 'She used to visit her in the home, quite often.'

'Did Turia absolutely hate being in such a place?' I asked.

'Perhaps not hate, but it didn't suit her temperament. She would get very *fiu* with the other old people. On the whole, those others were simple – not her type at all!'

'I don't suppose they were. What did she find to do all day?'

'She couldn't move about much, because of the arthritis. So she spent most of her time asleep.'

Asleep? Turia? It was unimaginable, she who, as I remembered her, was always so lively.

'Will we all be like that in the end?' I asked, expecting (and getting) the answer: 'Who knows?'

Turia had been ever-present during my second coming to Tahiti, not as intangibly as a *tupaupau*, but constantly recalled to mind; not exactly grieved over, but vainly regretted.

I said: 'This is what happens as the result of coming back to Paradise after too long away. You hear things you'd rather not hear; yet in the end you prefer always to know the truth.'

My last evening in Papeete was spent on my own. I watched the sun going down over the harbour, creating scarlet and mauve streaks in the sea under a scarlet and silver sky.

After a long reverie, I limped slowly towards the waterfront, intending to pick up a snack at some mobile stall, but turned aside to treat myself to a meal in comfort at a restaurant called Acajou, recommended by Med Kellum.

From my solitary table I saw a Frenchman similarly sitting on his own, so I went across with a *'Pardon M'sieu!'* and a suggestion that he join me. 'Thank you, but I prefer my own company!' he said firmly. Moments later, I saw another lone sitter and, nothing daunted, repeated my act. *'Quelle plaisir!'* was the reaction. We enjoyed a pleasant, impersonal meal together before parting on friendly terms. I thought to myself: *Some people would have been put off by the first failure. But that would have been silly. As with throwing dice, each result bears no relation to the one before, or the one after.* It had taken a lifetime of overcoming shyness to enable me to re-roll the dice and accost strangers without blushing, for which I was truly thankful.

I reflected upon the luck of that inexperienced idiot who'd come to the South Seas at just the right time after the war, when even beach-combers – young ones, especially – were a rarity. It had been before the days of back-packers, let alone tourists. Blessed chance had given me a field virtually to myself. Had I not been driven by a dream I would never have had the nerve to cut loose, without much money, from the first stirrings of a literary career in England. Inasmuch as luck entered the equation, it had been my good fortune to be sufficiently pig-headed to persevere in the face of opposition. Paradoxically, my time as a despised conchie had given me ample practice in how to stand up and fight.

As for equivocal sexuality, I couldn't judge how important it had been. Perhaps the fountain-head of every 'anti' idea since early child-hood? If so, far from cursing my fate, I had to thank God for making me what I was; otherwise how would I have fared, unwillingly, but without the strength to resist falling into line with rules of conduct as (apparently) unalterable as the laws of the Medes and Persians? I could almost feel sorry for those born or raised without obstacles to overcome; but I wasn't really sorry, because, if I'd learnt anything, it was that seizing an opportunity was what counted, not the fact that the opportunity happened to be there.

A return to Paradise had been needed in order to make me fully aware of what I'd been seeking, the first time round, as a young man; and above all, of what the search had taught me. It didn't greatly matter that I'd found so many things changed, for what else did I expect? Thank God, I'd known those islands before such changes took place.

I was due to leave early next morning, unattended, unmissed. This time my *adieu* to *Tahiti-nui marearea* was short, but without lasting regret. So many things had gone right that I had no real grounds for complaint. All the same, it would have been nice if there'd been just *one* person to rush forward with a glad cry of '*Iorana!*', and meaning it.

Back in London there would be rudimentary noises more golden than silence from Gian Carlo, interrupted by Silver's frantic barks. Nothing could surpass such a welcome. In the last resort, as in the first, there was no place like home.

————

125

In July 1991, I lay in an unfamiliar bed, at a friend's house, in Venice. I reflected on how desperately so many people spent their lives looking for, but seldom finding, real love.

I haven't told him clearly enough how important he's been, I decided. *Not just important, but vital. Nothing I've achieved in these last twenty-four years could have been achieved without him being there.* I might have spent too much time drifting around, picking up casual friends, inviting danger to the point of death. Even the fact that I'd had to work so hard to prevent him from sliding into alcoholism had been a sort of salvation for me, too. There was so much to be grateful to him for. Had I told him so, often enough?

I travelled back to Mamma Cesira's house in Mestre. LM had been moved permanently to the sitting-room sofa whilst I'd spent the night away, because he preferred being in the centre of things instead of being shut away in his bedroom. I wanted to tackle the conversation immediately; yet he was seldom left alone long enough for me to get a confidential word in edgeways. After one or two false starts I managed at last to unburden myself of the vitally important message. He reacted exactly as expected. I could understand every broken word: 'You're only saying that to cheer me up.'

'No, I promise I'm not. I ought to have said it hundreds of times before.'

'You really mean it?'

'With all my heart!' For once, I couldn't stop myself crying in front of him. His eyes gleamed.

Four months earlier, in March, Gian Carlo had developed a lump the size of a pea on his head. There had been chemotherapy which had been successful, until another lump appeared in May on his stomach. By June, the doctors said anything else they contrived to do would do more harm than good.

He died in August, Mamma Cesira and I taking it in turns to sit by his bedside, occasionally murmuring fondly into his ear, till all signs of recognition ceased.

I suppose that our life together was just too idyllic, it was so wonderful. How lucky to have had so long! That's what I tried my hardest to think. But I couldn't stop crying. It had been too awful seeing him struggling against the inevitable. He was so gallant and noble. I could never have achieved so high a standard, had it been required of me.

I thought back to our last Christmas together, so different in 1990 to 1989 when we'd been so terrified of this exact occasion. The Little Man had brought out all his traditional decorations – the paper-ruffles, the lights, the wreaths and favours – and hung them expertly round the rooms, festooning his Chiswick cottage with an even more extravagant display of coloured baubles.

I thought of how he'd said goodbye to Villa Marco when we'd come out to Italy, nodding his head at the lime trees, saying a silent goodbye to the house and the bees.

I thought of how only two years earlier I'd taken him to the Silver Vaults in Chancery Lane, where we'd chanced upon Langford's and I'd said there was no point in waiting another three years for a silver wedding anniversary. We'd found six complete place-settings of spoons and forks of 'fiddle' design. They weren't a set, but they were all Georgian or William and Mary, with modern knives to match. How glad I was that we'd done that; how strange it was too, as if we'd had the foresight that three years was beyond us, that we'd never make it to the auspicious occasion.

At the funeral, Morvyne came up trumps with her flowers. Her contribution was so lavish and dazzling that I was deeply touched, for I was unused to having my own family understand much about what made me tick.

In my diary I wrote: 'My life in ruins.' What else was there to say?

126

In a letter to Mavis, beautiful and beloved, her friend Cicely Hornby wrote how she felt about her husband's death: 'All goes on without him, and I do everything, going and coming, talking all normal and naturally and yet there is that great void which can never be filled.' I quoted it in my book because it seemed so true to life, little knowing that it was exactly how I would be feeling myself before many years had passed.

Shortly after coming back to London I had to think of taking honey from the hives at Gilston Lodge and Villa Marco, the date being fixed by the memory of Granny Rawnsley lying in bed at Claxby, stertorous with Cheyne-Stokes breathing, the ghastly noise interrupted only by the *thump-thump-thump* of an extractor being spun round by hand in the spare room downstairs. When I told the bees in Paxton Road that their multi-faceted eyes would never again form a blurred picture of their respected keeper, it was like throwing a final clod of earth on his coffin. I wondered whether I could bear to go through the same process, another year. Perhaps I could still keep the bees, whilst ignoring their wondrous harvest?

1991 moved creakingly towards its end; creaking for lack of a lubricant of love to make its progress smoother. The aftermath of my misery dragged on, promising nothing, solving nothing. When people talk of 'the dark night of the soul' they assume that the sun must eventually rise. But what if it takes its time doing so? At what point may despair give way to renewed hope? I tried to be grateful to God that an experience suffered by so many should be mine, at last, for otherwise I might never have known how dreadful the loss of an adored one could be. So perhaps there was something legitimately to be glad about, even in that darkest of all hours, before the dawn of an unwanted day.

Little flecks of humour, like mayflies, glittered briefly and were extinguished; glittered again and lasted longer. That was better, wasn't it? I wished I could believe my own words instead of merely pretending to. Seeking the truth in sorrow was harder than finding it in gladness; but that was no reason to call off the search.

Alleviation was slow in coming, but in time I felt as if I were on the long journey back, faint smiles breaking through the stabbing pains of loss. To accompany that journey, why not go on a real one?

A boat-trip on the waterways linking St Petersburg to Moscow attracted my attention and might be favoured by Ernest, too. Being a Professor of English, he was seldom at a loss for a poetic allusion – in which way, he was like me. In the late summer of 1992, Browning was pressed into service: '"We'll have a last ride together",' he said, 'if you're sure you can manage it?'

'I'll manage it somehow!' I said, gritting my teeth.

The best bargain was a tour being organised by Noble Caledonia on behalf of the *Daily Telegraph*, taking advantage of the travelling opportunity brought about by the extraordinary collapse of the Soviet Union only the year before. I'd been in Communist territory once before, a lifetime ago in '74, when my mother, Morvyne, Genissa, Michael and I had gone to Poland for a week. We'd also been joined by an old flame of Morvyne's: tall, with long white locks wisping from an otherwise bald head, who had once been Tom Newman but now went by the name

Violet. He* announced to us that in this life he was in the wrong body. Violet wasn't in the least effeminate and didn't think of himself as being in any way queer. In fact, no one could have guessed his secret, had he not been eager to disclose it. Being an artist and a person of intelligence, he was excellent company.

In Cracow, we had been served a breakfast of slices of ham and cheese that had been carefully counted, and handed tiny demi-tasses of coffee, being told we were not allowed a pot. Further evidence of Communism could be seen from the bus: public buildings, grim colourless blocks, Russianed neo-Egyptian in style; brownish-grey houses with peeling stucco exteriors deprived of paint for a generation; few cars except taxis; trams cram-jammed full, clanking down cobbled streets; old people in long, ragged coats, heads bowed against the pouring rain; young people in identical padded anoraks, the new student uniform. It was a shoddy 'World of the Future', state-controlled. Needless to say, few of us other than the blinkered found it in any way admirable.

I was therefore interested to see what state we would find Russia in. The flight out took no more than three and a half hours. On arrival, we were directed on to a dilapidated red bus and driven thirty-five kilometres to the riverside, where four huge white boats like elongated egg-boxes were tied up. Ours was *Russ*, apparently no different from the other three. The cabins were fairly large, the bathrooms (with hand-held shower) fairly small. We were shown to cabin 301, sandwiched between restaurant and bar, anything but the 'quiet' quarters requested in our booking. I soon got it exchanged for cabin 320. 'You can bet your bottom dollar, two men sharing always get given the worst!' said Ernest.

Next day we were bussed into, then out of, Peter the Great's city. The city outskirts were frankly frightful, depressing concrete blocks of flats, blown about with rubbish, their only saving grace the presence of trees planted along the roads, as on the outskirts of Beijing, but in less profusion. To come through that drab encirclement and into the roomy 'Georgian' magnificence of the city centre was like penetrating a barrier of thorns protecting a Sleeping Beauty. 'How *could* they have done it?' we asked ourselves – the 'it' being the sleazy setting of workers' flats, not the sparkling jewel in the centre. For inner St Petersburg was glorious

---

* Roddy used the masculine pronouns; it can be assumed that either Violet didn't mind or wanted to remain 'he'/'him', given that Roddy continued to refer to Violet as Violet throughout the rest of his stories about Poland, of which there were more in the original memoirs.

from every angle, especially along the Nevsky Prospekt; an extended architectural triumph.

Next day we were to 'do' the Hermitage, once the Winter Palace of the Tsars and one of the largest art museums in the world, as well as the Church of Alexander Nevsky, the Cathedral of St Nicholas and the Church of St Isaac. The blue, white and golden-domed confection known as the Alexander Nevsky Church hummed with activity. I bought a candle at the entrance for 5 roubles (160 roubles = $1) and stuck it in a holder in front of a Virgin icon which people were genuflecting and going down on their knees in front of before walking up over a kind of wooden bridge and approaching and kissing her robe (through glass – I bumped my nose on it). No one could fail to be impressed by the atmosphere, the number of people wandering purposefully, pausing to pray in front of this icon or that.

At the Cathedral of St Nicholas I saw a naive curiosity for the first time, though we were to encounter it often enough in the future: an icon of Our Lady with a tiny head of Christ set centrally in Her bosom in place of a heart – well worth a candle. On we went to St Isaac's, burial-place of the Romanovs, then retreated to the Astoria hotel for a rest. Said to be St Petersburg's finest, the hotel was of old-fashioned international standard – a pleasant surprise.

On to the Hermitage, the mint green, white and gold-columned extravaganza that seemed to stretch indefinitely down the Neva River. Once within, we found a guide in the 'Bureau': a man by the window looked up and on seeing Ernest, obviously American, smiled. He turned out to be the Assistant Curator and, like E, he spoke good German. Thankfully I noted: 'He was a gay middle-aged hunchback and he offered to take us round himself! What a triumph.'

Spouting fluently, the paragon led us rapidly through the Silver section (with its heavy candelabras, *épergnes* and the like) to the French Impressionists, to be confronted by a superb Van Gogh of two women talking, quite unlike anything else of his, also a Gauguin revelation – a Tahitian face, huge, seen through a window with apparently an Eye of God looking down from the centre of a room in Tahiti. Most extraordinary. There was the famous Matisse of female figures dancing in utter abandon against an orange background, and a less impressive one of dancing men; some lovely Vlamincks, too. Our expert guide whizzed us swiftly through what he called the less important sections, ending our tour with two small Leonardos and a Rembrandt of *The Return of the Prodigal Son*, itself recently returned from fresh authentication in Amsterdam.

Finally he took us, thirsty and exhausted, down to a small café in the basement for a late lunch, where we were told that they'd run out of everything to drink, including even water. They did still have bread spread with bogus caviar and sour cream and a few horrible stale buns, with which we made do. Then came the question of what to give such a big-wig as an Assistant Curator who asked for nothing. I had no doubts. 'Academics like him get paid a pittance, *if* they get paid at all,' I said. 'They're not like spivs or taxi-drivers. I suggest twenty dollars.'

'Isn't that overdoing it?' Ernest said.

'Of course it is. We'll be his lovely dream!'

Indeed, he was most hesitant and grateful. Translated into roubles, it might have represented as much as a week's salary. He was worth it. We could never have imagined having the services of such a guide to the finest museum in Russia all to ourselves.

Away from Lake Ladoga, *Russ* entered a wild-looking canal with banks of irregular red cliffs. Birch trees grew in profusion from every patch of flat land beyond. It was fine, sitting in our cabin with its large 'railway-carriage' window, gliding along, pursued by a 'wash' which sucked at the nearest bank. A full moon rose orange into the sky. We passed small settlements with steam-boats moored near them – tinted houses with nothing but tracks connecting them, roads being non-existent. The people in those settlements could probably see us and the other passengers all too easily lit up on deck as we passed by, like tarts in Amsterdam's red-light quarter, I imagined.

Russ reached Kizhi, on Lake Onega, late in the afternoon. There I had to endure a walk which was a mere nothing for the others: a fifteen-minute stroll along duck-boarding laid over uneven ground to a complex known as the Open-air Museum of Architecture. The pride of the museum's group of largely reconstructed wooden buildings was the famous eighteenth-century Church of the Transfiguration, with its twenty-two onion-domes like bunches of wooden balloons, looking as if waiting for a Russian Mary Poppins to float off with them into the sunset.

That night there was to be a Russian lesson, conducted by a girl so solidly built that she might have been the ship's gym-mistress, and as domineering as she looked. Her method was to bully us into learning how to express ourselves in Russian by publicly picking on this or that person for an answer. We had to stand up in front of the class and be reprimanded for a failure to follow. Though hardly pleasant, it was undeniably effective. We didn't dare *not* learn a few words, utterly unfamiliar because they weren't based on the twin pillars of Greek and Latin.

During the night, we arrived at Petrozavodsk, a provincial capital, though not looking much like one. At each place there were churches to be seen, and each church was full of icons and wall-paintings. We were already growing not exactly bored but satiated, even though, for an expert eye, recognising the slight differences between one set of 'illustrations' and the next was the point of the exercise. Petrozavodsk had a covered market to which we thankfully repaired after one more museum visit. Grapes were on sale for 75 roubles a kilo, apples were 10 roubles each, but other than fruit and some scraggy meat there seemed to be nothing at all to buy except some tattered clothing.

We began going through the locks of the Volga–Baltic canal on our way to Goritsy. It was only just wide enough to take *Russ*, presumably the determining factor in the boat's specification. The landscape underwent change, no longer lacustrine and marshy but with land looking like land and fir trees interspersed with birch, hills, etc. – much more civilised. Such a nice Victorian scene as we passed through the locks with their well-tended gardens, children rushing out to offer fruit, hoping for pens or sweets, putting me in mind of those far-off Oxford days when young Eckstein had hired a whole steamer to go to Abingdon and back, dispensing largesse to the multitude.

An ancient man whom I met on board mentioned that he'd known a Captain and Mrs Fenwick Owen at Bosham. Was I a relation? When I told him, 'The only son, by a different mother,' he said: 'George was a very strong, very forceful character. Beni did well for herself after that rather dim husband she had, first off.'

It was nice to hear my father praised. It occurred to me that I really knew very little about him, or indeed about anyone on that side of the family except for Roddy Owen. My mother had done too good a job of ensuring that her children looked on George as an ogre. I had never agreed with that verdict, but done practically nothing to find out more, when given the opportunity.

Such a mistake.

*

We were making for Yaroslavl, formerly the port for Moscow, which had lost importance since the completion of the Volga-Moscow canal. It sounded as though it might be rather nice and unspoiled on that account. By night we cruised on and on along the Volga, for once going up in a lock instead of down. *Russ* always looked incapable of fitting into such narrow spaces, but always (of course) just managed it. We passed slowly by an immense industrial complex, where the air was being visibly polluted by clumps of high factory chimneys, including some great low fat ones.

Whilst we were refuelling from a tanker out in mid-stream, the sky was alight with an evocative sunset – but evocative of what? I'd wandered round to the stern of *Russ* at 9 p.m. to watch a huge sun hanging low, an orange orb crossed by absolutely horizontal lines of cloud. In that dreamy state of supernaturally still air a ship loaded with logs of birch-wood steamed into the flat, lagoon-like water dotted with marker-buoys just as the sun was sinking into a bed of low cloud (probably pollution). It chugged into a distance already becoming faint and misty, the noise of its engine gradually dying away, leaving a luminous silence, filling me with melancholy. Somehow the small cargo-boat seemed to represent the dear friend of my heart going to his long rest, whilst I sat there watching, longing to help, summoning up all the powers of heaven and earth to help, yet unable to do anything to cure his tortured body. In that moment, my own life seemed to be flowing out into the sunset, towards the gathering gloom of eternity. Such a wonderful life!

I noted sadly: 'I felt very much an invalid today and wonder whether my own time isn't drawing to a close. I gradually pee slower and more often and wonder if this doesn't mean an obstruction – increasing in size.'

But when the sun had set (and I had not), sombre thoughts took wing and disappeared below the horizon. No doubt they would return, no doubt at all, but I would do well to keep them to myself, thanking God for whatever days were left, blaming nobody. Could such a lofty outlook survive the breakers ahead? I hoped so, although with very little basis for optimism other than Faith.

———

127

What a surprise was Moscow! A great city, bustling, crowded with cars, 'with visible shops all over the place, though I don't know how they are selling, or what', I noted. Someone arriving for a first time and seeing only Moscow would be getting an entirely wrong impression of the country; its vast bitty-ness, its primitive rurality.

Moscow's outskirts were as ugly as was to be expected: flats, flats, flats, in aggressively plain concrete blocks. In answer to my question 'Are there any nice houses, anywhere?' we were told: 'Nobody lives in a house in Moscow!' That one chill sentence seemed to sum up a whole lifetime of 'levelling down'. Houses, or dachas, even for the Party faithful, had only flourished where space was of little significance, in the wide-open country.

We went to a State Store, to see for ourselves what an appalling experience shopping for food was for ordinary Russians. The main thing in the store's favour was that goods were very cheap, honey, for instance, being only 13 roubles a jar. But oh, the palaver! To get it meant seeing the stuff and finding out what it cost, then queuing for a ticket and paying, then taking the ticket to the counter and handing it over. Certainly two if not three queues. In a 'free enterprise' shop close at hand goods could be bought directly for cash, as elsewhere in the world, but it had very little for sale: tinned fish; sweet biscuits, bagged higgledy-piggledy; and some fruit and veg of poor quality, the one exception being fresh raspberries. At that shop I made two purchases: a tiny wooden box with a portrait of a collie-dog like Silver on its lid, costing 6 shillings; and a set of dolls-within-dolls, for which I knew there would be a demand back home. The doll-monstrosity, well painted but still horrible, cost £7.

On entering Red Square we were inevitably exposed to a long walk before being directed into GUM, fancifully (and deceitfully) called the 'Harrods of Moscow'. GUM was nothing of the sort. It was the only multiple store of its kind in the country but was actually more like a vast prison which has been converted to selling shoddy goods – a 'Crystal Palace' roof in glass arches over a galleried complex of small shops which look at first as though they are all dealing in the same stuff, and that the sort of thing nobody wants. Rather than continue to mill round GUM, seeing nothing to buy and buying nothing, we preferred the spectacle of soldiers of the Red Army goose-stepping in front of Lenin's tomb – pompous, militaristic to an nth degree.

I'd assumed that we would be going into St Basil's Cathedral, a colourful feature of Red Square with its multi-pepper-potted, variegated domes, but it was closed. The nearby Kremlin seemed like a monstrous version of many of the other Kremlins we had encountered in smaller towns. Red walls and red internal towers were massive; domes thickly gilded, as if first coated with gesso.

Instead of going back to the boat with the others, Ernest and I chose to be dropped off at the Metropol, Moscow's best hotel, an art nouveau edifice conveniently just across the road from the Central Metro station. Amidst marble pillars strolled men in suits (unlike us in our tourist 'casuals') looking as if they were coming from one deal and going to another. Ernest chatted up an assistant manager called David, from England, who led us on a conducted tour which included the huge breakfast-room in Turkish red-plush style, with the gallery from which Lenin had made a famous speech. There was another restaurant, European, expensive, where £40 a head was the least a customer would have to spend; and a bistro downstairs, far cheaper.

We booked to eat there, then went off to find the Bath, said to be the finest in all Russia, nevertheless set inside a gloomy building with a massive staircase and two men sitting at a table issuing tickets at 300 roubles each. We were ushered into a wonderfully old-fashioned room of mahogany cubicles, each one shielded by golden curtains, each with two shortened beds covered in sheets. To be allotted one of those, we were asked for a further $3 more than for the Bath itself, although admittedly the extra included a bottle of beer.

The Bath had once been favoured by grossly sensual Rasputin, then by a mentally alert Soljhenitsyn,* so we were expecting something special in every sense – which was what we got. We undressed and went naked through into a large room where there were bunches of birch-twigs with their leaves still on and buckets of water, also some

---

* Aleksandr Solzhenitsyn, famous author of *One Day in the Life of Ivan Denisovich*.

four showers. Off it a hut room where you went upstairs into an even hotter place, off which men were lashing each other with the birch-twig bundles. It was fearfully hot, so we couldn't stay long. On beyond I found my favourite type of shower, the kind where jets came from all round instead of from just overhead – an intensely stimulating erotic experience. Beyond that, in a marble-slabbed room with water dripping from its ceiling, I was given one of the best massages ever.

For the sake of the experience, we wanted to travel on the Metro back to *Russ*, having learnt from St Petersburg exactly what to do: buy metal tokens (at 1 rouble each, all journeys costing the same); master the rapid moving-staircase; gape at the profusion of marble, the chandeliers sunk in domed ceilings; then wait opposite the right aperture for boarding a train. We knew in advance what to ask for, phonetically: '*Rechnoy Wahksal*', Water Terminal, nine stations away.

The grandeur of the stations was by no means matched by the condition of the trains, which were as dirty as London's, though wider and without straps to hold on to. We chatted to a youth, a student trumpeter who regularly supplemented his meagre earnings by travelling to Turkey to buy clothing which he sold in Moscow. He refused a packet of cigarettes, saying that he 'did physical culture', so didn't smoke or drink. It was then a long walk back to *Russ*, which exhausted me and caused me dreadful pains, but it was worth it for such an extraordinary day.

The next day should have been Kremlin day, but large sections of it were closed, for conflicting reasons: 'because it's Thursday'; 'because of a terrorist threat'; and so on. The result was, too many tourists converging on the one part remaining open, the Armoury, for which a long queue had already formed. It was chaos, and hot chaos at that because we all had coats on against the cold. In a semi-solid wedge we were taken shuffling past magnificent displays of massive silver, Fabergé eggs, richly embroidered garments, state coaches and the like, by a guide screaming her head off but still inaudible against the hubbub.

That afternoon the group was to proceed to the Pushkin Museum, a ploy utterly beyond me. I wanted only to get back to *Russ* and rest; I felt a cold coming on, and I felt that I'd had enough, the two things being connected. This *was* a last ride, no doubt about it. Pain was outweighing pleasure; not just sometimes, but on a daily basis. We were to be taken to Zagorsk next day, but I didn't want to face the long drive, with nose streaming, in order to be confronted with more examples of the splendid religious inheritance which the Communists had done their best to destroy. I never would have thought it possible, but yes, I'd really had enough.

––––––––––

128

With the realisation that my travelling days were over, I needed to sell Bettina in Malta. Morvyne and I went out once more, followed by a last trip with Ernest. I thought: *Growing old is really a long-drawn-out process of saying goodbye – to people, to things, to places. When young, you assume you'll come back soon, then 'perhaps one day'. Finally, 'probably never'.*

As it happened, during my span of life on Earth I'd been able to take a second glance at nearly every once-cherished scene; and I hadn't found the process disillusioning, so much as re-illusioning. Malta was the only place to which I'd returned so often that I could almost have been described as a commuter, and my days in Malta were at an end, over and done with. I need never go back, God willing – but oh, how sad!

We enjoyed the usual peaceful, unexacting time for the last time, and towards the end of our short stay I began to wonder if I shouldn't sell up but instead come out more often. Yet I knew that after a few days back in England I would wonder why I'd left London, where life required so much less effort. Throughout the years, one aspect had remained constant: each visit to Malta possessed the faculty of spreading out time, slowing it down by providing a multiplicity of people to be seen and things to be done, filling life with detail – and so, prolonging it. In London, the weeks seemed to fly by, habit providing the super-fuel to maintain their speed.

And hadn't life suddenly seemed to have flown by. By 1995 my two nephews and niece had produced eight great-nephews and -nieces between them: Jennifer, Rory, Peter, Clare, Susie, Sarah, Charlie, and Michael, the eldest, who I'd promised to 'put through' Eton. Come September that year he was duly taken by his father to Gailey's for the autumn 'half'. Next thing we knew, on 8 September a photograph appeared in the *Daily Telegraph* – and in hundreds of other newspapers and magazines throughout the world as well as on TV – of him walking with his House Master near the boy who was the real object of such fervent press coverage: the heir to the throne, HRH Prince William, also newly arriving at Eton that day.

Michael was asked: 'Will it be a problem, having the Prince boarding with you at the Manor?' Whatever his reply may have been, it was evidently considered especially satisfactory, for the next moment he and Andrew Wrightson (great-nephew of Oliver Wrightson, that old friend from Oxford who'd taken me to visit Peryl in 1940) were messing with the Prince and friend, under promise of maintaining complete confidentiality. Ralph Anstruther was also able to assure his employer that her royal grandson was not sitting at table with an unknown, but with the nephew of his god-daughter, my niece Mary. Approval was expressed all round.

Were I rash enough to look once more into a makeshift crystal, I would surely see tiny moving dots indicating myself in decline, avoiding only with the greatest difficulty the sin of minding too excessively. As for continuing to keep a diary, why chronicle gloom? Sundials can tell only of sunny hours, but a human recorder has to keep working when there are nothing but clouds, or risk misleading gentle readers.

Instead, I have written about the past in order to try and exorcise the present. I saved the £1000 Tops left me, deliberating for some time, waiting for what I knew must be invented in answer to an obvious demand; then got a Sharp Fontwriter 710, with one disc doing the work of forty or fifty of its Smith Corona predecessor, yet smaller, more portable, and printing, not typing. Whenever I use it, Tops is there, amused and trenchantly unshockable. I reflect how every passing moment sets Gian Carlo and I further and further asunder, yet how we have grown closer over the years, in large part thanks to this process of retrospection. Altogether it has made me agree with one of Kierkegaard's aphorisms: 'Life can only be understood backwards; it has to be lived forwards.' Seems obvious, doesn't it? But then the truth often is.

If asked for a parting valediction, it would be that the truth has been the alpha and omega of every word of these pages; except once or twice to protect others and for occasional reticence over sexual details. Even so, there will doubtless be many who may object to the inclusion of what they would call 'more than enough to be going on with'.

It isn't from shame. I have long considered it ludicrous – and said so, repeatedly – to treat the multi-faceted expression of such a universal experience – sex – as sinful. Why not appreciate and approve the power of a God-given urge common to us all, combatants, non-combatants and neutrals alike, gladly accepting the different solutions applied by different people? We might then stand some chance of getting to grips with the real problems of morality, of which there are plenty, heaven knows.

I can add little in condemnation of hypocrisy in general, having been myself guilty of so much of it in the past. I have to hope that these last words make up, to some extent, for all the half truths which have characterised everything else I have ever written.

The prospect of 'signing off', of no more travel, might once have plunged me into depths of gloom, but actually hasn't. Before long, the trumpets will be sounding for an old man already past the Biblical 'three score years and ten'. It is up to me to accept that situation without protest and make the best of what gentler exercises remain.

Truthfully, I don't want to be young, or even middle-aged, again; for what could possibly match the dazzling variety of ever-changing patterns which enriched my life so kaleidoscopically the first time round?

Afterword

I met Roddy thirty years ago, at more or less exactly the time that the story of this book ends. My cousin Tom, his doctor and friend for forty years, had taken me to lunch. This was eaten, as was usual at Gilston Lodge, in the kitchen; disconcertingly, at a table and chairs taken from a Victorian railway carriage, complete with wood panelling, cut glass lamps and a polished brass luggage rack. The view from the window by the table – of shrubbery, a laburnum and the gable of the house next door (which, much to Roddy's joy, had just been moved into by an American movie starlet) – gave no clue as to the date. Nor, really, did Roddy.

Although clearly no longer young, he seemed a curious blurring of ages. A recent (and unsuccessful) operation on his spine had left him stooped and in pain. It certainly had not slowed him down, however. Driving with a terrifying *brio*, he continued to race to Chiswick every day to walk his dogs there – an absent-minded collie who died soon after, and a shih tzu called Trooper who begged at table with goggle-eyed fury. This latter was admonished with the unconvincing rebuke, 'Oh, come *along*, sweetie', spoken in loving tones which the dog point-edly ignored.

Roddy's manners and vocabulary – courtly, bubbling, Etonian – seemed to come from another time. So, too, did Gilston Lodge. It was, for London, an unimaginably large house, with rooms leading off other rooms and the whole topped off with a tower like a widow's walk. On the three-and-a-half floors above the railway carriage kitchen, for fifty years had lived or stayed a whole cast of characters who recurred in Roddy's stories, but were now almost all dead. And yet Roddy did not seem cast down by all these ghosts. Side by side with a strong romantic streak was another of complete pragmatism: the dead were dead, and that was all.

Another unexpected side to him was a firm belief in an afterlife – not a specifically Christian one, although that too – so that his attachment to the saints whose images dotted Gilston Lodge was both breezy and real. And he loved to shock. As a rather embarrassable young gay man myself, I found his revelations about his love life, by no means all in the past, a source of terrible anguish. Roddy, spotting this, would follow up with stories even more hair-raising, revelling in my growing confusion. Even when, felled by a stroke in 2008, he was bedbound in Gilston Lodge's drawing room, he longed for gossip and naughtiness. I fear I must have been a terrible disappointment to him.

Roddy died of cancer in February 2011. His funeral, at St Mary's The Bolton's, outside his back gate, was conducted by the local vicar. The eulogy, though, was read by the much-loved Rabbi Lionel Blue, who Roddy had met in the Turkish baths of the Imperial Hotel, Russell Square – then a notorious gay cruising ground – sixty years before. Lionel spoke of him with a tenderness that was spiritual but not pious. He was, from memory, the last of the old guard present. Sir Richard Neville had died in 1994; Sir Ralph Anstruther in 2002; Gulzaman in 2003; my cousin Tom just six months before. Roddy was also the last of his immediate family, Genissa having died of Parkinson's and dementia in 2003, and Morvyne of cancer in 2008. After nearly sixty years of his living there, Gilston Lodge was sold. Roddy had paid £10,000 for it; it went on the market at £8.5 million. The world had changed.

By the time I got to know him, Roddy's travelling days were over; but then so was the golden age of freebooting. He had, in any case, been just about everywhere there was to go. Now, his wings clipped by infirmity, Roddy took refuge in his bees, his remaining friends and family, and set off on a voyage around himself. This, a decade in the finishing, took the form of three sequential volumes which were part autobiography, part travelogue, part genealogical chronicle. Roddy published the trilogy himself, giving it to family and close friends. This new work you have just finished is, among other things, a distillation of his experiences of those times. That these still have the power to shock would please Roddy mightily; as, indeed, would this book.

Charles Darwent, co-executor of Roderic Fenwick Owen's literary estate

Repeat Characters

Characters have been alphabetised by surname where surnames have been given; first names if not. The publishers would be interested to hear more information about what happened to any of the people listed below, particularly those denoted in bold.

A

Abdullah 'Moonface' – Sheikh Shakhbut's interpreter

Sheikh Ahmed – of the ruling al-Khalifa family in Bahrain

HRH Prince Alexander of Yugoslavia – Patricia Denny's lodger and lover

Ali – the guide who shows Roddy around the Luxor Temple during the war

al-Sharif, Abdul-Nabi – Roddy's young Bahraini facilitator

Anstruther, Sir Ralph – a good friend of Roddy's and later equerry to the Queen Mother

Azzopardi, Giuseppina 'Guse' – Roddy's charlady in Malta

B

Beeley, Sir Harold – Roddy's contact in Cairo during his *Roddy Owen's Africa* quest

Belgrave, Charles – the British adviser to the ruler of Bahrain

Belgrave, James and Enid – Charles's son and his wife

Benenson, Flora – Peter Benenson's impressive mother

Benenson, Peter – Roddy's Summer Fields, Eton and Balliol friend who went on to found Amnesty International

Berkeley, Maurice – Roddy's theatrical housemate on his return to London after the war

Birmingham, Sgt Joe – the GI Roddy meets in Naples, but bed bugs put paid to his plans

Bolton, Geoffrey 'Boltosh' – Roddy's villainous Summer Fields teacher

Braverman, Sylvia – Roddy's dress-designer lover that he meets on his journey back from New York

Brenda – Manzoor's wife and Manzoora and Gulzaman's sister-in-law

Burrows, Bernard – the British Political Resident, Persian Gulf (sometimes at odds with Charles Belgrave)

Busuttil, Guido – one of Roddy's guides when he first arrived in Malta; friend thereafter

C

Cacobau, Ratu George – the chief in Fiji

Cavendish-Bentinck, Group Captain Morven – the man who helps Roddy to join the RAF

Mamma Cesira – Gian Carlo's mother

Chetwynd, Bridget – Roddy's sometime lover and long-term friend, who Roddy met when he moved to London during the war

Chetwynd, Randolph – Bridget's understanding but straight-laced husband

Chris – the Spitfire pilot in Sorrento who Roddy chases Italian girls with

Connolly, Cyril – the literary critic and a friend of Roddy's

Cook, Joyce – Gian Carlo's speech therapist

Crane, Cornelius – the 'millionaire' in Tahiti who employs Turia

Mr Croft – Gian Carlo's surgeon

Cuthbert, Ian – the 'King of Das'

D

Damant, Dr Tom – Roddy's friend, doctor and fellow bee-keeper

Danielsson, Bengt – an adventurer from the *Kon-Tiki*, who Roddy and Turia entertained after they married

Denny, Patricia – Roddy's friend through Harry Nuttall; originally living with Gina Edwards and sleeping with Prince Alexander

Dobson, Meric – Wayland Dobson's brother; a financial adviser in Kuwait

Dobson, Wayland – a friend at Balliol who co-hosted a famous pretend husband and wife party

Domenico – the gardener at Dil Aram in Anacapri
Duryea, Otu – the bird-like friend in Tahiti who tutors the children
    of the Krainères and tells Roddy about Maison Edwards

E

Eden, John MP – a facilitator of Roddy's trip to Pakistan who Roddy
    meets through Bill McLean in the House of Commons
Edwards, Gina – originally Patricia Denny's friend; later Roddy's
    lodger
Elgood, Bonté – the honorary great-aunt in Heliopolis, Egypt who
    hosts Roddy during the war and is a big cheese in Anglo-Egyptian
    society
Ellul, Indri – of the Malta Gas Board, who helps Roddy with the
    house
England, Paul – artist in New York who lives with Hart
Essayan, Rita – a very rich friend Roddy makes in the 1950s
Great-Aunt Evie – left Roddy and his sisters £7000 each when she
    died

F

Fenwick Owen, Beni – Roddy's father's third wife
Fenwick Owen ('Mung'), Bettina – Roddy's mother
Fenwick Owen (later Harding), Genissa – Roddy's sister
Fenwick Owen, George – Roddy's father
Fenwick Owen, Maya – Roddy's paternal grandmother
Fenwick Owen, Morvyne – Roddy's sister
Fleming, Ward – primo ballerino, New York Negro Ballet
Fox, Hubert – Roddy's friend who he originally met at Oxford and
    was a fellow member of the University Ambulance Unit
Friend, Ann – social worker at the rehab wing of St Bernard's

G

Gaury, Gerald de – a friend of Mavis Mortimer Wheeler's who set up
    introductions for Roddy to take advantage of in Pakistan
**Gavoka, Adi 'Voka' – the respected estranged wife of Ratu
George Cacobau who supports Roddy in Fiji**

Gian Carlo – a barman originally at the Kensington Close Club; later Roddy's long-term partner

Gilmore, Bunny – a helpful friend to Roddy in Tahiti

Giuseppe – a lover Roddy met in a Spanish restaurant, introduced through Ernest Hofer

Gorakshakar, Vilasini 'Vil' – Roddy's friend over from India to study at the Slade School during the war

Gough, Sylvia – one of the vocal 'bar-flies' at the Fitzroy Tavern

Gregory, Norman – Niarchos shipping agent who Roddy hopes will help grant passage to Gulzaman

Grischotti, Marcus – Roddy's main Nassau Street lodger

Gulzaman – the Pakistani friend Roddy originally meets on Das Island

H

Hall, James Norman and Lala – the famous author living in Tahiti and his wife

Hamnett, Nina – one of the vocal 'bar-flies' at the Fitzroy Tavern

Harding, Charles and Margaret – Roddy's nephew and his wife

Harding, David and Marian – Roddy's nephew and his wife

Harding, Mary – Roddy's niece

Harding, Michael – Genissa's husband

Hart – the dancer, warehouseman and lover Roddy met at the Mount Morris Baths in New York

Henderson, Charles – the British Consul in Tahiti

Henderson, Edward – important in the conversations over the Buraimi Oasis dispute; Roddy originally meets him at the Adviserate in Bahrain

Hendra, Bob – Ann Friend's colleague

'Auntie' Herrington – Maud Rawnsley's housekeeper at Claxby Hall

Hiley, Peter – Roddy's often helpful school friend

Hillyard, Tim – BP manager in Abu Dhabi

Hofer, Ernest – Roddy's friend and travel partner

Howard, Brian – the famous poet and Roddy's friend when he moved to London during the war

Howard-Williams, Aelwyn – Roddy's cousin who lives in the basement of 94 Queen's Gate

Howson, Squadron Leader – Roddy's senior, who takes the Flying Control Refresher Course with him in Cairo

Hudson, Squadron Leader Tony – Roddy's senior in Vienna, when they try to get the Russians on side with regards Allied rules of aircraft safety

I

Ibrahim – one of Roddy's Bahraini friends
Ivanovic, Daška – Bill McLean's wife

J

James, Monty – author and Eton Provost who was at school with Roddy's grandfather
Jope, Ratu – the Buli of Bau who shows Roddy around
Jusuf – Roddy's Bahraini friend, member of the HEC

K

Kamran – Pakistani diplomat's son who stayed with Gulzaman
Kellum, Medford and Gladys – Turia's neighbours in Opunohu Bay; when Turia's house burned down, Med let Turia build on his land
Kerkhoff, Emilie van and Miss Suart – Roddy's Indonesian-Dutch friends in Anacapri
Sheikh Khaled – Sheikh Shakhbut's brother
Khaleq, Abdul – Roddy's contact in Abu Dhabi for his visit in 1989
King-Smith, Mike – Roddy's lodger both at 94 Queen's Gate and in Gilston Lodge
Kit the Purser – on *Clan Urquhart*, the ship that sailed Roddy to the South Seas
Knabenshue, Iona – A friend at Balliol who co-hosted a famous pretend husband and wife party
Krainère, Marcel and Pussy – the couple in Tahiti Roddy makes friends with

L

Lancaster, Terry – the journalist Roddy travels around Italy with at the end of the war, who was originally supposed to write the DAF history

Lowder-Downing, Jacqui – Roddy's first girlfriend, who he met when they both worked at Stoke Newington Rest Centre

Lubbock, Ian – son of the classical pianist Irene Scharrer who Roddy lives with at the end of the war

M

Mach, Budi von – the German au pair Roddy went to stay with in Ulm in 1939

Makonnen, Endalkachew and Inky – Ethiopian Embassy official Roddy met through an acquaintance made at the YMCA off Tottenham Court Road

Manzoor – Manzoora's brother

Manzoora – Gulzaman's wife

Margaret – Roddy's charlady at Gilston Lodge

McClanahan, Dale – the American heiress and friend Roddy first meets in Tahiti on his original trip

McDermid, Anne – Roddy's second literary agent

McKinley, Hazel 'H' – the famous Guggenheim who takes a liking to Roddy on his first night in New York

McLean, Bill – Roddy's long-term friend who he met at Eton

Medhurst, Air Marshal – introduced to Roddy by Bonté Elgood; provided Roddy with the 'magic carpet' needed to transport him around north Africa at the end of the war

Mohammed – carpenter and friend in Bahrain

Morris, Alun and Edith – vicar in Bahrain and his wife

Mortimer Wheeler, Mavis – Roddy's friend who he originally meets at a party of Bridget Chetwynd's when she was only recently released from prison

N

Nasreen – Manzoora's sister

Neville, Lady 'Bobbie' – Sir Richard Neville's mother

Neville, Sir Richard – one of Roddy's oldest school friends

Nuttall, Harry – Roddy's northern gay friend he first met at The Fitzroy

O

Orion – a spiritual person from Glastonbury on Roddy's Tibet tour

Ossorio, Alphonso – Roddy's absent host in New York; introduced to Roddy by Hubert Fox

Owen, Major Roddy – Roddy's great-uncle; a celebrity of his day for having won the Grand National

Oxley, Miss Evelyn 'Tocky' – originally Morvyne's governess

P

Peryl, Marchesa di Montagliari – Roddy's original lover during the war

Pollock, Jackson and Lee – the artists; Roddy stays with them on his trip to New York (facilitated by Alphonso Ossorio, through Hubert Fox)

Poroi, M. – the Mayor of Papeete in Tahiti

Prendergast, Geoffrey – a long-term friend Roddy makes in the 1950s

R

Rasac – Roddy's Persian-Bahraini friend who runs an import business

Rashid – Roddy's driver in Abu Dhabi in 1989

Rawnsley, Dick – Roddy's mother's brother and his uncle

Rawnsley, Canon Hardwicke and Eleanor – Roddy's mother's great-uncle, the co-creator of the National Trust, and his wife

Rawnsley, Maud – Roddy's maternal grandmother

Rawnsley, Noel and Violet (*née* Cutbill) – the owners of Dil Aram in Anacapri

Rawnsley, Susan – Dick's wife

Rawnsley, Walter – Roddy's maternal grandfather

Reasin, Purea – a Tahitienne who married an American; one of Turia and Roddy's friends after they married

Reeve, John – Aunt Susan Rawnsley's nephew

Richards, Brooks – Bernard Burrows' deputy

Mr Robson – the uncrowned 'King of Easter Island' who threw the legendary feast; Roddy's neighbour in Tahiti

S

Sheikha Salama – Sheikh Shakhbut's mother

Sheikh Salman – the ruler of Bahrain

Salmon, Melanie – Turia's sister

Salmon, Minou and Rozi – Turia's brother and his wife

Salmon, Turia – Roddy's wife

Scaretti, Marjorie (formerly Jebb) – Aunt Susan Rawnsley's friend who Roddy stays with in Rome during the war

Scharrer, Irene – Ian Lubbock's pianist mother

Scott, Ernest – owner of Kingston House estate, where Roddy lives after the family is 'ruined' after the Great Crash of 1929

Sheikh Shakhbut – the ruler of Abu Dhabi

Shamlan, Abdul-Aziz – the number 2 member of the HEC in Bahrain

Siemers, Carola – Hans' elegant daughter who takes Roddy to parties

Siemers, Georg – Hans' son who takes Roddy to the local red-light district

Siemers, Hans – the von Machs' friend who Roddy stays with in Hamburg in 1939

Mr Skinner – the Bapco chief in Bahrain

Spring-Rice, Stephen – the Eton senior who gets Roddy into trouble for smoking

Stanley-Smith, Mary – Roddy's friend in Oxford who taught him how to be a good host

Strickland, Miss Mabel – 'Queen of Malta' and proprietress of the *Times of Malta*

Sultan – Salman's servant

Mrs Sutton – Roddy's landlady in West Hartlepool when he's working in the Ambulance Service

Sykes, Daniel – Bridget Chetwynd's drug addict lover

T

Tara – a spiritual person from Glastonbury on Roddy's Tibet tour

Tedder, Arthur – Marshal of the RAF who allows Roddy to write his biography

Tedder, Toppy – wife of Arthur Tedder

Y

Yateem, Hussain – Roddy's Bahraini friend who helps him secure his first place to stay

Z

Sheikh Zayed – Sheikh Shakhbut's brother

Morvyne, Bettina, the author, Granny
Rawnsley, wicked Uncle Dick, cold Aunt Susan

The then Prince of
Wales and the author's
cherished Grandfather
Rawnsley

The author with beautiful and
beloved Mavis Mortimer Wheeler

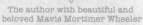

Uncle Roddy's memorial,
now submerged by the Nasser Dam

The author at Franklin's Furthest